736 Rapid Recipes For Busy Cooks

FUSS-FREE FOOD full of "from scratch" flavor is what you'll find in this sixth edition of the cookbook based on the recipes from *Quick Cooking* magazine.

This *2004 Quick Cooking Annual Recipes* cookbook conveniently gathers every fast-to-fix recipe published in *Quick Cooking* during 2003— that's 736 recipes in all—and combines them in one reader-friendly collection. This recipe-packed volume is filled with hundreds of mouth-watering photos so you can see what many of the dishes look like before you prepare them.

Here's what else you'll find inside:

Chapters That Meet Your Needs. With 21 chapters that correspond to popular features in *Quick Cooking* magazine, it's a snap to find a recipe that matches your family's taste and timetable. (See page 3 for a complete list of chapters.)

For example, when your family is eyeing the table and you're eyeing the clock, see the "30 Minutes to Mealtime" chapter for 12 complete meals that go from start to finish in less than half an hour.

Or when you have a mere 10 minutes to spare in the kitchen, rely on Creamed Chicken, Taco Turkey Wraps, Apple-Curry Tuna Melts, Cherry Chiffon Dessert or any of the 19 other timeless recipes in the "10 Minutes to the Table" chapter.

Award-Winning Recipes. You'll get all the palate-pleasing, quick-to-prepare foods that earned top honors in the six national recipe contests we held last year: Speedy Soups, Crunched-for-Time Casseroles, Glorious Grilling, Timely Trimmed-Down Dishes, Time-Saving Sandwiches and Fast Freezer Desserts.

Easy-to-Use Indexes. To make all 736 recipes easy to find, we've listed them in two indexes. (See page 332.) The general index lists every recipe by category and/or major food ingredient. The alphabetical listing is great for folks who are looking for a specific family favorite. In both indexes, you'll find a bold red checkmark (✓) in front of all recipes that use less fat, sugar or salt and include Nutritional Analysis and Diabetic Exchanges.

What's on the Menu? To make meal planning simple, our food editors grouped several recipes from various chapters to create a host of around-the-clock suggested menus. (This time-saving tool appears on page 4.)

Every rapid recipe and helpful hint in this *2004 Quick Cooking Annual Recipes* cookbook was specifically selected with the busy cook in mind. You're sure to enjoy this timeless treasury for years to come...and you'll be able to treat your loved ones to comforting, wholesome home cooking without spending all of your precious time in the kitchen.

2004 Quick Cooking Annual Recipes

Editor: Faithann Stoner

Art Director: Lori Arndt

Food Editor: Janaan Cunningham

Associate Editors: Heidi Reuter Lloyd, Jean Steiner

Graphic Art Associates: Ellen Lloyd, Catherine Fletcher

Cover Photography: Dan Roberts, Rob Hagen

Senior Food Photography Artist: Stephanie Marchese

Food Photography Artist: Julie Ferron,

Taste of Home Books
©2004 Reiman Media Group, Inc.
5400 S. 60th St., Greendale WI 53129

International Standard Book Number:
0-89821-388-6
International Standard Serial Number:
1522-6603

PICTURED ON THE COVER: Light Chicken Cordon Bleu (p. 226) and Strawberry Pie (p. 15).

To order additional copies of this book or any other Reiman Publications books, write: *Taste of Home* Books, P.O. Box 908, Greendale WI 53129; call toll-free 1-800/344-2560 to order with a credit card or visit our Web site at **www.reimanpub.com**.

Taste of Home's
QUICK COOKING

Executive Editor: Kathy Pohl
Editor: Julie Kastello
Food Editor: Janaan Cunningham
Associate Editor: Mark Hagen
Art Director: Brian Sienko
Associate Food Editor: Coleen Martin
Senior Recipe Editor: Sue A. Jurack
Copy Editors: Kristine Krueger, Scott K. Enk
Test Kitchen Director: Karen Johnson RD
Senior Home Economist: Amy Welk RD
Home Economists: Peggy Fleming RD, Sue Draheim, Tamra Duncan, Mark Morgan RD, Patricia Schmeling, Wendy Stenman, Karen Wright
Test Kitchen Assistants: Rita Krajcir, Megan Taylor
Editorial Assistants: Ursula Maurer, Mary Ann Koebernik
Food Photographers: Rob Hagen, Dan Roberts
Food Stylists: Kristin Koepnick, Joylyn Trickel
Senior Food Photography Artist: Stephanie Marchese
Food Photography Artist: Julie Ferron
Photo Studio Manager: Anne Schimmel
Graphic Art Associates: Ellen Lloyd, Catherine Fletcher
Chairman and Founder: Roy Reiman
President: Russell Denson

⏱ *Contents*

What's on The Menu?

GRAB A MENU from the best "fast food" place in town—your kitchen! The price is right, the atmosphere is relaxing, and the service couldn't be friendlier nor the guests more appreciative. And with the *2004 Quick Cooking Annual Recipes* book in your hands, you've already given yourself a generous tip!

Here's how to use the menu ideas featured here: Our food editors screened all the recipes that appear in this book, then "grouped" several from various chapters to make up menus for everyday and special-occasion family meals. Plus, you can mix and match recipes to make up menus of your own.

For even more complete meals, turn to the following chapters: The Busiest Cooks in the Country (p. 6), 30 Minutes to Mealtime (p. 20), Thinking Up a Theme (p. 34) and Company's Coming! (p. 298).

Six Breakfast Choices

Sixteen Lunch Choices

Thirty Dinner Choices

LIKE MOST BUSY COOKS, your day probably begins early in the morning and ends well after dark. Between work, family activities and all your other obligations, you probably pack as much as you can into each day.

It may seem that there's little time to feed your hungry family a wholesome, hearty dinner. But this chapter pleasantly proves that speedy yet memorable meals are within reach.

Six fellow frenzied cooks from across the country share their reliable rapid recipes, time-saving tips and menu-planning pointers, all of which are guaranteed to put you on the meal-making fast track in no time.

MEMORABLE MEAL. Clockwise from upper left: Strawberry Pie, Campfire Potatoes and Tarragon Chicken Bundles (all recipes on page 15).

Planning Makes For Satisfying Suppers

AS A MOTHER, elementary school assistant principal and college student, Sarah Burks is constantly racing against the clock.

"My husband, Jerry, and I have four children—Bryan, Brady, Brennen and Breanne," Sarah explains. "Jerry is a high school counselor, and between our kids' extracurricular activities and happenings at the schools we work for, we're always on the run."

However, a lively lifestyle doesn't stop this Wathena, Kansas mom from getting a homemade supper on the table. For Sarah, sit-down family dinners are just too important to miss.

"My mom and grandma taught me how to cook," she says, "but what I value most are the conversations we had while preparing meals. That's why I firmly believe cooking and eating should involve the whole family.

"Jerry and I think that there's a lot to be shared at the dinner table. In fact, the first piece of furniture we bought together was a dining room set."

The couple says they take a team approach to running their home...and that includes the kitchen duties.

"For example, I do most of the cooking and Jerry does most of the dishes. Sometimes he gets supper started for me, too," Sarah notes.

"The little ones even help with baking. Bryan is a freshman in college, and his siblings love to bake goodies to send to him.

"I like to think our children will someday recall fond memories of moments we shared while preparing and enjoying food together," Sarah says. "That's why we have sit-down meals regularly."

Finding the time to prepare those meals can be challenging. Sarah attends night school once a week, working toward her Education Specialist degree.

"On days I have class, I use my slow cooker to give me a head start on dinner," she says. "With a little planning, I can have a main course simmering while I'm at work. Then, when I get home, there's enough time to eat together before I leave for class."

Sarah sets aside one afternoon each month to bake casseroles that she stores in the freezer. "Freezing these entrees guarantees a good supper no matter how full our agenda gets," she explains. "Similarly, I make and freeze waffles for easy breakfasts."

These are a few of the handy strategies Sarah relies on when she has meetings with her Bible study group, parent-teacher association or honor society for educators.

"In addition to making life easier, these shortcuts leave more time to walk, camp or bike with my family," she adds.

One of the menus that Sarah depends on includes Slow-Cooked Swiss Steak.

"This is a favorite because I can flour and season the steaks and refrigerate them the night before," she explains. "The next morning, I put the ingredients in the slow cooker, and the dish is ready when I come home from work.

"The children eat every bite, particularly when I also add in a little spaghetti sauce and serve the tender meat over pasta."

Mixed Vegetable Casserole not only complements Sarah's slow-cooked specialty, but it's as pleasing to the eye as it is to the palate.

"While vacationing in France, I learned the importance of serving foods that look as good as they taste," she says. "This simple side dish is colorful and has guests asking for seconds."

To round out the meal, you can't beat Creamy Refrigerator Pie, which takes advantage of common convenience items.

"My sister-in-law gave me this recipe," notes Sarah. "It's so easy, and the sweet treat can even be prepared with reduced-fat ingredients."

Why not feature Sarah's recipes at a sit-down dinner in your home? You're likely to create some warm family memories of your own.

Beat-the-Clock Basics

- I buy items in bulk...chips, carrots, you name it. When I get home, I divide everything into small resealable plastic bags. This way, something is always available for the kids to munch on when they're hungry, and it's much more cost efficient than buying individual prepackaged snacks.

- When I purchase ground beef in bulk, I fry it all at once—often 10 pounds at a time. After I drain it, I divide it among several freezer-proof containers. When time is tight, it's great to have the cooked beef ready to add to dishes like casseroles and spaghetti sauce.

- We buy meat from a local meat locker, and I always request that some of the ground beef be made into patties. Not only do I save the time of forming the patties myself, but they're versatile enough to grill as burgers or serve smothered in a simple sauce.
  —Sarah Burks

Slow-Cooked Swiss Steak

Plan ahead...uses slow cooker

2 tablespoons all-purpose flour
1/2 teaspoon salt
1/4 teaspoon pepper
1-1/2 pounds boneless beef round steak, cut into six pieces
1 medium onion, cut into 1/4-inch slices
1 celery rib, cut into 1/2-inch slices
2 cans (8 ounces *each*) tomato sauce

In a large resealable plastic bag, combine the flour, salt and pepper. Add the steak; seal bag and toss to coat. Place the onion in a greased slow cooker. Top with the steak, celery and tomato sauce. Cover and cook on low for 6-8 hours or until meat is tender. **Yield:** 6 servings.

Mixed Vegetable Casserole

Ready in 45 minutes or less

1 package (16 ounces) frozen mixed vegetables, thawed
1 large onion, chopped
3 celery ribs, chopped
1 cup (4 ounces) shredded cheddar cheese
1 cup mayonnaise*
3/4 cup crushed butter-flavored crackers
1/4 cup butter *or* margarine, melted

In a bowl, combine the first five ingredients. Spoon into a greased 1-1/2-qt. baking dish. Toss the cracker crumbs and butter; sprinkle over the top. Bake, uncovered, at 350° for 30-35 minutes or until heated through. **Yield:** 6 servings.

Editor's Note: Reduced-fat or fat-free mayonnaise may not be substituted for regular mayonnaise in this recipe.

Creamy Refrigerator Pie

Plan ahead...needs to chill

2 packages (3 ounces *each*) cream cheese, softened
1 can (14 ounces) sweetened condensed milk
2 tablespoons lemon juice
2 cups whipped topping
1 graham cracker crust (9 inches)
1 can (21 ounces) peach pie filling *or* pie filling of your choice

In a large mixing bowl, beat cream cheese until smooth. Add the milk and lemon juice; mix well. Fold in whipped topping. Spoon into the crust. Cover and refrigerate for 4 hours or until set. Top with pie filling. **Yield:** 6-8 servings.

Freezing Food Is the Key to Easy Dining

LIFE IS NEVER DULL for Christi Gillentine. "Our home is always bursting with activity," she says.

"My husband, Clint, and I have three children—Tyler and twins Colton and Dana," explains the Tulsa, Oklahoma mother. "I'm a stay-at-home mom. But when I'm not chasing after the kids, I work as a freelance writer, volunteer with a support group for mothers of multiples and get together with friends to scrapbook."

Christi also teaches a class about freezer-friendly foods and recently wrote an Internet cookbook about freezer cooking on a budget (see the site www.30 daygourmet.com for details).

"I prepare and freeze entrees so I can spend more time with my family and less time in the kitchen," Christi notes. "Without having these meals in the freezer, dinnertime at our house would not run as smoothly as it does."

Christi credits her grandmother with introducing her to the convenience of frozen fare. "My grandma made large batches of waffles and froze them," recalls Christi. "That's when I realized a freezer is more than a place to store frozen vegetables."

In addition to freezing waffles for her own family, Christi sets aside 2 days each month to prepare dinners for the upcoming weeks.

"Cooking suppers ahead of time makes life so much easier," she says. "If you can't find the time to make several meals at once, try doubling recipes on a few nights and freezing the leftovers."

To maximize freezer space, Christi suggests using resealable freezer bags. "Remove as much air from the bag as possible and lay it flat in the freezer.

"And if you're freezing something like taco meat, why not attach a bag of shredded cheese to it?" she suggests. "Freezing additional ingredients that go with the main course can save you from making last-minute trips to the store."

Labeling freezer bags or containers with a permanent marker is an important step, too. "I also keep a list of the frozen dinners I have on hand. This eliminates

guesswork and makes meal planning a snap."

The menu Christi shares here features three popular freezer pleasers she fixes ahead of time. "On busy nights, whatever I serve must take only 30 minutes or less to prepare or I won't even try to cook it," she explains. "So freezer meals are ideal.

"Not only does Sausage Marinara Sauce freeze well, but it's a family favorite. I like to keep a few batches in the freezer. Then I simply cook the pasta, reheat the sauce and dinner is ready."

Chock-full of turkey sausage, peppers and onion, the skillet sensation is a surefire success whether you make extra to freeze or not.

Christi often serves Ranch Biscuits alongside the main dish. "I jazz up biscuit mix with ranch salad dressing mix, then brush the golden bites with garlic butter after baking," she shares.

"I bake several dozen at once and store them in the freezer. Whenever I need a few, I let them defrost before warming them in the microwave or oven. The parsley-flecked biscuits go well with any entree."

Christi caps off supper with a creamy no-bake dessert. Frosty Peanut Butter Pie calls for only a handful of ingredients but promises to deliver well-deserved compliments.

"Whenever I bring this make-ahead pie to get-togethers, I'm asked for the recipe," Christi says. "I hope other families will enjoy this freezer-friendly meal as much as we do."

Sausage Marinara Sauce

Ready in 45 minutes or less

✓ Uses less fat, sugar or salt. Includes Nutritional Analysis and Diabetic Exchanges.

1 pound turkey Italian sausage links, casings removed
1 medium onion, thinly sliced

Quick Cues for Cold Storage

- My husband prepares Saturday breakfast, so I stir up pancake batter and freeze it in quart-size freezer bags. I thaw a bag in the refrigerator on Friday night. The next day, he simply clips a corner off the bag and pours the batter onto a hot skillet. This method simplifies cleanup, too.

- I freeze uncooked chicken and meats in different marinades. I transfer the meat to the refrigerator a day or two before cooking to let it absorb the marinade as it thaws. So we always have seasoned meats available.

- Preparing meatballs and other family favorites in bulk cuts back drastically on prep time. I often make as many as five dinners' worth of meatballs in one evening. To serve, I drop a package of frozen cooked meatballs into simmering spaghetti sauce and heat through.

—*Christi Gillentine*

1 medium sweet red pepper, julienned
1 medium green pepper, julienned
1 teaspoon olive *or* canola oil
1 can (15 ounces) crushed tomatoes
1 cup chicken broth
5 tablespoons tomato paste
3 to 4 teaspoons sugar
1-1/2 teaspoons dried basil
1/4 teaspoon garlic powder
Hot cooked penne *or* pasta of your choice

Crumble sausage into a skillet. Add the onion, peppers and oil. Cook over medium heat until sausage is no longer pink and vegetables are tender; drain. Add the tomatoes, broth, tomato paste, sugar, basil and garlic powder; heat through. Serve over pasta. **Yield:** 6 servings.

Nutritional Analysis: One 3/4-cup serving (prepared with reduced-sodium chicken broth and 3 teaspoons sugar; calculated without pasta) equals 195 calories, 8 g fat (2 g saturated fat), 41 mg cholesterol, 675 mg sodium, 16 g carbohydrate, 3 g fiber, 16 g protein. **Diabetic Exchanges:** 2 lean meat, 1 starch.

Ranch Biscuits

Ready in 30 minutes or less

2 cups biscuit/baking mix
4 teaspoons dry ranch salad dressing mix
2/3 cup milk
2 tablespoons butter *or* margarine, melted
1 teaspoon dried parsley flakes
1/8 teaspoon garlic powder

In a bowl, stir the biscuit mix, salad dressing mix and milk until combined. Drop 2 in. apart onto a greased baking sheet. Bake at 425° for 10-15 minutes or until golden brown. In a small bowl, combine the butter, parsley and garlic powder; brush over warm biscuits. **Yield:** 9 biscuits.

Frosty Peanut Butter Pie

Plan ahead…needs to freeze

4 ounces cream cheese, softened
1/4 cup peanut butter
1/4 cup sugar
1 teaspoon vanilla extract
1 package (8 ounces) frozen whipped topping, thawed
1 chocolate crumb crust (8 inches)
2 teaspoons chocolate syrup

In a mixing bowl, beat the cream cheese, peanut butter, sugar and vanilla until smooth. Fold in the whipped topping. Spoon into the crust. Drizzle with chocolate syrup. Cover and freeze for 4 hours or until set. Remove from the freezer 30 minutes before serving. **Yield:** 6 servings.

She Serves Speedy Suppers With Sparkle

KITCHEN CLEANUP isn't a big chore for Melissa Mosness. As the owner and operator of a cleaning service, the wife and mother of two has plenty of tricks up her sleeve for keeping her work area tidy while preparing meals.

"I found it's best to clean as you go along," she explains. "The longer the food is stuck to the stovetop, the harder it is to clean up."

Melissa, who lives in Loveland, Colorado, has had lots of practice polishing her cleaning techniques. "I clean 12 homes by myself," she says. "I see some clients once a month and others once a week, but in general I visit at least one house a day.

"I also clean an office every Monday and Thursday at 3 a.m., and I work alternating weekends."

Even though Melissa's calendar gets a bit harried, she enjoys the fact that she can take son Bradley to some jobs while daughter Kelsea is at school.

"I spend time with my husband, Adrian, and our children as often as I can," she shares, "and we eat supper together every night."

Adrian works in construction, running heavy equipment for a local builder. "His workdays are at least 9-1/2 hours long and include some Saturdays," Melissa says.

"Between our work schedules and taking care of the kids, it can be a challenge to come up with a hearty dinner that's fast, too. I've found that I can speed things up, however, by preparing ingredients in advance.

"For example, if Kelsea is snacking on celery sticks, I dice up a few extra pieces and freeze them to add to chili later in the week."

"I also depend on my slow cooker quite a bit," Melissa says. "I can throw just about anything in it in the morning and when I get home from work, the meal is done. This gives me extra time to help our daughter with homework and tend to our house."

When she has a little free time, you might find Melissa busy with a scrapbook. "I love working on the scrapbooks that I've started for the kids," she

shares. She also works in her flower gardens.

Baking is another hobby of Melissa's. "Kelsea and I bake something nearly every Sunday," she notes. "It's heartwarming to see how proud she feels when her daddy goes hog-wild over our freshly baked goodies."

Melissa says that she does all of the cooking in her house. "The only thing Adrian makes for dinner is a phone call to the local pizza place," she says with a chuckle.

"Guests accused me of doing something similar, however, after they tasted my Seafood Alfredo. They couldn't believe I had prepared it myself."

This rich, creamy main dish features plenty of seafood flavors with a hint of garlic and lemon. Frozen peas and a jar of Alfredo sauce make it a simple supper that will be requested time and again.

Fresh greens always make a lovely accompaniment to a pasta entree, but Melissa's Artichoke Tossed Salad is particularly special.

"I used to care for an elderly woman who loved artichokes, so I created this salad especially for her," Melissa says. "Not only is it convenient to make with bottled Italian dressing, but you can dress it up with salad shrimp, too."

Classic Lemon Bars are a pleasant conclusion to this mouth-watering meal. The from-scratch dessert comes together in a snap, but can even be made with a prepared graham cracker crust when time is especially tight.

"These bars are simple enough for no-fuss dinners yet elegant enough for special celebrations," Melissa shares. "Regardless of when you serve them, I'm sure they'll be a hit at your home."

Seafood Alfredo

Ready in 30 minutes or less

1 package (12 ounces) bow tie pasta
2 garlic cloves, minced

Time-Saving Kitchen Tactics

- To keep sliced apples and other fruit from turning brown when making a snack or salad, I mix lemon juice with half as much water in a small squirt bottle reserved just for this purpose. Giving the cut fruit a few squirts keeps it looking fresh and bright until serving time.
- After I remove baked potatoes from the microwave oven, I immediately wipe down the inside of the microwave with a paper towel. The steam that builds up while the potatoes are baking helps remove cooked-on bits, so it's easy to clean my microwave without a lot of commercial products.
- I have a hard time getting the last of the mayonnaise out of the squeeze bottle. When it gets to that point, I add a tablespoon of milk to the bottle and shake it a few times. The remaining mayonnaise squeezes out easily.
  —*Melissa Mosness*

2 tablespoons olive *or* vegetable oil
1 package (8 ounces) imitation crabmeat, flaked
1 package (5 ounces) frozen cooked salad shrimp, thawed
1 tablespoon lemon juice
1/2 teaspoon pepper
1 jar (16 ounces) Alfredo sauce
1/2 cup frozen peas, thawed
1/4 cup shredded Parmesan cheese

Cook pasta according to package directions. Meanwhile, in a large skillet, saute garlic in oil until tender. Stir in the crab, shrimp, lemon juice and pepper. Cook and stir for 1 minute. Add Alfredo sauce and peas. Cook and stir until heated through. Drain pasta; top with the seafood mixture and sprinkle with Parmesan cheese. **Yield:** 4-6 servings.

Artichoke Tossed Salad

Ready in less than 15 minutes

2 cups *each* torn romaine, leaf and iceberg lettuce
1 jar (6-1/2 ounces) marinated artichoke hearts, drained and chopped
1 cup sliced fresh mushrooms
1 can (2-1/4 ounces) sliced ripe olives, drained
1/2 cup Italian salad dressing

In a salad bowl, combine the lettuce, artichokes, mushrooms and olives. Drizzle with salad dressing; toss to coat. Serve immediately. **Yield:** 6 servings.

Classic Lemon Bars

Ready in 1 hour or less

1/2 cup butter *or* margarine, softened
1/4 cup sugar
1 cup all-purpose flour
FILLING:
2 eggs
3/4 cup sugar
3 tablespoons lemon juice
2 tablespoons all-purpose flour
1/4 teaspoon baking powder
Confectioners' sugar

In a small mixing bowl, cream the butter and sugar; gradually add the flour. Press into an ungreased 8-in. square baking dish. Bake at 375° for 12 minutes. Cool slightly.

Meanwhile, in another mixing bowl, beat the eggs, sugar, lemon juice, flour and baking powder until frothy. Pour over warm crust. Bake for 15-20 minutes or until lightly browned. Cool on a wire rack. Dust with confectioners' sugar. Cut into bars. **Yield:** 9 servings.

Flame-Broiled Fare Suits Outdoor Lifestyle

ALTHOUGH Michelle Isenhoff enjoys her busy life in the city of Grand Rapids, Michigan, she much prefers the open spaces and fresh air of the countryside. So she and her husband, Troy, eagerly anticipate weekends when they can gather up daughter Emily and son Micah and head for the great outdoors. Troy does computer work for a pharmaceuticals company, and Michelle changed her career from substitute teacher to stay-at-home mom. "Although the children remain my highest priority, the kids and I are on the go more often than we're home," she says.

Michelle volunteers with her church, often with the little ones in tow. "I'm a director with our Bible Club, I sometimes play the flute and piano for services and I'm involved with the nursery program at church.

"In addition, I help cook and deliver meals to parishioners in need, and I volunteer at a local center that provides struggling mothers with baby food, clothes and toys."

Michelle's background in education comes in handy when she substitutes for Sunday school teachers.

"I also spend 1 day a week with a family that homeschools," she adds. "I help the mother with grading and lesson planning, and I occasionally evaluate the children's progress."

Michelle and Troy own a duplex and live in one side while renting out the other. "Maintaining a rental property has its challenges," she notes. "Making sure broken appliances are repaired, cleaning between occupants and advertising vacancies keeps me on my toes."

The energetic mom also baby-sits for two nephews weekly. "They are the same ages as our children, so when they visit, there are four toddlers in the house. I definitely have a new admiration for mothers of twins!" she says.

"When I have some free time and a quiet moment, I let my creative juices flow by writing short stories," explains Michelle. "I've even had a few items published recently."

By the time the weekend approaches, Michelle and her family eagerly anticipate camping somewhere far from the city.

"Nearly every weekend of the summer, we visit one of the campgrounds along Michigan's scenic lakeshore," she says.

"We all enjoy typical camping activities like hiking, fishing, swimming and sitting around the campfire. It's also fun to visit new campgrounds and explore the surrounding little towns."

The Isenhoffs certainly know how to make the most of warm weather. "We're an outdoor family," notes Michelle. "I keep our camping gear packed and our menus simple all summer long. In fact, I've adapted many of our favorite meals so they can be prepared while camping.

"Take Tarragon Chicken Bundles, for example. The foil-wrapped packets are convenient and make cleanup a snap. And with each serving wrapped individually, the ingredients can be adjusted to suit everyone's tastes."

Loaded with tender strips of chicken, yellow summer squash, zucchini, cherry tomatoes and other garden-fresh veggies, the robust entree will be a hit wherever you prepare it.

"The bundles are ideal for campfire cooking, but I also whip them up on the grill at home because Troy requests them often," Michelle says.

For a swift side dish, try Campfire Potatoes. "They are an excellent complement to the chicken," she recommends. "We look forward to the tender cheesy potatoes, which also cook easily in foil."

Michelle likes to complete summer meals with slices of Strawberry Pie. "The recipe came from my mother, and it's just as refreshing when made with peaches or blueberries," she suggests.

"I hope this simple menu helps families enjoy the outdoors as much as we do," Michelle says, "even if it's just in their own backyard."

Packing Camping Cuisine

- Inexpensive disposable storage containers are invaluable for carrying salads, pasta dishes and even desserts and snacks to the campsite. I also freeze and pack cooked ground beef in these compact containers to add to spaghetti sauce and use in other simple meals.

- I created a file of camping recipes by writing the recipes on colored index cards. Main courses are written on red cards, side dishes on green cards, etc. I punch a hole in the corner of each card, slip it onto a ring with the existing cards and store the whole thing in our picnic basket.

- Our picnic basket also holds some basic seasonings such as garlic powder, onion powder, salt, pepper and a few other staples. I keep a tiny notebook and pencil in the basket, so I can jot down anything I might run out of while away from home.
  —*Michelle Isenhoff*

Tarragon Chicken Bundles

(Also pictured on page 7)

Ready in 45 minutes or less

1 pound boneless skinless chicken breasts, cut into strips
2 medium carrots, julienned
1 medium yellow summer squash, julienned
1 medium zucchini, julienned
1 cup fresh mushrooms, halved
1 cup cherry tomatoes, halved
4 tablespoons butter *or* margarine
2 teaspoons dried tarragon
1 teaspoon salt
Pepper to taste

Divide the chicken strips and vegetables among four pieces of heavy-duty foil. Top each with 1 tablespoon butter, tarragon, salt and pepper. Fold foil over and seal tightly. Grill, covered, over medium heat for 15-20 minutes or until chicken juices run clear and vegetables are tender. **Yield:** 4 servings.

Campfire Potatoes

(Also pictured on page 7)

Ready in 45 minutes or less

5 medium potatoes, peeled and sliced
1/4 cup grated Parmesan cheese
2 teaspoons minced fresh parsley
3/4 teaspoon garlic powder
1/2 teaspoon salt

1/8 teaspoon pepper
1/4 cup butter *or* margarine, cubed

Place half of the potatoes on a large piece of heavy-duty foil. Sprinkle with Parmesan cheese, parsley, garlic powder, salt and pepper; dot with butter. Top with the remaining potatoes. Fold foil over and seal tightly. Grill, covered, over medium heat for 30-35 minutes or until the potatoes are tender. **Yield:** 4 servings.

Strawberry Pie

(Also pictured on page 6 and front cover)

Plan ahead...needs to chill

1 unbaked pastry shell (9 inches)
3/4 cup sugar
2 tablespoons cornstarch
1 cup water
1 package (3 ounces) strawberry gelatin
4 cups sliced fresh strawberries
Fresh mint, optional

Line unpricked pastry shell with a double thickness of heavy-duty foil. Bake at 450° for 8 minutes. Remove foil; bake 5 minutes longer. Cool on a wire rack.

In a saucepan, combine the sugar, cornstarch and water until smooth. Bring to a boil; cook and stir for 2 minutes or until thickened. Remove from the heat; stir in gelatin until dissolved. Refrigerate for 15-20 minutes or until slightly cooled. Meanwhile, arrange strawberries in the crust. Pour gelatin mixture over berries. Refrigerate until set. Garnish with mint if desired. **Yield:** 6-8 servings.

Fast Fabulous Feast Pampers Unexpected Guests

IT'S NO SURPRISE that Julia Trachsel can whip up a meal on a moment's notice. She's had plenty of practice.

The Victoria, British Columbia cook began stirring up cake batter at age 4 and remembers making her first solo batch of whole wheat bread when she was 7 years old.

"I misread the recipe and used salt instead of sugar," she recalls. "We each had one slice and tossed the rest into the yard for the hens. But even they didn't eat the salty morsels!"

Since then, Julia's skills in the kitchen have improved dramatically. These days, you'll likely find her baking a treat for her husband of 16 years.

"Derek is a pilot who flies firefighters to forest fire sites," Julia says. "As a captain, he is on call 12 hours a day during the spring and summer.

"We never know when he'll be called away, but when he is notified of a flight, I have to assemble, cook and serve his meal in 45 minutes—the amount of time he has before heading to the airport. So, tasty dishes that are quick are highly valued."

During the cold months, it's Derek's turn in the kitchen, and he prepares many of the couple's meals. "Regardless of who cooks, dinners must come together fast because I usually attend meetings after work," says Julia.

"I'm a career educator at the University of Victoria, where I help students prepare resumes, search for work and practice their interview skills," she says.

Julia is also an active member of two career development organizations and does freelance writing regarding job-search techniques.

"I love to cook, share recipes and collect old cookbooks," she says. "I've taught several cooking classes and wrote and edited two successful community cookbooks."

When Julia is responsible for dinner, she makes sit-down suppers every night of the week. When their schedules allow, the couple cuts back on kitchen time by helping each other. "If Derek makes the salad, vegetables or bread, I can focus on the main course."

In fact, similar teamwork played a part in the menu Julia shares here.

"Friends we hadn't seen for a while dropped by unexpectedly," she recalls. "They were on a tight schedule, and if I wanted them to stay for supper, I needed to fix something quickly. I didn't have time to make lasagna, so I created Spinach Lasagna Roll-Ups."

The savory spirals feature a creamy three-cheese filling and take advantage of convenience items such as jarred spaghetti sauce and frozen spinach. Plus, the enticing entree bakes in a fraction of the time that the traditional version takes.

"While I prepared the roll-ups, I asked my friend to toss together Pepper Cup Salad," Julia explains. In this side dish, a refreshing vegetable medley is coated with a simple dressing, then presented in crisp pepper halves.

"As my friend finished spooning the crunchy vegetables into the peppers, I worked on dessert," she says. Frozen pound cake, pudding mix and whipped topping made Five-Minute Trifle easy to assemble...and true to its name.

"Any type of cake can be used," Julia explains. "Then add your favorite berries or fruit and any flavor of pudding. Chocolate cake, canned cherry pie filling and chocolate pudding make a Black Forest variation that's delicious!

"Our friends left our home that night feeling cared for and well-fed," she says. "We all enjoyed the time this meal allowed us to spend together."

Spinach Lasagna Roll-Ups

Ready in 1 hour or less

12 lasagna noodles
 2 eggs, lightly beaten
2-1/2 cups ricotta cheese
2-1/2 cups shredded mozzarella cheese
 1/2 cup grated Parmesan cheese
 1 package (10 ounces) frozen chopped spinach, thawed and squeezed dry

Finding Freezer Space

I like to store foods in my chest freezer, but I'm not very tall, so it's hard to reach the items at the bottom...then I had a brain wave. Each year, I buy berries in bulk from local farms and freeze them. The berries come in deep, sturdy rectangular cardboard flats with slots on each end for carrying.

I placed each type of berry in its own resealable freezer bag, setting all of the bags into one flat. I then used one of the remaining flats to hold frozen seafood, another to hold nuts and so on.

The flats stack neatly inside of the freezer, and I don't have trouble pulling out the flats on the bottom of the stack. Now when I need something, I can reach it easily and find it quickly as similar foods are all stored together.

—Julia Trachsel

1/4 teaspoon salt
1/4 teaspoon pepper
1/4 teaspoon ground nutmeg
1 jar (26 ounces) meatless spaghetti
  sauce

Cook lasagna noodles according to package directions; drain. In a bowl, combine the eggs, cheeses, spinach, salt, pepper and nutmeg. Spread 1/3 cup cheese mixture over each noodle; carefully roll up.

Pour 1 cup spaghetti sauce into an ungreased 13-in. x 9-in. x 2-in. baking dish. Place roll-ups seam side down over sauce. Top with remaining sauce. Bake, uncovered, at 375° for 20-25 minutes or until heated through. **Yield:** 6 servings.

Pepper Cup Salad

Ready in 15 minutes or less

 Uses less fat, sugar or salt. Includes Nutritional Analysis and Diabetic Exchanges.

6 celery ribs, thinly sliced
2 medium tomatoes, diced
3 green onions, cut into 1/4-inch
  pieces
3 tablespoons vegetable *or* canola oil
1 tablespoon cider vinegar
3 large green peppers

In a bowl, combine the celery, tomatoes and onions. Combine oil and vinegar; drizzle over vegetables. With a sharp knife, cut peppers in half lengthwise; remove seeds. Cut a thin slice from bottom of pepper halves. Fill with vegetable mixture. Cover and refrigerate until serving. **Yield:** 6 servings.

Nutritional Analysis: One serving equals 102 calories, 7 g fat (1 g saturated fat), 0 cholesterol, 41 mg sodium, 9 g carbohydrate, 3 g fiber, 2 g protein. **Diabetic Exchanges:** 2 vegetable, 1 fat.

Five-Minute Trifle

2 cups cold milk
1 package (3.4 ounces) instant vanilla
  pudding mix
1 loaf (10-3/4 ounces) frozen pound
  cake, thawed
3 cups fresh *or* frozen raspberries,
  thawed
Whipped topping and additional raspberries

In a bowl, whisk milk and pudding mix for 2 minutes. Let stand for 2 minutes or until pudding is soft-set. Cut the cake into 1-in. cubes; place in a 2-qt. glass bowl. Top with raspberries and pudding.

Cover and refrigerate until serving. Garnish with whipped topping and additional raspberries. **Yield:** 6 servings.

Easy Weekday Dinner Is Dressy Enough for Company

STOP BY the Nevada, Ohio home of Tina Lust and you may find the energetic mom chasing after young son Clayton, working on the family farm, checking on a customer or canning home-grown produce.

"My husband, Tom, farms corn and soybeans with his dad, uncle and cousin," Tina says. "I also help out when I'm not busy selling corn and soybean seeds to area farmers."

For the past 3 years, Tina has run a home-based dealership for a national seed company.

In addition, Tina is a trustee with a Farm Bureau board and is a Certified Crop Advisor. She recently started a Farm Bureau advisory council with her husband and two friends, and she oversees the kitchen activities at an annual Farm Bureau breakfast for more than 1,000 people.

"I occasionally help with the nursery program during our church's Sunday service, play tennis when I get a chance, and enjoy scrapbooking and spending time in our flower and vegetable gardens," she adds.

With her garden bounty, Tina continues a family tradition. "I started canning pickles, relishes, jams and jellies several years ago, hoping to 'preserve' this disappearing art," she says.

"I'm so glad my mom showed me the canning techniques she learned from her mother, and both of my grandmothers gave me lots of helpful hints as well," Tina shares. "I recently compiled a scrapbook of canning and other heirloom recipes handwritten by my grandmothers."

Canned goods come in handy when Tina's designing weekly menus. "Time is of the essence when planning supper, especially on a weekday," she says. "Since I'm cooking for just the three of us, I often prepare a hearty casserole that serves several people and freeze the leftovers for later. Then I rely on canned fruits and vegetables to round out some of these meals.

Whether fixing dinner during the week or hosting a larger family gathering on a special occasion, Tina doesn't have hours to spend in the kitchen. That's why she depends on swift suppers like this one.

"I love to serve pork," says Tina. "Not only is it delicious, but it cooks up in no time. That's why Cranberry Pork Chops are popular in our house...particularly around the holidays.

"The entree is dressy enough for company yet can easily be served on weeknights. Tom likes the tender chops and I appreciate that the recipe calls for only five ingredients," she says.

While the pork browns on the stovetop, bottled French dressing and other convenience products make a sweet-tart sauce that comes together in the microwave with little fuss. "The sauce is also great on chicken," Tina adds.

Speedy Spinach Salad is the perfect accompaniment to the moist pork chops. "I created this recipe to make the most of the fresh spinach from our garden," she explains.

"I like using crushed crackers in place of croutons, but you can also top this salad with whatever fresh vegetables you have on hand."

Tina jazzes up refrigerated crescent rolls with sour cream and herbs to create Country Herb Croissants. "I keep the herbs on hand, but feel free to substitute dried cranberries, chopped walnuts and grated orange peel for rolls to serve with brunch," she suggests.

Tina tops off her meal with taste-tempting Pumpkin Pie Dessert, an easy alternative to the traditional treat served around the holidays.

"It's particularly quick when you need a special dessert," she says. "It doesn't require baking, which frees up the oven for the rest of your meal."

Cranberry Pork Chops

Ready in 30 minutes or less

4 boneless pork chops (about 1-1/2 pounds)
1 tablespoon vegetable oil
1 can (16 ounces) whole-berry cranberry sauce
1 cup French salad dressing
4 teaspoons dry onion soup mix

In a large skillet, cook pork chops in oil on both sides for 12-15 minutes or until juices run clear. Meanwhile, in a microwave-safe bowl, combine the cranberry sauce,

Extrordinary Organization

- Space is at a premium in my small kitchen, so I created a message center by attaching a cork board to the inside of a cupboard door. I tack my grocery list to it so it's always within easy reach, and I also keep important notes and messages there. This keeps them from cluttering up our refrigerator door and away from Clayton's little hands.
- All of my bulk dry ingredients, such as flour, sugar, cornmeal, baking mix and pasta, are kept in clear plastic storage containers. Not only does my pantry stay neat, but I can see at a glance when I'm running low.
  —*Tina Lust*

salad dressing and soup mix. Cover and microwave on high until heated through, about 2 minutes. Serve over pork chops. **Yield:** 4 servings.

Speedy Spinach Salad

Ready in 10 minutes or less

4 cups torn fresh spinach
1/2 cup shredded Monterey Jack cheese
1/2 cup coarsely crushed butter-flavored crackers (about 8)
Ranch salad dressing *or* dressing of your choice

Place spinach in a salad bowl; top with cheese and crackers. Serve with dressing. **Yield:** 4 servings.

Country Herb Croissants

Ready in 30 minutes or less

1 tube (8 ounces) refrigerated crescent rolls
1 tablespoon sour cream
1 tablespoon dried minced onion
1/2 teaspoon dried parsley flakes
1/2 teaspoon rubbed sage
1/4 teaspoon celery salt

Unroll crescent roll dough and separate into triangles. In a small bowl, combine the sour cream, onion, parsley, sage and celery salt; spread over dough. Roll up from the wide end and place pointed side down 2 in. apart on greased baking sheets. Curve ends down to form crescent shape. Bake at 375° for 11-13 minutes or until golden brown. Serve warm. **Yield:** 8 rolls.

Pumpkin Pie Dessert

Plan ahead…needs to chill

2-1/4 cups crushed butter-flavored crackers (about 50 crackers)
1/2 cup sugar
3/4 cup butter *or* margarine, melted
2 cups cold milk
2 packages (3.4 ounces *each*) instant vanilla pudding mix
1 can (15 ounces) solid-pack pumpkin
1 teaspoon pumpkin pie spice
1/2 teaspoon ground cinnamon
1/4 teaspoon ground ginger
1/4 teaspoon ground nutmeg
Whipped topping and chopped pecans

In a bowl, combine the cracker crumbs, sugar and butter. Press into a greased 13-in. x 9-in. x 2-in. dish; set aside. In a bowl, whisk milk and pudding mix for 2 minutes. Stir in pumpkin and spices. Spread over the crust. Refrigerate for 3 hours or until set. Garnish with whipped topping and nuts. **Yield:** 12-15 servings.

Chapter 2

WOULDN'T IT BE AWESOME, on busy days, to have an appealing assortment of menus that you can get on the table in only half an hour?

When your hectic schedule doesn't allow you to spend even an hour in the kitchen, rely on these 12 complete meals that you can put together in 30 minutes or less.

Each and every fast-to-fix favorite comes from the recipe file of a fellow busy cook. So your family is sure to enjoy each of these delicious dishes.

SPEEDY SUPPER. Clockwise from top right: Snowy Cherry Trifles, Asparagus Turkey Stir-Fry and Sweet Potato Pineapple Bake (all recipes on p. 33).

Microwave Hurries Hearty Menu

SATISFYING SUPPERS are simple to prepare when you take advantage of time-saving appliances. Our home economists compiled this meal that relies on your microwave and stove, so it can be made in half an hour.

"I love cooking in the microwave," declares Nicole Russman of Lincoln, Nebraska. "Once I really learned how to use my microwave, I found I can cook whole meals in it and they taste great.

"Here's a simple way to make individual meat loaves," she says. Moist Barbecued Onion Meat Loaves get plenty of flavor from barbecue sauce and dry onion soup mix.

"This recipe is also handy during the summer when I don't want to turn on the oven," Nicole says.

While the entree cooks, fix a speedy stovetop side dish of Spicy Carrots. "After my sister brought these carrots to a family gathering, my husband begged me to ask for the recipe," recalls Dawn Flanigan of Westville, Ohio.

Folks who like horseradish will enjoy the tangy-sweet combination. "It tastes too good to be so quick and easy," Dawn assures.

Since the meat loaves cook so quickly, your microwave will be free to fix sweet Coconut Macadamia Bars shared by Annette Lamle of Columbia City, Indiana.

"We found this recipe when working on our son Cody's 4-H microwave cooking project," she notes. "We made different versions of this treat 'til Cody decided which one he and his dad liked best. He received Reserve Grand Champion for his efforts."

Barbecued Onion Meat Loaves

    1 egg, beaten
 1/3 cup milk
    2 tablespoons plus 1/4 cup barbecue sauce, *divided*
 1/2 cup crushed stuffing
    1 tablespoon onion soup mix
1-1/4 pounds lean ground beef

In a bowl, combine the egg, milk, 2 tablespoons barbecue sauce, stuffing and onion soup mix. Crumble beef over mixture and mix well. Shape into five loaves; arrange around the edge of a microwave-safe dish.

Microwave, uncovered, on high for 6-7 minutes or until a meat thermometer reads 160°. Cover and let stand for 5-10 minutes. Top with the remaining barbecue sauce. **Yield:** 5 servings.

Editor's Note: This recipe was tested in an 850-watt microwave.

Spicy Carrots

3-1/2 cups fresh baby carrots
    2 tablespoons butter *or* margarine
    2 tablespoons sugar
    1 tablespoon prepared horseradish
    1 teaspoon dried parsley flakes
Salt and pepper to taste

Place carrots in a saucepan; cover with water. Bring to a boil. Reduce heat; cover and simmer 10-15 minutes or until tender. Drain; keep warm. In same pan, melt butter; stir in sugar, horseradish and parsley. Add carrots, salt and pepper; stir gently to coat. **Yield:** 5 servings.

Coconut Macadamia Bars

 1/3 cup butter *or* margarine
    1 cup graham cracker crumbs
    1 teaspoon sugar
1-1/4 cups flaked coconut, *divided*
 2/3 cup sweetened condensed milk
 1/2 cup chopped macadamia nuts
    1 cup vanilla *or* white chips
    1 teaspoon shortening

Place the butter in an 8-in. square microwave-safe dish. Cover and microwave on high until melted, about 1 minute. Stir in cracker crumbs and sugar; press firmly onto the bottom of the dish. Microwave, uncovered, on high for 1-1/2 minutes. Cool for 5 minutes.

In a bowl, combine 1 cup coconut, milk and nuts; spoon over the crust. Microwave, uncovered, on high for 1 minute. Rotate dish a half turn; cook 1 minute longer or until heated through.

In a small microwave-safe bowl, combine chips and shortening. Microwave, uncovered, at 70% power for 1 minute; stir. Heat 40 seconds longer or until melted, stirring once. Quickly pour over coconut mixture; spread evenly. Toast remaining coconut; sprinkle over top. Cool on a wire rack; cut into bars. **Yield:** 16 servings.

Editor's Note: This recipe was tested in an 850-watt microwave.

mother's years ago," she recalls. "I always have the ingredients on hand in case I need a quick dessert."

Cheesy Rice with Peas

✓ Uses less fat, sugar or salt. Includes Nutritional Analysis and Diabetic Exchanges.

2-1/4 cups cooked rice
   1 package (10 ounces) frozen peas, thawed
   1 jar (6 ounces) sliced mushrooms, drained
   6 ounces process cheese (Velveeta), cubed

In a bowl, combine all ingredients. Transfer to a greased 1-1/2-qt. baking dish. Cover and bake at 350° for 20 minutes or until heated through. Stir before serving. **Yield:** 6 servings.
   Nutritional Analysis: One 3/4-cup serving (prepared with reduced-fat process cheese) equals 167 calories, 3 g fat (2 g saturated fat), 12 mg cholesterol, 608 mg sodium, 24 g carbohydrate, 3 g fiber, 10 g protein. **Diabetic Exchanges:** 1-1/2 starch, 1 lean meat.

Crab Cake Sandwiches

   3 cans (6 ounces *each*) crabmeat, well drained
1/2 cup crushed butter-flavored crackers
   1 medium onion, chopped
1/2 cup chopped green pepper
1/4 cup mayonnaise
   1 egg
   1 teaspoon salt
   1 teaspoon ground mustard
   1 teaspoon Worcestershire sauce
1/2 teaspoon lemon juice
1/4 teaspoon garlic powder
1/4 cup all-purpose flour
1/4 cup vegetable oil
   6 hard rolls, split
Lettuce leaves, tomato and onion slices, optional

In a bowl, combine the crab, crushed crackers, onion, green pepper, mayonnaise, egg, salt, mustard, Worcestershire sauce, lemon juice and garlic powder. Shape into six 3-in. patties; coat with flour. In a large skillet, fry patties in oil for 5 minutes on each side or until browned. Serve on rolls with lettuce, tomato and onion if desired. **Yield:** 6 servings.

Creamy Fruit Medley

   1 carton (16 ounces) frozen whipped topping, thawed
   1 package (3 ounces) orange gelatin
   1 can (20 ounces) crushed pineapple, drained
   1 can (11 ounces) mandarin oranges, drained
   2 cups miniature marshmallows
1/2 cup chopped pecans

Set aside 1 cup whipped topping. Place remaining topping in a bowl; sprinkle with gelatin and stir until combined. Fold in pineapple, oranges, marshmallows and pecans. Garnish with reserved topping. **Yield:** 6 servings.

Fast Fare Features Seafood Sandwich

DAYS are filled with activity at Yvonne Bellomo's home in Ebensburg, Pennsylvania. The former teacher and her husband, Alan, have an energetic daughter, Brianna Lynn, who keeps them on their toes.
   Yet Yvonne finds time for church activities, woodworking projects, crafts, canning and preserving homegrown fruits and vegetables, and cooking, of course.
   Yvonne makes a point to make a sit-down dinner every night, even when Alan, who frequently travels for his job at the Department of Justice, can't join them. When he's home, the menu might feature the delicious dishes that Yvonne shares here.
   "I start by assembling Cheesy Rice with Peas, so it can bake while I work on the rest of the meal," she explains. "I usually use leftover cooked rice."
   "While it's in the oven, I prepare Crab Cake Sandwiches," Yvonne continues. She originally created the golden cakes to use up leftover crab, but you can use convenient canned crab.
   "I've also used the crab mixture to stuff mushroom caps and bake them as an appetizer," she adds.
   Last but not least, Yvonne tosses together an effortless sweet treat to cap off the meal. "I received the recipe for Creamy Fruit Medley from a friend of my

Lamb with Sauteed Veggies

3 tablespoons olive *or* vegetable oil, *divided*
2 tablespoons Dijon mustard
2 tablespoons balsamic *or* red wine vinegar
2 teaspoons dried thyme
2 garlic cloves, minced
1/4 teaspoon salt
1/4 teaspoon pepper
12 loin lamb chops (1 inch thick)
1 medium sweet red pepper, thinly sliced
2 small zucchini, thinly sliced
1 medium sweet onion, thinly sliced

In a small bowl, combine 2 tablespoons oil, mustard, vinegar, thyme, garlic, salt and pepper; set aside 1 tablespoon. Place the lamb chops on a broiler pan. Spread remaining mustard mixture over both sides of chops. Broil 4-6 in. from the heat for 5-6 minutes on each side or until a thermometer reaches 160°.

Meanwhile, in a large skillet, saute red pepper, zucchini and onion in remaining oil until crisp-tender. Stir in reserved mustard mixture; toss to coat. Serve with lamb chops. **Yield:** 6 servings.

Seasoned Couscous

2 cups water
1 tablespoon butter *or* margarine
1 tablespoon dried parsley flakes
2 teaspoons chicken bouillon granules
1/2 teaspoon dried minced onion
1/2 teaspoon dried basil
1/4 teaspoon pepper
1/8 teaspoon garlic powder
1 package (10 ounces) couscous

In a saucepan, combine the first eight ingredients; bring to a boil. Remove from the heat; stir in couscous. Cover and let stand for 5 minutes or until the liquid is absorbed. Fluff with a fork. **Yield:** 6 servings.

Brownie Sundaes

3/4 cup semisweet chocolate chips
1/2 cup evaporated milk
2 tablespoons brown sugar
2 teaspoons butter *or* margarine
1/2 teaspoon vanilla extract
6 prepared brownies (3 inches square)
6 scoops vanilla *or* chocolate fudge ice cream
1/2 cup chopped pecans

In a saucepan, combine the chocolate chips, evaporated milk and brown sugar. Cook and stir over medium heat for 5 minutes or until the chocolate is melted and sugar is dissolved. Remove from the heat; stir in butter and vanilla.

Spoon about 2 tablespoons warm chocolate sauce onto each dessert plate. Top with a brownie and a scoop of ice cream. Drizzle with additional chocolate sauce if desired. Sprinkle with pecans. **Yield:** 6 servings.

Luscious Lamb Speeds Up Supper

DAYS are jam-packed with activity for Ruth Lee, who lives in the close-knit farming village of Troy, Ontario.

Ruth and husband Doug run an electric fencing business that's open 24 hours a day, 7 days a week.

Besides sharing many of the duties of their home-based business, Doug also works at a local brewery.

"Since he works there full-time, it's usually my job to repair machines as well as sell supplies, do estimates and install fences," Ruth explains.

She also belongs to an agricultural society and chairs a public-speaking competition. "I help with church dinners, work on various committees and can over 150 jars of homegrown produce," she adds.

But spending time with family is important to Ruth, too. "We have two grown children and six grandchildren. They love to help in the kitchen when I'm preparing meals for get-togethers."

One of the streamlined suppers Ruth might serve at a family function is Lamb with Sauteed Veggies.

"My parents raised sheep for more than 30 years, so I have good lamb recipes," she says. "Not only are these chops tender, but they cook quickly."

While the lamb broils, Ruth sautes red pepper and zucchini to accompany it.

"People always comment on this great combination," she assures. "Partner it with delicious and speedy Seasoned Couscous, and you have a winner."

Ruth caps off dinner with Brownie Sundaes. "With prepared brownies, I can fix this sweet treat in a flash," she notes.

Packaged Products Help Trim Time

DELICIOUS DINNERS are only minutes away when you take advantage of frozen foods, canned vegetables and other pantry staples.

Our home economists combined the following reader recipes into this must-try menu. Thanks to popular convenience foods, this family-tested fare can be ready in just half an hour.

When time is tight, Beverly Menser whips up Pasta Meatball Soup in her Madisonville, Kentucky home.

The savory Italian soup relies on items most cooks have on hand, including pasta, prepared spaghetti sauce, canned and frozen vegetables and frozen meatballs. The chunky mixture needs to simmer for only minutes before it can be ladled into bowls.

Couple the spirit-warming specialty with crunchy Herbed French Bread. Karin Bailey of Golden, Colorado adds a little pizzazz to a store-bought loaf with only three ingredients. Freshly minced herbs liven up each buttery bite of the broiled slices.

Round out the fast feast with quick-to-fix Creamy Lettuce Salad.

"This recipe is a family favorite I recall my mom serving often when I was growing up," shares Jacquie Troutman of Zephyrhills, Florida. "She particularly liked it because it was so easy to make and called for things she usually had on hand."

A sweet dressing tops packaged salad greens that are dressed up with hard-cooked eggs, tomato and onion.

Once the salad's tossed, all you have to do is call your family to the table and sit down to a great meal.

Pasta Meatball Soup

1 cup uncooked spiral *or* shell pasta
32 frozen Italian meatballs (about 1 pound), thawed
2 cans (14-1/2 ounces *each*) chicken broth
1 can (28 ounces) diced tomatoes, undrained
1-1/2 cups frozen sliced carrots, thawed
1 can (16 ounces) kidney beans, rinsed and drained
1 jar (14 ounces) meatless spaghetti sauce
1 jar (4-1/2 ounces) sliced mushrooms, drained
1 cup frozen peas

Cook pasta according to package directions. Meanwhile, combine the remaining ingredients in a soup kettle or Dutch oven. Bring to a boil; cover and simmer for 5 minutes. Drain pasta and add to the soup; heat through. **Yield:** 10 servings (3 quarts).

Herbed French Bread

1 loaf (1 pound) French bread
1/2 cup butter *or* margarine, softened
1/4 cup minced fresh parsley
1/4 cup minced chives

Cut bread into 1-in. slices. In a small bowl, combine the butter, parsley and chives; spread over one side of each slice of bread. Place buttered side up on an ungreased baking sheet. Broil 4 in. from the heat for 1-2 minutes or until golden brown. **Yield:** 10 servings.

Creamy Lettuce Salad

3 hard-cooked eggs
1 package (16 ounces) ready-to-serve salad greens
1 medium tomato, diced
1/4 cup diced onion
DRESSING:
3/4 cup mayonnaise *or* salad dressing
3 to 4 tablespoons milk
2 tablespoons sugar
2 tablespoons cider vinegar

Cut one egg into wedges for garnish. Dice remaining eggs. In a salad bowl, combine the greens, tomato, onion and diced eggs. In a jar with a tight-fitting lid, combine the dressing ingredients; shake well. Pour over salad and toss to coat. Garnish with egg wedges. Serve immediately. **Yield:** 10 servings.

Turn to Your Stove For Speedy Dinner

YOU CAN CALL your family to dinner early when you serve this streamlined menu of reader recipes compiled by our Test Kitchen. By using your stovetop rather than your oven, you can have these skillet specialties on the table in half an hour or less.

Creamy Tortellini Carbonara from Cathy Croyle calls for only five ingredients and comes together in mere moments.

The Davidsville, Pennsylvania cook simmers a rich bacon and Parmesan cheese sauce in one pan while boiling packaged tortellini to perfection in another. Then she combines the two to create a memorable main dish.

"Add more cheese or additional parsley to the sauce to fit your family's taste," Cathy recommends.

Serve this classic pasta toss with Apricot-Glazed Green Beans from Nancy Mueller. "I like to add a little extra flavor to homegrown beans, and this is one of our favorite treatments," she explains from Bloomington, Minnesota.

Apricot preserves make the simple yet tasty coating for the veggies. Try this side dish alongside most any entree whenever time is tight.

Complete this made-in-minutes meal with Fruit Medley. "This recipe is an adaptation of a fruit salad from my husband's aunt," says Becky Hughes of Las Cruces, New Mexico.

"The original recipe calls for a homemade glaze, but I use canned peach pie filling to hurry along preparation.

"Since my husband, son and I have busy schedules, we are often in a rush to get dinner on the table so we can sit down and eat together. This can be whipped up in no time and makes a great side salad or dessert," she says.

"You can even mix the pie filling with the fruit early in the day and keep it in the refrigerator. Then just stir in the nuts and you're ready to bring it to the table," Becky suggests. "It disappears quickly at potlucks, too."

Tortellini Carbonara

　8　bacon strips, cooked and crumbled
　1　cup heavy whipping cream
1/2　cup minced fresh parsley
1/2　cup grated Parmesan *or* Romano cheese
　1　package (9 ounces) refrigerated cheese tortellini

In a large saucepan, combine the bacon, cream, parsley and cheese; cook until heated through. Meanwhile, prepare tortellini according to package directions; drain and transfer to a serving bowl. Drizzle cheese sauce over tortellini and toss to coat. Serve immediately. **Yield:** 4 servings.

Apricot-Glazed Green Beans

　1　pound fresh green beans, cut into 3-inch pieces
1/3　cup apricot preserves
　1　tablespoon butter *or* margarine
1/4　teaspoon salt

Place beans in a steamer basket in a saucepan over 1 in. of water. Bring to a boil; cover and steam for 7-8 minutes or until crisp-tender.

In a microwave-safe bowl, combine the preserves, butter and salt. Heat, uncovered, on high for 30 seconds or until butter is melted. Transfer beans to a serving bowl; add apricot mixture and toss to coat. **Yield:** 4 servings.

Fruit Medley

　1　can (21 ounces) peach pie filling
　1　can (20 ounces) pineapple chunks, drained
　1　can (11 ounces) mandarin oranges, drained
　1　jar (10 ounces) maraschino cherries, drained
　2　medium firm bananas, sliced
1/2　cup chopped pecans

In a bowl, combine the pie filling, pineapple, oranges, cherries and bananas. Cover and refrigerate. Just before serving, stir in pecans. **Yield:** 8-10 servings.

fried versions but with less mess," she reports.

Rounding out the meal are Breaded Tomato Slices. Garden-fresh tomatoes are sliced, breaded and browned in a skillet for a flavorful change of pace. "They're crunchy and well seasoned," she adds. "The mozzarella cheese perfectly complements the simple, tasty coating."

Patricia says cleanup for this dinner is quick, too. "Keith and I make a good team in the kitchen. I do all of the cooking and he does all of the dishes!"

Italian Beef Sandwiches

1 can (14-1/2 ounces) beef broth
2 garlic cloves, minced
1 teaspoon dried oregano
1/8 teaspoon pepper
1 medium green pepper, thinly sliced into rings
1 pound thinly sliced deli roast beef
6 hoagie *or* submarine sandwich buns, split

In a skillet, bring the broth, garlic, oregano and pepper to a boil. Add green pepper. Reduce heat; simmer, uncovered, until tender, about 5 minutes. Remove green pepper with a slotted spoon; keep warm.

Return broth to a boil. Add roast beef; cover and remove from the heat. Let stand for 2 minutes or until heated through. Place beef and green pepper on buns; serve with broth for dipping. **Yield:** 6 servings.

Seasoned Oven Fries

6 medium baking potatoes
2 tablespoons butter *or* margarine, melted
2 tablespoons vegetable oil
1 teaspoon seasoned salt

Cut each potato lengthwise into thirds; cut each portion into thirds. In a large resealable plastic bag, combine the butter, oil and seasoned salt. Add potatoes; shake to coat. Place in a single layer on a greased baking sheet. Bake, uncovered, at 450° for 20-25 minutes or until tender, turning once. **Yield:** 6 servings.

Breaded Tomato Slices

1/2 cup seasoned bread crumbs
1 tablespoon finely chopped green onion
1 tablespoon grated Parmesan cheese
1 teaspoon salt
1 teaspoon Italian seasoning
1/4 cup milk
4 medium tomatoes, cut into 1/2-inch slices
2 tablespoons olive *or* vegetable oil
1/3 to 1/2 cup shredded mozzarella cheese

In a shallow bowl, combine the bread crumbs, onion, Parmesan cheese, salt and Italian seasoning; mix well. Place milk in another bowl. Dip tomato slices in milk, then coat with crumb mixture. In a skillet, heat oil. Fry tomato slices for 2 minutes on each side or until golden brown. Sprinkle with mozzarella cheese. **Yield:** 6 servings.

Swift Sandwich Makes Meaty Meal

EVEN THOUGH Patricia and Keith Fredericks reside in Oak Creek—a city located in southeastern Wisconsin—you'll likely find them at their log cabin in the northern part of the state.

"That's where we spend our weekends," notes Patricia. "I go there to relax, ride our paddleboat, read and do needlework.

"Our children, Mandy and Matthew, are grown and on their own, but they often join us at the cabin," she says.

In order to keep weekends free for their treks up north, the couple stays busy during the week. Keith works in the commercial arts industry and Patricia is a school secretary. "I also work some evenings as a supervisor for a local research company," she says.

"Because my hours vary, Keith and I don't always have dinner at the same time. That's why it's important to plan meals that reheat well," she explains. "When we do eat together, I depend on recipes that need little preparation.

"Italian Beef Sandwiches are ready in a snap. I simply stop at the deli on the way home from work to pick up sliced roast beef and sandwich buns." Served with an au jus created by dressing up canned beef broth, the pepper-topped sandwiches make a perfect weeknight dinner.

For a swift side dish, Patricia bakes Seasoned Oven Fries. "These potato wedges are as tasty as the deep-

will your family request them again, but you'll appreciate the time you saved!

Herbed Orange Roughy

    4 orange roughy *or* red snapper fillets (6 ounces *each*)
  1/3 cup lemon juice
1-1/2 teaspoons minced fresh parsley
1-1/2 teaspoons minced fresh basil *or* 1/2 teaspoon dried basil
  1/2 teaspoon salt
  1/4 teaspoon garlic powder
  1/2 cup thinly sliced fresh mushrooms, optional
  1/8 teaspoon paprika

Place the fish fillets in a single layer in a large skillet. Sprinkle with lemon juice, parsley, basil, salt and garlic powder. Place mushrooms over fish if desired. Bring to a boil. Reduce heat; cover and simmer for 6-8 minutes or until fish flakes easily with a fork. Sprinkle with paprika. **Yield:** 4 servings.
    Nutritional Analysis: One serving equals 123 calories, 1 g fat (trace saturated fat), 34 mg cholesterol, 401 mg sodium, 2 g carbohydrate, trace fiber, 25 g protein. **Diabetic Exchange:** 4 very lean meat.

Green 'n' Gold Veggies

    2 cups cut fresh green beans (1-inch pieces)
  1/3 cup water
  1/4 cup thinly sliced green onions
  1/4 cup butter *or* margarine
1-1/2 cups frozen corn, thawed
  3/4 teaspoon salt
  1/2 teaspoon sugar
  1/2 teaspoon celery salt
  1/2 teaspoon paprika

In a large saucepan, bring beans and water to a boil. Reduce heat; cover and simmer for 5-7 minutes or until crisp-tender. Meanwhile, in a large skillet, saute onions in butter until tender. Stir in the corn, salt, sugar, celery salt and paprika. Drain beans; add to corn mixture. Cook and stir for 4 minutes or until heated through. **Yield:** 4 servings.

Cake with Lemon Sauce

    1 package (3 ounces) cream cheese, softened
1-3/4 cups cold milk
    1 package (3.4 ounces) instant lemon pudding mix
    4 slices pound cake *or* angel food cake
Fresh raspberries, optional

In a small mixing bowl, beat the cream cheese until smooth. Add milk and pudding mix; beat for 2 minutes or until smooth and thickened. Serve with cake. Garnish with raspberries if desired. **Yield:** 4 servings.

Keep Cool with Stovetop Cuisine

WARM SUMMER EVENINGS call for dinners that don't require hours in a hot kitchen. So our home economists put together the following reader recipes to create a mouth-watering menu that's both tempting and time-saving.

Because these dishes combine fresh vegetables and herbs with convenient packaged and frozen goods, the entire meal can be ready in a half hour.

Family-pleasing fish is never long in the making for Carla Weeks. Her Herbed Orange Roughy simmers quickly on the stove, keeping her St. Charles, Illinois home cool.

"My mother created this main dish, which is low in fat and calories," Carla notes. "I often use fresh scrod instead of orange roughy."

Serve the fast fillets alongside Green 'n' Gold Veggies shared by Opal Sanders of Glouster, Ohio. The buttery skillet side dish features beans, corn and green onions and works well with nearly any main course.

"I use canned corn and green beans when I'm really in a hurry," says Opal. "Fresh corn is nice when it's available, too. Regardless, the results are always well received at get-togethers."

Refreshing Cake with Lemon Sauce completes the delightful dinner. "This is a family favorite on hot summer nights," shares Claire Dion from Canterbury, Connecticut.

Cream cheese, milk and pudding mix are all that's needed for the sunny sauce drizzled over prepared pound cake and topped with a few berries.

"Sponge cake dessert shells instead of sliced pound cake are an easy option," Claire suggests.

Serve up these simple selections soon. Not only

Savory Stir-Fry Swiftly Satisfies

VARIETY is the spice of life for Lynn Mazza. The Colchester, Vermont mom likes diversity in the projects she volunteers for...as well as the meals she serves.

"While my husband, Mike, is busy at our auto parts store, I'm often working at the school our son, Erik, attends," she explains. "I'm a part-time substitute teacher and involved with a children's reading program there."

In addition, Lynn is president of the school's parent-teacher organization and serves on a superintendent's advisory committee. "I also like being involved with our church," she adds.

Furthermore, Lynn helps out at a nearby hospital and takes the family dog to visit an adult care program.

Despite such a full schedule, Lynn makes no less than five family meals a week. "I like to make a healthy main course and serve several veggies at each meal. But I try not to prepare the same thing for dinner more than once every 2 or 3 months," she says.

When fixing the menu shared here, Lynn starts with Orange Chicken Skillet, a succulent stir-fry that spotlights tender chicken and fresh vegetables.

"While the chicken is cooking, you can get the salad ready," suggests Lynn. Mixed greens, sliced cucumber and crunchy sunflower kernels make Sunflower Tossed Salad a certain success.

Smile-producing Ice Cream Sandwiches end this fast feast. "You need just two ingredients for these frosty treats," Lynn says.

The cookies can bake while you work on the rest of the meal, then assemble the sandwiches and pop them in the freezer until it's time for dessert.

Orange Chicken Skillet

1 pound boneless skinless chicken breasts, cut into 1-inch strips
2 medium carrots, thinly sliced
1 medium green pepper, chopped
1 medium onion, thinly sliced
2 tablespoons olive *or* vegetable oil
5 teaspoons all-purpose flour
1 tablespoon brown sugar
1 cup orange juice
1/3 cup chili sauce
Hot cooked pasta

In a large skillet, stir-fry the chicken, carrots, green pepper and onion in oil until chicken juices run clear and vegetables are crisp-tender. In a small bowl, combine the flour and brown sugar; stir in orange juice and chili sauce until smooth. Add to skillet. Bring to a boil; cook and stir for 2 minutes or until thickened. Serve over pasta. **Yield:** 4 servings.

Sunflower Tossed Salad

4 cups torn mixed salad greens
1 small cucumber, sliced
2 tablespoons sunflower kernels
TART VINAIGRETTE:
1/3 cup olive *or* vegetable oil
3 tablespoons balsamic *or* cider vinegar
2 tablespoons white wine vinegar *or* additional cider vinegar
1 tablespoon soy sauce
1 tablespoon Dijon mustard
1 tablespoon minced fresh thyme *or* 1 teaspoon dried thyme
1 garlic clove, minced

In a salad bowl, combine the greens, cucumber and sunflower kernels. In a jar with a tight-fitting lid, combine the vinaigrette ingredients; shake well. Pour over salad and toss to coat. **Yield:** 4 servings.

Ice Cream Sandwiches

1 tube (18 ounces) refrigerated chocolate chip cookie dough
4 cups peanut butter cup ice cream *or* flavor of your choice

Bake cookies according to package directions. Cool on baking sheets for 1-2 minutes before removing to wire racks. Cool for 5 minutes. Place 1/2 cup of ice cream on the bottoms of eight cookies; top each with another cookie and press down gently. Wrap each in plastic wrap. Freeze until serving. **Yield:** 8 servings.

Breakfast's Ready In Blink of an Eye

THE MOST IMPORTANT meal of the day just got easier! Thanks to this compilation of reader recipes selected by our home economists, you can beat the morning rush and serve a great breakfast.

Catherine Fontana kicks off the meal with full-flavored Mushroom Sausage Omelets. "When our children were young, I prepared this recipe regularly because it's fast and easy," says the Lake Villa, Illinois cook.

Loaded with cheese, Italian sausage, fresh mushrooms and garlic, the recipe makes two omelets, but the ingredients can easily be increased to suit larger families.

"Sometimes I leave out the sausage for a delicious meatless entree," Catherine shares.

Serve the hearty omelets alongside Strawberry Fruit Dip from Pat Habiger. The Spearville, Kansas cook dresses up strawberry cream cheese with honey and a touch of lemon peel. The creamy creation is perfect for dipping berries, sliced kiwi, cubed melon or most any fruit.

An easy addition to morning meals and brunch buffets, the combo also makes an appealing after-school snack or pretty party platter.

From Petersburg, West Virginia, Maureen Dongoski contributes Cinnamon Bread Shapes. The four-ingredient treats rely on convenient refrigerated breadstick dough and feature a tasty topping.

After the dough is dipped in a mixture of pecans, sugar and cinnamon, it can be tied in simple knots, coiled like cinnamon rolls or twisted into a variety of fun shapes. Then simply pop them in the oven until golden.

Wake up your family with these speedy sunrise selections soon. Everyone will be glad you did.

Mushroom Sausage Omelets

10 eggs
1/4 to 1/2 cup minced fresh parsley
1/2 cup grated Parmesan cheese
2 to 4 garlic cloves, minced
1/4 teaspoon pepper
2 tablespoons olive *or* vegetable oil
1/2 cup bulk Italian sausage, cooked and drained
1/2 cup sliced fresh mushrooms

In a large bowl, whisk eggs. Stir in the parsley, Parmesan cheese, garlic and pepper. Coat a 10-in. skillet with 1 tablespoon oil; place over medium-low heat. Add half of the egg mixture, sausage and mushrooms. As eggs set, lift edges, letting uncooked portion flow underneath. When the eggs are completely set, fold omelet over. Repeat for second omelet. **Yield:** 2 omelets (4 servings).

Strawberry Fruit Dip

✓ Uses less fat, sugar or salt. Includes Nutritional Analysis and Diabetic Exchanges.

1 carton (8 ounces) whipped strawberry cream cheese
1-1/2 teaspoons honey
1 teaspoon milk
1/2 teaspoon grated lemon peel
Assorted fresh fruit

In a small mixing bowl, beat the cream cheese, honey, milk and lemon peel. Serve with fruit. Refrigerate leftovers. **Yield:** 3/4 cup.

Nutritional Analysis: 2 tablespoons of dip (prepared with reduced-fat cream cheese and fat-free milk) equals 50 calories, 0 fat (0 saturated fat), 6 mg cholesterol, 253 mg sodium, 8 g carbohydrate, 1 g fiber, 5 g protein. **Diabetic Exchange:** 1/2 fruit.

Cinnamon Bread Shapes

1/4 cup finely chopped pecans
3 tablespoons sugar
1/2 teaspoon ground cinnamon
1 tube (11 ounces) refrigerated breadsticks

In a shallow bowl, combine the pecans, sugar and cinnamon. Separate breadsticks; dip into pecan mixture. Shape as desired. Place on a baking sheet lightly coated with nonstick cooking spray. Bake at 375° for 13-15 minutes or until golden brown. Immediately remove from pan. Serve warm. **Yield:** 1 dozen.

and they're out of the oven in just 10 minutes.

While the ham is baking, Mildred tosses together Avocado Fruit Salad. "This is simply delish!" she notes. "I'm glad a friend gave me the recipe. My family loves it...and so do I."

Besides the unusual addition of avocados, the refreshing medley includes chopped apple, sliced banana, grape halves and mandarin oranges. A light lemon dressing gives the final touch to this swift salad, making the sensational supper ready to serve.

Crunchy Ice Cream Dessert

2 cups crushed Rice Chex
2/3 cup packed brown sugar
1/2 cup chopped peanuts
1/2 cup flaked coconut
1/2 cup butter *or* margarine, melted
1/2 gallon vanilla ice cream*

In a bowl, combine the cereal, brown sugar, peanuts and coconut. Drizzle with butter; stir until combined. Press half of the mixture into an ungreased 13-in. x 9-in. x 2-in. dish. Cut ice cream into 3/4-in.-thick slices; arrange evenly over crust. Top with remaining crumb mixture; press down lightly. Cover and freeze until serving. **Yield:** 12-15 servings.

*Editor's Note: Purchase a rectangular-shaped package of ice cream for the easiest cutting.

Hawaiian Ham Steaks

2 boneless fully cooked ham steaks (about 1 pound *each*)
2 tablespoons brown sugar
1 tablespoon Dijon mustard
6 pineapple slices

Cut each ham steak into three serving-size pieces. Combine brown sugar and mustard; spread over ham. Top each piece with a pineapple slice. Place in an ungreased 15-in. x 10-in. x 1-in. baking pan. Bake at 375° for 10 minutes or until heated through. **Yield:** 6 servings.

Avocado Fruit Salad

3 medium avocados, pitted and peeled
2 tablespoons lemon juice
1/2 cup plain yogurt
2 tablespoons honey
1 teaspoon grated lemon peel
1 medium apple, chopped
1 medium firm banana, cut into
1/4-inch slices
1 cup halved seedless grapes
1 can (11 ounces) mandarin oranges, drained

Cut avocados into chunks; toss with lemon juice. Drain, reserving the lemon juice; set avocados aside. For dressing, in a small bowl, combine the yogurt, honey, lemon peel and reserved lemon juice. In a large bowl, toss the apple, banana, grapes, oranges and avocados. Serve with dressing. **Yield:** 6 servings.

Ham Steak Streamlines Supper

COOKING DINNER for her family without spending hours in the kitchen is old hat for Mildred Sherrer.

The Fort Worth, Texas mom has three sons—John, Henry and Van Craig—all married with families of their own.

For years, Mildred taught first through sixth grade, volunteered as a Sunday school instructor and gave students special help with various subjects over the summer. Even with this schedule, Mildred prepared family dinners nightly.

"Now that I'm retired, I fill my days by reading, occasionally helping out at church, spending time with my seven grandchildren and cooking," she explains.

With the 30-minute menu Mildred offers here, you can follow her lead and get supper on the table in a snap.

She starts by preparing dessert first. Crunchy Ice Cream Dessert features vanilla ice cream sandwiched by sweet layers of cereal, peanuts and coconut.

Mildred next turns her attention to the easy main course. Hawaiian Ham Steaks call for only four items

Fancy Fare Leaves You Time to Spare

WHEN the holidays are just around the corner, fuss-free meals are a busy cook's dream come true. That's why our home economists combined the following recipes into this streamlined supper that can be on the table in a half hour or less.

The entree and side dish depend on everyday ingredients, so you can avoid last-minute trips to the store. And if you keep a pound cake in the freezer, you'll have a head start on the luscious dessert.

From High Point, North Carolina, Barbara Arbuckle shares her secret for moist Curry Chicken Breasts. The palate-pleasing sauce combines the savory flavors of curry powder, Worcestershire sauce, garlic, chili sauce, onion and hot pepper sauce. Prepared on the stovetop, it's ready in no time.

For an easy accompaniment to the tender chicken, try pretty Lemon-Pepper Veggies. The must-try medley submitted by Linda Bernhagen of Plainfield, Illinois is a breeze to make in the microwave.

"Guests are surprised that this quick dish is so flavorful," says Linda.

Karen Gardiner completes the made-in-moments meal with Quick Coffee Torte. "This easy-to-prepare dessert really hits the spot," says the Eutaw, Alabama cook.

Curry Chicken Breasts

✓ Uses less fat, sugar or salt. Includes Nutritional Analysis and Diabetic Exchanges.

4 boneless skinless chicken breast halves (4 ounces *each***)**

1 tablespoon vegetable *or* canola oil
1/4 cup Worcestershire sauce
4 teaspoons chili sauce
1 to 2 teaspoons curry powder
1 teaspoon garlic salt *or* garlic powder
1/4 teaspoon hot pepper sauce
1/4 cup chopped onion
Hot cooked rice

In a large skillet, brown chicken on both sides in oil. In a bowl, combine the Worcestershire sauce, chili sauce, curry powder, garlic salt and hot pepper sauce. Pour over chicken. Add onion. Reduce heat; cover and simmer for 9-11 minutes or until chicken juices run clear. Serve with rice. **Yield:** 4 servings.

Nutritional Analysis: One serving (prepared with garlic powder; calculated without rice) equals 180 calories, 5 g fat (1 g saturated fat), 66 mg cholester-ol, 325 mg sodium, 6 g carbohydrate, trace fiber, 26 g protein. **Diabetic Exchanges:** 3 lean meat, 1 vegetable.

Lemon-Pepper Veggies

2 cups fresh broccoli florets
2 cups cauliflowerets
1 cup sliced carrots
2 tablespoons water
4-1/2 teaspoons butter *or* margarine, melted
1 teaspoon lemon-pepper seasoning
1/2 teaspoon garlic powder

In a microwave-safe bowl, combine the broccoli, cauliflower, carrots and water. Cover and microwave on high for 4-7 minutes or until crisp-tender; drain. Combine the remaining ingredients; drizzle over vegetables and toss to coat. **Yield:** 4 servings.

Editor's Note: This recipe was tested in an 850-watt microwave.

Quick Coffee Torte

1/4 cup sugar
1/4 cup water
1 tablespoon instant coffee granules
1-1/2 teaspoons butter *or* margarine
1/8 teaspoon rum extract
1 frozen pound cake (10-3/4 ounces), thawed
1 carton (8 ounces) frozen whipped topping, thawed
Grated chocolate, optional

In a small saucepan, combine the sugar, water and coffee. Bring to a boil; cook for 3 minutes, stirring occasionally. Remove from the heat; stir in butter and rum extract. Cool slightly.

Split cake into three horizontal layers. Place bottom layer on a serving plate. Brush with about 1 tablespoon coffee mixture; spread with 1 cup whipped topping. Repeat layers. Brush remaining coffee mixture over cut side of remaining cake layer; place coffee side down over topping. Spread remaining whipped topping over top of torte. Garnish with grated chocolate if desired. Chill until serving. **Yield:** 6-8 servings.

Seasonal Supper Stands Out

WHEN it comes to adventure, May Evans often finds it in the kitchen. "I love to cook and I love to try new recipes, even ones that have unusual names," she explains. "They usually turn out wonderfully."

May lives in the small rural town of Corinth, Kentucky with her husband, Scotty, and daughter Ashley.

"I've been a stay-at-home mom for a few years now and am very happy to have the extra time to spend with my family," she says.

May prepares sit-down dinners every night. And no matter how adventurous she gets, she keeps one thing in mind. "Ashley can be a picky eater, so it's important to me that meals I plan appeal to all of us," she explains.

The 30-minute menu May shares here is perfect for the holidays or any time of year.

"I start out by fixing dessert," she says. Snowy Cherry Trifles rely on store-bought angel food cake, canned pie filling and a few other convenience items for swift preparation.

Once the dessert is in the fridge, May easily assembles her Sweet Potato Pineapple Bake and pops it in the oven. "Not only is it yummy, but it's quick because it calls for canned yams," she says. "I got the idea from my sister...I just added the pineapple."

With the sweet potatoes baking, May begins fixing Asparagus Turkey Stir-Fry. "When people try this, they ask me for the recipe, just as I did when I first tasted it at the home of a church friend," she recalls.

Coated with a delicious lemon sauce, this simple skillet dish is sure to satisfy on the busiest of nights.

"It's an excellent way to use up turkey left over from Thanksgiving or Christmas," adds May. "I hope everyone will enjoy these tempting recipes as much as we do."

Snowy Cherry Trifles

4 ounces cream cheese, softened
1/4 cup sugar
2 tablespoons milk
1-3/4 cups whipped topping
4 cups cubed angel food cake
1 cup cherry pie filling
1/4 teaspoon almond extract

In a large mixing bowl, beat the cream cheese and sugar. Add milk; beat until smooth. Fold in whipped topping and cake cubes. Transfer to individual serving dishes. Combine pie filling and almond extract; spoon over cake mixture. Refrigerate until serving. **Yield:** 4 servings.

Sweet Potato Pineapple Bake

1 can (29 ounces) cut sweet potatoes, drained
1 can (8 ounces) crushed pineapple
3 tablespoons chopped pecans
2 tablespoons brown sugar
2 tablespoons butter *or* margarine, melted
3/4 cup miniature marshmallows

In a large bowl, mash the sweet potatoes. Stir in pineapple, pecans, brown sugar and butter. Transfer to a greased 2-qt. baking dish. Bake, uncovered, at 375° for 20 minutes. Sprinkle with marshmallows. Bake 5 minutes longer or until marshmallows are lightly browned. **Yield:** 4 servings.

Asparagus Turkey Stir-Fry

2 teaspoons cornstarch
1/4 cup chicken broth
1 tablespoon lemon juice
1 teaspoon soy sauce
1 pound turkey breast tenderloin, cut into 1/2-inch strips
1 garlic clove, minced
2 tablespoons vegetable oil, *divided*
1 pound fresh asparagus, trimmed and cut into 1-1/2-inch pieces
1 jar (2 ounces) sliced pimientos, drained

In a small bowl, combine the cornstarch, broth, lemon juice and soy sauce until smooth; set aside. In a large skillet or wok, stir-fry turkey and garlic in 1 tablespoon oil until meat is no longer pink; remove and keep warm.

Stir-fry asparagus in remaining oil until crisp-tender. Add pimientos. Stir broth mixture and add to the pan; cook and stir for 1 minute or until thickened. Return turkey to the pan; heat through. **Yield:** 4 servings.

Chapter 3

WHY NOT MAKE your next ordinary get-together with family and friends extraordinary?

Our *Quick Cooking* Test Kitchen staff has done the planning for you by creating six easy menus so you can have a fun, festive and fuss-free theme party.

From sensational sleepover fare, an appealing Easter brunch and a marvelous morning meal for Mother's Day, to a beachside supper, a back-to-school buffet and a super snack for Christmas Eve, you can easily create long-remembered occasions for your relatives and friends with just a short time spent in the kitchen.

BEAUTIFUL BREAKFAST. Crab Quiche, Blooming Sweet Rolls, and Butterscotch Coffee (all recipes on p. 41).

Successful Sleepovers Start with Festive Fare

FUN FINGER FOODS are as important to slumber parties as giggling, music and pillow fights. But fixing must-have morsels that are kid-friendly, too, shouldn't require hours in the kitchen.

That's why *Quick Cooking's* home economists assembled this munchable menu that offers lots of opportunities for make-ahead convenience.

Whip up the creamy dip for fruit a day early. Slice the fruit right before the kids arrive.

You can cook and shred chicken for the pizza the night before, too.

The easy cheesy breadsticks are fast to fix and pop in the oven. (While they bake, stir together rapid root beer floats.)

Round out this sleeping bag buffet with sweet blond brownies. Bake them in advance and frost them early in the day. Or, invite guests to doll up their own cute creations.

Dreamy Fruit Dip

Ready in 15 minutes or less

Everyone will love this thick creamy sensation. Chill leftover dip for a tasty topping for toast the next morning.
—*Anna Beiler, Strasburg, Pennsylvania*

    1 package (8 ounces) cream cheese, softened
1/2 cup butter *or* margarine, softened
1/2 cup marshmallow creme
    1 carton (8 ounces) frozen whipped topping, thawed
Assorted fresh fruit

In a small mixing bowl, beat cream cheese and butter until smooth. Beat in marshmallow creme. Fold in whipped topping. Serve with fruit. Store in the refrigerator. **Yield:** about 4 cups.

Slumber Party Pizza

Ready in 30 minutes or less

A prebaked crust, bottled barbecue sauce, shredded chicken and cheese make this one of the tastiest pizzas ever.

    1 prebaked Italian bread shell crust (14 ounces)
    3 cups shredded cooked chicken
    1 cup barbecue sauce
    1 cup (4 ounces) shredded mozzarella cheese
1/2 cup shredded cheddar cheese
Minced fresh parsley

Place the crust on a 14-in. pizza pan. Combine the chicken and barbecue sauce; spread over crust. Sprinkle with cheeses. Bake at 450° for 8-10 minutes or until cheese is melted. Sprinkle with parsley. **Yield:** 8 slices.

Late-Night Breadsticks

Ready in 45 minutes or less

Full of cheese flavor, these speedy snacks disappear fast. Serve with marinara or pizza sauce for dipping.

✓ Uses less fat, sugar or salt. Includes Nutritional Analysis and Diabetic Exchanges.

1/2 cup grated Parmesan cheese
1/4 cup finely shredded cheddar cheese
1/2 teaspoon Italian seasoning
1/2 teaspoon garlic powder
1/8 teaspoon onion powder
    1 loaf (1 pound) frozen white bread dough, thawed
1/4 cup butter *or* stick margarine, melted

In a shallow bowl, combine the first five ingredients; set aside. Divide dough into 16 pieces; roll each into a 6-in. rope. Dip ropes in butter, then roll in cheese mixture. Place 2 in. apart on a greased baking sheet. Let rest for 10 minutes. Bake at 400° for 10-12 minutes or until golden brown. **Yield:** 16 breadsticks.

Nutritional Analysis: One breadstick equals 123 calories, 5 g fat (1 g saturated fat), 4 mg cholesterol, 249 mg sodium, 15 g carbohydrate, 1 g fiber, 5 g protein. **Diabetic Exchanges:** 1 fat, 1 starch.

Sleeping Bag Brownies

Sharon Bickett sent her golden brownie recipe from Chester, South Carolina, and our staff dressed it up.

    1 cup butter *or* margarine, softened
    1 cup sugar
    1 cup packed brown sugar
    2 eggs
    2 teaspoons vanilla extract
    2 cups self-rising flour*
    2 cups chopped pecans, optional
1-1/2 cups white frosting
Black, green, orange, pink and blue gel food coloring
  16 mint parfait Andes candies
  16 gumballs (1/2 inch)

Line a 13-in. x 9-in. x 2-in. baking pan with foil; grease the foil. In a mixing bowl, cream butter and sugars. Beat in eggs and vanilla until combined. Add flour; mix well. Fold in pecans if desired. Pour into prepared pan. Bake at 325° for 35-40 minutes or until a toothpick comes out clean. Cool on a wire rack.

Using foil, lift brownies out of pan. Remove foil. Trim 1/2 in. from all sides of brownies; set aside for another use. Cut the remaining large rectangle into sixteen 3-in. x 1-1/2-in. bars. Tint 2 tablespoons frosting black; set aside.

Divide the remaining frosting between four small bowls; tint with green, orange, pink and blue food coloring. Frost four brownies with each color. Place remaining tinted frosting in small resealable plastic bags. Cut a small hole in the corner of bag; pipe a contrasting color around the edge of each brownie. Pipe designs on top.

For pillow, place an Andes candy, imprinted side down, on one end of brownie. Pipe a dab of frosting on pillow to attach gumball. With reserved black frosting, pipe eyes and mouth on each gumball. **Yield:** 16 brownies.

*Editor's Note: As a substitute for *each* cup of self-rising flour, place 1-1/2 teaspoons baking powder and 1/2 teaspoon salt in a measuring cup. Add all-purpose flour to measure 1 cup.

Eye-Appealing Easter Luncheon Is Easy, Too

WHEN WE ASKED the home economists in our Test Kitchen to surprise us with a fun Easter menu, we didn't need to egg them on. They hopped right to it and hatched up this easy special spring luncheon.

Springtime Lime Slushy

Plan ahead...needs to freeze

With its tangy flavor and slushy consistency, this lively lime beverage is cool and refreshing. —Joyce Minge-Johns Jacksonville, Florida

    2 packages (3 ounces *each*) lime gelatin
    2 cups boiling water
    2 cups cold water
    2 quarts lime sherbet
    3 cups ginger ale, chilled

In a freezer container, dissolve gelatin in boiling water. Stir in the cold water and sherbet until combined. Freeze for 4 hours or until set. Remove from the freezer 45 minutes before serving. For each serving, place 1 cup of slush mixture in a glass; add about 1/3 cup ginger ale. **Yield:** 8 servings.

Chickie Cheese Sandwiches

Ready in 30 minutes or less

Folks are sure to crack a smile when they see these irresistible open-faced sandwiches. Cheese and a few olive pieces create the cheery chick that sits atop each ham slice.

    8 slices bread
    4 to 8 teaspoons prepared mustard
    8 slices fully cooked ham
    8 slices mozzarella cheese
 1/2 cup finely shredded cheddar cheese
    4 pitted ripe olives

Place bread on an ungreased baking sheet. Spread each slice with mustard; top with ham. Using a 3-1/2-in. egg-shaped cutter, cut mozzarella cheese into egg shapes (discard trimmings or save for another use). Using a sharp knife, cut zigzags in the middle of each egg shape. Place on ham, leaving 1 in. of space between the two pieces.

For each chick, sprinkle cheddar cheese between the two egg pieces. Broil 4 in. from the heat for 2-3 minutes or until the cheese is melted. Cut olives into eight triangles for beaks and 16 small pieces for eyes. Arrange on chicks. **Yield:** 8 servings.

Easter Grass Slaw

Ready in 30 minutes or less

Chopped apple and shredded carrot add pretty color to this swift salad that uses packaged coleslaw mix to save time.

✓ Uses less fat, sugar or salt. Includes Nutritional Analysis and Diabetic Exchanges.

    6 cups coleslaw mix
    2 large carrots, shredded
    1 medium sweet yellow pepper, chopped
    1 large apple, chopped
    3 green onions, sliced
 1/2 cup chopped celery
    1 cup mayonnaise
 1/2 cup sugar
    2 tablespoons cider vinegar
    1 teaspoon salt
 1/4 teaspoon pepper

In a large bowl, combine the first six ingredients. In a small bowl, combine the mayonnaise, sugar, vinegar, salt and pepper. Pour over the cabbage mixture and toss to coat. Cover and refrigerate until serving. **Yield:** 8 servings.

Nutritional Analysis: One 1-cup serving (prepared with fat-free mayonnaise) equals 123 calories, 1 g fat (trace saturated fat), 3 mg cholesterol, 564 mg sodium, 29 g carbohydrate, 4 g fiber, 2 g protein. **Diabetic Exchanges:** 2 vegetable, 1 fruit.

Easter Basket Cake

Your guests won't guess how simple it is to cut and assemble this crowd-pleasing cake. Food coloring brightens the store-bought frosting that decorates the basket and eggs, and turns flaked coconut into green Easter grass.

    1 package (18-1/4 ounces) white cake mix
    4 cups vanilla frosting
 Pink, yellow, blue and purple gel *or* paste food
    coloring
    3 tablespoons flaked coconut
    3 drops green food coloring

Prepare cake mix according to package directions. Pour the batter into a greased 15-in. x 10-in. x 1-in. baking pan. Bake at 350° for 20-25 minutes or until a toothpick inserted near the center comes out clean. Cool on a wire rack for 10 minutes; invert cake onto a wire rack to cool completely.

Referring to the diagram below, cut cake into a basket, handle and six eggs. Arrange basket and handle on a 19-in. x 14-in. covered board. Place 1/4 cup of frosting in each of three bowls; tint one pink, one yellow and one blue. Place 1 cup of frosting in another bowl; tint purple. Leave the remaining frosting white.

Frost the basket purple. Frost the sides of the handle white. Cut a hole in the corner of a pastry or plastic bag; insert star tip #32. Fill with white frosting. Pipe a rope border on handle and on top and bottom of basket.

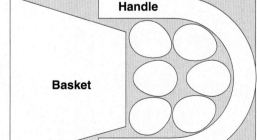

For grass, place coconut in a resealable plastic bag; add green food coloring. Seal bag and shake to tint. Sprinkle above the top of the basket.

Frost and decorate eggs as desired with white and tinted frosting. Arrange in and around basket. **Yield:** 8-10 servings.

Surprise Mom with Beautiful Breakfast

CELEBRATING Mom's special day is a cinch, particularly when Dad and his little helpers whip up this bountiful breakfast from our home economists.

Start her morning off with a steaming cup of butterscotch-flavored coffee.

Sweet rolls never looked more inviting than when arranged to resemble a flower. When the rolls turn golden, remove them from the oven and turn up the heat for the main course...a seafood quiche.

A refreshing fruit medley caps off the mouth-watering menu. Toss the lovely dish together the night before, and you'll have more time in the morning to let Mom know how much you appreciate her!

Butterscotch Coffee

Ready in 30 minutes or less

Five ingredients are all you'll need for this sweet sipper. Individual servings are topped with whipped cream and fun garnishes made from melted butterscotch chips.

    1 cup butterscotch chips, *divided*
    8 cups hot brewed coffee
    1/2 cup half-and-half cream
    5 to 8 tablespoons sugar
Whipped cream in a can

In a microwave-safe bowl, heat 1/2 cup butterscotch chips at 70% power for 2-3 minutes or until melted, stirring occasionally. Cut a small hole in the corner of a pastry or plastic bag; insert a #4 round tip. Fill with melted chips. Pipe "Mom" eight times onto a waxed paper-lined baking sheet. Refrigerate until set, about 10 minutes.

In a large bowl, stir the coffee and remaining butterscotch chips until chips are melted. Stir in half-and-half and sugar. Serve in mugs with whipped cream and "Mom" garnishes. **Yield:** 8 servings.

Blooming Sweet Rolls

Ready in 1 hour or less

Kids will have fun arranging prepared dough into a flower and decorating it with jelly and glaze.

    10 frozen bread dough dinner rolls, thawed
3-1/2 teaspoons currant jelly, *divided*
    1 teaspoon mint jelly, *divided*
    1 cup confectioners' sugar
    1 tablespoon milk
1-1/2 teaspoons butter *or* margarine, melted
    1/8 teaspoon almond extract

Place one roll in center of a greased baking sheet. Shape six rolls into ovals; place around center roll, forming a flower. For stem, roll one of remaining rolls into a 5-in. rope; place rope touching the flower. Shape remaining rolls into leaves; arrange on each side of stem. Cover and let rise in a warm place until doubled, about 30 minutes.

With the end of a wooden spoon handle, make an indentation in the center of each petal and flower center; fill with about 1/4 teaspoon currant jelly. Make an indentation in the center of each leaf; fill with about 1/4

teaspoon mint jelly.

Bake at 350° for 15-20 minutes or until golden brown. Carefully remove from pan to a wire rack. Fill indentations with remaining jelly. In a small bowl, whisk the confectioners' sugar, milk, butter and extract; drizzle over warm sweet rolls. **Yield:** 10 servings.

Crab Quiche

Chopped green onions and sweet red pepper bring a bit of color to this golden entree. The creamy filling features imitation crabmeat and Swiss cheese.

    1 unbaked pastry shell (9 inches)
    1 cup (4 ounces) shredded Swiss cheese, *divided*
    1/2 cup chopped sweet red pepper
    1/4 cup chopped green onions
    1 tablespoon butter *or* margarine
    3 eggs
1-1/2 cups half-and-half cream
    1/2 teaspoon salt
    1/4 teaspoon pepper
    3/4 cup flaked imitation crabmeat, chopped

Line unpricked pastry shell with a double thickness of heavy-duty foil. Bake at 450° for 5 minutes; remove foil. Bake 5 minutes longer. Immediately sprinkle 1/2 cup cheese over crust. Reduce heat to 375°. In a skillet, saute red pepper and onions in butter until tender. In a large bowl, whisk eggs, cream, salt and pepper. Stir in crab, red pepper mixture and remaining cheese. Pour into crust. Bake for 30-35 minutes or until a knife inserted near the center comes out clean. Let stand for 15 minutes before cutting. **Yield:** 6-8 servings.

Sparkling Fruit Salad

Plan ahead...needs to chill

Pineapple chunks, mandarin oranges, strawberries and grapes are treated to a dressing of wine and sparkling club soda in this delightful salad. Serve in dessert dishes or set the whole bowl on the table for a fetching presentation.

✓ Uses less fat, sugar or salt. Includes Nutritional Analysis and Diabetic Exchanges.

    1 fresh pineapple, peeled and cut into chunks
        or 1 can (20 ounces) pineapple chunks, drained
    1 can (11 ounces) mandarin oranges, drained
    1 cup halved fresh strawberries
    1 cup halved green grapes
    1 cup white wine *or* white grape juice
    1/2 cup chilled club soda

In a large serving bowl, combine the pineapple, oranges, strawberries and grapes. Combine wine or grape juice and club soda; pour over fruit. Cover and refrigerate for at least 2 hours, stirring occasionally. Serve with a slotted spoon. **Yield:** 8 servings.

Nutritional Analysis: One serving (3/4 cup) equals 93 calories, trace fat (trace saturated fat), 0 cholesterol, 6 mg sodium, 19 g carbohydrate, 2 g fiber, 1 g protein. **Diabetic Exchange:** 1 fruit.

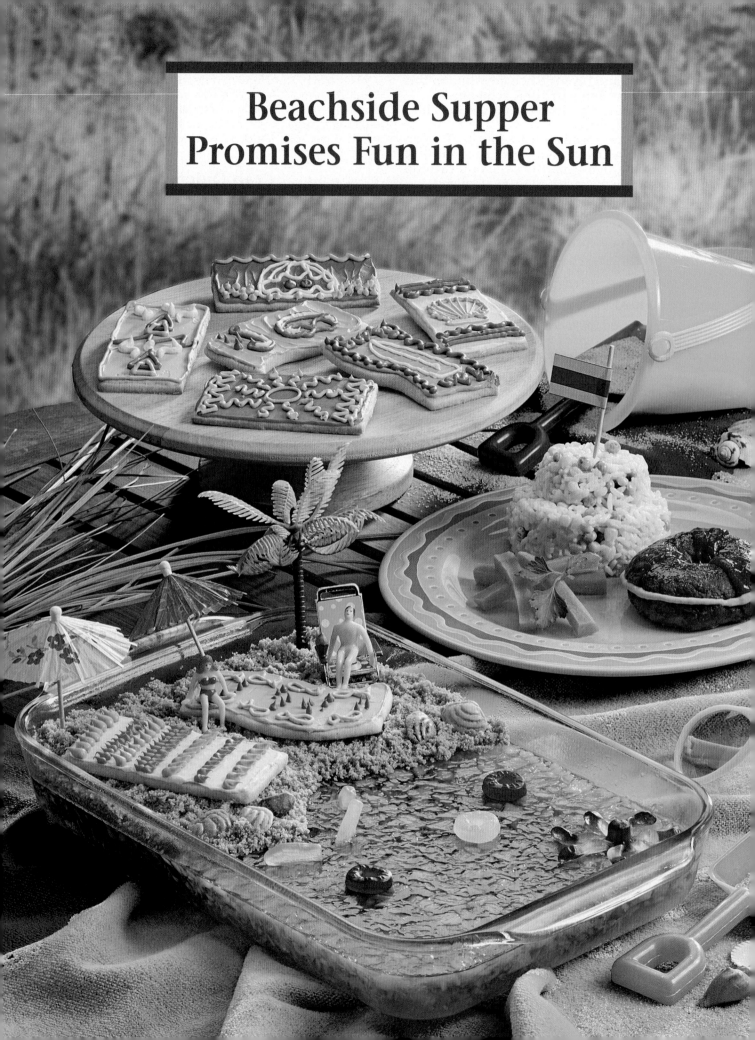

Beachside Supper Promises Fun in the Sun

HANKERING for a relaxing day at the beach? There's no need to go far...just head to your kitchen.

The home economists in *Quick Cooking*'s Test Kitchen cooked up this seaside-inspired menu that sets the scene so well, beachcombers of all ages will be able to imagine wriggling the sun-warmed sand between their toes!

Life Preserver Meat Loaves

Ready in 45 minutes or less

An old standby gets a new look when formed into rings to resemble life preservers. Place a little ketchup and mustard in separate resealable plastic bags to easily pipe fast, flavorful markings on the moist mini meat loaves.

✓ Uses less fat, sugar or salt. Includes Nutritional Analysis and Diabetic Exchanges.

    1 egg
    1 can (5-1/2 ounces) spicy-hot *or* picante V8
1/4 cup milk
    1 cup seasoned bread crumbs
1-1/2 teaspoons seasoned salt
    1 teaspoon chili powder
1-1/2 pounds lean ground beef
Ketchup and mustard

In a large bowl, combine the first six ingredients. Crumble beef over mixture and mix well. Shape into six balls; flatten slightly. Make a hole in the center of each ball with the end of a wooden spoon handle. Place in a greased 15-in. x 10-in. x 1-in. baking pan. Bake, uncovered, at 350° for 25-30 minutes or until meat is no longer pink and a meat thermometer reads 160°. Decorate with ketchup and mustard. **Yield:** 6 servings.

Nutritional Analysis: One serving (prepared with egg substitute and fat-free milk; calculated without ketchup and mustard) equals 274 calories, 11 g fat (4 g saturated fat), 41 mg cholesterol, 1,056 mg sodium, 15 g carbohydrate, 1 g fiber, 27 g protein. **Diabetic Exchanges:** 3 lean meat, 1 starch, 1/2 fat.

Seaside Gelatin Salad

Plan ahead...needs to chill

This busy beach scene is easy to create when you stir crushed pineapple into berry blue gelatin, chill, then top with graham cracker crumb "sand". Add fun details with simple store-bought items like gummy fish, chocolate seashells, paper umbrellas and more.

    4 packages (3 ounces *each*) berry blue gelatin
    3 cups boiling water
    3 cups cold water
    1 can (20 ounces) crushed pineapple, drained
1-3/4 cups graham cracker crumbs (about 28 squares)
    6 tablespoons butter *or* margarine, melted
1/4 cup sugar
Candies for decorating

In a large bowl, dissolve gelatin in boiling water. Stir in cold water and pineapple. Pour into a 13-in. x 9-in. x 2-in. dish. Refrigerate until set. In a bowl, combine the cracker crumbs, butter and sugar; cover and refrigerate. Just before serving, sprinkle cracker mixture over half of the gelatin to form a beach. Decorate as desired. **Yield:** 12-15 servings.

Rice Sand Castles

Ready in 30 minutes or less

Cooked rice and frozen vegetables hurry along the preparation of this savory side dish. Simply press the cheesy mixture into measuring cups with the back of a spoon and stack them to make individual sand castles.

3-3/4 cups cooked rice
    3/4 cup frozen peas, thawed
    3/4 cup frozen corn, thawed
    4 ounces process cheese (Velveeta), cubed
    1/4 teaspoon pepper

In a large microwave-safe bowl, combine all ingredients; mix well. Cover and microwave on high for 2-3 minutes or until heated through and cheese is melted, stirring twice. To make sand castles, pack rice mixture into 1/2-cup and 1/4-cup measures; unmold and stack on dinner plates. **Yield:** 6 servings.

Editor's Note: This recipe was tested in an 850-watt microwave.

Beach Blanket Sugar Cookies

Plan ahead...needs to chill

A hint of pumpkin pie spice in the homemade dough gives a mild taste twist to these crunchy sugar cookies. Canned frosting tinted with food coloring decorates the beach towel treats. (And don't forget to place one or two on the sandy area of the Seaside Gelatin Salad for a finishing touch.)

1/2 cup butter (no substitutes), softened
2/3 cup sugar
    1 egg
1-3/4 cups all-purpose flour
    1 teaspoon baking powder
1/4 teaspoon pumpkin pie spice
    1 can (16 ounces) vanilla frosting
Gel *or* liquid food coloring

In a mixing bowl, cream the butter and sugar. Beat in egg. Combine the flour, baking powder and pumpkin pie spice; gradually add to creamed mixture. Cover and refrigerate for 1 hour or until easy to handle.

Divide dough in half. On a lightly floured surface, roll each portion into a 15-in. x 8-in. rectangle. Cut in half lengthwise; cut widthwise into thirds, forming six strips. Place 1 in. apart on ungreased baking sheets. Bend slightly if desired to form curves in cookies.

Bake at 350° for 10-13 minutes or until edges are lightly browned. Remove to wire racks to cool. Tint frosting with food coloring; decorate cookies as desired. **Yield:** 2 dozen.

Back-to-School Buffet
Earns High Marks

CELEBRATING the first week of school? Surprise your favorite students with this special supper. Preparing the fast feast is elementary, because our Test Kitchen kept in mind the three R's...refreshingly rapid recipes.

Straight-A Salad

Ready in 15 minutes or less

This colorful salad with its mild mustard vinaigrette gets a gold star for versatility—it's ideal with most any entree.

    1/2 cup plus 2 tablespoons olive or vegetable oil
      3 tablespoons red wine vinegar or cider
        vinegar
      2 tablespoons sugar
      2 teaspoons spicy brown or horseradish
        mustard
    1/4 teaspoon onion salt
    1/8 teaspoon pepper
      6 cups torn salad greens
Tomato wedges and cucumber slices

For dressing, combine the first six ingredients in a blender; cover and process until smooth. In a salad bowl, combine the greens, tomato and cucumber; add dressing and toss to coat. **Yield:** 6-8 servings (3/4 cup dressing).

ABC Vegetable Soup

Ready in 30 minutes or less

All you need for this down-home soup is a handful of ingredients like fun alphabet pasta and frozen veggies.

    1/2 cup uncooked alphabet pasta
      3 cans (14-1/2 ounces each) beef broth
      1 package (16 ounces) frozen mixed
        vegetables
    1/2 teaspoon dried thyme
    1/2 teaspoon dried basil
    1/4 teaspoon pepper

Cook pasta according to package directions. In a large saucepan, combine the remaining ingredients. Bring to a boil. Reduce heat; cover and simmer for 5 minutes or until vegetables are tender. Drain pasta; stir into soup. **Yield:** 6-8 servings.

Ruler Stromboli

Ready in 1 hour or less

Filled with deli turkey, Swiss cheese and sauteed peppers, refrigerated pizza dough makes this super sandwich a snap to assemble.

    1/2 cup chopped green pepper
    1/2 cup chopped sweet red pepper
      1 tablespoon butter or margarine
      1 tube (10 ounces) refrigerated pizza dough
      6 slices Swiss cheese, *divided*
      8 ounces sliced deli turkey
      5 sweet red pepper strips (2-inch pieces)
     12 green pepper strips (1-inch pieces)
      2 ounces cream cheese, softened
    1/2 teaspoon milk

In a skillet, saute chopped peppers in butter until tender. On an ungreased baking sheet, pat dough into a 13-in. x 8-in. rectangle. Arrange four cheese slices lengthwise over half of the dough to within 1/2 in. of edge; top with turkey and sauteed peppers. Fold dough over filling; pinch edges to seal. Bake at 400° for 20-25 minutes or until golden brown.

Cut remaining cheese slices in half lengthwise; place along one long edge of the sandwich. Bake 1-2 minutes longer or until cheese is melted. Immediately press red pepper strips into the cheese to create inch marks and add green pepper strips for fractions. Let stand for 10 minutes.

In a small mixing bowl, beat cream cheese and milk until smooth. Spoon into a heavy-duty resealable plastic bag; cut a small hole in a corner of bag. Pipe numerals above red pepper strips. Slice and serve warm. **Yield:** 6-8 servings.

Schoolhouse Cake

You'll receive extra credit when you serve this sweet schoolhouse made from a boxed cake mix.

      1 package (18-1/4 ounces) yellow cake mix
      1 can (16 ounces) vanilla frosting
Red gel food coloring
      6 rectangular wafer sandwich cookies
      2 graham cracker squares
      2 milk chocolate M&M's
      1 yellow Chuckles candy

Line a greased 13-in. x 9-in. x 2-in. baking pan with waxed paper; grease and flour the paper. Prepare cake batter; pour into prepared pan. Bake according to package directions. Cool on a wire rack. Invert cooled cake onto a large platter or covered board. Carefully remove waxed paper.

Cut two triangles off of cake to form roofline (see Fig. 1). For bell tower, cut a square out of one triangle and place above peak of roof. Place remaining triangle above square. (Discard remaining cut cake pieces or save for another use.)

Tint frosting red; frost entire cake. Place wafer cookies along top edge of schoolhouse roof and bell tower roof. For door, place one graham cracker square at bottom of schoolhouse. For the doorknobs, attach M&M's on door with frosting. Cut the remaining cracker square in half; place on cake for windows. Flatten Chuckles candy to 1/4-in. thickness; cut out bell shape and place in bell tower. **Yield:** 12-15 servings.

Fig. 1 Cake cutting diagram

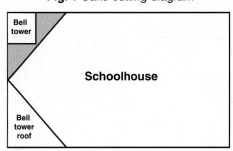

Elves of All Ages Will Savor Swift Snacks

'TIS the night before Christmas...and your children are eager to catch a glimpse of Santa as he comes down the chimney. But what can you do with their youthful energy in the meantime? Have them help whip up a merry menu for the jolly ol' elf himself.

The snacks dreamed up by the home economists in our Test Kitchen are sure to keep Santa, his reindeer and your family satisfied on this festive evening.

The speedy sandwiches can be made while the munchable snack mix bakes. And for dessert, take advantage of convenience items to hurry along the preparation of the cute coffee cups filled with mousse.

This fast and festive fare promises a merry Christmas to all...and to all a good night!

Ho-Ho-Ho Sandwiches

Ready in 15 minutes or less

It's a snap to jazz up deli meats and cheeses to create this satisfying stacker for Santa...or for anyone with a hearty appetite. A three-ingredient spread turns an ordinary sandwich into something special.

    1/2 cup mayonnaise
      2 tablespoons chopped ripe olives
      1 tablespoon spicy brown *or* horseradish
         mustard
      8 slices white bread
    1/4 pound thinly sliced deli ham
      4 slices provolone cheese
    1/4 pound thinly sliced deli salami
      4 slices mozzarella cheese

In a small bowl, combine the mayonnaise, olives and mustard. Spread about 1 tablespoon over each slice of bread. Layer ham, provolone cheese, salami and mozzarella cheese on four slices of bread; top with remaining bread. Serve immediately. **Yield:** 4 servings.

Reindeer Snack Mix

Rudolph and his pals will be dashing, dancing and prancing to gobble up this snack mix. Humans also will enjoy the buttery, perfectly seasoned and crunchy combination.

      2 cups Bugles
      2 cups cheese-flavored snack crackers
      2 cups pretzel sticks
      1 cup Corn Chex
      1 cup bite-size Shredded Wheat
      1 cup pecan halves
    1/2 cup butter *or* margarine, melted
      1 tablespoon maple syrup
    1-1/2 teaspoons Worcestershire sauce
    3/4 teaspoon Cajun seasoning
    1/4 teaspoon cayenne pepper

In a large bowl, combine the first six ingredients. In another bowl, combine the butter, syrup, Worcestershire sauce, Cajun seasoning and cayenne; pour over cereal mixture and toss to coat.

Transfer to an ungreased 15-in. x 10-in. x 1-in. baking pan. Bake, uncovered, at 250° for 1 hour, stirring every 15 minutes. **Yield:** about 9 cups.

Santa's Cup O' Mousse

You'll love this tempting treat. Waffle bowls—sold near the ice cream cones at the grocery store—are decorated with melted chocolate and filled with rich mocha mousse. Cookie dough forms the handles and saucers.

      3 ounces milk chocolate candy coating
    1-1/2 ounces white candy coating
      4 waffle bowls
      1 tube (18 ounces) refrigerated sugar cookie
         dough
      2 packages (2.8 ounces *each*) mocha mousse
         mix

In separate microwave-safe bowls, melt the milk chocolate and white candy coatings. Transfer each to a resealable plastic bag; cut a small hole in corner of bag. Invert waffle bowls; drizzle with coatings. Set aside.

For saucers, cut four 1/4-in. slices of cookie dough. Place on an ungreased baking sheet. Bake at 350° for 8-10 minutes or until edges are golden brown. Drape each warm cookie over an inverted 8-oz. custard cup; cool.

For cup handles, roll remaining cookie dough to 1/4-in. thickness. Cut out two hearts with a 2-1/4-in. heart-shaped cookie cutter. Cut a small heart in the center of each large heart with a 1-in. heart-shaped cutter. Remove center cutout; add to the remaining dough and save for another use. Place hearts on an ungreased

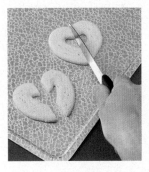

baking sheet. Bake at 350° for 5-7 minutes. Cut hearts in half (above left). Remove to wire racks to cool completely.

Turn waffle bowls right side up. Attach handles, using remaining white candy coating. Spread center of saucers with the remaining milk chocolate coating; let stand until set. Place cups on saucers. Prepare mousse mix according to package directions. Transfer to a large resealable plastic bag. Cut a hole in the corner of the bag; pipe mousse into cups. **Yield:** 4 servings.

Family Traditions

Do you enjoy a special activity on Christmas Eve?

If not, it's never too late to create your own Yuletide traditions. Consider one or more of these ideas:

• Bake gingerbread cookies
• Sing Christmas carols
• Put out snacks for Santa and his reindeer
• Rent a favorite holiday movie
• Allow each family member to open one gift
• Enjoy a special meal
• Learn about Christmas customs around the world
• Attend a church service
• Read aloud a classic Christmas poem or story

Chapter 4

⏱ *Give Me 5 or Fewer*

TODAY'S time-crunched cooks know from experience that recipes with fewer ingredients usually take less time to prepare.

So it's no mystery why busy cooks who steer clear of long lists of ingredients will turn to this chapter often.

With just five ingredients—or fewer—per recipe, each delicious dish is so simple to assemble.

But while these tasty entrees, side dishes, soups, salads and desserts are short on ingredients, they're long on flavor. So you can offer wholesome home-made foods your whole family will enjoy and appreciate.

SIMPLE YET SENSATIONAL. Honey-Mustard Potatoes, Baked Swiss Chicken and Cream Cheese Pineapple Pie (all recipes on pp. 56 and 57).

Tomato Macaroni Casserole

Ready in 30 minutes or less

I dress up cooked macaroni with four flavorful ingredients. This dish is one of my husband's favorites.
—*Karen Smith, Thornton, Colorado*

- 4 cups cooked elbow macaroni
- 1 can (14-1/2 ounces) diced tomatoes, drained
- 1 can (10 ounces) diced tomatoes and green chilies, undrained
- 1 cup (4 ounces) shredded Colby-Monterey Jack cheese, *divided*
- 6 bacon strips, cooked and crumbled

In a greased 11-in. x 7-in. x 2-in. microwave-safe dish, combine the macaroni, tomatoes and 3/4 cup cheese; mix well. Cover and microwave on high for 3 minutes; stir. Cover and heat 1 minute longer. Sprinkle with bacon and remaining cheese. Microwave, uncovered, for 30-45 seconds or until cheese is melted. Let stand for 5 minutes before serving. **Yield:** 4 servings.

Editor's Note: This recipe was tested in an 850-watt microwave.

Cherry Marble Cake

This recipe was given to me by a friend years ago. It's the perfect cake to mix up at the last minute. Choose any fruit pie filling, such as blueberry, peach or apple. If you use apple, sprinkle a little cinnamon on top. —*Tessa Downing*
Doylestown, Pennsylvania

- 1 package (18-1/4 ounces) yellow cake mix
- 1/4 cup vegetable oil
- 3 eggs
- 1/2 cup water
- 1 can (21 ounces) cherry pie filling

In a greased 13-in. x 9-in. x 2-in. baking pan, combine cake mix and oil. Combine eggs and water; stir into cake mix until blended. Drop tablespoonfuls of pie filling onto batter; cut through batter with a knife to swirl.

Bake at 350° for 30-35 minutes or until a toothpick inserted near the center comes out clean (top will have an uneven appearance). Cool on a wire rack. **Yield:** 16-20 servings.

Chewy Peanut Butter Cookies

Ready in 1 hour or less

I like to add candy bars to cookie dough for a change of pace. Crushed Clark bars give a boost of peanut butter and chocolate flavor to these flourless peanut butter cookies. I took them to work and they were a big hit.
—*Christine Beeman, Horseheads, New York*

- 1/2 cup peanut butter
- 1 cup sugar
- 1 egg
- 1 teaspoon vanilla extract
- 3 Clark candy bars (1-3/4 ounces *each*), crushed

In a mixing bowl, combine peanut butter and sugar; beat in egg and vanilla. Stir in candy bars. Roll into 1-in.

balls. Place 2 in. apart on ungreased baking sheets. Bake at 325° for 12-15 minutes or until golden brown. Remove to wire racks to cool. **Yield:** about 2 dozen.

Editor's Note: This recipe does not contain flour.

Spicy Ground Beef Stew

Ready in 30 minutes or less

I don't remember how I came up with the recipe for this swift stew, but it's so easy. It has good flavor from the spicy tomatoes and green chilies, and my co-workers love it.
—*Kelly Tyras, Houston, Texas*

- 1 pound ground beef
- 2 cans (10-1/2 ounces *each*) condensed vegetable beef soup, undiluted
- 1 can (10 ounces) diced tomatoes and green chilies, undrained

In a large saucepan, cook the beef over medium heat until no longer pink; drain. Stir in soup and tomatoes; heat through. **Yield:** 5 servings.

Pepperoni Quesadillas

Ready in 15 minutes or less

My husband, Nathan, first made these zippy "taco pizzas" for me after we got engaged. I was very impressed with his cooking. Now, 12 years and six kids later, fast recipes like this one are in demand at our house.
—*Annalee Wadsworth, Fallon, Nevada*

- 1 package (3-1/2 ounces) sliced pepperoni
- 6 flour tortillas (7 inches)
- 1-1/2 cups (6 ounces) shredded Colby-Monterey Jack *or* mozzarella cheese
- Shredded lettuce and picante sauce

Divide pepperoni among the tortillas; sprinkle with cheese. Place one tortilla at a time on a microwave-safe plate. Microwave, uncovered, at 50% power for 40-50 seconds or until cheese is melted. Top with lettuce and picante sauce; fold in half. **Yield:** 3-6 servings.

Editor's Note: This recipe was tested in an 850-watt microwave.

Ham 'n' Broccoli Hash

(Pictured at right)

Ready in 30 minutes or less

This meal-in-one skillet dish with potatoes, ham and broccoli is nice for brunch or as a light supper. I like to serve it with rolls and butter.
—*Brenda Ruse*
Truro, Nova Scotia

- 4 cups frozen O'Brien hash brown potatoes
- 2 cups cubed fully cooked ham
- 1/2 teaspoon salt
- 3 tablespoons vegetable oil
- 2 cups fresh broccoli florets

In a bowl, combine potatoes, ham and salt. In a large nonstick skillet, heat oil over medium-high heat. Add potato mixture and flatten with a spatula. Cover and cook for 2 minutes. Sprinkle with broccoli. Cover and cook 6-8 minutes longer or until potatoes are tender and lightly browned, stirring occasionally. Serve immediately. **Yield:** 3-4 servings.

French Onion Pan Rolls

(Pictured below)

A crusty topping of Parmesan cheese and onion soup mix adds lots of flavor to these golden brown rolls. They're great with a bowl of soup or a salad. I sometimes use frozen rolls to make preparation even easier.
—Anne Prince, Elkhorn, Wisconsin

    2 loaves (1 pound *each*) frozen bread dough, thawed
    1 cup grated Parmesan cheese
    1 envelope onion soup mix
  1/2 cup butter *or* margarine, melted

Divide the bread dough into 20 portions; shape each into a ball. In a bowl, combine the Parmesan cheese and soup mix. Place butter in another bowl. Roll each ball in butter, then in the cheese mixture. Arrange in a greased 13-in. x 9-in. x 2-in. baking dish. Cover and let rise in a warm place until doubled, about 45 minutes.
    Bake at 350° for 30-35 minutes or until golden brown. Remove from pan to a wire rack. Serve warm. **Yield:** 20 rolls.

Fruited Cranberry Gelatin

(Pictured below)

Plan ahead...needs to chill

This is our traditional Thanksgiving salad. But we don't limit it to just once a year. It's so easy to make that we have it with almost every meal that includes chicken.
—Lyn Chapman, Provo, Utah

    1 package (6 ounces) orange gelatin
    1 can (16 ounces) whole-berry cranberry sauce
    1 can (8 ounces) crushed pineapple, undrained
    1 can (12 ounces) ginger ale

In a saucepan over medium heat, cook the gelatin powder and cranberry sauce until gelatin is dissolved. Remove from the heat; stir in the pineapple and ginger ale until combined. Pour into a 1-1/2-qt. serving bowl. Chill until set, stirring after 1-1/2 hours. **Yield:** 6 servings.

French Onion Pan Rolls
Ham 'n' Broccoli Hash
Fruited Cranberry Gelatin

Honey Mustard Chicken
Sesame Green Beans
Cherry Mallow Dessert

Honey Mustard Chicken

(Pictured above)

Ready in 30 minutes or less

The whole family enjoys this saucy chicken served over rice, so I make it often. It cooks up so tender and juicy that I sometimes serve the chicken on rolls with lettuce and tomato. —Heather Wray, Portville, New York

 Uses less fat, sugar or salt. Includes Nutritional Analysis and Diabetic Exchanges.

> **4 boneless skinless chicken breast halves (4 ounces *each*)**
> **1 can (10-1/2 ounces) chicken gravy**
> **4 teaspoons Dijon mustard**
> **2 to 3 teaspoons honey**
> **Hot cooked rice, optional**

In a skillet coated with nonstick cooking spray, cook chicken over medium-high heat for 5 minutes on each side. Combine the gravy, mustard and honey; pour over chicken. Bring to a boil. Reduce heat; cover and simmer for 8-12 minutes or until chicken juices run clear. Serve over rice if desired. **Yield:** 4 servings.

Nutritional Analysis: One serving (prepared with fat-free gravy and 2 teaspoons honey; calculated without rice) equals 165 calories, 2 g fat (trace saturated fat), 72 mg cholesterol, 717 mg sodium, 7 g carbohydrate, trace fiber, 28 g protein. **Diabetic Exchanges:** 3 very lean meat, 1/2 starch.

Sesame Green Beans

(Pictured above)

Ready in 30 minutes or less

 *Looking for an ideal accompaniment to almost any entree? This is a simple side dish of fresh green beans mildly flavored with sesame seeds and garlic cloves.* —Linda Vietmeier Pittsburgh, Pennsylvania

Uses less fat, sugar or salt. Includes Nutritional Analysis and Diabetic Exchanges.

> **1 pound fresh green beans, trimmed**
> **1 tablespoon sesame seeds**
> **2 garlic cloves, minced**
> **2 tablespoons canola *or* vegetable oil**
> **Salt to taste, optional**

Place beans in a saucepan and cover with water; bring to a boil. Cook, uncovered, for 8-10 minutes or until crisp-tender. Meanwhile, in a skillet, saute the sesame seeds and garlic in oil. Drain beans; stir into garlic mixture. Season with salt if desired. **Yield:** 6 servings.

Nutritional Analysis: One 3/4-cup serving (prepared

without salt) equals 73 calories, 5 g fat (trace saturated fat), 0 cholesterol, 8 mg sodium, 5 g carbohydrate, 3 g fiber, 1 g protein. **Diabetic Exchanges:** 1 vegetable, 1 fat.

Cherry Mallow Dessert

(Pictured at left)

Plan ahead…needs to chill

For a swift sweet treat, I spread a homemade graham cracker crust with canned cherry pie filling, then top it with a fun marshmallow-and-whipped-cream layer. Also try it with blueberry pie filling. —Carol Heppner
Caronport, Saskatchewan

1-1/2 cups graham cracker crumbs (about 24 squares)
1/3 cup butter *or* margarine, melted
1 can (21 ounces) cherry pie filling
3 cups miniature marshmallows
1 cup heavy whipping cream, whipped

Set aside 1 tablespoon graham cracker crumbs for topping. Place the remaining crumbs in a bowl; stir in butter until combined. Press into a greased 9-in. square baking pan. Bake at 350° for 10-12 minutes or until lightly browned. Cool completely.

Spread pie filling over crust. Fold marshmallows into the whipped cream; spread over filling. Sprinkle with the reserved crumbs. Refrigerate for at least 6 hours. **Yield:** 9 servings.

Stuffing Meatballs

Ready in 30 minutes or less

This is one of my mother's most popular recipes. We loved it when she served these well-seasoned meatballs with sauce over spaghetti or egg noodles. —Dorothy Parrish
Kenly, North Carolina

1-1/2 pounds ground beef
2/3 cup crushed seasoned stuffing
1 tablespoon vegetable oil
1 jar (26 ounces) meatless spaghetti sauce

In a bowl, combine beef and stuffing mix. Shape into 1-in. balls. In a large skillet over medium heat, brown meatballs in oil in small batches; drain. Return all meatballs to the pan; add spaghetti sauce. Bring to a boil. Reduce heat; cover and simmer for 6-8 minutes or until meat is no longer pink. **Yield:** 6 servings.

Chili Cheese Toast

Ready in 15 minutes or less

A friend brought these savory snacks to lunch one day, and they've been a staple in our house ever since. The cheese-topped toast is great with a bowl of soup or chili, or served alongside a salad. —Alberta Frey
Shingletown, California

1 can (4 ounces) chopped green chilies
2 tablespoons mayonnaise
6 slices French bread, toasted
6 slices Monterey Jack *or* pepper Jack cheese

In a bowl, combine the chilies and mayonnaise. Spread over each slice of bread. Top each with a cheese slice. Broil 4 in. from the heat for 3-4 minutes or until cheese is melted. **Yield:** 3-6 servings.

Scotch Teas

Ready in 1 hour or less

When my kids were little, these sweet golden bars were standbys for hurry-up treats. They were often my contribution to work functions, too. —Jane Hacker
Milwaukee, Wisconsin

2 cups quick-cooking oats
3/4 cup packed brown sugar
1 teaspoon baking powder
1/4 teaspoon salt
1/2 cup butter *or* margarine, melted

In a large bowl, combine the oats, brown sugar, baking powder and salt; mix well. Stir in butter. Pat evenly into a greased 8-in. square baking dish. Bake at 350° for 20-25 minutes or until golden brown. Cool on a wire rack. Cut into bars. **Yield:** 20 bars.

Sausage Corn Bread Dressing

Ready in 30 minutes or less

I dress up stuffing mix with pork sausage and jarred mushrooms to create this in-a-dash dressing. The hearty side dish is terrific with chicken, turkey or pork. —Ruby Harman, Carrollton, Missouri

1 pound bulk pork sausage
3-1/2 cups water
1 jar (7 ounces) sliced mushrooms, drained
2 packages (6 ounces *each*) corn bread stuffing mix

In a large skillet, brown the sausage; drain. Add water and mushrooms. Bring to a boil. Remove from the heat; add the stuffing mix. Cover and let stand for 5 minutes. **Yield:** 8 servings.

Pantry Scalloped Potatoes

This was one of my favorite dishes when I was growing up. It's so easy to make with convenience items. I usually double the batch because we think the potatoes taste even better the next day. —Linda Schwarz
Bertrand, Nebraska

1 can (10-3/4 ounces) condensed golden mushroom soup, undiluted
1 can (10-3/4 ounces) condensed creamy onion soup, undiluted
1 can (10-3/4 ounces) condensed cheddar cheese soup, undiluted
8 medium potatoes, peeled and thinly sliced

In a bowl, combine soups; mix well. In a greased 13-in. x 9-in. x 2-in. baking dish, layer a third of the potatoes; top with a third of the soup mixture. Repeat layers twice. Cover and bake at 350° for 1 hour or until potatoes are tender. **Yield:** 6-8 servings.

Swiss Mushroom Pie

I needed a before-dinner snack, so I conjured this up with ingredients that I had at home. It was enjoyed by all. Rich wedges also would make a nice brunch dish or light lunch alongside a salad.
—Rita Weaver
Lakewood, Washington

1 package (15 ounces) refrigerated pie pastry
1 pound fresh mushrooms, sliced
1 teaspoon chopped onion
1 tablespoon butter *or* margarine
1 pound Swiss cheese, sliced

Line a 9-in. pie plate with bottom pastry; trim even with edge. In a skillet, saute the mushrooms and onion in butter; drain. Arrange half of the cheese slices in the crust. Top with half of the mushroom mixture; repeat layers.

Place remaining pastry over filling; trim, seal and flute edges. Cut slits in the top. Bake at 350° for 45-50 minutes or until golden brown. Let stand for 10 minutes. Cut into wedges. **Yield: 6-8 servings.**

Pineapple Cracker Spread

Plan ahead...needs to chill

I've been serving this thick mild-tasting mixture with snack crackers for more than 20 years. I usually have everything for the simple yet delicious dip on hand, so I can prepare it in a snap and refrigerate it for parties and get-togethers.
—Gloria Wark, Houston, Texas

✓ Uses less fat, sugar or salt. Includes Nutritional Analysis and Diabetic Exchanges.

1 can (8 ounces) crushed unsweetened pineapple
1 package (8 ounces) cream cheese, softened
1/2 cup chopped green pepper
2 to 3 green onions, chopped
Assorted crackers

Drain pineapple, reserving 1 teaspoon juice. In a small mixing bowl, beat cream cheese until smooth. Beat in the pineapple, green pepper, onions and reserved juice. Cover and chill for 1-1/2 hours. Serve with crackers. **Yield: 2 cups.**

Nutritional Analysis: 1/4 cup of spread (prepared with reduced-fat cream cheese) equals 59 calories, 3 g fat (2 g saturated fat), 10 mg cholesterol, 109 mg sodium, 5 g carbohydrate, trace fiber, 3 g protein. **Diabetic Exchanges:** 1/2 fruit, 1/2 fat.

Mandarin Cookie Salad

Ready in 1 hour or less

This yummy dessert is an all-time favorite with our family. I seldom bring home leftovers when I take it to potlucks or family gatherings. It's so easy, even the kids can make it!
—Karen Marcus, Renville, Minnesota

2 cups cold buttermilk
1 package (5.1 ounces) instant vanilla pudding mix
1 carton (12 ounces) frozen whipped topping, thawed
2 cans (11 ounces *each*) mandarin oranges, drained
1 package (11-1/2 ounces) fudge-striped shortbread cookies, coarsely crushed

In a bowl, whisk the buttermilk and pudding mix for 2 minutes. Let stand for 2 minutes or until soft-set. Fold in whipped topping and oranges. Cover and refrigerate until serving. Fold in crushed cookies. **Yield: 8 servings.**

Garlic Chicken 'n' Pasta

Ready in 30 minutes or less

A jar of store-bought Parmesan sauce makes it a breeze to toss together this chicken and pasta combo. I like to garnish the entree with crisp crumbled bacon and chopped fresh basil.
—Phyllis Schmalz, Kansas City, Kansas

1 package (8 ounces) spiral *or* penne pasta
4 boneless skinless chicken breast halves
1 teaspoon olive *or* vegetable oil
1 jar (16 ounces) roasted garlic Parmesan sauce
2 small tomatoes, seeded and chopped, *divided*

Cook pasta according to package directions. Meanwhile, in a large skillet, brown chicken in oil. Add the Parmesan sauce; cover and simmer for 8-10 minutes or until chicken juices run clear. Add half of the tomatoes. Drain pasta; top with chicken and sauce. Sprinkle with remaining tomatoes. **Yield: 4 servings.**

Club Salad

(Pictured at right)

Ready in 15 minutes or less

I first made this tossed chicken salad for my cousin's baby shower, and everyone loved it. It was special enough for my youngest daughter's baptism luncheon, yet it's easy enough to put together for dinner.
—Beth Martin Sine
Faulkner, Maryland

1 package (10 ounces) ready-to-serve salad
1 package (6 ounces) fully cooked chicken breast strips, cubed
10 to 15 cherry tomatoes, halved
8 bacon strips, cooked and crumbled
3/4 cup Italian salad dressing

In a large bowl, combine the salad, chicken, tomatoes and bacon. Drizzle with dressing and toss to coat. Serve immediately. **Yield: 6 servings.**

Mozzarella Ham Stromboli

(Pictured at right)

Ready in 45 minutes or less

The original recipe for this savory bread called for salami, but I use ham instead. People are always amazed that it only takes about 15 minutes to assemble. I usually serve it with tomato soup. —Janice Brightwell, Jeffersonville, Indiana

1 tube (11 ounces) refrigerated crusty French loaf
2 cups (8 ounces) shredded mozzarella cheese
1/4 pound thinly sliced deli ham
1 tablespoon butter *or* margarine, melted
1 tablespoon grated Parmesan cheese

On a lightly floured surface, unroll dough at seam. Pat dough into a 14-in. x 12-in. rectangle. Sprinkle mozzarella cheese over dough to within 1/2 in. of edges. Top with a single layer of ham. Roll up tightly from a short side; pinch seam to seal. Place seam side down on an ungreased baking sheet. Brush top of loaf with butter; sprinkle with Parmesan cheese.

Bake at 375° for 20-25 minutes or until golden brown. Cool on a wire rack for 5 minutes. Cut with a serrated knife. **Yield:** 6 servings.

Orange Cream Slush

(Pictured below)

Plan ahead...needs to freeze

I blend together these slushy beverages that taste just like orange Creamsicles. If you don't have time to freeze the orange juice, use orange sorbet instead. —Nina Hall
Citrus Heights, California

8 cups orange juice
8 scoops vanilla ice cream
8 orange slices, optional

Pour orange juice into 2-qt. freezer container; cover and freeze for 2 hours or until slushy, stirring twice.

To serve, pour slush into eight glasses. Add a scoop of ice cream to each glass. Garnish with orange slices if desired. **Yield:** 8 servings.

Orange Cream Slush
Club Salad
Mozzarella Ham Stromboli

Honey-Mustard Potatoes
Baked Swiss Chicken
Cream Cheese Pineapple Pie

Honey-Mustard Potatoes

(Pictured above and on page 49)

Ready in 30 minutes or less

I dish out these simply seasoned spuds after they've cooled. But the easy-to-prepare potatoes also taste terrific warm. They're great for barbecues and go well with a variety of foods.   —Debbi Gillotti, Mercer Island, Washington

> **8 medium red potatoes (about 2 pounds), cut into wedges**
> **1/2 cup honey-mustard vinaigrette salad dressing**
> **2 green onions, chopped**
> **1/2 teaspoon salt, optional**

Place the potatoes in a large saucepan and cover with water. Bring to a boil. Cook until tender, about 15 minutes; drain. In a large serving bowl, combine the warm potatoes, salad dressing, onions and salt if desired; toss gently. Serve warm or cold. **Yield:** 6 servings.

Baked Swiss Chicken

(Pictured above and on page 49)

Ready in 1 hour or less

Canned soup, white wine, Swiss cheese and crushed croutons dress up chicken breasts in this elegant entree. Ideal for unexpected guests, it requires only a few ingredients. The creamy sauce is excellent with garlic mashed potatoes or rice.
*   —Beverly Roberge*
Bristol, Connecticut

> **6 boneless skinless chicken breast halves (1-1/2 pounds)**
> **1 can (10-3/4 ounces) condensed cream of chicken soup, undiluted**
> **1/2 cup white wine *or* chicken broth**
> **6 slices Swiss cheese**
> **1 cup crushed seasoned croutons**

Place chicken in a greased 13-in. x 9-in. x 2-in. baking dish. In a bowl, combine the soup and wine or broth; pour over chicken. Top with cheese and sprinkle with croutons. Bake, uncovered, at 350° for 35-40 minutes or until chicken juices run clear. **Yield:** 6 servings.

Cream Cheese Pineapple Pie

(Pictured at left and on page 48)

Plan ahead…needs to freeze

I love pineapple and use it in all kinds of recipes. Not too sweet and not too tangy, the mild pineapple flavor in this frosty dessert comes through just right. —Raydonna Biles Clinton, Missouri

    1 unbaked pastry shell (9 inches)
    1 package (8 ounces) cream cheese, softened
    1 carton (16 ounces) vanilla yogurt
    1 cup pineapple preserves

Line unpricked pastry shell with a double thickness of heavy-duty foil. Bake at 450° for 8 minutes. Remove foil; bake 5 minutes longer. Cool on a wire rack.

In a mixing bowl, beat cream cheese until smooth. Add the yogurt and preserves; pour into crust. Cover and freeze for 8 hours or overnight. Remove from the freezer 30 minutes before cutting. **Yield:** 6-8 servings.

Maple Baked Beans

Ready in 30 minutes or less

Jazz up cans of beans with maple syrup and just a dash of cinnamon for a unique taste twist. This sweet and saucy side dish is a snap to fix in the microwave, so it's handy to add to summertime menus. —Susan Baxter Morgantown, Indiana

    2 cans (16 ounces *each*) pork and beans
    1/2 cup ketchup
    1/2 cup maple syrup
    Dash ground cinnamon

In a large microwave-safe bowl, combine all ingredients. Microwave, uncovered, on high for 15-20 minutes or until mixture reaches desired thickness, stirring every 5 minutes. Let stand for 5 minutes before serving. **Yield:** 4-6 servings.

Editor's Note: This recipe was tested in an 850-watt microwave.

Tortilla Ham Pinwheels

Plan ahead…needs to chill

Looking for an easy appetizer to bring to a party or get-together? These rapid roll-ups rely on an envelope of salad dressing mix for fast flair. It's pretty hard to eat just one. —Judy Addair, Bristol, Tennessee

    2 packages (one 8 ounces, one 3 ounces)
       cream cheese, softened
    1 envelope Italian salad dressing mix
    5 flour tortillas (7 inches)
    1 package (12 ounces) sliced fully cooked ham

In a small mixing bowl, combine the cream cheese and salad dressing mix. Spread over one side of each tortilla. Top with ham; roll up. Refrigerate for 1 hour. Cut into 1-in. slices. **Yield:** about 2-1/2 dozen.

Pink Cloud

Plan ahead…needs to chill

My grandmother made this colorful fluff for Christmas dessert, but it's delicious any time of the year. Replace the crunchy pecans with cubes of sponge cake for a fun change of pace. —Joanna Powell, Etobicoke, Ontario

    1 package (3 ounces) strawberry gelatin
    1 cup boiling water
    1 cup vanilla ice cream
    3/4 cup chopped fresh strawberries
    1/4 cup chopped pecans

In a mixing bowl, dissolve gelatin in boiling water. Cool until syrupy. Add ice cream; beat until blended. Refrigerate until partially set. Fold in strawberries and pecans. Spoon into individual serving dishes. Refrigerate until firm. **Yield:** 4 servings.

Green Chili Rice Casserole

Ready in 45 minutes or less

This cheesy bake is wonderful for church potlucks because it goes well with any main course. I often sprinkle a little paprika over the top for color. —Naomi Newkirk Sacramento, California

    4 cups cooked rice
    2 cans (4 ounces *each*) chopped green chilies
    1/2 teaspoon salt
    3/4 pound Monterey Jack cheese, cut into
       1/2-inch cubes
    2 cups (16 ounces) sour cream

In a bowl, combine all ingredients. Transfer to a greased 2-qt. baking dish. Cover and bake at 350° for 30 minutes or until heated through. **Yield:** 8 servings.

Fried Banana Sundaes

Ready in 15 minutes or less

This is a quick and creative dessert recipe. Lightly fried bananas are drizzled with honey, topped with scoops of vanilla ice cream and sprinkled with nutmeg. —Joyce Key, Snellville, Georgia

    3 medium ripe bananas, peeled and halved
       lengthwise
    2 tablespoons butter *or* margarine
    2 teaspoons honey
    Vanilla ice cream
    Ground nutmeg

In a large skillet, saute bananas in butter until light golden brown, turning once. Place on serving plates; drizzle with honey. Top with a scoop of ice cream; sprinkle with nutmeg. **Yield:** 6 servings.

Barbecued Steak Strips

Ready in 30 minutes or less

When our oven broke and I could use only the stove, I got creative with my skillet cooking! That's when I invented this treatment for sirloin steak. It makes a tasty meal with mashed potatoes and green beans.
—Lynnelle Nissen, Beaver Crossing, Nebraska

 1 pound boneless beef sirloin steak, cut into 1/2-inch strips
 1 tablespoon vegetable oil
 1 to 2 cups barbecue sauce
 2 tablespoons honey
 1 teaspoon sugar

In a large skillet, brown steak in oil over medium-high heat; drain. Combine the barbecue sauce, honey and sugar; pour over meat. Bring to a boil. Reduce heat; simmer, uncovered, for 10-15 minutes or until the sauce is slightly thickened and meat is tender. **Yield:** 3-4 servings.

Butterscotch Peanut Treats

I use pudding mix to stir up these sweet, crunchy no-bake bites. If you like butterscotch, you will love these delicious treats. *—Bernice Martinoni, Petaluma, California*

 1/2 cup corn syrup
 1/3 cup butter *or* margarine, cubed
 1 package (3.5 ounces) cook-and-serve butterscotch pudding mix
 4 cups cornflakes
 1 cup coarsely chopped dry roasted peanuts

In a large heavy saucepan, cook and stir the corn syrup and butter until butter is melted. Stir in pudding mix until blended. Cook and stir until mixture comes to a boil. Cook and stir 1 minute longer.

Remove from the heat. Cool for 1 minute, stirring several times. Stir in the cornflakes and peanuts until evenly coated. Drop by rounded tablespoonfuls onto waxed paper-lined baking sheets; cool. **Yield:** about 2-1/2 dozen.

Italian Salad Croutons

Ready in 30 minutes or less

These crisp buttery croutons are so good. I don't know where I got the recipe, but I've been using it for more than 10 years. Toss the croutons in a salad, garnish a bowl of soup with them or sprinkle them on top of a creamy casserole. *—Ellen Benninger, Greenville, Pennsylvania*

 1/4 cup butter *or* margarine, melted
1-1/2 teaspoons Italian seasoning
 1/2 teaspoon garlic powder
 5 slices bread, cut into 1/2-inch cubes

In a large bowl, combine the butter, Italian seasoning and garlic powder. Add bread cubes and toss to coat. Arrange in a single layer on an ungreased baking sheet. Bake at 325° for 15-20 minutes or until lightly browned, stirring occasionally. **Yield:** about 2 cups.

Ruby Pears

Ready in 1 hour or less

Cranberry sauce gives a sweet-tart taste to pear halves in this spiced side dish that's perfect for fall. It's excellent with chicken or pork dishes and can be enjoyed hot or cold.
—Kathy Ginn, Washington Court House, Ohio

 1 can (29 ounces) pear halves, drained
 1 can (16 ounces) whole-berry cranberry sauce
 1/4 cup sugar
 2 tablespoons lemon juice
 1/4 teaspoon ground cinnamon

Place pears cut side up in a greased 8-in. square baking dish. In a saucepan, combine cranberry sauce, sugar, lemon juice and cinnamon. Cook and stir until sugar is dissolved and mixture is heated through; spoon over pears. Bake, uncovered, at 350° for 25-30 minutes or until heated through. **Yield:** 5-6 servings.

Parmesan Ham Appetizers

Ready in 30 minutes or less

I first tried this simple snack bread at an office Christmas party. The easy recipe can be increased or decreased depending on the size of your guest list. It's wonderful when made with proscuitto (thinly sliced Italian ham).
—Marge Fisher, Arlington, Virginia

 1 carton (8 ounces) whipped cream cheese
 1 cup shredded Parmesan cheese
 1/4 pound deli ham, finely chopped
 1/2 to 1 teaspoon garlic powder
 1 unsliced loaf (1 pound) Italian bread

In a small mixing bowl, beat the cream cheese, Parmesan cheese, ham and garlic powder until blended.

Cut bread in half lengthwise; spread with cream cheese mixture. Cut into 1-1/2-in. slices. Place on an ungreased baking sheet. Broil 4 in. from heat for 3-5 minutes or until topping is lightly browned. **Yield:** about 1-1/2 dozen.

Pineapple Salad Dressing

(Pictured at right)

Ready in 15 minutes or less

Perk up an ordinary salad with this tangy mixture. With sweetness from pineapple juice and a bit of zip from cumin, this salad dressing is a refreshing change of pace.
—Shawn Nelson, Evansville, Indiana

✓ Uses less fat, sugar or salt. Includes Nutritional Analysis and Diabetic Exchanges.

 1/2 cup unsweetened pineapple juice
 1/4 cup white vinegar
 1 teaspoon ground cumin
 1 garlic clove, minced
Mixed salad greens

In a jar with a tight-fitting lid, combine the pineapple juice, vinegar, cumin and garlic; shake well. Serve with salad greens. Refrigerate leftovers; shake or stir before serving. **Yield:** 3/4 cup.

Nutritional Analysis: One serving (2 tablespoons dressing) equals 15 calories, trace fat (0 saturated fat), 0 cholesterol, 1 mg sodium, 4 g carbohydrate, trace fiber, trace protein. **Diabetic Exchange:** Free food.

German Chocolate Bars

(Pictured below)

Plan ahead...needs to chill

My mom gave me this recipe at Christmas when I wanted to make something simple, different and yummy for gifts. The chewy bars can be cut into larger pieces, but they're very rich. —Jennifer Sharp, Murfreesboro, Tennessee

    1 package (18-1/4 ounces) German chocolate
      cake mix
2/3 cup cold butter *or* margarine
    1 cup (6 ounces) semisweet chocolate chips
    1 can (15 ounces) coconut-pecan frosting
1/4 cup milk

Place cake mix in a bowl; cut in butter until crumbly. Press 2-1/2 cups into a greased 13-in. x 9-in. x 2-in. baking pan. Bake at 350° for 10 minutes; immediately sprinkle with chocolate chips. Drop frosting by tablespoonfuls over the chips. Stir milk into the remaining crumb mixture; drop by teaspoonfuls over top.

Bake 25-30 minutes longer or until bubbly around the edges and top is cracked. Cool on a wire rack. Refrigerate for 4 hours before cutting. **Yield:** 4 dozen.

Garlic Butter Shrimp

(Pictured below)

Ready in 30 minutes or less

Garlic and lemon lend a pleasant flavor to these speedy sauteed shrimp. It's an extra-special entree that takes hardly any effort. I like to serve them over wild rice mix from a box. —Sheryll Hughes-Smith Jackson, Mississippi

    1 pound uncooked medium shrimp, peeled
      and deveined
    2 to 3 garlic cloves, minced
1/4 cup butter *or* margarine
    3 tablespoons lemon juice
Hot cooked rice

In a large skillet, saute the shrimp and garlic in butter for 5 minutes or until shrimp turn pink. Add the lemon juice; heat through. Serve with rice. **Yield:** 4 servings.

Pineapple Salad Dressing
German Chocolate Bars
Garlic Butter Shrimp

Christmas Wreaths
Beef Sirloin Tip Roast
Creamy Mashed Potatoes

Creamy Mashed Potatoes

(Pictured above)

Ready in 30 minutes or less

I easily turn garlic-seasoned instant mashed potatoes in-to a comforting casserole that will earn raves. I stir in cream cheese before topping the dish with shredded cheese and broiling it until melted. —Debbie Pataky
Lookout Mountain, Georgia

> 3 cups water
> 1 cup milk
> 1 package (7.6 ounces) roasted garlic instant mashed potatoes
> 4 ounces cream cheese, cubed
> 1 cup (4 ounces) shredded Mexican cheese blend

In a large saucepan, bring water and milk to a rolling boil. Remove from the heat. Add the contents of both envelopes from the potato package. Let stand for 1 minute; whip with a fork.

Place the cream cheese in a microwave-safe bowl; cover and heat at 70% power for 45 seconds or until soft-ened. Stir into the potatoes. Transfer to a greased 1-qt. baking dish. Sprinkle with cheese. Broil 4 in. from the heat for 3-4 minutes or until cheese is melted. **Yield:** 6 servings.

Beef Sirloin Tip Roast

(Pictured above)

This meaty main course, served with a mouth-watering mushroom gravy, is a snap to assemble and pop in the oven. It is my husband's favorite. —Mrs. Burgess Marshbanks
Buies Creek, North Carolina

> 1 boneless beef sirloin tip roast (about 3 pounds)
> 1-1/4 cups water, *divided*
> 1 can (8 ounces) mushroom stems and pieces, drained
> 1 envelope onion soup mix
> 3 tablespoons cornstarch

Place a large piece of heavy-duty foil (21 in. x 17 in.) in a shallow roasting pan. Place roast on foil. Pour 1 cup water and mushrooms over roast. Sprinkle with soup mix. Wrap foil around roast; seal tightly. Bake at 350° for 2-1/2 to 3 hours or until meat reaches desired done-ness (for rare, a meat thermometer should read 140°; medium, 160°; well-done, 170°).

Remove roast to a serving platter and keep warm. Pour drippings and mushrooms into a saucepan. Com-bine cornstarch and remaining water until smooth; grad-ually stir into drippings. Bring to a boil; cook and stir for 2 minutes or until thickened. Serve with sliced beef. **Yield:** 10-12 servings.

Christmas Wreaths

(Pictured at left)

Ready in 1 hour or less

Cornflakes take the place of traditional crisp rice cereal in these sweet no-bake treats from our Test Kitchen. Dressed up with green food coloring and red candies, these wreaths are a fun addition to cookie platters and dessert buffets.

  20 large marshmallows
  2 tablespoons butter *or* margarine, cubed
Green food coloring
  3 cups cornflakes
  72 miniature red M&M baking bits

In a microwave-safe bowl, combine the marshmallows and butter. Microwave, uncovered, on high for 1 minute or until butter is melted and marshmallows are puffed. Add food coloring; mix well. Stir in the cornflakes. Shape into 3-in. wreaths on a waxed paper-lined baking sheet. Immediately press M&M's in three clusters of three for berries. Let stand until set. **Yield:** 8 wreaths.

Dried Beef Dip

Ready in 15 minutes or less

A friend shared this recipe with me about 10 years ago, and it continues to be a hit. Serve it with potato chips, crackers or raw veggies for a snack, or dollop it on baked potatoes at dinnertime. —Camie Schuiteman
Marion, Indiana

  1 package (8 ounces) cream cheese, softened
  2 cups (16 ounces) sour cream
  1 carton (16 ounces) French onion dip
  1 package (2-1/2 ounces) dried beef, chopped
Ridged potato chips

In a small mixing bowl, beat the cream cheese, sour cream and dip. Stir in the beef. Serve with chips. Refrigerate leftovers. **Yield:** about 5 cups.

Creamed Spinach Ham Pasta

Ready in 30 minutes or less

My kids think I improvise our weeknight meals…they're right! This taste-tempting creation is great with a fresh green salad and a loaf of crusty bread. —Brenda Andrew
San Antonio, Texas

  8 ounces uncooked small tube pasta
1-1/2 cups milk
  1 envelope carbonara pasta sauce mix
1-1/2 cups diced fully cooked ham
  1 package (10 ounces) frozen creamed spinach, thawed

Cook pasta according to package directions. Meanwhile, in a saucepan, whisk milk and sauce mix until blended. Bring to a boil over medium heat, stirring con-

stantly. Drain pasta; stir into sauce. Add ham and spinach; cook and stir until heated through. **Yield:** 4 servings.

Strawberry Bavarian Salad

Plan ahead…needs to chill

As a child, I asked my mother to make this colorful gelatin for birthdays. Now I fix it for my husband and son. You can leave out the marshmallows if you prefer.
—Lorna Northcutt, Gladstone, Oregon

  1 package (3 ounces) strawberry gelatin
  1 cup boiling water
  1 package (16 ounces) frozen sweetened sliced strawberries
  1 cup miniature marshmallows
  1/2 cup heavy whipping cream, whipped

In a large bowl, dissolve gelatin in water. Stir in the strawberries; fold in marshmallows and whipped cream. Transfer to a 5-cup serving bowl. Cover and refrigerate overnight. **Yield:** 6 servings.

Heavenly Hash Bars

Plan ahead…needs to chill

Chock-full of chips, nuts and mini marshmallows, these rich bars are a cinch to stir up. They make great Christmas treats, but I like to prepare them year-round.
—Peg Wilson, Elm Creek, Nebraska

  1 package (16 ounces) miniature marshmallows
  1 can (11-1/2 ounces) mixed nuts
  2 cups semisweet chocolate chips
  2 cups butterscotch chips
  1 cup peanut butter

Sprinkle marshmallows and nuts in a greased 13-in. x 9-in. x 2-in. pan; set aside. In a saucepan, melt chips and peanut butter over low heat, stirring constantly until smooth. Pour over marshmallows and nuts. Let stand 8-10 minutes. Gently stir to coat marshmallows. Refrigerate until set; cut into bars. **Yield:** 2-1/2 dozen.

Mexican Beef-Cheese Soup

Ready in 30 minutes or less

This hearty soup appeals to all ages and can be spiced up to suit individual tastes. I sometimes drain the can of tomatoes and add extra beef, serving it as a thick, cheesy dip. —Kim Gollin, Andover, Kansas

  1 pound ground beef
  1 medium onion, chopped
  1 can (14-1/2 ounces) diced tomatoes with green chilies, undrained
  1 can (11 ounces) Mexicorn, drained
  1 pound Mexican *or* plain process American cheese, cubed

In a large saucepan, cook beef and onion over medium heat until meat is no longer pink; drain. Stir in the tomatoes, corn and cheese. Cook and stir until cheese is melted. **Yield:** 6 servings.

Chapter 5

ON THE DAYS you're running behind schedule, 10 minutes may be all the time you have to prepare something delicious and satisfying for your family.

So the next time you're hungry and truly "down to the wire" on putting a homemade meal on the table, take a deep breath and count to 10.

Then turn to this time-saving chapter to quickly uncover a flavorful assortment of main dishes, sandwiches, side dishes, snacks, desserts and more. Each fantastic dish goes from start to finish in just about 10 minutes...but tastes like you spent hours in the kitchen.

ON-THE-RUN RECIPE. Chicken Pecan Wraps (p. 69).

Caramel Ice Cream Sauce

(Pictured at right)

I stir up this delightful dessert sauce on the stovetop. With its smooth texture and yummy taste from brown sugar, it's terrific drizzled over ice cream.   —Julee Wallberg
Reno, Nevada

   1/2 cup packed brown sugar
     1 tablespoon cornstarch
   1/3 cup half-and-half cream
     2 tablespoons water
     2 tablespoons light corn syrup
     1 tablespoon butter *or* margarine
   1/2 teaspoon vanilla extract
Ice cream

In a saucepan, combine the brown sugar and cornstarch. Stir in the cream, water and corn syrup until smooth. Bring to a boil; cook and stir for 2 minutes or until thickened. Remove from the heat; stir in the butter and vanilla until butter is melted. Serve warm or cold over ice cream. Refrigerate leftovers. **Yield:** about 1 cup.

Caramel Ice Cream Sauce

Cherry Chiffon Dessert

Pair cherry pie filling and pineapple tidbits to create this pretty pink fruit fluff. This dessert never lasts long around here.   —Louise Lawrence, Morgantown, Kentucky

     1 can (21 ounces) cherry pie filling
     1 can (20 ounces) pineapple tidbits, drained
     1 can (14 ounces) sweetened condensed milk
     1 cup miniature marshmallows
     1 carton (8 ounces) frozen whipped topping, thawed

In a bowl, combine the pie filling, pineapple, milk and marshmallows. Fold in whipped topping. Refrigerate until serving. **Yield:** 12 servings.

Creamed Chicken

I came up with this recipe as a variation to beef Stroganoff. I like to serve it over toasted English muffins or egg noodles.   —Debra Baker, Greenville, North Carolina

     1 pound boneless skinless chicken breasts, cut into 1/2-inch strips
     1 tablespoon vegetable oil
     1 can (10-3/4 ounces) condensed cream of chicken soup, undiluted
     1 cup water
   1/4 teaspoon salt
Pepper to taste
   1/2 cup sour cream
English muffins, split and toasted
Cayenne pepper *or* paprika

In a large skillet, saute the chicken in oil until no longer pink. Stir in the soup, water, salt and pepper. Bring to a boil. Remove from the heat and stir in sour cream. Serve over toasted English muffins. Sprinkle with cayenne or paprika. **Yield:** 4 servings.

Bacon 'n' Egg Tacos

Salsa perks up the flavor of this twist on a classic breakfast combo. This recipe can easily be divided to serve a few or doubled to serve a crowd. Just plan to use one egg for each taco.   —Wendy Matejek, Corpus Christi, Texas

     6 eggs
   1/4 cup crumbled cooked bacon
     2 tablespoons butter *or* margarine
     3 slices process American cheese, diced
   1/4 teaspoon salt
   1/4 teaspoon pepper
     6 flour tortillas (6 inches), warmed
Salsa, optional

In a bowl, beat the eggs; add bacon. Melt butter in a skillet over medium heat. Add egg mixture; cook and stir until the eggs are completely set. Stir in the cheese, salt and pepper. Spoon 1/4 cup down the center of each tortilla; fold sides over filling. Serve with salsa if desired. **Yield:** 6 servings.

Barbecue Kielbasa

I serve this mouth-watering main dish with corn bread and green beans. It can easily be tripled for potlucks. Serve the sweet sauce-covered sausage over hot cooked rice if time allows, or cut it into bite-size pieces for an appealing appetizer.   —Gina Slaven, Canfield, Ohio

     1 medium onion, halved and thinly sliced
     1 tablespoon butter *or* margarine
     1 pound fully cooked kielbasa *or* Polish sausage, cut into 1/4-inch slices
     1 cup ketchup
   1/3 to 1/2 cup packed brown sugar
     2 tablespoons Worcestershire sauce

In a large skillet, saute onion in butter until tender. Stir in the remaining ingredients. Bring to a boil. Reduce heat; simmer, uncovered, for 3 minutes or until sauce is slightly thickened, stirring occasionally. **Yield:** 4 servings.

Surprise Apple Salad

Chunks of Snickers candy bars are the sweet surprises in this fast fix. My busy daughter introduced me to this easy apple salad. My husband and I think it's great.
—*Elaine Sabacky, Litchfield, Minnesota*

- 3 **Snickers candy bars (2.07 ounces *each*), cut into 1/2-inch chunks**
- 3 **medium tart apples, peeled and chopped**
- 1 **carton (8 ounces) frozen whipped topping, thawed**

In a large bowl, combine all ingredients. Refrigerate until serving. **Yield:** 6-8 servings.

Grilled Cheese with Tomato

(Pictured below)

Put a tasty Italian twist on a lunchtime tradition. This speedy skillet sandwich features mozzarella, tomato slices, oregano and basil. —*Tricia Curley, Joliet, Illinois*

- 1 **tablespoon butter *or* margarine, softened**
- 2 **slices Italian bread**
- 1/3 **cup shredded mozzarella cheese**
- 2 **slices tomato**
- 1/4 **to 1/2 teaspoon dried oregano**
- 1/4 **to 1/2 teaspoon dried basil**

Spread butter on one side of each slice of bread. Place one slice, buttered side down, in a skillet; top with half of the cheese. Layer with tomato and remaining cheese; sprinkle with oregano and basil. Top with remaining bread, buttered side up. Cook over medium heat until golden brown on both sides. **Yield:** 1 serving.

Microwave Red Snapper

We fish a lot, so when I tried this recipe at a microwave cooking class, I knew it was a keeper. My husband requests it several times a month. —*Evelyn Gavin Cayucos, California*

- 4 **red snapper *or* haddock fillets (6 ounces *each*)**
- 3/4 **cup sour cream**
- 1/4 **cup mayonnaise**
- 3 **tablespoons milk**
- 1 **tablespoon prepared mustard**
- 1-1/2 **teaspoons dill weed**
Hot cooked rice

Cut fish into serving-size pieces; place in an ungreased shallow microwave-safe dish. Cover and microwave on high for 4 minutes. Drain liquid. Combine the sour cream, mayonnaise, milk, mustard and dill; drizzle 1/2 cup over the fish. Microwave, uncovered, on high for 4 minutes or until fish flakes easily with a fork. Serve over rice with remaining sauce. **Yield:** 6 servings.

Editor's Note: Reduced-fat or fat-free mayonnaise may not be substituted for regular mayonnaise in this recipe. It was tested in an 850-watt microwave.

Grilled Cheese with Tomato

Ham Coleslaw

(Pictured below)

Ham is an unusual addition to this crunchy slaw. To make this swift side dish even quicker, I use pimientos instead of chopping sweet red pepper. —Audrey Dee Benson
Flagler, Colorado

    2 cups shredded cabbage
    1 cup diced fully cooked ham
1/4 cup diced green pepper
    2 tablespoons diced sweet red pepper
1/4 cup vegetable oil
    2 tablespoons cider vinegar
    1 teaspoon sugar
1/2 to 1 teaspoon celery seed
1/4 teaspoon salt
1/4 teaspoon pepper
1/4 teaspoon paprika

In a bowl, toss the cabbage, ham and peppers. In a jar with a tight-fitting lid, combine the oil, vinegar, sugar, celery seed, salt, pepper and paprika; shake well. Pour over cabbage mixture and toss to coat. **Yield:** 5 servings.

Easy Chicken Barbecue

(Pictured below)

I have my family over for Sunday dinner once a month, so I'm always looking for new and different recipes to prepare. These simple sandwiches are quick and tasty. —Connie Perrone
Rockford, Illinois

Easy Chicken Barbecue
Ham Coleslaw

1/4 cup *each* chopped celery, green pepper and onion
    1 tablespoon butter *or* margarine
2/3 cup barbecue sauce
    1 can (10 ounces) chunk white chicken, drained
    3 sandwich rolls, split

In a saucepan, saute the celery, green pepper and onion in butter until tender. Stir in barbecue sauce and chicken; heat through. Serve on rolls. **Yield:** 3 servings.

Taco Turkey Wraps

I get lots of compliments whenever I bring these roll-ups to potluck lunches. Sour cream, taco seasoning and shredded Mexican cheese bring south-of-the-border flair to deli turkey in the rapid wraps. —Kathy Neidermann
Holland, Michigan

✓ Uses less fat, sugar or salt. Includes Nutritional Analysis and Diabetic Exchanges.

2/3 to 3/4 cup sour cream
    2 tablespoons taco seasoning
    6 flour tortillas (8 inches)
    1 cup (4 ounces) shredded Mexican cheese blend *or* cheddar cheese
1/2 pound thinly sliced deli turkey breast
Salsa, optional

In a bowl, combine the sour cream and taco seasoning. Spread over tortillas. Sprinkle with cheese. Top with turkey; roll up. Serve with salsa if desired. **Yield:** 6 servings.

    Nutritional Analysis: One serving (prepared with 2/3 cup fat-free sour cream and reduced-fat cheese; calculated without salsa) equals 282 calories, 8 g fat (3 g saturated fat), 33 mg cholesterol, 1,087 mg sodium, 34 g carbohydrate, 0 fiber, 19 g protein. **Diabetic Exchanges:** 2 starch, 2 lean meat.

Apple-Curry Tuna Melts

You'll want to make plenty of these delicious open-faced sandwiches because your family will come back for seconds. Curry powder puts a twist on traditional tuna salad, adding a colorful appearance and delightful taste. —Edie DeSpain, Logan, Utah

    1 can (6 ounces) tuna, drained and flaked
1/2 cup diced apple
1/4 cup mayonnaise
    1 tablespoon chopped green onion
    1 teaspoon Dijon mustard
1/2 teaspoon curry powder
    4 slices bread, toasted
1/4 cup chopped walnuts, toasted
    4 slices cheddar cheese

In a bowl, combine the first six ingredients; mix well. Spread 1/4 cup on each slice of toast; sprinkle with walnuts. Top with a slice of cheese. Broil 5 in. from the heat until cheese is melted. **Yield:** 4 servings.

Refreshing Fruit Dip

(Pictured at right)

I share this colorful dip made by blending peaches and strawberries from the freezer. Sometimes I don't completely thaw the fruit first, because I like the dip cold. —Jessica Humphrey
Fort Atkinson, Wisconsin

✓ Uses less fat, sugar or salt. Includes Nutritional Analysis and Diabetic Exchanges.

   1 package (16 ounces) frozen unsweetened sliced peaches, thawed
   1 package (10 ounces) frozen sweetened sliced strawberries, thawed
   1 tablespoon lemon juice
   1/4 teaspoon almond extract
Assorted fresh fruit

In a food processor, combine the first four ingredients; cover and process until smooth. Serve with fruit. **Yield:** 2-1/2 cups.
   Nutritional Analysis: One serving (1/4 cup dip) equals 75 calories, trace fat (0 saturated fat), 0 cholesterol, 8 mg sodium, 19 g carbohydrate, 2 g fiber, 1 g protein. **Diabetic Exchange:** 1 fruit.

Refreshing Fruit Dip

Eggplant with Tomato Sauce

Things don't get much quicker than this mouth-watering side dish. I broil sliced eggplant before topping it with a speedy garlic-seasoned tomato sauce and a little Parmesan cheese. —Edna Hoffman, Hebron, Indiana

   1 medium eggplant
   2 tablespoons butter *or* margarine, melted
Salt and pepper to taste
   1 can (8 ounces) tomato sauce
   1/4 teaspoon garlic powder
   1/4 cup grated Parmesan cheese, optional

Cut eggplant lengthwise into 1/2-in.-thick slices. Place on a broiler pan. Brush with butter; sprinkle with salt and pepper. Broil 4 in. from the heat for 3-4 minutes on each side or until tender. Meanwhile, heat the tomato sauce and garlic powder. Drizzle over eggplant. Sprinkle with Parmesan cheese if desired. **Yield:** 6-8 servings.

Summer Chicken Salad

Using a little imagination, I came up with this recipe for drop-in dinner guests one night. It's so versatile. You can leave out the grapes and add chopped apples or vegetables instead. —Diana Boschulte, Goodfield, Illinois

   2 cups cubed cooked chicken
   1 celery rib, thinly sliced
   1/2 cup seedless red grapes
   1/3 cup raisins
   1/2 cup mayonnaise
   1/2 teaspoon salt
   1/8 teaspoon pepper
   1/3 cup chopped pecans
Leaf lettuce
Tomato slices, optional

In a bowl, combine the chicken, celery, grapes and raisins. Add mayonnaise, salt and pepper; mix well. Stir in pecans. Serve on lettuce. Garnish with tomato if desired. **Yield:** 2-3 servings.

Ham 'n' Corn Scrambled Eggs

For a light lunch or dinner, try this skillet supper. Place a couple of potatoes in the microwave to "bake" while you're making this, so you have a complete meal. —Esther Shank, Harrisonburg, Virginia

   6 eggs, lightly beaten
   2 packages (10 ounces *each*) frozen corn in butter sauce, thawed
   1 teaspoon sugar
   1/2 teaspoon salt
   1/4 teaspoon pepper
1-1/2 cups cubed fully cooked ham
   2 tablespoons butter *or* margarine
   1 cup (4 ounces) shredded cheddar cheese

In a bowl, combine the first five ingredients; set aside. In a large skillet, cook ham in butter until heated through. Add egg mixture; cook and stir over medium heat until the eggs are completely set. Sprinkle with cheese. Cover and remove from the heat. Let stand for 3-5 minutes or until cheese is melted. **Yield:** 3-4 servings.

Italian Bread Salad

(Pictured at right)

It's easy to put dinner together on a busy night when you prepare this salad with its delicious pizza flavor. I often cut a block of mozzarella into cubes rather than using shredded cheese. —Sandra Castillo, Sun Prairie, Wisconsin

    1 prebaked Italian bread shell crust (14 ounces), cubed
1-1/2 cups diced fresh tomatoes
  1/2 cup thinly sliced fresh basil
  1/2 cup Italian salad dressing, *divided*
    7 cups ready-to-serve salad greens
    1 small green pepper, julienned
    1 cup sliced pepperoni
    1 cup (4 ounces) shredded mozzarella cheese
  1/2 cup grated Parmesan cheese
  1/2 cup sliced ripe olives

In a large salad bowl, combine bread cubes, tomatoes, basil and 1/4 cup salad dressing; let stand for 5 minutes. Add the salad greens, green pepper, pepperoni, mozzarella cheese, Parmesan cheese and olives. Add remaining salad dressing and toss to coat. **Yield:** 8-10 servings.

Italian Bread Salad

Chili-Cheese Mashed Potatoes

I jazz up instant mashed potatoes with garlic, green chilies and cheese to create this speedy side dish. It's really tasty and really quick. —Peter Halferty, Corpus Christi, Texas

 Uses less fat, sugar or salt. Includes Nutritional Analysis and Diabetic Exchanges.

2-3/4 cups water
    1 cup milk
1-1/2 teaspoons salt
    1 tablespoon butter *or* stick margarine
    3 garlic cloves, minced
    3 cups instant mashed potato flakes
    2 cans (4 ounces *each*) chopped green chilies
    1 cup (4 ounces) shredded Mexican cheese blend *or* cheddar cheese

In a large saucepan, bring the water, milk and salt to a boil. Add the butter, garlic, potato flakes and chilies; stir until thickened. Sprinkle with cheese. **Yield:** 6 servings.
    Nutritional Analysis: One 3/4-cup serving (prepared with fat-free milk and reduced-fat cheese) equals 169 calories, 5 g fat (3 g saturated fat), 13 mg cholesterol, 923 mg sodium, 23 g carbohydrate, 3 g fiber, 9 g protein. **Diabetic Exchange:** 1-1/2 starch.

Ginger Fruit Sundaes

The distinctive flavor of ginger steals the show in this tempting fruit-filled topping that I serve warm over ice cream. Use orange marmalade and canned fruit to streamline preparation. It's a real treat. —Heidi Wilcox
Lapeer, Michigan

    1 can (11 ounces) mandarin oranges
    1 tablespoon cornstarch
    1 can (8 ounces) crushed pineapple, undrained
  1/2 cup orange marmalade
  1/2 teaspoon ground ginger
Vanilla ice cream

Drain oranges, reserving 1/4 cup juice; set oranges aside. In a saucepan, combine cornstarch and reserved juice until smooth. Add the pineapple, marmalade and ginger. Bring to a boil; cook and stir for 2 minutes or until thickened. Remove from the heat; stir in oranges. Serve over ice cream. **Yield:** 4 servings.

Honey Peanut Apple Dip

Everyone just loves this dip...it never lasts long. The thick mixture is easy to scoop up with apple slices.
—Carolyn Sykora, Bloomer, Wisconsin

    1 package (8 ounces) cream cheese, softened
    1 cup finely chopped peanuts
  2/3 cup honey
    1 teaspoon vanilla extract
Sliced apples

In a small mixing bowl, beat cream cheese until smooth. Beat in the peanuts, honey and vanilla until combined. Serve with apples. Refrigerate leftovers. **Yield:** 2 cups.

Bagel Melts

I use whole wheat bagels or English muffins for these open-faced sandwiches. The quick combo is great for breakfast or alongside soup for dinner. —Linda Mincy
Counce, Tennessee

    4 tablespoons prepared mustard
    2 bagels, split

8 cheddar cheese slices
8 Canadian bacon slices
8 tomato slices

Spread 1 tablespoon mustard over each bagel half. Layer with one cheese slice, two Canadian bacon slices, two tomato slices and a second cheese slice. Place on an ungreased baking sheet. Bake at 350° for 4-6 minutes or until cheese is melted. Serve immediately. **Yield:** 4 servings.

Chicken Pecan Wraps

(Pictured below and on page 62)

Pecans add a touch of crunch to the warm chicken mixture in these speedy soft-shell tacos. Kick up the heat a notch or two by using medium or hot salsa.
—*Judy Frakes*
Blair, Nebraska

1 pound boneless skinless chicken breasts, cut into 1-inch cubes
1/4 cup chopped onion
1/4 teaspoon ground cumin
1 tablespoon butter *or* margarine
1/4 cup chopped pecans
3 tablespoons sour cream
4 flour tortillas (10 inches), warmed
1 cup (4 ounces) shredded cheddar cheese
1 cup salsa
Shredded lettuce, optional

In a large skillet, saute chicken, onion and cumin in butter until chicken juices run clear. Reduce heat to low. Add pecans and sour cream; cook and stir until heated through. Spoon about 1/2 cupful down the center of each tortilla; top with cheese, salsa and lettuce if desired. Fold in sides. **Yield:** 4 servings.

Crunchy Crab Salad

I frequently serve this cool salad at home and at social functions. It's super simple to make and has a unique taste that's delicious.
—*Stephanie Hamilton*
Rupert, Idaho

1 can (6 ounces) crabmeat, drained, flaked and cartilage removed
1 package (10 ounces) frozen peas, thawed
1 cup chopped celery
1 small onion, chopped
3/4 cup mayonnaise
1 tablespoon lemon juice
1 teaspoon soy sauce
1/4 teaspoon garlic salt
1/4 teaspoon curry powder
1 can (3 ounces) chow mein noodles
1/2 cup slivered almonds

In a bowl, combine the crab, peas, celery and onion; set aside. Combine the mayonnaise, lemon juice, soy sauce, garlic salt and curry powder; add to the crab mixture and toss to coat. Stir in the chow mein noodles and almonds. **Yield:** 6 servings.

Chicken Pecan Wraps

Chapter 6

WHEN YOU'RE at a loss for what to serve, a look in your pantry may be all that's needed to put together a mouth-watering meal fast!

A wide range of packaged convenience foods can help you find quick fixes to your dinner dilemmas.

It can be as simple as beefing up canned goods to make a comforting casserole, jazzing up frozen potatoes to fix an effortless entree or using a cake mix to create easy bars.

Or save even more time—and money, too—by making your own homemade mixes. The appealing assortment in this chapter is easy to assemble in advance and will provide a head start on your menu planning.

MIX MIRACLES. Left to right: Wild Rice Shrimp Bake and Walnut Carrot Cake (both recipes on p. 76).

Fast Fixes With Mixes

THE WORD IS OUT! Packaged convenience foods are a surefire way to save time in the kitchen. Big on flavor and low on fuss, today's boxed cake mixes, canned pie fillings, bottled sauces and other items give fast-to-fix dishes a down-home flavor the whole family enjoys.

So the next time you need a shortcut snack, easy entree or dessert in a dash, check your cupboard and whip up one of these speedy specialties.

Spinach Stuffing Balls

Ready in 30 minutes or less

These cute bites are a snap to fix with stuffing mix and frozen spinach. Over the years, we've held several appetizer parties for our family gatherings. These delicious spinach balls are always a big hit. —Janice Mitchell Aurora, Colorado

    6 eggs, lightly beaten
    1 package (6 ounces) stuffing mix
1/2 cup butter *or* margarine, melted
    1 cup grated Parmesan cheese
1/4 teaspoon salt
1/8 teaspoon pepper
    2 packages (10 ounces *each*) frozen chopped spinach, thawed and squeezed dry

In a bowl, combine eggs, stuffing mix, butter, Parmesan cheese, salt and pepper. Add spinach; mix well. Shape into 1-1/2-in. balls; place in an ungreased 15-in. x 10-in. x 1-in. baking pan. Bake at 350° for 12-15 minutes or until lightly browned. **Yield:** about 3-1/2 dozen.

Poppy Seed Blueberry Bread

(Pictured below left)

This was the first bread I made that my husband said was a "keeper". Poppy seeds and lemon perk up the flavor of these moist mini loaves. —Jennifer Miller, Avon, Indiana

    1 package (18-1/4 ounces) blueberry muffin mix
    1 egg
3/4 cup water
    3 tablespoons vegetable oil
    1 to 2 tablespoons poppy seeds
    2 to 3 teaspoons grated lemon peel
GLAZE:
1/2 cup confectioners' sugar
    1 to 2 tablespoons lemon juice

Drain and rinse blueberries from muffin mix; set aside. In a bowl, combine the muffin mix, egg, water, oil, poppy seeds and lemon peel just until blended. Fold in reserved blueberries. Pour into two greased 5-3/4-in. x 3-in. x 2-in. loaf pans. Bake at 350° for 40-45 minutes or until a toothpick inserted near the center comes out clean. Cool for 10 minutes before removing from pans to wire racks. Combine glaze ingredients; drizzle over warm loaves. **Yield:** 2 mini loaves.

Taco Pie

Ready in 45 minutes or less

This easy recipe combines tempting taco fixings with convenient biscuit mix to create a hearty zippy main-dish pie. You can flavor it as mild or as hot as you like. It goes well with a tossed salad. —Shelly Winkleblack Interlaken, New York

✓ Uses less fat, sugar or salt. Includes Nutritional Analysis and Diabetic Exchanges.

    1 pound ground beef
    1 large onion, chopped
1/2 cup salsa
    2 tablespoons taco seasoning
1/4 teaspoon pepper
    1 cup (4 ounces) shredded cheddar cheese
    2 eggs
    1 cup milk
1/2 cup biscuit/baking mix

In a large skillet, cook beef and onion over medium heat until meat is no longer pink; drain. Stir in salsa, taco seasoning and pepper. Transfer to a greased 9-in. pie plate; sprinkle with cheese. In a bowl, combine eggs, milk and biscuit mix just until blended; pour over cheese. Bake at 400° for 25-30 minutes or until a knife inserted near the center comes out clean. **Yield:** 6 servings.

Nutritional Analysis: One serving (prepared with lean ground beef, reduced-fat cheese, egg substitute, fat-free milk and reduced-fat biscuit mix) equals 276 calories, 12 g fat (6 g saturated fat), 42 mg cholesterol, 764 mg sodium, 16 g carbohydrate, 1 g fiber, 25 g protein. **Diabetic Exchanges:** 3 lean meat, 1 starch, 1 fat.

Poppy Seed Blueberry Bread

Chicken Spaghetti Casserole
Pear 'n' Apple Cobbler

Chicken Spaghetti Casserole

(Pictured above)

I first made this meal-in-one when I had unexpected guests. It's popular when I'm in a hurry, because it takes minutes to assemble. —Bernice Janowski
Stevens Point, Wisconsin

    8 ounces uncooked spaghetti
    1 carton (8 ounces) ricotta cheese
    1 cup (4 ounces) shredded mozzarella cheese, *divided*
    2 tablespoons grated Parmesan cheese
    1/2 teaspoon Italian seasoning
    1/2 teaspoon garlic powder
    1 jar (26 ounces) meatless spaghetti sauce
    1 can (14-1/2 ounces) Italian diced tomatoes, undrained
    1 jar (4-1/2 ounces) sliced mushrooms, drained
    4 breaded fully cooked chicken patties (10 to 14 ounces)

Cook spaghetti according to package directions. Meanwhile, in a bowl, combine the ricotta, 1/2 cup of mozzarella, Parmesan, Italian seasoning and garlic powder; set aside. In another bowl, combine the spaghetti sauce, tomatoes and mushrooms.

Drain spaghetti; add 2 cups spaghetti sauce mixture and toss to coat. Transfer to a greased 13-in. x 9-in. x 2-in. baking dish; top with cheese mixture. Arrange chicken patties over the top; drizzle with the remaining spaghetti sauce mixture. Sprinkle with the remaining mozzarella. Bake, uncovered, at 350° for 40-45 minutes or until bubbly. **Yield:** 4 servings.

Pear 'n' Apple Cobbler

(Pictured above)

Ready in 1 hour or less

Nutmeg lends a homey touch to apple pie filling and canned pears topped with tender biscuits. I've received many great comments about this dessert from my family and friends. Vanilla ice cream makes a wonderful addition to it. —Shirley Brown, Pocatello, Idaho

    2 teaspoons cornstarch
    1/4 teaspoon plus 1/8 teaspoon ground nutmeg, *divided*
    2/3 cup orange juice
    1 can (21 ounces) apple pie filling
    1 can (15-1/4 ounces) sliced pears, drained
1-1/2 cups biscuit/baking mix
    2 tablespoons plus 2 teaspoons sugar, *divided*
    1/2 cup milk
    2 tablespoons butter *or* margarine, melted

In a large saucepan, combine the cornstarch, 1/4 teaspoon of nutmeg and orange juice until smooth. Gently stir in pie filling and pears. Bring to a boil; cook and stir for 1-2 minutes or until thickened. Keep warm.

In a bowl, combine the biscuit mix, 2 tablespoons sugar, milk and butter just until blended. Pour hot filling into an ungreased 11-in. x 7-in. x 2-in. baking dish. Drop batter in six mounds onto fruit mixture. Combine the remaining sugar and nutmeg; sprinkle over the top.

Bake at 350° for 35-40 minutes or until bubbly and a toothpick inserted in the biscuit topping comes out clean. Serve warm. **Yield:** 6 servings.

Cocoa Cola Cake

Remove from the heat; stir in confectioners' sugar until smooth. Fold in pecans. Spread over cake. Let stand for 20 minutes before cutting. **Yield:** 12-15 servings.

Soft Macaroons

I bake 22 types of cookies at Christmas, and these macaroons are the most requested. People can't believe I use sherbet and cake mix to make the simple sweets.
—*Barbara Schindler, Napoleon, Ohio*

> 1 pint pineapple *or* orange sherbet, softened
> 2 teaspoons almond extract
> 1 package (18-1/4 ounces) white cake mix
> 6 cups flaked coconut

In a large mixing bowl, combine sherbet, almond extract and dry cake mix; mix well. Stir in the coconut. Drop by tablespoonfuls 2 in. apart onto greased baking sheets. Bake at 350° for 12-15 minutes or until edges are lightly browned. Remove to wire racks to cool. **Yield:** about 6 dozen.

Creamy Chicken Casserole

Ready in 1 hour or less

I need only four items for this comforting meal-in-one. If you'd like, add chopped broccoli to the rice for color. It's fast enough for weeknights yet tasty enough for company.
—*Sarah Larson, La Farge, Wisconsin*

> 2 packages (6.9 ounces *each*) chicken-flavored rice mix
> 4 cups cubed cooked chicken
> 2 cups (16 ounces) sour cream
> 2 cups chow mein noodles

Prepare rice mix according to package directions. Remove from the heat; stir in the chicken and sour cream. Transfer to a greased 13-in. x 9-in. x 2-in. baking dish. Sprinkle with the chow mein noodles. Bake, uncovered, at 350° for 25-30 minutes or until heated through. **Yield:** 6-8 servings.

BLT Pasta Salad

(Pictured at right)

Ready in 30 minutes or less

I make this easy salad for lots of potlucks and always come home with an empty dish. Crisp bacon, chopped tomato and fresh greens give a packaged pasta salad mix terrific flavor. —*Ellie Marsh, Lewistown, Pennsylvania*

> 1 package (6.2 ounces) pasta salad mix*
> 1 medium tomato, seeded and chopped
> 6 bacon strips, cooked and crumbled
> 5 cups torn lettuce

Prepare pasta salad mix according to package directions. Stir in the tomato and bacon. Serve over lettuce. **Yield:** 6 servings.

*Editor's Note: This recipe was tested with Betty Crocker Suddenly Salad Creamy Parmesan mix.

Cocoa Cola Cake

(Pictured above)

I love this tender cake because I usually have the ingredients on hand and it mixes up in a jiffy. Cola makes an interesting ingredient. The rich fudge frosting is easy to prepare, and the chopped pecans add nice crunch. —*Ellen Champagne New Orleans, Louisiana*

> 1 package (18-1/4 ounces) white cake mix
> 1 cup regular cola
> 2 eggs
> 1/2 cup buttermilk
> 1/2 cup butter *or* margarine, melted
> 1/4 cup baking cocoa
> 1 teaspoon vanilla extract
> 1-1/2 cups miniature marshmallows
> **FUDGE FROSTING:**
> 1/4 cup baking cocoa
> 1/2 cup butter *or* margarine, cubed
> 1/3 cup regular cola
> 4 cups confectioners' sugar
> 1 cup chopped pecans, toasted

In a large mixing bowl, combine the first seven ingredients. Beat on medium speed for 2 minutes. Fold in marshmallows. Pour into a greased 13-in. x 9-in. x 2-in. baking pan. Bake at 350° for 35-40 minutes or until a toothpick inserted near the center comes out clean. Cool on a wire rack for 15 minutes.

Meanwhile, for frosting, combine cocoa and butter in a saucepan. Cook over low heat until butter is melted. Stir in cola until blended. Bring to a boil, stirring constantly.

Hash Brown Pizza

(Pictured below)

Ready in 1 hour or less

Shredded hash browns make the golden crust for this family favorite. The tasty toppings include ground beef, sliced mushrooms and shredded cheese. Sometimes I add basil or oregano to the seasonings. —*Kim Rauhala Didsbury, Alberta*

1 package (30 ounces) frozen shredded hash brown potatoes, thawed
1 can (10-3/4 ounces) condensed cheddar cheese soup, undiluted
1 pound ground beef
3 celery ribs, chopped
1 medium onion, chopped
1 can (8 ounces) tomato sauce
1 jar (6 ounces) sliced mushrooms, drained
1-1/4 teaspoons chili powder
3/4 teaspoon seasoned salt
1/2 teaspoon garlic powder
1/4 teaspoon pepper
2 cups (8 ounces) shredded Colby-Monterey Jack cheese

In a large bowl, combine the hash browns and soup. Spread into a greased 15-in. x 10-in. x 1-in. baking pan. Bake at 400° for 30 minutes.

Meanwhile, in a large skillet, cook the beef, celery and onion over medium heat until meat is no longer pink and vegetables are tender; drain. Add the tomato sauce, mushrooms, chili powder, seasoned salt, garlic powder and pepper. Spread over the crust. Sprinkle with cheese. Bake 10 minutes longer or until the cheese is melted. **Yield:** 8 servings.

Hash Brown Pizza
BLT Pasta Salad

Wild Rice Shrimp Bake

(Pictured below and on page 70)

Ready in 45 minutes or less

Fresh shrimp lends a special touch to this effortless entree that starts out with a boxed wild rice mix. I top off the creamy casserole with a handful of crunchy croutons. It's a wonderful dish to serve company. —Lee Stearns, Mobile, Alabama

    1 package (6 ounces) long grain and wild rice mix
    1 pound uncooked medium shrimp, peeled and deveined
    1 medium green pepper, chopped
    1 medium onion, chopped
    1 can (4 ounces) mushroom stems and pieces, drained
1/4 cup butter *or* margarine
    1 can (10-3/4 ounces) condensed cream of chicken soup, undiluted
1/2 cup seasoned stuffing croutons

Prepare rice according to package directions. Meanwhile, in a large skillet, saute the shrimp, green pepper, onion and mushrooms in butter until shrimp turn pink. Add the soup to the rice; stir into the shrimp mixture. Transfer to a greased 2-qt. baking dish. Sprinkle with croutons. Bake, uncovered, at 350° for 20-25 minutes or until heated through. **Yield:** 6 servings.

Walnut Carrot Cake

(Pictured below left and on page 71)

I hope you enjoy this quicker version of carrot cake. To streamline it further, buy shredded carrots from the produce section and use prepared cream cheese frosting instead of homemade.
—Ardyce Piehl
Poynette, Wisconsin

    1 package (18-1/4 ounces) yellow cake mix
1-1/4 cups mayonnaise*
    4 eggs
1/4 cup water
    2 teaspoons ground cinnamon
    2 cups shredded carrots
1/2 cup chopped walnuts
FROSTING:
    1 package (8 ounces) cream cheese, softened
    5 tablespoons butter *or* margarine, softened
    4 cups confectioners' sugar
    2 tablespoons milk
    1 teaspoon vanilla extract
Orange gel food coloring and fresh parsley, optional

In a mixing bowl, combine the first five ingredients; mix well. Stir in carrots and nuts. Pour into a greased 13-in. x 9-in. x 2-in. baking pan. Bake at 350° for 40-45 minutes or until a toothpick inserted near the center comes out clean. Cool completely on a wire rack.

For frosting, in a small mixing bowl, beat cream cheese and butter until fluffy. Beat in confectioners' sugar, milk and vanilla until frosting reaches spreading consistency. If carrot decoration is desired, tint a small amount of frosting orange. Frost cake with plain frosting. Cut into squares. Pipe an orange carrot onto each square; add a parsley sprig for the carrot top. Store in the refrigerator. **Yield:** 12-15 servings.

*Editor's Note: Reduced-fat or fat-free mayonnaise may not be substituted for regular mayonnaise in this recipe.

Bacon Corn Bread

Ready in 1 hour or less

Central Illinois is one of the major corn and pork producing areas in the country, so why wouldn't this bread be a favorite here? I dress up a basic batter with corn, onion and cheese, then top it with poppy seeds and bacon.
—Carol Roper, Litchfield, Illinois

    1 package (8-1/2 ounces) corn bread/muffin mix
    1 egg
1/2 cup frozen corn, thawed
1/3 cup milk
1/4 cup shredded cheddar cheese
1/4 cup grated onion
    5 bacon strips, cooked and crumbled
1/2 teaspoon poppy seeds, optional
1/8 teaspoon paprika

In a bowl, combine the first six ingredients just until blended. Pour into a greased 8-in. square baking dish. Sprinkle with bacon, poppy seeds if desired and paprika. Bake at

Wild Rice Shrimp Bake
Walnut Carrot Cake

Rhubarb Berry Coffee Cake

375° for 20-25 minutes or until a toothpick inserted near the center comes out clean. Cut into squares; serve warm. **Yield:** 9 servings.

Rhubarb Berry Coffee Cake

(Pictured above)

I rely on a cake mix to stir up this moist streusel-topped dessert that pairs tart rhubarb with sweet strawberries. I prefer it without the frosting so that it doesn't get too sweet. —Jackie Heyer, Cushing, Iowa

1 package (18-1/4 ounces) yellow cake mix, *divided*
2/3 cup packed brown sugar
2 tablespoons cold butter *or* margarine
3/4 cup chopped walnuts
2 eggs
1 cup (8 ounces) sour cream
1-1/2 cups finely chopped fresh rhubarb
1-1/2 cups sliced fresh strawberries
1/2 cup cream cheese frosting, optional

In a bowl, combine 2/3 cup cake mix and sugar; cut in butter until crumbly. Add walnuts; set aside. Place remaining cake mix in another bowl; add the eggs and sour cream. Fold in rhubarb and strawberries. Spread into a greased 13-in. x 9-in. x 2-in. baking dish. Sprinkle with reserved crumb mixture.

Bake at 350° for 40-50 minutes or until a toothpick

inserted near the center comes out clean. Cool on a wire rack. If desired, place frosting in a microwave-safe bowl and heat for 15 seconds. Drizzle over cake. **Yield:** 12-15 servings.

Sloppy Joe Biscuit Bake

Ready in 45 minutes or less

Families are sure to gobble up this casserole. A meaty mixture flavored with sloppy joe seasoning is covered with cheese and refrigerated biscuits for a hearty main dish. —Kelli Nothern, Colorado Springs, Colorado

1 pound ground beef
1 small onion, chopped
1 envelope sloppy joe seasoning
2 cups spaghetti sauce
1 can (8 ounces) tomato sauce
1 cup (4 ounces) shredded mozzarella cheese
1 cup (4 ounces) shredded cheddar cheese
1 can (7-1/2 ounces) refrigerated buttermilk biscuits

In a large skillet, cook beef and onion over medium heat until meat is no longer pink; drain. Add sloppy joe seasoning, spaghetti sauce and tomato sauce; heat through. Transfer to a greased 13-in. x 9-in. x 2-in. baking dish. Sprinkle with cheeses. Place biscuits randomly over the top. Bake, uncovered, at 375° for 15-20 minutes or until biscuits are golden brown. **Yield:** 4 servings.

Creamy Watermelon Pie

PEANUT BUTTER DRIZZLE:
  2/3 cup confectioners' sugar
    2 tablespoons creamy peanut butter
    2 tablespoons plus 2 teaspoons water
CHOCOLATE DRIZZLE:
  2/3 cup confectioners' sugar
    2 tablespoons baking cocoa
    2 tablespoons plus 1 to 2 teaspoons water

Place the brownie mix, eggs, oil and water in a bowl. Beat with a spoon until combined. Stir in the pecans and chocolate chips. Pour into a greased 13-in. x 9-in. x 2-in. baking pan. Top with peanut butter cups.

Bake at 350° for 25-30 minutes or until a toothpick inserted near the center comes out clean. Cool on wire rack.

In a small mixing bowl, combine confectioners' sugar, peanut butter and water until smooth; drizzle over brownies. In a bowl, combine confectioners' sugar, cocoa and water until smooth; drizzle over brownies. Let set before cutting. **Yield:** 3-1/2 dozen.

Au Gratin Beef Bake

This swift savory supper is so full of down-home taste that no one will believe it's so easy. Canned tomato soup and packaged au gratin potatoes are baked with ground beef to create the comforting casserole.
—Margaret Schroeder
Cudahy, Wisconsin

    1 pound ground beef
    1 large onion, chopped
    2 celery ribs, chopped
1/2 cup chopped green pepper
    1 package (5-1/4 ounces) au gratin potatoes
    1 can (10-3/4 ounces) condensed tomato soup, undiluted
    1 teaspoon Worcestershire sauce
1-3/4 cups water
  2/3 cup milk

In a large skillet, cook the beef, onion, celery and green pepper until meat is no longer pink and vegetables are tender; drain. In a greased 2-1/2-qt. baking dish, combine beef mixture, potatoes with contents of sauce mix, soup and Worcestershire sauce. Stir in the water and milk. Bake, uncovered, at 400° for 45-50 minutes or until potatoes are tender. **Yield:** 6 servings.

Ham Muffinwiches

(Pictured at right)

Ready in 45 minutes or less

I concocted this fun recipe when looking for something to pack for lunch. I had leftover ham but no bread, so I got creative with corn bread mix. The tender muffins freeze well and are handy for an on-the-go breakfast or lunch.
—Jenny Wiebe, Villa Hills, Kentucky

    1 package (8-1/2 ounces) corn bread/muffin mix
1/8 teaspoon ground mustard
1/3 cup milk

Creamy Watermelon Pie

(Pictured above)

Plan ahead...needs to chill

This simple pie is so refreshing that it never lasts long on warm summer days. Watermelon and a few convenience items make it a delightful dessert that doesn't take much effort.
—Velma Beck, Carlinville, Illinois

    1 package (3 ounces) watermelon gelatin
1/4 cup boiling water
    1 carton (12 ounces) frozen whipped topping, thawed
    2 cups cubed seeded watermelon
    1 graham cracker crust (9 inches)

In a large bowl, dissolve gelatin in boiling water. Cool to room temperature. Whisk in whipped topping; fold in watermelon. Spoon into crust. Refrigerate for 2 hours or until set. **Yield:** 6-8 servings.

Fancy Fudge Brownies

I'm a true chocolate lover. To dress up brownies from a boxed mix, I added chips, nuts and mini peanut butter cups before baking, then drizzled them with both a chocolate and a peanut butter icing. They instantly became a family favorite. —Karen Wisner, Grafton, North Dakota

    1 package fudge brownie mix (13-inch x 9-inch pan size)
    3 eggs
1/2 cup vegetable oil
1/4 cup water
    1 cup chopped pecans
    1 cup (6 ounces) semisweet chocolate chips
1/2 cup milk chocolate chips
    18 miniature peanut butter cups, halved

1 tablespoon vegetable oil
1 egg
1 cup chopped fully cooked ham
1/4 cup thinly sliced green onions
2 tablespoons shredded cheddar cheese

In a bowl, combine corn bread mix, mustard, milk, oil and egg just until blended. Stir in the ham and onions. Fill greased or paper-lined muffin cups half full. Bake at 400° for 15-20 minutes or until a toothpick comes out clean. Immediately sprinkle with cheese. Cool for 5 minutes before removing from pan. Serve warm. **Yield:** 9 muffins.

Sausage Brunch Casserole

(Pictured below)

I've served this hearty dish to many guests, and they always ask for the recipe. It can even be assembled the night before and kept in the refrigerator. Just pop it in the oven in the morning. —Paula Christensen, Soldotna, Alaska

1 pound bulk pork sausage, cooked and drained
1/2 cup chopped green onions
1 can (4 ounces) mushroom stems and pieces, drained
2 medium tomatoes, chopped
2 cups (8 ounces) shredded mozzarella cheese
1 cup pancake mix
12 eggs
1 cup milk
1/2 teaspoon dried oregano
1/2 teaspoon salt
1/4 teaspoon pepper

In a greased 3-qt. baking dish, layer the sausage, onions, mushrooms, tomatoes and cheese. In a large bowl, whisk the pancake mix, eggs, milk, oregano, salt and pepper; pour over cheese.

Bake, uncovered, at 350° for 45-50 minutes or until top is set and lightly browned. Let stand for 10 minutes before serving. **Yield:** 6-8 servings.

Sausage Brunch Casserole
Ham Muffinwiches

Cheesy Chicken

Ready in 30 minutes or less

This is such a simple recipe, and leftovers make a great lunch the next day. The best part is that my young daughter, who can be a picky eater, just loves it!
—*Christine Burk, Tallahassee, Florida*

- 1 package (10 ounces) frozen broccoli in cheese sauce
- 1 package (6-1/2 ounces) broccoli au gratin rice mix
- 1 cup cubed cooked chicken
- 1/2 cup cubed process cheese (Velveeta)

Prepare broccoli according to package directions. In a large saucepan, prepare rice mix according to package directions. Stir in the broccoli, chicken and process cheese. Cook until cheese is melted. **Yield:** 4 servings.

Editor's Note: This recipe was tested with Green Giant Broccoli & Cheese Sauce and Rice-a-Roni Broccoli Au Gratin rice and pasta mix.

Lime Sherbet Molded Salad

(Pictured below)

Plan ahead...needs to chill

For an eye-appealing addition to a picnic, potluck or other gathering, try this molded gelatin salad. With its lovely color, creamy texture and refreshing flavor, it's sure to disappear in a jiffy. —*Cyndi Fynaardt, Oskaloosa, Iowa*

- 2 packages (3 ounces *each*) lime gelatin
- 2 cups boiling water
- 2 pints lime sherbet, softened
- 1 carton (8 ounces) whipped topping

In a large bowl, dissolve gelatin in boiling water. Stir in sherbet until well blended. Cool until syrupy. Spoon whipped topping into a large mixing bowl. Gradually

beat in the gelatin mixture on low speed until well blended. Pour into a 12-cup mold coated with nonstick cooking spray. Refrigerate for 6-8 hours or until set. **Yield:** 16 servings.

Artichoke Bean Salad

Ready in 15 minutes or less

You can stir up this colorful bean salad in no time. Two kinds of canned beans and a jar of artichokes pick up fast flavor when tossed with prepared salad dressing.
—*Dixie Terry, Goreville, Illinois*

- 1 can (16 ounces) kidney beans, rinsed and drained
- 1 can (14-1/2 ounces) cut green beans, drained
- 1 jar (6-1/2 ounces) marinated artichoke hearts, undrained
- 1-1/2 cups chopped red onion
- 1/2 cup chopped green pepper
- 1/2 cup Italian salad dressing

In a large bowl, toss all ingredients. Cover and refrigerate until serving. **Yield:** 10 servings.

Special Cookie Bars

I use four types of chips to create these yummy treats. I made these sweet bars when I needed quick holiday gifts for teachers. The teachers requested them over and over—even after our children were no longer their students!
—*Mary Haass Valstad, Casper, Wyoming*

- 2 cups finely crushed cornflakes
- 1/3 cup butter *or* margarine, melted
- 2 tablespoons sugar
- 1/4 cup *each* milk chocolate, peanut butter, semisweet chocolate and vanilla *or* white chips*
- 1 cup flaked coconut
- 1 cup chopped mixed nuts
- 1 can (14 ounces) sweetened condensed milk

In a bowl, combine the cornflake crumbs, butter and sugar. Press into a greased 13-in. x 9-in. x 2-in. baking pan. Sprinkle with chips, coconut and nuts. Drizzle with milk. Bake at 350° for 25 minutes. Cool on a wire rack before cutting. **Yield:** about 2 dozen.

*Editor's Note: Any combination of baking chips equal to 1 cup may be used.

Sunday Chops and Stuffing

(Pictured above right)

Ready in 1 hour or less

Our married children and their families come over for dinner most Sundays. This meal-in-one casserole with tender chops, apple slices and a moist stuffing has been a longtime favorite and is so easy to prepare. It's a memorable main dish we all enjoy.
—*Georgiann Franklin, Canfield, Ohio*

Lime Sherbet Molded Salad

2 cups water
2 celery ribs, chopped
7 tablespoons butter *or* margarine, *divided*
1/4 cup dried minced onion
6 cups seasoned stuffing croutons
6 bone-in pork loin chops (3/4 inch thick)
1 tablespoon vegetable oil
1/4 teaspoon salt
1/4 teaspoon pepper
2 medium tart apples, sliced
1/4 cup packed brown sugar
1/8 teaspoon pumpkin pie spice

In a saucepan, combine the water, celery, 6 table-spoons butter and onion. Bring to a boil. Remove from the heat; stir in croutons. Spoon into a greased 13-in. x 9-in. x 2-in. baking dish; set aside.

In a large skillet, brown pork chops on both sides in oil. Arrange over the stuffing. Sprinkle with salt and pepper. Combine the apples, brown sugar and pumpkin pie spice; spoon over pork chops. Dot with the remaining butter. Bake, uncovered, at 350° for 30-35 minutes or until a meat thermometer reads 160° and meat juices run clear. **Yield:** 6 servings.

No-Fuss Pumpkin Cake

(Pictured above)

This moist, old-fashioned cake goes together quickly. That's a plus for me, because I have a husband who loves desserts. —Nancy Heider, Larsen, Wisconsin

1 can (15 ounces) solid-pack pumpkin
3 eggs
1/3 cup sugar
1/3 cup vegetable oil
1 package (18-1/4 ounces) yellow cake mix
1 tablespoon pumpkin pie spice
1 can (16 ounces) vanilla frosting
1 package (3 ounces) cream cheese, softened

In a large mixing bowl, combine the pumpkin, eggs, sugar and oil; mix well. Add cake mix and pumpkin pie spice; beat for 2 minutes. Pour into a greased 15-in. x 10-in. x 1-in. baking pan. Bake at 350° for 25-35 minutes or until a toothpick inserted near the center comes out clean. Cool on a wire rack. In a mixing bowl, combine the frosting and cream cheese. Spread over cake. Store in the refrigerator. **Yield:** 20-24 servings.

Taco Bean Soup
Cheddar Garlic Biscuits

Cheddar Garlic Biscuits

(Pictured above)

Ready in 30 minutes or less

I get a lot of recipes from friends, and this one is no exception. Biscuit mix is combined with a little minced onion, garlic powder and cheese to create these golden drop biscuits that bake in a flash.
—*Frances Poste*
Wall, South Dakota

   2 cups biscuit/baking mix
1/2 cup shredded cheddar cheese
1/2 teaspoon dried minced onion
2/3 cup milk
1/4 cup butter *or* margarine, melted
1/2 teaspoon garlic powder

In a bowl, combine the biscuit mix, cheese and onion. Stir in milk until a soft dough forms; stir 30 seconds longer. Drop by rounded tablespoonfuls 2 in. apart onto ungreased baking sheets. Bake at 450° for 8-10 minutes or until golden brown. Combine butter and garlic powder; brush over biscuits. Serve warm. **Yield:** 15 biscuits.

Taco Bean Soup

(Pictured above)

Ready in 1 hour or less

This hearty three-bean soup is very easy to fix. You can add a can of green chilies if you like it hotter. I increase the amount of tomatoes and beans for large church get-togethers. —*Sharon Thompson, Hunter, Kansas*

   1 pound bulk pork sausage
   1 pound ground beef

   1 envelope taco seasoning
   4 cups water
   2 cans (16 ounces *each*) kidney beans, rinsed
    and drained
   2 cans (15 ounces *each*) pinto beans, rinsed
    and drained
   2 cans (15 ounces *each*) garbanzo beans,
    rinsed and drained
   2 cans (14-1/2 ounces *each*) stewed tomatoes
   2 cans (14-1/2 ounces *each*) Mexican diced
    tomatoes, undrained
   1 jar (16 ounces) chunky salsa
Sour cream, shredded cheddar cheese and sliced
  ripe olives, optional

In a soup kettle, cook sausage and beef over medium heat until no longer pink; drain. Add taco seasoning and mix well. Stir in the water, beans, tomatoes and salsa. Bring to a boil. Reduce heat; simmer, uncovered, for 30 minutes or until heated through, stirring occasionally. Garnish with sour cream, cheese and olives if desired. **Yield:** 12-14 servings.

Chocolate Upside-Down Cake

This dessert is out of this world. Coconut, chocolate chips, marshmallows and pecans turn a boxed cake mix into a delectable treat. All of your guests will agree that it's the best ever. Enjoy it with a scoop of vanilla ice cream.
—*Iola Egle, McCook, Nebraska*

1-1/4 cups water
  1/4 cup butter *or* margarine
   1 cup packed brown sugar
   1 cup flaked coconut
   2 cups (12 ounces) semisweet chocolate chips
   1 cup chopped pecans
   2 cups miniature marshmallows
   1 package (18-1/4 ounces) German chocolate
    cake mix

In a small saucepan, heat water and butter until butter is melted. Stir in brown sugar; mix well. Pour into a greased 13-in. x 9-in. x 2-in. baking pan. Sprinkle with coconut, chocolate chips, pecans and marshmallows.

  Prepare cake batter according to package directions; carefully pour over marshmallows. Bake at 325° for 55-60 minutes or until a toothpick inserted near the center comes out clean. Cool for 10 minutes before inverting cake onto a serving plate. **Yield:** 12-15 servings.

Apricot Cranberry Cake

(Pictured at right)

This cranberry and apricot cake is a nice treat for breakfast or brunch. —*Helen Borkoski, Silver Spring, Maryland*

   3 cups biscuit/baking mix
 3/4 cup sugar
   2 eggs, beaten
   1 cup (8 ounces) plain yogurt
  1/4 cup orange juice
  1/4 cup vegetable oil
1-1/2 teaspoons almond extract

    2 cups chopped fresh *or* frozen cranberries
3/4 cup chopped dried apricots
1/2 cup chopped almonds
GLAZE:
    1 cup confectioners' sugar
    4 teaspoons orange juice
1/2 teaspoon vanilla extract

In a bowl, combine biscuit mix and sugar. In another bowl, combine eggs, yogurt, orange juice, oil and almond extract. Stir into biscuit mixture just until combined. Fold in cranberries, apricots and almonds.

Transfer to a greased and floured 10-in. fluted tube pan. Bake at 350° for 50-55 minutes or until toothpick inserted near the center comes out clean. Cool for 10 minutes before removing to wire rack to cool completely. In a bowl, combine the glaze ingredients until smooth. Drizzle over cooled cake. **Yield:** 12-16 servings.

Tuna Patties

Ready in 45 minutes or less

My family likes anything that includes stuffing mix, so these tuna burgers are a popular request. —Sonya Sherrill Sioux City, Iowa

    2 eggs, beaten
    1 can (10-3/4 ounces) condensed cream of
        mushroom soup, undiluted, *divided*
3/4 cup milk, *divided*
    2 cups stuffing mix
    1 can (12 ounces) tuna, drained and flaked
    2 tablespoons butter *or* margarine

In a bowl, combine the eggs, a third of the soup and 1/4 cup milk; mix well. Stir in stuffing mix and tuna. Shape into eight patties. In a skillet, brown patties in butter for 3-4 minutes on each side or until heated through. Meanwhile, in a small saucepan, heat remaining soup and milk. Serve with patties. **Yield:** 4 servings.

Creamy Onion Potatoes

Ready in 45 minutes or less

French onion dip streamlines preparation and provides unbelievably rich flavor. —Betty Glasgow, Bolivar, Missouri

    6 cups cubed red potatoes, cooked
1/3 cup chopped green onions
    1 carton (16 ounces) French onion dip
White pepper to taste
    1 cup (4 ounces) shredded cheddar cheese

In a bowl, combine potatoes, onions, dip and pepper. Transfer to a greased 1-1/2-qt. baking dish; sprinkle with cheese. Bake, uncovered, at 350° for 20-25 minutes or until cheese melts and potatoes are heated through. **Yield:** 6 servings.

Handy Shaker

I have an extra shaker container that I fill with flour for flouring cake pans or flouring a board before rolling out dough. The shaker top lets out just the right amount of flour.
    —Mark Sisul
    Carol Stream, Illinois

Apricot Cranberry Cake

Homemade Mixes

BY KEEPING these homemade mixes on hand, you'll have made-in-minutes meals and time-saving treats at your fingertips whenever you need a quick fix.

And because these family-tested mixes are as economical as they are simple, you can put that boxed mix back on your grocer's shelf and put the money you save back in your wallet!

Editor's Note: The contents of mixes may settle during storage. When preparing the recipe, spoon the mix into a measuring cup.

Crumb Coating for Fish

(Pictured below)

Being a farm wife, I don't have much time to prepare meals. That's why I keep this mix for coating fish on hand.
—*Rosalie Mellott, Oakland, Maryland*

    1 cup crushed saltines (about 30 crackers)
    1 cup cornmeal
    2 tablespoons paprika
    5 teaspoons seafood seasoning
    2 teaspoons salt
    1 to 1-1/2 teaspoons pepper
ADDITIONAL INGREDIENT (for *each* batch):
    1 pound sole fillets

In a large resealable plastic bag, combine the first six ingredients. Store in a cool dry place for up to 6 months. **Yield:** 6 batches (2 cups total).

To prepare fish: Place 1/3 cup coating in a shallow bowl; coat both sides of the fillets. Place in a greased 13-in. x 9-in. x 2-in. baking dish. Bake, uncovered, at 400° for 12-15 minutes or until fish flakes easily with a fork. **Yield:** 4 servings.

Crumb Coating for Fish

Raisin Bran Muffin Mix

My husband likes to take muffins to work. And with this mix in my pantry, I can have muffins ready in minutes.
—*Darlene Markel, Salem, Oregon*

      2 cups all-purpose flour
  1-1/4 cups sugar
      1 cup nonfat dry milk powder
      6 teaspoons baking powder
      1 teaspoon salt
    1/2 teaspoon ground cinnamon
      1 cup shortening
  1-1/2 cups raisin bran cereal
      1 cup chopped almonds
ADDITIONAL INGREDIENTS (for *each* batch):
      1 egg
      1 cup water

In a large bowl, combine first six ingredients. Cut in shortening until crumbly. Stir in cereal and nuts. Store in an airtight container in a cool dry place or in the freezer for up to 2 months. **Yield:** 2 batches (8 cups total).

To prepare muffins: Place 4 cups of muffin mix in a bowl. Beat egg and water; stir into mix just until moistened. Fill greased muffin cups two-thirds full. Bake at 400° for 15-17 minutes or until a toothpick comes out clean. Cool for 5 minutes before removing from pan to a wire rack. **Yield:** 1 dozen.

Oatmeal Spice Mix

My daughters love packaged oatmeal flavored with maple and brown sugar. But because that oatmeal can be expensive, I created my own spice mix for oatmeal. The girls think it tastes better than the store-bought variety.
—*Marcy Waldrop, Pasadena, Texas*

    1/2 cup powdered nondairy creamer
    1/2 cup confectioners' sugar
    1/3 cup packed brown sugar
      1 teaspoon salt
    1/2 teaspoon ground cinnamon
    1/4 teaspoon pumpkin pie spice
    1/4 teaspoon ground nutmeg
ADDITIONAL INGREDIENTS (for *each* batch):
    2/3 cup quick-cooking oats
    1/3 to 1/2 cup boiling water
Brown sugar, optional

In a bowl, combine the first seven ingredients; mix well. Store in an airtight container in a cool dry place for up to 6 months. **Yield:** 9 batches (about 1 cup total).

To prepare oatmeal: In a bowl, combine oats and 2 tablespoons oatmeal spice mix. Add enough boiling water until oatmeal is desired consistency. Sprinkle with brown sugar if desired. **Yield:** 1 serving.

Flour Tortilla Mix

This recipe makes tasty homemade flour and spinach tortillas. Use them when a recipe calls for the packaged variety, or try them in the Southwestern suppers I also share here.   —*Katie Koziolek, Hartland, Minnesota*

8-1/2 cups all-purpose flour
2/3 cup nonfat dry milk powder
1 tablespoon baking powder
1 teaspoon salt
1 cup shortening
ADDITIONAL INGREDIENTS FOR FLOUR TORTILLAS:
1/2 cup plus 1 to 2 tablespoons water
ADDITIONAL INGREDIENTS FOR SPINACH TORTILLAS:
1/4 cup frozen chopped spinach, thawed and squeezed dry
1/3 cup plus 2 to 3 tablespoons water

In a large bowl, combine the flour, milk powder, baking powder and salt. With a pastry blender, cut in shortening until crumbly. Store in an airtight container in a cool dry place for up to 6 months. **Yield:** 4 batches (about 10 cups total).

To prepare flour tortillas: In a bowl, combine 2-1/2 cups tortilla mix and 1/2 cup water. Stir with a fork until mixture forms a ball, adding additional water if necessary. Turn onto a lightly floured surface; knead 6-8 times or until smooth and combined. Divide into 10 portions. Roll each piece into an 8-in. circle.

In a 10-in. ungreased nonstick skillet, cook each tortilla over medium-high heat for 30-45 seconds or until bubbles form. Turn tortilla, pressing bubbles down with a spatula. Cook about 30 seconds longer or until lightly browned. **Yield:** 10 tortillas (8 inches each).

To prepare spinach tortillas: In a blender, combine spinach and 1/3 cup water; cover and process until pureed. In a bowl, combine 2-1/2 cups tortilla mix and spinach mixture. Continue as directed for flour tortillas. **Yield:** 10 tortillas.

Taco Burritos

(Pictured above right)

Flour tortillas bake to a delightful crispness in this family-pleasing fare from Katie. Full of beef, peppers and south-of-the-border flair, the burritos are a great way to spice up dinnertime.

1-1/2 pounds ground beef *or* pork
1 green pepper, chopped
1 medium onion, chopped
2 garlic cloves, minced
1 envelope taco seasoning
1/4 cup water
8 flour tortillas
1 tablespoon vegetable oil
Taco toppings of your choice

In a large skillet, cook the meat, green pepper and onion over medium heat until meat is no longer pink; drain. Add the garlic, taco seasoning and water. Simmer, uncovered, for 2 minutes.

Place four tortillas on a microwave-safe plate; microwave on high for 20 seconds. Place 1/2 cup of meat mixture on each; fold over sides and ends. Place seam side down in a greased 13-in. x 9-in. x 2-in. baking dish. Repeat with remaining tortillas and filling.

Brush burritos with oil. Bake, uncovered, at 450° for

Taco Burritos
Fajita Tortilla Bowls

9-10 minutes or until lightly browned and slightly crisp. Serve with toppings. **Yield:** 8 servings.

Fajita Tortilla Bowls

(Pictured above)

When brushed with butter and baked over custard cups, Katie's spinach tortillas make crunchy bowls for lettuce salads topped with pork and peppers.

6 spinach tortillas
2 tablespoons butter *or* margarine, melted
1 tablespoon vegetable oil
1 pound boneless pork loin chops, cut into thin strips
1 envelope fajita seasoning mix
1 medium onion, thinly sliced
1 sweet red pepper, thinly sliced
1 green pepper, thinly sliced
4-1/2 cups shredded lettuce
1 medium tomato, chopped

Place six 10-oz. custard cups upside down in a shallow baking pan; set aside. Brush both sides of tortillas with butter; place in a single layer on ungreased baking sheets. Bake, uncovered, at 425° for 1 minute. Place a tortilla over each custard cup, pinching sides to form a bowl shape. Bake for 7-8 minutes or until crisp. Remove tortillas from cups to cool on wire racks.

Heat oil in a large skillet over medium-high heat. Add pork and seasoning mix; cook and stir until meat juices run clear. Remove pork with a slotted spoon. In the drippings, saute onion and peppers until crisp-tender. Place lettuce in tortilla bowls; top with pork, pepper mixture and tomato. **Yield:** 6 servings.

Editor's Note: 4-in.-diameter foil balls can be used instead of custard cups.

Microwave Cake Mix

Microwave Cake Mix

(Pictured above)

I rely on my microwave to bake this from-scratch cake in less than 15 minutes. I'm always looking for recipes that save minutes and money. This tasty chocolate cake mix does just that. —Sandy Shineldecker, Hart, Michigan

    3 cups sugar
    2 cups all-purpose flour
    2 cups baking cocoa
1-1/2 teaspoons baking powder
ADDITIONAL INGREDIENTS (for *each* **cake):**
    2 eggs
 1/2 cup mayonnaise
 1/2 cup milk
Frosting of your choice

In a bowl, combine the sugar, flour, cocoa and baking powder. Store in an airtight container in a cool dry place for up to 1 year. **Yield:** 3 batches (6 cups total).
    To prepare cake: In a bowl, combine 2 cups mix, eggs, mayonnaise and milk; mix until combined. Pour into a well-greased 8-in. round microwave-safe casserole dish. Microwave at 50% power for 7 minutes. Microwave on high 5-6 minutes longer or until a toothpick inserted near the center comes out clean. Cool for 10 minutes before removing from dish to a wire rack. Frost when completely cooled. **Yield:** 6-8 servings.
    Editor's Note: Reduced-fat or fat-free mayonnaise may not be substituted for regular mayonnaise in this recipe. It was tested in an 850-watt microwave.

Italian Meatball Seasoning

I serve these meatballs with spaghetti sauce over pasta or in Italian rolls. I also use the seasoning mix for meat loaf and veal Parmesan. —Kathy Nieratko
Fair Haven, Vermont

    8 slices day-old white bread, cut into thirds
    8 teaspoons dried oregano
    8 teaspoons dried parsley flakes
    4 teaspoons dried basil
    4 teaspoons dried marjoram
    3 teaspoons garlic powder
    2 teaspoons seasoned salt

ADDITIONAL INGREDIENTS (for *each* **batch of meatballs):**
    2 eggs
 1/2 cup milk
 1/2 cup grated Parmesan cheese
    1 garlic clove, minced
 1/8 teaspoon pepper
    1 pound ground beef
    2 tablespoons vegetable oil

Place bread on an ungreased baking sheet. Bake at 200° for 20 minutes. Turn; bake 15-20 minutes longer or until dried. Place bread in a blender or food processor; cover and process until crumbly. Add seasonings. Store in an airtight container in a cool dry place for up to 6 months. **Yield:** 2 batches (about 2 cups total).
    To prepare meatballs: In a bowl, combine eggs, milk, 1 cup seasoned bread crumbs, Parmesan cheese, garlic and pepper. Crumble beef over mixture and mix well. Shape into 1-1/2-in. balls. In a large skillet, brown meatballs in oil; cook until meat is no longer pink. Drain on paper towels. **Yield:** 2 dozen.

Hearty Pancake Mix

Wheat flour, crushed cornflakes and old-fashioned oats create the multigrain mixture for these filling flapjacks. Served with butter and syrup, the golden cakes will keep your family going. —Mavis Diment, Marcus, Iowa

    5 cups all-purpose flour
1-1/2 cups whole wheat flour
1-1/2 cups finely crushed cornflakes
    1 cup old-fashioned oats
    2 tablespoons sugar
    1 tablespoon baking powder
1-1/2 teaspoons baking soda
1-1/2 teaspoons salt
ADDITIONAL INGREDIENTS (for *each* **batch of pancakes):**
1-1/2 cups milk
    1 egg
    1 tablespoon vegetable oil

In a large bowl, combine the first eight ingredients; mix well. Store in an airtight container in a cool dry place for up to 6 months. **Yield:** 5 batches (7-1/2 cups total).
    To prepare pancakes: In a bowl, combine 1-1/2 cups mix, milk, egg and oil; whisk just until moistened. Pour batter by 1/4 cupfuls onto a lightly greased hot griddle. Turn when bubbles form on top of pancakes; cook until second side is golden brown. **Yield:** 10 pancakes.
    Editor's Note: Contents of pancake mix may settle during storage. When preparing recipe, spoon mix into measuring cup.

Rosemary Pork Chops

(Pictured at right)

Ready in 30 minutes or less

I'm glad my sister-in-law shared the recipe for this coating mix for pork. It comes in handy when unexpected guests drop by, and it's wonderful on chicken, too. I usually bake

the tender chops, but it's even quicker to cook them on the stovetop. —Margaret Welder, Madrid, Iowa

1-1/2 cups dry bread crumbs
1/2 cup all-purpose flour
1-1/2 teaspoons salt
1 to 1-1/2 teaspoons dried rosemary, crushed
1 teaspoon paprika
1/4 teaspoon onion powder
3 tablespoons vegetable oil
ADDITIONAL INGREDIENTS (for *each* batch of pork chops):
6 bone-in pork loin chops (1/2 inch thick)
Vegetable oil

In a bowl, combine the first six ingredients; stir in oil until crumbly. Store in a covered container in the refrigerator. **Yield:** 3 batches (2-1/4 cups total).

To prepare pork chops: Place 3/4 cup coating mix in a resealable plastic bag. Place a small amount of water in a shallow bowl. Dip pork chops in water; place in the bag and shake to coat. In a skillet, cook chops in oil over medium heat for 4 minutes on each side or until juices run clear. **Yield:** 6 servings.

Ready Gravy Mix

(Pictured below)

Ready in 15 minutes or less

Surprise a beginner cook with a jar of this homemade gravy mix. Attach a wooden spoon and a label with the directions for making the gravy. It's a thoughtful and useful gift. —Edie DeSpain, Logan, Utah

1 jar (2-1/4 ounces) instant chicken *or* beef bouillon powder*
1-1/2 cups all-purpose flour
3/4 to 1 teaspoon pepper
ADDITIONAL INGREDIENTS (for *each* batch of gravy):
3 tablespoons butter *or* margarine
1-1/2 cups cold water

In a bowl, combine the bouillon, flour and pepper. Store in an airtight container in a cool dry place for up to 6 months. **Yield:** 8 batches (2 cups total).

To prepare gravy: In a saucepan, melt butter. Add 1/4 cup gravy mix. Cook and stir until lightly browned, about 1 minute. Whisk in water until smooth. Bring to a boil; cook and stir for 2 minutes or until thickened. **Yield:** 1-1/2 cups.

***Editor's Note:** This recipe was tested with Wyler's Shakers.

Frozen Fudge Pops

Plan ahead...needs to freeze

Kids of all ages will enjoy these cool chocolaty treats. Our children really love them on hot summer days. The frosty fudge pops start with a homemade mix that can be stored in the fridge or freezer. —Angie Hall
Newport, North Carolina

4 cups nonfat dry milk powder
1-1/2 cups sugar
1 cup all-purpose flour
1/2 cup baking cocoa
1/2 cup cold butter *or* margarine
ADDITIONAL INGREDIENTS (for *each* batch of fudge pops):
2-1/2 cups water
1 teaspoon vanilla extract

In a large bowl, combine the milk powder, sugar, flour and cocoa. Cut in butter until the mixture resembles coarse crumbs. Freeze in an airtight container for up to 6 months or refrigerate for up to 3 months. **Yield:** 3 batches (6-1/2 cups total).

To prepare fudge pops: In a saucepan, whisk 2 cups mix and water. Bring to a boil. Reduce heat; simmer for 1-2 minutes or until thickened, stirring frequently. Remove from the heat; stir in vanilla. Cool slightly. Fill 3-oz. molds or cups three-fourths full; top with holders or insert Popsicle sticks. Freeze for up to 3 months. **Yield:** 10 fudge pops.

**Rosemary Pork Chops
Ready Gravy Mix**

Butter Muffin Mix

(Pictured below)

I use a basic muffin mix to create both sweet and savory treats. The mild almond and apricot muffins are great for breakfast, while the savory beef and onion muffins make a nice dinner accompaniment.
—Lois Stiteley
Sun City West, Arizona

5-1/2 cups all-purpose flour
1/2 cup sugar
1/4 cup baking powder
1-1/2 teaspoons salt
3/4 cup cold butter *or* margarine
ADDITIONAL INGREDIENTS FOR APRICOT MUFFINS:
2 tablespoons sugar
1 egg
3/4 cup plus 1 tablespoon milk
1/4 teaspoon almond extract
1/4 cup chopped dried apricots
1/4 cup chopped slivered almonds, toasted
ADDITIONAL INGREDIENTS FOR BEEF AND ONION MUFFINS:
1 egg
3/4 cup plus 1 tablespoon milk
1 package (2-1/2 ounces) thinly sliced roast beef, finely chopped
1/4 cup chopped green onions

In a large bowl, combine the flour, sugar, baking powder and salt. Cut in butter until the mixture resembles coarse crumbs. Store in an airtight container in the refrigerator for up to 3 months. **Yield:** 3 batches (about 7 cups mix).

To prepare Apricot Muffins: In a large bowl, combine 2-1/3 cups muffin mix and sugar. Combine the egg, milk and extract; stir into dry ingredients just until moistened. Fold in apricots and almonds. Fill greased or paper-lined muffin cups two-thirds full. Bake at 425° for 10-13 minutes or until a toothpick comes out clean. Cool for 5 minutes before removing from pan to a wire rack. **Yield:** 1 dozen.

To prepare Beef and Onion Muffins: Place 2-1/3 cups muffin mix in a bowl. Combine egg and milk; stir into mix just until moistened. Fold in beef and onions. Fill greased or paper-lined muffin cups two-thirds full. Bake at 425° for 10-13 minutes or until a toothpick comes out clean. Cool for 5 minutes before removing from pan to a wire rack. **Yield:** 1 dozen.

Breakfast Cake Mix

This delightful crumb cake has a brown sugar topping featuring raisins, pecans and chocolate chips. A friend gave me this mix for Christmas. All I had to do was mix it and bake it in the pan she also provided. —Lucile Proctor
Panguitch, Utah

8-1/2 cups all-purpose flour
6 cups sugar
2 cups nonfat dry milk powder
1/4 cup baking powder
1-1/2 teaspoons salt
2-1/2 cups shortening
TOPPING:
3 cups raisins
3 cups packed brown sugar
2 cups chopped pecans
2 cups (12 ounces) semisweet chocolate chips
2 tablespoons ground cinnamon
ADDITIONAL INGREDIENTS (for *each* cake):
1 egg, lightly beaten
1 cup water

In a large bowl, combine the flour, sugar, milk powder, baking powder and salt; cut in shortening until crumbly. Store in airtight containers in a cool dry place for up to 6 months. In a large bowl, combine the topping ingredients. Store in airtight containers in a cool dry place for up to 6 months. **Yield:** 7 batches (21 cups cake mix and 10-1/2 cups topping mix).

To prepare cake: In a large bowl, combine 3 cups breakfast cake mix, egg and water; mix well. Pour into a greased 9-in. square baking pan. Sprinkle with 1-1/2 cups topping mix. Bake at 350° for 30-35 minutes or until a toothpick inserted near the center comes out clean. Cool on a wire rack. **Yield:** 9 servings.

Hot Roll Mix

(Pictured above right)

A friend who is a home economist gave me the recipe for this mix that can be used to make dinner rolls or cinnamon rolls. The buttery dinner rolls make a super accompaniment to any entree, and the sweet cinnamon rolls are perfect with coffee. —Barbara Morse, Spirit Lake, Iowa

10 cups (2-1/2 pounds) bread flour
3/4 cup nonfat dry milk powder
3/4 cup sugar
4-1/2 teaspoons salt
3/4 cup butter-flavored shortening

Butter Muffin Mix

Hot Roll Mix
Creamy Coffee Mix

ADDITIONAL INGREDIENTS FOR DOUGH:
    1 package (1/4 ounce) active dry yeast
    1 cup warm water (110° to 115°)
    1 egg
    1/4 to 1/2 cup bread flour
ADDITIONAL INGREDIENTS FOR CINNAMON ROLLS:
    3 tablespoons butter *or* margarine, softened
    3/4 cup packed brown sugar
    3/4 teaspoon ground cinnamon
    1 cup confectioners' sugar
    1/4 teaspoon vanilla extract
    1 to 2 tablespoons milk

In a large bowl, combine the flour, milk powder, sugar and salt; cut in shortening until crumbly. Store in an airtight container in a cool dry place for up to 6 months. **Yield:** 4 batches (about 13-1/3 cups total).

To prepare dough for dinner rolls or cinnamon rolls: In a mixing bowl, dissolve yeast in warm water. Add egg and 3-1/3 cups hot roll mix; beat until smooth. Add enough bread flour to form a soft dough. Turn onto a floured surface; knead until smooth and elastic, about 6-8 minutes. Place in a greased bowl, turning once to grease top. Cover and let rise in a warm place until doubled, about 45 minutes.

For dinner rolls: Punch the dough down; turn onto a lightly floured surface. Divide into 12 pieces; shape each into a ball. Place 2 in. apart on a greased baking sheet. Cover and let rise until doubled, about 30 minutes. Bake at 350° for 18-22 minutes or until golden brown. Remove to wire racks to cool. **Yield:** 1 dozen rolls per batch.

For cinnamon rolls: Punch dough down; turn onto a lightly floured surface. Roll into a 15-in. x 12-in. rectangle. Spread butter to within 1/2 in. of edges. Combine brown sugar and cinnamon; sprinkle over butter.

Roll up jelly-roll style, starting with a long side; pinch seam to seal. Cut into 1-1/2-in. slices. Place cut side down in a greased 13-in. x 9-in. x 2-in. baking pan. Cov-

er and let rise until doubled, about 30 minutes.

Bake at 350° for 30-35 minutes or until golden brown. Cool on a wire rack. For glaze, combine the confectioners' sugar, vanilla and milk; drizzle over rolls. **Yield:** 1 dozen rolls per batch.

Creamy Coffee Mix

(Pictured above)

Cinnamon and a little sugar dress up instant coffee granules in this easy blend. —Jane Fraser
Gig Harbor, Washington

    7 tablespoons instant coffee granules
    1/4 cup powdered nondairy creamer
    3 tablespoons sugar
    3 tablespoons nonfat dry milk powder
    1 teaspoon ground cinnamon
ADDITIONAL INGREDIENTS (for *each* batch):
    1 cup boiling water
Cinnamon stick, optional

In an airtight container, combine the coffee granules, creamer, sugar, milk powder and cinnamon. Store in a cool dry place for up to 2 months. **Yield:** 5 batches (about 1 cup total).

To prepare coffee: In a mug, dissolve about 3 tablespoons mix in boiling water; stir well. Serve with a cinnamon stick if desired. Yield: 1 serving.

Creative Croutons

Instead of adding croutons to our salads, I sprinkle on stuffing mix for some extra crunch. We like the corn bread stuffing mix, but I use whatever kind I have on hand. —Ann Shingleton, Fort Worth, Texas

Chapter 7

Look Ahead for Lively Leftovers

LEFTOVERS can make for quick-and-easy meals—without looking or tasting the same the second or even the third time around.

For example, start by offering the Herbed Pork and Potatoes pictured at left and featured on page 96. (Like all the weekend dishes that supply the main ingredient for the weekday recipes, its title is highlighted in a colored box.) Later, surprise your family with such lively leftovers as Snow Pea Pork Medley and Pork Salad Croissants.

The results taste so good that no one will realize they're eating leftovers!

NEXT-DAY DISHES. Clockwise from top: Herbed Pork and Potatoes, Snow Pea Pork Medley, Pork Salad Croissants (all recipes on pp. 96 and 97).

Homemade Refried Beans

These special refried beans are full of homemade flair. And because the recipe makes a big batch, you can sprinkle some with cheese to serve as a Southwestern side dish and use the rest in the two dinners that follow.
—Myra Innes, Auburn, Kansas

    1 large onion, chopped
    4 garlic cloves, minced
    6 tablespoons olive *or* vegetable oil, *divided*
    5 cans (15 ounces *each*) pinto beans, rinsed
        and drained
1-1/2 teaspoons ground cumin
    1 teaspoon salt
  1/2 teaspoon ground coriander
  1/4 teaspoon pepper
  1/4 teaspoon hot pepper sauce
    1 cup (4 ounces) shredded Monterey
        Jack cheese

In a large skillet, saute the onion and garlic in 2 table-spoons oil. Place 2 tablespoons oil in a blender or food processor; add half of the onion mixture, and half of the beans, cumin, salt, coriander, pepper, hot pepper sauce and cheese. Cover and process until smooth. Repeat with remaining ingredients.

Heat through in a skillet or microwave. Leftover refried beans may be frozen for up to 3 months. **Yield:** 7 cups.

Two-Bean Chili

Ready in 30 minutes or less

I was sure to learn the secrets behind my mom's zesty chili before I got married. Steaming bowls of it are great in the winter with coleslaw and corn bread or muffins. Surprise your gang with this snappy supper tonight.
—Deborah Heatwole, Waynesboro, Georgia

    1 pound ground beef
    1 large onion, chopped
    3 cans (16 ounces *each*) kidney beans, rinsed
        and drained
    1 can (46 ounces) tomato juice
    2 cans (14-1/2 ounces *each*) diced tomatoes,
        undrained
    2 cups refried beans
    3 tablespoons sugar
    3 tablespoons chili powder
    1 teaspoon salt
  1/4 teaspoon cayenne pepper
Dash pepper

In a soup kettle or Dutch oven, cook the beef and onion over medium heat until meat is no longer pink; drain. Stir in the remaining ingredients; cook until heated through. **Yield:** 15 servings.

Bean 'n' Beef Crescent Pie

Ready in 1 hour or less

My husband loves this meal. Convenient crescent roll dough is the quick crust for this savory south-of-the-border sensation. —Marla Miller, Englewood, Tennessee

1-1/4 pounds ground beef
    1 envelope taco seasoning
  1/3 cup salsa
    1 tube (8 ounces) refrigerated crescent rolls
    4 ounces cream cheese, softened
  1/2 cup refried beans
    1 cup (4 ounces) shredded Mexican cheese
        blend *or* cheddar cheese

In a large skillet, cook the beef over medium heat until no longer pink; drain. Add taco seasoning and salsa; simmer, uncovered, until thickened. Meanwhile, unroll crescent roll dough. Press onto the bottom and up the sides of an ungreased 13-in. x 9-in. x 2-in. baking dish; seal perforations. Spread cream cheese over the dough.

Stir the refried beans into beef mixture. Spoon over cream cheese layer. Bake, uncovered, at 375° for 20-25 minutes or until crust is golden brown. Sprinkle with cheese; bake 5 minutes longer or until the cheese is melted. **Yield:** 6-8 servings.

Baked Spiral Ham

(Pictured at right)

This is one of our favorite ham recipes. It will deliciously feed a crowd, or use what's remaining in the two recipes offered here. No one groans about having to eat ham leftovers when these items are on the menu.
—Marilou Robinson
Portland, Oregon

    1 large onion, sliced
    2 tablespoons butter *or* margarine
    1 fully cooked spiral ham (7 to 9 pounds)
1-1/2 cups chicken broth
    1 cup red wine *or* additional chicken broth

In a small skillet, saute the onion in butter until tender; transfer to a roasting pan. Place ham on top. Pour the broth and wine or additional broth over ham. Bake, uncovered, at 325° for 2-3 hours or until a meat thermometer reads 140° and ham is heated through. **Yield:** 12-15 servings.

Colorful Ham Strata

(Pictured above right)

Plan ahead...start the night before

Marilou's make-ahead breakfast bake is a cinch, particularly when leftover ham is used. Chock-full of peppers, onions and cheese, the eye-opener makes an ideal contribution to brunch buffets and is a great way to start the day.

    2 medium onions, quartered and sliced
  3/4 cup *each* julienned green and sweet
        red pepper
    1 teaspoon olive *or* vegetable oil
    1 loaf (1 pound) French bread, cut into 1/2-
        inch cubes
1-1/2 cups diced fully cooked ham (3/4 pound)
    1 cup (4 ounces) shredded Monterey
        Jack cheese

Baked Spiral Ham
Colorful Ham Strata
Greek Ham Wraps

6 eggs
2 cups milk
1 teaspoon salt
1/2 teaspoon pepper

In a large skillet, saute onions and peppers in oil. Place half of the bread cubes in a greased 13-in. x 9-in. x 2-in. baking dish. Sprinkle with half of the onion mixture, ham and cheese. Repeat layers. In a bowl, beat the eggs, milk, salt and pepper. Pour over bread mixture. Cover and refrigerate overnight.

Remove from the refrigerator 30 minutes before baking. Bake, uncovered, at 350° for 30-35 minutes or until a knife inserted near the center comes out clean. **Yield:** 6-8 servings.

Greek Ham Wraps

(Pictured above)

Ready in 30 minutes or less

Feta cheese and black olives give Greek flavor to julienned ham in these tasty handheld specialties. Marilou sometimes adds slices of roasted red pepper before wrapping everything in the tortilla. The green onion tie is a simple way to turn an ordinary lunch into something special.

6 tablespoons mayonnaise
2 tablespoons minced fresh basil *or* 2 teaspoons dried basil
6 flour tortillas (8 inches)
6 lettuce leaves
3 cups julienned fully cooked ham (1-1/2 pounds)
1 can (4-1/2 ounces) sliced ripe olives, drained
6 tablespoons crumbled feta cheese
6 green onions, chopped
Additional green onions, optional
1 cup water, optional

In a small bowl, combine the mayonnaise and basil; spread over each tortilla. Top with lettuce, ham, olives, feta cheese and chopped onions; roll up.

For optional onion ties, cut white portion off additional onions; save for another use. In a saucepan, bring water to a boil. Add green onion tops; boil for 1 minute or until softened. Drain and immediately place onion tops in ice water; drain and pat dry. Tie around wraps. **Yield:** 6 servings.

Fudgy Brownies
(Pictured below)

I've made these moist brownies many times and they're always a hit. If your family doesn't gobble up the whole pan, you can use the leftovers in the sweet treats that follow. —June Formanek, Belle Plaine, Iowa

    4 squares (1 ounce *each*) unsweetened chocolate
    1 cup butter (no substitutes), cubed
    4 eggs
    2 cups sugar
    1 teaspoon vanilla extract
    1 cup all-purpose flour
    1 cup (6 ounces) semisweet chocolate chips
    1 cup chopped pecans, optional
Confectioners' sugar

In a microwave, melt unsweetened chocolate and butter; stir until smooth. In a mixing bowl, beat eggs, sugar and vanilla for 1-2 minutes or until light and lemon-colored. Beat in the chocolate mixture. Add flour; beat just until combined. Fold in the chocolate chips and pecans if desired.

Transfer to a greased 13-in. x 9-in. x 2-in. baking pan. Bake at 350° for 25-30 minutes or until a toothpick inserted near the center comes out with moist crumbs. Cool on a wire rack. Dust with confectioners' sugar. **Yield:** 16-20 servings.

Mocha Mousse Brownie Trifle
(Pictured below)

Our Test Kitchen used some of the extra brownies to create this tempting, time-saving trifle. It's a snap to assemble with a packaged mousse mix and whipped topping, yet it looks so special that folks will think you fussed.

    5 cups cubed brownies (1/2-inch cubes)
    1 package (2.8 ounces) mocha mousse mix
    1 carton (12 ounces) frozen whipped topping, thawed
  1/4 cup English toffee bits *or* almond brickle chips
Grated chocolate

Place half of the cubed brownies in a 2-qt. serving bowl. Prepare mousse mix according to package directions. Spread half over the brownies. Top with half of the whipped topping; sprinkle with toffee bits. Repeat layers of brownies, mousse and whipped topping. Sprinkle with grated chocolate. Refrigerate until serving. **Yield:** 10-12 servings.

Brownie Cheesecake
Mocha Mousse Brownie Trifle
Fudgy Brownies

Brownie Cheesecake

(Pictured below left)

Plan ahead...needs to chill

I don't remember where I got this recipe, but it's so good! Before baking the smooth and creamy chocolate cheesecake, I stir crumbled brownies into the batter for a delectable touch. —Dorothy Olivares, El Paso, Texas

1-1/2 cups crushed vanilla wafers (about 45 cookies)
 6 tablespoons confectioners' sugar
 6 tablespoons baking cocoa
 6 tablespoons butter *or* margarine, melted
FILLING:
 3 packages (8 ounces *each*) cream cheese, softened
 1/4 cup butter *or* margarine, softened
 1 can (14 ounces) sweetened condensed milk
 3 teaspoons vanilla extract
 1/2 cup baking cocoa
 4 eggs
1-1/2 cups crumbled brownies
Whipped topping and pecan halves, optional

In a bowl, combine the wafer crumbs, confectioners' sugar and cocoa. Stir in the butter until blended. Press onto the bottom of a greased 9-in. springform pan. In a mixing bowl, beat the cream cheese and butter until fluffy. Add the milk and vanilla; mix well. Add cocoa; mix well. Beat in the eggs just until combined. Fold in brownies. Spoon into crust.

Place pan on a baking sheet. Bake at 350° for 50-55 minutes or until center is almost set. Cool on a wire rack for 10 minutes. Carefully run a knife around the edge of pan to loosen. Cool 1 hour longer. Refrigerate overnight. Garnish with whipped topping and pecans if desired. **Yield:** 10-12 servings.

Corned Beef Dinner

Plan ahead...uses slow cooker

This flavorful meal is a must for St. Patrick's Day but great any time of year. While I usually cook it on the stovetop, a slow cooker makes it even easier. It serves four nicely with enough leftover meat for Reuben sandwiches or other dishes. —Michelle Rhodes
Cleveland, Ohio

 4 to 5 medium red potatoes, quartered
 2 cups fresh baby carrots, halved lengthwise
 3 cups chopped cabbage
 1 corned beef brisket (3-1/2 pounds) with spice packet
 3 cups water
 1 tablespoon caraway seeds

Place the potatoes, carrots and cabbage in a 5-qt. slow cooker. Cut brisket in half; place over vegetables. Add the water, caraway seeds and contents of spice packet. Cover and cook on low for 9-10 hours or until the meat and vegetables are tender. **Yield:** 4-6 servings plus leftovers.

Reuben Monte Cristos

I use leftover corned beef for this twist on a traditional Reuben. I dip the sandwiches in egg and crushed corn chips before grilling them to crunchy perfection. These tasty sandwiches are great with a cup of soup.
—Helen Jay, Arkansas City, Kansas

 2 eggs
 1 tablespoon milk
2-1/2 cups corn chips, crushed
 8 slices rye bread
1/2 cup Thousand Island salad dressing
 12 slices cooked corned beef
 8 slices Swiss cheese
 1 cup sauerkraut, rinsed and well drained

In a shallow bowl, beat the eggs and milk. Place chips in another shallow bowl. Dip one side of four slices of bread in the egg mixture, then in the chips. Place chip side down on a greased baking sheet. Spread with salad dressing. Top with corned beef, Swiss cheese and sauerkraut.

Dip the remaining bread slices in egg mixture and chips; place chip side up on sandwiches. Cook on a medium-hot griddle until lightly browned, turning once. **Yield:** 4 servings.

Corned Beef Omelet

I was raised on a farm, where we had chickens as well as other farm animals, so we ate a lot of egg dishes. We usually served this simple omelet for breakfast with toast on the side. —Kitty Jones, Chicago, Illinois

 2 green onions, sliced
 2 tablespoons butter *or* margarine
 6 eggs
1/4 cup milk
 1 cup cubed cooked corned beef
1/2 cup shredded cheddar cheese
Dash pepper

In a large skillet, saute the onions in butter. In a bowl, lightly beat eggs and milk; pour over the onions. Cook over medium heat; as the eggs set, lift edges, letting uncooked portion flow underneath.

When the eggs are nearly set, sprinkle with the corned beef, cheese and pepper. Remove from the heat; cover and let stand for 1-2 minutes or until the cheese is melted. Cut into wedges. **Yield:** 4 servings.

Corned Beef Basics

Corned beef is a type of beef brisket that has been cured in a salt brine and treated with spices.

Fresh beef brisket is a boneless cut of meat that often requires long, slow cooking to achieve optimum tenderness. It is sold as a flat or point cut. The flat cut is usually leaner, but the point cut is a bit more flavorful.

Coney Island Sauce

Ready in 30 minutes or less

Put the ketchup aside! I turn ground beef, chopped onion, tomato sauce and chili powder into a zippy topping ideal for hot dogs. Grill two packages of hot dogs at your next barbecue and save the extras for the following dishes.
—Shirley Heston, Pickerington, Ohio

```
1/2  pound ground beef
1/4  cup chopped onion
  2  tablespoons chopped celery
  1  can (8 ounces) tomato sauce
  2  tablespoons brown sugar
  1  tablespoon lemon juice
2-1/4 teaspoons Worcestershire sauce
3/4  teaspoon chili powder
1/2  teaspoon prepared mustard
1/4  teaspoon salt
 20  hot dogs
  8  hot dog buns, split
```

In a skillet, cook beef, onion and celery over medium heat until meat is no longer pink; drain. Stir in tomato sauce, brown sugar, lemon juice, Worcestershire sauce, chili powder, mustard and salt. Bring to a boil. Reduce heat; simmer, uncovered, for 15-20 minutes or until sauce is thickened, stirring occasionally.

Grill or cook hot dogs according to package directions. Place eight hot dogs in buns; top with sauce. Refrigerate remaining hot dogs. **Yield:** 8 servings with sauce plus leftover hot dogs.

Cheesy Mac 'n' Dogs

Ready in 1 hour or less

I've made this casserole for 25 years and my family never gets tired of it. I like to assemble it the night before, then pop it in the oven after work. A tossed salad completes the meal nicely. —Sue Gonzales, Fortson, Georgia

```
  1  package (8 ounces) elbow macaroni
  1  small onion, finely chopped
1/4  cup butter or margarine
1/4  cup all-purpose flour
  1  teaspoon salt
1/2  teaspoon ground mustard
2-1/2 cups milk
3/4  teaspoon Worcestershire sauce
 12  ounces process cheese (Velveeta), cubed
  7  cooked hot dogs, diced
1/4  cup dry bread crumbs
```

Cook macaroni according to package directions. Meanwhile, in a large skillet, saute onion in butter until tender. Stir in the flour, salt and mustard. Gradually add milk. Bring to a boil; cook and stir for 2 minutes or until thickened. Stir in the Worcestershire sauce and cheese until cheese is melted.

Drain macaroni; stir into the cheese sauce. Add the hot dogs. Transfer to a greased 2-1/2-qt. baking dish. Sprinkle with bread crumbs. Bake, uncovered, at 350° for 20-25 minutes or until bubbly. **Yield:** 6-8 servings.

Hearty German Potato Salad

Ready in 1 hour or less

This is a tasty take on German potato salad. I add sliced hot dogs to the bacon, cider vinegar and potatoes found in this classic. —Michelle Beran, Claflin, Kansas

```
  4  bacon strips, diced
1/4  cup chopped onion
  1  tablespoon all-purpose flour
1/2  cup water
1/4  cup cider vinegar
  1  tablespoon sugar
3/4  teaspoon salt
1/2  teaspoon celery seed
Dash pepper
  2  medium potatoes (about 1-1/2 pounds),
       cooked, peeled, halved and sliced
  5  cooked hot dogs, sliced
```

In a large skillet, cook bacon over medium heat until crisp. Remove with a slotted spoon to paper towels. In the drippings, saute the onion until tender. Stir in flour until blended. Gradually stir in water, vinegar, sugar, salt, celery seed and pepper. Bring to a boil; cook and stir for 2 minutes or until thickened.

Stir in the potatoes, hot dogs and reserved bacon. Transfer to a greased 1-qt. baking dish. Bake, uncovered, at 350° for 20-25 minutes or until heated through. **Yield:** 4 servings.

Herbed Pork and Potatoes

(Pictured at right and on page 90)

Ready in 1 hour or less

I know you're going to enjoy preparing and serving this mouth-watering meal-in-one. The Test Kitchen crew tripled the number of rosemary-seasoned tenderloins, so you can serve one with the potatoes for a family dinner, then save the leftover pork for the next two recipes.
—Denise Dowd, St. Louis, Missouri

```
3/4  cup olive or vegetable oil
4-1/2 teaspoons minced fresh thyme or 1-1/2
       teaspoons dried thyme
  6  garlic cloves, minced
  1  tablespoon dried minced onion
  1  tablespoon minced fresh rosemary or 1
       teaspoon dried rosemary, crushed
1-1/2 teaspoons seasoned salt
1-1/2 teaspoons coarsely ground pepper
1-1/2 teaspoons ground mustard
  3  pork tenderloins (1 pound each)
  1  pound small red potatoes, quartered
```

In a bowl, combine the first eight ingredients. Place the pork in a large shallow baking pan. Drizzle with three-fourths of the herb mixture. Toss potatoes with remaining herb mixture; place around pork.

Bake, uncovered, at 375° for 40-45 minutes or until a meat thermometer reads 160° and potatoes are tender. Let pork stand for 5 minutes before slicing. **Yield:** 3-4 servings with potatoes plus leftover pork.

Herbed Pork and Potatoes
Snow Pea Pork Medley
Pork Salad Croissants

Snow Pea Pork Medley

(Pictured above and on page 91)

Last night's pork and a microwave oven make this mild main dish a snap to prepare. This is a favorite in our home.
—Gloria Bisek, Deerwood, Minnesota

    2 tablespoons cornstarch
    3 tablespoons soy sauce
    1 teaspoon chicken bouillon granules
  1/2 cup water
  1/4 teaspoon ground ginger, optional
    1 can (8 ounces) sliced water chestnuts,
      drained
    1 can (8 ounces) bamboo shoots, drained
    1 package (6 ounces) frozen snow peas, thawed
  1/2 cup sliced green onions
  1/2 cup sliced onion
    2 cups sliced cooked pork tenderloin (1/4 inch
      thick)
Hot cooked rice

In a large microwave-safe bowl, combine the cornstarch, soy sauce, bouillon, water and ginger if desired until smooth. Cover and microwave on high for 2 minutes, stirring once.

Add the water chestnuts, bamboo shoots, peas and onions. Cover and cook on high for 4-5 minutes or until vegetables are crisp-tender, stirring occasionally. Stir in

pork; cook 2-3 minutes longer or until heated through. Serve over rice. **Yield:** 4 servings.

Editor's Note: This recipe was tested in an 850-watt microwave.

Pork Salad Croissants

(Pictured above and on page 90)

Looking for a tasty change of pace from traditional chicken or tuna salad sandwiches? Try this rapid recipe from our Test Kitchen. It combines apple chunks, grapes, chopped walnuts and cubed pork with ginger, chutney and mayonnaise for a lunchtime lifesaver. This sandwich is sure to be a hit at your house.

    2 cups diced cooked pork tenderloin
    1 medium tart apple, diced
  1/2 cup halved seedless red grapes
  1/2 cup mayonnaise
    2 tablespoons chopped walnuts
    2 tablespoons chutney
  1/2 teaspoon salt
  1/4 teaspoon ground ginger
Lettuce leaves
    4 croissants, split

In a bowl, combine the first eight ingredients; mix well. Serve on lettuce-lined croissants. **Yield:** 4 servings.

Grilled Sesame Chicken

(Pictured below)

Plan ahead...needs to marinate

Chicken gets great flavor from a soy marinade and basting sauce. Grilling really says summer. Enjoy some chicken for dinner and use the extra in the two recipes that follow. —Catherine Allan, Twin Falls, Idaho

- 1 cup olive *or* vegetable oil
- 1 cup white grape juice
- 1 cup soy sauce
- 1 cup chopped green onions
- 1/3 cup sesame seeds, toasted
- 2 tablespoons ground mustard
- 1-1/2 teaspoons ground ginger *or* 2 tablespoons grated fresh gingerroot
- 2 teaspoons pepper
- 8 garlic cloves, minced
- 12 boneless skinless chicken breast halves

In a large resealable plastic bag, combine the first nine ingredients. Remove 1/2 cup for basting; cover and refrigerate. Add chicken to the bag; seal and turn to coat. Refrigerate for 6-8 hours.

Drain and discard marinade from chicken. Grill, covered, over medium heat for 6 minutes. Turn and cook 6-8 minutes longer or until meat juices run clear, basting occasionally with the reserved marinade. **Yield:** 6 servings plus 6 leftover chicken breast halves.

Grilled Chicken Salad

(Pictured below)

Ready in 30 minutes or less

I liked the tangy dressing on a Hawaiian chicken salad I tried once at a restaurant, so I devised my own through trial and error. I make this tempting refreshing salad at least once a week. You can also add mandarin oranges or pineapple chunks. —Lynn Merrifield, Watrous, Saskatchewan

Grilled Sesame Chicken
Grilled Chicken Salad
Chicken Primavera

4 grilled boneless skinless chicken breast halves
1/4 cup Catalina salad dressing
1/2 teaspoon lemon-pepper seasoning
1/2 teaspoon garlic powder
1/3 cup olive *or* vegetable oil
1/4 cup lemon juice
1/4 cup honey
1/4 cup honey mustard
1 garlic clove, minced
1/4 teaspoon dried tarragon
1/4 teaspoon dried rosemary, crushed
1 bunch romaine, torn
2 medium tomatoes, seeded and chopped
1 cup sliced cucumber
3 green onions, sliced

Place the chicken in a microwave-safe dish. Combine the salad dressing, lemon-pepper and garlic powder; pour over chicken. Cover and microwave at 50% power for 2-3 minutes or until heated through.

Meanwhile, in a jar with a tight-fitting lid, combine the oil, lemon juice, honey, mustard, garlic, tarragon and rosemary; shake well. On four plates, arrange the romaine, tomatoes, cucumber and onions. Top with chicken and drizzle with dressing. **Yield:** 4 servings.

Editor's Note: As a substitute for honey mustard, combine 2 tablespoons Dijon mustard and 2 tablespoons honey. This recipe was tested in an 850-watt microwave.

Chicken Primavera

(Pictured at left)

Ready in 30 minutes or less

A creamy homemade sauce seasoned with basil and garlic coats this terrific combination of leftover chicken, pepper strips and pasta. I love to make this dish...it's fast and easy. —Lisa Dato, Franklin Park, Illinois

1 cup julienned sweet red pepper
1 cup sliced fresh mushrooms
1/4 cup chopped green onions
3 garlic cloves, minced
1/4 cup butter *or* margarine
2 cups heavy whipping cream
1 teaspoon dried basil
2 grilled boneless skinless chicken breast halves, thinly sliced
1/2 teaspoon salt
Hot cooked angel hair pasta

In a large skillet, saute the red pepper, mushrooms, onions and garlic in butter. Add the cream, basil, chicken and salt; cook and stir until slightly thickened. Serve over pasta. **Yield:** 4 servings.

Homemade Hash Browns

Hosting a large brunch gathering? A big batch of these hearty hash browns from our Test Kitchen is sure to be popular. The recipe makes a lot, so if you're feeding just a few, use the leftovers in the two dishes that follow.

6 pounds medium potatoes
2 cups chopped green pepper
2 cups chopped sweet red pepper
1 large onion, chopped
1/2 cup butter *or* margarine
1 teaspoon salt
1 teaspoon pepper

Place potatoes in a Dutch oven and cover with water. Bring to a boil; cover and simmer for 15-20 minutes or until potatoes are tender but still firm. Cool slightly; peel and shred. In the Dutch oven, saute the peppers and onion in butter. Add the shredded potatoes; sprinkle with salt and pepper. Cook until golden brown. **Yield:** 12 cups.

Mexican Meat Loaf

Being a working mother with a small budget and little time, I make lots of dishes using ground beef. When our son complained about having meat loaf again, I came up with this taco-seasoned version. The whole family loves it served with sour cream and extra salsa.
—Alice McCauley
Beaumont, Texas

4 cups cooked hash brown potatoes
1/4 cup salsa
1 egg, lightly beaten
2 tablespoons vegetable soup mix
2 tablespoons taco seasoning
2 cups (8 ounces) shredded cheddar cheese, *divided*
2 pounds ground beef

In a large bowl, combine the hash browns, salsa, egg, soup mix, taco seasoning and 1 cup cheese. Crumble beef over mixture and mix well. Shape into a 12-in. loaf. Place in a 13-in. x 9-in. x 2-in. baking dish.

Bake, uncovered, at 350° for 1 hour or until a meat thermometer reads 160°. Sprinkle with the remaining cheese; bake 5 minutes longer or until cheese is melted. Let stand for 10 minutes before slicing. **Yield:** 6-8 servings.

Bacon Hash Brown Bake

About 15 years ago, a co-worker brought these rich potatoes to a potluck, and they were an instant hit. I've been bringing them to gatherings ever since.
—Patricia Monahan, Smithfield, Rhode Island

1 package (3 ounces) crumbled cooked bacon
6 cups cooked hash brown potatoes
1 cup mayonnaise*
1/2 cup process cheese sauce

Set aside 1/4 cup bacon for topping. In a bowl, combine the hash browns, mayonnaise, cheese sauce and remaining bacon. Transfer to a greased 11-in. x 7-in. x 2-in. baking dish. Sprinkle with the reserved bacon. Bake, uncovered, at 350° for 20-25 minutes or until heated through. **Yield:** 6-8 servings.

*Editor's Note: Reduced-fat or fat-free mayonnaise may not be substituted for regular mayonnaise in this recipe.

Roundup Beef Roast

Plan ahead...needs to marinate

I made this roast for my husband's birthday party and everyone loved it. Enjoy the juicy roast for one meal and beat the clock another day by using the leftovers in the two recipes that follow. —Shannon Jones, Trail, British Columbia

    1/4 cup sherry *or* apple juice
    1/4 cup red wine vinegar *or* cider vinegar
      4 garlic cloves, minced
      1 tablespoon soy sauce
      1 tablespoon honey
      1 teaspoon dried rosemary, crushed
    1/2 teaspoon dried thyme
3-1/2 pounds boneless beef rump roast
      1 tablespoon Dijon mustard

In a large resealable plastic bag, combine the first seven ingredients; add the roast. Seal bag and turn to coat; refrigerate overnight.

Drain and discard marinade. Place roast on a rack in a shallow roasting pan. Brush with mustard. Bake, uncovered, at 450° for 10 minutes. Reduce heat to 325°. Bake for 2 to 2-1/2 hours or until meat reaches desired doneness (for rare, a meat thermometer should read 140°; medium, 160°; well-done, 170°). Let stand for 10 minutes; thinly slice against the grain. **Yield:** 3-4 servings plus 4-1/2 cups leftover roast beef.

Asparagus Beef Stir-Fry

Ready in 45 minutes or less

As appealing to the eye as it is to the palate, this stovetop specialty features lots of vegetables, beef and crunchy cashews. —Joyce Huebner, Marinette, Wisconsin

      2 tablespoons cornstarch
      1 cup beef broth
      3 tablespoons soy sauce
    1/2 teaspoon sugar
      2 tablespoons vegetable oil
      2 whole garlic cloves
      2 pounds fresh asparagus, trimmed and cut into 2-1/2-inch pieces
      2 medium onions, halved and thinly sliced
      1 medium sweet red pepper, julienned
      1 large carrot, cut into 2-1/2-inch strips
2-1/2 cups sliced cooked roast beef (2-1/2-inch strips)
      1 cup salted cashew halves
Hot cooked rice

In a small bowl, combine cornstarch and broth until smooth. Stir in the soy sauce and sugar; set aside. In a wok or large skillet, heat oil; add garlic. Cook and stir for 2 minutes or until lightly browned; discard garlic.

Stir-fry the asparagus, onions, red pepper and carrot for 15-20 minutes or until crisp-tender. Add roast beef; heat through. Stir reserved sauce; add to the pan. Bring to a boil; cook and stir for 2 minutes or until thickened. Sprinkle with cashews. Serve with rice. **Yield:** 4-6 servings.

Roast Beef Burritos

Ready in 45 minutes or less

I rely on cumin, taco sauce and red pepper flakes to season these savory south-of-the-border sensations. The recipe is a great way to spice up leftover roast. —Ann Nolte Hampton, Virginia

      1 medium onion, chopped
      1 garlic clove, minced
      1 tablespoon vegetable oil
      4 medium tomatoes, chopped
      2 cups chopped cooked roast beef
      1 bottle (8 ounces) taco sauce
      1 can (4 ounces) chopped green chilies
    1/2 teaspoon ground cumin
    1/8 teaspoon crushed red pepper flakes, optional
      6 flour tortillas (7 inches), warmed
Shredded cheddar cheese and lettuce, optional

In a large skillet, saute onion and garlic in oil until tender. Stir in the tomatoes, roast beef, taco sauce, chilies, cumin and red pepper flakes if desired. Bring to a boil. Reduce heat; simmer, uncovered, for 25 minutes or until thickened.

Spoon about 2/3 cup down the center of each tortilla; fold over sides and ends. Serve with cheese and lettuce if desired. **Yield:** 6 servings.

Homemade Pizza Sauce

Ready in 45 minutes or less

Flavored with garlic, basil and Italian seasoning, this versatile sauce from our Test Kitchen staff will give Italian flair to all kinds of appetizing entrees. In fact, our home economists came up with the following two dishes that spotlight the zesty mixture.

      3 garlic cloves, minced
      3 tablespoons olive *or* vegetable oil
      1 can (29 ounces) tomato puree
      1 can (28 ounces) crushed tomatoes
      2 tablespoons brown sugar
      1 tablespoon Italian seasoning
      1 teaspoon dried basil
    1/2 teaspoon salt
    1/2 teaspoon crushed red pepper flakes

In a large saucepan, saute garlic in oil until tender. Stir in the remaining ingredients. Bring to a boil. Reduce heat; simmer, uncovered, for 30 minutes or until sauce reaches desired thickness. Use in Deep-Dish Sausage Pizza, Tomato Artichoke Chicken or any recipe that calls for pizza sauce. Sauce may be refrigerated for up to 1 week. **Yield:** 5-1/2 cups.

Tomato Artichoke Chicken

(Pictured above right)

Ready in 30 minutes or less

Preparing the pizza sauce early in the week sure saves time later when it's used in this fast dinner. Tender chicken,

Deep-Dish Sausage Pizza
Tomato Artichoke Chicken

roasted red peppers and marinated artichoke hearts put a flavorful spin on the red sauce that's served over pasta.

- 1 jar (12 ounces) marinated artichoke hearts
- 4 boneless skinless chicken breast halves
- 1 tablespoon olive *or* vegetable oil
- 2 cups pizza sauce
- 1 jar (7-1/4 ounces) roasted sweet red peppers, drained and cut into strips

Hot cooked fettuccine

Drain artichoke hearts, reserving 1/4 cup liquid. Cut artichokes into quarters. In a large skillet, brown chicken in oil. Add pizza sauce, artichokes, red peppers and reserved artichoke liquid. Bring to a boil. Reduce heat; cover and simmer for 8-10 minutes or until chicken juices run clear. Serve over fettuccine. **Yield:** 4 servings.

Deep-Dish Sausage Pizza

(Pictured above)

Ready in 1 hour or less

This hearty pizza pie is sure to become a supper staple in your house. Frozen bread dough is pressed into a springform pan to make an easy crust, then spread with the superb homemade sauce and topped with sausage, green pepper and cheese.

- 1 loaf (1 pound) frozen bread dough, thawed
- 2 teaspoons cornmeal
- 1-3/4 cups pizza sauce
- 1/2 pound bulk Italian sausage, cooked and drained
- 1-1/2 cups (6 ounces) shredded mozzarella cheese, *divided*
- 1 teaspoon dried oregano

Green pepper rings

On a lightly floured surface, roll and stretch dough into a 9-in. circle. Cover with plastic wrap; let rest for 10 minutes. Roll and stretch the dough into a 12-in. circle. Sprinkle cornmeal into a greased 9-in. springform pan. Place dough in pan and press 1 in. up the sides of the pan.

Spread pizza sauce over crust. Top with sausage, 1 cup of cheese, oregano and green pepper. Sprinkle with remaining cheese. Bake at 425° for 20-25 minutes or until crust is golden brown. Remove to a wire rack; let stand for 5 minutes before removing sides of pan. **Yield:** 6 servings.

Slimmer Sausage

Before you use cooked pork sausage, drain, rinse and pat dry with paper towels to cut the calories and fat.

Teriyaki Turkey Breast

(Pictured below)

Plan ahead...needs to marinate

Marinating this turkey breast overnight gives it great flavor and a juicy tenderness. This is the best turkey you will ever eat. Leftovers—if there are any—taste terrific in the two delicious dishes that follow. —Marvin Hayes
Delano, Minnesota

- 1 cup packed brown sugar
- 3/4 cup soy sauce
- 1/2 cup sherry *or* apple juice
- 1/4 cup olive *or* vegetable oil
- 1 tablespoon ground ginger
- 1 tablespoon ground mustard
- 1 teaspoon garlic powder
- 1 bone-in turkey breast (8 pounds)

In a bowl, combine the first seven ingredients; mix well. Pour 1 cup marinade into a large resealable plastic bag; add the turkey. Seal bag and turn to coat; refrigerate overnight. Cover and refrigerate remaining marinade.

Drain and discard marinade from the turkey. Place on a rack in a shallow roasting pan. Bake, uncovered, at 350° for 2 to 2-1/2 hours or until a meat thermometer reads 170°, basting every 30 minutes with reserved marinade. Let stand for 10 minutes before slicing. **Yield:** 8-10 servings plus carcass and 3 cups cubed leftover turkey.

Turkey Soup

(Pictured below)

I make the most of my turkey by simmering the carcass to create this soup that's warm and comforting on a cold winter's day. The golden broth is full of rice, barley and colorful veggies. —Myrna Sisel, Green Bay, Wisconsin

- 1 leftover turkey breast carcass (from an 8-pound turkey breast)
- 3 quarts water

Teriyaki Turkey Breast
Turkey Soup
Turkey Macaroni Bake

4 teaspoons chicken bouillon granules
2 bay leaves
1/2 cup uncooked instant rice
1/2 cup uncooked quick-cooking barley
1-1/2 cups sliced carrots
1 cup chopped onion
1 cup sliced celery
1 garlic clove, minced
1 teaspoon salt
1/4 teaspoon pepper
1 cup cubed cooked turkey
2 tablespoons minced fresh parsley *or* 2 teaspoons dried parsley flakes

Place the carcass, water, bouillon and bay leaves in a Dutch oven or soup kettle; bring to a boil. Reduce heat; cover and simmer for 1-1/2 hours. Remove carcass; cool. Remove meat from bones and cut into bite-size pieces; set meat aside. Discard bones. Strain broth and skim fat; discard bay leaves.

Add rice and barley to broth; bring to a boil. Reduce heat; cover and simmer for 30 minutes. Add the carrots, onion, celery, garlic, salt and pepper; cover and simmer 20-25 minutes longer or until the vegetables are tender. Add cubed turkey, parsley and reserved turkey; heat through. **Yield:** 12 servings.

Turkey Macaroni Bake

(Pictured at left)

A co-worker gave me this recipe when we were discussing quick-and-easy ways to use leftover turkey. The mild cheesy casserole is a hit with my family. And it doesn't get much easier than this…you don't even have to cook the macaroni first! —Cherry Williams, St. Albert, Alberta

2 cups cubed cooked turkey
1-1/2 cups uncooked elbow macaroni
2 cups (8 ounces) shredded cheddar cheese, *divided*
1 can (10-3/4 ounces) condensed cream of chicken soup, undiluted
1 cup milk
1 can (8 ounces) mushroom stems and pieces, drained
1/4 teaspoon pepper

In a large bowl, combine the turkey, macaroni, 1-1/2 cups cheese, soup, milk, mushrooms and pepper. Pour into a greased 2-qt. baking dish. Cover and bake at 350° for 60-65 minutes or until macaroni is tender. Uncover; sprinkle with remaining cheese. Bake 5-10 minutes longer or until cheese is melted. **Yield:** 6 servings.

Sugar 'n' Spice Cranberries

Plan ahead…needs to chill

My grandmother gave me the recipe for this tangy cranberry dish more than 30 years ago. It's a nice accompaniment to a traditional turkey dinner, but it also goes well with pork. I save a portion to make the cranberry gelatin salad for the next day. —Jill Alpert, Kansas City, Missouri

3 packages (12 ounces *each*) fresh *or* frozen cranberries
3-1/2 cups sugar
1-1/2 cups water
1/2 cup cider vinegar
1-1/2 teaspoons ground cinnamon
3/4 teaspoon ground allspice *or* cloves

In a Dutch oven, combine all of the ingredients. Bring to a boil. Reduce heat; simmer, uncovered, for 35-40 minutes or until the cranberries pop and mixture is thickened. Cover and refrigerate until chilled. **Yield:** 7 cups.

Molded Cranberry Salad

Plan ahead…needs to chill

To create this pretty salad mold, Jill combines the extra spiced cranberry sauce with fresh fruit, and some celery and nuts for crunch. This dish is great with leftover turkey sandwiches.

2 envelopes unflavored gelatin
2-1/2 cups chilled cranberry juice
1 cup sugar
3 cups Sugar 'n' Spice Cranberries (recipe below left)
1 small apple, peeled and finely chopped
1 medium navel orange, peeled and chopped
1/2 cup halved red seedless grapes
1/2 cup chopped walnuts, optional
1/4 cup finely chopped celery, optional

In a large saucepan, sprinkle gelatin over the cranberry juice; let stand for 1 minute. Cook over low heat, stirring until gelatin is completely dissolved. Stir in sugar until dissolved. Add the cranberries, apple, orange, grapes, walnuts and celery if desired.

Pour into an 8-cup ring mold coated with nonstick cooking spray. Refrigerate until set. Unmold onto a serving plate. **Yield:** 8-10 servings.

Cranberry Chicken Dinner

This meal in one pan combines chicken breasts with frozen sugar snap peas and leftover spiced cranberry sauce. For an easy dinner anytime, use a can of whole-berry cranberry sauce instead. I prepared this over the holidays and it was so good. —Sally Huzyak, Incline Village, Nevada

2 cups frozen pearl onions
2 cups frozen sugar snap peas
4 bone-in chicken breast halves
1-1/2 cups Sugar 'n' Spice Cranberries (recipe at left)
1/2 cup chopped pecans
1/4 cup olive *or* vegetable oil
1 envelope onion soup mix

Arrange the onions and peas in an ungreased 13-in. x 9-in. x 2-in. baking dish. Top with chicken. Combine the cranberries, pecans, oil and soup mix; spoon over chicken. Bake, uncovered, at 375° for 45-50 minutes or until chicken juices run clear. **Yield:** 4 servings.

Chapter 8

⏱ *Freezer Pleasers*

ON ACTION-PACKED DAYS when your schedule heats up, cool down the dinnertime rush with make-ahead meals from the freezer.

By doing a lot of the prep work on more leisurely days, it's easy to pop an already-assembled entree in the oven after a long day. Soon you'll have a hot and homemade dinner on the table without a lot of fuss—and all the while keeping your cool in the kitchen.

In addition to main dishes, this chapter features time-easing and crowd-pleasing recipes for appetizers, salads and desserts you can freeze to make mealtime a breeze.

FAST FREEZER FARE. Veggie Calzones and Hamburger Stew (recipes on pp. 116 and 117).

Ground Beef Mix

I season a batch of ground beef, divide it into meal-size portions and keep it in the freezer. With a few additional ingredients, I can quickly whip up the three entrees that follow. —Candace Robinson, Newark, Ohio

3 eggs
1-1/4 cups milk
2 cups crushed saltines (about 30 crackers)
2 large onions, chopped
2 teaspoons salt
1/2 teaspoon pepper
3-1/2 pounds ground beef

In a bowl, combine the eggs, milk, cracker crumbs, onions, salt and pepper; mix well. Crumble beef over mixture and mix well. Divide into three freezer containers. May be frozen for up to 1 month. **Yield:** 3 portions (14 cups total).

Beef-Stuffed Shells
Bacon Meat Loaf

Beef-Stuffed Shells

(Pictured below left)

To assemble this easy casserole, Candace fills jumbo pasta shells with her beef mixture, then tops them off with spaghetti sauce and mozzarella cheese. Add a green salad and breadsticks for a made-in-minutes meal.

20 jumbo pasta shells
1 jar (26 ounces) spaghetti sauce, *divided*
1 portion Ground Beef Mix (recipe on previous page), thawed
1-1/2 to 2 cups (6 to 8 ounces) shredded mozzarella cheese

Cook pasta shells according to package directions; drain. Spread about 1 cup of spaghetti sauce in a greased 13-in. x 9-in. x 2-in. baking dish. Fill shells with beef mix; place in pan. Top with the remaining spaghetti sauce.

Cover and bake at 350° for 30 minutes. Uncover; sprinkle with cheese. Bake 10 minutes longer or until meat is no longer pink. **Yield:** 6-8 servings.

Bacon Meat Loaf

(Pictured at left)

For this fast family fare, Candace thaws a portion of Ground Beef Mix, shapes it into a loaf and covers it with tomato sauce and bacon. Since there's little preparation before popping it in the oven, this main dish is ideal for busy weeknights.

1 portion Ground Beef Mix (recipe on previous page), thawed
1 can (8 ounces) tomato sauce
4 bacon strips, halved

Shape beef mix into a loaf; place in a greased 11-in. x 7-in. x 2-in. baking dish. Top with tomato sauce. Bake at 350° for 45 minutes. Cook bacon until almost done; place over loaf. Bake 10 minutes longer or until meat is no longer pink and a meat thermometer reads 160°. Let stand for 10 minutes before slicing. **Yield:** 4 servings.

Meatballs with Gravy

Preparing comfort food is a cinch when you have a batch of Ground Beef Mix in the freezer. Here, Candace tops hot cooked noodles with mouth-watering meatballs smothered in a savory sauce.

1 portion Ground Beef Mix (recipe on previous page), thawed
1 cup boiling water
1 teaspoon beef bouillon granules
1 can (10-3/4 ounces) condensed cream of mushroom soup, undiluted
Browning sauce, optional
Hot cooked noodles

Shape beef mix into 30 meatballs, about 1 in. each. In a large saucepan, bring the water, bouillon and soup to a boil; cook and stir until bouillon is dissolved. Add the meatballs and browning sauce if desired; cook until heated through and meat is no longer pink. Serve over noodles. **Yield:** 6-8 servings.

Orange Ice Cream Pie

This dessert is so good that you'll fix it often. The five-ingredient pie gets its refreshing taste from soft drink mix. We like orange Kool-Aid best, but feel free to try it with your family's favorite flavor. —Barbara Sigwald
Baltimore, Maryland

1/2 cup sweetened orange soft drink mix
1/2 cup warm water
2 cups vanilla ice cream, softened
1 carton (8 ounces) frozen whipped topping, thawed
1 graham cracker crust (8 *or* 9 inches)

In a large bowl, stir drink mix and water until dissolved. Add ice cream; mix well. Fold in whipped topping. Pour into the crust. Freeze until firm. May be frozen for up to 2 months. **Yield:** 6-8 servings.

Cheddar Turkey Bake

This recipe makes two creamy casseroles. Serve one for dinner and freeze the second for a night when you're racing against the clock. If you prefer, you can use chicken for the turkey and corn instead of peas. —Carol Dilcher
Emmaus, Pennsylvania

2 cups chicken broth
2 cups water
4 teaspoons dried minced onion
2 cups uncooked long grain rice
2 cups frozen peas, thawed
4 cups cubed cooked turkey
2 cans (10-3/4 ounces *each*) condensed cheddar cheese soup, undiluted
2 cups milk
1 teaspoon salt
2 cups finely crushed butter-flavored crackers (about 60 crackers)
6 tablespoons butter *or* margarine, melted

In a large saucepan, bring the broth, water and onion to a boil. Reduce heat. Add rice; cover and simmer for 15 minutes. Remove from the heat; fluff with a fork. Divide rice between two greased 9-in. square baking dishes. Sprinkle each with peas and turkey.

In a bowl, combine the soup, milk and salt until smooth; pour over turkey. Toss the cracker crumbs and butter; sprinkle over the top. Cover and freeze one casserole for up to 3 months. Bake the remaining casserole, uncovered, at 350° for 35 minutes or until golden brown. **Yield:** 2 casseroles (4-6 servings each).

To use frozen casserole: Thaw in the refrigerator for 24 hours. Bake, uncovered, at 350° for 70 minutes or until heated through.

Coconut Ice Cream Squares

I use cereal, coconut and pecans to create a crunchy top and bottom crust for this ice cream dessert. This is great to have in the freezer when unexpected guests arrive.
—Trudy Vincent, Valles Mines, Missouri

3-1/2 cups crushed Cinnamon Life cereal
    1 cup flaked coconut
  3/4 cup packed brown sugar
  1/2 cup chopped pecans
  1/2 cup butter *or* margarine, melted
  1/2 gallon vanilla ice cream, softened

In a bowl, combine the cereal, coconut, brown sugar and pecans. Drizzle with butter; stir until combined. Press half into an ungreased 13-in. x 9-in. x 2-in. dish. Carefully spread with ice cream. Sprinkle with remaining cereal mixture; gently press down. Cover and freeze until firm. Remove from the freezer 10 minutes before cutting. May be frozen for up to 2 months. **Yield:** 12-15 servings.

Italian Chicken Strips

This moist chicken goes from stove to freezer to table without losing flavor or texture. I usually get two frying pans going and have four cookie sheets full of chicken when I'm done. The hardest part is keeping my fellas out of it 'til dinnertime.   *—Barbara Eberlein, Belleville, Illinois*

    1 package (15 ounces) dry bread crumbs
    1 package (8 ounces) grated Parmesan cheese
    2 tablespoons Italian seasoning
    2 teaspoons garlic salt, *divided*
    6 eggs
  1/4 cup water
2-1/2 pounds boneless skinless chicken breasts, cut into 1/2-inch strips
Vegetable oil for deep-fat frying

In a large resealable plastic bag, combine the bread crumbs, Parmesan cheese, Italian seasoning and 1 teaspoon garlic salt. In a shallow bowl, beat eggs, water and remaining garlic salt. Dip chicken strips into egg mixture, then shake in crumb mixture.

In an electric skillet or deep-fat fryer, heat 1 in. of oil to 375°. Fry chicken in batches until golden brown, about 4 minutes. Drain on paper towels. Serve immediately; or cool and freeze for up to 3 months. **Yield:** 10-12 servings.

To use frozen chicken strips: Bake on ungreased baking sheets at 350° for 15 minutes or until heated through.

Ham 'n' Cheese Quiche

(Pictured at far right)

When I was expecting our daughter, I made and froze these cheesy quiches. After her birth, it was nice to have dinner in the freezer when we were too tired to cook.
—Christena Palmer, Green River, Wyoming

  2 pastry shells (9 inches)
  2 cups diced fully cooked ham
  2 cups (8 ounces) shredded sharp cheddar cheese

  2 teaspoons dried minced onion
  4 eggs
  2 cups half-and-half cream
1/2 teaspoon salt
1/4 teaspoon pepper

Line unpricked pastry shells with a double thickness of heavy-duty foil. Bake at 400° for 5 minutes. Remove foil; bake 5 minutes longer.

Divide ham, cheese and onion between the shells. In a bowl, whisk eggs, cream, salt and pepper. Pour into shells. Cover and freeze for up to 3 months. Or cover edges with foil and bake at 400° for 35-40 minutes or until a knife inserted near the center comes out clean. Let stand for 5-10 minutes before cutting. **Yield:** 2 quiches (6 servings each).

To use frozen quiche: Completely thaw in the refrigerator. Remove from the refrigerator 30 minutes before baking as directed.

Strawberry Lemonade Slush

(Pictured at right)

This refreshing fruity slush really perks up the taste buds. It has a nice sweet-tart flavor. I have made it for Christmas, Valentine's Day, summer potlucks and other occasions, and there is seldom any left.
—Sue Jorgensen
Rapid City, South Dakota

  1 package (10 ounces) frozen sweetened sliced strawberries, thawed
3/4 cup pink lemonade concentrate
3/4 cup water
3/4 cup ice cubes
  1 cup club soda

In a blender, combine the strawberries, lemonade concentrate, water and ice cubes. Cover and process until smooth. Pour into a freezer container. Cover and freeze for at least 12 hours or up to 3 months. Let stand at room temperature for 1 hour before serving. Stir in club soda. **Yield:** 4 servings.

Caramelized Bacon Twists

(Pictured at right)

A friend gave me this recipe to use at a bridal shower brunch, and the sweet chewy bacon strips were a big hit. Lining the pan with foil before baking helps cut down on cleanup.   *—Jane Paschke, Duluth, Minnesota*

  1 pound sliced bacon
1/2 cup packed brown sugar
  2 teaspoons ground cinnamon

Cut each bacon strip in half widthwise. Combine brown sugar and cinnamon. Dip bacon strips in sugar mixture; twist. Place on a foil-lined 15-in. x 10-in. x 1-in. baking pan. Bake at 350° for 15-20 minutes or until crisp. Serve; or cool and freeze in an airtight container for up to 1 month. **Yield:** 3 dozen.

To use frozen bacon: Bake at 350° for 6-8 minutes or until heated through.

Ham 'n' Cheese Quiche
Strawberry Lemonade Slush
Caramelized Bacon Twists

Pizza Snacks

(Pictured below)

Since pizza is a big favorite with my teenagers, I like to keep these crispy snacks on hand. Loaded with toppings, they go right from the freezer to the oven with little time and effort. And they're always a hit. —Ruby Williams
Bogalusa, Louisiana

- 1/2 cup shredded cheddar cheese
- 1/2 cup shredded mozzarella cheese
- 1 jar (4-1/2 ounces) sliced mushrooms, drained
- 1/3 cup chopped pepperoni
- 1/3 cup mayonnaise
- 1/4 cup chopped onion
- 3 tablespoons chopped ripe olives
- 5 English muffins, split

In a bowl, combine the first seven ingredients; mix well. Spread over cut side of each muffin half. Cover and freeze for up to 2 months. **Yield:** 10 snacks.

To use frozen snacks: Place on an ungreased baking sheet. Bake at 350° for 20 minutes or until cheese is melted.

Coconut Cream Dessert

(Pictured below)

Butter-flavored crackers make the crunchy crust for this frozen take on coconut cream pie. A mixer works great to easily combine the ice cream, milk and pudding mix. Try sprinkling chopped nuts or cracker crumbs on top instead of the coconut. —Carol Beamer, Glenville, West Virginia

- 2-1/2 cups crushed butter-flavored crackers (about 68 crackers)
- 1/2 cup plus 2 tablespoons butter *or* margarine, melted
- 1/2 gallon vanilla ice cream, softened
- 1/2 cup cold milk
- 2 packages (3.4 ounces *each*) instant coconut cream pudding mix

Coconut Cream Dessert
Pizza Snacks

1 carton (8 ounces) frozen whipped topping, thawed
1/3 cup flaked coconut, toasted

In a bowl, combine the cracker crumbs and the butter; mix well. Press into an ungreased 13-in. x 9-in. x 2-in. dish.

In a mixing bowl, combine the ice cream, milk and pudding mixes. Spread over the crust; top with whipped topping and coconut. Cover and freeze for up to 2 months. Remove from the freezer 15 minutes before serving. **Yield:** 12-15 servings.

Turkey Ham Loaf

This flavorful recipe produces two moist ham loaves that are topped with a sweet homemade sauce. I sometimes serve one loaf and freeze individual slices of the other. The slices are great for fast sandwiches at lunchtime.
—Mary Stretchbery, Weston, Ohio

      3 eggs
1-1/2 cups milk
      2 cups graham cracker crumbs (about 32 squares)
  1/2 teaspoon salt
  1/2 teaspoon ground allspice
      3 pounds fully cooked smoked turkey ham, ground
      1 pound ground turkey
SAUCE:
      1 can (10-3/4 ounces) condensed tomato soup, undiluted
  1/2 cup packed brown sugar
  1/2 cup cider vinegar
1-1/2 teaspoons prepared mustard

In a large bowl, combine the eggs, milk, cracker crumbs, salt and allspice. Crumble turkey ham and turkey over mixture; mix well. Pat into two ungreased 9-in. x 5-in. x 3-in. loaf pans.

In a bowl, combine the sauce ingredients; place half in a freezer container. Cover and freeze one loaf and container of sauce for up to 2 months. Pour about 1/2 cup of remaining sauce over the second loaf. Bake at 350° for 45 minutes. Baste with remaining sauce. Bake 35-45 minutes longer or until a meat thermometer reads 165°. Drain. **Yield:** 2 loaves (6-8 servings each).

To use frozen ham loaf and sauce: Thaw in the refrigerator overnight; bake as directed.

Hamburger Goulash

Goulash over mashed potatoes was my birthday meal of choice when I was growing up. Now I make my mother's tangy recipe for my family, and they like it, too.
—Jennifer Willingham, Kansas City, Missouri

2-1/2 pounds ground beef
      1 medium onion, chopped
      2 cups water
  3/4 cup ketchup
      2 tablespoons Worcestershire sauce

      2 teaspoons paprika
      1 to 2 teaspoons sugar
      1 teaspoon salt
  1/2 teaspoon ground mustard
  1/4 teaspoon garlic powder
      2 tablespoons all-purpose flour
  1/4 cup cold water
Hot cooked noodles *or* mashed potatoes

In a Dutch oven, cook beef and onion over medium heat until meat is no longer pink; drain. Add the water, ketchup, Worcestershire sauce, paprika, sugar, salt, mustard and garlic powder. Bring to a boil. Reduce heat; simmer, uncovered, for 20 minutes.

In a bowl, combine flour and cold water until smooth; stir into the meat mixture. Bring to a boil; cook and stir for 2 minutes or until thickened. Serve over noodles or potatoes; or cool and freeze for up to 3 months. **Yield:** 6 cups.

To use frozen goulash: Thaw in the refrigerator; place in a saucepan and heat through.

Chicken Lasagna Rolls

Take pasta to new heights with this clever creation. I roll a cheesy mixture of chicken and broccoli into lasagna noodles, making enough for two dinners. It's nice to have a pan of these roll-ups in the freezer for unexpected company.
—Darlene Markel, Salem, Oregon

      1 small onion, chopped
      3 tablespoons butter *or* margarine
      3 tablespoons all-purpose flour
      1 can (14-1/2 ounces) chicken broth
      1 cup milk
1-1/2 cups (6 ounces) shredded Monterey Jack cheese
      3 cups diced cooked chicken
      2 packages (10 ounces *each*) frozen chopped broccoli, thawed and drained
      2 eggs, beaten
  3/4 cup dry bread crumbs
      1 jar (6-1/2 ounces) diced pimientos, drained
  1/4 cup minced fresh parsley
  1/2 teaspoon salt, optional
     12 lasagna noodles, cooked and drained

In a saucepan, saute onion in butter until tender. Stir in flour until blended. Gradually add broth and milk. Bring to a boil; cook and stir for 2 minutes. Remove from the heat; stir in cheese. Pour 1/3 cup each into two greased 8-in. square baking dishes; set aside.

In a bowl, combine 1 cup cheese sauce, chicken, broccoli, eggs, bread crumbs, pimientos, parsley and salt if desired. Spread about 1/2 cup over each noodle. Roll up jelly-roll style, beginning with a short side; secure ends with toothpicks. Place six roll-ups curly end down in each baking dish. Top with remaining cheese sauce.

Cover and freeze one casserole for up to 3 months. Cover and bake second casserole at 350° for 40 minutes. Uncover; bake 5 minutes longer. Discard the toothpicks before serving. **Yield:** 2 casseroles (3 servings each).

To use frozen casserole: Cover and bake at 350° for 1-1/4 hours. Uncover; bake 5 minutes longer or until heated through.

Freezer Coleslaw

Plan ahead...needs to chill

Every year, we go on a week-long camping trip and plan ahead for all of our meals. I always prepare and freeze this versitile salad beforehand. It stays fresh and delicious right through to the very last day.
—Lynn Johnson, Alexandria, Minnesota

1 large head cabbage, shredded
3 medium carrots, shredded
1 medium green pepper, shredded
1 small onion, shredded
3/4 cup sugar
1 cup cider vinegar
3/4 cup vegetable oil
3 teaspoons salt
1 teaspoon ground mustard
1 teaspoon celery seed

In a large bowl, combine cabbage, carrots, green pepper and onion. Add sugar; toss to coat. In a saucepan, combine vinegar, oil, salt, mustard and celery seed. Bring to a boil. Pour over cabbage mixture; toss to coat. Cover; refrigerate for at least 2 hours before serving. Coleslaw may be frozen up to 3 months; remove from the freezer 2 hours before serving. **Yield:** 12-16 servings.

Broccoli Bites

Ready in 45 minutes or less

Herb stuffing and Parmesan cheese add nice flavor to the broccoli in these cute appetizers. The recipe makes several dozen, so you can just take out of the freezer as many as you need. —Laurie Todd, Columbus, Mississippi

2 packages (10 ounces *each*) frozen chopped broccoli
2 cups crushed seasoned stuffing
1 cup grated Parmesan cheese
6 eggs, lightly beaten
1/2 cup butter *or* margarine, softened
1/2 teaspoon salt
1/4 teaspoon pepper

Cook broccoli according to package directions; drain and place in a bowl. Add the remaining ingredients; mix well. Shape into 1-in. balls. Place in a greased 15-in. x 10-in. x 1-in. baking pan. Bake at 350° for 11-12 minutes or until golden brown. Or place in a single layer in a freezer container and freeze for up to 1 month. **Yield:** about 5 dozen.

To use frozen appetizers: Place in a greased 15-in. x 10-in. x 1-in. baking pan. Bake at 350° for 16-18 minutes or until golden brown.

Mushroom Pasta Sauce

Ready in 30 minutes or less

When I'm out of spaghetti sauce and don't have time to make it from scratch, I rely on this easy recipe that
makes the most of canned items. It has a sweet taste that kids enjoy. —Louise Graybiel, Toronto, Ontario

2 cans (14-1/2 ounces *each*) diced tomatoes, undrained
2 cans (10-3/4 ounces *each*) condensed tomato soup, undiluted
2 cans (7 ounces *each*) pizza sauce
1 can (8 ounces) mushroom stems and pieces, drained
1 teaspoon dried oregano
1 teaspoon dried basil
1 garlic clove, minced

In a large saucepan, combine all ingredients. Bring to a boil, stirring frequently. Reduce heat. Simmer, uncovered, for 15 minutes; cool. Transfer to freezer bags or containers. Freeze for up to 3 months. **Yield:** about 7 cups.

To use frozen sauce: Thaw in the refrigerator overnight. Heat and serve.

Cheddar Beef Enchiladas

(Pictured at right)

Ready in 1 hour or less

I created these enchiladas to satisfy several picky eaters in our house. They were an instant hit and are now requested at least once a week. I especially like that we can enjoy this meal twice by freezing half for a later (and busier) day.
—Stacy Cizek, Conrad, Iowa

1 pound ground beef
1 envelope taco seasoning
1 cup water
2 cups cooked rice
1 can (16 ounces) refried beans
2 cups (8 ounces) shredded cheddar cheese, *divided*
10 to 12 flour tortillas (8 inches)
1 jar (16 ounces) salsa
1 can (10-3/4 ounces) condensed cream of chicken soup, undiluted

In a skillet, cook beef over medium heat until no longer pink; drain. Stir in taco seasoning and water. Bring to a boil. Reduce heat; simmer, uncovered, for 5 minutes. Stir in rice. Cook and stir until liquid is evaporated. Spread about 2 tablespoons of refried beans, 1/4 cup beef mixture and 1 tablespoon cheese down the center of each tortilla; roll up. Place seam side down in two greased 13-in. x 9-in. x 2-in. baking dishes.

Combine salsa and soup; pour down the center of enchiladas. Sprinkle with remaining cheese. Bake one casserole, uncovered, at 350° for 20-25 minutes or until heated through and cheese is melted. Cover and freeze remaining casserole for up to 3 months. **Yield:** 2 casseroles (5-6 enchiladas each).

To use frozen casserole: Thaw in the refrigerator overnight. Cover and bake at 350° for 30 minutes. Uncover; bake 5-10 minutes longer or until heated through and cheese is melted.

Cheddar Beef Enchiladas
Chocolate Ice Cream Pie

Chocolate Ice Cream Pie

(Pictured above)

Plan ahead...needs to freeze

I keep the ingredients for these frosty chocolate pies on hand during the summer. They're so quick to assemble. My husband and kids love them. —Wendy Bognar
Sparks, Nevada

2 quarts vanilla ice cream, melted

1 package (5.9 ounces) instant chocolate pudding mix
2 graham cracker crusts (10 inches *each*)
Whipped topping, optional

In a bowl, whisk melted ice cream and pudding mix for 2 minutes. Pour into crusts. Freeze until firm. Pies may be frozen for up to 2 months. Remove from the freezer 10 minutes before serving. Garnish with whipped topping if desired. **Yield:** 2 pies (6-8 servings each).

Chicken Potpie

(Pictured below)

Chock-full of chicken, potatoes, peas and corn, this autumn favorite makes two golden pies, so you can serve one at supper and save the other for a busy night.
—Karen Johnson, Torrance, California

2 cups diced peeled potatoes
1-3/4 cups sliced carrots
2/3 cup chopped onion
1 cup butter *or* margarine
1 cup all-purpose flour
1-3/4 teaspoons salt
1 teaspoon dried thyme
3/4 teaspoon pepper
3 cups chicken broth
1-1/2 cups milk
4 cups cubed cooked chicken
1 cup frozen peas
1 cup frozen corn
Pastry for two double-crust pies (9 inches)

Place potatoes and carrots in a large saucepan; cover with water. Bring to a boil. Reduce heat; cover and simmer for 8-10 minutes or until crisp-tender. Drain and set aside. In a large skillet, saute onion in butter until tender. Stir in the flour, salt, thyme and pepper until blended. Gradually stir in broth and milk. Bring to a boil; cook and stir for 2 minutes or until thickened. Add the chicken, peas, corn, potatoes and carrots; remove from the heat.

Line two 9-in. pie plates with bottom pastry; trim even with edge of plate. Fill pastry shells with chicken mixture. Roll out remaining pastry to fit top of pies. Cut slits or decorative cutouts in pastry. Place over filling; trim, seal and flute edges.

Bake one potpie at 425° for 35-40 minutes or until crust is lightly browned. Let stand for 15 minutes before cutting. Cover and freeze remaining potpie for up to 3 months. **Yield:** 2 potpies (6-8 servings each).

To use frozen potpie: Shield frozen pie crust edges with foil; place on a baking sheet. Bake at 425° for 30 minutes. Reduce heat to 350°; bake 70-80 minutes longer or until crust is golden brown.

Chicken Potpie
Coconut Pumpkin Loaves

Coconut Pumpkin Loaves

(Pictured below left)

A friend shared the recipe for this moist bread years ago. Because the big batch makes three scrumptious loaves, I can give one loaf to a neighbor, enjoy one with my family and freeze one for later.
—Anne Smithson, Cary, North Carolina

5 eggs
2 cups canned pumpkin
2 cups sugar
1-1/4 cups vegetable oil
3 cups all-purpose flour
2 packages (3.4 ounces *each*) instant coconut pudding mix
3 teaspoons ground cinnamon
2 teaspoons baking soda
1 teaspoon ground nutmeg
3/4 cup chopped pecans

In a large mixing bowl, beat the eggs and pumpkin until smooth. Add sugar and oil; mix well. Combine the flour, pudding mixes, cinnamon, baking soda and nutmeg; add to the pumpkin mixture. Stir in nuts.

Transfer to three greased and floured 8-in. x 4-in. x 2-in. loaf pans. Bake at 350° for 60-65 minutes or until a toothpick inserted near the center comes out clean. Cool for 10 minutes before removing from pans to wire racks to cool completely. Wrap and freeze for up to 6 months. **Yield:** 3 loaves.

Bing Cherry Delight

Featuring cherries, pecans and a cookie-crumb topping, this frosty dessert has a refreshing flavor that'll have guests asking for seconds. *—Carol Jackson, Burleson, Texas*

1 can (14 ounces) sweetened condensed milk
7 tablespoons lemon juice
1 can (16-1/2 ounces) pitted dark sweet cherries, drained
1 cup heavy whipping cream
1 cup chopped pecans
1/2 cup vanilla wafer crumbs

In a large bowl, combine milk and lemon juice. Fold in cherries. In a mixing bowl, beat cream until stiff peaks form. Gently fold cream and pecans into cherry mixture. Spread into an ungreased 11-in. x 7-in. x 2-in. dish; sprinkle with wafer crumbs. Cover and freeze overnight or until firm. May be frozen for up to 2 months. Remove from the freezer 15 minutes before cutting. **Yield:** 8 servings.

Creamy Lasagna Casserole

Satisfy your gang with this casserole. Whip up a rich combination of cream cheese, sour cream and cheddar cheese and layer with lasagna noodles and a beefy sauce.
—Shelly Korell, Eaton, Colorado

2 pounds ground beef
1 can (29 ounces) tomato sauce
1 teaspoon salt
1/2 teaspoon pepper
1/2 teaspoon garlic powder
2 packages (3 ounces *each*) cream cheese, softened
2 cups (16 ounces) sour cream
2 cups (8 ounces) shredded cheddar cheese, *divided*
4 green onions, chopped
12 to 14 lasagna noodles, cooked and drained

In a Dutch oven, cook beef over medium heat until no longer pink; drain. Add the tomato sauce, salt, pepper and garlic powder. Bring to a boil. Reduce heat; simmer, uncovered, for 15 minutes. In a mixing bowl, beat cream cheese until smooth. Add sour cream, 1 cup cheddar cheese and onions; mix well.

Spread about 1/2 cup meat sauce into two greased 8-in. square baking dishes. Place two to three noodles in each dish, trimming to fit if necessary. Top each with about 1/2 cup cream cheese mixture and about 2/3 cup meat sauce. Repeat layers twice. Sprinkle 1/2 cup cheddar cheese over each.

Cover and freeze one casserole for up to 1 month. Bake remaining casserole, uncovered, at 350° for 25-30 minutes or until bubbly and heated through. Let stand for 15 minutes before cutting. **Yield:** 2 casseroles (4-6 servings each).

To use frozen casserole: Thaw in the refrigerator for 18 hours. Remove casserole from the refrigerator 30 minutes before baking. Bake, uncovered, at 350° for 40-50 minutes or until heated through.

Editor's Note: Reduced-fat or fat-free cream cheese and sour cream are not recommended for this recipe.

Candy Bar Ice Cream

Three ingredients are all I need to create this treat for two. It tastes just like it came from an ice cream parlor.
—Myra Innes, Auburn, Kansas

2-1/2 cups vanilla ice cream, softened
1 tablespoon fudge ice cream topping
2 Snickers candy bars (2.07 ounces *each*), chopped

In a blender, combine the ice cream and fudge topping; cover and process until smooth. Stir in the candy bars. Transfer to a freezer container; freeze for 4 hours or until firm. May be frozen for up to 2 months. **Yield:** 2 servings.

Create a Freezer List

Because I was tired of digging through my freezer for items I eventually realized I didn't have, I decided to use my computer to develop a list of frozen foods I had on hand. I keep the list posted on the freezer, and when I use something from the freezer, I cross it off the list. Items added to the freezer are added to the list. I update the list on my computer once a week, print a new one and place it on the freezer. *—Betty Gregerson*
Big Sandy, Texas

Lemon Lime Dessert

This make-ahead treat offers a wonderfully refreshing blend of citrus flavors. Topped with a smooth lemon sauce, it's the perfect ending to any meal. Using an electric mixer makes it easy to combine the lime sherbet and vanilla ice cream. —Marsha Schindler
Fort Wayne, Indiana

1-1/2 cups graham cracker crumbs (about 24
     squares)
   14 tablespoons butter *or* margarine, melted,
     divided
1-1/4 cups sugar, *divided*
  1/2 gallon vanilla ice cream, softened
   1 quart lime sherbet, softened
   2 eggs, beaten
  1/4 cup lemon juice

In a bowl, combine the cracker crumbs, 7 tablespoons butter and 1/4 cup sugar; mix well. Press into an ungreased 13-in. x 9-in. x 2-in. dish; freeze. In a mixing bowl, combine ice cream and sherbet; pour over crust. Freeze until firm.

In a heavy saucepan, combine the eggs and remaining sugar. Stir in the lemon juice and remaining butter. Cook over low heat until mixture is thickened and reaches 160°. Cover and refrigerate until cool. Spread over ice cream mixture. Cover and freeze for 3 hours or overnight. May be frozen for up to 2 months. Just before serving, remove from the freezer and cut into squares. **Yield:** 12-15 servings.

Chicken Tetrazzini

This is my revised version of a recipe a friend shared with me 35 years ago. It's nice to give to friends who are unable to cook. —Helen McPhee, Savoy, Illinois

   1 package (12 ounces) spaghetti
  1/3 cup butter *or* margarine
  1/3 cup all-purpose flour
  3/4 teaspoon salt
  1/4 teaspoon white pepper
   1 can (14-1/2 ounces) chicken broth
1-1/2 cups half-and-half cream
   1 cup heavy whipping cream
   4 cups cubed cooked chicken
   3 cans (4 ounces *each*) mushroom stems and
     pieces, drained
   1 jar (4 ounces) sliced pimientos, drained
  1/2 cup grated Parmesan cheese

Cook spaghetti according to package directions. Meanwhile, in a Dutch oven, melt butter. Stir in flour, salt and pepper until smooth. Gradually add the broth, half-and-half and whipping cream. Bring to a boil; cook and stir for 2 minutes or until thickened. Remove from the heat. Stir in the chicken, mushrooms and pimientos. Drain spaghetti; add to the chicken mixture and toss to coat.

Transfer to two greased 11-in. x 7-in. x 2-in. baking dishes. Sprinkle with Parmesan cheese. Cover and freeze one casserole up to 2 months. Bake second casserole, uncovered, at 350° for 20-25 minutes or until heated through. **Yield:** 2 casseroles (3-4 servings each).

To use frozen casserole: Thaw in the refrigerator overnight. Cover and bake at 350° for 30 minutes. Uncover; bake 15-20 minutes longer or until heated through. Stir before serving.

Dilly Cheddar Cubes

This is a delicious crowd-pleasing appetizer. I make it for all my parties by request of my guests. The cheese cubes are so easy to prepare ahead of time, then just remove them from the freezer and pop them in the oven for a few minutes. —Lisa Lovitz, Lockport, New York

   1 cup (4 ounces) shredded cheddar cheese
  1/4 cup butter *or* margarine, cubed
   1 package (3 ounces) cream cheese, cubed
   2 teaspoons minced chives
   1 teaspoon dill weed
   2 egg whites
  24 cubes French bread (1-inch cubes)

Line a baking pan with waxed paper; set aside. In a small saucepan, combine the first five ingredients. Cook and stir over medium-low heat until cheese is melted. Remove from the heat.

In a small mixing bowl, beat the egg whites until stiff peaks form; fold into cheese mixture. Using a fork, dip bread cubes into cheese mixture and place on prepared pan. Freeze, uncovered, until firm. Transfer to a resealable plastic freezer bag; freeze for up to 3 months. **Yield:** 2 dozen.

To use frozen appetizers: Arrange bread cubes 1 in. apart on greased baking sheets. Bake at 425° for 10-12 minutes or until lightly browned. Serve warm.

Hamburger Stew

(Pictured above right and on page 104)

A lady in our church first gave me this recipe as a way to use our bounty of home-canned tomatoes. My husband loves the hearty combination of ingredients. I like that it's easy to warm up for a carefree dinner in the winter months. —Marcia Clay, Truman, Minnesota

   2 pounds ground beef
   2 medium onions, chopped
   4 cans (14-1/2 ounces *each*) stewed tomatoes
   8 medium carrots, thinly sliced
   4 celery ribs, thinly sliced
   2 medium potatoes, peeled and cubed
   2 cups water
  1/2 cup uncooked long grain rice
   1 to 2 tablespoons salt
   1 to 2 teaspoons pepper
ADDITIONAL INGREDIENT (for each batch of stew):
   1 cup water

Veggie Calzones
Hamburger Stew

In a Dutch oven, cook beef and onions over medium heat until meat is no longer pink; drain. Add the tomatoes, carrots, celery, potatoes, water, rice, salt and pepper; bring to a boil. Reduce heat; cover and simmer for 30 minutes or until vegetables and rice are tender.

Uncover; simmer 20-30 minutes longer or until thickened. Freeze in 3-cup portions for up to 3 months. **Yield:** about 5 batches (15 cups total).

To use frozen stew: Thaw in the refrigerator for 24 hours. Transfer to a saucepan; add water. Cook until hot and bubbly.

Veggie Calzones

(Pictured above and on page 105)

Bread dough makes it a breeze to assemble these savory turnovers. If you have a favorite pizza dough, use it instead. These freeze well and once they are frozen, they can be heated in half an hour. —Lee Ann Arey, Gray, Maine

  1/2 **pound fresh mushrooms, chopped**
    1 **medium onion, chopped**
    1 **medium green pepper, chopped**
    2 **tablespoons vegetable oil**
    3 **plum tomatoes, seeded and chopped**
    1 **can (6 ounces) tomato paste**

    1 **cup (4 ounces) shredded mozzarella cheese**
    1 **cup (4 ounces) shredded Monterey Jack cheese**
  1/2 **cup grated Parmesan cheese**
    2 **loaves (1 pound** *each***) frozen bread dough, thawed**
    1 **egg**
    1 **tablespoon water**

In a large skillet, saute the mushrooms, onion and green pepper in oil until tender. Add tomatoes; cook and stir for 3 minutes. Stir in tomato paste; set aside.

Combine cheeses and set aside. On a lightly floured surface, divide dough into eight pieces. Roll each piece into a 7-in. circle. Spoon a scant 1/2 cup mushroom mixture and 1/4 cup cheese mixture over one side of each circle. Brush edges of dough with water; fold dough over filling and press edges with a fork to seal. Place calzones 3 in. apart on greased baking sheets. Cover and let rise in a warm place for 20 minutes.

Combine egg and water; brush over calzones. Bake at 375° for 15 minutes. Cool desired number of calzones; freeze for up to 3 months. Bake the remaining calzones 18-22 minutes longer or until golden brown. Serve immediately. **Yield:** 8 servings.

To use frozen calzones: Place calzones 2 in. apart on a greased baking sheet. Bake at 350° for 30-35 minutes or until golden brown.

Macadamia Berry Dessert

Macadamia Berry Dessert

(Pictured above)

My family and friends love this dessert, and I've shared the recipe several times. The crunchy nut crust and colorful raspberry filling make it special enough for guests. During the holidays, I substitute a can of whole-berry cranberry sauce for the raspberries. —Louise Watkins
Sparta, Wisconsin

- 1 cup crushed vanilla wafers (about 32 wafers)
- 1/2 cup finely chopped macadamia nuts
- 1/4 cup butter *or* margarine, melted
- 1 can (14 ounces) sweetened condensed milk
- 3 tablespoons orange juice
- 3 tablespoons lemon juice
- 1 package (10 ounces) frozen sweetened raspberries, thawed
- 1 carton (8 ounces) frozen whipped topping, thawed

Fresh raspberries and additional whipped topping, optional

Combine the wafer crumbs, nuts and butter. Press onto the bottom of a greased 9-in. springform pan. Bake at 375° for 8-10 minutes or until golden brown. Cool completely.

In a mixing bowl, beat the milk, orange juice and lemon juice on low speed until well blended. Add raspberries; beat on low until blended. Fold in whipped topping. Pour over the crust. Cover and freeze for 3 hours or until firm. May be frozen for up to 3 months.

Remove from the freezer 15 minutes before serving. Carefully run a knife around edge of pan to loosen. Remove sides of pan. Garnish with raspberries and whipped topping if desired. **Yield:** 12 servings.

Fancy Frozen Fruit Cups

(Pictured below)

In the summer, I make a big batch of these delicious slushy fruit cups and store them in the freezer. They make great snacks and are wonderful to have on hand when friends stop by. We also like them with blueberries, raspberries, muskmelon and cherries. —Alyce Wyman
Pembina, North Dakota

✓ Uses less fat, sugar or salt. Includes Nutritional Analysis and Diabetic Exchanges.

- 2 cups water
- 3/4 cup sugar
- 3/4 cup orange juice concentrate
- 3/4 cup lemonade concentrate
- 1 can (20 ounces) pineapple tidbits, drained
- 2 medium firm bananas, cut into 1/2-inch slices
- 1-1/2 cups watermelon chunks
- 1-1/2 cups green grapes
- 1-1/2 cups quartered strawberries
- 1-1/2 cups cubed peaches
- 2 kiwifruit, peeled, quartered and sliced

In a small saucepan, bring water and sugar to a boil, stirring constantly. Remove from the heat; stir in orange juice and lemonade concentrates. In a large bowl, combine the pineapple, bananas, watermelon, grapes, strawberries and peaches. Add juice mixture and mix well.

Place about 1/2 cup fruit mixture in 5-oz. disposable plastic wine glasses with removable bottoms or 5-oz. disposable cups. Top each with four kiwi pieces. Cover and freeze until firm. May be frozen for up to 1 month. Remove from the freezer about 1-3/4 hours before serving. **Yield:** 18 servings.

Fancy Frozen Fruit Cups

Coffee Ice Cream Torte

Chocolate Mint Torte

This frozen treat comes together in a snap. I melt chocolate-covered mint candies and mix them into the creamy filling for refreshing flavor. A cookie-crumb crust and a sprinkling of extra mint candies make it fun any time of the year. —Joni Mehl, Grand Rapids, Michigan

  27 cream-filled chocolate sandwich cookies, crushed
1/3 cup butter *or* margarine, melted
1/3 cup chocolate-covered mint candies*
1/4 cup milk
   1 jar (7 ounces) marshmallow creme
   2 cups heavy whipping cream, whipped
Additional whipped cream and chocolate-covered mint candies

In a bowl, combine cookie crumbs and butter. Press onto the bottom and 1-1/2 in. up the sides of a greased 9-in. springform pan. Chill for at least 30 minutes.

In a small saucepan, heat mint candies and milk over low heat until mints are melted; stir until smooth. Cool for 10-15 minutes. Place marshmallow creme in a mixing bowl; gradually beat in mint mixture. Fold in whipped cream. Transfer to prepared crust. Cover and freeze until firm. May be frozen for up to 2 months.

Remove from the freezer about 30 minutes before serving. Remove sides of pan. Garnish with additional whipped cream and candies. **Yield:** 12 servings.

*Editor's Note: This recipe was tested with Junior Mints.

Cookie Ice Cream Cake

I discovered this recipe on-line and changed it a little to suit my family's tastes. It always gets lots of compliments because people love the hot fudge topping and unique cookie crust. My husband says it's the best ice cream cake he's ever had. —Heather McKillip Aurora, Illinois

  44 miniature chocolate chip cookies*
1/4 cup butter *or* margarine, melted
   1 cup hot fudge topping, *divided*
   1 quart vanilla ice cream, softened
   1 quart chocolate ice cream, softened

Crush 25 cookies; set remaining cookies aside. In a bowl, combine cookie crumbs and butter. Press onto the bottom of a greased 10-in. springform pan. Freeze for 15 minutes.

In a microwave-safe bowl, heat 3/4 cup hot fudge topping on high for 15-20 seconds or until pourable; spread over crust. Arrange reserved cookies around the edge of pan. Freeze for 15 minutes. Spread vanilla ice cream over fudge topping; freeze for 30 minutes. Spread

with chocolate ice cream. Cover and freeze until firm. May be frozen for up to 2 months.

Remove from the freezer 10 minutes before serving. Remove sides of pan. Warm remaining hot fudge topping; drizzle over top. **Yield:** 10-12 servings.

*Editor's Note: This recipe was tested with Famous Amos chocolate chip cookies.

Coffee Ice Cream Torte

(Pictured above)

Not only does this make-ahead dessert go over big with company, but it calls for only four ingredients. If you can't find coffee-flavored ice cream, dissolve instant coffee granules in warm water and stir into vanilla ice cream. —Janet Hutts, Gainesville, Georgia

   2 packages (3 ounces *each*) ladyfingers
   1 cup chocolate-covered English toffee bits *or* 4 Heath candy bars (1.4 ounces *each*), crushed, *divided*
1/2 gallon coffee ice cream, softened
   1 carton (8 ounces) frozen whipped topping, thawed

Place ladyfingers around the edge of a 9-in. springform pan. Arrange remaining ladyfingers to line the bottom of the pan. Stir 1/2 cup toffee bits into the ice cream; spoon into prepared pan. Cover with plastic wrap; freeze overnight or until firm. May be frozen for up to 2 months.

Just before serving, remove sides of pan. Garnish with the whipped topping and remaining toffee bits. **Yield:** 12-16 servings.

Cran-Orange Ribbon Dessert

I dress up vanilla ice cream with cream cheese and orange juice concentrate before spreading it over a quick homemade crust. The delicate ribbon of cranberry sauce adds a touch of elegance to each serving.
—Deborah Bills, Paducah, Kentucky

1-2/3 cups graham cracker crumbs (about 26 squares)
  1/4 cup ground pecans
    3 tablespoons sugar
    6 tablespoons butter *or* margarine, melted
    1 package (8 ounces) cream cheese, softened
  1/2 gallon vanilla ice cream
    1 can (12 ounces) frozen orange juice concentrate, thawed
    1 can (16 ounces) whole-berry cranberry sauce
  1/2 teaspoon almond extract

In a bowl, combine the cracker crumbs, pecans and sugar. Add butter; mix well. Press into a greased 13-in. x 9-in. x 2-in. baking dish. Bake at 350° for 8-10 minutes or until set. Cool on a wire rack.

In a large mixing bowl, beat cream cheese until smooth. Add ice cream; mix well. Gradually beat in orange juice concentrate; spread half over crust. Cover and freeze for 1 hour. Refrigerate remaining ice cream mixture.

In a food processor or blender, process the cranberry sauce and almond extract until blended; spread half over ice cream layer. Cover and freeze for at least 30 minutes. Spread with the remaining ice cream mixture and cranberry mixture. Cover and freeze until firm. May be frozen for up to 2 months. Remove from the freezer about 30 minutes before serving. **Yield:** 12-15 servings.

Three-Fruit Frozen Yogurt

(Pictured below)

I received this super-easy recipe from a friend. It takes just minutes to combine the bananas, strawberries and pineapple with a few other ingredients before popping everything in the freezer. I've been told the luscious mixture tastes even better than ice cream. —Wendy Hilton
Laurel, Mississippi

    2 medium ripe bananas
    1 package (10 ounces) frozen sweetened sliced strawberries, thawed and drained
    1 can (8 ounces) crushed pineapple, drained
    1 carton (6 ounces) strawberry yogurt
  1/2 cup sugar
    1 carton (8 ounces) frozen whipped topping, thawed

In a large bowl, mash the bananas and strawberries. Stir in the pineapple, yogurt and sugar. Fold in whipped topping. Cover and freeze until firm. May be frozen for up to 1 month. **Yield:** 1-1/2 quarts.

Apple Pie a la Mode

Here is a family favorite that combines apple pie filling and butter pecan ice cream with caramel topping and chopped nuts. I created it when trying to think up a rich dessert to complete a dinner party menu. —Trisha Kruse
Boise, Idaho

    1 can (21 ounces) apple pie filling
    1 graham cracker crust (8 inches)
    1 pint butter pecan ice cream, softened
    1 jar (12 ounces) caramel ice cream topping
  1/4 cup chopped pecans, toasted

Spread half of the pie filling over crust. Top with half of the ice cream; cover and freeze for 30 minutes. Drizzle with half of the caramel topping; cover and freeze for 30 minutes. Top with remaining pie filling; cover and freeze for 30 minutes. Top with remaining ice cream; cover and freeze until firm. May be frozen for up to 2 months.

Remove from the freezer about 30 minutes before serving. Warm remaining caramel topping; drizzle some on serving plates. Top with a slice of pie; drizzle remaining caramel topping over pie and sprinkle with pecans. **Yield:** 6-8 servings.

Ice Cream Party Roll

This tempting take on the much-loved cake roll features a from-scratch chocolate cake, vanilla ice cream and a layer of berry jam. Garnished with hot fudge and whipped topping, the slices are hard to resist. —Laura Andrews
Mantee, Mississippi

    4 eggs, *separated*
  3/4 cup sugar, *divided*
  1/2 cup cake flour
  1/3 cup baking cocoa
    1 teaspoon baking powder
  1/4 teaspoon salt
  1/2 cup strawberry *or* raspberry jam
    2 cups vanilla ice cream, softened
Confectioners' sugar
Hot fudge topping and whipped topping

Three-Fruit Frozen Yogurt

Strawberry Banana Pie

In a bowl, combine the crushed ice cream cones, pecans and butter. Press onto the bottom and up the sides of a greased 10-in. pie plate. Refrigerate for at least 30 minutes.

In a bowl, combine vanilla ice cream and mashed bananas. Spread over the crust; cover and freeze for 30 minutes. Arrange sliced bananas over ice cream; cover and freeze for 30 minutes. Top with strawberry ice cream; cover and freeze for about 45 minutes.

Hull and halve strawberries; place around edge of pie. Mound or pipe whipped topping in center of pie. Cover and freeze for up to 1 month. Remove from the freezer about 30 minutes before serving. **Yield:** 8-10 servings.

Grape Ice

(Pictured below)

When I was growing up, this slushy dessert was a popular request at our house, and Mom stirred it up in no time. Loaded with grape flavor, frosty servings are perfect for entertaining. —Sharron Kemp, High Point, North Carolina

> 3-1/2 cups water
> 3/4 cup sugar
> 1 can (12 ounces) frozen grape juice concentrate, thawed
> 1 tablespoon lemon juice

In a microwave-safe bowl, combine water and sugar. Cover and microwave on high for 1-2 minutes; stir until sugar is dissolved. Stir in grape juice concentrate and lemon juice. Pour into a 1-1/2-qt. freezer container. Cover and freeze for at least 12 hours, stirring several times. May be frozen for up to 3 months. Just before serving, break apart with a large spoon. **Yield:** 6 servings.

Editor's Note: This recipe was tested in an 850-watt microwave.

In a mixing bowl, beat egg whites until soft peaks form. Gradually add 1/4 cup sugar, beating until stiff peaks form. In another mixing bowl, beat egg yolks and remaining sugar until thick and lemon-colored, about 5 minutes. Combine the flour, cocoa, baking powder and salt; add to yolk mixture and mix well. Fold in egg white mixture.

Line a greased 15-in. x 10-in. x 1-in. baking pan with waxed paper; grease the paper. Spread batter evenly in pan. Bake at 375° for 10-12 minutes or until cake springs back when lightly touched. Cool for 5 minutes. Invert cake onto a kitchen towel dusted with confectioners' sugar. Gently peel off paper. Roll up cake in towel jelly-roll style, starting with a short side. Cool on a wire rack.

Unroll cake; spread jam to within 1/2 in. of edges. Top with ice cream. Roll up without towel. Place seam side down on a platter. Cover and freeze for at least 4 hours before slicing. May be frozen for up to 2 months. Sprinkle with confectioners' sugar; serve with hot fudge topping and whipped topping. **Yield:** 12 servings.

Strawberry Banana Pie

(Pictured above)

With its sugar-cone crust and layers of bananas and strawberry ice cream, this pretty pie never seems to last long...especially when our grandchildren visit.
—Bernice Janowski, Stevens Point, Wisconsin

> 1 package (5-1/4 ounces) ice cream sugar cones, crushed
> 1/4 cup ground pecans
> 1/3 cup butter *or* margarine, melted
> 2 cups vanilla ice cream, softened
> 2 medium ripe bananas, mashed
> 2 large firm bananas, cut into 1/4-inch slices
> 2 cups strawberry ice cream, softened
> 1 pint fresh strawberries
> 1 carton (8 ounces) frozen whipped topping, thawed

Grape Ice

Chapter 9

◉ *Easy Morning Eye-Openers*

HURRYING OFF to work, school and other activities leaves precious little time to prepare and enjoy a satisfying morning meal.

Too often, folks either rush to their nearest fast-food drive-thru or, worse, forgo a good breakfast altogether.

This chapter steers you to quick and tasty recipes that will help get your family's day off to a delicious, nutritious start in short order. You can even serve them as a beautiful brunch for weekend guests.

Families on the go will make time for these fast-to-fix egg dishes, beverages, pancakes, fruit salads and more.

MORNING MARVELS. Clockwise from center top: Fruited Sausage, Apple Grape Drink and Fluffy Waffles (all recipes on p. 133).

Orange Peach Smoothies
Chili-Cheese Rice Frittata
Apple-Sausage French Toast

Chili-Cheese Rice Frittata

(Pictured at left)

Ready in 45 minutes or less

You don't need to fuss with a crust when you fix this hearty breakfast bake that makes the most of leftover rice. It's pretty, tasty and always gets raves. —Betty Archibald Boise, Idaho

    1 medium green pepper, julienned
    1 medium red onion, chopped
  1/2 cup sliced green onions
    1 tablespoon butter *or* margarine
1-1/2 cups cooked rice
1-1/2 cups (6 ounces) shredded cheddar cheese
    1 medium tomato, seeded and chopped
    1 can (4 ounces) chopped green chilies
    5 eggs
  1/3 cup milk
    1 teaspoon Worcestershire sauce
  1/2 teaspoon salt
  1/4 teaspoon hot pepper sauce
Picante sauce *or* salsa

In a 10-in. ovenproof skillet, saute the green pepper and onions in butter. Remove from the heat; stir in the rice, cheese, tomato and chilies. In a bowl, combine the eggs, milk, Worcestershire sauce, salt and hot pepper sauce. Stir into the rice mixture.

Bake, uncovered, at 350° for 20-25 minutes or until a knife inserted near the center comes out clean. Cut into wedges; serve with picante sauce or salsa. **Yield:** 4-6 servings.

Orange Peach Smoothies

(Pictured at left)

Ready in 15 minutes or less

This refreshing shake is wonderful in summer when peaches are in season, but canned or frozen peaches work well, too. I've had several requests for the recipe, and everyone is surprised to discover almond extract is the mystery ingredient. —Kara Cook, Elk Ridge, Utah

✓ Uses less fat, sugar or salt. Includes Nutritional Analysis and Diabetic Exchanges.

    2 cups frozen unsweetened peach slices,
      thawed
    1 cup milk
    1 can (6 ounces) frozen orange juice
      concentrate, thawed
  1/4 teaspoon almond extract
    1 pint vanilla ice cream *or* frozen yogurt
    3 drops *each* red and yellow food coloring,
      optional

In a blender, combine the peaches, milk, orange juice concentrate and extract. Add ice cream; cover and process until smooth. Add food coloring if desired. Pour into glasses; serve immediately. **Yield:** 4 servings.

Nutritional Analysis: One 1-cup serving (prepared with fat-free milk and reduced-fat frozen yogurt) equals 228 calories, 2 g fat (1 g saturated fat), 11 mg cholesterol, 104 mg sodium, 47 g carbohydrate, 2 g fiber, 8 g protein. **Diabetic Exchanges:** 2 fruit, 1 starch, 1/2 fat.

Apple-Sausage French Toast

(Pictured at left)

Plan ahead...start the night before

Sandwiching sausage and apples between bread slices makes this baked French toast a bit different. I like to serve it to overnight guests. It's a great way to get them going in the morning. —Renee Olson, Kendrick, Idaho

  3/4 pound bulk pork sausage
    2 medium apples, peeled and cut into 1/4-inch
      slices
    6 eggs
2-1/2 cups milk
  1/3 cup maple syrup
  1/2 teaspoon ground nutmeg
   18 slices French bread (1/2 inch thick)

In a skillet, cook sausage over medium heat until no longer pink; drain. Remove and set aside. Add apples to the skillet; cover and cook for 3-5 minutes or until tender, stirring occasionally.

In a bowl, lightly whisk the eggs, milk, syrup and nutmeg until combined. In a greased 13-in. x 9-in. x 2-in. baking dish, arrange half of the bread. Top with the sausage, apples and remaining bread. Pour egg mixture over the top. Cover and refrigerate for 8 hours or overnight.

Remove from the refrigerator 30 minutes before baking. Bake, uncovered, at 350° for 45-50 minutes or until eggs are set and bread is golden. **Yield:** 9 servings.

Maple Breakfast Rolls

Ready in 1 hour or less

Maple syrup, brown sugar and walnuts create the sweet glaze that covers these cream cheese-filled rolls. They look like you fussed, but they're very easy to make with refrigerated biscuits. —Nadine Brissey, Jenks, Oklahoma

  1/4 cup butter *or* margarine, melted
    1 cup packed brown sugar
  1/2 cup chopped walnuts
  1/3 cup maple syrup
    1 package (8 ounces) cream cheese, softened
  1/2 cup confectioners' sugar
    4 tubes (6 ounces *each*) refrigerated
      buttermilk biscuits

In a small bowl, combine the butter, brown sugar, nuts and syrup. Spread into a greased 13-in. x 9-in. x 2-in. baking dish; set aside. In a small mixing bowl, beat the cream cheese and confectioners' sugar until smooth.

On a lightly floured surface, roll out each biscuit into a 4-in. circle. Spread 1 tablespoon of cream cheese mixture down the center of each biscuit. Bring dough from opposite sides over filling just until edges meet; pinch to seal. Place seam side down over nut mixture. Bake at 350° for 25-30 minutes or until golden brown. Immediately invert onto a serving plate. Serve warm. **Yield:** 8-10 servings.

Fruit Slush Cups

(Pictured at right)

Plan ahead...needs to freeze

This frosty favorite is a great brunch basic. Pour the batch into one container to freeze, then scoop out single servings. Or spoon the colorful medley into individual plastic cups before freezing. —Betty Webb, Nauvoo, Illinois

 Uses less fat, sugar or salt. Includes Nutritional Analysis and Diabetic Exchanges.

    4 cups water
    1 to 1-1/2 cups sugar
  3/4 cup orange juice concentrate
  3/4 cup lemonade concentrate
    3 medium firm bananas, sliced
    1 can (20 ounces) unsweetened pineapple
      tidbits, undrained
    1 can (11 ounces) mandarin oranges,
      drained
  1/2 cup halved maraschino cherries

In a saucepan, combine the water, sugar and concentrates. Cook and stir over medium heat until sugar is dissolved. Stir in the fruit. Pour into a shallow 3-qt. freezer container. Cover and freeze for 8 hours or overnight. Remove from the freezer 1 hour before serving. **Yield:** 12 servings.
  Nutritional Analysis: One serving (prepared with 1 cup sugar) equals 185 calories, trace fat (trace saturated fat), 0 cholesterol, 6 mg sodium, 47 g carbohydrate, 2 g fiber, 1 g protein. **Diabetic Exchange:** 3 fruit.

Skillet Scramble

(Pictured at right)

Ready in 30 minutes or less

 When we have baked potatoes for dinner, I often bake a couple extra to use in this hearty breakfast. This delicious recipe is so versatile that you can always use up whatever leftovers you have on hand. —Linda Wakefield, Mulino, Oregon

    2 large potatoes, baked and cubed
  1/2 cup chopped green pepper
    1 small onion, chopped
    2 tablespoons olive *or* vegetable oil
  1/2 teaspoon *each* onion powder, garlic powder
      and seasoned salt
    8 eggs, lightly beaten
  1/2 pound cubed fully cooked ham
  1/4 cup water
  1/4 cup salsa
  1/2 teaspoon salt
  1/4 teaspoon pepper
  1/2 cup shredded cheddar cheese

In a skillet, saute potatoes, green pepper and onion in oil. Sprinkle with onion powder, garlic powder and seasoned salt; mix well. In a bowl, combine the eggs, ham, water, salsa, salt and pepper. Add to potato mixture. Cook until eggs are set. Sprinkle with cheese; cook 2 minutes longer or until cheese is melted. **Yield:** 6-8 servings.

Pecan Sweet Roll Rings

(Pictured at right)

Ready in 45 minutes or less

 I rely on tubes of convenient refrigerated crescent roll dough to create these tender treats. Loaded with chopped pecans, cinnamon and nutmeg, the eye-appealing rings feature a sweet glaze. —Jill Cooley Raleigh, North Carolina

    2 tubes (8 ounces *each*) refrigerated crescent
      rolls
    4 tablespoons butter *or* margarine, melted,
      divided
  1/2 cup chopped pecans
  1/4 cup sugar
    1 teaspoon ground cinnamon
  1/2 teaspoon ground nutmeg
  1/2 cup confectioners' sugar
    2 tablespoons maple syrup

Unroll crescent dough and separate into eight rectangles; seal perforations. Brush with 2 tablespoons butter. Combine the pecans, sugar, cinnamon and nutmeg; mix well. Sprinkle 1 tablespoon over each rectangle; gently press into dough. Roll up jelly-roll style, starting at a long side. Pinch seams to seal. Twist two or three times.
  Cut six shallow diagonal slits in each roll. Shape each into a ring; pinch ends together. Place on a greased baking sheet; brush with remaining butter. Bake at 375° for 12-14 minutes or until golden brown. Combine confectioners' sugar and syrup until smooth; drizzle over the warm rolls. **Yield:** 8 rolls.

Pancake Pizza

Ready in 30 minutes or less

This "pancake" is large enough to satisfy several folks. Because everyone wants seconds, I frequently double the recipe to make two of the golden nut-topped rounds. —Francy Glessner, Stafford, Virginia

    2 cups biscuit/baking mix
    2 eggs
    1 cup milk
    1 tablespoon vegetable oil
    1 teaspoon pancake syrup
    1 cup granola without raisins
    1 cup chopped walnuts
Additional pancake syrup

Place biscuit mix in a bowl. Combine the eggs, milk, oil and syrup; add to biscuit mix and mix well. Spread onto a greased 14-in. pizza pan; sprinkle with granola and walnuts. Bake at 425° for 12-15 minutes or until golden brown. Cut into wedges. Serve with additional syrup. **Yield:** 8 servings.

Fruit Slush Cups
Skillet Scramble
Pecan Sweet Roll Rings

Maple Bacon Muffins
Spinach Frittata
Delightful Fruit Compote

Spinach Frittata

(Pictured at left)

Ready in 30 minutes or less

My mom served this dish years ago. It is one of my favorite ways to use spinach. —Paula Tuduri, Bozeman, Montana

    1/2 cup julienned sweet red pepper
    1/2 cup chopped onion
      2 tablespoons olive *or* vegetable oil
      3 eggs
    1/2 cup milk
      1 cup chopped cooked chicken, optional
      1 package (10 ounces) frozen chopped
        spinach, thawed and squeezed dry
    1/2 cup shredded mozzarella cheese
      1 tablespoon grated Parmesan cheese
    1/2 teaspoon salt
    1/4 teaspoon pepper

In a skillet, saute the red pepper and onion in oil until tender. In a bowl, beat eggs and milk. Stir in chicken if desired, 1/2 cup spinach, mozzarella and Parmesan cheeses, salt and pepper (save remaining spinach for another use). Add to the skillet. Cover and cook over medium heat for 7-10 minutes or until completely set. Cut into wedges. **Yield:** 4 servings.

Maple Bacon Muffins

(Pictured at left)

Ready in 45 minutes or less

Maple and bacon—my two favorite breakfast flavors—are combined in these grab-and-go muffins.
                    —Trisha Kruse, Boise, Idaho

      2 cups all-purpose flour
      8 bacon strips, cooked and crumbled
      3 teaspoons baking powder
    1/4 teaspoon salt
      1 egg
    1/2 cup milk
    1/2 cup vegetable oil
    2/3 cup maple syrup

In a large bowl, combine flour, bacon, baking powder and salt. In another bowl, whisk egg, milk, oil and syrup until combined. Stir into dry ingredients just until moistened.

Fill greased or paper-lined muffin cups two-thirds full. Bake at 400° for 20-25 minutes or until a toothpick comes out clean. Cool for 5 minutes before removing from pan to a wire rack. Refrigerate leftovers. **Yield:** 1 dozen.

Delightful Fruit Compote

(Pictured at left)

Ready in 30 minutes or less

Apple jelly lightly glazes this bright medley of fresh and frozen fruits.   —Janet Doherty, Belpre, Ohio

✓ Uses less fat, sugar or salt. Includes Nutritional Analysis and Diabetic Exchanges.

      2 medium ripe peaches, sliced
      1 cup fresh *or* frozen blueberries
      1 cup quartered fresh strawberries
      2 kiwifruit, peeled and sliced
    3/4 cup seedless red *or* green grapes
      3 tablespoons apple jelly
      4 teaspoons water
    Vanilla yogurt and sliced almonds, optional

In a bowl, combine the peaches, berries, kiwi and grapes. In a microwave-safe bowl, combine the jelly and water. Microwave, uncovered, on high for 45 seconds or until jelly is melted; stir until smooth. Drizzle over fruit. Top with yogurt and sprinkle with almonds if desired. **Yield:** 8 servings.

Nutritional Analysis: One 3/4-cup serving (calculated without yogurt and almonds) equals 80 calories, trace fat (0 saturated fat), 0 cholesterol, 5 mg sodium, 20 g carbohydrate, 2 g fiber, 1 g protein. **Diabetic Exchange:** 1-1/2 fruit.

Ham Griddle Cakes

Ready in 30 minutes or less

Looking for a different way to use up leftover ham? Try these golden pancakes. I've served them to company with rave reviews.   —Virginia Cullen, Sarasota, Florida

      1 cup all-purpose flour
    1-1/2 teaspoons baking powder
      2 eggs
    3/4 cup milk
      1 cup ground fully cooked ham
    Pancake syrup

In a large bowl, combine flour and baking powder. In another bowl, beat eggs and milk. Stir into dry ingredients just until moistened. Fold in ham. Pour batter by 1/4 cupfuls onto a lightly greased hot griddle. Turn when pancakes begin to brown on the edges; cook until second side is golden. Serve with syrup. **Yield:** 8 pancakes.

Peeling Kiwifruit

There is a quick and simple way to peel kiwifruit with a teaspoon. This method works best with fruit that is ripe but not too soft.

First, cut off both ends of a kiwi. Then slip a teaspoon just under the skin, matching the spoon's curve to the curve of the fruit.

Now slide the spoon around the kiwi to separate the fruit from the skin, being careful not to dig the spoon into the flesh. Once the spoon has been completely run around the fruit, it will easily slip out of the skin in one smooth piece!

Strawberry Peach Cups

(Pictured at right)

Ready in 15 minutes or less

To dress up breakfast, I toss together a fruit medley, then dollops it with citrus-flavored topping. I sometimes serve the orange cream as a dip alongside fruit.
—*Romaine Wetzel, Ronks, Pennsylvania*

2 cups sliced fresh strawberries
2 cups fresh *or* frozen sliced peaches, thawed
1 package (3 ounces) cream cheese, softened
3 tablespoons orange juice
1/4 teaspoon grated orange peel
1/2 cup whipped topping

Divide strawberries and peaches among four small dishes. In a small mixing bowl, beat the cream cheese, orange juice and peel; fold in whipped topping. Dollop over fruit. **Yield:** 4 servings.

Sausage Breakfast Loaf

(Pictured at right)

Ready in 45 minutes or less

The recipe for this sausage roll has been in my family for years. A tube of refrigerated pizza dough makes it quick and easy, but it tastes like it took hours to prepare.
—*Luella Drake, Auburn, Indiana*

1 pound smoked kielbasa *or* Polish sausage, julienned
1-1/2 cups (6 ounces) shredded mozzarella cheese
2 eggs
1-1/2 teaspoons minced fresh parsley
1/2 teaspoon onion salt
1/2 teaspoon garlic salt
1 tube (10 ounces) refrigerated pizza dough

In a large skillet, saute the sausage; cool. In a bowl, combine the sausage, cheese, one egg, parsley, onion salt and garlic salt; mix well.

Unroll pizza dough; roll into a 12-in. x 8-in. rectangle. Spread sausage mixture down the center of dough. Bring dough over filling; pinch seams to seal. Place seam side down on a greased baking sheet; tuck ends under. Beat remaining egg; brush over top. Bake at 350° for 25-30 minutes or until golden brown. Let stand for 5 minutes before slicing. **Yield:** 6 servings.

Zucchini Egg Bake

(Pictured at right)

Ready in 1 hour or less

This wonderfully moist brunch dish can be made a day early and stored in the refrigerator to save time. Loaded with zucchini, herbs and cheese, it goes well with croissants and fresh fruit. —*Kim Hafner, East Walpole, Massachusetts*

3 cups chopped peeled zucchini
1 large onion, chopped
2 garlic cloves, minced
1/4 cup butter *or* margarine

4 eggs
1/2 cup grated Parmesan cheese
1/4 cup minced fresh parsley
1-1/2 teaspoons minced fresh basil *or* 1/2 teaspoon dried basil
1-1/2 teaspoons minced fresh marjoram *or* 1/2 teaspoon dried marjoram
1/2 teaspoon salt
1/2 cup shredded Monterey Jack cheese

In a large skillet, saute the zucchini, onion and garlic in butter until tender; set aside. In a large bowl, whisk the eggs, Parmesan cheese, parsley, basil, marjoram and salt. Stir in zucchini mixture and Monterey Jack cheese.

Pour into a greased 1-qt. baking dish. Bake at 350° for 20-25 minutes or until a knife inserted near the center comes out clean. Let stand for 5 minutes before serving. **Yield:** 6 servings.

French Toasted Buns

Ready in 30 minutes or less

Being a frugal mom, I take pride in feeding my family creative foods on a budget. This is a favorite of our four children and a fantastic way to use up leftover hamburger buns. It's also a big hit when we're camping.
—*Sharon Strouse Millersburg, Ohio*

4 eggs
1/2 cup milk
1 teaspoon sugar
1/2 teaspoon vanilla extract
1/4 teaspoon salt
1/4 teaspoon ground cinnamon
6 day-old hamburger buns, split
1 cup maple syrup
1/3 cup chopped dried fruit

In a shallow bowl, combine the first six ingredients; mix well. Dip both sides of each bun in egg mixture. Cook on a greased hot griddle until golden brown on both sides. Meanwhile, in a saucepan, combine the syrup and dried fruit; cook over medium heat until heated through. Serve with French Toasted Buns. **Yield:** 6 servings.

Pancake Pointers

- My daughter-in-law has a unique way of making pancakes for her family of six. She pours pancake batter into a 15-inch x 10-inch baking pan and bakes it at 400° for about 20 minutes. She then cuts the pancakes into squares and serves them. You could also bring a little fun to breakfast by cutting the pancakes into shapes with large cookie cutters.
—*Ruth Gunderson, Menominee, Michigan*

- Blenders are great for mixing up pancake batter. The batter pours onto the griddle nicely, and cleaning is a breeze since there are no beaters or bowls to wash.
—*Michelle Lindgren, Moorhead, Minnesota*

Sausage Breakfast Loaf
Zucchini Egg Bake
Strawberry Peach Cups

**Fruited Sausage
Apple Grape Drink
Fluffy Waffles**

Apple Grape Drink

(Pictured at left and on page 123)

Ready in 15 minutes or less

Why settle for plain juice at brunch when you can sip this fizzy morning beverage by stirring together just four ingredients? Everyone loves the taste of this refreshing punch. —Deborah Butts, Union Bridge, Maryland

6 cups apple juice, chilled
3 cups white grape juice, chilled
1 can (12 ounces) frozen lemonade
  concentrate, thawed
1 liter club soda, chilled

In a large container, combine the juices and lemonade concentrate; mix well. Stir in club soda. Serve immediately. **Yield:** 3-3/4 quarts.

Fruited Sausage

(Pictured at left and on page 122)

Ready in 15 minutes or less

A glazed combination of sausage and fruit is a welcome addition to a breakfast buffet. I've also served it over noodles or rice as a skillet supper. —Roseann Loker Vicksburg, Michigan

1 can (20 ounces) pineapple chunks, undrained
1 package (16 ounces) fully cooked kielbasa *or*
  Polish sausage, cut into chunks
1/4 cup packed brown sugar
2 tablespoons cornstarch
1 can (11 ounces) mandarin oranges, drained
1 cup fresh *or* frozen blueberries

In a large skillet, bring the pineapple and sausage to a boil. Combine the brown sugar and cornstarch; add to the skillet. Stir in the oranges and blueberries. Return to a boil; cook and stir for 1-2 minutes or until thickened. **Yield:** 5 servings.

Fluffy Waffles

(Pictured at left and on page 122)

Ready in 45 minutes or less

A friend shared the recipe for these light and delicious waffles. The cinnamon cream syrup is a delicious change of pace from maple syrup...and it keeps quite well in the fridge. Our two children also like it on toast. —Amy Gilles Ellsworth, Wisconsin

2 cups all-purpose flour
1 tablespoon sugar
2 teaspoons baking powder
1/2 teaspoon salt
3 eggs, *separated*
2 cups milk
1/4 cup vegetable oil
CINNAMON CREAM SYRUP:
1 cup sugar

1/2 cup light corn syrup
1/4 cup water
1 can (5 ounces) evaporated milk
1 teaspoon vanilla extract
1/2 teaspoon ground cinnamon

In a bowl, combine the flour, sugar, baking powder and salt. Combine the egg yolks, milk and oil; stir into dry ingredients just until moistened. In a small mixing bowl, beat egg whites until stiff peaks form; fold into batter. Bake in a preheated waffle iron according to manufacturer's directions.

Meanwhile, for syrup, combine the sugar, corn syrup and water in a saucepan. Bring to a boil over medium heat; cook and stir for 2 minutes or until thickened. Remove from the heat; stir in the milk, vanilla and cinnamon. Serve with the waffles. **Yield:** 8-10 waffles (6-1/2 inches) and 1-2/3 cups syrup.

Orange Cranberry Oatmeal

Ready in 15 minutes or less

I never liked oatmeal until I jazzed it up with fruit and nuts. Wheat germ adds a great flavor and a nice nutritional boost. —Jenni Oyler, Poughkeepsie, New York

2 cups water
3 tablespoons orange juice concentrate
1 cup quick-cooking oats
1/3 cup toasted wheat germ
1/4 cup dried cranberries
1 can (11 ounces) mandarin oranges, drained
3 tablespoons brown sugar
1/4 cup chopped walnuts, optional

In a large saucepan, bring the water and orange juice concentrate to a boil. Stir in the oats, wheat germ and cranberries. Return to a boil; cook and stir for 2 minutes. Remove from the heat. Stir in oranges, brown sugar and walnuts if desired. **Yield:** 4 servings.

Broccoli Hash Brown Quiche

I prepare this flavorful quiche for breakfast or dinner. Since we have six children, I rely on quick nutritious dishes like this one. I like to vary it by adding ham or bacon. —Joy Vincent, Goldsboro, North Carolina

3 cups frozen shredded hash brown potatoes,
  thawed
1-1/2 cups frozen broccoli cuts, thawed
4 eggs
1 cup (8 ounces) sour cream
1/2 teaspoon salt
1 cup (4 ounces) shredded Colby-Monterey
  Jack cheese

Press the hash browns onto the bottom and up the sides of a greased 9-in. pie plate, forming a shell. Sprinkle with broccoli. In a bowl, beat the eggs, sour cream and salt; stir in cheese. Pour over broccoli. Bake at 350° for 55-65 minutes or until a knife inserted near the center comes out clean. Let stand for 5 minutes before cutting. **Yield:** 6 servings.

Grapefruit Orange Medley

(Pictured at right)

Ready in 45 minutes or less

Our Test Kitchen staff lets the natural flavor of three kinds of fruit shine through in this refreshing recipe.

> 2 tablespoons sugar
> 1 tablespoon cornstarch
> 1/2 cup lemon-lime soda
> 2 cans (11 ounces *each*) mandarin oranges, drained
> 2 medium grapefruit, peeled and sectioned
> 1-1/2 cups green grapes

In a small saucepan, combine sugar and cornstarch. Whisk in soda until smooth. Bring to a boil; cook and stir for 1 minute or until thickened. Cover and refrigerate until cool. In a large bowl, combine the oranges, grapefruit and grapes. Add sauce; stir to coat. **Yield:** 5 servings.

Egg Blossoms

(Pictured at right)

Ready in 1 hour or less

These cute phyllo dough shells and savory filling are served atop a warm homemade salsa.
—*Barbara Nowakowski, North Tonawanda, New York*

> 4 sheets phyllo dough (14 inches x 9 inches)
> 2 tablespoons butter *or* margarine, melted
> 4 teaspoons grated Parmesan cheese
> 4 eggs
> 4 teaspoons finely chopped green onion
> 1/4 teaspoon salt
> 1/8 teaspoon pepper
> SALSA:
> 1 can (14-1/2 ounces) diced tomatoes, undrained
> 1 small onion, chopped
> 1-1/2 teaspoons sugar
> 1-1/2 teaspoons white wine vinegar *or* cider vinegar
> 1 garlic clove, minced
> 1/2 teaspoon salt
> 1/4 teaspoon dried oregano

Place one sheet of phyllo dough on a work surface; brush with butter. Top with another sheet of phyllo; brush with butter. Cut into six 4-1/2-in. squares. (Keep remaining phyllo dough covered with plastic wrap to avoid drying out.) Repeat with remaining phyllo and butter.

Stack three squares of layered phyllo in each of four greased muffin cups, rotating squares so corners do not overlap. Sprinkle 1 teaspoon of the cheese into each cup. Top with one egg. Sprinkle with green onion, salt and pepper. Place on a baking sheet. Bake at 350° for 25-30 minutes or until eggs are completely set and pastry is golden brown.

Meanwhile, combine the salsa ingredients in a saucepan. Bring to a boil over medium heat. Reduce heat; simmer, uncovered, for 10 minutes or until onion is tender. Serve with egg cups. **Yield:** 4 servings.

Overnight Coffee Cake

(Pictured at right)

Plan ahead...start the night before

This is a wonderful time-saver because it's assembled the night before. My kids think that the nutty cinnamon topping, sweet glaze and from-scratch cake make it the ultimate treat. —*Cindy Harris, San Antonio, Texas*

> 3/4 cup butter *or* margarine, softened
> 1 cup sugar
> 2 eggs
> 2 cups all-purpose flour
> 1 teaspoon baking soda
> 1 teaspoon ground nutmeg
> 1/2 teaspoon salt
> 1 cup (8 ounces) sour cream
> 3/4 cup packed brown sugar
> 1/2 cup chopped pecans *or* walnuts
> 1 teaspoon ground cinnamon
> 1-1/2 cups confectioners' sugar
> 3 tablespoons milk

In a large mixing bowl, cream butter and sugar. Add eggs, one at a time, beating well after each addition. Combine the flour, baking soda, nutmeg and salt; add to the creamed mixture alternately with sour cream. Pour into a greased 13-in. x 9-in. x 2-in. baking dish.

In a small bowl, combine the brown sugar, pecans and cinnamon; sprinkle over coffee cake. Cover and refrigerate overnight.

Remove from the refrigerator 30 minutes before baking. Bake, uncovered, at 350° for 35-40 minutes or until a toothpick inserted near the center comes out clean. Cool on a wire rack for 10 minutes. Combine confectioners' sugar and milk; drizzle over warm coffee cake. **Yield:** 12-15 servings.

Cranberry Butter

Ready in 15 minutes or less

I'm pleased to share the recipe for this easy four-ingredient berry and citrus spread. It's great on toast or bagels.
—*Marlene Muckenhirn, Delano, Minnesota*

> 3/4 cup butter (no substitutes), softened
> 1 teaspoon grated orange peel
> Dash to 1/8 teaspoon almond extract
> 1 cup whole-berry cranberry sauce

In a small mixing bowl, cream butter, orange peel and almond extract. Beat in the cranberry sauce until blended. Store in the refrigerator. **Yield:** about 1-3/4 cups.

'Grate A-peel'

Grating fresh orange peel is a lot easier when you place the orange in the freezer the night before. I also wear a pair of clean gloves to prevent cutting my fingertips on the grater.
—*Jennifer Benson*
Sheboygan, Wisconsin

Overnight Coffee Cake
Grapefruit Orange Medley
Egg Blossoms

Chapter 10

⏱ *Casseroles and Skillet Suppers*

FOR FOLKS who have little extra time on their hands, convenience is often the key to success in the kitchen.

That's why all-in-one casseroles are so appealing. This "comfort food" is packed with a blend of meat, vegetables, pasta, rice and sauces, and can be tossed together while you wait for the oven to preheat. In no time at all, you'll be dishing out hearty helpings of a warm, hearty main course or side dish.

For even faster preparation, turn to this chapter's assortment of skillet suppers that require just a single pan and only a few minutes to make. You'll surely file these in-a-dash dinners under "F" for filling, flavorful...and flat-out fast!

HEAVENLY HOTDISHES. Clockwise from top right: Chicken Ham Casserole (p. 144), Italian Bow Tie Bake (p. 143), Blueberry Brunch Bake (p. 144) and Taco Lasagna (p. 145).

Catchall Casseroles

WHETHER you call them casseroles, bakes or hot dishes, these comforting oven-baked standbys satisfy hunger in a hurry. And they don't take hours to put together. Most can be assembled while you wait for the oven to preheat.

Cashew Chicken

(Pictured below)

I love to cook and bake for my family and friends. I season this chicken and rice casserole with ground ginger, then stir in some crunchy cashews. —Bonnie DeVries
Brainerd, Minnesota

1 pound boneless skinless chicken breasts, cut into 1-inch cubes
1 medium onion, chopped
2 cups frozen broccoli cuts
1-3/4 cups boiling water
1 cup uncooked long grain rice
1 jar (6 ounces) sliced mushrooms, drained
1 tablespoon chicken bouillon granules
1/2 to 1 teaspoon ground ginger
Pepper to taste
3/4 cup salted cashews, *divided*

In a large bowl, combine the first nine ingredients. Transfer to a greased shallow 1-1/2-qt. baking dish. Cover and bake at 375° for 45-55 minutes or until rice is tender and chicken is no longer pink. Stir in 1/2 cup of cashews. Sprinkle with remaining cashews. **Yield:** 4 servings.

Cashew Chicken

Ham and Bean Bake

Ready in 1 hour or less

My mother shared the recipe for this hearty corn bread-topped meal with me. —Rita Maddix, Nelsonville, Ohio

1 medium onion, chopped
1 small green pepper, chopped
2 garlic cloves, minced
2 tablespoons butter *or* margarine
2 cups cubed fully cooked ham
1 can (16 ounces) kidney beans rinsed and drained
1 can (15 ounces) pinto beans, rinsed and drained
1 can (14-1/2 ounces) Italian diced tomatoes, undrained
1 can (8 ounces) tomato sauce
1 teaspoon chili powder
1 teaspoon prepared mustard
1/2 teaspoon salt
1/2 teaspoon pepper
1/4 teaspoon hot pepper sauce
CORN BREAD TOPPING:
1 cup cornmeal
1 cup all-purpose flour
2-1/2 teaspoons baking powder
1/2 to 1 teaspoon salt
1-1/4 cups milk
1 egg
3 tablespoons vegetable oil
1 can (8-1/4 ounces) cream-style corn

In a large skillet, saute onion, green pepper and garlic in butter until tender. Stir in ham, beans, tomatoes, tomato sauce, chili powder, mustard, salt, pepper and hot pepper sauce. Bring to a boil. Meanwhile, in a bowl, combine the cornmeal, flour, baking powder and salt. In another bowl, combine the milk, egg and oil; stir in corn. Add to cornmeal mixture just until combined.

Transfer the hot bean mixture to a greased 13-in. x 9-in. x 2-in. baking dish. Drop corn bread batter by spoonfuls over the top. Bake, uncovered, at 375° for 30-35 minutes or until bubbly and a toothpick inserted near the center of topping comes out clean. **Yield:** 6-8 servings.

Broccoli Corn Stuffing

Ready in 1 hour or less

Broccoli, creamed corn and stuffing croutons combine in this side dish. We've even cooked it in the microwave with great results. —Mary Bondegard, Brooksville, Florida

 Uses less fat, sugar or salt. Includes Nutritional Analysis and Diabetic Exchanges.

1 tablespoon chopped onion
3 tablespoons butter *or* stick margarine, *divided*
1 can (14-3/4 ounces) cream-style corn
1 package (10 ounces) frozen chopped broccoli, thawed

1 egg, lightly beaten
1/4 teaspoon salt, optional
1/4 teaspoon pepper
1 cup seasoned stuffing croutons, *divided*

In a skillet, saute the onion in 1 tablespoon butter. In a bowl, combine the corn, broccoli, egg, salt if desired and pepper; mix well. Add the onion mixture and 3/4 cup of croutons. Spoon into a greased 1-qt. baking dish.

Melt the remaining butter; toss with remaining croutons. Sprinkle over the top. Bake, uncovered, at 350° for 30-35 minutes or until heated through. **Yield:** 4 servings.

Nutritional Analysis: One 3/4-cup serving (prepared with 1/4 cup egg substitute and without salt) equals 302 calories, 11 g fat (6 g saturated fat), 23 mg cholesterol, 1,054 mg sodium, 46 g carbohydrate, 5 g fiber, 8 g protein. **Diabetic Exchanges:** 2-1/2 starch, 2 fat, 1 vegetable.

Pineapple Chicken Casserole

Ready in 30 minutes or less

I love to cook, but with teaching school, playing handbells at church and juggling my husband's and teenage twins' schedules, I have little time in the kitchen. I'm always looking for one-dish dinners like this one that save time and cleanup.
—Susan Warren
North Manchester, Indiana

2 cups cubed cooked chicken
1 can (10-3/4 ounces) condensed cream of mushroom soup, undiluted
1 cup pineapple tidbits
2 celery ribs, chopped
1 tablespoon chopped green onion
1 tablespoon soy sauce
1 can (3 ounces) chow mein noodles, *divided*

In a large bowl, combine the first six ingredients. Fold in 1 cup chow mein noodles. Transfer to a greased shallow 2-qt. baking dish. Sprinkle with remaining noodles. Bake, uncovered, at 350° for 20-25 minutes or until heated through. **Yield:** 4-6 servings.

Hominy Beef Bake

Ready in 1 hour or less

I received this recipe from a friend many years ago and have been using it ever since. Corn chips create a tasty topping on a nicely spiced mixture of ground beef, hominy and chili. Even my meat-and-potatoes husband likes it!
—Jean Stokes, Sacramento, California

1 pound ground beef
1 small onion, chopped
2 garlic cloves, minced
1 can (15-1/2 ounces) hominy, drained
1 can (15 ounces) chili with beans
1 can (8 ounces) tomato sauce
1/2 cup water
3 teaspoons chili powder
Salt and pepper to taste
1 package (10-1/2 ounces) corn chips, crushed

Baked Chops and Fries

In a large skillet, cook beef, onion and garlic over medium heat until meat is no longer pink; drain. Stir in the hominy, chili, tomato sauce, water, chili powder, salt and pepper. Transfer to a greased 13-in. x 9-in. x 2-in. baking dish. Sprinkle with corn chips. Bake, uncovered, at 350° for 30 minutes or until heated through. **Yield:** 4-6 servings.

Baked Chops and Fries

(Pictured above)

Convenience items like frozen vegetables and a jar of cheese sauce make it a snap to assemble this comforting pork chop supper. It's an easy meal-in-one that goes over well every time I make it.
—Gregg Voss, Emerson, Nebraska

6 bone-in pork loin chops (1 inch thick)
1 tablespoon olive *or* vegetable oil
1/2 teaspoon seasoned salt
1 jar (8 ounces) process cheese sauce
1/2 cup milk
4 cups frozen cottage fries
1 can (2.8 ounces) french-fried onions, *divided*
1 package (10 ounces) frozen broccoli florets

In a large skillet, brown pork chops in oil; sprinkle with seasoned salt. In a bowl, combine the cheese sauce and milk until blended; spread into a greased 13-in. x 9-in. x 2-in. baking dish. Top with cottage fries and half of the onions. Arrange broccoli and pork chops over the top.

Cover and bake at 350° for 45 minutes. Sprinkle with remaining onions. Bake 10 minutes longer or until the meat is no longer pink and the broccoli is tender. **Yield:** 6 servings.

Pineapple Ham Casserole

Artichoke Spinach Shells

Ready in 1 hour or less

I discovered this recipe several years ago. If you're looking for a vegetarian meal, it's wonderful as the main course. We like to serve it with hot dinner rolls and a salad.
—Rachel Balsamo, Lewiston, Maine

    4 cups uncooked medium pasta shells
  10 ounces fresh spinach, chopped
    3 cups (12 ounces) shredded cheddar cheese
    1 can (14-1/2 ounces) Italian stewed tomatoes
    1 can (14 ounces) water-packed artichoke
       hearts, drained and quartered
    1 cup (8 ounces) sour cream
1/2 teaspoon garlic salt

In a Dutch oven, cook pasta in boiling water for 5 minutes. Add spinach; cook, uncovered, for 6-8 minutes or until pasta is tender. Drain. In a large bowl, combine the remaining ingredients. Stir in pasta mixture until blended. Transfer to a 3-qt. baking dish. Bake, uncovered, at 350° for 30-35 minutes or until heated through. **Yield: 6-8 servings.**

Pineapple Ham Casserole

(Pictured above)

Ready in 1 hour or less

I turn to this recipe when I want to use leftover ham. The slightly sweet combination of ham, pineapple tidbits, rice and Swiss cheese is popular at my house. We even featured this recipe in our family cookbook.
—Gail Earman
Alpharetta, Georgia

    1 can (20 ounces) pineapple tidbits
1/2 cup mayonnaise*
    1 teaspoon salt
    1 teaspoon prepared mustard
1/4 teaspoon pepper
    3 cups cooked rice
    2 cups cubed fully cooked ham
    1 cup chopped green pepper
1-1/2 cups (6 ounces) shredded Swiss cheese,
      divided
1/3 cup chopped onion

Drain the pineapple, reserving 1/2 cup juice; set pineapple aside. In a large bowl, combine the mayonnaise, salt, mustard, pepper and reserved pineapple juice; mix well. Fold in the rice, ham, green pepper, 1 cup of Swiss cheese, onion and pineapple.

Transfer to a greased 2-qt. baking dish. Cover and bake at 350° for 30 minutes. Sprinkle with remaining cheese. Bake, uncovered, for 10 minutes or until heated through and the cheese is melted. **Yield: 6 servings.**

*Editor's Note: Reduced-fat or fat-free mayonnaise may not be substituted for regular mayonnaise in this recipe.

Tomato-Orange Beef Patties

Ready in 1 hour or less

I love to cook. When I decided to try a recipe prepared by a chef on TV, my husband didn't believe the combination of ingredients would be good. With its mild sweet-and-sour taste, this dish is now a favorite.
—Evelyn Eisenhuth, Knox, Pennsylvania

    2 pounds ground beef
    3 large onions, sliced and separated into rings
    2 tablespoons butter *or* margarine
    1 tablespoon all-purpose flour
Salt and pepper to taste
    1 cup orange juice
    2 tablespoons white wine vinegar *or* cider
      vinegar
    4 medium tomatoes, peeled, seeded and
      chopped

Shape beef into eight oval patties. In a large skillet, cook patties and onions over medium heat until meat is no longer pink; drain. Transfer to a greased 13-in. x 9-in. x 2-in. baking dish.

In a large saucepan, melt butter over medium heat. Stir in the flour, salt and pepper until smooth. Gradually stir in orange juice and vinegar. Bring to a boil; cook and stir for 2 minutes or until thickened. Stir in tomatoes. Pour over beef patties. Cover and bake at 350° for 25-30 minutes or until hot and bubbly. **Yield: 8 servings.**

Sweet Potato Apple Bake

This slightly sweet side dish is perfect for fall. Apples and sweet potatoes are topped with brown sugar, oats, maple syrup and a sprinkling of spices for flavorful results.
—Vicki Schurk, Hamden, Connecticut

6 medium tart apples, peeled and thinly sliced
2 medium sweet potatoes, peeled, halved
   and thinly sliced
1 cup quick-cooking oats
1/2 cup packed brown sugar
1/4 teaspoon *each* ground cinnamon, ginger
   and nutmeg
1/2 cup maple syrup
2 tablespoons butter *or* margarine, melted

In a greased shallow 2-1/2-qt. baking dish, combine the apples and sweet potatoes. Combine the remaining ingredients; sprinkle over apple mixture. Cover and bake at 350° for 40 minutes. Uncover; bake 15-20 minutes longer or until apples and potatoes are tender. **Yield:** 6-8 servings.

Beef Broccoli Supper

Ready in 1 hour or less

When I put together a cookbook for our family reunion, my sister submitted this recipe. My husband and our boys usually don't care for broccoli, but they enjoy it in this dish. —Nita Graffis, Dove Creek, Colorado

3/4 cup uncooked long grain rice
1 pound ground beef
1-1/2 cups fresh broccoli florets
1 can (10-3/4 ounces) condensed broccoli
   cheese soup, undiluted
1/2 cup milk
1 teaspoon salt-free seasoning blend
1 teaspoon salt
1/2 teaspoon pepper
1/2 cup dry bread crumbs
2 tablespoons butter *or* margarine, melted

Cook rice according to package directions. Meanwhile, in a large skillet, cook beef over medium heat until no longer pink; drain. Add the rice, broccoli, soup, milk, seasoning blend, salt and pepper; stir until combined. Transfer to a greased 2-qt. baking dish.

Toss bread crumbs and butter; sprinkle over beef mixture. Cover and bake at 350° for 30 minutes. Uncover; bake 5-10 minutes longer or until heated through. **Yield:** 4-6 servings.

Brat 'n' Tot Bake

(Pictured at right)

Ready in 1 hour or less

Our town is dubbed the bratwurst capital of America. As a volunteer at our annual Bratwurst Festival, I could not have someone in my family who disliked bratwurst, so I developed this cheesy casserole for our son. It's the only way he will eat them. —Jodi Gobrecht, Bucyrus, Ohio

1 pound uncooked bratwurst, casings removed
1 medium onion, chopped
1 can (10-3/4 ounces) condensed cream of
   mushroom soup, undiluted
1 package (32 ounces) frozen Tater Tots
2 cups (16 ounces) sour cream
2 cups (8 ounces) shredded cheddar cheese

Crumble bratwurst into a large skillet; add onion. Cook over medium heat until meat is no longer pink; drain. Stir in the soup. Transfer to a greased 13-in. x 9-in. x 2-in. baking dish. Top with Tater Tots and sour cream. Sprinkle with cheese.

Bake, uncovered, at 350° for 35-40 minutes or until heated through and cheese is melted. Let stand for 5 minutes before serving. **Yield:** 6 servings.

Reheating Cheese-Topped Servings

I have a tip you can use for reheating one serving of lasagna (or other cheese-topped leftovers) in the microwave. I put the lasagna in a microwave-safe dish and stick a toothpick into the center of the lasagna. Then I "tent" a microwave-safe paper towel over the top. After reheating, there's very little mess in my microwave, and the cheese is not stuck to the paper towel. —*Cynthia Woodrow, Moreno Valley, California*

Brat 'n' Tot Bake

Chicken Stuffing Bake

Cheesy Green Bean Casserole

Ready in 45 minutes or less

This is a variation of a recipe I used in home ec class when I was in middle school. I made it a lot for our family of seven when I was growing up. Now I fix it frequently for my family of five. I usually use canned green beans, and there's seldom any left over. —Paula Magnus
Republic, Washington

  1 package (16 ounces) frozen French-style
    green beans
  2 cups diced fully cooked ham
  2 cans (10-3/4 ounces *each*) condensed cream
    of celery soup, undiluted
1/2 cup mayonnaise *or* salad dressing
  2 teaspoons Dijon mustard
  2 cups (8 ounces) shredded cheddar cheese
  1 cup (4 ounces) shredded mozzarella cheese
1/2 cup dry bread crumbs
  2 tablespoons butter *or* margarine, melted

In an ungreased 13-in. x 9-in. x 2-in. baking dish, layer the green beans and ham. Combine the soup, mayonnaise and mustard; pour over ham. Sprinkle with cheeses. Toss bread crumbs and butter; sprinkle over the top. Bake, uncovered, at 350° for 25-30 minutes or until heated through and cheese is melted. **Yield:** 8-10 servings.

Tuna Noodle Casserole

Ready in 1 hour or less

Our sons really like this quick casserole because it tastes special. The creamy main dish is easy to assemble with pantry items such as canned tuna, egg noodles, cream soup and pimientos. —Florence Munger, Malone, New York

  3 cups uncooked egg noodles
  1 cup chopped celery
1/3 cup chopped onion
1/4 cup chopped green pepper
  1 tablespoon vegetable oil
  1 can (10-3/4 ounces) condensed cream of
    mushroom soup, undiluted
  1 cup (4 ounces) shredded cheddar cheese
  1 cup milk
  1 can (12 ounces) tuna, drained and flaked
1/2 cup mayonnaise*
  1 jar (2 ounces) diced pimientos, drained
1/2 teaspoon salt

Cook noodles according to package directions. Meanwhile, in a skillet, saute the celery, onion and green pepper in oil until tender; set aside. In a saucepan, combine the soup, cheese and milk. Cook and stir over low heat until cheese is melted.

Drain noodles; place in a large bowl. Add the celery mixture, soup mixture, tuna, mayonnaise, pimientos and salt. Pour into a greased 8-in. square baking dish. Bake, uncovered, at 350° for 25-30 minutes or until heated through. **Yield:** 4-6 servings.

*Editor's Note: Reduced-fat or fat-free mayonnaise is not recommended for this recipe.

Chicken Stuffing Bake

(Pictured above)

Ready in 45 minutes or less

I love to cook but just don't have much time. This casserole is both good and fast—which makes it my favorite kind of recipe. I serve it with a green salad.
—Jena Coffey, Sunset Hills, Missouri

 Uses less fat, sugar or salt. Includes Nutritional Analysis and Diabetic Exchanges.

  1 can (10-3/4 ounces) condensed cream of
    mushroom soup, undiluted
  1 cup milk
  1 package (6 ounces) stuffing mix
  2 cups cubed cooked chicken breast
  2 cups fresh broccoli florets, cooked
  2 celery ribs, finely chopped
1-1/2 cups (6 ounces) shredded Swiss cheese,
    divided

In a large bowl, combine soup and milk until blended. Add the stuffing mix with contents of seasoning packet, chicken, broccoli, celery and 1 cup cheese. Transfer to greased 13-in. x 9-in. x 2-in. baking dish. Bake, uncovered, at 375° for 20 minutes or until heated through. Sprinkle with remaining cheese; bake 5 minutes longer or until cheese is melted. **Yield:** 8 servings.

Nutritional Analysis: One 1-cup serving (prepared with reduced-fat reduced-sodium soup, fat-free milk and reduced-fat cheese) equals 247 calories, 7 g fat (4 g saturated fat), 42 mg cholesterol, 658 mg sodium, 24 g carbohydrate, 3 g fiber, 22 g protein. **Diabetic Exchanges:** 2 lean meat, 1-1/2 starch.

Italian Bow Tie Bake

(Pictured at right and on page 137)

Ready in 45 min. or less

Served with a green salad and garlic bread, this is the easiest dinner I prepare for my family. They love the four-ingredient main dish and think I worked on it for hours. They don't even miss the meat! —Lisa Blackwell Henderson, North Carolina

8 ounces uncooked bow tie pasta
1 jar (16 ounces) garlic and onion spaghetti sauce
1 envelope Italian salad dressing mix
2 cups (8 ounces) shredded mozzarella cheese

Cook pasta according to package directions; drain. In a bowl, combine the spaghetti sauce and salad dressing mix; add pasta and toss to coat. Transfer to a greased shallow 2-qt. baking dish. Sprinkle with cheese. Bake, uncovered, at 400° for 15-20 minutes or until heated through. **Yield:** 4 servings.

Italian Bow Tie Bake

Colorful Chicken and Rice

(Pictured below)

Ready in 1 hour or less

Topped with crushed corn chips, shredded lettuce and chopped tomatoes, this marvelous meal-in-one is as pretty as it is tasty. I serve it to company along with bread and dessert, and it always gets compliments. —Dana Wise Quinter, Kansas

1 can (10-3/4 ounces) condensed cream of chicken soup, undiluted
1 cup (8 ounces) sour cream
1/2 cup small-curd cottage cheese
1 package (3 ounces) cream cheese, cubed
3 cups cubed cooked chicken
3 cups cooked rice
1-1/2 cups (6 ounces) shredded Monterey Jack *or* mozzarella cheese
1 can (4 ounces) chopped green chilies
1 can (2-1/4 ounces) sliced ripe olives, drained
1/8 teaspoon garlic salt
1-1/2 cups crushed corn chips
2 cups shredded lettuce
2 medium tomatoes, chopped

In a blender or food processor, combine soup, sour cream, cottage cheese and cream cheese; cover and process until smooth. Transfer to a large bowl. Stir in chicken, rice, Monterey Jack cheese, chilies, olives and garlic salt.

Pour into a greased 2-qt. baking dish. Bake, uncovered, at 350° for 25-30 minutes or until heated through. Just before serving, top with corn chips, lettuce and tomatoes. **Yield:** 6-8 servings.

Colorful Chicken and Rice

Cheese Savvy

- Opened cheese should be wrapped with waxed paper, then wrapped again with a tight seal of plastic wrap or foil. Mozzarella cheese stored this way in the refrigerator at a temperature of 34° to 38° will keep for several weeks. If mold develops, trim off the mold plus 1/2 inch extra of cheese and discard it. The rest of the cheese can be eaten. —*Test Kitchen*

- Cheese used to spoil before we used it up. Now, I purchase an economical 2-pound block of cheese, quickly shred the whole thing with my salad shooter and store the cheese in the freezer. Since I can take out just the amount I need, I never have to throw any away. —*Joanne Dyk, Ellensburg, Washington*

- Shredding cheese is easier (and so is cleanup!) when I spritz some nonstick cooking spray on my cheese grater. —*Sherry Barber, Whittier, California*

Blueberry Brunch Bake

Three-Cheese Spirals

Ready in 1 hour or less

Sour cream and three kinds of cheese create the creamy coating for this tasty "twist" on macaroni and cheese. It calls for only six ingredients and can be served as an entree or a side dish. —Deb Collette, Holland, Ohio

> 1 package (16 ounces) spiral pasta
> 1 egg
> 1-1/2 cups (12 ounces) sour cream
> 1-1/2 cups (12 ounces) small-curd cottage cheese
> 1 pound process American cheese, cubed
> 2 cups (8 ounces) shredded cheddar cheese

Cook pasta according to package directions. Meanwhile, in a blender, combine the egg, sour cream and cottage cheese; cover and process until smooth. Transfer to a large bowl; add American and cheddar cheeses. Drain pasta; stir into cheese mixture until evenly coated.

Transfer to a greased shallow 3-qt. baking dish. Bake, uncovered, at 350° for 15 minutes; stir. Bake 15-20 minutes longer or until bubbly and edges begin to brown. **Yield:** 8-10 servings.

Blueberry Brunch Bake

(Pictured above and on page 136)

Plan ahead...start the night before

This recipe is especially nice for overnight company. It's simple to make the day before and then pop in the oven in the morning. Just sit back and enjoy your guests and a great breakfast. —Carol Forcum, Marion, Illinois

> 1 loaf (1 pound) day-old French bread, cut into 1/2-inch cubes
> 1-1/2 cups blueberries
> 12 ounces cream cheese, softened
> 8 eggs
> 1/2 cup plain yogurt
> 1/3 cup sour cream
> 1 teaspoon vanilla extract
> 1/2 teaspoon ground cinnamon
> 1/2 cup milk
> 1/3 cup maple syrup
> Additional blueberries, optional
> Additional maple syrup

Place half of the bread cubes in a greased shallow 3-qt. baking dish. Sprinkle with blueberries. In a mixing bowl, beat cream cheese until smooth. Beat in the eggs, yogurt, sour cream, vanilla and cinnamon. Gradually add milk and 1/3 cup syrup until blended. Pour half over the bread. Top with the remaining bread and cream cheese mixture. Cover and refrigerate overnight.

Remove from the refrigerator 30 minutes before baking. Cover and bake at 350° for 30 minutes. Uncover; bake 20-25 minutes longer or until a knife inserted near the center comes out clean. Sprinkle with additional blueberries if desired. Let stand for 5 minutes. Serve with syrup. **Yield:** 6-8 servings.

Chicken Ham Casserole

(Pictured below and on page 137)

I am retired and always looking for fast-to-fix foods to serve when my children or grandchildren stop by. Leftover chicken, ham and a wild rice mix make this comforting dish quick to assemble. If you have extra turkey, you can use it instead of the chicken.
—Lovetta Breshears, Nixa, Missouri

Chicken Ham Casserole

1 package (6 ounces) long grain and wild
   rice mix
2 cups cubed cooked chicken
1 cup cubed fully cooked ham
1 can (10-3/4 ounces) condensed cream of
   chicken soup, undiluted
1 can (12 ounces) evaporated milk
1 cup (4 ounces) shredded Colby cheese
1/8 teaspoon pepper
1/4 cup grated Parmesan cheese

Cook rice mix according to package directions. Transfer to a greased 2-qt. baking dish. Top with chicken and ham. In a bowl, combine the soup, milk, Colby cheese and pepper; pour over chicken mixture. Sprinkle with the Parmesan. Bake, uncovered, at 350° for 25-30 minutes or until bubbly. **Yield:** 6 servings.

Taco Lasagna

(Pictured at right and on page 136)

Ready in 1 hour or less

If you like foods with Southwestern flair, this might become a new favorite. —Terri KeenanTuscaloosa, Alabama

1 pound ground beef
1/2 cup chopped green pepper
1/2 cup chopped onion
2/3 cup water
1 envelope taco seasoning
1 can (15 ounces) black beans, rinsed and
   drained
1 can (14-1/2 ounces) Mexican diced
   tomatoes, undrained
6 flour tortillas (8 inches)
1 can (16 ounces) refried beans
3 cups (12 ounces) shredded Mexican cheese
   blend

In a large skillet, cook the beef, green pepper and onion over medium heat until meat is no longer pink; drain. Add water and taco seasoning; bring to a boil. Reduce heat; simmer, uncovered, for 2 minutes. Stir in the black beans and tomatoes. Simmer, uncovered, for 10 minutes.

Place two tortillas in a greased 13-in. x 9-in. x 2-in. baking dish. Spread with half of the refried beans and beef mixture; sprinkle with 1 cup cheese. Repeat layers. Top with remaining tortillas and cheese. Cover and bake at 350° for 25-30 minutes or until heated through and cheese is melted. **Yield:** 9 servings.

Shoepeg Corn Casserole

Ready in 45 minutes or less

This comforting side dish makes a creamy accompaniment to most any main course. —Lori Talamo
Baton Rouge, Louisiana

2 cans (11 ounces *each*) shoepeg *or* white
   corn, drained
1 can (10-3/4 ounces) condensed cream of
   celery soup, undiluted

Taco Lasagna

1 cup (8 ounces) sour cream
1 cup (4 ounces) shredded cheddar cheese
1/2 cup chopped onion
1/2 cup chopped celery
1/4 cup chopped green pepper
3/4 cup crushed butter-flavored crackers (about
   18 crackers)
2 tablespoons butter *or* margarine, melted

In a large bowl, combine the first seven ingredients. Transfer to a greased 2-qt. baking dish. Sprinkle with the cracker crumbs; drizzle with butter. Bake, uncovered, at 350° for 20-25 minutes or until bubbly. **Yield:** 6 servings.

Efficient Cooking

• When cooking or baking, I often grab an extra dishwasher-safe bowl and set it on the counter within easy reach. I use it as my "garbage bowl" for egg shells, wrappers, etc.

Then, when I'm finished, I simply dump the contents of the bowl into the trash and place the bowl in the dishwasher. It saves time by eliminating multiple messy trips to the garbage.
      —*Jennifer Leisenheimer, Bemidji, Minnesota*

• When I reduce a recipe that makes several servings, I often need only half of an onion or pepper or just one rib of celery. The rest goes to waste. I solved this by visiting my local supermarket's salad bar. There, I can get as much sliced onion, pepper or celery as I need for my meal with no fuss or waste.

At first glance, it seems more expensive, but not when compared to unused food that would eventually be thrown out. It's time saving, too, because I don't have to clean or chop the items.
      —*Bob Sulenski, Silver Spring, Maryland*

Southwestern Spaghetti

(Pictured below)

Ready in 1 hour or less

A close friend made this Mexican-Italian bake for me almost 20 years ago, and I've prepared it regularly ever since. It comes together in a snap because it relies largely on convenience items I keep on hand. We like it with a loaf of crusty bread.

—Rose Turner Minnick
Christiansburg, Virginia

    12 ounces uncooked spaghetti
1-1/2 pounds ground beef
    1 small onion, chopped
    1 envelope taco seasoning
    1 jar (26 ounces) spaghetti sauce
    1 jar (4-1/2 ounces) sliced mushrooms,
      drained
    1 can (2-1/4 ounces) sliced ripe olives, drained
    2 cups (8 ounces) shredded cheddar cheese
Shredded lettuce, diced tomatoes, sour cream and salsa *or* picante sauce

Cook spaghetti according to package directions. Meanwhile, in a large skillet, cook beef and onion over medium heat until meat is no longer pink; drain. Stir in the taco seasoning, spaghetti sauce, mushrooms and olives. Drain spaghetti; stir into the beef mixture.

Transfer to a greased shallow 3-qt. baking dish; sprinkle with cheese. Bake, uncovered, at 350° for 25-30 minutes or until heated through. Serve with lettuce, tomatoes, sour cream and salsa. **Yield:** 8 servings.

Broccoli Turkey Supreme

Broccoli Turkey Supreme

(Pictured above)

I do a lot of catering, and this easy rice casserole always gets rave reviews from clients as well as friends and family. It is loaded with turkey, broccoli and water chestnuts. I'm asked for the recipe over and over.

—Marcene Christopherson, Miller, South Dakota

✓ Uses less fat, sugar or salt. Includes Nutritional Analysis and Diabetic Exchanges.

    4 cups cubed cooked turkey breast
    1 can (10-3/4 ounces) condensed cream of
      chicken soup, undiluted
    1 package (10 ounces) frozen broccoli florets,
      thawed and drained
    1 package (6.9 ounces) chicken-flavored rice
      mix
1-1/3 cups milk
    1 cup chicken broth
    1 cup chopped celery
    1 can (8 ounces) sliced water chestnuts,
      drained
    3/4 cup mayonnaise
    1/2 cup chopped onion

In a large bowl, combine all of the ingredients. Transfer to a greased 3-qt. baking dish. Cover and bake at 325° for 1 hour. Uncover; bake 15-20 minutes longer or until rice is tender. **Yield:** 8 servings.

Nutritional Analysis: One serving (prepared with reduced-fat reduced-sodium soup, fat-free milk, reduced-sodium chicken broth and fat-free mayonnaise) equals 268 calories, 3 g fat (1 g saturated fat), 67 mg cholesterol, 1,031 mg sodium, 32 g carbohydrate, 3 g fiber, 28 g protein. **Diabetic Exchanges:** 2 lean meat, 1-1/2 starch, 1 vegetable.

Southwestern Spaghetti

Cheesy Sausage Penne

Ready in 1 hour or less

This lasagna-like entree takes me back to my childhood. I got the recipe from a friend's mother, who fixed it for us when we were kids. I made a few changes to it, but it's still quick and delicious. —Dallas McCord, Reno, Nevada

- 1 pound bulk Italian sausage
- 1 garlic clove, minced
- 1 jar (26 ounces) spaghetti sauce
- 1 package (1 pound) penne *or* medium tube pasta
- 1 package (8 ounces) cream cheese, softened
- 1 cup (8 ounces) sour cream
- 4 green onions, sliced
- 2 cups (8 ounces) shredded cheddar cheese

In a large skillet, cook the sausage and garlic over medium heat until meat is no longer pink; drain. Stir in spaghetti sauce; bring to a boil. Reduce heat; cover and simmer for 20 minutes. Meanwhile, cook pasta according to package directions; drain. In a small mixing bowl, combine the cream cheese, sour cream and onions.

In a greased shallow 3-qt. baking dish, layer half of the pasta and sausage mixture. Dollop with half of the cream cheese mixture; sprinkle with half of the cheddar cheese. Repeat layers. Bake, uncovered, at 350° for 30-35 minutes or until bubbly. **Yield:** 12 servings.

Lobster Newburg

Ready in 30 minutes or less

We live in Maine, so we like to use fresh lobster in this time-honored recipe. However, it can also be made with frozen, canned or imitation lobster. No matter how you prepare it, guests will think you fussed when you treat them to these rich individual seafood casseroles.
—Wendy Cornell, Hudson, Maine

- 3 cups fresh, frozen *or* canned flaked lobster meat *or* imitation lobster chunks
- 3 tablespoons butter *or* margarine
- 1/4 teaspoon paprika
- 3 cups heavy whipping cream
- 1/2 teaspoon Worcestershire sauce
- 3 egg yolks, lightly beaten
- 1 tablespoon sherry *or* water
- 1/4 teaspoon salt
- 1/3 cup crushed butter-flavored crackers (about 8 crackers)

In a large skillet, saute the lobster in butter and paprika for 3-4 minutes; set aside. In a large saucepan, bring cream and Worcestershire sauce to a gentle boil. Meanwhile, in a bowl, combine the egg yolks, sherry or water and salt.

Remove cream from the heat; stir a small amount into egg yolk mixture. Return all to the pan, stirring constantly. Bring to a gentle boil; cook and stir for 5-7 minutes or until slightly thickened. Stir in the lobster.

Divide lobster mixture between four 10-oz. individual baking dishes. Sprinkle with cracker crumbs. Broil 6 in. from the heat for 2-3 minutes or until golden brown. **Yield:** 4 servings.

Cheddar Taters

(Pictured below)

Ready in 45 minutes or less

Potato chips are the fun topping that's sprinkled over this irresistible treatment for Tater Tots. With its garlic, onion and cheese flavors, you're not likely to have much left over. To cut preparation and cleanup time, try mixing the ingredients right in the baking dish.
—Ruth Van Nattan, Kingston, Tennessee

- 1 can (10-3/4 ounces) condensed cream of chicken soup, undiluted
- 1 can (12 ounces) evaporated milk
- 1 cup (8 ounces) sour cream
- 1/2 cup butter *or* margarine, melted
- 1 teaspoon garlic powder
- 1 teaspoon onion powder
- 1 package (32 ounces) frozen Tater Tots
- 1-1/2 cups (6 ounces) shredded cheddar cheese
- 1 cup crushed potato chips

In a large bowl, combine the first six ingredients. Gently stir in the Tater Tots. Transfer to a greased 13-in. x 9-in. x 2-in. baking dish. Sprinkle with cheese and potato chips. Bake, uncovered, at 350° for 30-35 minutes or until bubbly. **Yield:** 8-10 servings.

Cheddar Taters

Tasty Turkey Skillet

saute rice in butter until lightly browned. Stir in water, cayenne and contents of seasoning packet.

Bring to a boil. Reduce heat; cover and simmer for 15 minutes. Stir in corn, broccoli, red pepper if desired and turkey. Return to a boil. Reduce heat; cover and simmer for 6-8 minutes or until the rice and vegetables are tender. **Yield:** 4-6 servings.

Italian Chicken Stew

Ready in 30 minutes or less

My husband enjoys preparing this satisfying stew because it's so easy to make. With warm Italian bread, it's a winner on a cold day. —Jo Calizzi, Vandergrift, Pennsylvania

✓ Uses less fat, sugar or salt. Includes Nutritional Analysis and Diabetic Exchanges.

    1 pound boneless skinless chicken breasts, cubed
    4 medium potatoes, peeled and cut into 1/4-inch cubes
    1 medium sweet red pepper, chopped
    2 garlic cloves, minced
    1 to 2 tablespoons olive *or* canola oil
    1 jar (26 ounces) meatless spaghetti sauce
1-3/4 cups frozen cut green beans
    1 teaspoon dried basil
 1/4 to 1/2 teaspoon salt
 1/4 teaspoon crushed red pepper flakes
Pepper to taste

In a large skillet, cook the chicken, potatoes, red pepper and garlic in oil until chicken is no longer pink and vegetables are tender. Stir in the remaining ingredients; cook and stir until heated through. **Yield:** 4 servings.
    Nutritional Analysis: One 1-1/2-cup serving (prepared with 1 tablespoon oil and 1/4 teaspoon salt) equals 475 calories, 13 g fat (3 g saturated fat), 63 mg cholesterol, 995 mg sodium, 62 g carbohydrate, 11 g fiber, 31 g protein. **Diabetic Exchanges:** 4 starch, 3 very lean meat, 1 fat.

Dash in the Pan

YOU'VE COME to the right place if "going steady" with your stove doesn't fit your active lifestyle. Many of the mouth-watering recipes in this section take a half hour or less to put on the table. That's not all—afterward, cleanup's quick, too!

Tasty Turkey Skillet

(Pictured above)

Ready in 30 minutes or less

I like using boxed rice and pasta mixes as the basis for quick meals. This colorful dish is simple to cook on the stovetop. —Betty Kleberger, Florissant, Missouri

    1 pound turkey breast tenderloins, cut into 1/4-inch strips
    1 package (5.3 ounces) Oriental fried rice mix
    1 tablespoon butter *or* margarine
    2 cups water
 1/8 teaspoon cayenne pepper
1-1/2 cups frozen corn, thawed
    1 cup frozen broccoli cuts, thawed
    2 tablespoons chopped sweet red pepper, optional

In a nonstick skillet coated with nonstick cooking spray, saute turkey until no longer pink; drain. Remove and keep warm. Set aside seasoning packet from rice. In the skillet,

Meatball Stroganoff

Ready in 30 minutes or less

It takes mere minutes to fix this comforting combination that's delicious over noodles or rice. A little sour cream adds richness to the flavorful from-scratch sauce that deliciously dresses up frozen meatballs. —Alpha Wilson Roswell, New Mexico

    1 small onion, sliced
    1 garlic clove, minced
4-1/2 teaspoons butter *or* margarine
    4 fresh mushrooms, sliced
4-1/2 teaspoons all-purpose flour
 1/2 teaspoon salt
    1 cup milk
Hot pepper sauce to taste
   16 frozen cooked meatballs, thawed
    2 tablespoons sour cream
Hot cooked noodles

In a large saucepan, saute the onion and garlic in butter until tender. Add mushrooms; cook for 1 minute. Stir in flour and salt until blended. Gradually add the milk and hot pepper sauce. Bring to a boil; cook and stir for 2 minutes or until thickened.

Reduce heat; add the meatballs and sour cream. Heat through (do not boil). Serve over the noodles. **Yield:** 4 servings.

Chili Jack Chicken

Ready in 30 minutes or less

I'm a mother, military wife and full-time pharmacist, so I appreciate quick recipes. I increase the recipe for this flavorful chicken when company comes.
—*Karen Dunavant, Aiea, Hawaii*

2 boneless skinless chicken breast halves
1 tablespoon butter *or* margarine
1 tablespoon vegetable oil
1/2 cup chicken broth
1 can (4 ounces) chopped green chilies
1 teaspoon prepared mustard
1 garlic clove, minced
Salt to taste
1/2 cup heavy whipping cream
1/2 cup shredded Monterey Jack cheese
Hot cooked rice

In a large skillet, brown chicken in butter and oil for 10 minutes; drain. Add the broth, chilies, mustard, garlic and salt. Simmer, uncovered, for 10 minutes or until chicken juices run clear. Stir in the cream; simmer until thickened. Sprinkle with cheese. Cover and cook until the cheese is melted. Serve over rice. **Yield:** 2 servings.

Bratwurst Potato Skillet

Ready in 30 minutes or less

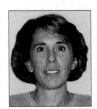

Apples are a sweet and surprising addition to tender potatoes and leftover bratwurst in this stovetop supper. Having grown up in the Midwest, I love a meat-and-potatoes meal. If I can make it all in one pot, it's an added bonus. —*Marcia Graves-Wilbur Indian Harbour Beach, Florida*

3 medium red potatoes, cubed
1 cup beef broth
5 fully cooked bratwurst, cut into 1/2-inch slices
2 medium tart apples, peeled and cubed
1 medium onion, chopped
1 teaspoon salt
2 tablespoons sugar
3 tablespoons butter *or* margarine

In a skillet, bring potatoes and broth to a boil. Reduce heat; simmer, uncovered, for 10 minutes. Add bratwurst, apples, onion and salt; cook for 5-10 minutes or until potatoes are tender and broth has evaporated.

Push bratwurst mixture to the sides of pan. Place sugar in the center of pan; cook until sugar is melted and golden brown. Add butter; cook and stir until butter is melted. Toss with the bratwurst mixture; serve immediately. **Yield:** 6-8 servings.

Ravioli Primavera

(Pictured below)

Ready in 30 minutes or less

I rely on convenient frozen vegetables and ravioli to hurry along this tasty, colorful main dish. It's pleasantly seasoned with minced garlic and fresh parsley. It's a nice light entree or a versatile side dish.
—*Lois McAtee, Oceanside, California*

4 cups frozen miniature cheese ravioli
1 package (16 ounces) frozen Italian vegetables, thawed
2 garlic cloves, minced
1/4 cup olive *or* vegetable oil
1/4 cup chicken *or* vegetable broth
2 tablespoons minced fresh parsley
1/4 teaspoon salt
1/4 teaspoon pepper

Prepare ravioli according to package directions. Meanwhile, in a skillet, saute vegetables and garlic in oil for 4 minutes. Stir in the broth. Simmer, uncovered, for 2 minutes. Stir in parsley, salt and pepper; cook 2 minutes longer or until vegetables are tender. Drain pasta; add to vegetable mixture and toss to coat. **Yield:** 4 servings.

Ravioli Primavera

Zucchini and Kielbasa

(Pictured below)

Ready in 30 minutes or less

For a skillet supper that's hearty enough to satisfy the biggest appetites in your house, try this savory recipe. It's chock-full of vegetables and sliced sausage. I like to serve this dish with corn bread muffins. —Norma Fick
Decatur, Illinois

2 small zucchini, cut into 1/8-inch slices
1 small onion, chopped
1/2 cup chopped green pepper
2 tablespoons olive *or* vegetable oil
1 pound kielbasa *or* Polish sausage, halved lengthwise and cut into 1/2-inch slices
1 can (15-1/4 ounces) whole kernel corn, drained
1 can (8 ounces) tomato sauce
2 teaspoons Italian seasoning
1/8 teaspoon crushed red pepper flakes

In a large skillet, saute the zucchini, onion and green pepper in oil until crisp-tender. Stir in the remaining ingredients; cook until heated through. **Yield:** 6 servings.

Sausage Cabbage Skillet

Ready in 45 minutes or less

For a one-dish dinner, simmer together this hearty combination. Sometimes I use sauerkraut in place of the cabbage. When time allows, you can also bake it in the oven rather than cook it on the stovetop. —Yvette Rothrock
Winslow, Indiana

1 pound smoked kielbasa *or* Polish sausage, cut into 1/4-inch slices
1 small head cabbage, chopped
1 medium green pepper, chopped
1 medium sweet onion, chopped
2 medium potatoes, thinly sliced
2 teaspoons Worcestershire sauce
1 garlic clove, minced
Salt and pepper to taste

In a large skillet, brown the sausage; drain. Stir in the remaining ingredients. Cover and cook for 15 minutes or until the vegetables are tender. **Yield:** 6 servings.

Hamburger Rice Skillet

Ready in 30 minutes or less

I use onion soup mix to mildly and conveniently flavor this kid-pleasing mixture of ground beef, instant rice and fresh vegetables. It's good as a main meal or a side dish. —Suzanne Dolata
Ripon, Wisconsin

1 pound ground beef
3 cups water
2 medium carrots, cut into 1/4-inch slices
1 celery rib, chopped
1 envelope onion soup mix
2 cups uncooked instant rice

In a large skillet, cook beef over medium heat until no longer pink; drain. Stir in the water, carrots, celery and soup mix. Bring to a boil. Reduce heat; cover and simmer for 8 minutes or until vegetables are tender. Return to a boil; add the rice. Remove from the heat; let stand for 5 minutes or until rice is tender. **Yield:** 4 servings.

Veggie Mac 'n' Cheese

Ready in 30 minutes or less

I plant a nice-sized garden every year. I came up with this quick combination when trying to think of a different way to fix an abundance of zucchini and yellow squash. Everyone enjoyed it, so I fixed it again the next week and it was just as good. —Barbie Noffsinger

Reno, Nevada

Zucchini and Kielbasa

1 medium carrot, thinly sliced
2 tablespoons butter *or* margarine
1 medium onion, chopped
1 medium zucchini, sliced
1 medium yellow summer squash, halved lengthwise and sliced
1 can (10-3/4 ounces) condensed cheddar cheese soup, undiluted
1/3 cup milk
1/4 teaspoon salt
1/8 teaspoon pepper
1-2/3 cups cooked elbow macaroni
3/4 cup shredded cheddar cheese
4 bacon strips, cooked and crumbled

In a large skillet, saute carrot in butter for 2 minutes. Add onion; cook and stir 2 minutes longer. Add zucchini and summer squash; cook for 5 minutes or until vegetables are tender.

In a bowl, combine the soup, milk, salt and pepper. Stir into skillet. Add macaroni; heat through. Sprinkle with cheese. Cover and cook for 2 minutes or until cheese is melted. Sprinkle with bacon. **Yield:** 4 servings.

Onion Turkey Meatballs

Onion Turkey Meatballs

(Pictured at right)

Ready in 1 hour or less

This is one of my "experiments". I came up with it when trying to figure out a new taste for ground turkey, since we eat a lot of it. But I didn't want to run to the grocery store, so I used ingredients I had on hand. It's now one of our family's favorites.   —Regina Davis, Griffin, Georgia

1 cup soft bread crumbs
1 envelope onion soup mix, *divided*
1-1/2 pounds ground turkey
3 cups water, *divided*
3 tablespoons all-purpose flour
Hot cooked noodles *or* rice

In a bowl, combine the bread crumbs, half of the soup mix and the turkey; mix well. Shape into 1-in. balls. In a large skillet, brown meatballs in batches over medium heat, turning frequently. Stir in 2-1/2 cups water and remaining soup mix. Bring to a boil. Reduce heat; cover and simmer for 10 minutes or until juices run clear.

In a bowl, combine the flour and remaining water until smooth; add to the skillet. Bring to a boil; cook for 2 minutes or until thickened. Serve over noodles or rice. **Yield:** 6 servings.

Hurry-Up Tuna Supper

Ready in 15 minutes or less

All kinds of convenience products—including canned tuna and frozen vegetables and instant rice—are used to prepare this satisfying supper.   —Dorothy Pritchett Wills Point, Texas

1 package (10 ounces) frozen mixed vegetables
2 cups water

2 tablespoons dried minced onion
1/2 teaspoon salt
1 can (10-3/4 ounces) condensed cream of celery soup, undiluted
1-1/3 cups uncooked instant rice
1 can (6 ounces) tuna, drained and flaked
2 teaspoons dried parsley flakes
3/4 teaspoon dried marjoram
1 teaspoon lemon juice

In a skillet, combine the vegetables, water, onion and salt. Bring to a boil over medium heat. Stir in the soup, rice, tuna, parsley and marjoram. Reduce heat; cover and simmer for 5-10 minutes or until the rice is tender and the liquid is absorbed. Stir in lemon juice. Serve immediately. **Yield:** 4 servings.

Italian Seasoning Savvy

Italian seasoning can be found in the spice aisle of most grocery stores. A basic blend might contain marjoram, thyme, rosemary, sage, oregano and basil. If your grocery store does not carry Italian seasoning, ask the manager if it can be ordered.

Or, mix up your own. If you don't have all the ingredients on your spice shelf, you can blend just a few of them with good results. Try substituting 1/4 teaspoon each of basil, thyme, rosemary and oregano for each teaspoon of Italian seasoning called for in a recipe.

Apple Chicken and Rice

(Pictured below)

Ready in 1 hour or less

The first time we tried this lightly sweet chicken, I knew I'd be making it for a long time to come. I serve it with a salad and bread.
—Nadene MacLeod
Springfield, Massachusetts

✓ Uses less fat, sugar or salt. Includes Nutritional Analysis and Diabetic Exchanges.

- 1 pound boneless skinless chicken breasts, cut into 1-inch cubes
- 2 tablespoons butter *or* stick margarine, *divided*
- 1 package (6 ounces) chicken-flavored rice mix
- 1-1/4 cups water
- 1/2 cup chicken broth
- 1/2 cup apple juice
- 1 medium apple, chopped
- 1 cup sliced fresh mushrooms
- 1/2 cup chopped onion
- 1/4 cup dried cranberries *or* raisins

In a large skillet, brown chicken in 1 tablespoon butter until juices run clear; remove and keep warm. Set seasoning packet from rice mix aside. In the same skillet, saute rice mix in remaining butter for 5 minutes or until golden brown.

Add the water, broth, apple juice, apple, mushrooms, onion, cranberries and contents of rice seasoning packet; bring to a boil. Reduce heat; cover and simmer for 15-20 minutes or until rice is tender, stirring occasionally. Return chicken to the pan; heat through. **Yield:** 4 servings.

Nutritional Analysis: One 1-1/4-cup serving (prepared with reduced-sodium broth) equals 391 calories, 8 g fat (4 g saturated fat), 81 mg cholesterol, 818 mg sodium, 48 g carbohydrate, 3 g fiber, 32 g protein. **Diabetic Exchanges:** 3 lean meat, 2 starch, 1 fruit.

Pineapple Pork Chop Suey

Ready in 1 hour or less

This sweet-and-sour entree combines tender pork, tangy pineapple, crunchy water chestnuts and colorful pepper strips. It has superb flavor, and friends love it.
—Eva Doucet, Bathurst, New Brunswick

- 4 tablespoons all-purpose flour, *divided*
- 2 teaspoons ground ginger
- 1 teaspoon salt
- 1/4 teaspoon pepper
- 1 pound pork chop suey meat
- 2 tablespoons vegetable oil
- 1 can (20 ounces) pineapple chunks
- 1/4 cup sugar
- 1/4 cup cider vinegar
- 1/4 cup soy sauce
- 1 tablespoon Worcestershire sauce
- 1 tablespoon chili sauce
- 1 small green pepper, julienned
- 1 can (8 ounces) sliced water chestnuts, drained
- 1 cup canned bean sprouts
- Hot cooked rice

In a large resealable plastic bag, combine 2 tablespoons flour, ginger, salt and pepper. Add the pork and shake to coat. In a large skillet or wok over medium-high heat, stir-fry the pork in oil for 5-7 minutes or until no longer pink.

Drain pineapple, reserving juice; set pineapple aside. Place the remaining flour in a bowl; stir in reserved juice until smooth. Add sugar, vinegar, soy sauce, Worcestershire sauce and chili sauce. Stir into pork. Add green pepper, water chestnuts, bean sprouts and pineapple. Bring to a boil; cook and stir for 2 minutes. Serve over rice. **Yield:** 4 servings.

Skillet Beef 'n' Rice

Ready in 30 minutes or less

Even picky children enjoy this economical dish. Our kids agree it's one of their favorites. If you leave out the onion and pepper, it's still delicious.
—Lori Thompson
New London, Texas

✓ Uses less fat, sugar or salt. Includes Nutritional Analysis and Diabetic Exchanges.

- 1 package (6.8 ounces) beef-flavored rice mix
- 1 pound ground beef
- 1 small onion, chopped
- 1 small green pepper, chopped
- 2 tablespoons plus 1-1/2 teaspoons Worcestershire sauce
- 1 teaspoon garlic powder

Apple Chicken and Rice

Cook rice mix according to package directions. Meanwhile, in a large skillet, cook the beef, onion and green pepper over medium heat until the meat is no longer pink; drain. Stir in the rice mixture, Worcestershire sauce and garlic powder; mix well. **Yield:** 4 servings.

Nutritional Analysis: One 1-1/4-cup serving (prepared with lean ground beef) equals 351 calories, 9 g fat (3 g saturated fat), 56 mg cholesterol, 883 mg sodium, 40 g carbohydrate, 2 g fiber, 27 g protein. **Diabetic Exchanges:** 3 lean meat, 2-1/2 starch.

Ham Spaghetti Skillet

Ham Spaghetti Skillet

(Pictured at right)

Ready in 30 minutes or less

This satisfying skillet consists of ham, chicken and spaghetti that's tossed in a creamy sauce. For make-ahead convenience, assemble it in a casserole the day before and store it in the fridge.   —Edna Shaver, San Antonio, Texas

   6 ounces thin spaghetti, broken into 2-inch pieces
   6 green onions, chopped
   1 jar (4-1/2 ounces) sliced mushrooms, drained
1/4 cup butter *or* margarine
1-1/2 cups cubed fully cooked ham
   1 cup cubed cooked chicken
   1 cup (8 ounces) sour cream
   1 cup (8 ounces) small-curd cottage cheese
1/2 teaspoon celery salt
1/2 teaspoon salt
1/8 teaspoon pepper
Shredded cheddar cheese

Cook spaghetti according to package directions. Meanwhile, in a large skillet, saute onions and mushrooms in butter until tender; reduce heat to low. Drain spaghetti. Add the spaghetti, ham, chicken, sour cream, cottage cheese, celery salt, salt and pepper to the skillet. Cook and stir until heated through. Remove from the heat. Sprinkle with cheese. **Yield:** 4 servings.

Meatballs Monte Carlo

Ready in 1 hour or less

I need just one pan to prepare this easy entree. Once the meatballs have browned, the egg noodles cook in the tomatoey sauce right along with them.   —Margaret Wilson Hemet, California

1/3 cup evaporated milk
1/4 cup dry bread crumbs
   1 small onion, chopped
1/4 teaspoon salt
Dash pepper
   1 pound ground beef
   1 envelope spaghetti sauce mix
   4 cans (11-1/2 ounces *each*) tomato juice
   1 cup water
   5 cups uncooked extra wide egg noodles
   1 can (2-1/4 ounces) sliced ripe olives, drained

In a large bowl, combine milk, bread crumbs, onion, salt and pepper. Crumble beef over mixture and mix well. Shape into 1-1/2-in. balls.

In a large skillet over medium-high heat, brown meatballs; drain. Combine the spaghetti sauce mix, tomato juice and water; pour over the meatballs. Bring to a boil. Stir in the noodles and olives. Reduce heat; cover and simmer for 20-25 minutes or until noodles are tender, stirring occasionally. **Yield:** 6 servings.

Creamy Shrimp Stir-Fry

Ready in 15 minutes or less

Looking for a speedy supper that's perfect for family or company? Try this saucy stir-fry. This recipe is a favorite with guests.   —Ruth Andrewson, Leavenworth, Washington

✓ Uses less fat, sugar or salt. Includes Nutritional Analysis and Diabetic Exchanges.

1/2 pound fresh mushrooms, sliced
   1 can (8 ounces) sliced water chestnuts, drained
   1 small onion, halved and sliced
   1 medium carrot, cut into 1/4-inch slices
   1 celery rib, cut into 1/4-inch slices
   2 tablespoons butter *or* stick margarine
1-1/2 pounds uncooked medium shrimp, peeled and deveined
   1 cup (8 ounces) sour cream
1/2 cup plain yogurt
1/4 teaspoon pepper
Hot cooked rice

In a large skillet or wok, stir-fry vegetables in butter until crisp-tender. Add shrimp; cook and stir for 2-3 minutes or until shrimp turn pink. Reduce heat to low. Add the sour cream, yogurt and pepper; cook and stir until heated through (do not boil). Serve over rice. **Yield:** 6 servings.

Nutritional Analysis: One 3/4-cup serving (prepared with reduced-fat sour cream and fat-free yogurt; calculated without rice) equals 254 calories, 11 g fat (6 g saturated fat), 202 mg cholesterol, 258 mg sodium, 13 g carbohydrate, 3 g fiber, 27 g protein. Diabetic Exchanges: 3 lean meat, 1 starch, 1/2 fat.

Chapter 11

FLUFFY ROLLS...fruit-filled muffins...sweet coffee cakes...and savory loaves. Cooks agree breads make great accompaniments to a delicious breakfast, hearty lunch or speedy supper.

You can enjoy home-baked items such as these without spending hours in the kitchen.

The quick breads featured here promise oven-fresh flavor without the work traditional yeast breads require. Just mix the batter, fill the pan and pop it in the oven.

Don't think you have the time to make old-fashioned homemade bread from scratch? Think again!

Thanks to today's bread machines, yummy yeast breads can be quick and easy, too.

A BOUNTY OF BREADS. Cranberry Coffee Cake and Apple Cinnamon Bismarcks (recipes on pp. 164 and 165).

Oven-Fresh Quick Breads

MERINGUE-topped muffins...super spice breads...savory onion biscuits and more. You can enjoy the old-fashioned goodness of items like these without spending hours in the kitchen.

The recipes we feature here promise fresh-from-the-oven flavor without the work traditional yeast breads require. The results are quick accompaniments to breakfast, lunch or supper!

Honey Corn Bread

Ready in 1 hour or less

This recipe for sweet corn bread is a combination of many trials and errors. I tried to duplicate an extraordinary corn bread I sampled in another town. Adding honey to a combination of recipes finally did the trick. —Kristy Kent Wind Gap, Pennsylvania

1 cup all-purpose flour
3/4 cup cornmeal
1/4 cup sugar
1 teaspoon baking powder
1 teaspoon baking soda
Dash salt
1-1/3 cups half-and-half cream
1 cup frozen corn
1/4 cup butter *or* margarine, melted
1/4 cup honey
1 egg
3 teaspoons vanilla extract

In a bowl, combine the flour, cornmeal, sugar, baking powder, baking soda and salt. In another bowl, combine the remaining ingredients; stir into dry ingredients just until moistened.

Pour into a greased 9-in. ovenproof skillet. Bake at 425° for 30-35 minutes or until a toothpick inserted near the center comes out clean. Cut into wedges; serve warm. **Yield:** 6-8 servings.

Onion Cheese Biscuits

Ready in 30 minutes or less

I received the recipe for these pretty biscuits from a neighbor. She called me 10 years later to ask for the recipe because she had lost her copy. She was so glad she'd shared it with me! —Joann Alexander, Center, Texas

1/2 cup milk
1 egg
1 tablespoon butter *or* margarine, melted
1-1/2 cups biscuit/baking mix

3/4 cup shredded cheddar cheese, *divided*
1/2 cup finely chopped onion
1 tablespoon poppy seeds

In a bowl, combine the milk, egg and butter. Add biscuit mix, 1/2 cup cheese and onion. Spoon into six greased muffin cups. Sprinkle with the poppy seeds and remaining cheese. Bake at 400° for 12-14 minutes or until a toothpick comes out clean. Cool for 5 minutes before removing from pan to a wire rack. **Yield:** 6 biscuits.

Orange Mini Muffins

It doesn't take long to fix these bite-size citrus muffins. Not only are they delicious and moist, but they fill the house with a fabulous aroma. —Amy Karp Spanish Fork, Utah

1-3/4 cups all-purpose flour
2/3 cup packed brown sugar
2-1/2 teaspoons baking powder
1/4 teaspoon salt
1 egg
3/4 cup orange juice
1/2 cup sour cream
1/4 cup vegetable oil
1 tablespoon grated orange peel
1-1/2 teaspoons vanilla extract

In a large bowl, combine the dry ingredients. In another bowl, beat the egg, orange juice, sour cream, oil, orange peel and vanilla. Stir into dry ingredients just until moistened. Fill greased or paper-lined miniature muffin cups two-thirds full. Bake at 350° for 18-20 minutes or until a toothpick comes out clean. Cool for 5 minutes before removing from pans to wire racks. **Yield:** 4 dozen.

Editor's Note: 12 regular-size muffin cups may be used instead; bake for 23-25 minutes.

Pecan Apricot Bread

Pecans, apricots and bananas share the stage in this bread. I use allspice, cinnamon and vanilla to give the loaves comforting flavor. —Kathleen Smith, Hayesville, Ohio

2-1/4 cups all-purpose flour
3/4 cup sugar
3/4 cup quick-cooking oats
1 tablespoon buttermilk blend powder
1 teaspoon baking powder
1 teaspoon salt
1 teaspoon ground allspice
1 teaspoon ground cinnamon
1/2 teaspoon baking soda
3 eggs
1-1/2 cups mashed ripe bananas (about 3 medium)
1/2 cup vegetable oil
3 teaspoons vanilla extract
1 cup chopped dried apricots
1 cup chopped pecans

In a large bowl, combine the dry ingredients. In a mixing bowl, beat the eggs, bananas, oil and vanilla. Stir into dry ingredients just until combined. Stir in apricots and pecans.

Swirled Spice Loaves
Banana Meringue Muffins

Pour into two greased 8-in. x 4-in. x 2-in. loaf pans.

Bake at 350° for 45-50 minutes or until a toothpick inserted near the center comes out clean. Cool for 10 minutes before removing from pans to wire racks. **Yield:** 2 loaves.

Swirled Spice Loaves

(Pictured above)

Pumpkin pie spice and molasses season these two down-home loaves. The tender marbled slices taste as great as they look. The lovely loaves sell well at bake sales, too.
—Nancy Zimmerman
Cape May Court House, New Jersey

        2 cups all-purpose flour
 1-1/3 cups sugar
        2 teaspoons baking powder
     3/4 teaspoon salt
        3 eggs
 1-1/4 cups heavy whipping cream
        2 tablespoons molasses
        3 teaspoons vanilla extract
 1-1/2 teaspoons pumpkin pie spice

In a bowl, combine the flour, sugar, baking powder and salt. Beat the eggs and cream; stir into dry ingredients just until combined. Remove 1-1/2 cups batter to another bowl; stir in the molasses, vanilla and pumpkin pie spice until blended.

Spoon a fourth of the molasses batter into each of two greased 8-in. x 4-in. x 2-in. loaf pans. Top each with a fourth of the plain batter. Repeat layers; cut through batter with a knife to swirl.

Bake at 350° for 45-50 minutes or until a toothpick inserted near the center comes out clean. Cool for 10

minutes before removing from pans to wire racks. **Yield:** 2 loaves.

Banana Meringue Muffins

(Pictured above)

Ready in 45 minutes or less
My daughter was young when I first baked these treats filled with bananas, cherries and walnuts. She liked them so much that she surprised us one Easter morning with a batch she whipped up by herself.
—James Bogdanovitch, Rutland, Vermont

      2 cups biscuit/baking mix
   1/4 cup plus 1/3 cup sugar, *divided*
      2 eggs, *separated*
   2/3 cup milk
      2 tablespoons vegetable oil
     12 slices ripe banana
     12 maraschino cherries, halved
     12 walnut halves
   2/3 cup flaked coconut

In a bowl, combine biscuit mix and 1/4 cup sugar. In another bowl, beat the egg yolks, milk and oil; stir into dry ingredients just until moistened. Spoon 1-1/2 tablespoons of batter into 12 paper-lined muffin cups. Place a banana slice, cherry half and walnut half in each cup. Top with remaining batter.

In a small mixing bowl, beat the egg whites until soft peaks form. Gradually add remaining sugar, beating until stiff peaks form. Fold in the coconut. Spoon over batter. Top with remaining cherry halves. Bake at 400° for 14-18 minutes or until a toothpick comes out clean. Cool for 5 minutes before removing from pan to a wire rack. Store in the refrigerator. **Yield:** 1 dozen.

Butter Dip Breadsticks
Lemon Blueberry Coffee Cake

Butter Dip Breadsticks

(Pictured above)

Ready in 30 minutes or less

This recipe has been in my family for as long as I can remember. It can easily be halved to accommodate smaller families. The buttery breadsticks always appear on our menu for holidays and special occasions.
—*Martha Rhoades, Fayetteville, Arkansas*

  1/3 cup butter *or* margarine, melted
2-1/4 cups all-purpose flour
3-1/2 teaspoons baking powder
    3 teaspoons sugar
1-1/2 teaspoons salt
    1 cup milk

Place butter in an ungreased 15-in. x 10-in. x 1-in. baking pan. In a bowl, combine the flour, baking powder, sugar and salt; mix well. Stir in the milk just until moistened. Turn onto a floured surface; knead 10 times. Roll into a 12-in. x 9-in. rectangle. Cut into 9-in. x 1/2-in. strips.

Dip each side of strips in butter in prepared pan; arrange in the pan (do not allow sides to touch). Bake at 450° for 15-20 minutes or until golden brown. **Yield:** 2 dozen.

Lemon Blueberry Coffee Cake

(Pictured above)

Ready in 1 hour or less

Baking mix eases preparation of this quick coffee cake. Fresh blueberries, lemon peel and a quick glaze really perk up the flavor. It's among the quick treats I make for guests and family. —*Nancy Brown, Dahinda, Illinois*

    1 egg, lightly beaten
  1/3 cup sugar
    1 teaspoon grated lemon peel
  2/3 cup milk
2-1/4 cups biscuit/baking mix
    1 cup fresh *or* frozen blueberries*
  3/4 cup confectioners' sugar
    4 teaspoons lemon juice

In a bowl, combine the egg, sugar, lemon peel and milk; mix well. Stir in the biscuit mix just until moistened. Fold in blueberries. Pour into a greased 9-in. round baking pan.

Bake at 350° for 25-30 minutes or until a toothpick inserted near the center comes out clean. Cool for 10 minutes before removing from pan to a wire rack. Combine the confectioners' sugar and lemon juice until smooth; drizzle over warm cake. Cut into wedges. **Yield:** 6-8 servings.

*Editor's Note: If using frozen blueberries, do not thaw before adding to the batter.

Cinnamon Chip Muffins

Ready in 45 minutes or less

I made quite a few changes to an Amish friendship bread recipe to come up with these sweet muffins. They freeze well, so I usually make a double batch and save some for later.
—Kelly Sellers
Tallahassee, Florida

✓ Uses less fat, sugar or salt. Includes Nutritional Analysis and Diabetic Exchanges.

  2-1/2 cups all-purpose flour
    1 package (3.4 ounces) instant French vanilla
      pudding mix
    2 teaspoons ground cinnamon
  1/2 teaspoon baking powder
  1/2 teaspoon baking soda
  1/2 teaspoon salt
    3 eggs
    1 cup buttermilk
  1/2 cup vegetable oil
  1/2 cup honey
    1 teaspoon vanilla extract
    1 cup miniature semisweet chocolate chips

In a large bowl, combine flour, pudding mix, cinnamon, baking powder, baking soda and salt. In another bowl, combine eggs, buttermilk, oil, honey and vanilla; add to dry ingredients. Whisk for 1-2 minutes or until combined. Fold in chocolate chips.

Fill greased or paper-lined muffin cups two-thirds full. Bake at 350° for 20-25 minutes or until a toothpick comes out clean. Cool for 5 minutes before removing from pans to wire racks. **Yield:** 1-1/2 dozen.

Nutritional Analysis: One muffin equals 218 calories, 10 g fat (3 g saturated fat), 38 mg cholesterol, 142 mg sodium, 29 g carbohydrate, 1 g fiber, 4 g protein. **Diabetic Exchanges:** 2 starch, 1 fat.

Pineapple Carrot Bread

If you like carrot cake, you'll surely enjoy the taste of this lovely loaf. Each moist slice is chock-full of shredded carrot, crushed pineapple and crunchy chopped walnuts.
—Sue Yount, McBain, Michigan

    3 cups all-purpose flour
    1 teaspoon salt
    1 teaspoon baking soda
    1 teaspoon ground cinnamon
    3 eggs
    2 cups sugar
  3/4 cup vegetable oil
    1 cup finely shredded carrot
    1 can (8 ounces) crushed pineapple, undrained
    2 teaspoons vanilla extract
    1 cup chopped walnuts

In a bowl, combine dry ingredients. In a mixing bowl, beat eggs, sugar and oil; add carrot, pineapple and vanilla. Stir into dry ingredients just until moistened. Fold in walnuts. Pour into two greased 8-in. x 4-in. x 2-in. loaf pans.

Bake at 350° for 55-60 minutes or until a toothpick comes out clean. Cool for 10 minutes before removing from pans to wire racks. **Yield:** 2 loaves.

Cinnamon-Sugar Fan Biscuits

Ready in 45 minutes or less

I love to bake. These layered homemade biscuits are so easy when you need a breakfast treat for company.
—Doris Heath, Franklin, North Carolina

    2 cups all-purpose flour
    3 tablespoons sugar
    4 teaspoons baking powder
  1/2 teaspoon salt
  1/2 teaspoon cream of tartar
  1/2 cup shortening
  2/3 cup milk
FILLING:
    3 tablespoons butter *or* margarine, softened
    3 tablespoons sugar
    1 teaspoon ground cinnamon

In a bowl, combine the flour, sugar, baking powder, salt and cream of tartar. Cut in shortening until mixture resembles coarse crumbs. Stir in milk just until moistened. Turn onto a lightly floured surface; knead 8-10 times. Roll or pat into a 12-in. x 10-in. rectangle. Spread with butter. Combine sugar and cinnamon; sprinkle over butter.

Cut into five 2-in. strips; stack strips on top of each other. Cut into six 2-in. pieces; place cut side down in six greased muffin cups. Bake at 425° for 11-14 minutes or until golden brown. Remove from pan to wire racks. Serve warm. **Yield:** 6 biscuits.

Walnut Date Loaf

I discovered this nutty bread when my aunt gave our family a bunch of dates and we didn't know what to do with them. I love it! —Karen-Jean Coxe, Ione, California

    1 cup chopped dates
    1 cup boiling water
    1 tablespoon vegetable oil
    1 cup packed brown sugar
    1 egg
    1 teaspoon vanilla extract
    2 cups all-purpose flour
    1 teaspoon baking soda
  1/4 teaspoon salt
    1 cup chopped walnuts

In a bowl, combine the dates, water and oil; let stand for 10 minutes (do not drain). Add the brown sugar, egg and vanilla; mix well. Combine the flour, baking soda and salt; stir into date mixture just until combined. Fold in walnuts.

Transfer to a greased 8-in. x 4-in. x 2-in. loaf pan. Bake at 350° for 60-65 minutes or until golden brown and a toothpick comes out clean. Cool for 10 minutes before removing from pan to a wire rack. **Yield:** 1 loaf.

Coconut Biscuits

Ready in 30 minutes or less

These sweet biscuits are wonderful with coffee in the morning...or alongside chicken for dinner. Sometimes I even top them with fresh pineapple or mango chunks and whipped cream for a delicious dessert. It's my grandmother's recipe. —Howie Wiener, Spring Hill, Florida

    2 cups all-purpose flour
    2 tablespoons sugar
2-1/2 teaspoons baking powder
    1/2 teaspoon salt
    1/3 cup shortening
    1 cup milk
    1/2 teaspoon vanilla extract
    3/4 cup flaked coconut, toasted

In a large bowl, combine the flour, sugar, baking powder and salt; cut in shortening until crumbly. Combine milk and vanilla; stir into dry ingredients just until moistened. Fold in coconut. Drop by 2 tablespoonfuls 2 in. apart onto greased baking sheets. Bake at 425° for 8-10 minutes or until golden brown. Serve warm. **Yield:** about 1-1/2 dozen.

Swedish Sugar Toast

Ready in 30 minutes or less

The recipe for this tasty spiced toast comes from a dear friend, and I've shared it with many people.
—Helen Applequist, St. Louis Park, Minnesota

    1/2 cup sugar
    1 teaspoon ground cinnamon
    1/2 teaspoon ground cardamom
    1/4 teaspoon ground cloves
Butter *or* margarine, softened
    1 loaf white bread, thinly sliced (about 18 slices)

In a small bowl, combine sugar, cinnamon, cardamom and cloves. Spread butter on one side of each slice of bread; sprinkle sugar mixture on buttered side. Cut in half diagonally. Place on ungreased baking sheets. Bake at 350° for 10 minutes. **Yield:** about 3 dozen.

Mexicorn Muffins

Ready in 45 minutes or less

I use bacon, jalapeno pepper and a few other favorite items to put a different twist on a corn muffin mix. The moist bites complement a breakfast of scrambled eggs. They freeze well, too, but with my household of three guys, I can't keep them in the freezer for very long. —Judy Foley Ridgeway, Virginia

 Uses less fat, sugar or salt. Includes Nutritional Analysis and Diabetic Exchanges.

    1 package (8-1/2 ounces) corn bread/muffin
      mix
    1 egg
    1/3 cup milk
    3/4 cup salsa

    1 can (8-3/4 ounces) whole kernel corn, drained
    1/2 cup shredded Mexican cheese blend *or*
      cheddar cheese
    1/2 cup sour cream
    3 bacon strips, cooked and crumbled
    2 tablespoons chopped seeded jalapeno pepper*

In a bowl, combine corn bread mix, egg and milk just until blended. Stir in salsa, corn, cheese, sour cream, bacon and jalapeno. Fill greased or paper-lined muffin cups three-fourths full. Bake at 400° for 15-20 minutes or until a toothpick comes out clean. Cool for 5 minutes before removing from pan to a wire rack. Serve warm. **Yield:** 1 dozen.
    Nutritional Analysis: One muffin (prepared with fat-free milk, reduced-fat cheese and reduced-fat sour cream) equals 146 calories, 5 g fat (2 g saturated fat), 29 mg cholesterol, 355 mg sodium, 21 g carbohydrate, 1 g fiber, 5 g protein. **Diabetic Exchanges:** 1-1/2 starch, 1/2 fat.
    ***Editor's Note:** When cutting or seeding hot peppers, use rubber or plastic gloves to protect your hands. Avoid touching your face.

Pecan Zucchini Bread

 Sour cream makes this the best zucchini bread I've ever come across. I add plenty of chopped pecans for a fun crunch that enhances the loaf's zucchini flavor. It's a pleasure to share a loaf of this yummy bread. —Audrey Lavoie, Centerville, Ohio

    3 cups all-purpose flour
    2 cups sugar
    1 teaspoon baking soda
    1 teaspoon salt
    1 teaspoon ground cinnamon
    1/4 teaspoon baking powder
    3 eggs
    1/2 cup vegetable oil
    1/2 cup sour cream
    1 teaspoon vanilla extract
    2 cups shredded zucchini
    1 cup chopped pecans

In a large bowl, combine the first six ingredients. In another bowl, beat the eggs, oil, sour cream and vanilla. Stir into dry ingredients just until moistened. Fold in zucchini and nuts.
    Transfer to two greased 9-in. x 5-in. x 3-in. loaf pans. Bake at 350° for 60-65 minutes or until a toothpick inserted near the center comes out clean. Cool for 15 minutes before removing from pans to wire racks to cool completely. **Yield:** 2 loaves.

Dilled Biscuit Ring

(Pictured above right)

Ready in 1 hour or less

I rely on convenient refrigerated buttermilk biscuits to streamline the preparation of this savory pull-apart loaf. Fabulously flavored with dill, Parmesan cheese

Dilled Biscuit Ring
Cheddar Bacon Toasts

and garlic powder, this golden biscuit ring makes an ideal addition to most meals. It's also an easy and scrumptious potluck offering. —Lisa Bender
Windber, Pennsylvania

- 2 tubes (12 ounces *each*) refrigerated buttermilk biscuits
- 1/4 cup butter *or* margarine, melted
- 1/4 cup grated Parmesan cheese
- 1 teaspoon dill weed
- 1/4 teaspoon garlic powder

Separate each tube of biscuits into 10 biscuits. Cut each biscuit in half; set aside. In a small bowl, combine the remaining ingredients; drizzle half into a greased 10-in. fluted tube pan. Place half of the biscuits in pan; drizzle with the remaining butter mixture. Top with remaining biscuits.

Bake at 350° for 30-35 minutes or until golden brown. Cool for 5 minutes before removing from pan. Serve warm. **Yield:** 10-12 servings.

Cheddar Bacon Toasts

(Pictured above)

Ready in 30 minutes or less

Four ingredients are all you need to bake up these scrumptious appetizers. Everyone enjoys the creamy combination of cheese and bacon on crisp toast. They go great with a bowl of soup or can be served as an after-school snack.
—Mary Martin, Columbus, Kansas

- 2 cups (8 ounces) finely shredded cheddar cheese
- 3/4 cup mayonnaise
- 1/3 cup crumbled cooked bacon
- 1 loaf French bread (1 pound)

In a bowl, combine the cheese, mayonnaise and bacon. Cut the bread into 24 slices, about 1/2 in. each. Spread the cheese mixture on one side of each slice. Place on a baking sheet. Bake at 425° for 8-10 minutes or until golden brown. **Yield:** 2 dozen.

Parmesan Herb Loaves
Confetti Corn Muffins

Confetti Corn Muffins

(Pictured above)

Ready in 45 minutes or less

Green pepper and shredded carrot add color to these home-made corn muffins. They are a nice change from sweeter muffins and very good to serve with soup and salad.
—Dolores Hurtt, Florence, Montana

 Uses less fat, sugar or salt. Includes Nutritional Analysis and Diabetic Exchanges.

1-1/4 cups all-purpose flour
  3/4 cup cornmeal
    2 tablespoons sugar
    3 teaspoons baking powder
    1 teaspoon salt
    1 egg
    1 cup milk
  1/4 cup butter *or* stick margarine, melted
    1 medium carrot, shredded
  1/3 cup chopped green pepper

In a large bowl, combine flour, cornmeal, sugar, baking powder and salt. In another bowl, combine egg, milk and butter; stir into dry ingredients just until moistened. Fold in carrot and green pepper.

Fill greased or paper-lined muffin cups two-thirds full. Bake at 425° for 14-18 minutes or until a toothpick comes out clean. Cool for 5 minutes before removing from pan to a wire rack. Serve warm. **Yield:** 1 dozen.

Nutritional Analysis: One muffin (prepared with fat-free milk) equals 139 calories, 5 g fat (3 g saturated fat), 28 mg cholesterol, 312 mg sodium, 21 g carbohydrate, 1 g fiber, 4 g protein. **Diabetic Exchange:** 1-1/2 starch.

Parmesan Herb Loaves

(Pictured above)

I dress up frozen bread dough with herbs and Parmesan cheese to create two savory home-baked loaves. Let them rise while you prepare the rest of the meal.
—Shirley Sibit Rudder, Burkeville, Texas

    2 loaves (1 pound *each*) frozen bread dough
  1/2 cup shredded Parmesan cheese
    1 tablespoon dried parsley flakes
    1 tablespoon dried minced garlic
  1/2 teaspoon dill weed
  1/2 teaspoon salt
    2 tablespoons butter *or* margarine, melted

Place dough in two greased 8-in. x 4-in. x 2-in. loaf pans. Thaw according to package directions. In a small bowl, combine the Parmesan cheese, parsley, garlic, dill and salt. Brush dough with butter; sprinkle with cheese mixture. Cover and let rise in a warm place until nearly doubled, about 2-1/2 hours. Bake at 350° for 20-25 minutes or until golden brown. **Yield:** 2 loaves.

Strawberry Coffee Cake

Ready in 1 hour or less

With two busy children, I like to have recipes that get me out of the kitchen fast. Our neighboring town hosts a strawberry festival every June, so strawberry recipes are popular in our area. This one is simple and delicious. Serve it warm. —Rose Palsgrove, Piqua, Ohio

   1 cup all-purpose flour
1/2 cup sugar
   2 teaspoons baking powder
1/2 teaspoon salt
   1 egg
1/2 cup milk
   2 tablespoons butter *or* margarine, melted
1-1/2 cups sliced fresh strawberries
TOPPING:
1/2 cup all-purpose flour
1/2 cup sugar
1/4 cup cold butter *or* margarine
1/4 cup chopped pecans, optional

In a large bowl, combine the dry ingredients. In another bowl, combine the egg, milk and butter; stir into dry ingredients just until moistened. Pour into a greased 8-in. square baking dish. Top with strawberries.

For topping, combine flour and sugar in a bowl; cut in butter until crumbly. Stir in pecans if desired; sprinkle over strawberries. Bake at 375° for 30-35 minutes or until a toothpick inserted near the center comes out clean. Cut into squares; serve warm. **Yield:** 9 servings.

Kiwifruit Muffins

Ready in 1 hour or less

I received this recipe while living in New Zealand with a friend. His wife prepared a batch of these moist muffins for him. I "sampled" so many that the next time, she doubled the recipe so there were plenty for both of us. —Tim Fink
Steamboat Springs, Colorado

   1 cup all-purpose flour
1/2 cup sugar
1/2 teaspoon baking soda
1/2 teaspoon ground cinnamon
1/4 teaspoon ground allspice
Dash salt
   1 egg
1/2 cup milk
   2 tablespoons butter *or* margarine, melted
   2 kiwifruit, peeled and chopped
1/2 cup raisins

In a bowl, combine the dry ingredients. In another bowl, beat the egg, milk and butter. Stir into dry ingredients just until moistened. Fold in kiwi and raisins. Fill paper-lined muffin cups three-fourths full. Bake at 425° for 15-18 minutes or until a toothpick comes out clean. Cool for 5 minutes before removing from pan to a wire rack. **Yield:** 10 muffins.

Orange Yogurt Scones

This recipe from my mother produces a wonderful light scone. Use any flavor fruit yogurt if you don't have orange. —Hollye Chapman, Corvallis, Oregon

   2 cups all-purpose flour
1/3 cup plus 2 teaspoons sugar, *divided*
2-1/2 teaspoons baking powder
1/4 teaspoon baking soda
1/4 teaspoon salt
   3 tablespoons cold butter *or* margarine
   1 carton (6 ounces) orange yogurt
1/4 cup orange juice
   2 teaspoons grated orange peel

In a bowl, combine the flour, 1/3 cup sugar, baking powder, baking soda and salt; cut in butter until crumbly. In another bowl, whisk the yogurt, orange juice and peel; stir into dry ingredients just until moistened. Turn onto a floured surface; knead 10 times.

Transfer dough to a greased baking sheet. Pat into an 8-in. circle. Cut into eight wedges, but do not separate. Sprinkle with remaining sugar. Bake at 400° for 15-20 minutes or until golden brown. Serve warm. **Yield:** 8 servings.

Nutty Peach Quick Bread

A crunchy topping of brown sugar and oats covers these mini loaves that have little chunks of peaches throughout. You can substitute three peeled and diced pears or 1-1/2 cups fresh blueberries, raspberries or blackberries for the peaches. —Ron Gardner, Grand Haven, Michigan

1/2 cup butter *or* margarine, softened
1/2 cup sugar
1/3 cup packed brown sugar
   2 eggs
   2 tablespoons honey
   1 teaspoon vanilla extract
1-3/4 cups all-purpose flour
   1 teaspoon baking powder
   1 teaspoon ground cinnamon
1/2 teaspoon baking soda
1/8 teaspoon salt
1/2 cup milk
1-1/2 cups diced peeled ripe peaches (3 medium)
1/2 cup chopped pecans
TOPPING:
1/3 cup quick-cooking oats
1/3 cup packed brown sugar

In a large mixing bowl, cream the butter and sugars. Add eggs, one at a time, beating well after each addition. Beat in honey and vanilla. Combine the flour, baking powder, cinnamon, baking soda and salt; add to creamed mixture alternately with milk. Fold in peaches and pecans.

Spoon into three greased 5-3/4-in. x 3-in. x 2-in. loaf pans. Combine the oats and brown sugar; sprinkle over batter and gently press in. Bake at 350° for 45-50 minutes or until a toothpick comes out clean. Cool for 20 minutes before removing from pans to wire racks to cool completely. **Yield:** 3 mini loaves.

Honey Chip Muffins

Ready in 30 minutes or less

I dress up a packaged chocolate chip muffin mix with a few pantry staples. I love peanut butter, so I added it to a muffin mix with a little honey. My family loves the results.
—Mary Young, Stroudsburg, Pennsylvania

> 1 package (17.8 ounces) chocolate chip muffin mix
> 1 tablespoon baking cocoa
> 2 tablespoons honey
> 1 tablespoon peanut butter
> 1 egg
> 3/4 cup water
> 1/4 cup semisweet chocolate chips

In a large bowl, combine the muffin mix and cocoa. In a small bowl, combine honey and peanut butter; add the egg and water. Stir into dry ingredients with a spoon just until moistened, about 50 strokes (batter will be slightly lumpy). Stir in chocolate chips.

Fill foil- or paper-lined muffin cups two-thirds full. Bake at 400° for 17-20 minutes or until a toothpick comes out clean. Cool for 5 minutes before removing from the pan to a wire rack. **Yield:** 1 dozen.

Cheddar-Salsa Biscuit Strips

Ready in 30 minutes or less

A few ingredients are all you'll need for these tender breadsticks that get their kick from salsa. I brought them to a wedding shower and got rave reviews. They're an excellent finger food for parties and equally good alongside soup or chili. —Peggy Key, Grant, Alabama

> 1-2/3 cups self-rising flour*
> 1 cup (4 ounces) shredded cheddar cheese
> 1/2 cup salsa
> 1/4 cup butter *or* margarine, melted
> 1/4 cup water
> Additional melted butter, optional

In a bowl, combine the flour and cheese. Stir in the salsa, butter and water just until combined. Knead 6-8 times or until smooth. On a floured surface, roll out dough into a 12-in. x 6-in. rectangle. Cut into 2-in. x 1-in. strips. Place on a greased baking sheet. Bake at 425° for 6-8 minutes or until golden brown. Brush with butter if desired. **Yield:** about 3 dozen.

*Editor's Note: As a substitute for 1 cup of self-rising flour, place 1-1/2 teaspoons baking powder and 1/2 teaspoon salt in a measuring cup. Add all-purpose flour to measure 1 cup. As a substitute for 2/3 cup of self-rising flour, place 1 teaspoon baking powder and 1/4 teaspoon salt in a measuring cup. Add all-purpose flour to measure 2/3 cup.

Cherry Pistachio Bread

The red maraschino cherries and green pistachio pudding mix echo the colors of Christmas. But their pleasant taste makes them appropriate any time of year.
—Rose Harman, Hays, Kansas

> 1 package (18-1/4 ounces) yellow cake mix
> 1 package (3.4 ounces) instant pistachio pudding mix
> 4 eggs
> 1 cup (8 ounces) sour cream
> 1/4 cup vegetable oil
> 2 tablespoons water
> 4 drops green food coloring, optional
> 3/4 cup halved maraschino cherries
> 1/2 cup chopped pecans
> 1/4 cup sugar
> 1 teaspoon ground cinnamon

In a mixing bowl, combine cake and pudding mixes. Combine the eggs, sour cream, oil, water and food coloring if desired; add to dry ingredients. Beat until blended (batter will be thick). Fold in cherries and pecans.

Combine sugar and cinnamon; sprinkle 1 tablespoon over the bottom and up the sides of two greased 8-in. x 4-in. x 2-in. loaf pans. Add batter; sprinkle with remaining cinnamon-sugar. Bake at 350° for 40-50 minutes or until a toothpick inserted near the center comes out clean. Cool for 10 minutes before removing from pans to wire racks. **Yield:** 2 loaves.

Pepperoni Pizza Muffins

Ready in 45 minutes or less

Loaded with pizza flavor, these moist muffins are served at home regularly. They're great for lunch but also make good appetizers when baked in mini muffin cups. Try adding chopped mushrooms or green pepper to the batter.
—Andrea McGee, Port Alsworth, Alaska

> 3 cups biscuit/baking mix
> 1 can (10-3/4 ounces) condensed tomato soup, undiluted
> 3/4 cup water
> 1/2 cup shredded mozzarella cheese
> 1/2 cup shredded cheddar cheese
> 1/2 cup diced pepperoni
> 2 tablespoons chopped ripe olives
> 1 tablespoon dried minced onion
> 1 teaspoon Italian seasoning

Place the biscuit mix in a large bowl. Combine the remaining ingredients; stir into biscuit mix just until moistened. Fill greased muffin cups three-fourths full. Bake at 350° for 17-20 minutes or until a toothpick comes out clean. Cool for 5 minutes before removing from the pans to wire racks. Serve warm. **Yield:** 14 muffins.

Apple Cinnamon Bismarcks

(Pictured above right and on page 154)

Ready in 30 minutes or less

I use convenience items to speed the preparation of these down-home treats. I pipe a bit of apple pie filling into baked biscuits topped with a comforting combination of sugar and cinnamon. —Leigh Ann Baird, Knoxville, Tennessee

> 1 tube (16.3 ounces) large refrigerated flaky biscuits

Cranberry Coffee Cake
Apple Cinnamon Bismarcks

1/2 cup sugar
1/2 teaspoon ground cinnamon
1/4 cup butter *or* margarine, melted
1 cup apple pie filling

Bake biscuits according to package directions. In a shallow bowl, combine the sugar and cinnamon. Brush warm biscuits with butter, then roll in cinnamon-sugar.

In a small mixing bowl, beat the pie filling until smooth. Cut a small hole in the corner of a pastry or plastic bag; insert a large round tip. Fill bag with the pie filling. Push the tip through the top of each biscuit to fill. **Yield:** 8 servings.

Cranberry Coffee Cake

(Pictured above and on page 155)

Ready in 45 minutes or less

This recipe was given to me by a former neighbor. The yummy cake relies on baking mix, canned cranberry sauce and an easy nut topping, so it's truly a quick bread.
—Doris Brearley, Vestal, New York

2 cups biscuit/baking mix
2 tablespoons sugar
2/3 cup milk
1 egg, beaten
2/3 cup jellied cranberry sauce
TOPPING:
1/2 cup chopped walnuts
1/2 cup packed brown sugar
1/2 teaspoon ground cinnamon
GLAZE:
1 cup confectioners' sugar
2 tablespoons milk
1/4 teaspoon vanilla extract

In a large bowl, combine the biscuit mix, sugar, milk and egg. Pour into a greased 8-in. square baking dish. Drop cranberry sauce by teaspoonfuls over batter. Combine topping ingredients; sprinkle over cranberry sauce. Bake at 400° for 18-23 minutes or until a toothpick inserted near the center comes out clean. Cool on a wire rack.

In a small bowl, combine the glaze ingredients; drizzle over coffee cake. **Yield:** 9 servings.

Christmas Banana Bread
Frosted Pumpkin Muffins

Frosted Pumpkin Muffins

(Pictured above)

I jazz up pound cake mix with some canned pumpkin and pumpkin pie spice to create these sweet muffins. They're so good, even picky eaters cannot seem to get enough. They're also delicious without frosting or nuts. —Samantha Callahan Muncie, Indiana

  1 package (16 ounces) pound cake mix
  2 eggs
  1 cup canned pumpkin
1/3 cup water
  2 teaspoons pumpkin pie spice
  1 teaspoon baking soda
  1 can (16 ounces) cream cheese frosting
1/2 cup finely chopped pecans, optional

In a mixing bowl, combine the cake mix, eggs, pumpkin, water, pumpkin pie spice and baking soda. Beat on medium speed for 3 minutes. Fill greased or paper-lined muffin cups two-thirds full. Bake at 350° for 18-22 minutes or until a toothpick comes out clean. Cool for 5 minutes before removing from pans to wire racks.

Frost cooled muffins. Sprinkle with pecans if desired. Store in the refrigerator. **Yield:** 1-1/2 dozen.

Christmas Banana Bread

(Pictured above)

This bread is a pretty addition to the table during the holidays. Cherries, walnuts and chocolate chips give fast festive flair to the loaf of moist banana bread.
—Phyllis Schmalz, Kansas City, Kansas

  1/2 cup butter *or* margarine, softened
    1 cup sugar
    2 eggs
    2 cups all-purpose flour
    1 teaspoon baking soda
  1/4 teaspoon salt
1-1/4 cups mashed ripe bananas (about 3 medium)
  1/2 cup chopped walnuts
  1/2 cup semisweet chocolate chips
  1/4 cup chopped maraschino cherries

In a large mixing bowl, cream butter and sugar. Add eggs, one at a time, beating well after each addition. Combine the flour, baking soda and salt; gradually add to creamed mixture. Beat in the bananas just until combined. Stir in the walnuts, chocolate chips and cherries.

Pour into a greased 9-in. x 5-in. x 3-in. loaf pan. Bake at 350° for 70-80 minutes or until a toothpick inserted near the center comes out clean. Cool for 10 minutes before removing from pan to a wire rack. **Yield:** 1 loaf.

Herb Sausage Biscuits

Ready in 30 minutes or less

Flavored with sausage and cheese, these savory drop biscuits make a nice accompaniment to almost any meal. The leftovers are great for breakfast—warm in the microwave in the morning when everyone is on the run.
—*Marion Lowery, Medford, Oregon*

1/4 pound bulk Italian sausage
2 cups biscuit/baking mix
1/4 cup shredded cheddar cheese
2 teaspoons minced fresh oregano
  or 3/4 teaspoon dried oregano
2 teaspoons dried minced onion
1/2 teaspoon minced fresh cilantro *or* parsley
1 egg, beaten
2/3 cup milk

In a small skillet, cook sausage over medium heat until no longer pink; drain. In a bowl, combine the biscuit mix, cheese, oregano, onion and cilantro. Combine the egg and milk; stir into dry ingredients just until moistened. Stir in the sausage.

Drop by heaping tablespoonfuls onto greased baking sheets. Bake at 425° for 8-10 minutes or until lightly browned. Serve warm. Refrigerate any leftovers. **Yield:** 14 biscuits.

Currant Drop Scones

Ready in 30 minutes or less

The scones have become a favorite in our home because they're so quick and easy to prepare. I like to serve them warm. —*Lois Smyth, Pincher Creek, Alberta*

4 cups all-purpose flour
1 cup sugar
3 teaspoons baking powder
1 teaspoon salt
1/2 teaspoon baking soda
1 cup shortening
1 cup dried currants *or* raisins
1-1/2 cups buttermilk
Additional sugar

In a large bowl, combine the flour, sugar, baking powder, salt and baking soda. Cut in shortening until mixture resembles coarse crumbs. Fold in currants. Stir in buttermilk just until moistened.

Drop by tablespoonfuls 1 in. apart onto greased baking sheets; sprinkle with additional sugar. Bake at 400° for 12-15 minutes or until the edges are golden brown. Serve warm. **Yield:** about 2-1/2 dozen.

Peanut Butter Oat Bread

When our children were growing up, I made this bread quite often. They loved it. —*Nola Laughery, Connellsville, Pennsylvania*

1-1/2 cups all-purpose flour
1 cup quick-cooking oats
1 cup sugar
1 tablespoon baking powder
1/2 teaspoon salt
3/4 cup chunky peanut butter
1 egg
1 cup milk
1 teaspoon vanilla extract

In a bowl, combine the flour, oats, sugar, baking powder and salt. Cut in the peanut butter until crumbly. Combine the egg, milk and vanilla; stir into dry ingredients just until moistened.

Transfer to a greased 9-in. x 5-in. x 3-in. loaf pan. Bake at 350° for 55-60 minutes or until a toothpick inserted near the center comes out clean. Cool for 10 minutes before removing from pan to a wire rack. **Yield:** 1 loaf.

Fig Coffee Cake

My mother-in-law shared this interesting coffee cake recipe with me. I have reinvented it by using different flavors of Fig Newtons. My favorite version is made with apple-cinnamon, but be sure to try the raspberry, too. It's a terrific treat to serve for brunch. —*Barbara Angel Retherford Laughlin, Nevada*

1/3 cup butter *or* margarine, softened
1/2 cup sugar
1 egg
1 teaspoon vanilla extract
1-1/4 cups all-purpose flour
1-1/2 teaspoons baking powder
1/2 teaspoon salt
1/2 cup milk
FILLING:
2/3 cup packed brown sugar
1 teaspoon ground cinnamon
2 tablespoons cold butter *or* margarine
15 Fig Newton cookies, crumbled

In a mixing bowl, cream butter and sugar. Beat in egg and vanilla. Combine the flour, baking powder and salt; add to creamed mixture alternately with milk. In another bowl, combine brown sugar and cinnamon; cut in butter until crumbly. Fold in crumbled cookies.

Spread a third of the batter into a greased 8-in. square baking dish. Top with half of the filling. Repeat layers. Top with remaining batter. Bake at 350° for 35-40 minutes or until golden brown. Cool completely on a wire rack before cutting. **Yield:** 9 servings.

Currant Clues

- Dried currants are actually small dark seedless Zante grapes that grow in clusters on vines. After they've been dried, they are usually used in baked goods. They can be found in most supermarkets near the raisins.
- Fresh red, black or golden currants, on the other hand, grow in clusters on shrubs. They are often used to make preserves and syrups and can sometimes be found at farmers markets.

Bread at The Touch Of a Button

BREAD MACHINES make it more convenient to bake bread at home than pick it up at the supermarket. It takes only minutes to put your ingredients in the pan, flick a few switches and make a simple check. Soon, the wonderful aroma of just-baked bread will fill your kitchen!

Crusty Mini Loaves

(Pictured below)

These little loaves are so easy to make yet taste so good.
—Caroline Knox Fnnington, Ontario

✓ Uses less fat, sugar or salt. Includes Nutritional Analysis and Diabetic Exchanges.

　 1 cup plus 1 tablespoon water (70° to 80°)
　 3 teaspoons sugar
1-1/2 teaspoons salt
2-1/2 cups bread flour
　 1/2 cup 7-grain cereal*
1-1/2 teaspoons active dry yeast

Crusty Mini Loaves

　 1 egg yolk
　 1 teaspoon cold water
Sesame *or* poppy seeds, optional

In bread machine pan, place the first six ingredients in order suggested by manufacturer. Select dough setting (check dough after 5 minutes of mixing; add 1 to 2 tablespoons of water or flour if needed).

When the cycle is completed, turn dough onto a lightly floured surface. Divide into four portions; shape into 6-in. loaves. Place on a greased baking sheet. Cut slits in the top of each loaf. Cover and let rise in a warm place until doubled, about 30 minutes.

In a small bowl, beat the egg yolk and water; brush over dough. Sprinkle with sesame or poppy seeds if desired. Bake at 375° for 18-20 minutes or until golden brown. **Yield:** 4 loaves.

Nutritional Analysis: One serving (half of a loaf) equals 182 calories, 1 g fat (trace saturated fat), 27 mg cholesterol, 449 mg sodium, 35 g carbohydrate, 1 g fiber, 6 g protein. **Diabetic Exchange:** 2-1/2 starch.

*Editor's Note: This recipe was tested with Bob's Red Mill 7-grain cereal.

Country Cornmeal Bread

We grow over 1,000 acres of corn on our farm, so guests expect to enjoy some when they visit. This country bread is a favorite when served warm.
—Arlene Riensche
Jesup, Iowa

2-3/4 cups bread flour
　 1/2 cup cornmeal
　 1 cup plus 2 tablespoons warm buttermilk (70° to 80°)
　 2 tablespoons butter *or* margarine, softened
　 2 tablespoons sugar
　 1 teaspoon salt
2-1/4 teaspoons active dry yeast

In a bowl, combine the flour and cornmeal until well blended. In bread machine pan, place all ingredients in order suggested by manufacturer. Select basic bread setting. Choose crust color and loaf size if available. Bake according to bread machine directions (check dough after 5 minutes of mixing; add 1 to 2 tablespoons of water or flour if needed). Serve warm. **Yield:** 1 loaf (1-1/2 pounds).

Editor's Note: Warmed buttermilk will appear curdled. If your bread machine has a time-delay feature, we recommend you do not use it for this recipe.

Peanut Butter Bread

This moist peanut butter bread is terrific toasted and served with jelly or used in sandwiches. Make a grilled cheese, but substitute peanut butter for the cheese and add sliced banana. The gooey treat goes well with a glass of cold milk.
—Barbara Hileman, Cortland, Ohio

1 cup plus 1 tablespoon water (70° to 80°)
1/2 cup peanut butter*
　 3 tablespoons brown sugar
　 1 teaspoon salt

3 cups bread flour
2-1/4 teaspoons active dry yeast

In bread machine pan, place all ingredients in order suggested by manufacturer. Select basic bread setting. Choose crust color and loaf size if available. Bake according to bread machine directions (check dough after 5 minutes of mixing; add 1 to 2 tablespoons of water or flour if needed). **Yield:** 1 loaf (1-1/2 pounds).

*Editor's Note: Reduced-fat or generic brands of peanut butter are not recommended for this recipe.

Buttermilk Wheat Rolls

Tropical Sweet Bread

This Hawaiian-style bread is an elegant addition to any meal. It features pineapple, banana, coconut and macadamia nuts. It makes a delightful hostess gift, too.
—*Camie Schuiteman, Marion, Indiana*

1/4 cup warm buttermilk (70° to 80°)
1/4 cup pineapple juice
3 tablespoons butter *or* margarine, softened
1 egg
1/2 cup pineapple tidbits
1/2 cup sliced ripe banana
3 cups bread flour
1/4 cup whole wheat flour
1/2 cup flaked coconut
4-1/2 teaspoons sugar
1 teaspoon salt
1/4 teaspoon baking soda
1-1/2 teaspoons active dry yeast
1/3 cup chopped macadamia nuts

In bread machine pan, place the first 13 ingredients in order suggested by manufacturer. Select basic bread setting. Choose crust color and loaf size if available. Bake according to bread machine directions (check dough after 5 minutes of mixing; add 1 to 2 tablespoons water or flour if needed).

Just before the final kneading (your machine may audibly signal this), add the macadamia nuts. **Yield:** 1 loaf (2 pounds).

Editor's Note: Warmed buttermilk will appear curdled. If your bread machine has a time-delay feature, we recommend you do not use it for this recipe.

Buttermilk Wheat Rolls

(Pictured above right)

This recipe produces light, tender rolls, considering the amount of whole wheat flour it calls for. I bake them for company and parties. —*Beth Zaring, Wellston, Ohio*

✓ Uses less fat, sugar or salt. Includes Nutritional Analysis and Diabetic Exchanges.

1-1/2 cups warm buttermilk (70° to 80°)
1/4 cup vegetable *or* canola oil
1 teaspoon lemon juice
2 tablespoons sugar
1-1/2 teaspoons salt
1/4 teaspoon baking soda

1/2 cup toasted wheat germ
2 cups whole wheat flour
1-1/4 cups bread flour
2 teaspoons active dry yeast
2 tablespoons butter *or* margarine, melted, optional

In bread machine pan, place the first 10 ingredients in order suggested by manufacturer. Select dough setting (check dough after 5 minutes of mixing; add 1 to 2 tablespoons of water or flour if needed).

When cycle is completed, turn dough onto a lightly floured surface and punch down. Divide into 24 pieces; shape each into a ball. Place on two greased baking sheets. Cover and let rise in a warm place until doubled, about 30 minutes. Brush with butter if desired. Bake at 350° for 12-14 minutes or until golden brown. Remove from pans to wire racks to cool. **Yield:** 2 dozen.

Nutritional Analysis: One roll (prepared with 1% buttermilk and without butter) equals 96 calories, 3 g fat (trace saturated fat), 1 mg cholesterol, 177 mg sodium, 15 g carbohydrate, 2 g fiber, 4 g protein. **Diabetic Exchange:** 1 starch.

Editor's Note: Warmed buttermilk will appear curdled. If your bread machine has a time-delay feature, we recommend you do not use it for this recipe.

For the Best Bread...

- Bread machines vary depending on the manufacturer. Before making new recipes, try those provided in your manual—they were developed specifically for your machine.
- When trying any new recipe, be sure to stay within the limits of the maximum flour amounts listed in the recipes in your machine's manual.
- Add the ingredients only in the order recommended by the manufacturer (which isn't always how they may appear in a recipe here).
- Your bread machine does the mixing and kneading, so you must learn to judge the bread with your eyes and ears to decide if a recipe needs adjusting.

  If your bread machine sounds labored as it kneads the dough, it might be too dry. Add 1 to 2 tablespoons of water. If the dough is flat and wet-looking, add 1 to 2 tablespoons of flour.

Dilly Onion Bread

(Pictured above)

I adapted a recipe for herb bread to come up with this flavorful version that's become one of our favorites. My bread machine makes a smaller size loaf, which is perfect for my husband and me. —LeAne Swanson Chab
Palmdale, California

3/4 cup water (70° to 80°)
1 tablespoon butter *or* margarine, softened
2 tablespoons sugar
3 tablespoons dried minced onion
2 tablespoons dried parsley flakes
1 tablespoon dill weed
1 teaspoon salt
1 garlic clove, minced
2 cups bread flour
1/3 cup whole wheat flour
1 tablespoon nonfat dry milk powder
2 teaspoons active dry yeast

In bread machine pan, place all ingredients in order suggested by manufacturer. Select basic bread setting. Choose crust color and loaf size if available. Bake according to bread machine directions (check dough after 5 minutes of mixing; add 1 to 2 tablespoons of water or flour if needed). **Yield:** 1 loaf (about 1-1/2 pounds).

Herbed Sandwich Buns

I use the dough setting on my bread machine to make these nicely seasoned buns. We like to use them for burgers and sandwiches. —Patty Thompson, Jefferson, Iowa

1/4 cup water (70° to 80°)
1/4 cup warm milk (70° to 80°)
1 egg

2/3 cup small-curd cottage cheese
1/4 cup grated Parmesan cheese
3 tablespoons sugar
1-1/2 teaspoons salt
3 cups bread flour
2-1/4 teaspoons active dry yeast
1 teaspoon Italian seasoning
1/2 teaspoon dried minced garlic
1/4 teaspoon dried basil
1/4 cup chopped onion
4-1/2 teaspoons butter *or* margarine

In bread machine pan, place the first 12 ingredients in order suggested by manufacturer. In a small skillet, saute onion in butter until tender; add to bread machine pan. Select dough setting (check dough after 5 minutes of mixing; add 1 to 2 tablespoons of water or flour if needed).

When cycle is completed, turn dough onto a lightly floured surface. Divide into 10 pieces; shape each into a ball. Place 2 in. apart on a greased baking sheet. Cover and let rise until doubled, about 30 minutes. Bake at 375° for 10-12 minutes or until golden brown. **Yield:** 10 buns.

Editor's Note: If your bread machine has a time-delay feature, we recommend you do not use it for this recipe.

Buttermilk Bread

This bread reminds me of sourdough without the trouble of having to prepare and replenish the starter. Buttermilk gives a light tartness to the chewy loaf. It's a great all-purpose bread. —Nita Anderson, Florence, Alabama

✓ Uses less fat, sugar or salt. Includes Nutritional Analysis and Diabetic Exchanges.

1/2 cup plus 2 tablespoons water (70° to 80°)
1/2 cup warm buttermilk (70° to 80°)
1 teaspoon lemon juice
2 tablespoons butter *or* stick margarine, softened
2 tablespoons brown sugar
1 teaspoon salt
3 cups bread flour
2-1/4 teaspoons active dry yeast

In bread machine pan, place all ingredients in order suggested by manufacturer. Select basic bread setting. Choose crust color and loaf size if available. Bake according to bread machine directions (check dough after 5 minutes of mixing; add 1 to 2 tablespoons of water or flour if needed). **Yield:** 1 loaf (1-1/2 pounds, 16 slices).

Nutritional Analysis: One slice equals 99 calories, 1 g fat (1 g saturated fat), 4 mg cholesterol, 166 mg sodium, 19 g carbohydrate, 1 g fiber, 3 g protein. **Diabetic Exchange:** 1 starch.

Editor's Note: If your bread machine has a time-delay feature, we recommend you do not use it for this recipe.

Apricot Yeast Bread

This fruity bread is good throughout the day. It is wonderful to have with coffee in the morning, later as a snack or most any time. —Barbara Lorensen, Mexico, Missouri

1 cup plus 2 tablespoons water (70° to 80°)
1 teaspoon vegetable oil
1/4 cup apricot jam
2 tablespoons butter *or* stick margarine, cut into 4 pieces
1-1/2 teaspoons salt
2 tablespoons nonfat dry milk powder
3 cups bread flour
3/4 cup dried apricots, chopped
3 teaspoons active dry yeast

In bread machine pan, place all ingredients in order suggested by manufacturer. Select basic bread setting. Choose crust color and loaf size if available. Bake according to bread machine directions (check dough after 5 minutes of mixing; add 1 to 2 tablespoons of water or flour if needed). **Yield:** 1 loaf (about 1-1/2 pounds, 16 slices).

Nutritional Analysis: One slice equals 128 calories, 2 g fat (1 g saturated fat), 4 mg cholesterol, 242 mg sodium, 25 g carbohydrate, 1 g fiber, 4 g protein. **Diabetic Exchange:** 1-1/2 starch.

Editor's Note: If your bread machine has a time-delay feature, we recommend you do not use it for this recipe.

Focaccia Bread

(Pictured below)

Rosemary, garlic salt and Parmesan cheese give incredible flavor to this round loaf. Crusty on the outside and chewy on the inside, it's great with Italian food. I serve warm slices along with peppered olive oil. —Patty Lashbrook
San Jose, California

1 cup plus 3 tablespoons water (70° to 80°)
1 tablespoon olive *or* vegetable oil
1 teaspoon salt
3 cups bread flour
1-1/2 teaspoons active dry yeast
Additional olive *or* vegetable oil
1 tablespoon grated Parmesan cheese
1-1/2 teaspoons minced fresh rosemary
1/2 to 1 teaspoon garlic salt
DIPPING SAUCE:
1/4 cup olive *or* vegetable oil
1/2 teaspoon coarsely ground *or* cracked pepper

In bread machine pan, place the first five ingredients in order suggested by manufacturer. Select dough setting (check the dough after 5 minutes of mixing; add 1 to 2 tablespoons of water or flour if needed).

When cycle is complete, let dough rest in pan for 5 minutes. Transfer dough to a greased baking sheet. Pat into an 8-in. circle about 3/4 in. high. Brush with oil; sprinkle with the Parmesan cheese, rosemary and garlic salt. Bake at 425° for 20-25 minutes or until golden brown. In a small bowl, combine dipping sauce ingredients; serve with warm bread. **Yield:** 1 loaf (1-1/2 pounds).

Focaccia Bread

Soft Garlic Breadsticks

(Pictured below)

I rely on a bread machine to mix the dough for these buttery golden breadsticks that are mildly seasoned with garlic and basil. I like to use this dough when making pizza, too. It makes two 12-inch crusts. —Charles Smith
Baltic, Connecticut

 Uses less fat, sugar or salt. Includes Nutritional Analysis and Diabetic Exchanges.

> 1 cup plus 2 tablespoons water (70° to 80°)
> 2 tablespoons olive *or* canola oil
> 3 tablespoons grated Parmesan cheese
> 2 tablespoons sugar
> 3 teaspoons garlic powder
> 1-1/2 teaspoons salt
> 3/4 teaspoon minced fresh basil *or* 1/4 teaspoon dried basil
> 3 cups bread flour
> 2 teaspoons active dry yeast
> 1 tablespoon butter *or* stick margarine, melted

In bread machine pan, place the first nine ingredients in order suggested by manufacturer. Select dough setting (check dough after 5 minutes of mixing; add 1 to 2 tablespoons of water or flour if needed).

When cycle is completed, turn dough onto a lightly floured surface. Divide into 20 portions. Shape each into a ball; roll each into a 9-in. rope. Place on greased baking sheets. Cover and let rise in a warm place for 40 minutes or until doubled. Bake at 350° for 18-22 minutes or until golden brown. Remove to wire racks. Brush warm breadsticks with butter. **Yield:** 20 breadsticks.

Nutritional Analysis: One breadstick equals 88 calories, 2 g fat (1 g saturated fat), 2 mg cholesterol, 196 mg sodium, 15 g carbohydrate, 1 g fiber, 3 g protein. **Diabetic Exchange:** 1 starch.

Soft Garlic Breadsticks

Pear Yeast Bread

Because I have a busy schedule, I revamped this recipe so I could use my bread machine. I also substituted canned pears, which make preparation even easier. We like it for a weekend breakfast treat. —Maureen De Garmo
Martinez, California

> 1 can (15 ounces) pear halves, undrained
> 1/2 teaspoon almond extract
> 2 tablespoons butter *or* margarine, softened
> 1 tablespoon brown sugar
> 1-1/2 teaspoons salt
> 1 teaspoon ground cinnamon
> 1/4 teaspoon ground nutmeg
> 3-1/2 cups bread flour
> 2-1/4 teaspoons active dry yeast

In a blender or food processor, combine the pears and extract; cover and process until pureed. Pour into bread machine pan.

Add the remaining ingredients in order suggested by manufacturer. Select basic bread setting. Choose crust color and loaf size if available. Bake according to bread machine directions (check dough after 5 minutes of mixing; add 1 to 2 tablespoons water or flour if needed). **Yield:** 1 loaf (1-1/2 pounds).

Almond-Honey Wheat Bread

I have two bread machines, and I keep both of them going when the grandkids come to visit. Featuring plenty of crunchy almonds, this bread is the best of any we've tried. We think it's particularly good toasted. —Ray Rowe
Cadiz, Kentucky

> 1-1/4 cups water (70° to 80°)
> 1/4 cup honey
> 2 tablespoons butter *or* margarine, softened
> 2 teaspoons salt
> 2 cups bread flour
> 2 cups whole wheat flour
> 2/3 cup slivered almonds, toasted
> 3 teaspoons active dry yeast

In bread machine pan, place all ingredients in order suggested by manufacturer. Select basic bread setting. Choose crust color and loaf size if available. Bake according to bread machine directions (check the dough after 5 minutes of mixing; add 1 to 2 tablespoons of water or flour if needed). **Yield:** 1 loaf (1-1/2 pound).

Ale Bread

For a tender white loaf that's a bit moister and denser than other breads, try this simple recipe. It's equally good whether you use beer or ginger ale. —Jeannine Norder
Eaton Rapids, Michigan

> 1 cup warm beer *or* ginger ale (70° to 80°)
> 1/3 cup water (70° to 80°)
> 2 tablespoons vegetable oil
> 3 tablespoons sugar
> 1-1/2 teaspoons salt

3 cups bread flour
2-1/4 teaspoons active dry yeast

In bread machine pan, place all ingredients in order suggested by manufacturer. Select basic bread setting. Choose crust color and loaf size if available. Bake according to bread machine directions (check dough after 5 minutes of mixing; add 1 to 2 tablespoons of water or flour if needed). **Yield:** 1 loaf (about 1-1/2 pounds).

Stuffing Bread

(Pictured at right)

When you are in a hurry and want to get that loaf going quick, a bread machine sure does the trick. Whenever I bake this bread, everyone says, "It smells like Thanksgiving." —Barbara Adams, Redford, Michigan

1-1/4 cups water (70° to 80°)
   1 egg
   3 tablespoons dried minced onion
   1 tablespoon butter *or* margarine, softened
   1 tablespoon sugar
   1 tablespoon dried parsley flakes
1-1/2 teaspoons poultry seasoning
   1 teaspoon salt
  1/2 teaspoon celery seed
3-1/2 cups bread flour
2-1/4 teaspoons active dry yeast

In bread machine pan, place all ingredients in order suggested by manufacturer. Select basic bread setting. Choose crust color and loaf size if available. Bake according to bread machine directions (check dough after 5 minutes of mixing; add 1 to 2 tablespoons of water or flour if needed). **Yield:** 1 loaf (1-1/2 pounds).

Editor's Note: If your bread machine has a time-delay feature, we recommend you do not use it for this recipe.

Golden Pan Rolls

I use a bread machine to fix these delightfully light rolls. There's no need to serve butter with the moist tender rolls, because they are brushed with butter before baking. —Phalice Ayers, Spokane, Washington

   1 can (11 ounces) mandarin oranges, drained
  1/2 cup small-curd cottage cheese
   2 tablespoons water
   2 tablespoons vegetable oil
   2 tablespoons honey
  1/2 teaspoon salt
  1/2 teaspoon baking soda
   3 cups bread flour
   1 cup quick-cooking oats
2-1/2 teaspoons active dry yeast
   1 tablespoon butter *or* stick margarine, melted

In bread machine pan, place the first 10 ingredients in order suggested by manufacturer. Select dough setting. Check dough after 5 minutes of mixing (dough should be stiff). Add 1 to 2 tablespoons of water or flour if needed.

Stuffing Bread

When cycle is completed, turn dough onto a lightly floured surface. Cover and let rest for 15 minutes. Roll or pat to 1/2-in. thickness. Cut with a 2-in. biscuit cutter. Place in a greased 13-in. x 9-in. x 2-in. baking pan. Brush with butter. Cover and let rise in warm place until doubled, about 1 hour. Bake at 350° for 20-25 minutes or until golden brown. Serve warm. **Yield:** 2 dozen.

Editor's Note: If your bread machine has a time-delay feature, we recommend you do not use it for this recipe.

Tomato Basil Bread

I tasted a tomato basil bread at a restaurant and tried to duplicate it in my bread machine. I combined several recipes to come up with this loaf. We love slices topped with smoked turkey, but it also makes plain bologna taste like a treat! —Julie Barta, Hiawatha, Iowa

   1 can (8 ounces) tomato sauce
  1/4 cup water (70° to 80°)
   2 tablespoons nonfat dry milk powder
   2 tablespoons olive *or* vegetable oil
   1 tablespoon sugar
1-1/2 teaspoons salt
1-1/2 teaspoons dried minced onion
1-1/2 teaspoons dried basil
   1 teaspoon dried marjoram
   1 teaspoon dried thyme
   3 cups all-purpose flour
1-3/4 teaspoons active dry yeast

In bread machine pan, place all ingredients in order suggested by manufacturer. Select basic bread setting. Choose crust color and loaf size if available. Bake according to bread machine directions (check dough after 5 minutes of mixing; add 1 to 2 tablespoons of water or flour if needed). **Yield:** 1 loaf (about 1-1/2 pounds).

Chapter 12

☼ Snappy Soups, Salads & Sandwiches

LICKETY-SPLIT LUNCHES and speedy suppers are just minutes away when you start with fast-to-fix soups, salads and sandwiches. For time-pressed cooks, these mouth-watering mainstays are ideal.

Meal planning is a snap when you add one or more of these rapid recipes to your menu.

All of the simple-to-make soups, snappy salads and short-cut sandwiches here are family favorites, undeniably delicious and surprisingly filling.

SURE TO SATISFY. Clockwise from top right: Pita Pocket Chicken Salad (p. 192), Boston Subs (p. 179), Grilled Roast Beef Sandwiches (p. 180) and Pizza Loaf (p. 192).

Artichoke Melts

Ready in 15 minutes or less

These open-faced egg and artichoke melts are a favorite. The Dijon mustard adds a nice zip, making them more exciting than plain grilled cheese. —Jill Gross, Roselle, Illinois

 1 can (14 ounces) water-packed artichoke hearts, drained and chopped
 1-1/2 cups (6 ounces) shredded cheddar cheese
 3 tablespoons mayonnaise
 1 tablespoon Dijon mustard
 1/2 teaspoon dried thyme
 6 slices rye *or* pumpernickel bread
 3 hard-cooked eggs, sliced

In a bowl, combine the artichokes, cheese, mayonnaise, mustard and thyme; set aside. Place bread on a baking sheet; broil 4 in. from the heat until toasted. Turn over. Place egg slices on untoasted side of bread; spread with artichoke mixture. Broil for 3-5 minutes or until cheese is melted and top is golden brown. **Yield:** 3-6 servings.

Ham 'n' Cheese Stromboli

(Pictured at right)

I sometimes make several of these savory loaves to keep in my freezer for quick meals. —Susan Brown Lithonia, Georgia

 1 loaf (1 pound) frozen white bread dough, thawed
 1/2 pound sliced Swiss cheese
 1/2 pound thinly sliced deli ham
 1 cup (4 ounces) shredded cheddar cheese
 1 cup (4 ounces) shredded Colby cheese
 1 package (16 ounces) frozen chopped broccoli, thawed and drained
 1/2 teaspoon garlic powder

On a floured surface, roll dough into an 18-in. x 12-in. rectangle. Layer with Swiss cheese, ham, cheddar cheese, Colby cheese and broccoli to within 1 in. of edges; sprinkle with garlic powder. Roll up jelly-roll style, starting with a long side; seal seams and ends.

Place seam side down on a greased 15-in. x 10-in. x 1-in. baking pan. Bake, uncovered, at 400° for 20 minutes. Cover loosely with foil; bake 15-20 minutes longer. Let stand for 10 minutes before slicing. **Yield:** 6-8 servings.

Crunchy Veggie Toss

(Pictured at right)

Plan ahead...needs to chill

Crisp carrots, green beans, water chestnuts, garbanzo beans and more combine with bottled dressing in this sensational salad. —Ronda Leuth, Le Claire, Iowa

✓ Uses less fat, sugar or salt. Includes Nutritional Analysis and Diabetic Exchanges.

 1 pound carrots, julienned
 1 package (16 ounces) frozen French-style green beans, thawed

 2 cans (15 ounces *each*) garbanzo beans *or* chickpeas, rinsed and drained
 2 cans (8 ounces *each*) sliced water chestnuts, drained
 1 can (14 ounces) bean sprouts, drained
 1 cup slivered almonds, toasted
 1 bottle (8 ounces) Italian *or* vinegar and oil salad dressing

In a bowl, combine first five ingredients; mix well. Add almonds and salad dressing; toss to coat. Cover and refrigerate for 4 hours before serving. **Yield:** 12 servings.
 Nutritional Analysis: One 3/4-cup serving (prepared with fat-free Italian dressing) equals 194 calories, 5 g fat (1 g saturated fat), 1 mg cholesterol, 524 mg sodium, 31 g carbohydrate, 8 g fiber, 7 g protein. **Diabetic Exchanges:** 2 starch, 1 fat.

New England Clam Chowder

(Pictured at right)

Ready in 15 minutes or less

This shortcut clam chowder has the traditional flavor of the original. —Rosann McWherter, Dublin, California

 1 can (10-3/4 ounces) condensed New England clam chowder, undiluted
 1-1/3 cups milk
 1 can (6-1/2 ounces) chopped clams, drained
 2 tablespoons sherry *or* chicken broth
 1 tablespoon butter *or* margarine
Shredded cheddar cheese, optional

In a saucepan, combine first five ingredients. Bring to a boil. Reduce heat; cover and simmer for 5 minutes. Garnish with cheese if desired. **Yield:** 3 servings.

Hearty Grilled Cheese

Ready in 30 minutes or less

A quick-to-fix cheese sauce makes this simple sandwich extra special. —Catherine Brennan, Denver, Colorado

 12 slices dark rye bread
 6 slices *each* American cheese, Swiss cheese, fully cooked ham and fully cooked turkey
 1/4 cup butter *or* margarine, softened
CHEESE SAUCE:
 1 can (10-3/4 ounces) condensed cheddar cheese soup, undiluted
 2/3 cup water
 1/4 teaspoon liquid smoke, optional
 1/8 to 1/4 teaspoon onion powder
 1/8 to 1/4 teaspoon garlic powder
 1/4 teaspoon cayenne pepper, optional

On six slices of bread, layer one slice of American cheese, Swiss cheese, ham and turkey. Top with remaining bread. Butter outsides of bread; set aside.

In a small saucepan, combine the sauce ingredients. Cook over medium heat until heated through, stirring occasionally. Meanwhile, toast sandwiches on a hot griddle for 2-3 minutes on each side or until lightly browned. Serve with cheese sauce. **Yield:** 6 servings.

Crunchy Veggie Toss
New England Clam Chowder
Ham 'n' Cheese Stromboli

Ham and Pea Salad
Chicken Salad Sandwiches
Cream of Spinach Soup

Ham and Pea Salad

(Pictured at left)

Ready in 15 minutes or less

I need just five ingredients to create this quick colorful salad. I work 10-hour days, so I look for all the short-cuts I can find. —Laura Whitney, Ephrata, Washington

1 package (16 ounces) frozen peas, thawed
1/2 pound fully cooked ham, julienned
1 cup (4 ounces) shredded cheddar cheese
1 cup chopped red onion
1/3 to 1/2 cup ranch salad dressing

In a serving bowl, combine the peas, ham, cheese and onion. Pour dressing over the top; toss to coat evenly. **Yield:** 6-8 servings.

Cream of Spinach Soup

(Pictured at left)

Ready in 15 minutes or less

This rich, creamy soup tastes like it's made by a professional chef. —Patricia Bradley, Rohnert Park, California

1 package (1.8 ounces) leek soup and dip mix
1 package (10 ounces) frozen leaf spinach, thawed, drained and chopped
1 cup (8 ounces) sour cream
1/4 teaspoon ground nutmeg
Lemon slices

Prepare soup mix according to package directions. Stir in spinach. Cover and simmer for 2 minutes. Remove from the heat; stir in sour cream and nutmeg. Garnish with lemon slices. **Yield:** 4 servings.

Chicken Salad Sandwiches

(Pictured at left)

Ready in 15 minutes or less

I entered this recipe in a contest that our local newspaper holds each year, and it won first place in the salad division. Toasted almonds and celery add crunch to the flavorful filling. —Judy Kisch-Keuten, Beatrice, Nebraska

 Uses less fat, sugar or salt. Includes Nutritional Analysis and Diabetic Exchanges.

2 cups cubed cooked chicken
2 celery ribs, chopped
1/2 cup chopped green pepper
1/2 cup mayonnaise
1/3 cup slivered almonds, toasted
1/4 cup sweet pickle relish
1/4 cup chopped stuffed olives
2 tablespoons chopped onion
2 teaspoons prepared mustard
3/4 to 1-1/4 teaspoons salt
1/4 teaspoon pepper
12 English muffins, split and toasted
12 lettuce leaves
12 thin tomato slices

In a bowl, combine the first 11 ingredients; [...] 12 muffin halves with lettuce leaves; spre[...] en salad. Top with tomato slices and remai[...] halves. **Yield:** 12 servings.
  Nutritional Analysis: One serving (prepared with fat-free mayonnaise and 3/4 teaspoon salt) equals 213 calories, 4 g fat (1 g saturated fat), 21 mg cholesterol, 635 mg sodium, 31 g carbohydrate, 3 g fiber, 13 g protein. **Diabetic Exchanges:** 2 starch, 1 lean meat.

Boston Subs

(Pictured on page 175)

Ready in 30 minutes or less

My mother has been making these wonderful sandwiches since she left her hometown of Boston many years ago. They're quick to prepare and travel well if tightly wrapped in plastic wrap. The recipe is great for parties if you use a loaf of French or Italian bread instead of the individual rolls. —Sue Erdos, Meriden, Connecticut

1/2 cup mayonnaise
12 submarine sandwich buns, split
1/2 cup Italian salad dressing, *divided*
4 ounces *each* thinly sliced bologna, deli ham, hard salami, pepperoni and olive loaf
4 ounces thinly sliced Provolone cheese
1 medium onion, diced
1 medium tomato, diced
1/2 cup diced dill pickles
1 cup shredded lettuce
1 teaspoon dried oregano

Spread mayonnaise on inside of buns. Brush with half of the salad dressing. Layer deli meats and cheese on bun bottoms. Top with onion, tomato, pickles and lettuce. Sprinkle with oregano and drizzle with remaining dressing. Replace bun tops. **Yield:** 12 servings.

Dressed-Up Tuna Salad

Ready in 30 minutes or less

My family has enjoyed this pretty salad for many years. To save time, use prepared balsamic dressing instead of making it yourself. —Shelly Kaiser, Louisville, Kentucky

1 head romaine, torn
1 pint cherry tomatoes, halved
4 hard-cooked eggs, cut into wedges
4 ounces Swiss cheese, julienned
2 cans (6 ounces *each*) tuna, drained
1/2 cup sliced red onion
1/2 cup olive *or* vegetable oil
3 tablespoons balsamic *or* red wine vinegar
1 teaspoon dried oregano
1 teaspoon salt
1/2 teaspoon pepper

Arrange romaine on four salad plates. Top with the tomatoes, eggs, cheese, tuna and onion. In a jar with a tight-fitting lid, combine the oil, vinegar, oregano, salt and pepper. Drizzle over salads. Serve immediately. **Yield:** 4 servings.

Southwestern Bean Soup

mushrooms are sandwiched between slices of sourdough bread, then toasted on a griddle to buttery perfection.
—Jolie Goddard, Elko, Nevada

　1　medium onion, sliced
　1　medium green pepper, sliced
1/2　pound fresh mushrooms, sliced
　2 to 3　garlic cloves, minced
　2　tablespoons vegetable oil
1/4　teaspoon salt
1/8　teaspoon pepper
　8　slices sourdough bread
　16　slices Colby-Monterey Jack *or* Swiss cheese, divided
　8　slices deli roast beef
1/2　cup butter *or* margarine, softened
Garlic salt, optional

In a large skillet, saute the onion, green pepper, mushrooms and garlic in oil until tender; sprinkle with salt and pepper. On four slices of bread, layer two slices of cheese, two slices of beef and a fourth of the vegetable mixture. Top with the remaining cheese and bread.

　Butter outsides of bread; sprinkle with garlic salt if desired. On a hot griddle, toast sandwiches for 3-4 minutes on each side or until golden brown. **Yield:** 4 servings.

Ham and Corn Chowder

Ready in 30 minutes or less

I'm always on the lookout for easy soups because my husband and I love them, particularly in the winter months. This creamy chowder gets a little kick from cayenne and chopped jalapeno pepper. Extra servings freeze very well.　　—*Sharon Price, Caldwell, Idaho*

✓ Uses less fat, sugar or salt. Includes Nutritional Analysis and Diabetic Exchanges.

　2　celery ribs, chopped
1/4　cup chopped onion

Grilled Roast Beef Sandwiches

Southwestern Bean Soup

(Pictured above)

Ready in 30 minutes or less

When a friend needs a night off from cooking, I make this one-pot meal. I deliver it with tortilla chips, shredded cheese and sour cream for garnish.　　—*Jackie Hacker Seville, Ohio*

　1　large onion, chopped
　1　teaspoon vegetable oil
　2　cans (15 ounces *each*) black beans, rinsed and drained
　2　cans (14-1/2 ounces *each*) diced tomatoes with garlic and onion, undrained
　2　cans (14-1/2 ounces *each*) chicken broth
　1　can (16 ounces) kidney beans, rinsed and drained
　1　can (15 ounces) cannellini *or* white kidney beans, rinsed and drained
1-1/2　cups fresh *or* frozen corn
　4　garlic cloves, minced
1-1/2　teaspoons ground cumin
1-1/2　teaspoons chili powder
1/8 to 1/4　teaspoon hot pepper sauce

In a Dutch oven or soup kettle, saute the onion in oil until tender. Stir in the remaining ingredients; bring to a boil. Reduce heat; simmer, uncovered, for 5 minutes or until heated through. **Yield:** 12 servings (3 quarts).

Grilled Roast Beef Sandwiches

(Pictured at right and on page 174)

Ready in 30 minutes or less

This fast favorite hits the spot when we're short on time. Roast beef, cheese, and sauteed onion, green pepper and

1 jalapeno pepper, seeded and chopped*
2 tablespoons butter *or* stick margarine
2 tablespoons all-purpose flour
3 cups milk
2 cups cubed fully cooked ham
2 cups cubed cooked potatoes
1-1/2 cups fresh *or* frozen corn
1 can (14-3/4 ounces) cream-style corn
3/4 teaspoon minced fresh thyme *or* 1/4
 teaspoon dried thyme
1/8 to 1/4 teaspoon cayenne pepper
1/8 teaspoon salt

In a large saucepan, saute the celery, onion and jalapeno in butter until vegetables are tender. Stir in the flour until blended. Gradually add milk. Bring to a boil; cook and stir for 2 minutes or until thickened. Stir in the remaining ingredients. Bring to a boil. Reduce heat; cover and simmer for 10 minutes or until heated through. **Yield:** 8 servings (2 quarts).

Nutritional Analysis: One 1-cup serving (prepared with fat-free milk and lean ham) equals 216 calories, 5 g fat (2 g saturated fat), 20 mg cholesterol, 673 mg sodium, 31 g carbohydrate, 2 g fiber, 14 g protein. **Diabetic Exchanges:** 2 starch, 1 lean meat.

*Editor's Note: When cutting or seeding hot peppers, use rubber or plastic gloves to protect your hands. Avoid touching your face.

Italian Peasant Soup

(Pictured above right)

Ready in 45 minutes or less

My father shared this recipe with me, and I use it whenever I need a hearty, healthy meal. It's my sons' favorite. Loaded with sausage, chicken, beans and spinach, the quick soup is nice for special occasions, too.
—*Kim Knight, Hamburg, Pennsylvania*

 Uses less fat, sugar or salt. Includes Nutritional Analysis and Diabetic Exchanges.

1 pound Italian sausage links, casings removed
 and cut into 1-inch slices
2 medium onions, chopped
6 garlic cloves, chopped
1 pound boneless skinless chicken breasts, cut
 into 1-inch cubes
2 cans (15 ounces *each*) cannellini *or* white
 kidney beans, drained
2 cans (14-1/2 ounces *each*) chicken broth
2 cans (14-1/2 ounces *each*) diced tomatoes,
 undrained
1 teaspoon dried basil
1 teaspoon dried oregano
6 cups fresh spinach leaves, chopped
Shredded Parmesan cheese, optional

In a Dutch oven or soup kettle, cook sausage over medium heat until no longer pink; drain. Add onions and garlic; saute until tender. Add chicken; cook and stir until no longer pink. Stir in the beans, broth, tomatoes, basil and oregano. Cook, uncovered, for 10 minutes. Add spinach and heat just until wilted. Serve with Parmesan

Italian Peasant Soup

cheese if desired. **Yield:** 11 servings (2-3/4 quarts).

Nutritional Analysis: One 1-cup serving (prepared with turkey Italian sausage and reduced-sodium chicken broth; calculated without Parmesan cheese) equals 220 calories, 5 g fat (2 g saturated fat), 48 mg cholesterol, 598 mg sodium, 20 g carbohydrate, 5 g fiber, 22 g protein. **Diabetic Exchanges:** 2-1/2 lean meat, 1 starch.

French Market Sandwiches

Ready in 30 minutes or less

I first tasted this warm ham and cheese sandwich at a luncheon, and it quickly became a favorite in our house. I keep some in the freezer for fast meals. My bridge club enjoys them with soup and fresh fruit.
—*Florence McNulty, Montebello, California*

1/2 cup butter *or* margarine, softened
1/2 cup Dijon mustard
2 tablespoons chopped green onions
1/2 teaspoon poppy seeds
1/4 teaspoon curry powder
10 croissants, split
10 slices deli ham
10 slices Swiss cheese

In a bowl, combine the butter, mustard, onions, poppy seeds and curry powder. Spread over cut sides of croissants. Place a slice of ham and cheese on each croissant; replace tops. Wrap individually in foil. Bake at 325° for 15-20 minutes or until heated through. Serve immediately. **Yield:** 10 servings.

Basil Tomato Soup

(Pictured at right)

Ready in 30 minutes or less

After bringing this soup to a teachers' function, I had lots of recipe requests. —Sarah Perkins, Southlake, Texas

> 2 cans (28 ounces *each*) crushed tomatoes
> 1 can (14-1/2 ounces) chicken broth
> 18 to 20 fresh basil leaves, minced
> 1 teaspoon sugar
> 1 cup heavy whipping cream
> 1/2 cup butter *or* margarine

In a saucepan, bring tomatoes and broth to a boil. Reduce heat; cover and simmer for 10 minutes. Add basil and sugar. Reduce heat to low; stir in cream and butter. Cook until butter is melted. **Yield:** 9 servings.

Chicken Salad Pitas

(Pictured at right)

Ready in 30 minutes or less

This Mediterranean-inspired sandwich is a treat to eat. It's real tasty. —Janice Conway, Reynolds, Illinois

✓ Uses less fat, sugar or salt. Includes Nutritional Analysis and Diabetic Exchanges.

> 1-1/2 cups cubed cooked chicken
> 1 medium carrot, julienned
> 1/2 cup julienned cucumber
> 1/4 cup sliced radishes
> 1/4 cup sliced ripe olives
> 1/4 cup cubed mozzarella cheese (1/2-inch cubes)
> 1/3 to 1/2 cup Italian salad dressing
> 5 pita breads (6 inches), halved
> Lettuce leaves

In a bowl, combine the chicken, carrot, cucumber, radishes, olives and cheese. Add dressing and toss to coat. Line pita breads with lettuce leaves. Stuff about 1/3 cup of chicken mixture into each half. **Yield:** 5 servings.

Nutritional Analysis: One serving (prepared with part-skim mozzarella cheese and 1/3 cup fat-free salad dressing) equals 276 calories, 4 g fat (1 g saturated fat), 39 mg cholesterol, 674 mg sodium, 38 g carbohydrate, 2 g fiber, 20 g protein. **Diabetic Exchanges:** 2-1/2 starch, 2 lean meat.

Greek Pasta Salad

(Pictured at right)

Plan ahead...needs to chill

This full-flavored cold pasta salad is as attractive as it is delicious. —Dawna Waggoner, Minong, Wisconsin

> 3 cups uncooked tricolor spiral pasta
> 1 medium tomato, cut into wedges
> 1 small sweet red pepper, julienned
> 1 small green pepper, julienned
> 4 ounces crumbled feta cheese
> 1/2 cup sliced ripe olives

DRESSING:
> 2/3 cup olive *or* vegetable oil
> 1/4 cup minced fresh basil
> 3 tablespoons white vinegar
> 2 tablespoons chopped green onions
> 2 tablespoons grated Parmesan cheese
> 1/2 teaspoon salt
> 1/4 teaspoon pepper
> 1/4 teaspoon dried oregano

Cook the pasta according to package directions; rinse in cold water and drain. Place in a large serving bowl; add the tomato, peppers, feta cheese and olives.

In a blender, combine the dressing ingredients; cover and process until smooth. Pour over salad; toss to coat. Cover and refrigerate for 2 hours or overnight. Toss before serving. **Yield:** 10-12 servings.

Barley Chicken Chili

Ready in 30 minutes or less

For a deliciously different chicken dish, give this zesty chili a try. —Kayleen Grew, Essexville, Michigan

> 1 cup chopped onion
> 1/2 cup chopped green pepper
> 1 teaspoon olive *or* vegetable oil
> 2-1/4 cups water
> 1 can (15 ounces) tomato sauce
> 1 can (14-1/2 ounces) chicken broth
> 1 can (10 ounces) diced tomatoes and green chilies, undrained
> 1 cup quick-cooking barley
> 1 tablespoon chili powder
> 1/2 teaspoon ground cumin
> 1/4 teaspoon garlic powder
> 3 cups cubed cooked chicken

In a large saucepan, saute onion and green pepper in oil until tender. Add water, tomato sauce, broth, tomatoes, barley, chili powder, cumin and garlic powder; bring to a boil. Reduce heat; cover and simmer 10 minutes. Add chicken. Cover and simmer 5 minutes longer or until barley is tender. **Yield:** 9 servings (about 2 quarts).

Cutting Fresh Basil

FRESH BASIL is a wonderful addition to recipes and can be a pretty garnish, too. But chopping one leaf at a time can be tedious. To quickly chop a lot of basil, try this:

Before cutting the basil, sprinkle a few drops of vegetable oil on the leaves and gently rub to evenly coat the leaves. This will prevent them from darkening.

Stack several basil leaves and roll them into a tight tube. Slice the leaves widthwise into narrow pieces to create long thin strips. If you'd like smaller pieces, simply chop the strips.

Greek Pasta Salad
Basil Tomato Soup
Chicken Salad Pitas

Tortellini Vegetable Soup

Tortellini Vegetable Soup

(Pictured above)

Ready in 30 minutes or less

Tomatoes, carrots, green beans, potatoes, corn and celery are the perfect complements to convenient frozen tortellini in this heartwarming soup. Add a crusty loaf of bread and a green salad, and dinner is ready in no time.
—Deborah Hutchinson, Enfield, Connecticut

- 1 large onion chopped
- 2 celery ribs, chopped
- 2 tablespoons vegetable oil
- 2 cans (14-1/2 ounces *each*) beef broth
- 1 cup *each* frozen corn, sliced carrots and cut green beans
- 1 cup diced uncooked potatoes
- 1 teaspoon dried basil
- 1 teaspoon dried thyme
- 1/2 teaspoon minced chives
- 2 cans (14-1/2 ounces *each*) diced tomatoes, undrained
- 2 cups frozen beef *or* cheese tortellini

In a Dutch oven or soup kettle, saute the onion and celery in oil. Add the broth, corn, carrots, beans, potatoes, basil, thyme and chives; bring to a boil. Reduce heat; cover and simmer for 10-15 minutes or until potatoes are tender.

Add the tomatoes and tortellini. Simmer, uncovered, for 4-5 minutes or until tortellini is heated through. **Yield:** 10 servings (2-1/2 quarts).

Easy Baked Potato Soup

Ready in 30 minutes or less

I came up with this comforting soup one day when I was crunched for time and wanted to use up leftover baked potatoes. Since then, it has become a mealtime staple.

Its wonderful aroma always gets cheers from my husband when he arrives home from work. —Julie Smithouser
Colorado Springs, Colorado

- 3 to 4 medium baking potatoes, baked
- 5 bacon strips, diced
- 2 cans (10-3/4 ounces *each*) condensed cream of potato soup, undiluted
- 1 can (10-3/4 ounces) condensed cheddar cheese soup, undiluted
- 3-1/2 cups milk
- 2 teaspoons garlic powder
- 2 teaspoons Worcestershire sauce
- 1/2 teaspoon onion powder
- 1/4 teaspoon pepper
- Dash liquid smoke, optional
- 1 cup (8 ounces) sour cream
- Shredded cheddar cheese

Peel and dice the baked potatoes; set aside. In a Dutch oven or soup kettle, cook the bacon over medium heat until crisp. Using a slotted spoon, remove to paper towels. Drain, reserving 1-1/2 teaspoons drippings.

Add the soups, milk, garlic powder, Worcestershire sauce, onion powder, pepper, liquid smoke if desired and reserved potatoes to the drippings. Cook, uncovered, for 10 minutes or until heated through, stirring occasionally. Stir in sour cream; cook for 1-2 minutes or until heated through (do not boil). Garnish with cheddar cheese and bacon. **Yield:** 10 servings (2-1/2 quarts).

Seafood Bisque

(Pictured below)

Ready in 30 minutes or less

We live on the Gulf Coast, where fresh seafood is plentiful. I adapted several recipes to come up with this rich bisque. It's great as a first course or an entree, and it can be made with just shrimp or just crabmeat.
—Pat Edwards, Dauphin Island, Alabama

Seafood Bisque

2 cans (10-3/4 ounces *each*) condensed cream
   of mushroom soup, undiluted
1 can (10-3/4 ounces) condensed cream of
   celery soup, undiluted
2-2/3 cups milk
4 green onions, chopped
1/2 cup finely chopped celery
1 garlic clove, minced
1 teaspoon Worcestershire sauce
1/4 teaspoon hot pepper sauce
1-1/2 pounds uncooked medium shrimp, peeled
   and deveined
1 can (6 ounces) crabmeat, drained, flaked
   and cartilage removed
1 jar (4-1/2 ounces) whole mushrooms, drained
3 tablespoons Madeira wine *or* chicken broth
1/2 teaspoon salt
1/2 teaspoon pepper
Minced fresh parsley

In a Dutch oven or soup kettle, combine the first eight ingredients; mix well. Bring to a boil. Reduce heat; add the shrimp, crab and mushrooms. Simmer, uncovered, for 10 minutes. Stir in the wine or broth, salt and pepper; cook 2-3 minutes longer. Garnish with parsley. **Yield:** 10 servings (2-1/2 quarts).

Mushroom Crab Melts

Pizza Soup

Ready in 45 minutes or less

This robust soup is a family favorite, and it's a big hit with my canasta group as well. I top each bowl with a slice of toasted bread and cheese, but you can have fun incorporating other pizza toppings such as cooked sausage.
     —Jackie Brossard, Kitchener, Ontario

2 cans (14-1/2 ounces *each*) diced tomatoes,
   undrained
2 cans (10-3/4 ounces *each*) condensed
   tomato soup, undiluted
2-1/2 cups water
1 package (3-1/2 ounces) sliced pepperoni,
   quartered
1 medium sweet red pepper, chopped
1 medium green pepper, chopped
1 cup sliced fresh mushrooms
2 garlic cloves, minced
1/2 teaspoon rubbed sage
1/2 teaspoon dried basil
1/2 teaspoon dried oregano
Salt and pepper to taste
10 slices French bread, toasted
1-1/2 cups (6 ounces) shredded mozzarella
   cheese

In a Dutch oven or soup kettle, bring the tomatoes, soup and water to a boil. Reduce heat; cover and simmer for 15 minutes. Mash with a potato masher. Add the pepperoni, red and green peppers, mushrooms, garlic, sage, basil, oregano, salt and pepper. Cover and simmer for 10 minutes or until vegetables are tender.
   Ladle into ovenproof bowls. Top each with a slice of bread and sprinkle with cheese. Broil 4 in. from the

heat until cheese is melted and bubbly. **Yield:** 10 servings (about 2-1/2 quarts).

Mushroom Crab Melts

(Pictured above)

Ready in 45 minutes or less

I received this recipe from my grandmother. The rich open-faced treats are great with a green salad, but I've also cut them into quarters to serve as hors d'oeuvres. To save time, make the crab-mushroom topping early in the day and store it in the refrigerator.
     —Jean Bevilacqua
     Rhododendron, Oregon

3 bacon strips, diced
1 cup sliced fresh mushrooms
1/4 cup chopped onion
1 can (6 ounces) crabmeat, drained, flaked
   and cartilage removed *or* 1 cup chopped
   imitation crabmeat
1 cup (4 ounces) shredded Swiss cheese
1/2 cup mayonnaise
1/3 cup grated Parmesan cheese
2 tablespoons butter *or* margarine, softened
6 English muffins, split
Dash *each* cayenne pepper and paprika

In a skillet, cook bacon over medium heat until crisp; remove to paper towels. Drain, reserving 2 tablespoons drippings. Saute mushrooms and onion in drippings until tender. In a large bowl, combine the crab, Swiss cheese, mayonnaise, mushroom mixture, Parmesan cheese and bacon.
   Spread butter over muffin halves. Top with crab mixture; sprinkle with cayenne and paprika. Place on an ungreased baking sheet. Bake at 400° for 10-15 minutes or until lightly browned. **Yield:** 6 servings.

Cheesy Potato Soup
Creamy Salad Dressing
Hot Pizza Sub

Creamy Salad Dressing

(Pictured at left)

Ready in 15 minutes or less

This mild salad dressing was popular at our local bowling alley many years ago when they served meals. Most everyone asked for the recipe. It's very good.
—Dotty Egge, Pelican Rapids, Minnesota

1-1/4 cups heavy whipping cream
1/2 cup vegetable oil
1/4 cup cider vinegar
2 tablespoons sugar
1/2 teaspoon salt
1/4 teaspoon pepper
Salad greens and vegetables of your choice

In a jar with a tight-fitting lid, combine the cream, oil, vinegar, sugar, salt and pepper; shake well. Serve with salad. Refrigerate leftovers. **Yield:** 2 cups.

Hot Pizza Sub

(Pictured at left)

Ready in 30 minutes or less

I stack this warm sub so high with yummy ingredients, you'll have to open wide to take a bite! Slices are hearty with ham, gooey with melted cheese and spicy with salami and pepperoni. —Anna Whelan, Crystal, North Dakota

1 unsliced loaf (1 pound) Italian bread
1/4 cup pizza sauce
1-1/2 teaspoons Italian seasoning
1 medium green pepper, thinly sliced
4 slices fully cooked ham
10 slices salami
30 slices pepperoni
4 slices *each* cheddar, mozzarella and American cheese

Slice bread in half horizontally. Spread bottom half with pizza sauce; sprinkle with Italian seasoning. Top with green pepper, ham, salami, pepperoni and cheese; replace bread top. Place on a baking sheet. Bake at 425° for 12-15 minutes or until cheese is melted. **Yield:** 4 servings.

Cheesy Potato Soup

(Pictured at left)

Ready in 1 hour or less

It doesn't take long to put bowls of this comforting soup on the table. Convenience items such as canned soup and process cheese simplify the preparation.
—Tammy Condit, League City, Texas

1 medium onion, chopped
2 tablespoons butter *or* margarine
6 medium potatoes, peeled and cubed
5 cups water
2 cups milk

1 can (10-3/4 ounces) condensed cream of chicken soup, undiluted
1/2 teaspoon garlic salt
1/8 teaspoon pepper
12 ounces process American cheese (Velveeta), cubed
Minced fresh parsley

In a large saucepan or soup kettle, saute onion in butter. Add potatoes and water. Bring to a boil. Reduce heat; cover and simmer for 15 minutes or until potatoes are tender. Stir in the milk, soup, garlic salt and pepper; heat through. Add cheese; stir until cheese is melted. Garnish with parsley. **Yield:** 10 servings (2-1/2 quarts).

Roast Beef Sandwich Supreme

Ready in 15 minutes or less

An easy five-ingredient spread adds great flavor to these roast beef sandwiches. We made these many Sunday evenings when we wanted a simple supper. Add a beverage and light dessert for an easy meal. —June Formanek, Belle Plaine, Iowa

1/2 cup sour cream
1 tablespoon dry onion soup mix
2 teaspoons prepared horseradish, drained
1/8 teaspoon salt
1/8 teaspoon pepper
12 slices rye *or* pumpernickel bread
12 slices deli roast beef (about 1 pound)
6 lettuce leaves

In a small bowl, combine sour cream, soup mix, horseradish, salt and pepper. Spread over six slices of bread; top with beef, lettuce and remaining bread. **Yield:** 6 servings.

Egg Cauliflower Salad

Plan ahead...needs to chill

For a crunchy alternative to potato salad, try this well-dressed medley of cauliflower, peppers and celery. Add a half cup of shredded carrots and chopped broccoli as well as a cup of peas for a colorful presentation.
—Victoria Zmarzley-Hahn, Northampton, Pennsylvania

2 cups cauliflowerets
4 hard-cooked eggs, chopped
1/2 cup chopped celery
1/4 cup *each* chopped onion, green pepper and sweet red pepper
1/2 cup mayonnaise *or* salad dressing
1/2 teaspoon salt
1/4 teaspoon garlic powder
1/8 teaspoon pepper

In a serving bowl, combine the cauliflower, eggs, celery, onion and peppers. In a small bowl, combine the remaining ingredients. Add to cauliflower mixture and mix well. Cover and refrigerate for at least 2 hours. Serve with a slotted spoon. **Yield:** 6 servings.

Reunion Steak Sandwiches

Ready in 45 minutes or less

Every year, my grandma hosts a family reunion where these flank steak subs steal the show. They're topped with a "special sauce" that requires only three ingredients. For a quick dinner, serve them with coleslaw and macaroni salad from the deli. —Jane Clark, Ridgewood, New Jersey

    1 beef flank steak (1-1/2 pounds)
1/4 teaspoon salt
1/4 teaspoon pepper
    2 tablespoons butter *or* margarine, softened
    6 sesame submarine sandwich buns, split
    2 medium tomatoes, thinly sliced
    1 medium onion, thinly sliced
    6 slices American cheese
MUSTARD SAUCE:
1/2 cup mayonnaise
    2 tablespoons Dijon mustard
4-1/2 teaspoons Worcestershire sauce

Sprinkle steak with salt and pepper. Grill, covered, over medium-hot heat for 6-10 minutes on each side or until meat reaches desired doneness (for rare, a meat thermometer should read 140°; medium, 160°; well-done, 170°). Let stand for 5 minutes before thinly slicing.

Spread butter over inside of buns. Place the tomatoes, onion, sliced steak and cheese on bun bottoms. Broil 5-6 in. from the heat for 2-3 minutes or until cheese is melted. In a small bowl, whisk the mayonnaise, mustard and Worcestershire sauce until blended; spoon over cheese. Replace bun tops. **Yield:** 6 servings.

Turkey Salad on Wheat

(Pictured below)

Ready in 15 minutes or less

Turkey Salad on Wheat

Inspired by the turkey salad at a local deli, I developed this version to suit my family's tastes. You can serve it on whole-grain bread for a filling meal or on croissants for an elegant luncheon. Precooked bacon and leftover turkey make it a snap to fix. —Merrijane Rice Bountiful, Utah

✓ Uses less fat, sugar or salt. Includes Nutritional Analysis and Diabetic Exchanges.

    2 cups chopped romaine
1-1/4 cups diced cooked turkey
1/2 cup shredded Swiss cheese
    2 green onions, thinly sliced
    6 bacon strips, cooked and crumbled
1/3 cup frozen peas, thawed
1/2 cup mayonnaise *or* salad dressing
1/4 teaspoon pepper
  12 slices whole wheat bread

In a bowl, combine the first six ingredients; mix well. Add mayonnaise and pepper; toss to coat. Spread on six slices of bread; top with remaining bread. Serve immediately. **Yield:** 6 servings.

Nutritional Analysis: One sandwich (prepared with reduced-fat Swiss cheese and fat-free mayonnaise) equals 268 calories, 8 g fat (2 g saturated fat), 36 mg cholesterol, 618 mg sodium, 31 g carbohydrate, 5 g fiber, 20 g protein. **Diabetic Exchanges:** 2 starch, 2 lean meat.

Cauliflower Soup

Ready in 45 minutes or less

Cauliflower and carrots share the stage in this cheesy soup that's sure to warm you up on the chilliest of nights. We like it with hot pepper sauce; however, it can be omitted with equally tasty results. —Debbie Ohlhausen Chilliwack, British Columbia

    1 medium head cauliflower, broken into florets
    1 medium carrot, shredded
1/4 cup chopped celery
2-1/2 cups water
    2 teaspoons chicken bouillon granules
    3 tablespoons butter *or* margarine
    3 tablespoons all-purpose flour
3/4 teaspoon salt
1/8 teaspoon pepper
    2 cups milk
    1 cup (4 ounces) shredded cheddar cheese
1/2 to 1 teaspoon hot pepper sauce, optional

In a large saucepan, combine the cauliflower, carrot, celery, water and bouillon. Bring to a boil. Reduce heat; cover and simmer for 12-15 minutes or until vegetables are tender (do not drain).

In another large saucepan, melt butter. Stir in the flour, salt and pepper until smooth. Gradually add milk. Bring to a boil over medium heat; cook and stir for 2 minutes or until thickened. Reduce heat. Stir in the cheese until melted. Add hot pepper sauce if desired. Stir into the cauliflower mixture. **Yield:** 8 servings (about 2 quarts).

Chilled Berry Soup

(Pictured at right)

Plan ahead...needs to chill

I sampled a cool delicious strawberry soup while visiting Walt Disney World. I enjoyed it so much that the restaurant shared the recipe with me, but I eventually found this tasty combination, which I like even better. The ginger ale adds a special zing. —Lisa Watson, Sparta, Michigan

 Uses less fat, sugar or salt. Includes Nutritional Analysis and Diabetic Exchanges.

- 1 quart fresh strawberries, hulled
- 1/3 cup ginger ale
- 1/4 cup milk
- 1/3 cup sugar
- 1 tablespoon lemon juice
- 1 teaspoon vanilla extract
- 1 cup (8 ounces) sour cream

Place strawberries in a food processor or blender; cover and process until smooth. Add ginger ale, milk, sugar, lemon juice and vanilla; cover and process until blended. Pour into a bowl; whisk in sour cream until smooth. Cover and refrigerate until thoroughly chilled, about 2 hours. **Yield:** 4 servings.

Nutritional Analysis: One 3/4-cup serving (prepared with diet ginger ale, fat-free milk and reduced-fat sour cream) equals 189 calories, 5 g fat (4 g saturated fat), 19 mg cholesterol, 55 mg sodium, 32 g carbohydrate, 3 g fiber, 5 g protein. **Diabetic Exchanges:** 1-1/2 fruit, 1 fat-free milk.

Chilled Berry Soup

Meatball Sandwich Slices

Ready in 45 minutes or less

These sandwiches are ideal for everything from hurried family dinners to movie nights with friends. Three types of cheese give each slice a savory lasagna flavor, while frozen meatballs and jarred spaghetti sauce keep preparation simple. —Heidi Coomer, Fort Smith, Arkansas

- 2-1/4 cups shredded mozzarella cheese, *divided*
- 1 cup ricotta cheese
- 3 tablespoons grated Parmesan cheese
- 1 tablespoon Italian seasoning
- 1/2 teaspoon garlic powder
- Salt and pepper to taste
- 1 unsliced loaf (1 pound) Italian bread
- 12 frozen fully cooked Italian meatballs, thawed
- 1 jar (14 ounces) meatless spaghetti sauce
- Pickled pepper rings, optional

In a bowl, combine 1/4 cup mozzarella, ricotta, Parmesan, Italian seasoning, garlic powder, salt and pepper; set aside. Cut loaf of bread in half lengthwise. Cut a 2-in.-wide strip down the center of each half to within an inch of the bottom of the bread. Remove cut portion and save for another use. If desired, toast bread under the broiler until lightly browned.

Spread the cut side of bread with cheese mixture.

Place six meatballs in each half; top with spaghetti sauce. Place on a baking sheet. Bake at 400° for 20-25 minutes or until heated through. Sprinkle with remaining mozzarella cheese. Cut into slices; top with pepper rings if desired. **Yield:** 6-8 servings.

Cheeseburger Chowder

Ready in 30 minutes or less

After tasting a wonderful chowder at a restaurant, I dressed up a can of cheese soup to see if I could capture the same flavors. I then took things a step further by adding chilies and Southwestern spices. I hope you enjoy it as much as I do. —Lori Risdal, Sioux City, Iowa

- 1/2 pound ground beef
- 1 can (10-3/4 ounces) condensed cheddar cheese soup, undiluted
- 1-3/4 cups milk
- 1 cup frozen shredded hash brown potatoes
- 1 can (4 ounces) chopped green chilies
- 1 tablespoon taco seasoning
- 1 tablespoon dried minced onion
- 1/2 teaspoon chili powder
- Coarsely crushed corn chips, shredded Monterey Jack cheese and chopped green onions, optional

In a large saucepan, cook beef over medium heat until no longer pink; drain. Stir in soup, milk, potatoes, chilies, taco seasoning, onion and chili powder until blended. Bring to a boil. Reduce heat; simmer, uncovered, for 5 minutes or until heated through. Garnish with corn chips, cheese and green onions if desired. **Yield:** 4 servings.

Grilled Fish Sandwiches

(Pictured at right)

Ready in 30 minutes or less

I season fish fillets with lime juice and lemon-pepper before charbroiling them on the grill. A simple mayonnaise and honey-mustard sauce puts the sandwiches a step ahead of the rest. —Violet Beard, Marshall, Illinois

 Uses less fat, sugar or salt. Includes Nutritional Analysis and Diabetic Exchanges.

  4 cod fillets (4 ounces *each*)
  1 tablespoon lime juice
  1/2 teaspoon lemon-pepper seasoning
  1/4 cup mayonnaise
  2 teaspoons Dijon mustard
  1 teaspoon honey
  4 hamburger buns, split
  4 lettuce leaves
  4 tomato slices

Brush both sides of fillets with lime juice; sprinkle with lemon-pepper. Coat grill rack with nonstick cooking spray before starting the grill. Grill fillets, covered, over medium heat for 5-6 minutes on each side or until fish flakes easily with a fork.

In a small bowl, combine the mayonnaise, mustard and honey. Spread over the bottom of each bun. Top with a fillet, lettuce and tomato; replace bun tops. **Yield:** 4 servings.

Nutritional Analysis: One sandwich (prepared with fat-free mayonnaise) equals 241 calories, 3 g fat (1 g saturated fat), 49 mg cholesterol, 528 mg sodium, 28 g carbohydrate, 2 g fiber, 24 g protein. **Diabetic Exchanges:** 3 very lean meat, 2 starch.

This 'n' That Salad

(Pictured at right)

Plan ahead...needs to chill

While entertaining one night, I threw together this crunchy vegetable salad with items I had on hand. My guests loved it, and my mother even asked me for the recipe.
—Annette Marie Young, West Lafayette, Indiana

  1 pound fresh broccoli, cut into florets
  1 can (15 ounces) whole baby corn, rinsed, drained and halved *or* 1-1/2 cups frozen corn, thawed
  1 package (10 ounces) frozen peas, thawed
  1 can (8 ounces) sliced water chestnuts, drained
  1 small green pepper, chopped
  3 green onions, sliced
  3/4 cup mayonnaise
  1/2 cup ranch salad dressing
Salt and pepper to taste
Lettuce leaves
  2 hard-cooked eggs, sliced
  1 cup halved cherry tomatoes

In a large bowl, combine the first six ingredients. In a small bowl, combine the mayonnaise, salad dressing, salt and pepper. Pour over vegetable mixture and stir to combine.

Cover and refrigerate for 2 hours. Serve on lettuce-lined plates; garnish with eggs and tomatoes. **Yield:** 10 servings.

Italian Chicken Rice Soup

(Pictured at right)

Ready in 30 minutes or less

I created this soup so my family and I could enjoy a satisfying sit-down meal on busy nights. It's ready in no time but tastes like it simmered all day. —Wendy Sorensen Logan, Utah

  1 can (49-1/2 ounces) chicken broth
  1 jar (26 ounces) meatless spaghetti sauce
1-1/2 cups cubed cooked chicken
  2 tablespoons minced fresh parsley
  1/2 to 1 teaspoon dried thyme
  3 cups cooked rice
  1 teaspoon sugar

In a Dutch oven, combine broth, spaghetti sauce, chicken, parsley and thyme. Bring to a boil. Reduce heat; simmer, uncovered, for 10 minutes. Stir in rice and sugar. Simmer, uncovered, for 10 minutes or until heated through. **Yield:** 10 servings (2-1/2 quarts).

Dumpling Vegetable Soup

Delicious rice dumplings give a homemade touch to this soup that takes advantage of canned goods, frozen vegetables and dry soup mix. —Peggy Linton, Cobourg, Ontario

  1/2 pound ground beef
  4 cups water
  1 can (28 ounces) diced tomatoes, undrained
  1 package (10 ounces) frozen mixed vegetables
  1 envelope dry onion soup mix
  1/2 teaspoon dried oregano
  1/4 teaspoon pepper
RICE DUMPLINGS:
 1-1/4 cups all-purpose flour
  1 teaspoon baking powder
  1/2 teaspoon salt
  1 tablespoon shortening
  1/3 cup cooked rice, room temperature
  1 tablespoon minced fresh parsley
  1 egg, lightly beaten
  1/2 cup milk

In a Dutch oven, cook beef over medium heat until no longer pink; drain. Add the water, tomatoes, vegetables, soup mix, oregano and pepper; bring to a boil. Reduce heat; cover and simmer for 30-40 minutes or until the vegetables are tender.

For dumplings, combine the flour, baking powder and salt in a bowl. Cut in shortening until the mixture resembles coarse crumbs. Add rice and parsley; toss. In a small bowl, combine egg and milk. Add to rice mixture; stir just until moistened. Drop by teaspoonfuls onto simmering soup. Cover and simmer for 15 minutes or until a toothpick inserted in a dumpling comes out clean (do not lift the cover while simmering). Serve immediately. **Yield:** 6-8 servings (2 quarts).

This 'n' That Salad
Italian Chicken Rice Soup
Grilled Fish Sandwiches

Pita Pocket Chicken Salad

(Pictured below and on page 175)

Ready in 15 minutes or less

We wanted something cool for lunch one summer day, so I tossed together whatever I had in the refrigerator. This wonderful salad was the result. Guests enjoy the sweet grapes, tender chicken and crunchy almonds...and they always ask for the recipe. —Natasha Randall, Austin, Texas

  2 cups cubed cooked chicken
1-1/2 cups seedless red grapes, halved
  1 cup chopped cucumber
  3/4 cup sliced almonds
  3/4 cup shredded mozzarella cheese
  1/2 cup poppy seed salad dressing
  6 pita breads (6 inches), halved
Leaf lettuce, optional

In a large bowl, combine the chicken, grapes, cucumber, almonds and mozzarella cheese. Add dressing and toss to coat. Line pita breads with lettuce if desired; fill with chicken salad. **Yield:** 6 servings.

Pizza Loaf

(Pictured on page 174)

Ready in 1 hour or less

This savory stromboli relies on frozen bread dough, so it comes together in no time. The golden loaf is stuffed with cheese, pepperoni, mushrooms, peppers and olives. I often add a few thin slices of ham, too. It's tasty served with warm pizza sauce for dipping. —Jenny Brown
West Lafayette, Indiana

  1 loaf (1 pound) frozen bread dough, thawed
  2 eggs, *separated*
  1 tablespoon grated Parmesan cheese
  1 tablespoon olive *or* vegetable oil

Pita Pocket Chicken Salad

  1 teaspoon minced fresh parsley
  1 teaspoon dried oregano
  1/2 teaspoon garlic powder
  1/4 teaspoon pepper
  8 ounces sliced pepperoni
  2 cups (8 ounces) shredded mozzarella cheese
  1 can (4 ounces) mushroom stems and pieces, drained
  1/4 to 1/2 cup pickled pepper rings
  1 medium green pepper, diced
  1 can (2-1/4 ounces) sliced ripe olives, drained
  1 can (15 ounces) pizza sauce

On a greased baking sheet, roll out dough into a 15-in. x 10-in. rectangle. In a bowl, combine the egg yolks, Parmesan cheese, oil, parsley, oregano, garlic powder and pepper. Brush over the dough. Sprinkle with pepperoni, mozzarella cheese, mushrooms, pepper rings, green pepper and olives. Roll up, jelly-roll style, starting with a long side; pinch seam to seal and tuck ends under.

Place seam side down; brush with egg whites. Do not let rise. Bake at 350° for 35-40 minutes or until golden brown. Warm the pizza sauce; serve with sliced loaf. **Yield:** 10-12 slices.

Turkey Meatball Soup

Ready in 45 minutes or less

You don't need to cook the tender homemade meatballs or boil the egg noodles separately, so you can easily stir up this savory soup in no time. I usually double the recipe for our family of seven. —Carol Losier, Baldwinsville, New York

✓ Uses less fat, sugar or salt. Includes Nutritional Analysis and Diabetic Exchanges.

  2 cans (14-1/2 ounces *each*) chicken broth
  1 celery rib with leaves, thinly sliced
  1 medium carrot, thinly sliced
  1/4 cup chopped onion
  1 tablespoon butter *or* stick margarine
  1 egg, beaten
  1/2 cup dry bread crumbs
  2 tablespoons dried parsley flakes
  1 tablespoon Worcestershire sauce
  1/4 teaspoon pepper
  1/2 pound lean ground turkey
  1 cup uncooked egg noodles

In a large saucepan, bring the broth, celery and carrot to a boil. Reduce heat; cover and simmer for 10 minutes. Meanwhile, in a small skillet, saute onion in butter until tender. Transfer to a large bowl. Add the egg, bread crumbs, parsley, Worcestershire sauce and pepper. Crumble turkey over mixture and mix well. Shape into 1-in. balls.

Add meatballs to the simmering broth. Bring to a boil. Reduce heat; cover and simmer for 15 minutes. Add noodles. Cover and simmer for 5 minutes or until noodles are tender. **Yield:** 5 servings.

Nutritional Analysis: One serving (1 cup) equals 212 calories, 11 g fat (4 g saturated fat), 94 mg cholesterol, 919 mg sodium, 16 g carbohydrate, 1 g fiber, 13 g protein. **Diabetic Exchanges:** 2 fat, 1 starch, 1 lean meat.

Caesar Chicken Wraps

Caesar Chicken Wraps

(Pictured above)

Ready in 30 minutes or less

When we have chicken for dinner, I cook extra for these full-flavored roll-ups. Featuring Caesar salad dressing, cream cheese, red pepper, black olives and a hint of garlic, the wraps are perfect alongside corn on the cob and a green vegetable. —*Christi Martin, Elko, Nevada*

    1/2 cup Caesar salad dressing
    1/2 cup grated Parmesan cheese, *divided*
      1 teaspoon lemon juice
      1 garlic clove, minced
    1/4 teaspoon pepper
      1 package (8 ounces) cream cheese, softened
      3 cups shredded romaine
    1/2 cup diced sweet red pepper
      1 can (2-1/4 ounces) sliced ripe olives, drained
      5 flour tortillas (10 inches)
  1-3/4 cups cubed cooked chicken

In a small bowl, combine the salad dressing, 1/4 cup Parmesan cheese, lemon juice, garlic and pepper. In a small mixing bowl, beat cream cheese until smooth. Add half of the salad dressing mixture and mix well; set aside.

In a large bowl, combine the romaine, red pepper and olives. Add the remaining salad dressing mixture; toss to coat. Spread about 1/4 cup cream cheese mixture on each tortilla. Top with the romaine mixture and chicken; sprinkle with remaining Parmesan cheese. Roll up; cut in half. **Yield:** 5 servings.

Raspberry Grilled Cheese

(Pictured at right)

Ready in 15 minutes or less

My favorite appetizer is a raspberry-glazed cheese ball, so I used similar ingredients to dress up a plain grilled cheese sandwich. The quick combination was unique but delicious, and it became a popular request in my house. —*Jane Beers, Siloam Springs, Arkansas*

      2 tablespoons seedless red raspberry preserves
      4 slices sourdough bread
      2 tablespoons chopped pecans
      1 to 2 tablespoons sliced green onion
      4 slices Muenster *or* baby Swiss cheese
      3 tablespoons butter *or* margarine, softened

Spread preserves on two slices of bread; top with the pecans, onion and cheese. Top with remaining bread; butter outsides of bread. Toast on a hot griddle for 3-4 minutes on each side or until golden brown. **Yield:** 2 servings.

Cranberry Turkey Burgers

Ready in 1 hour or less

These turkey burgers are so good that you might give up traditional beef hamburgers altogether. The thick grilled patties are topped with prepared cranberry sauce and served on toasted English muffins for a nice change of pace. —*Barbara Lindauer, New Athens, Illinois*

      1 small tart apple, peeled and finely chopped
      1 celery rib, chopped
      1 small onion, chopped
      1 teaspoon poultry seasoning
    3/4 teaspoon salt
    1/4 teaspoon pepper
  1-1/4 pounds ground turkey
    1/2 cup mayonnaise
      6 English muffins, split and toasted
      6 lettuce leaves
      1 cup whole-berry cranberry sauce

In a bowl, combine the first six ingredients. Crumble turkey over mixture and mix well. Shape into six patties. Coat grill rack with nonstick cooking spray before starting the grill. Grill patties, covered, over medium heat for 10 minutes on each side or until a meat thermometer reads 165°.

Spread mayonnaise over the muffin halves. Place lettuce, turkey burgers and cranberry sauce on muffin bottoms; replace tops. **Yield:** 6 servings.

Raspberry Grilled Cheese

Buffet Sandwich

(Pictured at right)

Ready in 1 hour or less

The first time I took this beautiful sandwich "centerpiece" to a church potluck, it disappeared so fast, I was sorry I hadn't brought two. I have often added sliced tomatoes to it. —Margaret Rhodes, Coaldale, Alberta

1 loaf unsliced French bread
    (1 pound, 20 inches long)
3 to 4 tablespoons mayonnaise
2 tablespoons butter *or* margarine, softened
1 tablespoon prepared mustard
10 lettuce leaves
5 thin slices fully cooked ham, halved
5 slices pimiento loaf, halved, optional
10 slices salami
10 slices Swiss cheese, halved
5 slices mozzarella cheese, halved
10 thinly sliced sweet red *or* green pepper rings

Cut bread into 22 slices, leaving slices attached at the bottom. Cut off and discard the end pieces. In a small bowl, combine the mayonnaise, butter and mustard until blended. Spread over every other slice of bread.

Between the slices spread with the mayonnaise mixture, place a lettuce leaf, a half slice of ham, a half slice of pimiento loaf if desired, one salami slice, two Swiss cheese halves, a half slice of mozzarella cheese and one pepper ring. To serve, cut completely through the bread between the plain slices. **Yield:** 10 servings.

Chili Cheese Soup

(Pictured at right)

Ready in 30 minutes or less

To cut down on last-minute preparation, I chop the vegetables for this rich soup the night before and store them in the fridge. It has become one of our favorite comfort foods. —Kyle Gray, Glendale, Arizona

1 large onion, chopped
2 celery ribs, chopped
2 medium carrots, shredded
1/2 cup butter *or* margarine
1/2 cup all-purpose flour
2 teaspoons ground mustard
2 teaspoons paprika
2 teaspoons Worcestershire sauce
2 cans (14-1/2 ounces *each*) chicken broth
3 cups milk
2 cans (4 ounces *each*) chopped green chilies
1/2 to 1 teaspoon Liquid Smoke, optional
1 jar (16 ounces) process cheese sauce

In a Dutch oven, saute the onion, celery and carrots in butter until tender. Stir in the flour, mustard, paprika and Worcestershire sauce until blended. Gradually add broth and milk. Bring to a boil; cook and stir for 2 minutes or until thickened. Reduce heat; stir in chilies and Liquid Smoke if desired. Stir in cheese sauce until melted. **Yield:** 10 servings (about 2 quarts).

Festive Tossed Salad

(Pictured at right)

Ready in 10 minutes or less

This is a nice salad for company because it's special, easy and goes with anything. —Kate Hilts Fort Wainwright, Alaska

1/2 cup olive *or* vegetable oil
1/4 cup balsamic *or* red wine vinegar
3 tablespoons water
1 envelope Italian salad dressing mix
2 packages (10 ounces *each*) Italian-blend salad greens
2 medium tomatoes, seeded and chopped
1 small red onion, thinly sliced
1 cup (4 ounces) crumbled feta cheese *or* shredded mozzarella cheese
3/4 cup dried cranberries

In a jar with a tight-fitting lid, combine the oil, vinegar, water and salad dressing mix; shake well. In a large salad bowl, combine the greens, tomatoes, onion, cheese and cranberries. Serve with dressing. **Yield:** 10-12 servings.

Winter Warm-Up Soup

Ready in 1 hour or less

This savory vegetable soup hits the spot on cold days. —Miriam Appelbaum, Manalapan, New Jersey

1 medium onion, chopped
1/2 pound fresh mushrooms, sliced
1 tablespoon vegetable oil
1 can (49-1/2 ounces) chicken broth
4 medium carrots, chopped
1 large potato, peeled and cubed
1 teaspoon dried basil
1 teaspoon dried oregano
1/2 to 1 teaspoon salt
1 cup uncooked bow tie pasta
1 can (15-1/4 ounces) whole kernel corn *or* 1-1/2 cups frozen corn
4 plum tomatoes, thinly sliced and quartered

In a Dutch oven, saute onion and mushrooms in oil until tender. Add broth, carrots, potato and seasonings. Bring to a boil. Reduce heat; cover and simmer 15 minutes.

Meanwhile, cook pasta according to package directions; drain. Add the pasta, corn and tomatoes to soup; cook 5 minutes longer or until heated through and the vegetables are tender. **Yield:** 10 servings (2-1/2 quarts).

Easier Spreading

I use slices of frozen bread when making my daughter's peanut butter and jelly sandwiches for her school lunches. The peanut butter spreads easily and there's no tearing of the bread. At lunch, the bread has defrosted and is ready to eat. —Bonnie Williams Cincinnati, Ohio

Festive Tossed Salad
Buffet Sandwich
Chili Cheese Soup

Chapter 13

TIME-EASING TREATS like these are sure to end your dinners on a sweet note. Folks will think you fussed when you serve any of these impressive—yet easy-to-make—cakes, cookies, pies and other desserts.

Each tempting treat featured here looks and tastes special enough to serve weekend company. Yet they're so fast to fix you'll find yourself whipping them up for family and drop-in guests during the week.

The memorable results will have them asking for more!

SPEEDY SWEETS. Clockwise from upper left: Punch Bowl Trifle, Brownie Mallow Bars and Grasshopper Pie (all recipes on p. 201).

Coconut Cream Torte

(Pictured at right)

This three-layer cake is rich and yummy. Sour cream is the secret ingredient in the creamy frosting that's chock-full of coconut and pecans. If you fix this dessert a day ahead, it tastes even better. Just cover and refrigerate it.
—*Carol Barton, Bowling Green, Kentucky*

  1 package (18-1/2 ounces) butter recipe
     golden cake mix
  2 cups (16 ounces) sour cream
  1 package (10 ounces) flaked coconut
  1 cup chopped pecans, toasted
  1/2 cup sugar

Prepare cake batter according to package directions. Pour into three greased and floured 9-in. baking pans. Bake at 350° for 20-25 minutes or until a toothpick inserted near the center comes out clean. Cool for 10 minutes before removing from pans to wire racks to cool completely.

In a bowl, combine the sour cream, coconut, pecans and sugar. Place one cake on a serving platter; spread with a third of the sour cream mixture. Repeat layers twice. Store in the refrigerator. **Yield:** 12-16 servings.

Raspberry Cream Cheese Bars

(Pictured at right)

Make the most of an effortless oat mixture to form the crunchy crust and crumbly topping for these sweet bars. You can choose any flavor of preserves to suit your family's tastes.
—*Lisa Corroo, Madison, Wisconsin*

  3/4 cup butter *or* margarine, softened
    1 cup packed brown sugar
 1-1/2 cups quick-cooking oats
 1-1/2 cups all-purpose flour
  1/2 teaspoon baking soda
  1/2 teaspoon salt
    2 packages (one 8 ounces, one 3 ounces)
     cream cheese, softened
  1/2 cup sugar
    2 eggs
    1 teaspoon vanilla extract
    1 jar (18 ounces) red raspberry preserves
  1/3 cup chopped slivered almonds

In a mixing bowl, cream the butter and brown sugar. Combine the oats, flour, baking soda and salt; add to creamed mixture and mix well. Press three-fourths of the mixture into a greased 13-in. x 9-in. x 2-in. baking pan. Bake at 350° for 11-13 minutes or until set and edges just begin to brown.

Meanwhile, in a small mixing bowl, beat cream cheese and sugar. Add eggs and vanilla; mix well. Spread over crust. Drop preserves by spoonfuls over cream cheese mixture; carefully spread evenly. Combine almonds and remaining oat mixture; sprinkle over preserves.

Bake for 25-30 minutes or until set and edges are golden brown. Cool before cutting. Store in the refrigerator. **Yield:** 2-1/2 dozen.

Mint Candy Cookies

(Pictured at right)

Because you start with a store-bought cookie mix, it takes no time at all to make these minty treats. I usually drizzle melted chocolate chips over the cookie tops, but pink candy coating looks lovely for Valentine's Day.
—*Christina Hitchcock, Blakely, Pennsylvania*

    1 package (17-1/2 ounces) sugar cookie mix
  40 to 45 mint Andes candies
    6 ounces pink candy coating disks*
Heart-shaped decorating sprinkles, optional

Prepare the cookie dough according to package directions. Cover and chill for 15-30 minutes or until easy to handle. Pat a scant tablespoonful of dough in a thin layer around each mint candy. Place 2 in. apart on ungreased baking sheets. Bake at 375° for 7-9 minutes or until set. Cool for 1 minute before removing from pans to wire racks to cool completely.

In a microwave-safe bowl, melt candy coating; stir until smooth. Drizzle over cookies. Top with decorating sprinkles if desired. **Yield:** about 3-1/2 dozen.

***Editor's Note:** White candy coating tinted with red food coloring may be substituted for the pink candy coating.*

Mix-in-the-Pan Cake

You don't need a bowl to stir up this chocolate cake, so cleanup is a snap. I serve warm squares of the moist cake with scoops of coffee ice cream.
—*Diane Hixon*
Niceville, Florida

1-1/2 cups all-purpose flour
    1 cup packed brown sugar
  1/4 cup baking cocoa
    1 teaspoon baking soda
  1/2 teaspoon salt
  1/3 cup vegetable oil
    1 tablespoon lemon juice
    1 teaspoon vanilla extract
    1 cup strong brewed coffee, room temperature

In a greased 8-in. square baking dish, combine the flour, brown sugar, cocoa, baking soda and salt. Make a well in the center; add oil, lemon juice and vanilla. Stir just until moistened. Add coffee; stir until batter is smooth.

Bake at 350° for 25-30 minutes or until a toothpick inserted near the center comes out clean. Cool on a wire rack. **Yield:** 9 servings.

Get the Scoop

When baking, I use a gravy ladle to scoop flour out of the bag or canister and into a measuring cup. The flour piles up and sits nicely in the ladle, reducing spills and cutting back on kitchen messes.
—*Shirley Schilly, Bluffton, South Carolina*

Coconut Cream Torte
Raspberry Cream Cheese Bars
Mint Candy Cookies

Punch Bowl Trifle
Brownie Mallow Bars
Grasshopper Pie

Punch Bowl Trifle

(Pictured at left and on page 196)

I threw this dessert together when I needed something quick to take to my in-laws' house. Because it's beautiful, everyone thought I fussed, but it's very easy. And since it makes a lot, it's perfect for potlucks and large get-togethers. —Kristi Judkins Morrison, Tennessee

1 package (18-1/4 ounces) chocolate cake mix
1 quart fresh whole strawberries
1 carton (15 ounces) strawberry glaze
2 cartons (12 ounces *each*) frozen whipped topping, thawed, *divided*
1 cup chocolate frosting
Shaved chocolate

Prepare and bake cake according to package directions, using a 13-in. x 9-in. x 2-in. baking pan. Cool completely on a wire rack.

Set aside five strawberries for garnish. Slice remaining strawberries. Cut cake into 1-in. cubes. Place half of the cubes in a 6-qt. glass punch bowl. Top with half of the sliced strawberries; drizzle with half of the strawberry glaze. Spread with 3-1/2 cups whipped topping.

In a microwave-safe bowl, heat frosting on high for 20-30 seconds or until pourable, stirring often; cool slightly. Drizzle half over the whipped topping. Repeat layers of cake, berries, glaze, whipped topping and frosting. Top with remaining whipped topping. Cover and refrigerate until serving. Garnish with shaved chocolate and reserved strawberries. **Yield:** 24-28 servings.

Brownie Mallow Bars

(Pictured at left and on page 197)

Plan ahead...needs to chill

These yummy bars are a hit wherever I take them. A brownie mix streamlines assembly of the chewy bars, which are topped with mini marshmallows and a decadent layer of chocolate, peanut butter and crisp cereal. —Stacy Butler Lees Summit, Missouri

1 package fudge brownie mix (13-inch x 9-inch pan size)*
1 package (10-1/2 ounces) miniature marshmallows
2 cups (12 ounces) semisweet chocolate chips
1 cup peanut butter
1 tablespoon butter *or* margarine
1-1/2 cups crisp rice cereal

Prepare brownie batter according to package directions for fudge-like brownies. Pour into a greased 13-in. x 9-in. x 2-in. baking pan. Bake at 350° for 28-30 minutes. Top with marshmallows; bake 3 minutes longer (marshmallows will not be completely melted). Cool on a wire rack.

In a saucepan, combine the chocolate chips, peanut

butter and butter. Cook and stir over low heat until smooth. Remove from the heat; stir in cereal. Spread over brownies. Refrigerate for 1-2 hours or until firm before cutting. **Yield:** 2-1/2 dozen.

*Editor's Note: This recipe was tested with Betty Crocker fudge brownie mix.

Grasshopper Pie

(Pictured at left and on page 196)

Plan ahead...needs to freeze

I need only six ingredients to whip up this fluffy, refreshing treat. I usually make two, since we all go back for seconds. —LouCinda Zacharias, Spooner, Wisconsin

2 packages (3 ounces *each*) cream cheese, softened
1 can (14 ounces) sweetened condensed milk
15 drops green food coloring
24 chocolate-covered mint cookies, *divided*
2 cups whipped topping
1 chocolate crumb crust (9 inches)

In a large mixing bowl, beat the cream cheese until fluffy. Gradually beat in milk until smooth. Beat in the food coloring. Coarsely crush 16 cookies; stir into the cream cheese mixture. Fold in whipped topping. Spoon into the crust. Cover and freeze overnight. Remove from the freezer 15 minutes before serving. Garnish with remaining cookies. **Yield:** 8 servings.

Orange Drop Cookies

This recipe comes from a nursing home where I worked, so it makes a big batch. The cookie's delicate citrus flavor was loved by all. —Grace Nevlis, Steubenville, Ohio

1 cup butter (no substitutes), softened
2 cups sugar
3 eggs
1/3 cup orange juice
1 tablespoon grated orange peel
4 cups all-purpose flour
2 teaspoons baking powder
1 teaspoon baking soda

In a mixing bowl, cream butter and sugar. Beat in eggs, orange juice and peel. Combine the flour, baking powder and baking soda; gradually add to creamed mixture and mix well. Drop by teaspoonfuls 2 in. apart onto greased baking sheets. Bake at 350° for 12-14 minutes or until edges begin to brown. Remove to wire racks to cool. **Yield:** about 8 dozen.

No More Messy Measuring

I like to wipe a bit of vegetable oil inside my measuring cup when I'm measuring peanut butter or molasses. This keeps the sticky ingredients from clinging to the cup, making cleanup a snap. —Lynn Hayes St. John, New Brunswick

Chocolate Chip Cookie Tart

(Pictured at right)

Plan ahead...needs to chill

Convenient refrigerated cookie dough is a delightful crust for a creamy peanut butter filling in this yummy dessert. It's so simple to prepare, and everyone loves it.
—*Peg Gerhard, Latrobe, Pennsylvania*

  1 tube (18 ounces) refrigerated chocolate chip cookie dough
  1 package (8 ounces) cream cheese, softened
  2 tablespoons creamy peanut butter
  1 tablespoon butter *or* margarine, softened
  2 cups confectioners' sugar
1/4 cup milk chocolate chips, melted and cooled

Press cookie dough onto the bottom of an ungreased 9-in. springform pan. Bake at 350° for 20-24 minutes or until golden brown. Cool on a wire rack.

In a small mixing bowl, beat cream cheese, peanut butter and butter until smooth. Beat in confectioners' sugar. Remove sides of springform pan; place crust on a serving plate. Spread cream cheese mixture over crust to within 1/2 in. of edge. Drizzle with melted chocolate. Refrigerate for 1 hour or until set. **Yield:** 10-12 servings.

Mint Cake

(Pictured at right)

Plan ahead...needs to chill

My sister and I liked to bake this "cool" mint cake when we were learning to cook...and I still enjoy making it today. —*Sue Gronholz, Beaver Dam, Wisconsin*

 Uses less fat, sugar or salt. Includes Nutritional Analysis and Diabetic Exchanges.

    1 package (18-1/4 ounces) yellow cake mix
  1/2 teaspoon mint extract, *divided*
1-1/2 cups cold milk
    1 package (3.9 ounces) instant chocolate pudding mix
    1 carton (8 ounces) frozen whipped topping, thawed
    4 to 5 drops green food coloring

Prepare cake mix according to package directions. Add 1/4 teaspoon mint extract to batter; beat well. Pour into a greased 13-in. x 9-in. x 2-in. baking pan. Bake at 350° for 25-30 minutes or until a toothpick inserted near the center comes out clean. Cool completely on a wire rack.

In a bowl, whisk milk and pudding mix for 2 minutes. Let stand for 2 minutes or until soft-set. Using the end of a wooden spoon handle, poke 24 holes in cake. Spread pudding evenly over cake. Combine the whipped topping, food coloring and remaining extract; spread over pudding. Cover and refrigerate for at least 2 hours. **Yield:** 15 servings.

Nutritional Analysis: One serving (prepared with fat-free milk, sugar-free pudding and reduced-fat whipped topping) equals 217 calories, 6 g fat (2 g saturated fat), 1 mg cholesterol, 456 mg sodium, 37 g carbohydrate, 1 g fiber, 3 g protein. **Diabetic Exchanges:** 1-1/2 fruit, 1 starch, 1 fat.

Creamy Strawberry Dessert

(Pictured at right)

Plan ahead...needs to chill

The recipe for this fruity gelatin dessert is a summertime staple. It's so convenient to prepare it the day before I want to serve it. Because it's absolutely scrumptious, it disappears really fast. —*Rhonda Butterbaugh*
Weatherford, Oklahoma

1-1/2 cups crushed vanilla wafers (about 40 wafers)
  1/2 cup sugar
  1/2 cup packed brown sugar
  1/2 cup butter *or* margarine, melted
    2 packages (3 ounces *each*) strawberry gelatin
    1 cup boiling water
    1 package (16 ounces) frozen sweetened sliced strawberries, thawed
    1 can (14 ounces) sweetened condensed milk
    1 carton (12 ounces) frozen whipped topping, thawed

In a bowl, combine the wafer crumbs, sugars and butter; press into an ungreased 13-in. x 9-in. x 2-in. dish. Refrigerate for 30 minutes. Meanwhile, in a bowl, dissolve gelatin in boiling water. Stir in strawberries and milk. Refrigerate for 30 minutes or until partially set.

Fold whipped topping into strawberry mixture. Spread over prepared crust. Refrigerate for 2 hours or until set. Cut into squares. **Yield:** 15 servings.

Macadamia Cocoa Cookies

Ready in 1 hour or less

My mother made these soft and chewy chocolate cookies often. They're quick and easy to assemble, and we gobble them up quickly, too! —*Frances Gassen*
Rotonda West, Florida

3/4 cup butter *or* margarine, softened
1/2 cup confectioners' sugar
1/3 cup sugar
  1 teaspoon vanilla extract
  1 cup all-purpose flour
1/2 cup baking cocoa
2/3 cup macadamia nuts *or* pecans, chopped

In a mixing bowl, cream butter and sugars. Add vanilla. Combine flour and cocoa; gradually add to creamed mixture. Stir in nuts. Shape into 1-1/2-in. balls. Place 2 in. apart on ungreased baking sheets. Flatten with a fork. Bake at 350° for 12-14 minutes or until surface cracks. Remove to wire racks to cool. **Yield:** 2-1/2 dozen.

**Chocolate Chip Cookie Tart
Mint Cake
Creamy Strawberry Dessert**

Banana Cheesecake Dessert
Frosted Butter Cookies
Raspberry Brownies a la Mode

Frosted Butter Cookies

(Pictured at left)

These crisp cookies melt in your mouth…even when they're not frosted. —Sharon Pickerd, Sparta, Michigan

2 cups butter (no substitutes), softened
1-3/4 cups sugar
1 egg yolk
4 cups all-purpose flour
Prepared vanilla frosting
Food coloring and decorating sprinkles, optional

In a large mixing bowl, cream butter and sugar. Beat in egg yolk. Gradually add flour. Roll into 1-in. balls. Place 2 in. apart on ungreased baking sheets. Flatten with a glass dipped in flour. Bake at 375° for 8-10 minutes or until lightly browned. Remove to wire racks to cool.

Tint frosting with food coloring if desired. Frost cookies. Decorate as desired. **Yield:** 4-1/2 dozen.

Raspberry Brownies a la Mode

(Pictured at left)

Guests will think you fussed over the raspberry sauce on each fudgy wedge. —Denise Elder, Hanover, Ontario

5 squares (1 ounce *each*) unsweetened chocolate, coarsely chopped
2/3 cup butter (no substitutes)
3 eggs
2-3/4 cups sugar, *divided*
2 teaspoons vanilla extract
1 cup all-purpose flour
1 cup (6 ounces) semisweet chocolate chips
3 cups fresh raspberries
1 tablespoon lemon juice
Vanilla ice cream

In a microwave-safe bowl, combine unsweetened chocolate and butter. Cover; cook on high 1 minute; stir. Microwave 1 minute longer; stir until smooth. Cool 10 minutes.

In a mixing bowl, beat eggs, 1-3/4 cups sugar and vanilla for 3 minutes. Beat in melted chocolate. Add flour; beat until combined. Stir in chocolate chips. Pour into two greased 9-in. pie plates. Bake at 350° for 25-30 minutes or until a toothpick inserted in the center comes out clean. Cool on wire racks.

In a bowl, combine raspberries and remaining sugar; mash gently. Place in a sieve and press with back of a spoon; discard seeds and pulp. Add lemon juice to puree; refrigerate until serving. Cut brownies into wedges; serve with ice cream and sauce. **Yield:** 12-16 servings.

Banana Cheesecake Dessert

(Pictured at left)

Plan ahead…needs to chill

I use convenience items to create this delicious layered crowd-pleaser. —Jessica Simerly, New Castle, Indiana

2 packages (21.4 ounces *each*) strawberry no-bake cheesecake mix
3/4 cup butter *or* margarine, melted

1/4 cup sugar
3 cups cold milk
1 can (8 ounces) crushed pineapple, well drained
3 medium firm bananas, sliced
1/2 cup chocolate ice cream topping, warmed, *divided*
1/2 cup caramel ice cream topping, *divided*
1 carton (8 ounces) frozen whipped topping, thawed
1/3 cup chopped pecans
Maraschino cherries with stems

Set aside filling and strawberry topping packets from cheesecake mixes. Place contents of crust mix packets in a large bowl; add butter and sugar. Press into an ungreased 13-in. x 9-in. x 2-in. dish. In a mixing bowl, combine milk and contents of filling packets. Beat on low speed until blended. Beat on high for 3 minutes or until slightly thickened. Spread over crust. Chill for 1 hour.

Spread contents of strawberry topping packets over cheesecake. Top with pineapple and bananas. Drizzle with 1/4 cup of chocolate topping and 1/4 cup caramel topping. Spread with whipped topping (dish will be full). Refrigerate for 2 hours or until set. Before serving, drizzle with remaining chocolate and caramel toppings. Top with pecans and cherries. **Yield:** 16-20 servings.

Apple Cheese Crisp

Ready in 30 minutes or less

I use the microwave for this crisp, which can also be made in individual dishes. —Annette Norton, Prescott, Ontario

6 cups sliced peeled tart apples
1/3 cup sugar
2 tablespoons all-purpose flour
1 tablespoon lemon juice
1 teaspoon ground cinnamon
1/4 teaspoon salt
FILLING:
4 ounces cream cheese, softened
1/4 cup sugar
1 egg
1 tablespoon all-purpose flour
1 tablespoon milk
TOPPING:
3/4 cup quick-cooking oats
2/3 cup all-purpose flour
1/2 cup packed brown sugar
1 teaspoon ground cinnamon
5 tablespoons cold butter

In a 2-qt. microwave-safe dish, toss the first six ingredients. Microwave, uncovered, on high for 8 minutes, stirring once. In a mixing bowl, beat cream cheese and sugar. Add egg, flour and milk; mix well. Spread over apples.

In a bowl, combine the oats, flour, brown sugar and cinnamon. Cut in butter until crumbly. Sprinkle over filling. Microwave, uncovered, on high for 6 minutes or until apples are tender, rotating dish twice. Serve warm. **Yield:** 6 servings.

Editor's Note: This recipe was tested in an 850-watt microwave.

Jack-o'-Lantern Brownies

(Pictured at right)

Hosting a Halloween party? Use a cookie cutter to easily cut these tempting homemade chocolate brownies into pumpkin shapes, then give them personality with orange, black and green frosting. Our grandchildren thought these were great! —Flo Burtnett, Gage, Oklahoma

1-1/2 cups sugar
3/4 cup butter *or* margarine, melted
1-1/2 teaspoons vanilla extract
3 eggs
3/4 cup all-purpose flour
1/2 cup baking cocoa
1/2 teaspoon baking powder
1/4 teaspoon salt
1 can (16 ounces) vanilla frosting
Orange paste food coloring
Green and black decorating gel

In a large mixing bowl, combine the sugar, butter and vanilla. Beat in the eggs until well blended. Combine the flour, cocoa, baking powder and salt; gradually add to sugar mixture. Line a greased 13-in. x 9-in. x 2-in. baking pan with waxed paper; grease the paper. Spread batter evenly in pan. Bake at 350° for 18-22 minutes or until brownies begin to pull away from sides of pan. Cool on a wire rack.

Run a knife around edge of pan. Invert brownies onto a work surface and remove waxed paper. Cut brownies with a 3-in. pumpkin cookie cutter, leaving at least 1/8 in. between each shape. (Discard scraps or save for another use.) Tint frosting with orange food coloring; frost brownies. Use green gel to create the pumpkin stems and black gel to decorate the faces. **Yield:** about 1 dozen.

Coconut Chocolate Cake

(Pictured at right)

I tuck a coconut filling into this moist chocolate Bundt cake. It's easy to assemble with convenience products, including a boxed cake mix, instant pudding mix and canned frosting. —Renee Schwebach, Dumont, Minnesota

4 eggs
3/4 cup vegetable oil
3/4 cup water
1 teaspoon vanilla extract
1 package (18-1/4 ounces) chocolate cake mix
1 package (3.9 ounces) instant chocolate pudding mix
FILLING:
2 cups flaked coconut
1/3 cup sweetened condensed milk
1/4 teaspoon almond extract
1 can (16 ounces) chocolate frosting

In a mixing bowl, beat the eggs, oil, water and vanilla. Add the cake and pudding mixes; beat for 5 minutes. Pour 3 cups into a greased and floured 10-in. fluted tube pan. Combine the coconut, milk and extract; mix well. Drop by spoonfuls onto batter. Cover with remaining batter.

Bake at 350° for 50-60 minutes or until a toothpick inserted near the center comes out clean. Cool for 10 minutes before removing from pan to a wire rack to cool completely. Frost with chocolate frosting. **Yield:** 12-15 servings.

Spiderweb Cheesecake

(Pictured at right)

Plan ahead...needs to chill

The trick to this tempting treat is pulling a toothpick through rings of melted chocolate to create the web effect. This no-bake cream cheese pie goes together quickly and tastes delicious. It's fun to serve, too, because it never fails to draw comments. —Jan White, Plainview, Nebraska

1 envelope unflavored gelatin
1/4 cup cold water
2 packages (8 ounces *each*) cream cheese, softened
1/2 cup sugar
1/2 cup heavy whipping cream
1 teaspoon vanilla extract
1 chocolate crumb crust (8 *or* 9 inches)
2 tablespoons semisweet chocolate chips
1 tablespoon butter *or* margarine

In a small saucepan, sprinkle gelatin over water; let stand for 1 minute. Heat gelatin; stir until dissolved. Remove from the heat; cool slightly. In a mixing bowl, beat the cream cheese and sugar until smooth. Gradually beat in cream, vanilla and gelatin mixture until smooth. Pour into crust.

In a microwave, melt chocolate chips and butter; stir until smooth. Transfer to a heavy-duty resealable plastic bag; cut a small hole in a corner of bag. Pipe a circle of chocolate in center of cheesecake. Pipe evenly spaced thin concentric circles about 1/2 in. apart over filling. Beginning with the center circle, gently pull a toothpick through circles toward outer edge. Wipe toothpick clean. Repeat to complete web pattern. Cover; refrigerate at least 2 hours before cutting. **Yield:** 6-8 servings.

Why Cakes Sink

There are several factors that may cause a cake to sink in the center after baking. The most important one is oven temperature. An oven that is not hot enough can cause the cake to rise and then sink. Check the accuracy of your oven temperature with an oven thermometer.

Too short of a baking time can cause similar results. Use a toothpick to check the cake's doneness. A toothpick inserted near the center of the cake should come out clean, and the sides of the cake may start pulling away from the pan.

An incorrect proportion of ingredients may cause a cake to sink. Too much sugar, liquid or leavening or too little flour could be the culprit as well.

Other reasons a cake may sink include undermixing the batter, moving the cake during baking or baking in a pan that's too small for the amount of batter.

Coconut Chocolate Cake
Spiderweb Cheesecake
Jack-o'-Lantern Brownies

Peanut Butter Kiss Cookies

(Pictured at left)

Ready in 1 hour or less

These are great for little ones, and they keep adults guessing as to how they can be made with only five ingredients. —*Dee Davis, Sun City, Arizona*

    1 cup peanut butter
    1 cup sugar
    1 egg
    1 teaspoon vanilla extract
    24 milk chocolate kisses

In a mixing bowl, cream peanut butter and sugar. Add the egg and vanilla; beat until blended. Roll into 1-1/4-in. balls. Place 2 in. apart on ungreased baking sheets. Bake at 350° for 10-12 minutes or until tops are slightly cracked. Immediately press one chocolate kiss into the center of each cookie. Cool for 5 minutes before removing from pans to wire racks. **Yield:** 2 dozen.

Editor's Note: This recipe does not contain flour. Reduced-fat or generic brands of peanut butter are not recommended for this recipe.

Christmas Gift Cake

(Pictured at left)

Our home economists had a fun time "wrapping" up this extra-special dessert. Boxed cake mixes make it a snap to prepare while a fast frosting, fruit roll bow and fun candies add festive flair.

    2 packages (18-1/4 ounces *each*) chocolate
        cake mix
    1 cup butter, softened
    1 cup shortening
    8 cups confectioners' sugar
    6 to 8 tablespoons milk
    2 teaspoons vanilla extract
Red gel food coloring
    2 pieces (about 36 inches *each*) cherry
        fruit-by-the-foot fruit roll
Assorted candies

Line two 15-in. x 10-in. x 1-in. baking pans with waxed paper. Prepare one cake mix according to package directions; pour into one prepared pan. Repeat with remaining cake mix. Bake at 350° for 20-25 minutes or until a toothpick inserted near the center comes out clean. Cool for 5 minutes before removing to wire racks to cool completely. Gently peel waxed paper from cakes. Trim tops to level cakes.

In a large mixing bowl, cream butter and shortening. Beat in confectioners' sugar alternately with milk. Beat in vanilla. Remove 2 cups frosting to a bowl; tint red. Referring to diagram above right, cut each cake. (Save remaining cake pieces for another use.)

Place one large cake layer on a 16-in. x 12-in. covered board. Frost top with 1/3 cup white frosting; top with second large layer. Frost top and sides white. Top with one medium cake layer; frost top with 1/3 cup of white frosting. Top with remaining medium layer; frost top and sides red. Top with small cake layer; spread top with white frosting. Top with remaining small layer; frost top and sides white.

For ribbon, cut one fruit roll into a 19-in.-long strip; set aside remaining piece. Starting at the bottom short side of the cake, center fruit roll and drape over each layer, ending at bottom of opposite side. Cut another fruit roll into a 15-in. strip; set aside remaining piece. Repeat draping for the long side.

For bow, cut a 12-in. and a 3-in. strip from a reserved fruit strip. Loop each end of the 12-in. strip toward center; pinch together to seal. With the 3-in. strip, form a circle. Place in center of bow and press to hold. Place on cake. Insert 1-1/4-in. foil balls inside bow loops and a 3/4-in. foil ball inside center loop to hold open. Cut the remaining fruit strip into four 3-1/2-in. strips; cut a "V" in one end of each. Tuck straight ends under base of bow. Decorate cake with candies. Remove foil balls just before serving. **Yield:** 12-14 servings.

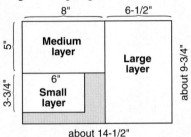

Fig. 1 Cutting diagram for baked cakes

Holiday Sugar Cookies

For make-ahead convenience, freeze the dough up to 3 months, then thaw in the fridge before baking the cookies. —*Katie Koziolek, Hartland, Minnesota*

    2 cups butter (no substitutes), softened
    2 cups sugar
    3 eggs
    1 tablespoon grated lemon peel
    2 teaspoons vanilla extract
    6 cups all-purpose flour
    1 teaspoon baking soda
FROSTING:
    3 cups confectioners' sugar
    3 tablespoons butter, melted
    1/4 cup milk
Green food coloring
Red-hot candies

In a large mixing bowl, cream butter and sugar. Add eggs, one at a time, beating well after each addition. Beat in lemon peel and vanilla. Combine flour and baking soda; gradually add to creamed mixture. Shape into three 10-in. rolls; wrap each in plastic wrap. Refrigerate for 4 hours or until firm.

Unwrap and cut into 1/4-in. slices. Place 2 in. apart on ungreased baking sheets. Bake at 350° for 10-15 minutes or until edges are lightly browned. Remove to wire racks.

In a bowl, combine confectioners' sugar, butter, milk and food coloring; transfer to a resealable plastic bag. Cut a small hole in corner of bag; drizzle over cookies in the shape of a Christmas tree. Place one red-hot at the top of each tree. **Yield:** about 9-1/2 dozen.

Chapter 14

ON-THE-GO GOODIES, such as cookies, bars and snack mixes, are always in demand for bake sales at school, church or other gatherings.

Time-crunched cooks will appreciate the standout specialties in this chapter because they offer make-ahead convenience, travel well and feed a crowd.

Check out these pages when you need sensational snacks that are taste-tested and family approved.

One of these taste-tempting treats is sure to steal the show at your next bake sale—and sell out in minutes!

SOON-TO-SELL-OUT. Kiddie Crunch Mix and Chocolate Caramel Cookies (both recipes on p. 215).

St. Patrick's Day Cupcakes
Chocolate Chip Mint Cookies

20 graham cracker squares, broken in half, *divided*
1 cup graham cracker crumbs (about 14 squares)
3/4 cup sugar
1/2 cup packed brown sugar
1/2 cup butter, cubed
1/3 cup milk
1/2 cup semisweet chocolate chips
1/4 cup creamy peanut butter

Line the bottom of a greased 11-in. x 7-in. x 2-in. dish with half of the graham crackers; set aside. In a 2-qt. microwave-safe bowl, combine the crumbs, sugars, butter and milk. Microwave, uncovered, on high for 1 minute; stir. Microwave on high 2 to 2-1/2 minutes longer. Immediately pour half over crackers in prepared pan. Top with the remaining graham crackers; spread with remaining sugar mixture.

In a small microwave-safe bowl, heat chocolate chips and peanut butter, uncovered, on high for 45-60 seconds or until chips are melted. Stir until smooth and blended. Spread evenly over bars. Cover and refrigerate for 1-1/2 hours before cutting. **Yield:** 20 bars.

St. Patrick's Day Cupcakes

(Pictured above)

On St. Patrick's Day, our family gets together for a special dinner and other festivities. Green is dominant in most of the food we serve, so these cupcakes tinted with pistachio pudding mix are a perfect addition. —Susan Frantz
Pittsburgh, Pennsylvania

1-3/4 cups all-purpose flour
1 package (3.4 ounces) instant pistachio pudding mix
2/3 cup sugar
2-1/2 teaspoons baking powder
1/2 teaspoon salt
3/4 cup miniature semisweet chocolate chips
2 eggs
1-1/2 cups milk
1/2 cup vegetable oil
1 teaspoon vanilla extract
1 cup cream cheese frosting
Green colored sugar *and/or* sprinkles

In a bowl, combine the flour, pudding mix, sugar, baking powder and salt. Stir in chocolate chips. In another bowl, combine the eggs, milk, oil and vanilla. Stir into dry ingredients until well mixed.

Fill foil- or paper-lined muffin cups two-thirds full. Bake at 375° for 18-20 minutes or until a toothpick comes out clean. Cool for 10 minutes before removing from pans to wire racks to cool completely. Frost and decorate as desired. **Yield:** about 1-1/2 dozen.

Peanut Butter Graham Bars

Plan ahead...needs to chill

I rely on my microwave to hurry along assembly of these yummy make-ahead bars. With their pleasant peanut butter and chocolate flavor, they're sure to disappear quickly. —Mina Dyck, Boissevain, Manitoba

Chocolate Chip Mint Cookies

(Pictured above left)

Ready in 1 hour or less

I jazz up a packaged cookie mix, then let Junior Mints melt on top of the warm treats to create an easy frosting. These delicious cookies are requested at every gathering. —Patricia Kaseta, Brockton, Massachusetts

1 package (17-1/2 ounces) chocolate chip cookie mix
3 tablespoons water
1 egg
1/4 cup vegetable oil
1/2 cup semisweet chocolate chips
1/2 cup vanilla *or* white chips
1/2 cup chopped walnuts
1 package (5-1/2 ounces) Junior Mints

In a mixing bowl, combine cookie mix, water, egg and oil; mix well. Stir in the chips and nuts. Drop by tablespoonfuls 2 in. apart onto ungreased baking sheets. Bake at 350° for 7-9 minutes or until edges are golden brown. Remove from the oven; place one candy on each cookie. Remove from pans to wire racks. When candy is melted, spread over cookie. Cool completely. **Yield:** 4 dozen.

Sweet Snack Mix

Ready in 1 hour or less

Friends of ours from Texas gave us this recipe that they call "Texas Trash". We think the white chocolate-coated mixture of crunchy cereal, pretzels and nuts is the best "trash" we've ever had! —Maureen Di Napoli
Hopkinton, Massachusetts

3 cups Honey Grahams cereal
1 cup miniature pretzels
1 cup salted peanuts

1 cup pecan halves
1 package (10 to 12 ounces) vanilla *or* white chips

In a large bowl, combine the cereal, pretzels and nuts; set aside. In a microwave-safe bowl, heat the chips at 70% power for 1 minute; stir. Microwave 30-45 seconds longer or until chips are melted; stir until smooth. Immediately pour over the cereal mixture and toss to coat evenly. Spread on waxed paper-lined baking sheets to cool; break into pieces. **Yield:** about 8-1/2 cups.

Editor's Note: This recipe was tested in an 850-watt microwave.

Banana Nut Cupcakes

Ready in 1 hour or less

These moist cupcakes taste like little loaves of banana bread. I keep ripe bananas in the freezer, so I can whip up these cupcakes whenever I need them for a bake sale or party. I like to top them with cream cheese frosting.
—Vicki Abrahamson, Seabeck, Washington

1/3 cup butter-flavored shortening
2/3 cup sugar
  1 cup mashed ripe bananas (about 3 medium)
  2 eggs
  2 tablespoons milk
  1 tablespoon vanilla extract
1-1/3 cups all-purpose flour
  2 teaspoons baking powder
1/2 teaspoon baking soda
1/4 teaspoon salt
1/4 cup chopped nuts

In a mixing bowl, cream shortening and sugar. Beat in the bananas, eggs, milk and vanilla. Combine the flour, baking powder, baking soda and salt; gradually add to creamed mixture until combined. Stir in nuts.

Fill paper-lined muffin cups two-thirds full. Bake at 350° for 18-20 minutes or until a toothpick comes out clean. Cool for 5 minutes before removing from pans to wire racks. **Yield:** 15 cupcakes.

Gumdrop Cereal Bars

(Pictured at right)

Ready in 1 hour or less

I was planning to make traditional marshmallow treats but didn't have enough Rice Krispies on hand, so I used Corn Pops instead. I added gumdrops for color, and the result was spectacular. —Laura Tryssenaar, Listowel, Ontario

5 cups Corn Pops cereal
1 cup gumdrops
4 cups miniature marshmallows
1/4 cup butter *or* margarine
1 teaspoon vanilla extract

Place cereal and gumdrops in a large bowl; set aside. In a microwave-safe bowl, heat the marshmallows and butter on high for 2 minutes; stir until melted. Stir in vanilla. Pour over cereal mixture and toss to coat. Spread into a greased 9-in. square pan. Cool on a wire

rack. Cut with a buttered knife. **Yield:** 16 bars.

Editor's Note: This recipe was tested in an 850-watt microwave.

Butterscotch Raisin Cookies

(Pictured below)

Ready in 1 hour or less

These chewy oatmeal cookies are full of butterscotch chips and raisins. Every so often I add a half cup of chopped pecans to a batch for something different.
—Victoria Zmarzley-Hahn, Northampton, Pennsylvania

  1 cup butter *or* margarine, softened
3/4 cup packed brown sugar
1/4 cup sugar
  2 eggs
  3 cups quick-cooking oats
1-1/2 cups all-purpose flour
  1 package (3.4 ounces) instant butterscotch pudding mix
  1 teaspoon baking soda
  1 cup raisins
1/2 cup butterscotch chips

In a large mixing bowl, cream butter and sugars. Add eggs; beat well. Combine the oats, flour, dry pudding mix and baking soda; gradually add to the creamed mixture. Stir in the raisins and butterscotch chips (dough will be stiff).

Drop by tablespoonfuls 2 in. apart onto ungreased baking sheets. Bake at 375° for 9-11 minutes or until lightly browned. Remove to wire racks to cool. **Yield:** 3-1/2 dozen.

Gumdrop Cereal Bars
Butterscotch Raisin Cookies

Frosted Cake Brownies

(Pictured below)

I dress up a boxed mix to create these moist brownies with from-scratch taste. This recipe is so good, it has to be shared. It uses about half of a can of prepared frosting. Save the rest, because you'll make them again. —Mary Fox Forest City, Iowa

    1 package fudge brownie mix (13-inch
      x 9-inch pan size)
    1 cup (8 ounces) sour cream
    1 cup milk chocolate chips
  1/2 cup chopped walnuts
    1 cup milk chocolate frosting

Prepare brownie mix according to package directions. Fold the sour cream, chocolate chips and walnuts into batter. Pour into a greased 13-in. x 9-in. x 2-in. baking pan. Bake at 350° for 30-35 minutes or until a toothpick inserted near the center comes out clean. Cool completely on a wire rack. Frost. Cut into bars. **Yield:** 2-1/2 dozen.

Smiling Sugar Cookies

(Pictured below)

These cute cookie pops are a big hit at bake sales. I sell them for $1 a piece and they disappear! The bright and cheery faces catch the kids' eyes, making them sure-fire sellers. —Brenda Bawdon, Alpena, South Dakota

  1/2 cup butter (no substitutes), softened
  1/2 cup sugar
  1/2 cup packed brown sugar
    1 egg
  1/3 cup milk
    2 teaspoons vanilla extract

    3 cups all-purpose flour
    2 teaspoons cream of tartar
    1 teaspoon baking soda
  1/2 teaspoon salt
About 24 Popsicle sticks
    1 cup vanilla frosting
Red, blue and green paste food coloring
Assorted small candies

In a large mixing bowl, cream the butter and sugars. Beat in the egg, milk and vanilla. Combine the flour, cream of tartar, baking soda and salt; gradually add to creamed mixture. Roll the dough into 1-1/2-in. balls; insert a wooden stick in the center of each.

Place 2 in. apart on lightly greased baking sheets; flatten slightly. Bake at 375° for 8-10 minutes or until lightly browned. Remove to wire racks to cool.

Divide frosting between three bowls; tint one red, one blue and one green. Place each color of frosting in a resealable plastic bag; cut a small hole in a corner of bag. Pipe hair and mouths onto cookies; use a dab of frosting to attach small candies for noses and eyes. Let dry for at least 30 minutes. **Yield:** about 2 dozen.

Peanutty Chocolate Cookies

Ready in 1 hour or less

I have never taken these cookies anywhere without a request for the recipe. For an attractive look, I reserve some chocolate and nuts to press into each cookie before baking. If I make them for church or school, I usually double the batch. —Brenda Jackson, Garden City, Kansas

    1 cup chunky peanut butter
    2 tablespoons vegetable oil
    2 eggs
    1 package fudge brownie mix (13-inch
      x 9-inch pan size)
  1/2 cup water
   12 ounces milk chocolate candy bars, coarsely
      chopped
  1/2 cup unsalted peanuts

In a large mixing bowl, cream peanut butter and oil. Beat in eggs just until combined. Stir in brownie mix and water. Fold in the chopped candy bars and peanuts. Drop by heaping tablespoonfuls 2 in. apart onto greased baking sheets. Bake at 350° for 12-14 minutes or until lightly browned. Remove to wire racks to cool. **Yield:** about 3-1/2 dozen.

Pecan Coconut Clusters

Crisp rice cereal and chopped pecans add crunch to these no-bake bites. This recipe is quick to fix, and the results are truly rich. —Norene Wright, Manilla, Indiana

    1 cup chopped pecans
    1 cup crisp rice cereal
  3/4 cup flaked coconut
    1 package (10 to 12 ounces) vanilla *or* white
      chips, melted

Place pecans in a 9-in. microwave-safe pie plate. Microwave, uncovered, on high for 3-4 minutes or until

Smiling Sugar Cookies
Frosted Cake Brownies

pecans are toasted, stirring every 45 seconds. In a bowl, combine the pecans, cereal and coconut. Add melted chips; mix well. Drop by rounded teaspoonfuls onto waxed paper-lined baking sheets. Let stand until set. **Yield:** about 3-1/2 dozen.

Editor's Note: This recipe was tested in an 850-watt microwave.

Kiddie Crunch Mix

(Pictured above and on page 210)

Ready in 15 minutes or less

This no-bake snack mix is a real treat for kids, and you can easily increase the amount to fit your needs. Place it in individual plastic bags or pour some into colored ice cream cones and cover with plastic wrap for a fun presentation. —Kara De la Vega, Suisun City, California

- 1 cup animal crackers
- 1 cup miniature teddy bear-shaped chocolate graham crackers
- 1 cup miniature pretzels
- 1 cup salted peanuts
- 1 cup M&M's
- 1 cup chocolate- *or* yogurt-covered raisins

In a bowl, combine all ingredients; mix well. Store in an airtight container. **Yield:** 6 cups.

Chocolate Caramel Cookies

(Pictured above and on page 211)

I rely on a convenient cake mix and chocolate-covered caramels to fix these cookies. They are very quick to prepare, yet taste so good when served fresh from the oven. People are surprised to bite into this crisp cookie and find a gooey caramel center. —Melanie Steele, Plano, Texas

- 1 package (18-1/4 ounces) devil's food cake mix

- 1 egg
- 1/4 cup water
- 3 tablespoons vegetable oil
- 38 Rolo candies
- Chopped hazelnuts

In a bowl, combine the cake mix, egg, water and oil; mix well. Roll rounded teaspoonfuls of dough into balls. Press a candy into each; reshape balls. Dip tops in hazelnuts. Place on ungreased baking sheets. Bake at 350° for 8-10 minutes or until tops are cracked. Cool for 2 minutes before removing from pans to wire racks. **Yield:** 3 dozen.

Editor's Note: If the dough is sticky, spray hands lightly with nonstick cooking spray before rolling into balls.

Chewy Walnut Bars

These rich nutty bars are so tasty, we doubled the recipe to serve a crowd! Our family has been making these yummy treats for years. We especially like to eat them with a dish of vanilla ice cream. —Tori Dunton Acme, Pennsylvania

- 2 eggs
- 2 cups packed brown sugar
- 2 teaspoons vanilla extract
- 1 cup all-purpose flour
- 1/2 teaspoon baking soda
- 1/2 teaspoon salt
- 1 cup chopped walnuts

In a mixing bowl, beat the eggs, brown sugar and vanilla. Combine the flour, baking soda and salt; add to the egg mixture. Stir in walnuts. Pour into a greased 13-in. x 9-in. x 2-in. baking pan. Bake at 350° for 20-25 minutes or until bars pull away from edges of the pan. Cool on a wire rack. **Yield:** 3 dozen.

Editor's Note: This recipe contains no butter or shortening.

Santa Claus Cookies
Chocolate Chip Brownies

2 tubes (18 ounces *each*) refrigerated
  chocolate chip cookie dough*
3/4 cup flaked coconut, *divided*
1 package brownie mix (8-inch square pan size)
1/2 cup semisweet chocolate chips
1/2 cup chopped pecans

Press cookie dough into a greased 13-in. x 9-in. x 2-in. baking pan. Sprinkle with 1/2 cup coconut and press firmly into dough.

Prepare brownie mix according to package directions; spread batter over coconut. Sprinkle with remaining coconut; top with chocolate chips and pecans. Bake at 350° for 45-50 minutes or until a toothpick inserted near the center comes out clean. Cool on a wire rack. **Yield:** 2 dozen.

*Editor's Note: If desired, 4-1/2 cups of your favorite chocolate chip cookie dough can be substituted for the refrigerated dough.

PB&J Bars

Ready in 1 hour or less

Big and little kids alike will love these four-ingredient bars that offer a cookie crust, a layer of jam and a crunchy peanut butter and granola topping. The delicious treats are also great for picnics or for packing into bag lunches.
—*Mitzi Sentiff, Alexandria, Virginia*

1 package (18 ounces) refrigerated sugar
  cookie dough, *divided*
2/3 cup strawberry jam
3/4 cup granola cereal without raisins
3/4 cup peanut butter chips

Line a 9-in. square baking pan with foil and grease the foil. Press two-thirds of the cookie dough into prepared pan. Spread jam over dough to within 1/4 in. of edges. In a mixing bowl, beat the granola, peanut butter chips and remaining dough until blended. Crumble over jam.

Bake at 375° for 25-30 minutes or until golden brown. Cool on a wire rack. Using foil, lift out of pan. Cut into bars and remove from foil. **Yield:** 9-12 servings.

Santa Claus Cookies

(Pictured above)

Ready in 1 hour or less

I need just six ingredients to create these cute Kris Kringle confections. Store-bought peanut butter sandwich cookies turn jolly with white chocolate, colored sugar, mini chips and red-hots. —*Mary Kaufenberg, Shakopee, Minnesota*

2 packages (6 ounces *each*) white baking
  chocolate, chopped
1 package (1 pound) Nutter Butter sandwich
  cookies
Red colored sugar
32 vanilla *or* white chips
64 miniature semisweet chocolate chips
32 red-hot candies

In a heavy saucepan over low heat, melt white chocolate, stirring occasionally. Dip one end of each cookie into melted chocolate. Place on wire racks. For Santa's hat, sprinkle red sugar on top part of chocolate. Press one vanilla chip off-center on hat for pom-pom; let stand until set.

Dip other end of each cookie into melted chocolate for beard, leaving center of cookie uncovered. Place on wire racks. With a dab of melted chocolate, attach semisweet chips for eyes and a red-hot for nose. Place on waxed paper until chocolate sets. **Yield:** 32 cookies.

Chocolate Chip Brownies

(Pictured above)

We call these "magic bars" because they're fast and easy to make, and they disappear quickly when finished—just like magic! —*Beverly Wilkerson, Crocker, Missouri*

Cocoa Chocolate Chip Cookies

Crisp outside but chewy inside, these sweet sensations will disappear in a hurry. I home-school our six children. The kids always have friends over, so I like to keep snacks on hand. They love these cookies. —*Mary Dudek
Alliance, Ohio*

2/3 cup butter *or* margarine, softened
1/2 cup vegetable oil
1 cup sugar
1 cup packed brown sugar
1 package (3.9 ounces) instant chocolate
  pudding mix
2 eggs
3 tablespoons water
3 cups all-purpose flour
1 teaspoon baking soda
1 teaspoon salt

1 package (12 ounces) miniature semisweet chocolate chips

In a large mixing bowl, beat the butter, oil and sugars until light and fluffy. Add pudding mix, eggs and water; mix well. Combine the flour, baking soda and salt; gradually add to the chocolate mixture (dough will be stiff). Stir in the chocolate chips.

Roll into 1-in. balls. Place 2 in. apart on ungreased baking sheets. Bake at 350° for 9-11 minutes or until set and edges are firm. Cool for 2 minutes before removing to wire racks. **Yield:** about 8-1/2 dozen.

Chocolate Lemon Cream Bars

A jazzed-up chocolate cake mix forms the layers that sandwich a lemony cream cheese center in these bars. I took these treats to the office, and they were a big hit with my co-workers. —Renee Schwebach, Dumont, Minnesota

1 package (18-1/4 ounces) devil's food cake mix
1/2 cup butter *or* margarine, softened
1 egg
1/2 cup chopped walnuts
FILLING:
1 package (8 ounces) cream cheese, softened
1 can (14 ounces) sweetened condensed milk
1 egg
3 tablespoons lemon juice
2 to 3 teaspoons grated lemon peel

In a large mixing bowl, beat the cake mix, butter and egg on low speed until combined. Stir in walnuts. Set aside 1 cup for topping. Press the remaining mixture into a greased 13-in. x 9-in. x 2-in. baking pan. Bake at 350° for 8-10 minutes or until set. Cool for 5 minutes.

In a mixing bowl, beat cream cheese until smooth. Add milk, egg, lemon juice and peel; mix well. Pour over the crust. Crumble reserved cake mixture over the top. Bake for 18-22 minutes or until set. Cool completely before cutting. Store in the refrigerator. **Yield:** 4 dozen.

Pecan Pie Bars

Ready in 1 hour or less

For a time-saving take on pecan pie, I turn to convenient crescent roll dough. Served with coffee, the thin golden squares are ideal as a sweet breakfast treat or a rich after-dinner dessert. —Shirley Conklin
Salsbury Cove, Maine

1 tube (8 ounces) refrigerated crescent rolls
1 egg
1/2 cup sugar
1/2 cup chopped pecans
1/2 cup corn syrup
1 tablespoon butter *or* margarine, melted
1/2 teaspoon milk

Unroll the crescent dough into a rectangle; press onto the bottom and 1/2 in. up the sides of a greased 13-in. x 9-in. x 2-in. baking pan. Seal the seams and perfora-

tions. Bake at 375° for 5 minutes.

Meanwhile, in a bowl, combine the remaining ingredients. Pour over the crust. Bake for 16-20 minutes or until golden brown and bubbly. Cool completely before cutting. **Yield:** 2 dozen.

Cereal Cookie Bars

(Pictured below)

Ready in 1 hour or less

These chewy crowd-pleasers feature all sorts of goodies, including chocolate chips, raisins, coconut and candy-coated baking bits. For a more colorful look, press the baking bits on top of the bars instead of stirring them into the cereal mixture. —Connie Craig, Lakewood, Washington

9 cups crisp rice cereal
6-1/2 cups quick-cooking oats
1 cup cornflakes
1 cup flaked coconut
2 packages (one 16 ounces, one 10-1/2 ounces) miniature marshmallows
1 cup butter *or* margarine, cubed
1/2 cup honey
1/2 cup chocolate chips
1/2 cup raisins
1/2 cup M&M miniature baking bits

In a large bowl, combine the cereal, oats, cornflakes and coconut; set aside. In a large saucepan, cook and stir the marshmallows and butter over low heat until melted and smooth. Stir in honey. Pour over cereal mixture; stir until coated. Cool for 5 minutes.

Stir in chocolate chips, raisins and baking bits. Press into two greased 15-in. x 10-in. x 1-in. pans. Cool for 30 minutes before cutting. **Yield:** 6 dozen.

Cereal Cookie Bars

Chapter 15

⊕ *Fast, Delicious...and Nutritious*

LOOKING for fast-to-fix dishes that fit today's healthy lifestyle? Then you've turned to the right chapter. If you're counting calories or trying to reduce fat, sugar or salt in your diet (and doing all this while keeping one eye on the clock), the lighter fare featured here is ideal.

These rapid recipes have less fat, calories, sugar and salt but still have full flavor. Each recipe includes a Nutritional Analysis and Diabetic Exchanges.

Anyone on a special diet—and even those who aren't—will enjoy these delicious and nutritious dishes.

(All the quick good-for-you foods in this book are flagged with a red checkmark in the indexes beginning on page 332.)

SLIMMED-DOWN DELICIOUS. Clockwise from top right: Cream Cheese Swirl Brownies, Light Chicken Cordon Bleu, Three-Bean Soup and Pork with Pineapple Salsa (all recipes on pp. 226-227).

219

Balsamic Salad Dressing
Spinach Tomato Linguine

substitute penne pasta and add cooked chicken for a heartier main meal. Using garlic-flavored feta cheese is a great touch. —Rosemary Averkamp, Genoa, Wisconsin

    8 ounces uncooked linguine
    3 cups chopped seeded plum tomatoes
    1 package (10 ounces) frozen chopped
        spinach, thawed and squeezed dry
1/2 cup chopped green onions
    1 tablespoon olive or canola oil
1/4 teaspoon salt
1/4 teaspoon garlic salt
    4 ounces crumbled feta cheese

Cook linguine according to package directions. Meanwhile, in a large nonstick skillet, saute the tomatoes, spinach and onions in oil until tomatoes are softened. Sprinkle with salt and garlic salt. Reduce heat. Stir in feta; heat until warmed. Drain linguine; toss with tomato mixture. Serve immediately. **Yield:** 4 servings.
   Nutritional Analysis: One serving (1 cup) equals 357 calories, 11 g fat (5 g saturated fat), 25 mg cholesterol, 646 mg sodium, 52 g carbohydrate, 6 g fiber, 15 g protein. **Diabetic Exchanges:** 2-1/2 starch, 2 vegetable, 1 lean meat, 1 fat.

Tender Chicken Nuggets

Ready in 30 minutes or less

Four ingredients are all it takes to create these moist golden bites that are healthier than fast food. I serve them with ranch salad dressing and barbecue sauce for dipping.

1/2 cup seasoned bread crumbs
    2 tablespoons grated Parmesan cheese
    1 egg white
    1 pound boneless skinless chicken breasts, cut
        into 1-inch cubes

In a large resealable plastic bag, combine the bread crumbs and Parmesan cheese. In a shallow bowl, beat the egg white. Dip chicken pieces in egg white, then place in bag and shake to coat. Place in a 15-in. x 10-in. x 1-in. baking pan coated with nonstick cooking spray. Bake, uncovered, at 400° for 12-15 minutes or until chicken is no longer pink, turning once. **Yield:** 4 servings.
   Nutritional Analysis: One serving (6 nuggets) equals 194 calories, 3 g fat (1 g saturated fat), 68 mg cholesterol, 250 mg sodium, 10 g carbohydrate, trace fiber, 30 g protein. **Diabetic Exchanges:** 3 lean meat, 1/2 starch.

Turkey Roll-Ups

Ready in 15 minutes or less

Whether served whole for lunch or cut into bite-size appetizers, these light wraps are always a hit. We prefer this blend of herbs, but feel free to use any combination you'd like. —Paula Alf, Cincinnati, Ohio

    1 package (8 ounces) fat-free cream cheese
1/2 cup reduced-fat mayonnaise
1/4 teaspoon dried basil

 All recipes in this chapter use less fat, sugar or salt and include Nutritional Analysis and Diabetic Exchanges.

Balsamic Salad Dressing

(Pictured above)

Ready in 15 minutes or less

This tomato juice-based dressing offers a nice combination of tangy and tart with only a trace of fat. We like our salad dressing tart, but you may want to add a little more sugar if that suits your family's tastes better.
—Alice Coate, Bryan, Texas

3/4 cup tomato juice
1/4 cup balsamic or red wine vinegar
    1 envelope Italian salad dressing mix
    2 teaspoons sugar

In a jar with a tight-fitting lid, combine all ingredients; shake well. Store in the refrigerator. **Yield:** 1 cup.
   Nutritional Analysis: One serving (2 tablespoons) equals 18 calories, trace fat (0 saturated fat), 0 cholesterol, 397 mg sodium, 4 g carbohydrate, trace fiber, trace protein. **Diabetic Exchange:** Free food.

Spinach Tomato Linguine

(Pictured above)

Ready in 30 minutes or less

Chock-full of garden freshness, this colorful toss makes an excellent side dish or meatless entree. Sometimes I

1/4 teaspoon dried oregano
1/4 teaspoon dill weed
1/4 teaspoon garlic powder
10 flour tortillas (7 inches), warmed
1 medium onion, chopped
10 slices deli turkey breast (1 ounce *each*)
Shredded lettuce

In a small mixing bowl, combine the first six ingredients; beat until smooth. Spread over the tortillas. Sprinkle with onion; top with turkey and lettuce. Roll up tightly jelly-roll style; serve immediately. **Yield:** 10 servings.

Nutritional Analysis: One serving equals 259 calories, 9 g fat (2 g saturated fat), 17 mg cholesterol, 701 mg sodium, 33 g carbohydrate, 2 g fiber, 13 g protein. **Diabetic Exchanges:** 2 starch, 1 lean meat, 1 fat.

Apricot Oat Muffins

Ready in 1 hour or less

Not only are these muffins quick and easy, but they're good for you, too. They're nicely seasoned with pumpkin pie spice and dotted with bits of dried apricots and chopped walnuts. —Roland Long, Silver Creek, Washington

2 cups all-purpose flour
1/2 cup quick-cooking oats
1/2 cup packed dark brown sugar
1/4 cup sugar
3 teaspoons baking powder
1-1/2 to 2 teaspoons pumpkin pie spice
1/2 teaspoon salt
1-1/2 cups fat-free milk
1/3 cup canola oil
1/4 cup egg substitute
3/4 cup chopped dried apricots
1/3 cup chopped walnuts

In a bowl, combine the flour, oats, sugars, baking powder, pumpkin pie spice and salt. In another bowl, combine milk, oil and egg substitute until blended; stir into dry ingredients just until blended (batter will be thin). Fold in the apricots and walnuts.

Fill greased or paper-lined muffin cups two-thirds full. Bake at 350° for 20-25 minutes or until a toothpick comes out clean. Cool for 5 minutes before removing from pans to wire racks. **Yield:** 15 muffins.

Nutritional Analysis: One muffin equals 206 calories, 7 g fat (1 g saturated fat), 1 mg cholesterol, 149 mg sodium, 32 g carbohydrate, 1 g fiber, 4 g protein. **Diabetic Exchanges:** 2 starch, 1 fat.

No-Bake Strawberry Dessert

(Pictured at right)

Plan ahead...needs to chill

Convenience items such as store-bought angel food cake, frozen strawberries and instant pudding mix make preparing this refrigerated delight as simple as can be. I whip up this refreshing dessert all year-round. It's particularly attractive when served in a glass dish. —Sherri Daniels Clark, South Dakota

1 loaf (10-1/2 ounces) angel food cake, cut into 1-inch cubes
2 packages (.3 ounce *each*) sugar-free strawberry gelatin
2 cups boiling water
1 package (20 ounces) frozen unsweetened whole strawberries, thawed
2 cups cold 1% milk
1 package (1 ounce) sugar-free instant vanilla pudding mix
1 carton (8 ounces) frozen reduced-fat whipped topping, thawed

Arrange cake cubes in a single layer in a 13-in. x 9-in. x 2-in. dish. In a bowl, dissolve gelatin in boiling water; stir in strawberries. Pour over cake and gently press cake down. Refrigerate until set, about 1 hour.

In a bowl, whisk milk and pudding mix for 2 minutes or until slightly thickened. Spoon over gelatin layer. Spread with whipped topping. Refrigerate until serving. **Yield:** 20 servings.

Nutritional Analysis: One serving equals 92 calories, 2 g fat (1 g saturated fat), 2 mg cholesterol, 172 mg sodium, 16 g carbohydrate, 1 g fiber, 2 g protein. **Diabetic Exchange:** 1 starch.

Salad Saver

I work full-time and often bring a salad for lunch. Before I put my salad fixings into a plastic bowl, I pour dressing in the bottom of the bowl. Then I add my lettuce and other veggies and pop on the lid.

At lunch, I mix up a fresh salad without the lettuce being wilted from the dressing. Plus, I only use one bowl, so I don't have to wash out a small container that held the dressing. This saves cleanup time.

—*Kathy Witowski, Hanover Park, Illinois*

No-Bake Strawberry Dessert

Asparagus Chicken Fajitas

(Pictured below)

Plan ahead...needs to marinate

When my children visited their aunt, she served these colorful fajitas. They were so impressed, they brought the recipe home to me. It's a great way to get them to eat vegetables. —Marlene Mohr, Cincinnati, Ohio

- 1 pound boneless skinless chicken breasts, cut into strips
- 3/4 cup fat-free Italian salad dressing
- 1 tablespoon canola *or* vegetable oil
- 1 pound fresh asparagus, trimmed and cut into 2-inch pieces
- 1 medium sweet red pepper, julienned
- 1 medium sweet yellow pepper, julienned
- 1/2 cup fresh *or* frozen corn
- 1/4 cup diced onion
- 2 tablespoons lemon juice
- 1/2 teaspoon garlic salt
- 1/8 teaspoon pepper
- 12 flour tortillas (7 inches), warmed

Place chicken in a large resealable plastic bag; add salad dressing. Seal bag and turn to coat; refrigerate for 4 hours, turning several times.

Drain and discard marinade. In a large nonstick skillet, saute chicken in oil for 3 minutes. Add the asparagus, peppers, corn and onion. Cook and stir for 7 minutes or until the chicken juices run clear and vegetables are crisp-tender. Stir in the lemon juice, garlic salt and pepper. Spoon 1/2 cup on each tortilla; fold in sides. **Yield:** 6 servings.

Nutritional Analysis: One serving (2 fajitas) equals 350 calories, 6 g fat (1 g saturated fat), 45 mg cholesterol, 715 mg sodium, 46 g carbohydrate, 5 g fiber, 29 g protein. **Diabetic Exchanges:** 3 starch, 2 lean meat.

Spanish Rice with Bacon

(Pictured below left)

Ready in 45 minutes or less

I add bacon to this zippy rice dish for a flavorful change of pace. Being big fans of Mexican food, my family loves this recipe. —David Bias, Siloam Springs, Arkansas

- 6 bacon strips, diced
- 1 tablespoon canola *or* vegetable oil
- 1 medium onion, chopped
- 1 cup uncooked long grain rice
- 1-3/4 cups water
- 2 large tomatoes, chopped
- 1 medium green pepper, chopped
- 2 jalapeno peppers, seeded and chopped*
- 1 to 1-1/2 teaspoons chili powder
- 1/2 teaspoon salt

In a large skillet, cook bacon over medium heat until crisp. Remove to paper towels. Add oil to the drippings; saute onion for 3 minutes. Add rice; stir until golden brown, about 5 minutes. Stir in the remaining ingredients. Bring to a boil. Reduce heat; cover and simmer for 30 minutes or until rice is tender. Sprinkle with bacon. **Yield:** 6 servings.

Nutritional Analysis: One serving (3/4 cup) equals 287 calories, 12 g fat (4 g saturated fat), 16 mg cholesterol, 514 mg sodium, 34 g carbohydrate, 2 g fiber, 10 g protein. **Diabetic Exchanges:** 2 starch, 2 fat, 1 vegetable.

***Editor's Note:** When cutting or seeding hot peppers, use rubber or plastic gloves to protect your hands. Avoid touching your face.

Lo-Cal Cheese Dip

Plan ahead...needs to chill

Working in a local deli and retail outlet that sells herbs and spices gives me a chance to create many recipes. Cottage cheese is the main ingredient in this creamy dip that's terrific with raw veggies or crackers. —Joyce Montague Wichita, Kansas

- 1 carton (16 ounces) 2% cottage cheese
- 1 tablespoon reduced-sodium beef bouillon granules
- 1 tablespoon dried minced onion
- 2 teaspoons lemon juice
- Raw vegetables *or* crackers

In a blender, combine cottage cheese, bouillon, onion and lemon juice; cover and process until smooth. Cover and chill for at least 1 hour. Serve with vegetables or crackers. **Yield:** 1-3/4 cups.

Nutritional Analysis: One serving (1/4 cup dip)

Spanish Rice with Bacon
Asparagus Chicken Fajitas

equals 68 calories, 2 g fat (1 g saturated fat), 6 mg cholesterol, 291 mg sodium, 3 g carbohydrate, trace fiber, 9 g protein. **Diabetic Exchange:** 1 lean meat.

Ham Noodle Casserole

Ready in 45 minutes or less

My mom used to make the original version of this mild curry casserole, which I loved. It didn't fit my healthier eating habits until I made a few changes. Now our whole family can enjoy it without the guilt. —Sheri Switzer Crawfordsville, Indiana

  6 cups uncooked no-yolk medium noodles
  1 can (10-3/4 ounces) reduced-fat reduced-sodium condensed cream of celery soup, undiluted
  1 cup cubed fully cooked lean ham
2/3 cup cubed reduced-fat process American cheese
1/2 cup fat-free milk
1/4 cup thinly sliced green onions
1/2 teaspoon curry powder

Cook noodles according to package directions; drain and place in a large bowl. Stir in the remaining ingredients. Transfer to a 2-1/2-qt. baking dish coated with nonstick cooking spray. Cover and bake at 375° for 20-30 minutes or until heated through. **Yield:** 6 servings.

Nutritional Analysis: One serving (1 cup) equals 241 calories, 4 g fat (2 g saturated fat), 20 mg cholesterol, 725 mg sodium, 35 g carbohydrate, 3 g fiber, 15 g protein. **Diabetic Exchanges:** 2-1/2 starch, 1 lean meat.

Warm Dijon Potato Salad

Ready in 45 minutes or less

This satisfying potato salad has so much wonderful taste, no one will ever guess it's light. The Dijon mustard really comes through. —LaVerne Kaeppel Vero Beach, Florida

  5 medium red potatoes (about 2 pounds)
1/4 cup reduced-fat mayonnaise
  1 tablespoon grated Parmesan cheese
  1 green onion, sliced
  2 teaspoons cider vinegar
  1 teaspoon Dijon mustard
1/2 teaspoon salt
1/4 teaspoon pepper

Place potatoes in a large saucepan and cover with water. Bring to a boil. Reduce heat; cover and simmer for 20 minutes or until tender.

In a large bowl, combine the remaining ingredients. Drain potatoes and cut into cubes; add to the mayonnaise mixture and gently toss to coat. Serve immediately. **Yield:** 8 servings.

Nutritional Analysis: One serving (3/4 cup) equals 119 calories, 3 g fat (1 g saturated fat), 3 mg cholesterol, 240 mg sodium, 21 g carbohydrate, 2 g fiber, 3 g protein. **Diabetic Exchanges:** 1-1/2 starch, 1/2 fat.

Tangy Lemonade Pie

Tangy Lemonade Pie

(Pictured above)

Plan ahead...needs to chill

I really enjoy lemon pie, but I have to watch my sugar intake. So I experimented with sugar-free gelatin and lemonade mix to come up with this light pie that's absolutely delicious. —Carol Anderson West Chicago, Illinois

  1 package (.3 ounce) sugar-free lemon gelatin
  1 package (8 ounces) reduced-fat cream cheese, cubed
1-3/4 teaspoons sugar-free lemonade drink mix*
  1 reduced-fat graham cracker crust (8 inches)
  6 tablespoons reduced-fat whipped topping

Prepare gelatin according to package directions. Refrigerate until almost set. Transfer to a blender or food processor. Add the cream cheese and lemonade mix; cover and process until smooth. Pour into the crust. Refrigerate overnight. Serve with whipped topping. **Yield:** 6 servings.

Nutritional Analysis: One serving (1 piece with 1 tablespoon whipped topping) equals 243 calories, 11 g fat (6 g saturated fat), 21 mg cholesterol, 273 mg sodium, 26 g carbohydrate, 0 fiber, 6 g protein. **Diabetic Exchanges:** 2 fat, 1 fat-free milk, 1 fruit.

*Editor's Note:** This recipe was tested with Crystal Light drink mix.

Tender Turkey Meatballs
Cauliflower Salad

Nutritional Analysis: One serving (5 meatballs with sauce and 1 cup spaghetti) equals 312 calories, 7 g fat (2 g saturated fat), 60 mg cholesterol, 1,047 mg sodium, 40 g carbohydrate, 5 g fiber, 22 g protein. **Diabetic Exchanges:** 2-1/2 starch, 2 lean meat.

Cauliflower Salad

(Pictured at left)

Plan ahead...needs to chill

Reduced-fat Italian salad dressing is the minute-saving marinade in this cold vegetable medley. I've made this easy salad for the past 40 years and it's still a family favorite. You can also use fresh green beans instead of frozen. —Dorothy Acker, Fort Wayne, Indiana

    1 medium head cauliflower, broken into florets
      and sliced
    1 package (16 ounces) frozen French-style
      green beans, thawed
1/2 pound fresh mushrooms, sliced
    1 large red onion, sliced and separated into
      rings
    1 teaspoon dried basil
    1 teaspoon dried oregano
    1 bottle (8 ounces) reduced-fat Italian salad
      dressing

In a large bowl, combine the first six ingredients. Add dressing and toss to coat. Cover and refrigerate for at least 2 hours before serving. **Yield:** 13 servings.
Nutritional Analysis: One serving (3/4 cup) equals 58 calories, 3 g fat (trace saturated fat), trace cholesterol, 144 mg sodium, 7 g carbohydrate, 2 g fiber, 2 g protein. **Diabetic Exchanges:** 1 vegetable, 1/2 fat.

Melon with Ice Cream

Ready in 15 minutes or less

Three items are all you need for this cool creation. It's particularly yummy on hot days. No granola in the pantry? Top off individual servings with chopped nuts or toasted coconut. —Tina Meekins, Port Orchard, Washington

    1 medium cantaloupe, cut into 4 wedges
    1 pint fat-free sugar-free vanilla ice cream
    4 tablespoons reduced-fat granola cereal
      without raisins

Place cantaloupe wedges in individual bowls. Top each with a scoop of ice cream and 1 tablespoon granola. Serve immediately. **Yield:** 4 servings.
Nutritional Analysis: One serving equals 156 calories, trace fat (trace saturated fat), 0 cholesterol, 98 mg sodium, 34 g carbohydrate, 1 g fiber, 6 g protein. **Diabetic Exchanges:** 2 fruit, 1/2 fat-free milk.

Chicken Cacciatore Skillet

Ready in 1 hour or less

I'm always experimenting with different ways to fix chicken. This was an instant success the first time I tried it. —Norma Lavanchy, Douglas, Arizona

Tender Turkey Meatballs

(Pictured above)

Ready in 1 hour or less

I changed one of my meatball recipes to come up with this healthier version. Whether they're offered as appetizers, packed cold for picnics or served over spaghetti at dinner, these moist marjoram-seasoned meatballs are well-received. —Jane Thoma, Monroe, Michigan

1/2 cup chopped onion
1/4 cup egg substitute
1/4 cup toasted wheat germ
1/4 cup chopped green pepper
1/4 cup ketchup
    1 teaspoon chili powder
1/2 teaspoon dried marjoram
1/2 teaspoon pepper
    1 pound lean ground turkey
    1 package (12 ounces) spaghetti
    5 cups meatless spaghetti sauce

In a bowl, combine the first eight ingredients. Crumble turkey over mixture and mix well. Shape into 30 balls, about 1 in. each. Place in a 15-in. x 10-in. x 1-in. baking pan coated with nonstick cooking spray. Bake at 400° for 13-16 minutes or until juices run clear.
    Meanwhile, cook spaghetti according to package directions. Transfer meatballs to a large saucepan; add spaghetti sauce. Heat through. Drain spaghetti; top with meatballs and sauce. **Yield:** 6 servings.

1/2 pound boneless skinless chicken breasts, cut into 1-inch cubes
1/4 cup chopped onion
2 garlic cloves, minced
1-1/2 cups low-sodium chicken broth, *divided*
3/4 cup chopped green pepper
1 can (4 ounces) mushroom stems and pieces, drained
1 bay leaf
1/4 teaspoon dried oregano
1/4 teaspoon dried basil
1/4 teaspoon pepper
3/4 cup uncooked long grain rice
1 cup meatless spaghetti sauce

In a large skillet, cook the chicken, onion and garlic in 3 tablespoons broth until chicken juices run clear. Stir in the green pepper, mushrooms, bay leaf, oregano, basil, pepper and remaining broth. Bring to a boil. Add the rice. Reduce heat; cover and simmer for 20-25 minutes or until the rice is tender. Add the spaghetti sauce; heat through. Discard bay leaf before serving. **Yield:** 4 servings.

Nutritional Analysis: One serving (1 cup) equals 250 calories, 1 g fat (trace saturated fat), 33 mg cholesterol, 641 mg sodium, 40 g carbohydrate, 3 g fiber, 19 g protein. **Diabetic Exchanges:** 2 starch, 2 vegetable, 1 lean meat.

Salsa Potato Salad

Plan ahead...needs to chill

Summer is a wonderful time to enjoy potato salad, but preparing it with regular mayonnaise adds too much fat. Salsa perks up this deliciously different version and disguises the fact that it uses fat-free items.
—Janet Lewis
Bangor, Pennsylvania

1/3 cup fat-free mayonnaise
2 tablespoons fat-free sour cream
1/4 cup salsa
1 tablespoon minced fresh parsley
3 cups cubed cooked unpeeled potatoes
1 celery rib, thinly sliced
1/4 cup chopped onion
1/2 cup reduced-fat shredded cheddar cheese

In a bowl, combine mayonnaise, sour cream, salsa and parsley. In a bowl, combine potatoes, celery and onion. Add dressing; toss to coat. Stir in cheese. Cover; chill for at least 1 hour before serving. **Yield:** 7 servings.

Nutritional Analysis: One serving (1/2 cup) equals 92 calories, 2 g fat (1 g saturated fat), 8 mg cholesterol, 212 mg sodium, 15 g carbohydrate, 2 g fiber, 4 g protein. **Diabetic Exchange:** 1 starch.

Berry Banana Smoothies

(Pictured at right)

Ready in 15 minutes or less

I keep several bananas in the freezer so that I'm always ready to whip up this thick beverage for a quick breakfast or a tasty treat. Frozen fruit gives it a great consistency...it's like drinking a berry milk shake! —Brenda Strohm
Omaha, Nebraska

1 cup reduced-fat vanilla yogurt
1 medium ripe banana, peeled, cut into chunks and frozen
1/4 cup *each* frozen unsweetened strawberries, blueberries, raspberries and blackberries
1 cup fat-free milk

In a blender or food processor, combine all ingredients; cover and process until smooth. Pour into chilled glasses; serve immediately. **Yield:** 3 servings.

Nutritional Analysis: One serving (1-1/4 cups) equals 161 calories, 1 g fat (1 g saturated fat), 6 mg cholesterol, 98 mg sodium, 31 g carbohydrate, 2 g fiber, 8 g protein. **Diabetic Exchanges:** 1 fruit, 1 reduced-fat milk.

Sneaky Nutrition

When my children were small, they hated kidney beans in their chili, but I wanted to make sure they got all the protein and fiber the beans provide. So I'd puree three-fourths of the beans and half a can of tomato sauce in the blender. I added this mixture to the chili along with the whole beans I'd set aside.

While they would still pick the whole beans out of their chili, I knew they were getting the benefits of the beans. The pureed mixture made the chili extra thick and tasty, too. —*Lorri Simmons, Minden City, Michigan*

Berry Banana Smoothies

Light Chicken Cordon Bleu

(Pictured below, on page 219 and front cover)

I love chicken cordon bleu, but since I'm watching my cholesterol, I couldn't afford to indulge in it often. Then I trimmed down a recipe that I received in my high school home economics class years ago. The creamy sauce makes it extra special. —Shannon Strate, Salt Lake City, Utah

   8 boneless skinless chicken breast halves
     (4 ounces *each*)
1/2 teaspoon pepper
   8 slices (1 ounce *each*) lean deli ham
1-1/2 cups (6 ounces) shredded part-skim
     mozzarella cheese
2/3 cup fat-free milk
   1 cup crushed cornflakes
   1 teaspoon paprika
1/2 teaspoon garlic powder
1/4 teaspoon salt
SAUCE:
   1 can (10-3/4 ounces) reduced-fat reduced-
     sodium condensed cream of chicken soup,
     undiluted
1/2 cup fat-free sour cream
   1 teaspoon lemon juice

Flatten chicken to 1/4-in. thickness. Sprinkle with pepper; place a ham slice and 3 tablespoons of cheese down the center of each piece. Roll up and tuck in ends; secure with toothpicks. Pour milk into a shallow bowl. In another bowl, combine the cornflakes, paprika, garlic powder and salt. Dip chicken in milk, then roll in crumbs.

Place in a 13-in. x 9-in. x 2-in. baking dish coated with nonstick cooking spray. Bake, uncovered, at 350° for 25-30 minutes or until juices run clear. Meanwhile, in a small saucepan, whisk the soup, sour cream and lemon juice until blended; heat through. Discard toothpicks from chicken; serve with sauce. **Yield:** 8 servings.

Nutritional Analysis: One serving (with 2 tablespoons sauce) equals 306 calories, 7 g fat (3 g saturated fat), 91 mg cholesterol, 990 mg sodium, 16 g carbohydrate, trace fiber, 41 g protein. **Diabetic Exchanges:** 3 lean meat, 1 starch, 1 fat.

Pork with Pineapple Salsa

(Pictured on page 218)

Ready in 1 hour or less

Not only does this easy entree taste awesome, but it's good for you, too. A little brown sugar, ground ginger and Dijon mustard help give the moist tenderloin its incredible flavor, and the tangy salsa can be made in no time.
—Nicole Pickett, Oro Valley, Arizona

   1 can (20 ounces) unsweetened pineapple
     tidbits
   1 pork tenderloin (1-1/4 pounds)
   3 tablespoons brown sugar, *divided*
   2 tablespoons Dijon mustard
   1 teaspoon paprika
1/2 teaspoon ground ginger
1/3 cup finely chopped sweet red *or* green
     pepper
1/4 cup chopped green onions
1/8 teaspoon crushed red pepper flakes,
     optional

Drain pineapple, reserving 1/4 cup juice. Set aside 1 cup of pineapple (save remaining pineapple for another use). Place the pork on a rack in a shallow roasting pan. Combine 2 tablespoons brown sugar, mustard, paprika and ginger. Spread half over the pork. Bake, uncovered, at 450° for 15 minutes. Spread with remaining brown sugar mixture. Bake 15-20 minutes longer or until a meat thermometer reads 160°.

Meanwhile, for salsa, combine the red pepper, onions, pepper flakes if desired, remaining brown sugar and reserved pineapple and juice in a bowl. Let pork stand for 5 minutes before slicing. Serve with salsa. **Yield:** 4 servings.

Nutritional Analysis: One serving (4 ounces cooked pork with 1/4 cup salsa) equals 259 calories, 6 g fat (2 g saturated fat), 84 mg cholesterol, 255 mg sodium, 19 g carbohydrate, 1 g fiber, 31 g protein. **Diabetic Exchanges:** 4 lean meat, 1 fruit.

Three-Bean Soup

(Pictured on page 218)

Ready in 30 minutes or less

This chili-like soup is delicious and very low in fat. Salsa, cumin and chili powder give it plenty of flavor while several canned items make it fast to throw together on busy nights. —Joni Voit, Champlin, Minnesota

   1 large onion, chopped
   1 medium green pepper, chopped

Light Chicken Cordon Bleu

4 garlic cloves, minced
2 teaspoons olive *or* canola oil
1 can (16 ounces) kidney beans, rinsed and drained
1 can (16 ounces) fat-free refried beans
1 can (15 ounces) black beans, rinsed and drained
1 can (14-1/2 ounces) reduced-sodium chicken broth
1 can (14-1/2 ounces) stewed tomatoes, cut up
3/4 cup salsa
2 teaspoons chili powder
1/2 teaspoon pepper
1/4 teaspoon ground cumin

In a large saucepan, saute the onion, green pepper and garlic in oil until tender. Add the remaining ingredients; mix well. Bring to a boil. Reduce heat; cover and simmer for 10 minutes. **Yield:** 8 servings.

Nutritional Analysis: One serving (1 cup) equals 187 calories, 2 g fat (trace saturated fat), 0 cholesterol, 975 mg sodium, 33 g carbohydrate, 10 g fiber, 10 g protein. **Diabetic Exchanges:** 2 starch, 1 lean meat.

Catfish Po'boys

Ready in 30 minutes or less

When my neighbor prepared these large full-flavored sandwiches, I had to have the recipe. Strips of catfish are treated to a zesty Cajun cornmeal breading, then served on a bun with packaged broccoli coleslaw mix dressed in a homemade sauce. —Mildred Sherrer, Fort Worth, Texas

2 tablespoons fat-free mayonnaise
1 tablespoon fat-free sour cream
1 tablespoon white wine vinegar *or* cider vinegar
1 teaspoon sugar
2 cups broccoli coleslaw mix
1 pound catfish fillets, cut into 2-1/2-inch strips
2 tablespoons fat-free milk
1/4 cup cornmeal
2 teaspoons Cajun seasoning
1/2 teaspoon salt
1/8 teaspoon cayenne pepper
2 teaspoons olive *or* canola oil
4 kaiser rolls, split

In a small bowl, whisk the mayonnaise, sour cream, vinegar and sugar until smooth. Add coleslaw mix; toss. Set aside. In a shallow bowl, toss the catfish with milk. In a large resealable plastic bag, combine cornmeal, Cajun seasoning, salt and cayenne. Add catfish, a few pieces at a time, and shake to coat.

In a large nonstick skillet, heat oil over medium heat. Cook catfish for 4-5 minutes on each side or until fish flakes easily with a fork and coating is golden brown. Spoon coleslaw onto rolls; top with catfish. **Yield:** 4 servings.

Nutritional Analysis: One serving equals 364 calories, 8 g fat (1 g saturated fat), 53 mg cholesterol, 1,001 mg sodium, 44 g carbohydrate, 4 g fiber, 28 g protein. **Diabetic Exchanges:** 3 starch, 2-1/2 lean meat.

Cream Cheese Swirl Brownies

Cream Cheese Swirl Brownies

(Pictured above and on page 219)

I'm a chocolate lover, and this treat has satisfied my cravings many times. No one guesses the brownies are light because their chewy texture and rich chocolate taste can't be beat. My family requests them often, and I'm happy to oblige. —Heidi Johnson, Worland, Wyoming

3 eggs
6 tablespoons reduced-fat stick margarine*
1 cup sugar, *divided*
3 teaspoons vanilla extract
1/2 cup all-purpose flour
1/4 cup baking cocoa
1 package (8 ounces) reduced-fat cream cheese

Separate two eggs, putting each white in a separate bowl (discard yolks or save for another use); set aside. In a small mixing bowl, beat margarine and 3/4 cup sugar until crumbly. Add the whole egg, one egg white and vanilla; mix well. Combine the flour and cocoa; add to the egg mixture and beat until blended. Pour into a 9-in. square baking pan coated with nonstick cooking spray; set aside.

In a mixing bowl, beat cream cheese and remaining sugar until smooth. Beat in the second egg white. Drop by rounded tablespoonfuls over the batter; cut through batter with a knife to swirl. Bake at 350° for 25-30 minutes or until set and edges pull away from sides of pan. Cool on a wire rack. **Yield:** 1 dozen.

Nutritional Analysis: One brownie equals 167 calories, 7 g fat (3 g saturated fat), 28 mg cholesterol, 108 mg sodium, 23 g carbohydrate, trace fiber, 4 g protein. **Diabetic Exchanges:** 1-1/2 starch, 1 fat.

*Editor's Note: This recipe was tested with Parkay Light stick margarine.

Bacon Ranch Dip

Bacon Ranch Dip

(Pictured above)

Plan ahead...needs to chill

I used reduced-fat items to lighten up this Parmesan and bacon dip. Not only is it a snap to mix up the night before a party, but the proportions can easily be adjusted for smaller or larger groups. I get requests for the recipe whenever I serve it. —Pam Garwood, Lakeville, Minnesota

  1/2 cup reduced-fat mayonnaise
  1/2 cup reduced-fat ranch salad dressing
  1/2 cup fat-free sour cream
  1/2 cup shredded Parmesan cheese
  1/4 cup crumbled cooked bacon
Assorted fresh vegetables

In a bowl, combine the first five ingredients; mix well. Cover and refrigerate for at least 1 hour before serving. Serve with vegetables. **Yield:** 1-1/2 cups.
  Nutritional Analysis: One serving (1/4 cup dip) equals 172 calories, 11 g fat (3 g saturated fat), 18 mg cholesterol, 542 mg sodium, 13 g carbohydrate, trace fiber, 7 g protein. **Diabetic Exchanges:** 2 fat, 1 starch.

Chicken Caesar Salad Pizza

Ready in 45 minutes or less

This delectable cold pizza proves that you can eat well even when you're eating healthy. A tube of refrigerated pizza crust is baked, spread with some seasoned cream cheese and topped with nicely dressed salad fixings and moist chicken. —Amber Zurbrugg, Alliance, Ohio

  1 tube (10 ounces) refrigerated pizza crust
  3/4 pound boneless skinless chicken breasts, cut into strips
  2 teaspoons canola *or* vegetable oil
  1/2 cup fat-free Caesar salad dressing
  1/2 cup shredded Parmesan cheese, *divided*
  1 teaspoon salt-free lemon pepper seasoning
  1 garlic clove, minced
  1 package (8 ounces) fat-free cream cheese, cubed
  4 cups thinly sliced romaine
  1/2 cup diced sweet red pepper
  1 can (2-1/4 ounces) sliced ripe olives, drained

Unroll pizza crust onto a 12-in. pizza pan coated with nonstick cooking spray; flatten dough and build up edges slightly. Prick with a fork. Bake at 400° for 11 minutes or until lightly browned. Cool on a wire rack.
  In a nonstick skillet, cook chicken in oil over medium heat until no longer pink; cool. In a small bowl, combine the dressing, 1/4 cup Parmesan, lemon-pepper and garlic. Combine cream cheese and half of the dressing mixture until well blended.
  Combine romaine, red pepper and olives. Add remaining dressing mixture; toss. Spread cream cheese mixture over crust. Top with romaine mixture, chicken and remaining Parmesan. **Yield:** 6 servings.
  Nutritional Analysis: One serving equals 280 calories, 6 g fat (1 g saturated fat), 43 mg cholesterol, 952 mg sodium, 28 g carbohydrate, 2 g fiber, 25 g protein. **Diabetic Exchanges:** 2 lean meat, 1-1/2 starch, 1 vegetable, 1/2 fat.

Applesauce Oat Muffins

Ready in 45 minutes or less

My grandmother passed this recipe down to me, and I'm eager to share it with my children. The down-home muffins are tender on the inside and have a crispy topping of oats, brown sugar and cinnamon. I've even added raisins and cranberries to the batter for a different taste. —Hannah Barringer, Loudon, Tennessee

1-1/2 cups quick-cooking oats
1-1/4 cups all-purpose flour
  1/2 cup packed brown sugar
  1 teaspoon baking powder
  3/4 teaspoon baking soda
  3/4 teaspoon ground cinnamon
  1/2 teaspoon salt
  1 cup unsweetened applesauce
  1/2 cup fat-free milk
  3 tablespoons canola *or* vegetable oil
  1 egg white
TOPPING:
  1/4 cup quick-cooking oats
  1 tablespoon brown sugar
  1/8 teaspoon ground cinnamon
  1 tablespoon butter *or* stick margarine, melted

In a large mixing bowl, combine the first seven ingredients. In another bowl, combine the applesauce, milk, oil and egg white. Stir into dry ingredients just until moistened. Fill muffin cups coated with nonstick cooking spray three-fourths full.

Combine topping ingredients; sprinkle over batter. Bake at 400° for 16-18 minutes or until a toothpick comes out clean. Cool for 10 minutes before removing to a wire rack. **Yield:** 10 muffins.

Nutritional Analysis: One muffin equals 222 calories, 6 g fat (1 g saturated fat), 3 mg cholesterol, 265 mg sodium, 37 g carbohydrate, 2 g fiber, 5 g protein. **Diabetic Exchanges:** 2 starch, 1 fat, 1/2 fruit.

Garden Frittata

I created this dish one day to use up some fresh yellow squash, zucchini and tomato. It's so easy to make because you don't have to fuss with a crust. Give it a different twist by trying it with whatever veggies you have on hand.
—Catherine Michel, O'Fallon, Missouri

    1 small yellow summer squash, thinly sliced
    1 small zucchini, thinly sliced
    1 small onion, chopped
    1 cup (4 ounces) shredded part-skim
        mozzarella cheese
    1 medium tomato, sliced
  1/4 cup crumbled feta cheese
    4 eggs
    1 cup fat-free milk
    2 tablespoons minced fresh basil
    1 garlic clove, minced
  1/2 teaspoon salt
  1/4 teaspoon pepper
  1/4 cup shredded Parmesan cheese

In a microwave-safe bowl, combine the squash, zucchini and onion. Cover and microwave on high for 7-9 minutes or until the vegetables are tender; drain well. Transfer to a 9-in. pie plate coated with nonstick cooking spray. Top with the mozzarella, tomato and feta cheese.

In a bowl, whisk the eggs, milk, basil, garlic, salt and pepper; pour over the cheese and tomato layer. Sprinkle with Parmesan cheese. Bake, uncovered, at 375° for 45-50 minutes or until a knife inserted near the center comes out clean. Let stand for 10 minutes before serving. **Yield:** 8 servings.

Nutritional Analysis: One serving equals 126 calories, 7 g fat (4 g saturated fat), 121 mg cholesterol, 316 mg sodium, 6 g carbohydrate, 1 g fiber, 11 g protein. **Diabetic Exchanges:** 1 lean meat, 1 vegetable, 1 fat.

Harvest Soup

(Pictured at right)

Ready in 1 hour or less

Loaded with ground beef, squash, tomatoes and two kinds of potatoes, this hearty soup makes a great family meal on a busy night. Go ahead and substitute any of the vegetables with those that better suit your tastes.
—Janice Mitchell, Aurora, Colorado

    1 pound lean ground beef
  3/4 cup chopped onion

    2 garlic cloves, minced
3-1/2 cups water
2-1/4 cups chopped peeled sweet potatoes
    1 cup chopped red potatoes
    1 cup chopped peeled acorn squash
    2 teaspoons beef bouillon granules
    2 bay leaves
  1/2 teaspoon chili powder
  1/2 teaspoon pepper
  1/8 teaspoon ground allspice
  1/8 teaspoon ground cloves
    1 can (14-1/2 ounces) diced tomatoes,
        undrained

In a large saucepan, cook the beef, onion and garlic over medium heat until meat is no longer pink; drain well. Add the water, potatoes, squash, bouillon, bay leaves, chili powder, pepper, allspice and cloves. Bring to a boil. Reduce heat; cover and simmer for 15-20 minutes or until vegetables are tender.

Add the tomatoes. Cook and stir until heated through. Discard bay leaves. **Yield:** 6 servings.

Nutritional Analysis: One serving (1-1/2 cups) equals 241 calories, 7 g fat (3 g saturated fat), 28 mg cholesterol, 493 mg sodium, 26 g carbohydrate, 4 g fiber, 18 g protein. **Diabetic Exchanges:** 2 lean meat, 2 vegetable, 1 starch.

Harvest Soup

Arctic Orange Pie

(Pictured below)

Plan ahead...needs to freeze

This dessert is very easy to make. I have tried lemonade, mango and pineapple juice concentrates instead of orange, and my family loves every variety. It's nice to know that it's low in fat and calories.
—Marie Przepierski
Erie, Pennsylvania

  1 package (8 ounces) fat-free cream cheese
  1 can (6 ounces) frozen orange juice
    concentrate, thawed
  1 carton (8 ounces) frozen reduced-fat
    whipped topping, thawed
  1 reduced-fat graham cracker crust (8 inches)
  1 can (11 ounces) mandarin oranges, drained

In a mixing bowl, combine the cream cheese and orange juice concentrate until smooth. Fold in whipped topping; pour into crust. Cover and freeze for 4 hours or until firm. Remove from the freezer about 10 minutes before cutting. Garnish with oranges. **Yield:** 8 servings.

Nutritional Analysis: One serving equals 241 calories, 7 g fat (4 g saturated fat), 2 mg cholesterol, 251 mg sodium, 36 g carbohydrate, 1 g fiber, 6 g protein. **Diabetic Exchanges:** 1-1/2 fat, 1 starch, 1 fruit.

Strawberry Cheesecake Ice Cream

I found the recipe for this creamy and refreshing dessert in an old cookbook. Made in an ice cream freezer, it's wonderful for family gatherings. We love how it tastes like a berry-topped cheesecake.
—Karen Maubach
Fairbury, Illinois

  3 cups sliced fresh strawberries
  6 ounces reduced-fat cream cheese
  2 cans (12 ounces each) fat-free evaporated
    milk
  1 can (14 ounces) fat-free sweetened
    condensed milk
  1 teaspoon vanilla extract
  1 cup reduced-fat whipped topping

Place strawberries in a blender or food processor; cover and process until smooth. In a large mixing bowl, beat cream cheese until smooth. Add evaporated milk and condensed milk, vanilla and pureed strawberries; mix well. Fold in whipped topping.

Fill cylinder of ice cream freezer two-thirds full; freeze according to manufacturer's directions. Refrigerate remaining mixture until ready to freeze. Allow to ripen in ice cream freezer or firm up in your refrigerator freezer for 2-4 hours before serving. **Yield:** 2 quarts.

Nutritional Analysis: One serving (3/4 cup) equals 234 calories, 4 g fat (3 g saturated fat), 15 mg cholesterol, 171 mg sodium, 38 g carbohydrate, 1 g fiber, 11 g protein. **Diabetic Exchanges:** 1-1/2 fruit, 1 fat-free milk, 1 fat.

Little Meat Loaves

Ready in 1 hour or less

I've wanted to reduce the fat in my meat loaf for many years, so I finally came up with this recipe. By starting with lean ground beef and not adding any milk or egg yolks, I reduced the total fat considerably. Making individual loaves cuts the cooking time by almost half.
—Paul Soper, Sierra Vista, Arizona

    3 egg whites
  1/2 cup fat-free plain yogurt
    1 can (6 ounces) tomato paste
    1 tablespoon Worcestershire sauce
  1/2 cup quick-cooking oats
    1 small onion, chopped
    2 tablespoons dried parsley flakes
    1 teaspoon salt
    1 teaspoon poultry seasoning
  1/2 teaspoon garlic powder
  1/2 teaspoon pepper
    2 pounds lean ground beef
  1/2 cup ketchup

In a large bowl, combine the first 11 ingredients. Crumble beef over mixture and mix well. Shape into eight loaves. Place on a rack coated with nonstick cooking spray in a shallow baking pan. Bake, uncovered, at 350° for 30 minutes. Spoon ketchup over the loaves. Bake 15 minutes longer or until a meat thermometer reads 160° and meat is no longer pink. **Yield:** 8 servings.

Nutritional Analysis: One serving equals 264 calories, 11 g fat (4 g saturated fat), 42 mg cholesterol, 633 mg sodium, 15 g carbohydrate, 2 g fiber, 27 g protein. Diabetic Exchanges: 3 lean meat, 1 starch, 1/2 fat.

Baked Blueberry French Toast

Plan ahead...start the night before

I like that this breakfast entree can be prepared ahead of time. Since you can use fresh or frozen blueberries, it's great any time of year. It makes a warm rich start to any morning.
—Suzanne Strocsher, Bothell, Washington

 24 slices day-old French bread (1/2 inch thick)
  1 package (8 ounces) reduced-fat cream
    cheese, cubed

Arctic Orange Pie

2/3 cup fat-free milk
1/2 cup reduced-fat sour cream
1/2 cup fat-free plain yogurt
1/3 cup maple syrup
1 teaspoon vanilla extract
1 teaspoon ground nutmeg
1/2 teaspoon ground cinnamon
2 cups egg substitute
2 cups fresh *or* frozen blueberries
Confectioners' sugar

Place 12 slices of bread in a 13-in. x 9-in. x 2-in. baking dish coated with nonstick cooking spray. In a blender or food processor, combine cream cheese, milk, sour cream, yogurt, syrup, vanilla, nutmeg and cinnamon. Add egg substitute; cover and process until smooth. Pour half of the egg mixture over bread; sprinkle with blueberries. Top with the remaining bread and egg mixture. Cover and refrigerate for 8 hours or overnight.

Remove from the refrigerator 30 minutes before baking. Cover and bake at 350° for 30 minutes. Uncover; bake 20-30 minutes longer or until a knife inserted near the center comes out clean. Let stand for 10 minutes before serving. Dust with confectioners' sugar. **Yield:** 12 servings.

Nutritional Analysis: One serving (2 slices) equals 228 calories, 5 g fat (3 g saturated fat), 14 mg cholesterol, 391 mg sodium, 33 g carbohydrate, 2 g fiber, 11 g protein. **Diabetic Exchanges:** 1 starch, 1 fat-free milk, 1/2 fruit.

Glazed Spiced Apples

(Pictured above right)

Ready in 45 minutes or less

My husband and I are watching our fat intake, so I came up with this recipe that's a great side dish with pork. It was a real success. —Mary Jo Duckworth, Denver, Colorado

1/2 cup packed brown sugar
3 tablespoons cornstarch
1 can (12 ounces) diet cream soda
1/4 cup honey
1/4 teaspoon apple pie spice
1/4 teaspoon ground cinnamon
1/8 teaspoon ground nutmeg
8 large apples, peeled and sliced

In a microwave-safe bowl, combine the brown sugar and cornstarch. Stir in the soda, honey, apple pie spice, cinnamon and nutmeg until smooth. Microwave, uncovered, on high for 5 minutes or until thickened, stirring after each minute.

Place apples in a 3-qt. microwave-safe dish; pour sauce over apples. Cover and cook on high for 7-1/2 minutes; stir. Cook, uncovered, 7-10 minutes longer or until apples are tender; stir. Let stand for 5 minutes. Serve warm. **Yield:** 10 servings.

Nutritional Analysis: One serving (2/3 cup) equals 187 calories, 1 g fat (1 g saturated fat), 0 cholesterol, 11 mg sodium, 47 g carbohydrate, 5 g fiber, trace protein.

Editor's Note: This recipe was tested in an 850-watt microwave.

Glazed Spiced Apples
Honey Chicken Stir-Fry

Honey Chicken Stir-Fry

(Pictured above)

Ready in 30 minutes or less

I'm a new mom, and my schedule is very dependent upon our young son. So I like meals that can be ready in as little time as possible. This all-in-one stir-fry with a hint of sweetness from honey is a big time-saver.
—*Caroline Sperry, Shelby, Michigan*

1 pound boneless skinless chicken breasts, cut into 1-inch pieces
1 garlic clove, minced
3 teaspoons olive *or* canola oil, *divided*
3 tablespoons honey
2 tablespoons reduced-sodium soy sauce
1/8 teaspoon salt
1/8 teaspoon pepper
1 package (16 ounces) frozen broccoli stir-fry vegetables
2 teaspoons cornstarch
1 tablespoon cold water
Hot cooked rice

In a large nonstick skillet or wok, stir-fry chicken and garlic in 2 teaspoons oil. Add the honey, soy sauce, salt and pepper. Cook and stir until chicken is lightly browned and juices run clear. Remove and keep warm.

In the same pan, stir-fry the vegetables in remaining oil for 4-5 minutes or until heated through. Return chicken to the pan; mix well. Combine cornstarch and cold water until smooth; stir into chicken mixture. Bring to a boil; cook and stir for 1 minute or until thickened. Serve over rice. **Yield:** 4 servings.

Nutritional Analysis: One serving (1 cup stir-fry mixture; calculated without rice) equals 243 calories, 5 g fat (1 g saturated fat), 66 mg cholesterol, 470 mg sodium, 19 g carbohydrate, 3 g fiber, 28 g protein. **Diabetic Exchanges:** 3 lean meat, 3 vegetable.

Grilled Salmon Steaks

Grilled Salmon Steaks

(Pictured above)

Ready in 30 minutes or less

Salmon is a popular fish that's rich in nutrients. Seasoned with herbs and lemon juice, these flame-broiled steaks are excellent. Sprinkle the hot coals with rosemary for additional flavor or quickly prepare the entree indoors using your broiler. —Robert Bishop, Lexington, Kentucky

  3 tablespoons dried rosemary, crushed, *divided*
  1 tablespoon rubbed sage
1/4 teaspoon white pepper
  1 tablespoon lemon juice
  1 tablespoon olive *or* canola oil
  6 salmon steaks (6 ounces *each*)

In a bowl, combine 4-1/2 teaspoons rosemary, sage, pepper, lemon juice and oil. Brush over both sides of salmon steaks. Coat grill rack with nonstick cooking spray before starting the grill. Sprinkle the remaining rosemary over hot coals for added flavor.

Place salmon on grill rack. Grill, covered, over medium heat for 5 minutes. Turn; grill 7-9 minutes longer or until fish flakes easily with a fork. **Yield:** 6 servings.

Nutritional Analysis: One serving equals 334 calories, 20 g fat (5 g saturated fat), 112 mg cholesterol, 81 mg sodium, 2 g carbohydrate, 1 g fiber, 34 g protein. **Diabetic Exchanges:** 5 lean meat, 1 fat.

Zucchini Sausage Pasta

Ready in 45 minutes or less

My husband and I enjoy the hearty flavor combinations in this meal. I often make it with orzo and use a can of zucchini in tomato sauce to speed preparation even more. —Karen Martis, Merrillville, Indiana

  1 pound Italian turkey sausage links, casings removed

  2 medium zucchini, sliced
  1 can (15 ounces) tomato sauce
  1 cup picante sauce
  2 green onions, chopped
  2 garlic cloves, minced
  2 teaspoons sugar
  1 teaspoon Italian seasoning
  2 cups cooked small shell pasta
1/4 cup grated Parmesan cheese
3/4 cup shredded part-skim mozzarella cheese

In a large nonstick skillet, cook and crumble sausage over medium heat until no longer pink. Add zucchini; saute 2 minutes longer. Drain. Stir in tomato sauce, picante sauce, onions, garlic, sugar and Italian seasoning. Reduce heat; simmer, uncovered, for 5 minutes.

Stir in pasta and Parmesan cheese; heat through. Remove from the heat. Sprinkle with mozzarella cheese; cover and let stand for 5 minutes or until cheese is melted. **Yield:** 7 servings.

Nutritional Analysis: One serving (1 cup) equals 240 calories, 9 g fat (4 g saturated fat), 44 mg cholesterol, 1,090 mg sodium, 20 g carbohydrate, 2 g fiber, 18 g protein. **Diabetic Exchanges:** 2 lean meat, 1 starch, 1 vegetable, 1/2 fat.

Gran's Apple Cake

Our grandmother occasionally brought over this wonderful cake warm from the oven. Its spicy apple flavor combined with the sweet cream cheese frosting was always welcome. Even though I've lightened it up, it's still a family favorite. —Lauris Conrad, Turlock, California

1-2/3 cups sugar
  2 eggs
1/2 cup unsweetened applesauce
  2 tablespoons canola *or* vegetable oil
  2 teaspoons vanilla extract
  2 cups all-purpose flour
  2 teaspoons baking soda
  2 teaspoons ground cinnamon
3/4 teaspoon salt
  6 cups chopped peeled tart apples (about 5 medium)
1/2 cup chopped pecans
FROSTING:
  4 ounces reduced-fat cream cheese
  2 tablespoons butter (no substitutes), softened
  1 teaspoon vanilla extract
  1 cup confectioners' sugar

In a mixing bowl, combine the sugar, eggs, applesauce, oil and vanilla. Beat for 2 minutes on medium speed. Combine the flour, baking soda, cinnamon and salt; add to applesauce mixture and beat until combined. Fold in apples and pecans.

Transfer to a 13-in. x 9-in. x 2-in. baking dish coated with nonstick cooking spray. Bake at 350° for 35-40 minutes or until top is golden brown and a toothpick inserted near center comes out clean. Cool on a wire rack.

For frosting, combine cream cheese, butter and vanilla in a small mixing bowl until smooth. Gradually beat in confectioners' sugar (mixture will be soft). Spread over cooled cake. **Yield:** 18 servings.

Nutritional Analysis: One piece equals 241 calories, 8 g fat (2 g saturated fat), 32 mg cholesterol, 283 mg sodium, 42 g carbohydrate, 2 g fiber, 3 g protein. **Diabetic Exchanges:** 2 starch, 1-1/2 fat, 1 fruit.

Almond Bran Muffins

Ready in 45 minutes or less

Almond flavor takes center stage in these moist treats. I decided to make up my own version of bran muffins, and this recipe was the tasty result. —Sandra Castillo
Sun Prairie, Wisconsin

1-3/4 cups All-Bran
1-1/4 cups fat-free evaporated milk
1/4 cup unsweetened applesauce
1/4 cup butter *or* stick margarine, melted
1/2 teaspoon almond extract
1 cup whole wheat flour
1/4 cup packed brown sugar
1-1/2 teaspoons baking powder
1-1/4 teaspoons ground cinnamon
1/2 teaspoon baking soda
2 egg whites, lightly beaten

In a bowl, combine the bran, milk, applesauce, butter and almond extract; let stand for 5 minutes. Meanwhile, combine the dry ingredients in a large bowl; stir in egg whites and bran mixture. Fill muffin cups coated with nonstick cooking spray two-thirds full.

Bake at 350° for 16-20 minutes or until a toothpick comes out clean. Cool for 5 minutes before removing from pan to a wire rack. Serve warm. **Yield:** 1 dozen.

Nutritional Analysis: One muffin equals 151 calories, 4 g fat (2 g saturated fat), 10 mg cholesterol, 219 mg sodium, 26 g carbohydrate, 5 g fiber, 5 g protein. **Diabetic Exchanges:** 1-1/2 starch, 1 fat.

Garlic Green Beans

(Pictured at right)

Ready in 30 minutes or less

Because this recipe is easy to prepare, healthy and delicious, it has become the only way I make green beans. The versatile beans feature plenty of garlic and Italian seasoning and complement most any entree. —Clara Saxe
Colorado Springs, Colorado

1-1/2 pounds fresh green beans
2 tablespoons olive *or* canola oil
3 garlic cloves, minced
2 teaspoons Italian seasoning
1/8 teaspoon salt
1/8 teaspoon pepper

In a 15-in. x 10-in. x 1-in. baking pan, toss green beans, oil, garlic and Italian seasoning until beans are well coated. Bake, uncovered, at 450° for 12-15 minutes or until beans are crisp-tender and lightly browned, stirring occasionally. Sprinkle with salt and pepper. **Yield:** 6 servings.

Nutritional Analysis: One serving (1/2 cup) equals 79 calories, 5 g fat (1 g saturated fat), 0 cholesterol, 203 mg sodium, 9 g carbohydrate, 1 g fiber, 2 g protein. **Diabetic Exchanges:** 1 vegetable, 1 fat.

Apple-Onion Pork Chops

(Pictured below)

Ready in 1 hour or less

I simmer these tender chops with a sweet-and-sour medley of onions and apple. This goes nicely with parsley potatoes and a crisp salad. —Jean McCormick
Deer Park, New York

4 lean boneless pork loin chops (4 ounces *each*)
1/2 teaspoon salt
1/4 to 1/2 teaspoon pepper
2 tablespoons olive *or* canola oil, *divided*
2 cups sliced red onions (1/2-inch slices)
1 large tart apple, peeled and chopped
3 tablespoons red wine vinegar *or* cider vinegar
1/3 cup reduced-sodium chicken broth

Sprinkle both sides of pork chops with salt and pepper. In a large nonstick skillet, brown chops in 1 tablespoon oil on both sides over medium-high heat. Remove and keep warm. In the same skillet, cook onions and apple in remaining oil over low heat until golden brown, about 30 minutes.

Return pork chops to the pan. Add vinegar; cook for 2 minutes. Stir in the broth. Bring to a boil. Reduce heat; cover and simmer for 18-20 minutes or until meat is tender. **Yield:** 4 servings.

Nutritional Analysis: One serving (1 pork chop with 1 cup onion mixture) equals 300 calories, 14 g fat (4 g saturated fat), 63 mg cholesterol, 383 mg sodium, 16 g carbohydrate, 3 g fiber, 26 g protein. **Diabetic Exchanges:** 3 lean meat, 1 vegetable, 1 fat, 1/2 fruit.

Garlic Green Beans
Apple-Onion Pork Chops

Chapter 16

Centsible Foods—Fast and Frugal

A GOOD QUICK MEAL doesn't have to strain the household budget.

Look here for "centsible" express-eating alternatives instead of relying on convenient yet costly restaurant carryout meals and store-bought packaged foods. These speedy recipes are as easy on the wallet as they are appetizing.

Our Test Kitchen has figured the cost per serving for each delicious dish. So these fast and frugal recipes will result in prompt meals and a plumper pocketbook.

SWIFT 'N' THRIFTY. Tomato Spinach Spirals and Lime Sherbet (recipes on p. 238).

Ranchero Supper

(Pictured below)

Ready in 30 minutes or less

This hearty dish is quick and easy to fix after a busy work-day. We like to use hickory and bacon baked beans and serve it with fruit or a green salad for a complete meal.
—Karen Roberts, Lawrence, Kansas

1-1/2 pounds ground beef
1 can (28 ounces) baked beans
1 can (11 ounces) whole kernel corn, drained
1/4 cup barbecue sauce
2 tablespoons ketchup
1 tablespoon prepared mustard
3/4 cup shredded cheddar cheese
Sliced green onions and sour cream, optional
7 cups tortilla chips

In a large skillet, cook beef over medium heat until no longer pink; drain. Stir in the baked beans, corn, barbecue sauce, ketchup and mustard; heat through. Sprinkle with cheese; cook until melted. Top with onions and sour cream if desired. Serve with tortilla chips. **Yield:** 7 servings (98¢ per serving).

Pepper Jack Potatoes

I make these nicely seasoned potatoes all the time...they seem to go with anything. This side dish is sure to satisfy several guests without straining your budget.
—Barbara Nowakowski, North Tonawanda, New York

6 medium potatoes, peeled and cut into 1/4-inch slices
1 medium onion, sliced

1/3 cup butter *or* margarine, melted
1/2 teaspoon salt
1/4 teaspoon chili powder
1/8 teaspoon cayenne pepper
1/8 teaspoon pepper
2-1/2 cups (10 ounces) shredded pepper Jack *or* Monterey Jack cheese, *divided*
Salsa, optional

In a large bowl, combine the potatoes and onion. Combine the butter and seasonings; drizzle over the potato mixture and toss to coat. Place half in a greased 13-in. x 9-in. x 2-in. baking dish. Sprinkle with half of the cheese; top with remaining potato mixture.

Cover and bake at 400° for 45-50 minutes or until potatoes are tender. Uncover; sprinkle with remaining cheese. Bake 5 minutes longer or until cheese is melted. Serve with salsa if desired. **Yield:** 10 servings (42¢ per serving).

Corny Coleslaw

Plan ahead...needs to chill

Corn and cabbage are a deliciously different combo in this creamy coleslaw sprinkled with peanuts. This salad is especially tasty when I use homegrown corn I've cut off the cob. This tasty dish always draws compliments.
—Patrice Ehrlich Merced, California

5 cups shredded cabbage
1-1/2 cups whole kernel corn
2 tablespoons finely chopped onion
1/2 cup sour cream
1/2 cup mayonnaise
2 tablespoons sugar
2 tablespoons lemon juice
1 teaspoon prepared mustard
1/2 teaspoon salt
1/2 cup chopped salted peanuts

In a bowl, combine cabbage, corn and onion. In a bowl, combine sour cream, mayonnaise, sugar, lemon juice, mustard and salt. Pour over cabbage mixture; toss to coat. Cover; refrigerate for 1 hour. Stir in peanuts just before serving. **Yield:** 6 servings (39¢ per serving).

Asian Turkey Burgers

Ready in 30 minutes or less

I use garlic, ginger and soy sauce to turn ground turkey into moist tender patties. They're winners at my house.
—Jeanette Saskowski, Antioch, Tennessee

1 egg white
1 tablespoon soy sauce
1/2 cup dry bread crumbs
1 tablespoon finely chopped onion
1 garlic clove, minced
1/4 teaspoon ground ginger
1/8 teaspoon pepper
12 ounces ground turkey

Ranchero Supper

Pepper Steak Fettuccine

In a bowl, combine the first seven ingredients. Crumble turkey over mixture and mix just until combined. Shape into four patties. Cook in a nonstick skillet coated with nonstick cooking spray until no longer pink. **Yield:** 4 servings (45¢ per serving).

Cabbage Chicken Salad

Plan ahead...needs to chill

We were on a tight budget when I was little, so my mother often made this refreshing salad that fit our pocketbook as well as our taste buds. It can be a light supper or a crunchy complement to sandwiches.
—*Heather Myrick*
Southaven, Mississippi

    1 package (3 ounces) chicken ramen noodles
    2 cups shredded cabbage
    1 cup cubed cooked chicken
1/4 cup sliced green onions
    3 tablespoons sesame seeds, toasted
1/3 cup white vinegar
    2 tablespoons sugar
    2 tablespoons water
    4 teaspoons vegetable oil
1/4 teaspoon salt
1/8 teaspoon pepper

Set seasoning packet from noodles aside. Crumble the noodles into a large bowl; add the cabbage, chicken, onions and sesame seeds. In a jar with a tight-fitting lid, combine the vinegar, sugar, water, oil, salt, pepper and contents of seasoning packet; shake well. Pour over cabbage mixture and toss to coat. Cover and refrigerate for 8 hours or overnight. **Yield:** 4 servings (48¢ per serving).

Pepper Steak Fettuccine

(Pictured above)

Ready in 45 minutes or less

My husband is a pasta lover, so I created this tangy dish for him. Strips of round steak, green pepper and onion make it hearty. —*Crystal West, New Straitsville, Ohio*

1-1/4 pounds boneless beef round steak (1/2 inch thick), cut into thin strips
    1 medium green pepper, julienned
    1 medium onion, julienned
    2 tablespoons stick margarine
    2 cans (15 ounces *each*) tomato sauce
    1 can (4 ounces) mushroom stems and pieces, drained
1-1/2 teaspoons salt
    1 teaspoon dried basil
1/4 teaspoon pepper
    1 package (16 ounces) fettuccine
1/3 cup shredded Parmesan cheese

In a large skillet, saute the steak, green pepper and onion in margarine until meat is no longer pink. Stir in tomato sauce, mushrooms, salt, basil and pepper. Bring to a boil. Reduce heat; cover and simmer for 20-25 minutes or until meat is tender. Cook fettuccine according to package directions; drain. Top with steak mixture; sprinkle with Parmesan cheese. **Yield:** 6 servings (99¢ per serving).

Tomato Spinach Spirals

(Pictured below and on page 234)

Ready in 30 minutes or less

A great side dish or meatless main course, this pasta pleaser comes together in a snap. It is tasty, quick and easy.
—*Janet Montano, Temecula, California*

    1 package (8 ounces) spiral pasta
    1 package (10 ounces) frozen creamed spinach
    1 can (15 ounces) diced tomatoes, undrained
    3 tablespoons grated Romano cheese, *divided*
    3 tablespoons grated Parmesan cheese, *divided*
    1/2 teaspoon salt

Cook pasta according to package directions. Meanwhile, prepare spinach according to package directions. Drain pasta; place in a bowl. Add the spinach, tomatoes, 2 tablespoons of Romano cheese, 2 tablespoons of Parmesan cheese and salt; toss. Sprinkle with the remaining cheeses. **Yield:** 6 servings (63¢ per serving).

Lime Sherbet

(Pictured below and on page 235)

Plan ahead…needs to freeze

This frozen treat is just as refreshing when it's made with orange or raspberry gelatin. My family especially enjoys it in the summer. —*Julie Benkenstein, Arcola, Indiana*

    1 package (3 ounces) lime gelatin *or* flavor of your choice
    1 cup sugar
    1 cup boiling water
    2 tablespoons lemon juice

    1-1/2 teaspoons grated lemon peel
    4 cups cold milk

In a bowl, dissolve gelatin and sugar in boiling water. Add lemon juice and peel. Whisk in milk; mix well. Pour into an ungreased 9-in. square pan. Cover and freeze for 2 hours.

Transfer to a mixing bowl; beat for 2 minutes. Return to the pan. Cover and freeze for 1 hour; stir. Freeze 1 hour longer or until firm. Let stand for 10 minutes before serving. **Yield:** 8 servings (20¢ per serving).

Bean 'n' Rice Burritos

Ready in 15 minutes or less

One night I wanted to make something different for dinner. I started with black beans and added things I thought would taste good. The end result was as delicious as it was economical. —*Susie Kohler, Union, Missouri*

    1 can (15 ounces) black beans, rinsed and drained
    1 can (14-1/2 ounces) diced tomatoes, drained
    2 teaspoons garlic powder
    1 teaspoon ground cumin
    2 cups cooked rice
    12 flour tortillas (7 inches), warmed
    4 ounces process cheese (Velveeta), cut into 12 slices
    1 cup (8 ounces) sour cream

In a large skillet, combine the beans, tomatoes, garlic powder and cumin; heat through. Stir in the rice. Spoon about 1/3 cupful off-center on each tortilla. Top with cheese. Fold sides and ends over filling and roll up. Serve with sour cream. **Yield:** 6 servings (89¢ per serving).

Tomato Spinach Spirals
Lime Sherbet

Taco Salad

(Pictured at right)

Ready in 30 minutes or less

I found this recipe in an old school cookbook. It's always a favorite at potlucks. I prepare the rest of the ingredients while the ground beef is browning, so dinner is ready in minutes. —Sandy Fynaardt, New Sharon, Iowa

Taco Salad

- 1 envelope taco seasoning
- 1 pound ground beef
- 1 head iceberg lettuce, torn
- 1 can (16 ounces) kidney beans, rinsed and drained
- 1 large red onion, chopped
- 4 medium tomatoes, seeded and diced
- 2 cups (8 ounces) shredded cheddar cheese
- 1 package (7-1/2 ounces) tortilla chips, crushed
- 1 bottle (8 ounces) Thousand Island salad dressing
- 2 tablespoons taco sauce

Set aside 1 tablespoon taco seasoning. In a large skillet, cook beef over medium heat until no longer pink; drain. Stir in remaining taco seasoning. In a large bowl, layer the beef, lettuce, beans, onion, tomatoes, cheese and tortilla chips. In a small bowl, combine the salad dressing, taco sauce and reserved taco seasoning; serve with salad. **Yield:** 12 servings (83¢ per serving).

Spinach Combo

Ready in 45 minutes or less

My mother and I get recipe ideas from watching TV cooking shows and looking through magazines, then substitute ingredients we prefer. That's how we created this tasty and colorful side dish. —Amy Brosnan, Kansas City, Missouri

- 3/4 cup chopped onion
- 2 tablespoons vegetable oil
- 1 package (10 ounces) frozen chopped spinach, thawed
- 1 cup uncooked long grain rice
- 2-1/4 cups water
- 2 medium tomatoes, diced
- 1 teaspoon salt
- 1/8 teaspoon pepper

In a skillet, saute onion in oil until tender. Add the spinach, rice and water. Bring to a boil. Reduce heat; cover and simmer for 20-25 minutes or until rice is tender and water is absorbed. Stir in the tomatoes, salt and pepper; heat through. **Yield:** 6 servings (30¢ per serving).

Chili Chicken 'n' Rice

Ready in 45 minutes or less

Tender chicken breasts on top of hearty chili and rice make for a filling and frugal meal-in-one. Choose mild or hot chili to suit your family's taste. —Kathy Duke, Anchorage, Alaska

- 4 boneless skinless chicken breast halves
- 2 cups cooked rice
- 1 can (15 ounces) chili with beans
- 2 tablespoons taco seasoning
- 4 slices process American cheese

In a nonstick skillet, brown chicken over medium heat. Spread rice in a greased 11-in. x 7-in. x 2-in. baking dish. Combine the chili and taco seasoning; spoon over the rice. Top with chicken.

Cover and bake at 350° for 25 minutes. Top with cheese slices. Bake, uncovered, for 5 minutes or until juices run clear. **Yield:** 4 servings (85¢ per serving).

Shortbread Meltaways

You'll need just five everyday ingredients to stir up a batch of these bite-size cookies. They're rich and melt-in-your-mouth good. —Ruth Whittaker, Wayne, Pennsylvania

- 1 cup butter (no substitutes), softened
- 1/2 cup confectioners' sugar
- 1 teaspoon vanilla extract
- 1 cup all-purpose flour
- 2/3 cup cornstarch

In a small mixing bowl, cream butter and confectioners' sugar. Beat in vanilla. Combine the flour and cornstarch; gradually add to creamed mixture. Drop by 1/2 teaspoonfuls onto ungreased baking sheets. Bake at 350° for 11-13 minutes or until bottoms are lightly browned. Cool for 5 minutes before removing from pans to wire racks. **Yield:** 7 dozen (4¢ per serving).

Mushroom Ham Fettuccine

This rich entree is one of our favorite pasta dishes and elegant enough for company.
—Renee Reyes
Owensboro, Kentucky

1/2 pound thinly sliced fully cooked ham, cut into strips
1 cup sliced fresh mushrooms
2 garlic cloves, minced
3 tablespoons plus 1/2 cup butter *or* margarine, *divided*
1 package (12 ounces) fettuccine
1 cup grated Parmesan cheese
1 cup (8 ounces) sour cream
1/4 teaspoon pepper

In a skillet, saute the ham, mushrooms and garlic in 3 tablespoons butter. Meanwhile, cook fettuccine according to package directions; drain. Melt the remaining butter in a large saucepan. Stir in the fettuccine, Parmesan cheese, sour cream and pepper. Add the ham mixture; toss to coat. **Yield:** 8 servings (92¢ per serving).

Lemon Cheese Bars

(Pictured below)

Cake mix speeds along the crust and topping for these special squares. With just a handful of ingredients, the bars are so easy to assemble.   —Janie Dennis, Evansville, Indiana

1 package (18-1/4 ounces) yellow cake mix
2 eggs
1/3 cup vegetable oil
1 package (8 ounces) cream cheese, softened
1/3 cup sugar
1 teaspoon lemon extract

In a bowl, combine the dry cake mix, one egg and oil until crumbly. Set aside 1 cup for topping. Press the remaining crumb mixture into a greased 13-in. x 9-in. x 2-in. baking pan. Bake at 350° for 15 minutes.

In a small mixing bowl, beat cream cheese until smooth; add the sugar, extract and remaining egg. Spread over crust. Sprinkle with reserved crumb mixture. Bake for 25-30 minutes or until golden brown. Cool on a wire rack. Refrigerate leftovers. **Yield:** 2-1/2 dozen (11¢ per serving).

Baked Salisbury Steak

Ready in 45 minutes or less

I bake ground beef patties in a savory mushroom soup gravy to create this mild, moist main course. It's a satisfying classic dish. The recipe is easy and quick. I get compliments whenever I serve it.
—Elsie Epp, Newton, Kansas

2 eggs, lightly beaten
1 cup quick-cooking oats
1/2 cup each diced green pepper, celery and onion
1/2 teaspoon salt
2 pounds ground beef
1 can (10-3/4 ounces) condensed golden mushroom *or* cream of mushroom soup, undiluted
3/4 cup water
1/4 teaspoon pepper

In a large bowl, combine the eggs, oats, green pepper, celery, onion and salt. Crumble beef over mixture and mix well. Shape into eight oval patties. In a large skillet, brown patties on both sides.

Place patties in an ungreased 13-in. x 9-in. x 2-in. baking dish. Combine soup, water and pepper; pour over beef. Cover; bake at 350° for 30-35 minutes or until meat is no longer pink. **Yield:** 8 servings (66¢ per serving).

Cream Cheese Potato Soup

Ready in 1 hour or less

I came up with this soup after I had tried something similar at a restaurant. Using chicken bouillon and frozen hash browns makes it easy to fix. It's good with sourdough bread.
—Stacy Bockelman
California, Missouri

6 cups water
7 teaspoons chicken bouillon granules
2 packages (8 ounces *each*) cream cheese, cubed
1 package (30 ounces) frozen cubed hash brown potatoes, thawed
1-1/2 cups cubed fully cooked ham
1/2 cup chopped onion
1 teaspoon garlic powder
1 teaspoon dill weed

In a Dutch oven, combine the water and bouillon. Add the cream cheese; cook and stir until cheese is melted. Stir in the remaining ingredients. Simmer, uncovered, for 18-20 minutes or until vegetables are tender. **Yield:** 12 servings (about 3 quarts) (47¢ per serving).

Lemon Cheese Bars

Hot Cranberry Drink

Hot Cranberry Drink

(Pictured above)

Ready in 1 hour or less

Red-hot candies, cinnamon and cloves add a little spice to this rosy beverage that's perfect for holiday buffets or winter potlucks. Serve it hot or cold. —Ruth Hastings
Louisville, Illinois

    4 quarts water, *divided*
    5 cups fresh *or* frozen cranberries
2-1/2 cups sugar
    1/2 cup red-hot candies
    3 tablespoons lemon juice
    12 whole cloves
    3 cinnamon sticks
Lemon slices and additional cinnamon sticks

In a large saucepan, bring 1 qt. of water and cranberries to a boil. Reduce heat; cover and simmer for 8-10 minutes or until berries begin to pop. Drain, reserving liquid and berries. Put berries through a fine strainer or food mill. In a Dutch oven or large kettle, combine the sugar, red-hots, lemon juice, cranberry liquid and pulp, and remaining water.

Place cloves and cinnamon sticks on a double thickness of cheesecloth. Bring up corners of cloth and tie with string to form a bag; add to pan. Bring to a boil; stir until sugar and candies are dissolved. Discard spice bag. Strain the juice through a fine sieve or cheesecloth. Serve hot with lemon slices and additional cinnamon sticks. **Yield:** 14 servings (3-1/2 quarts) (28¢ per serving).

Cherry Date Cookies

You can fix these chewy old-fashioned drop cookies with five ingredients. I received this recipe from a friend more than 40 years ago and have made these cookies every Christmas since. —Charlotte Moore
Parkersburg, West Virginia

2-1/4 cups graham cracker crumbs (about 27
        squares)
    1 can (14 ounces) sweetened condensed milk
    2 cups chopped dates
    2 cups chopped walnuts
    27 red *or* green maraschino cherries, halved

In a bowl, combine cracker crumbs and milk; let stand for 10 minutes. Stir in dates and walnuts (mixture will be very thick). Drop by tablespoonfuls 2 in. apart onto greased baking sheets. Top each with a cherry half. Bake at 350° for 10-15 minutes or until set and edges are lightly browned. Cool for 1 minute before removing from pans to wire racks. **Yield:** 4-1/2 dozen (16¢ per serving).

Chapter 17

KIDS hurry to the kitchen when they're invited to help prepare fun food. They'll be especially eager to get involved when they see the fast, flavorful foods in this chapter.

From speedy snacks and hearty entrees to tasty side dishes and sweet desserts, younger children can mix and measure ingredients while older ones help you get a head start on dinner.

Your children or grandchildren are sure to appreciate the hands-on experience, and you'll enjoy the quality time spent together.

Best of all, the entire family will be pleased—and proud—to sit down to a delectable dinner they helped make.

FUN, FESTIVE FARE. Sugar Cone Spruce Trees and Sledding Snacks (both recipes on p. 254).

Mini Cherry Cobblers

(Pictured below)

Ready in 30 minutes or less

Cinnamon and sugar add a sweet touch to the biscuits that top these warm fruit treats. The individual servings are a great way to surprise your family with dessert...even on the busiest of days. —Dixie Terry, Goreville, Illinois

> 1 can (21 ounces) cherry pie filling
> 1 tube (6 ounces) refrigerated buttermilk biscuits, separated into 5 biscuits
> 1 tablespoon butter *or* margarine, melted
> 2 teaspoons sugar
> 2 teaspoons brown sugar
> 1/8 to 1/4 teaspoon ground cinnamon

Set aside some of the pie filling, including five cherries, for garnish. Divide the remaining filling among five ungreased 6-oz. ramekins or custard cups. Top each with a biscuit; brush with butter. Combine sugars and cinnamon; sprinkle over biscuits. Bake at 375° for 14-18 minutes or until biscuits are browned. Top with reserved pie filling. **Yield:** 5 servings.

Cheesy Tuna Mac
Mini Cherry Cobblers

Cheesy Tuna Mac

(Pictured below left)

Ready in 45 minutes or less

This comforting casserole is a snap to fix, and my two boys gobble it up. —Stephanie Martin, Macomb, Michigan

> 1 package (7-1/4 ounces) macaroni and cheese mix
> 1/2 cup milk
> 1 tablespoon butter *or* margarine
> 1 can (10-3/4 ounces) condensed cream of broccoli soup, undiluted
> 1 can (6 ounces) tuna, drained and flaked
> 3/4 cup frozen peas
> 2 tablespoons finely chopped onion
> 1 tablespoon process cheese sauce

Cook the macaroni according to package directions; drain. Stir in the milk, butter and contents of cheese packet. Add the soup, tuna, peas, onion and cheese sauce. Spoon into a greased 1-1/2-qt. baking dish. Cover and bake at 350° for 20 minutes. Uncover; bake 5-10 minutes longer or until heated through. **Yield:** 4 servings.

Cheese Quesadillas

Ready in 15 minutes or less

Three ingredients are all you need for a Mexican twist on grilled cheese. The tasty wedges are ideal as an after-school snack or with soup at lunchtime. —Luke Walker Unionville, Ontario

> 4 flour tortillas (7 inches)
> 1/2 cup salsa
> 2/3 cup shredded cheddar cheese

Place two tortillas on a greased baking sheet. Top each with salsa, cheese and remaining tortillas. Broil 4 in. from the heat for 3 minutes on each side or until golden brown. Cut into wedges. **Yield:** 2-4 servings.

Crispy Dogs

Ready in 30 minutes or less

Hot dogs become more popular than ever when wrapped in corn tortillas and fried to golden perfection. —Christy Schroeder, Fremont, Nebraska

> 8 corn tortillas (6 inches)
> 8 hot dogs
> **Oil for deep-fat frying**
> **Ketchup and mustard, optional**

Place the tortillas on a microwave-safe plate. Cover with waxed paper; microwave on high for 10-20 seconds or until warm. Wrap a tortilla around each hot dog; secure with a toothpick.

In an electric skillet or deep-fat fryer, heat 1 in. of oil to 375°. Fry hot dogs, in two batches, for 3 minutes or until tortillas are golden brown and crispy, turning once. Drain on paper towels; discard toothpicks. Serve with ketchup and mustard if desired. **Yield:** 8 servings.

Pleasing Pops Promise to Be Popular

SWEET SUCCESS at bake sales is a sure thing when you fix these delightful handheld snacks from Linda Dyches of Round Rock, Texas. Her must-have Marshmallow Treat Pops are short on time yet long on appeal and fun!

Linda simply shapes a marshmallow-cereal mixture into balls and inserts a Popsicle stick in each. The munchable morsels are then dipped in melted chocolate or white candy coating and decorated with colorful sprinkles.

"My son took these to his first bake sale at school and was the hit of the class," Linda shares.

She wrapped the pops in clear plastic wrap, tied them with decorative ribbon and stuck the sticks into a piece of Styrofoam for an attractive display. The Styrofoam board also made them easy to transport.

Try these pops the next time your little baker needs a nifty nibble for a birthday treat or bake sale. "But watch out," Linda warns, "these cute creations are sure to draw a crowd."

Marshmallow Treat Pops

Ready in 45 minutes or less

3 tablespoons butter *or* margarine
4 cups miniature marshmallows
6 cups crisp rice cereal
24 Popsicle sticks
9 ounces milk chocolate candy coating
Decorating sprinkles
9 ounces white candy coating

In a large saucepan, combine the butter and marshmallows. Cook and stir over low heat until melted and smooth. Place the cereal in a large bowl; add the marshmallow mixture and stir until combined. Shape into 2-in. balls; gently insert a Popsicle stick into the center of each ball.

In a microwave-safe bowl, heat the milk chocolate

Marshmallow Treat Pops

candy coating until melted; stir until smooth. Dip half of the treats in chocolate; decorate with sprinkles. Repeat with the white candy coating and remaining treats and decorating sprinkles. Place on waxed paper until firm. **Yield:** 2 dozen.

Better Idea for Frozen Snack Popped into His Head

BECKY VAN BEEK of Bismark, North Dakota likes to keep speedy snacks on hand for her family. She learned a tasty, time-saving tip from her 10-year-old son, Daniel.

"I was explaining to him how we could make homemade pudding pops," she recalls. "I suggested pouring instant pudding into molds and freezing them.

"He looked at me and asked, 'Can we just put Popsicle sticks into the snack containers of pudding we buy

and freeze them instead?'

"Of course, I said yes. What an easy idea! We picked up a package of wooden craft sticks and have made these frosty snacks several times. They're delicious," Becky says.

"Once they're frozen, they pop right out of the plastic containers. It's nice to have a healthy snack on hand that keeps in the freezer for days."

Bunny Treats Will Hop into Hearts

Easter Bunny Treats

SWEET-TOOTHED TYKES will beg to build a bunch of these becoming bunnies at Easter. The remarkable rabbit recipe relies on just a few ingredients.

"Our son and daughter wanted to create something special for Easter," says Holly Jost of Manitowoc, Wisconsin. "I came up with these Easter Bunny Treats that are so simple, the kids can do most of the work.

"We used large marshmallows for the bunny's head and body," she explains. "Then we cut large marshmallows into quarters to make the ears and used mini ones for the legs and tail."

Canned vanilla frosting was used to glue the marshmallows to each other, and then some was tinted pink to create each bunny's face and ears.

Holly suggests heart-shaped candy sprinkles for the eyes and nose, but feel free to try mini chocolate chips, candy-coated baking pieces or other small store-bought sweets to dress up the marshmallow morsels.

"These treats were easy for our kids to assemble, and the whole family had fun making them," she says.

Easter Bunny Treats

> 2/3 cup vanilla frosting
> 30 large marshmallows
> Pink gel *or* paste food coloring
>   Red and pink heart-shaped decorating sprinkles
>   60 miniature marshmallows

Frost the tops of 12 large marshmallows; stack a large marshmallow on top of each. Quarter the remaining large marshmallows; set aside for ears. Tint 1/4 cup frosting pink. Cut a small hole in the corner of a pastry or plastic bag; place pink frosting in bag. Pipe a ribbon between the stacked marshmallows for bow tie. With white frosting, attach red hearts for eyes and a pink heart for nose. Pipe pink whiskers and smile.

For ears, pipe the center of quartered marshmallows pink; attach to head with white frosting. With the remaining white frosting, attach the miniature marshmallows for legs and tail. Let stand until dry. **Yield:** 1 dozen.

Potato-Stuffed Kielbasa

Ready in 45 minutes or less

Flavorful sausages are topped with mashed potatoes and cheese for this hearty meal-in-one. This is a quick dish to prepare, and everyone likes it. —Margery Bryan
Royal City, Washington

> 1 pound fully cooked kielbasa *or* Polish sausage
> 2 cups mashed potatoes
> 2 tablespoons thinly sliced green onion
> 1 teaspoon prepared mustard
> 1/2 cup shredded cheddar cheese

Cut sausage into four pieces; cut each piece lengthwise to within 1/2 in. of opposite side. Open sausage pieces so they are flat; place in a greased 11-in. x 7-in. x 2-in. baking dish. In a bowl, combine the potatoes, onion and mustard; spoon in mounds over sausage. Sprinkle with cheese. Bake, uncovered, at 350° for 20-25 minutes or until heated through. **Yield:** 4 servings.

Grandma's Spoiler Sandwich

Ready in 15 minutes or less

There are all kinds of sweet goodies in this gooey grilled sandwich that can be served for breakfast, as an after-school snack or even for dessert! My grandma used to make this special sandwich for my cousins and me when we would stay with her. It's really good with a cup of hot chocolate. —Michal Wooten, Greenville, Ohio

2 slices cinnamon bread
2 tablespoons peanut butter
4-1/2 teaspoons miniature marshmallows
1 tablespoon miniature chocolate chips
1 tablespoon butter *or* margarine

Spread one side of both slices of bread with peanut butter. Sprinkle one slice with marshmallows and chocolate chips; top with the second slice. Butter outsides of bread. In a skillet over medium heat, toast sandwich on both sides until bread is lightly browned and chips and marshmallows are melted. **Yield:** 1 serving.

Pinto Bean Turnovers

(Pictured below right)

Ready in 45 minutes or less

I pat cheese into dough, then tuck in store-bought bean dip to fix these tasty turnovers. They're easy to assemble with prepared pie crusts. —Sue Seymour, Valatie, New York

3/4 cup pinto bean dip*
1/3 cup chopped onion
1/3 cup chopped green pepper
Pastry for a double-crust pie (9 inches)
1/2 cup finely shredded cheddar cheese
1/2 teaspoon chili powder
Salsa and sour cream, optional

In a bowl, combine bean dip, onion and green pepper; set aside. On a lightly floured surface, roll pastry to 1/8-in. thickness. Sprinkle with half of cheese; press lightly with fingers. Turn pastry over; sprinkle with remaining cheese and press lightly. Cut into 3-in. circles.

Place about 2 teaspoons bean mixture in the center of each circle. Fold over; press edges with a fork to seal. Sprinkle with chili powder. Place on lightly greased baking sheets. Bake at 350° for 15-18 minutes or until golden brown. Serve with salsa and sour cream if desired. **Yield:** 2-1/2 dozen.

*Editor's Note: This recipe was tested with La Preferida canned bean dip.

Waffle Fry Nachos

(Pictured at right)

Ready in 45 minutes or less

My husband and two grown sons really enjoy these appetizers when we're camping. They can devour a platter of them in no time. They're also fun to fix when friends come over. —Debra Morgan, Idaho Falls, Idaho

1 package (22 ounces) frozen waffle fries
10 bacon strips, cooked and crumbled
3 green onions, sliced
1 can (6 ounces) sliced ripe olives, drained
2 medium tomatoes, seeded and chopped
2/3 cup salsa
1-1/2 cups (6 ounces) shredded cheddar cheese
1-1/2 cups (6 ounces) shredded Monterey Jack cheese
Sour cream

Bake fries according to package directions. Transfer to a 10-in. ovenproof skillet. Top with the bacon, onions, olives, tomatoes, salsa and cheeses. Return to the oven for 5 minutes or until cheese is melted. Serve with sour cream. **Yield:** 6-8 servings.

Nutty Soup

Years ago, we visited Williamsburg, Virginia and tried peanut soup. Now we're in our 70s, and I told my husband, Earl, that I wish I had a cup of that soup.

He whisked together a can of condensed cream of chicken soup, a can of milk and 2 heaping tablespoons of peanut butter. Then he heated it up until it was bubbly, stirring occasionally.

I hope other people will love this soup as much as my grandchildren and I do.

—Jean Wehr
Ashland, Ohio

Waffle Fry Nachos
Pinto Bean Turnovers

Mini Chicken Kabobs

(Pictured below)

Ready in 45 minutes or less

I first tried these kabobs when my daughter-in-law made them for my granddaughter's birthday party. Full of soy sauce, ginger and pineapple flavors, these appetizers are popular when I serve them at get-togethers.
—Norma Wells, Cookson, Oklahoma

> 1/4 cup soy sauce
> 2 teaspoons sugar
> 1/2 teaspoon salt
> Dash *each* pepper, garlic powder and ground ginger
> 1/2 pound boneless skinless chicken breasts, cut into 1-inch cubes
> 1 small green pepper, cut into 1/2-inch pieces
> 2 cans (8 ounces *each*) pineapple chunks, drained
> 1 teaspoon honey

In a bowl, combine the soy sauce, sugar, salt, pepper, garlic powder and ginger. Remove half of the marinade to a small bowl; set aside for basting. Add chicken to the remaining marinade; stir to coat. Cover and refrigerate for 20-30 minutes.

Drain and discard marinade from the chicken. Thread chicken, green pepper and pineapple onto wooden toothpicks. Place on a microwave-safe plate. Add honey to the reserved marinade. Microwave kabobs on high for 5-6 minutes or until chicken juices run clear, turning occasionally. Baste with reserved marinade during the last minute of cooking. **Yield:** 3 dozen.

Editor's Note: This recipe was tested in an 850-watt microwave.

Orange Pops

(Pictured below left)

Plan ahead...needs to freeze

Five ingredients are all you'll need for these fruity frozen pops. When my sister and I were raising our families, we looked for economical recipes. Our kids loved making and eating these refreshing treats. —JoAnn Skarivoda Manitowoc, Wisconsin

> 1 package (3 ounces) orange gelatin
> 1 envelope (.15 ounce) unsweetened orange soft drink mix
> 1 cup sugar
> 2 cups boiling water
> 2 cups cold water

In a bowl, dissolve the gelatin, soft drink mix and sugar in boiling water. Stir in cold water. Pour into molds or paper cups; insert Popsicle sticks. Freeze until firm. **Yield:** 16-18 servings.

Cheesy Pizza Macaroni

Ready in 1 hour or less

A work associate gave me this layered casserole recipe that jazzes up a boxed mix. I added more cheese to the dish, and my family loved it. I try to make this hearty meal at least once a month. —Kathryn McCaffery Camdenton, Missouri

> 1-1/2 pounds ground beef
> 2 packages (7-1/4 ounces *each*) macaroni and cheese
> 2 cans (15 ounces *each*) pizza sauce
> 2 cups (8 ounces) shredded cheddar cheese
> 2 cups (8 ounces) shredded mozzarella cheese

In a large skillet, cook the beef until no longer pink; drain. Prepare macaroni and cheese according to package directions. Spread one can of pizza sauce into a greased 13-in. x 9-in. x 2-in. baking dish; layer with half of the beef, macaroni and cheese, and cheddar and mozzarella cheeses. Repeat layers (dish will be full). Bake, uncovered, at 350° for 30-35 minutes or until bubbly. **Yield:** 10-12 servings.

Mini Chicken Kabobs
Orange Pops

Tuna Boat Sandwiches Picnic-Perfect

IF YOU WANT to get your kids into the kitchen, ask them for help planning an outdoor meal!

Janell Aguda of Chicago, Illinois says that her son, Cody, has enjoyed preparing food since he was little. (Cody was 9 years old when the photo above was taken.)

"I think the key to inspiring young cooks is involving them in the process of making and serving a meal," Janell says. "And picnics are a great way to do that.

"When Cody and I plan a picnic, I let him choose a theme," she says. "Together, we select foods that fit the theme and are ideal for outdoor dining.

"Next, I take Cody grocery shopping for the items we need. This introduces him to a variety of fruits and vegetables and gets him excited about fixing the meal," she explains.

"Sometimes our picnics involve submarine sandwiches, simple fruit salads and other items Cody can easily put together.

"On other occasions, we come up with fun foods that allow him to get creative, like Tuna Boats."

Cody's sea-cruising cuisine features a fast tuna salad stuffed into lettuce-lined rolls. Kids will love assembling the simple sails out of cheese slices and wooden skewers.

"We like to serve the boats on blue paper plates with fish-shaped crackers sprinkled around for a cute presentation," Janell concludes.

Tuna Boats

Tuna Boats

Ready in 30 minutes or less

 2 cans (6 ounces *each*) tuna, drained and flaked
 1 hard-cooked egg, chopped
 3 tablespoons finely chopped celery
 1 tablespoon finely chopped onion
 1/2 cup mayonnaise *or* salad dressing
 1 teaspoon sweet pickle relish
 4 submarine sandwich *or* hoagie buns
 4 lettuce leaves
 4 slices cheddar cheese
 8 wooden skewers
Fish-shaped crackers

In a bowl, combine the tuna, egg, celery and onion. Stir in the mayonnaise and pickle relish; set aside. Make a 2-in.- wide V-shaped cut in the center of each bun to within an inch of the bottom. Remove cut portion and save for another use. Line each bun with a lettuce leaf and fill with tuna mixture.

Cut cheese slices in half diagonally. For sails, carefully insert a wooden skewer into the top center of each cheese triangle. Bend cheese slightly; push skewer through bottom center of cheese. Insert two skewers into each sandwich. Place on a serving plate. Sprinkle fish crackers around boats. **Yield:** 4 servings.

Peanut Butter Stuffed Celery

Plan ahead...needs to chill

I found this idea in a magazine several years ago. I have shared it with many people and everyone enjoys it. The crisp celery sticks stuffed with peanut butter filling are dressy enough for holidays. —Irene Wilson
Grand Junction, Colorado

 2 packages (3 ounces *each*) cream cheese, softened
 1/4 cup creamy peanut butter
 2 tablespoons half-and-half cream
 1 tablespoon chopped onion
 5 to 6 celery ribs, cut into thirds
Chopped salted peanuts, optional

In a small mixing bowl, beat the cream cheese, peanut butter and cream until smooth; stir in the onion. Stuff or pipe into celery; sprinkle with peanuts if desired. Refrigerate for at least 1 hour. **Yield:** 6-8 servings.

Cute Cakes Hit the Right Note

Xylophone Cakes

"Our son, Alex, came home from school telling me it was his turn to bring in a snack for his class," Michele explains. "The snacks had to use the letter of the week, which happened to be 'X'.

"My husband came up with this idea that delighted Alex's classmates and his teacher," she says.

You need just a few convenience items to assemble Xylophone Cakes. Simply slice frozen pound cake, trim the slices to create the proper shape, then decorate with tinted frosting and colorful baking bits.

For the fun final touch, use pretzel sticks and miniature marshmallows to make the mallets for the yummy musical instruments.

Xylophone Cakes

Ready in 45 minutes or less

2 loaves (10-3/4 ounces *each*) frozen pound
    cake, thawed
Yellow, green, orange and red gel food coloring
    1 can (16 ounces) vanilla frosting
M&M miniature baking bits
    28 miniature marshmallows
    28 pretzel sticks

Cut each cake widthwise into seven 1-in. slices. Trim a diagonal slice from the long sides of each slice, angling slightly, leaving 1 in. wide at a short end.

Use food coloring to tint the frosting. Carefully spread or pipe stripes on cake slices; top with miniature baking bits. For mallets, press a miniature marshmallow into one end of each pretzel stick. **Yield:** 14 cakes.

NEED A TASTY TREAT that's in tune with your child's active schedule? Try these noteworthy no-bake nibbles shared by Michele Cascais of Mendham, New Jersey.

Mom Tucks Love into Cookbook for Daughter

ANNETTE MCCLAIN has fond memories of her mother's cooking, but her mom didn't get the chance to hand down her special recipes.

"My mother passed away when I was only 15," says the Altoona, Pennsylvania cook. "Mom was a fantastic cook. Unfortunately for us kids, she didn't have her recipes written down...they were all in her head.

"I vowed when I had a daughter, she would never have to go through what I did trying to remember how Mom made certain dishes," Annette says.

"So when my daughter was small, I started a cookbook for her. I bought a three-ring binder, notebook paper and a package of sheet protectors. The plastic protectors help keep the recipes clean and easy to wipe off," she explains.

"I also use convenient stick-on tabs to label each recipe category for easy reference.

"My daughter is in her 20s now and has her own place," Annette notes. "But I still have the cookbook because I use it myself and continue to add recipes to it every time I come across something really good.

"She knows that it's hers when I'm gone. In the meantime, she calls me and asks how to make this or that. I share my recipes with her but remind her to add that one very special ingredient—love. I say if you cook with love, it will always taste good!"

"There's nothing like Mom's cooking," Annette says. "I still miss my mom's cooking to this day. If mothers would create a cookbook like this, it might help keep family traditions alive."

Banana Nut Salad

Ready in 15 minutes or less

I combine two kid-friendly flavors in this speedy salad. Children can help out by slicing and arranging the bananas. Then just stir up the dressing and serve in minutes.
—Sharon Mensing, Greenfield, Iowa

    2 medium ripe bananas, sliced
Leaf lettuce
  1/4 cup mayonnaise
    1 tablespoon peanut butter
    1 tablespoon honey
  1/4 cup chopped peanuts

Place bananas on lettuce-lined salad plates. In a small bowl, combine the mayonnaise, peanut butter and honey. Spoon over bananas; sprinkle with peanuts. **Yield:** 4 servings.

Two-Tater Shepherd's Pie

I love shepherd's pie, but our oldest son, Andrew, doesn't like some of the ingredients. So I adjusted my recipe to come up with this version the whole family loves.
—Cindy Rebain, Robertsdale, Alabama

1-1/2 pounds ground beef
    1 can (10-3/4 ounces) condensed cream of
       mushroom soup, undiluted
  1/2 teaspoon garlic salt
  1/4 teaspoon pepper
    6 cups frozen Tater Tots
    2 cups frozen French-style green beans, thawed
    3 cups hot mashed potatoes
    1 cup (4 ounces) shredded Colby cheese

In a large skillet, cook beef over medium heat until no longer pink; drain. Stir in soup, garlic salt and pepper. Place Tater Tots in a greased 13-in. x 9-in. x 2-in. baking dish. Top with beef mixture and green beans. Spread mashed potatoes over the top; sprinkle with cheese. Bake, uncovered, at 350° for 40-45 minutes or until heated through. **Yield:** 8 servings.

Lemon Pineapple Fizz

(Pictured at right)

Ready in 15 minutes or less

I blend together this fruity beverage in a jiffy. It's refreshing, delicious and a great energy booster when it comes to mowing the lawn or working in the garden.
—Nella Parker, Hersey, Michigan

    1 can (6 ounces) pineapple juice, chilled
    1 cup vanilla ice cream
  1/2 cup lemon sherbet
    1 to 2 drops yellow food coloring, optional
    1 cup lemon-lime soda, chilled

In a blender, combine the pineapple juice, ice cream, sherbet and food coloring if desired; cover and process until smooth. Pour into chilled glasses; stir in soda. **Yield:** 2 servings.

Pizza Pancakes

(Pictured below)

Ready in 30 minutes or less

I clipped this recipe from our local paper a few years ago. It's a tasty lunch treat for hearty appetites. Plan on doubling the recipe for hungry grandkids. *—Maxine Smith Owanka, South Dakota*

    2 cups biscuit/baking mix
    2 teaspoons Italian seasoning
    2 eggs
    1 cup milk
  1/2 cup shredded mozzarella cheese
  1/2 cup chopped pepperoni
  1/2 cup chopped plum tomatoes
  1/4 cup chopped green pepper
    1 can (8 ounces) pizza sauce, warmed

In a large bowl, combine the biscuit mix and Italian seasoning. Combine eggs and milk; stir into dry ingredients just until moistened. Fold in the cheese, pepperoni, tomatoes and green pepper.

Pour batter by 1/4 cupfuls onto a lightly greased hot griddle. Turn when bubbles form on top; cook until the second side is golden brown. Serve with pizza sauce. **Yield:** 14 pancakes.

Lemon Pineapple Fizz
Pizza Pancakes

Oodles of Noodles Soup

(Pictured below)

Ready in 1 hour or less

When my godchild, Alex Van Ackeren, was young, I often gave her a children's cookbook for her birthday or other special occasions. We'd plan an entire menu from the books, prepare the meal together and serve it to her family. This soup recipe was a favorite. —Lorri Reinhard
Big Bend, Wisconsin

       3/4 **pound boneless skinless chicken breasts, cubed**
         2 **medium carrots, sliced**
         1 **small onion, chopped**
         2 **celery ribs, sliced**
         1 **garlic clove, minced**
         5 **cups water**
       1/4 **teaspoon pepper**
         2 **packages (3 ounces *each*) chicken ramen noodles**

In a large saucepan coated with nonstick cooking spray, saute the chicken, carrots, onion, celery and garlic until chicken is no longer pink. Add water, pepper and contents of seasoning packets from the noodles. Bring to a boil. Reduce heat; cover and simmer for 15-20 minutes or until carrots are tender.

Break noodles into pieces and add to soup; cover and cook for 3 minutes or until tender. **Yield:** 6 servings.

Pecan Cereal Clusters

(Pictured below left)

Plan ahead...needs to chill

Featuring crunchy cereal, colorful candies, pecans and loads of peanut butter flavor, these chocolaty bites offer plenty of make-ahead convenience. They're easy to whip up when you're in a hurry. —Debbie Zorn, Vidalia, Georgia

       3/4 **cup peanut butter***
         1 **cup (6 ounces) semisweet chocolate chips**
         3 **cups Cheerios**
         1 **package (14 ounces) milk chocolate M&M's**
       3/4 **cup pecan halves**

Line three 15-in. x 10-in. x 1-in. baking pans with waxed paper. In a large heavy saucepan over low heat, cook and stir the peanut butter and chocolate chips until chips are melted. Remove from the heat; stir in Cheerios, M&M's and pecans until evenly coated. Drop by rounded tablespoonfuls onto prepared pans. Refrigerate for 4 hours or until firm. **Yield:** about 5 dozen.

***Editor's Note:** Reduced-fat or generic brands of peanut butter are not recommended for this recipe.

Banana French Toast

Ready in 15 minutes or less

I like serving bananas with traditional French toast. I created this version when we were out of bread but had leftover hot dog buns on hand. Try it with confectioners' sugar in place of the maple syrup, or top it with sliced strawberries. —Don Johnson, Southfield, Michigan

         1 **egg**
       1/4 **cup milk**
         2 **hot dog buns, split**
         1 **tablespoon butter *or* margarine**
         2 **medium ripe bananas, sliced**
Maple syrup

In a shallow bowl, whisk egg and milk. Open buns so they lie flat; dip both sides in the egg mixture. In a nonstick skillet, melt butter over medium heat. Cook buns for 2 minutes on each side or until golden brown. Fill with banana slices. Drizzle with syrup. **Yield:** 2 servings.

Pizza English Muffins

Ready in 1 hour or less

My mother prepared these individual pizzas for me from the time I started elementary school until I entered college. They're a big hit with all ages. —Lea Deluca
St. Paul, Minnesota

         2 **pounds ground beef**
     1-1/2 **pounds bulk pork sausage**

Pecan Cereal Clusters
Oodles of Noodles Soup

Cat Cookies Are 'Purr-fect' Fun

TRICK-OR-TREATERS of all ages will gobble up these adorable Halloween Cat Cookies conjured up by our Test Kitchen. The tasty treats can be served as a swift after-school snack, an appealing addition to a fall bake sale, or a quick contribution to a classroom celebration or ghoulish get-together.

Our staff made sure the cute cookies are easy to make, so even young kids can help assemble them. Simply use refrigerated dough to bake a batch of chocolate chip cookies, then spread the cooled cookies with canned chocolate frosting.

Use colorful candy and store-bought cookies to decorate each cat. Candy corn forms the eyes and button nose while red shoestring licorice becomes the whimsical whiskers. For the fast final touch, create the ears by cutting thin wafer cookies into quarters.

If you don't have these convenience items on hand, get creative with whatever no-fuss fixings you do have. The results are sure to be unforgettable.

Halloween Cat Cookies

Halloween Cat Cookies

  1 tube (18 ounces) refrigerated chocolate chip
    cookie dough
54 pieces candy corn
  1 can (16 ounces) chocolate frosting
Red shoestring licorice, cut into 1-3/8-inch pieces
  9 thin chocolate wafers (2-1/4-inch diameter),
    quartered

Bake cookies according to package directions. Cool on wire racks. Cut off yellow tips from 18 pieces of candy corn (discard orange and white portion or save for another use). Frost cookies with chocolate frosting. Immediately decorate with two whole candy corns for eyes, a yellow candy corn tip for nose, six licorice pieces for whiskers and two wafer quarters for ears. **Yield:** 1-1/2 dozen.

  1 medium onion, chopped
  1 can (6 ounces) tomato paste
  1 teaspoon garlic salt
  1 teaspoon dried oregano
1/2 teaspoon cayenne pepper
  3 packages (12 ounces *each*) English muffins,
    split
  3 cups (12 ounces) shredded mozzarella cheese
  2 cups (8 ounces) shredded cheddar cheese
  2 cups (8 ounces) shredded Swiss cheese

In a Dutch oven, cook the beef, sausage and onion over medium heat until meat is no longer pink; drain. Stir in the tomato paste, garlic salt, oregano and cayenne. Spread over the cut side of each English muffin. Place on baking sheets. Combine the cheeses; sprinkle over meat mixture.

Freeze for up to 3 months or bake at 350° for 15-20 minutes or until heated through. **Yield:** 6 dozen.

  To use frozen Pizza English Muffins: Bake at 350° for 30 minutes.

Eye Appeal

I know how to bring smiles to little ones in the morning. I use large metal cookie cutters to shape our breakfast pancakes.

I clip a clean wooden clothespin on the rim of a cookie cutter in a hot skillet. Then I carefully pour pancake batter inside the cutter. When bubbles form on top of the batter, I remove the cutter by lifting the clothespin and flip the pancake.
          —*Marcie Nor*
          Macungie, Pennsylvania

Create a Winter Wonderland

SEARCHING for a fun activity to celebrate the season? Assemble these incredible edible evergreens from Carla Harris of Trenton, Tennessee.

"I came up with this idea when my mother-in-law brought our children horns of plenty for Thanksgiving," she recalls. "She poured a little melted chocolate into sugar cones and filled them with candy corn and candy pumpkins, then placed them on grass made from green-tinted frosting."

Carla capitalized on the idea at Christmastime by sprucing up ice cream cones to fashion some frosted firs. "I made 30 of these Sugar Cone Spruce Trees for a school Christmas party," she notes. She spread each cone with green frosting and placed it on a layer of white frosting "snow" on a disposable foam dessert plate.

"I used red-hots for ornaments, placed a star-shaped piece of cereal on the top of each tree and arranged foil-wrapped candy around the base of the trees to look like Christmas presents," she explains. "The kids loved them!"

Our home economists added powdered sugar to the prepared frosting to improve its consistency for decorating. Younger kids can use a butter knife to spread the green frosting on the cones while adults may want to pipe it on with a decorating tip to give the trees a more finished look.

"Start these the night before and store them in a cool place to harden the frosting slightly," Carla suggests.

To complement the trees, our Test Kitchen constructed simple Sledding Snacks. Store-bought frosting is used to attach mini candy cane "runners" to the graham cracker sleds.

For festive finishing touches, the frosted sleds are decorated with colored sprinkles and tied with red shoestring licorice "ropes".

These downhill delights are adorable when arranged on a plate with the Sugar Cone Spruce Trees to create a snowy scene, as shown in the photo at left. Or use both treats alongside a gingerbread house for extra atmosphere.

They can also be served individually at children's parties or used to add a holiday touch to meal trays at hospitals and retirement homes.

Sugar Cone Spruce Trees

(Pictured at left and on page 242)

Ready in 1 hour or less

    8 sugar ice cream cones
    1 can (16 ounces) vanilla frosting, *divided*
    1/2 cup confectioners' sugar
Green gel food coloring
Assorted candy decorations

Using a serrated knife, carefully score and cut ice cream cones to desired heights. In a small bowl, combine 3/4 cup frosting and confectioners' sugar; tint green. Set remaining frosting aside.

Cut a hole in the corner of a pastry or plastic bag; insert star tip #77. Fill with green frosting. Pipe frosting in overlapping rows over cones. Decorate with candies. When frosting on trees is dry, spread white frosting over a large serving platter to resemble snow. Arrange trees on frosted platter. **Yield:** 8 trees.

Sledding Snacks

(Pictured above left and on page 242)

Ready in 30 minutes or less

    3 whole graham crackers (about 5 inches x
        2-1/2 inches)
    1/2 cup vanilla frosting
    24 miniature candy canes
Assorted candy decorations
    12 pieces red shoestring licorice (12 inches *each*)

Break or cut each graham cracker along perforations into four pieces. Spread a small amount of frosting over both sides of crackers. Immediately press two candy canes into frosting on one side; press assorted decorations into the other side. Let stand until set. Tie ends of licorice together and loop around candy canes. **Yield:** 1 dozen.

Hot Dog Pie

Hot Dog Pie

(Pictured above)

Ready in 30 minutes or less

I received this recipe from a co-worker who loves hot dogs. It's a big hit for family get-togethers. It's so convenient, I usually double this recipe and put one pie in the freezer for times when we need a fast meal.
—Amy Bullis, Henryville, Pennsylvania

  1/2 pound ground beef
    4 hot dogs, cut in half lengthwise and sliced
    1 can (16 ounces) baked beans
  1/2 cup ketchup
    2 tablespoons brown sugar
    2 tablespoons prepared mustard
    2 ounces process cheese (Velveeta), cubed
    1 unbaked deep-dish pastry shell (9 inches)
    4 slices American cheese

In a large saucepan, cook beef over medium heat until no longer pink; drain. Add the hot dogs, beans, ketchup, brown sugar, mustard and cheese cubes. Cook and stir until cheese is melted.

  Meanwhile, prick pastry shell with a fork. Bake at 400° for 10 minutes. Fill with hot beef mixture. Cut each cheese slice into four strips; make a lattice topping over pie. Bake 5-10 minutes longer or until cheese is melted. **Yield:** 4-6 servings.

Baked Bean Corn Bread

Ready in 45 minutes or less

Our daughter Kaitlin created this moist bread. She loves to fix it for our family along with hot dogs and a salad. It's quick, simple, delicious and kid-friendly.
—Lauren McBride, Houston, Texas

    2 packages (8-1/2 ounces *each*) corn
      bread/muffin mix

  2/3 cup milk
    2 eggs, lightly beaten
    1 can (10 ounces) baked beans

In a large mixing bowl, combine the corn bread mixes, milk and eggs. Pour 1-1/2 cups of batter into a greased 9-in. pie plate. Spread with baked beans. Spread with remaining batter. Bake, uncovered, at 400° for 25-30 minutes or until a toothpick inserted into corn bread comes out clean. Serve warm. **Yield:** 4-6 servings.

Apple Peanut Salad

Ready in 15 minutes or less

I need just three items to toss together this sweet side dish. It's crunchy from crisp apples and peanuts yet sweet and fluffy from whipped topping.
—Heidi Wilcox
Lapeer, Michigan

    4 medium apples, diced
    3 cups salted dry roasted peanuts
    1 carton (8 ounces) frozen whipped topping,
      thawed

In a large bowl, combine the apples, peanuts and whipped topping. Cover and refrigerate until serving. **Yield:** 10 servings.

More Fun Food Ideas

- Make nifty necklaces with string and dry wagon wheel or tube pasta. Or use laces of licorice and doughnut-shaped cereal to create colorful bracelets or fun Hawaiian leis.
- Work together to plan a silly supper menu where the meal is served backward. Start with a favorite dessert, then enjoy an easy-to-assemble entree followed by an appealing appetizer.

Chapter 18

 ⟨🕐⟩ *Timeless Recipes with Kitchen Tools*

SLOW COOKERS, grills and microwaves are the convenient tools busy cooks use to get themselves out of the kitchen fast when time is tight.

You can easily assemble all the ingredients for wonderful recipes in your slow cooker with just a little preparation. Then simply put on the lid, switch on the pot...and go!

When it comes to putting a meal on the table in a hurry, grilling is "hot" no matter what the season.

Time-conscious cooks know the magic of a microwave. Now you can use yours for more than warming coffee and reheating leftovers.

SUPER SLOW-COOKED SUPPER.
Sausage Dressing and Turkey in a Pot
(recipes on p. 267).

Slow-Cooked Specialties

Nothing says "welcome home" like the aroma of a comforting dinner greeting you when you walk through the door.

By adding a few ingredients to your slow cooker in the morning, you're well on your way to having supper ready for you at the end of the day. Simply put on the lid...switch on the pot...and go!

This handy appliance slowly simmers foods to full-flavored perfection while you're gone. When you come home, your family can enjoy a hearty home-made meal—without fussing over last-minute details.

Mushroom Chicken Cacciatore

I give an Italian treatment to chicken by slow-cooking it in a zesty tomato sauce and serving it over spaghetti. It's great for company because it frees up time to spend with guests. Toss a salad and you're ready to eat.
—Jane Bone
Cape Coral, Florida

    4 boneless skinless chicken breast halves
       (about 1-1/2 pounds)
    2 tablespoons vegetable oil
    1 can (15 ounces) tomato sauce
    2 cans (4 ounces *each*) sliced mushrooms,
       drained
    1 medium onion, chopped
  1/4 cup red wine *or* chicken broth
    2 garlic cloves, minced
1-1/4 teaspoons dried oregano
  1/2 teaspoon dried thyme
  1/8 to 1/4 teaspoon salt
  1/8 teaspoon pepper
Hot cooked spaghetti

In a large skillet, brown chicken in oil on both sides. Transfer to a slow cooker. In a bowl, combine the tomato sauce, mushrooms, onion, wine or broth, garlic, oregano, thyme, salt and pepper; pour over chicken. Cover and cook on low for 4-5 hours or until chicken juices run clear. Serve over spaghetti. **Yield:** 4 servings.

Red Bean Vegetable Soup

The addition of Cajun seasoning boosts the flavor of this brothy soup. The easy recipe makes a big batch that's loaded with fresh vegetable chunks and canned beans.
—Ronnie Lappe, Brownwood, Texas

✓ Uses less fat, sugar or salt. Includes Nutritional Analysis and Diabetic Exchanges.

    3 large sweet red peppers, chopped
    3 celery ribs, chopped
    2 medium onions, chopped
    4 cans (16 ounces *each*) red kidney beans,
       rinsed and drained
    4 cups chicken broth
    2 bay leaves
  1/2 to 1 teaspoon salt
  1/2 to 1 teaspoon Cajun seasoning
  1/2 teaspoon pepper
  1/4 to 1/2 teaspoon hot pepper sauce

In a 5-qt. slow cooker, combine the peppers, celery, onions and beans. Stir in the remaining ingredients. Cover and cook on low for 6 hours or until vegetables are tender. Discard bay leaves before serving. **Yield:** 12 servings (3 quarts).

Nutritional Analysis: One 1-cup serving (prepared with reduced-sodium chicken broth, 1/2 teaspoon salt and 1/4 teaspoon hot pepper sauce) equals 156 calories, 1 g fat (trace saturated fat), 1 mg cholesterol, 688 mg sodium, 28 g carbohydrate, 7 g fiber, 10 g protein. **Diabetic Exchange:** 2 starch.

Sausage Pepper Sandwiches

Peppers and onions add a fresh taste to this zippy sausage filling for sandwiches. My mother gave me this recipe. It's simple to assemble, and it's gobbled up quickly.
—Suzette Gessel, Albuquerque, New Mexico

    5 uncooked Italian sausage links (about 20
       ounces)
    1 medium green pepper, cut into 1-inch pieces
    1 medium sweet red pepper, cut into 1-inch
       pieces
    1 large onion, cut into 1-inch pieces
    1 can (8 ounces) tomato sauce
  1/8 teaspoon pepper
    6 hoagie *or* submarine sandwich buns, split

In a large skillet, brown sausage links over medium heat. Cut into 1/2-in. slices; place in a slow cooker. Stir in the peppers, onion, tomato sauce and pepper. Cover and cook on low for 8 hours or until sausage is no longer pink and vegetables are tender. Use a slotted spoon to serve on buns. **Yield:** 6 servings.

Old-Fashioned Pot Roast

(Pictured above right)

We raise beef and have a large garden, so I try to find new ways to use these ingredients to make nutritious meals. Simmered in a brown gravy flecked with veggies, this roast is fork-tender when sliced.
—Joan Airey
Rivers, Manitoba

    1 boneless beef rump roast (3-1/2 to 4
       pounds)
    1 tablespoon vegetable oil
    1 teaspoon pepper
    2 medium carrots, grated
    1 medium onion, thinly sliced
    2 garlic cloves, minced

Old-Fashioned Pot Roast
Sausage Spanish Rice

1 can (8 ounces) tomato sauce
1/4 cup red wine *or* beef broth
1 tablespoon Worcestershire sauce
1/2 teaspoon salt
1/2 teaspoon *each* dried basil, marjoram, oregano and thyme
3 tablespoons cornstarch
3 tablespoons cold water

Cut roast in half; brown in a Dutch oven in oil on all sides. Sprinkle with pepper. Place the carrots, onion and garlic in a 5-qt. slow cooker; top with the roast. In a bowl, combine the tomato sauce, wine or broth, Worcestershire sauce and seasonings; pour over roast. Cover and cook on low for 8-10 hours or until meat is tender.

Remove meat and keep warm. Skim fat from cooking juices; pour into a saucepan. Bring to a boil. In a small bowl, combine the cornstarch and water until smooth; stir into cooking juices. Return to a boil; cook and stir for 1-2 minutes or until thickened. Serve with sliced beef. **Yield:** 12-14 servings.

Sausage Spanish Rice

(Pictured above)

My husband and I both work the midnight shift, so I'm always on the lookout for slow-cooker recipes. This one couldn't be easier. It's good as a side dish, but we often enjoy it as the main course because it's so hearty and filling. —Michelle McKay, Garden City, Michigan

✓ Uses less fat, sugar or salt. Includes Nutritional Analysis and Diabetic Exchanges.

1 pound fully cooked kielbasa *or* Polish sausage, cut into 1/4-inch slices
2 cans (14-1/2 ounces *each*) diced tomatoes, undrained
2 cups water
1-1/2 cups uncooked converted rice*
1 cup salsa
1 medium onion
1/2 cup chopped green pepper
1/2 cup chopped sweet red pepper
1 can (4 ounces) chopped green chilies
1 envelope taco seasoning

In a slow cooker, combine all ingredients; stir to blend. Cover and cook on low for 5-6 hours or until rice is tender. **Yield:** 9 servings.

Nutritional Analysis: One 1-cup serving (prepared with turkey sausage) equals 247 calories, 5 g fat (2 g saturated fat), 27 mg cholesterol, 1,153 mg sodium, 40 g carbohydrate, 3 g fiber, 12 g protein. **Diabetic Exchanges:** 2 starch, 1 meat, 1 vegetable.

*Editor's Note: This recipe was tested with Uncle Ben's converted rice.

Slow-Cooked Ham

(Pictured below)

Entertaining doesn't get much easier than when you serve this tasty five-ingredient entree. I first prepared it for Christmas with great results. Leftovers are delicious in casseroles.
—Heather Spring
Sheppard Air Force Base, Texas

      1/2 cup packed brown sugar
         1 teaspoon ground mustard
         1 teaspoon prepared horseradish
         4 tablespoons regular cola, *divided*
         1 boneless smoked ham (5 to 6 pounds),
              cut in half

In a bowl, combine the brown sugar, mustard, horse-radish and 2 tablespoons cola; mix well. Rub over ham. Place in a 5-qt. slow cooker; pour remaining cola over ham. Cover and cook on low for 8-10 hours or until a meat thermometer reads 140°. **Yield:** 15-20 servings.

Creamy Red Potatoes

(Pictured below)

I put my slow cooker to work to fix these saucy spuds. The delightful side dish features cubed red potatoes that are cooked in a creamy, cheesy coating until they are tender.

Be sure to stir the mixture before serving to help the sauce thicken.
—Elaine Ryan, Holley, New York

         7 cups cubed uncooked red potatoes
         1 cup (8 ounces) small-curd cottage cheese
      1/2 cup sour cream
      1/2 cup cubed process cheese (Velveeta)
         1 tablespoon dried minced onion
         2 garlic cloves, minced
      1/2 teaspoon salt
Paprika and minced chives, optional

Place the potatoes in a slow cooker. In a blender or food processor, puree cottage cheese and sour cream until smooth. Transfer to a bowl; stir in the process cheese, onion, garlic and salt. Pour over potatoes and mix well.

Cover and cook on low for 5-6 hours or until potatoes are tender. Stir well before serving. Garnish with paprika and chives if desired. **Yield:** 8 servings.

Southwestern Chicken Soup

This slow cooker recipe brings people back for seconds. Chock-full of chicken, corn, tomatoes, peppers and chilies, the savory soup is sure to put a little zip in mealtime.
—Harold Tartar
West Palm Beach, Florida

Slow-Cooked Ham
Creamy Red Potatoes

1-1/4 pounds boneless skinless chicken breasts, cut into thin strips
1 to 2 tablespoons canola *or* vegetable oil
2 cans (14-1/2 ounces *each*) chicken broth
1 package (16 ounces) frozen corn, thawed
1 can (14-1/2 ounces) diced tomatoes, undrained
1 medium onion, chopped
1 medium green pepper, chopped
1 medium sweet red pepper, chopped
1 can (4 ounces) chopped green chilies
1-1/2 teaspoons seasoned salt, optional
1 teaspoon ground cumin
1/2 teaspoon garlic powder

In a large skillet, saute the chicken in oil until lightly browned. Transfer to a 5-qt. slow cooker with a slotted spoon. Stir in the remaining ingredients. Cover and cook on low for 7-8 hours. Stir before serving. **Yield:** 10 servings.
Nutritional Analysis: One 1-cup serving (prepared with 1 tablespoon oil and reduced-sodium broth and without seasoned salt) equals 144 calories, 3 g fat (trace saturated fat), 33 mg cholesterol, 350 mg sodium, 15 g carbohydrate, 3 g fiber, 16 g protein. **Diabetic Exchanges:** 2 very lean meat, 1 starch.

Round Steak Supper

Here's a meat-and-potatoes dinner that will help you stick to your budget. Inexpensive round steak and potatoes are simmered for hours in an onion-flavored gravy to create the satisfying supper. —Sandra Castillo
Sun Prairie, Wisconsin

4 large potatoes, peeled and cut into 1/2-inch cubes
1-1/2 pounds boneless beef round steak
1 can (10-3/4 ounces) condensed cream of mushroom soup, undiluted
1/2 cup water
1 envelope onion soup mix
Pepper and garlic powder to taste

Place the potatoes in a slow cooker. Cut beef into four pieces; place over potatoes. In a bowl, combine the soup, water, soup mix, pepper and garlic powder. Pour over the beef. Cover and cook on low for 6-8 hours or until meat and potatoes are tender. **Yield:** 4 servings.

Saucy Pork Chops

I serve these tender chops a couple of times a month because we just love them. The tangy sauce is delicious over mashed potatoes, rice or noodles. —Sharon Polk
Lapeer, Michigan

8 boneless pork chops (1/2 inch thick)
2 tablespoons vegetable oil
1/4 teaspoon salt
1/8 teaspoon pepper
2 cans (10-3/4 ounces *each*) condensed cream of chicken soup, undiluted
1 medium onion, chopped
1/2 cup ketchup
2 tablespoons Worcestershire sauce
Mashed potatoes *or* hot cooked rice

In a large skillet, cook pork chops in oil until lightly browned on each side. Sprinkle with salt and pepper. Transfer to a slow cooker. In a bowl, combine the soup, onion, ketchup and Worcestershire sauce; pour over chops. Cover and cook on high for 4-5 hours or until meat juices run clear. Serve over potatoes or rice. **Yield:** 8 servings.

Crunchy Candy Clusters

Before I retired, I took these yummy peanut butter bites to work for special occasions. They're so simple. I still make them for holidays because my family looks forward to the coated cereal and marshmallow clusters.
—Faye O'Bryan, Owensboro, Kentucky

2 pounds white candy coating, broken into small pieces
1-1/2 cups peanut butter
1/2 teaspoon almond extract, optional
4 cups Cap'n Crunch cereal
4 cups crisp rice cereal
4 cups miniature marshmallows

Place candy coating in a 5-qt. slow cooker. Cover and cook on high for 1 hour. Add peanut butter. Stir in extract if desired. In a large bowl, combine the cereals and marshmallows. Stir in the peanut butter mixture until well coated. Drop by tablespoonfuls onto waxed paper. Let stand until set. Store at room temperature. **Yield:** 6-1/2 dozen.

Hearty Beans with Beef

My husband raved about this sweet bean dish after tasting it at a party, so I knew I had to get the recipe. It's perfect for get-togethers because you can mix it up a day early and toss it in the slow cooker a few hours before your guests arrive.
—Jan Biehl, Leesburg, Indiana

1 pound ground beef
1 medium onion, chopped
1 can (16 ounces) baked beans, undrained
1 can (15-1/2 ounces) chili beans, undrained
1 can (15-1/2 ounces) butter beans, rinsed and drained
1/2 cup ketchup
1/3 cup packed brown sugar
1 tablespoon barbecue sauce
1/4 teaspoon Worcestershire sauce

In a large skillet, cook beef and onion over medium heat until meat is no longer pink; drain. Transfer to a slow cooker. Stir in the remaining ingredients. Cover and cook on high for 3-4 hours or until heated through. **Yield:** 8-10 servings.

Cabbage Kielbasa Supper

If you're a fan of German food, you'll enjoy this traditional combination of sausage, cabbage and potatoes. This hearty main dish is so good. All you need is a bowl of fruit and dinner's ready. —Margery Bryan, Royal City, Washington

- 8 cups coarsely shredded cabbage
- 3 medium potatoes, cut into 1/2-inch cubes
- 1 medium onion, chopped
- 1-3/4 teaspoons salt
- 1/4 teaspoon pepper
- 1 can (14-1/2 ounces) chicken broth
- 2 pounds fully cooked kielbasa *or* Polish sausage, cut into serving-size pieces

In a 5-qt. slow cooker, combine the cabbage, potatoes, onion, salt and pepper. Pour broth over all. Place sausage on top (slow cooker will be full, but cabbage will cook down). Cover and cook on low for 8-9 hours or until vegetables are tender and sausage is heated through. **Yield:** 6-8 servings.

Creamy Herbed Chicken

I'm a nurse and work nights, so when I get home in the morning, I put this chicken on to cook. At the end of the day, the chicken is moist and tender, and the rich sauce seasoned with garlic and thyme is delicious. —Mary Humeniuk-Smith Perry Hall, Maryland

- 4 boneless skinless chicken breast halves
- 1 can (10-3/4 ounces) condensed cream of chicken soup, undiluted
- 1 cup milk
- 1 envelope garlic and herb pasta sauce mix*
- 1 teaspoon dried thyme
- 1 teaspoon dried parsley flakes
- Hot cooked fettuccine

Place chicken in a slow cooker. Combine the soup, milk, sauce mix, thyme and parsley; pour over chicken. Cover and cook on low for 4-5 hours or until chicken juices run clear. Serve over fettuccine. **Yield:** 4 servings.
  *Editor's Note: This recipe was tested with Knorr Garlic Herb Pasta Sauce Mix.

Slow-Cooked Stroganoff

I've been preparing this delicious Stroganoff in the slow cooker for more than 20 years. Once you've done it this way, you'll never cook it on the stovetop again. It's great for family or company. —Karen Herbert Placerville, California

- 3 pounds boneless beef round steak
- 1/2 cup all-purpose flour
- 1-1/2 teaspoons salt
- 1/2 teaspoon ground mustard
- 1/8 teaspoon pepper
- 1 medium onion, sliced and separated into rings

- 2 cans (4 ounces *each*) mushroom stems and pieces, drained
- 1 can (10-1/2 ounces) condensed beef broth, undiluted
- 1-1/2 cups (12 ounces) sour cream
- Hot cooked noodles

Cut round steak into 3-in. x 1/2-in. strips. In a large resealable plastic bag, combine flour, salt, mustard and pepper. Add beef in batches; toss to coat.
  In a 5-qt. slow cooker, layer the onion, mushrooms and beef. Pour broth over all. Cover and cook on low for 8-10 hours or until meat is tender. Just before serving, stir in the sour cream. Serve over noodles. **Yield:** 8-10 servings.

Ham and Bean Stew

Only five ingredients are needed to fix this thick, flavorful stew. It's very easy to make and a favorite with my family. I top bowls of it with grated cheese. —Teresa D'Amato, East Granby, Connecticut

- 2 cans (16 ounces *each*) baked beans
- 2 medium potatoes, peeled and cubed
- 2 cups cubed fully cooked ham
- 1 celery rib, chopped
- 1/2 cup water

In a slow cooker, combine all ingredients; mix well. Cover and cook on low for 7 hours or until the potatoes are tender. **Yield:** 6 servings.

Pork Chop Dinner

Canned soup creates a comforting gravy for tender pork and potatoes in this simple meal-in-one. Feel free to vary the amount of onion soup mix in the recipe to suit your family's tastes. —Mike Avery Battle Creek, Michigan

- 6 to 8 medium carrots (1 pound), coarsely chopped
- 3 to 4 medium potatoes, cubed
- 4 boneless pork loin chops (3/4 inch thick)
- 1 large onion, sliced
- 1 envelope onion soup mix
- 2 cans (10-3/4 ounces *each*) condensed cream of mushroom soup, undiluted

Place carrots and potatoes in a slow cooker. Top with the pork chops, onion, soup mix and soup. Cover and cook on low for 6-8 hours or until meat and vegetables are tender. **Yield:** 4 servings.

Sweet and Savory Ribs

(Pictured above right)

My husband, Randy, and I love barbecued ribs, but with our conflicting schedules, we rarely have time to fire up the grill. So we let the slow cooker do the work for us. By the time we get home from work, the ribs are tender, juicy and ready to devour. —Kandy Bingham, Green River, Wyoming

Chocolate Bread Pudding
Sweet and Savory Ribs

1 large onion, sliced and separated into rings
2-1/2 to 3 pounds boneless country-style
    pork ribs
1 bottle (18 ounces) honey barbecue sauce
1/3 cup maple syrup
1/4 cup spicy brown mustard
1/2 teaspoon salt
1/4 teaspoon pepper

Place the onion in a 5-qt. slow cooker. Top with the ribs. Combine the barbecue sauce, syrup, mustard, salt and pepper; pour over ribs. Cover and cook on low for 8-9 hours or until the meat is tender. **Yield:** 6-8 servings.

Chocolate Bread Pudding

(Pictured above)

I love chocolate and berries, so I was thrilled to come across this recipe that combines the two. I like to use egg bread when making this dessert. Since it cooks in the slow cooker, I can tend to other things. —Becky Foster, Union, Oregon

6 cups cubed day-old bread (3/4-inch cubes)
1-1/2 cups semisweet chocolate chips
1 cup fresh raspberries
4 eggs
1/2 cup heavy whipping cream
1/2 cup milk
1/4 cup sugar
1 teaspoon vanilla extract
Whipped cream and additional raspberries, optional

In a greased slow cooker, layer half of the bread cubes, chocolate chips and raspberries. Repeat layers. In a bowl, whisk eggs, cream, milk, sugar and vanilla. Pour over bread mixture.

Cover and cook on high for 2-1/4 to 2-1/2 hours or until a thermometer reads 160°. Let stand for 5-10 minutes. Serve with whipped cream and additional raspberries if desired. **Yield:** 6-8 servings.

Creamy Corn

(Pictured below)

A handful of ingredients and a slow cooker are all you'll need for this rich side dish. I first tasted it at a potluck with our camping club. It's easy to assemble and frees up time to prepare the main course. —Judy McCarthy
Derby, Kansas

 2 packages (16 ounces *each*) frozen corn
 1 package (8 ounces) cream cheese, cubed
 1/3 cup butter *or* margarine, cubed
 1/2 teaspoon garlic powder
 1/2 teaspoon salt
 1/4 teaspoon pepper

In a slow cooker, combine all ingredients. Cover and cook on low for 4 hours or until heated through and cheese is melted. Stir well before serving. **Yield:** 6 servings.

No-Fuss Swiss Steak

(Pictured below)

I received the recipe for this dish from my cousin. I make it regularly because our children love the savory steak, tangy gravy and fork-tender veggies. —Sharon Morrell
Parker, South Dakota

 3 pounds boneless beef round steak, cut into serving-size pieces
 2 tablespoons vegetable oil
 2 medium carrots, cut into 1/2-inch slices
 2 celery ribs, cut into 1/2-inch slices
 1-3/4 cups water

 1 can (11 ounces) condensed tomato rice soup, undiluted
 1 can (10-1/2 ounces) condensed French onion soup, undiluted
 1/2 teaspoon pepper
 1 bay leaf

In a large skillet, brown beef in oil over medium-high heat; drain. Transfer to a 5-qt. slow cooker. Add carrots and celery. Combine the remaining ingredients; pour over meat and vegetables. Cover and cook on low for 6-8 hours or until meat is tender.

Discard the bay leaf before serving. Thicken cooking juices if desired. **Yield:** 8-10 servings.

Old-Fashioned Peach Butter

Using the slow cooker to make this tasty spread eliminates much of the stirring required when simmering fruit butter on the stovetop. —Marilou Robinson, Portland, Oregon

 14 cups coarsely chopped peeled fresh *or* frozen peaches (about 5-1/2 pounds)
 2-1/2 cups sugar
 4-1/2 teaspoons lemon juice
 1-1/2 teaspoons ground cinnamon
 3/4 teaspoon ground cloves
 1/2 cup quick-cooking tapioca

In a large bowl, combine the peaches, sugar, lemon juice, cinnamon and cloves; mix well. Transfer to a 5-qt. slow cooker. Cover and cook on low for 8-10 hours or until peaches are very soft, stirring occasionally.

Stir in tapioca. Cook, uncovered, on high for 1 hour

Creamy Corn
No-Fuss Swiss Steak

or until thickened. Pour into jars or freezer containers; cool to room temperature, about 1 hour. Refrigerate or freeze. **Yield:** 9 cups.

Vegetable-Stuffed Peppers

I like to fix meatless main dishes for a change of pace. This flavorful combination has become a monthly mainstay for my family. —Sandra Allen, Austin, Texas

    2 cans (14-1/2 ounces *each*) diced tomatoes, undrained
    1 can (16 ounces) kidney beans, rinsed and drained
1-1/2 cups cooked rice
    2 cups (8 ounces) shredded cheddar cheese, *divided*
    1 package (10 ounces) frozen corn, thawed
1/4 cup chopped onion
    1 teaspoon Worcestershire sauce
3/4 teaspoon chili powder
1/2 teaspoon pepper
1/4 teaspoon salt
    6 medium green peppers

In a large bowl, combine the tomatoes, beans, rice, 1-1/2 cups cheese, corn, onion, Worcestershire sauce, chili powder, pepper and salt; mix well. Remove and discard tops and seeds of green peppers. Fill each pepper with about 1 cup of the vegetable mixture. Place in a 5-qt. slow cooker. Cover and cook on low for 8 hours.

Sprinkle with remaining cheese. Cover and cook 15 minutes longer or until peppers are tender and cheese is melted. **Yield:** 6 servings.

Slow-Cooked Italian Chicken

With its nicely seasoned tomato sauce, this enticing chicken entree is especially good over pasta or rice.
—Deanna D'Auria, Banning, California

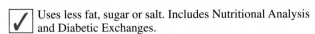 Uses less fat, sugar or salt. Includes Nutritional Analysis and Diabetic Exchanges.

    4 boneless skinless chicken breast halves (4 ounces *each*)
    1 can (14-1/2 ounces) chicken broth
    1 can (14-1/2 ounces) stewed tomatoes, cut up
    1 can (8 ounces) tomato sauce
    1 medium green pepper, chopped
    1 green onion, chopped
    1 garlic clove, minced
    3 teaspoons chili powder
    1 teaspoon ground mustard
1/2 teaspoon garlic salt *or* garlic powder
1/2 teaspoon onion salt *or* onion powder
1/2 teaspoon pepper
1/3 cup all-purpose flour
1/2 cup cold water
Hot cooked noodles

Place the chicken in a slow cooker. In a bowl, combine the next 11 ingredients; pour over chicken. Cover and cook on low for 4-5 hours or until chicken juices run clear.

Remove chicken and keep warm. Pour cooking juices into a saucepan; skim fat. Combine flour and cold water until smooth; stir into juices. Bring to a boil; cook and stir for 2 minutes or until thickened. Serve over chicken and noodles. **Yield:** 4 servings.

Nutritional Analysis: One chicken breast half with 1/2 cup sauce (prepared with reduced-sodium broth, garlic powder and onion powder; calculated without noodles) equals 241 calories, 2 g fat (trace saturated fat), 66 mg cholesterol, 1,003 mg sodium, 25 g carbohydrate, 4 g fiber, 31 g protein. **Diabetic Exchanges:** 2-1/2 lean meat, 1-1/2 starch.

Sweet-and-Sour Smokies

This warm appetizer is so simple to make but so tasty. I use cherry pie filling, chunks of pineapple and a little brown sugar to create a fruity sauce that's just perfect for mini sausage links. —Debi Hetland, Rochelle, Illinois

    2 packages (16 ounces *each*) miniature smoked sausage links
    2 cans (21 ounces *each*) cherry pie filling
    1 can (20 ounces) pineapple chunks, drained
    3 tablespoons brown sugar

Place sausages in a slow cooker. In a bowl, combine the pie filling, pineapple and brown sugar; pour over sausages. Cover and cook on low for 4 hours. **Yield:** 16-20 servings.

Flank Steak Fajitas

The slow cooker tenderizes the flank steak for these filling fajitas, which have just the right amount of spice.
—Twila Burkholder, Middleburg, Pennsylvania

1-1/2 to 2 pounds beef flank steak, cut into thin strips
    1 can (10 ounces) diced tomatoes and green chilies, undrained
    2 garlic cloves, minced
    1 jalapeno pepper, seeded and chopped*
    1 tablespoon minced fresh cilantro *or* parsley
    1 teaspoon chili powder
1/2 teaspoon ground cumin
1/4 teaspoon salt
    1 medium sweet red pepper, julienned
    1 medium green pepper, julienned
    8 to 10 flour tortillas (7 to 8 inches)
Sour cream, salsa and shredded cheddar cheese, optional

Place beef in a slow cooker. In a bowl, combine the tomatoes, garlic, jalapeno, cilantro, chili powder, cumin and salt; pour over beef. Cover and cook on low for 7-8 hours. Stir in red and green peppers. Cook 1 hour longer or until meat and peppers are tender. Thicken juices if desired.

Using a slotted spoon, place about 1/2 cup beef mixture down the center of each tortilla; fold sides over filling. Serve with sour cream, salsa and cheese if desired. **Yield:** 8-10 servings.

*Editor's Note: When cutting or seeding hot peppers, use rubber or plastic gloves to protect your hands.

Melt-in-Your-Mouth Meat Loaf

When my husband and I were first married, he refused to eat meat loaf because he said it was bland and dry. Then I prepared this version, and it became his favorite meal.   —Suzanne Codner, Starbuck, Minnesota

          2 eggs
      3/4 cup milk
      2/3 cup seasoned bread crumbs
          2 teaspoons dried minced onion
          1 teaspoon salt
      1/2 teaspoon rubbed sage
  1-1/2 pounds ground beef
      1/4 cup ketchup
          2 tablespoons brown sugar
          1 teaspoon ground mustard
      1/2 teaspoon Worcestershire sauce

In a large bowl, combine the first six ingredients. Crumble beef over mixture and mix well (mixture will be moist). Shape into a round loaf; place in a 5-qt. slow cooker. Cover and cook on low for 5-6 hours or until a meat thermometer reads 160°.

In a small bowl, whisk the ketchup, brown sugar, mustard and Worcestershire sauce. Spoon over the meat loaf. Cook 15 minutes longer or until heated through. Let stand for 10-15 minutes before cutting. **Yield:** 6 servings.

Slow-Cooked White Chili

This satisfying slow-simmered chili features chicken, two kinds of beans and crunchy corn. It's quick, easy and tastes great. It's a family favorite that we enjoy with corn bread.   —Lori Weber
Wentzville, Missouri

✓ Uses less fat, sugar or salt. Includes Nutritional Analysis and Diabetic Exchanges.

      3/4 pound boneless skinless chicken breasts,
          cubed
          1 medium onion, chopped
          1 garlic clove, minced
          1 tablespoon vegetable *or* canola oil
  1-1/2 cups water
          1 can (15 ounces) white kidney *or* cannelini
          beans, rinsed and drained
          1 can (15 ounces) garbanzo beans, rinsed and
          drained
          1 can (11 ounces) whole kernel white corn,
          drained *or* 1-1/4 cups frozen shoepeg corn
          1 can (4 ounces) chopped green chilies
          1 to 2 teaspoons chicken bouillon granules
          1 teaspoon ground cumin

In a large skillet, saute chicken, onion and garlic in oil until onion is tender. Transfer to a slow cooker. Stir in the remaining ingredients. Cover and cook on low for 7-8 hours or until chicken juices run clear and flavors are blended. **Yield:** 8 servings (2 quarts).

Nutritional Analysis: One 1-cup serving (prepared with frozen corn and 1 teaspoon bouillon) equals 196 calories, 4 g fat (trace saturated fat), 25 mg cholesterol, 361 mg sodium, 25 g carbohydrate, 6 g fiber, 15 g protein. **Diabetic Exchanges:** 2 very lean meat, 1-1/2 starch.

Pork and Veggie Soup

Looking for a change from typical vegetable beef soup? Try this hearty combination. A tasty broth has tender chunks of pork and a bounty of veggies, including carrots, green beans, diced tomatoes and corn.   —Jennifer Honeycutt
Nashville, Tennessee

          2 pounds boneless pork, cubed
          2 tablespoons vegetable oil
          2 cups water
          4 medium carrots, cut into 1-inch pieces
          1 can (14-1/2 ounces) diced tomatoes,
          undrained
  1-1/2 cups frozen corn
  1-1/2 cups frozen cut green beans
          1 large onion, chopped
          1 jar (8 ounces) salsa
          1 can (4 ounces) chopped green chilies
          1 tablespoon minced fresh parsley
          2 garlic cloves, minced
          2 teaspoons beef bouillon granules
          2 teaspoons ground cumin
      1/2 teaspoon salt
      1/2 teaspoon pepper

In a large skillet, brown pork in oil over medium heat; drain. Transfer to a slow cooker. Stir in the remaining ingredients. Cover and cook on low for 7-8 hours or until meat juices run clear and vegetables are tender. **Yield:** 9 servings.

Mushroom Potatoes

I jazz up sliced potatoes with mushrooms, onions, canned soup and cheese to create this versatile side dish. With its comforting flavor, it's a nice accompaniment to most meats.   —Linda Bernard, Golden Meadow, Louisiana

          7 medium potatoes, peeled and thinly sliced
          1 medium onion, sliced
          4 garlic cloves, minced
          2 green onions, chopped
          1 can (8 ounces) mushroom stems and pieces,
          drained
      1/4 cup all-purpose flour
          2 teaspoons salt
      1/2 teaspoon pepper
      1/4 cup butter *or* margarine, cubed
          1 can (10-3/4 ounces) condensed cream of
          mushroom soup, undiluted
          1 cup (4 ounces) shredded Colby-Monterey
          Jack cheese

In a slow cooker, layer half of the potatoes, onion, garlic, green onions, mushrooms, flour, salt, pepper and butter. Repeat layers. Pour soup over the top. Cover and cook on low for 6-8 hours or until potatoes are tender; sprinkle with cheese during the last 30 minutes of cooking time. **Yield:** 8-10 servings.

Sausage Dressing
Turkey in a Pot

Turkey in a Pot

(Pictured above and on page 256)

I use this recipe often for an easy Sunday dinner. The turkey breast gets a "holiday treatment" when served with cranberry gravy seasoned with cinnamon, cloves and allspice. —Lois Woodward, Okeechobee, Florida

  1 boneless turkey breast (3 to 4 pounds), halved
  1 can (16 ounces) whole-berry cranberry sauce
1/2 cup sugar
1/2 cup apple juice
  1 tablespoon cider vinegar
  2 garlic cloves, minced
  1 teaspoon ground mustard
1/2 teaspoon ground cinnamon
1/4 teaspoon ground cloves
1/4 teaspoon ground allspice
  2 tablespoons all-purpose flour
1/4 cup cold water
1/4 teaspoon browning sauce, optional

Place the turkey skin side up in a 5-qt. slow cooker. Combine the cranberry sauce, sugar, apple juice, vinegar, garlic, mustard, cinnamon, cloves and allspice; pour over turkey. Cover and cook on low for 5-6 hours or until a meat thermometer reads 170°.

Remove turkey to a cutting board; keep warm. Strain cooking juices. In a saucepan, combine flour and water until smooth; gradually stir in strained juices. Bring to a boil; cook and stir for 2 minutes or until thickened. Stir in browning sauce if desired. Serve with sliced turkey. **Yield:** 12-16 servings.

Sausage Dressing

(Pictured above and on page 256)

I relied on this slow cooker recipe at Thanksgiving when there was no room in my oven to bake stuffing. The results were fantastic—very moist and flavorful. Even family members who don't usually eat stuffing had some. There were no leftovers. —Mary Kendall, Appleton, Wisconsin

  1 pound bulk pork sausage
  1 large onion, chopped
  2 celery ribs, chopped
  1 package (14 ounces) seasoned stuffing
     croutons
  1 can (14-1/2 ounces) chicken broth
  1 large tart apple, chopped
  1 cup chopped walnuts *or* pecans
1/2 cup egg substitute
1/4 cup butter *or* margarine, melted
1-1/2 teaspoons rubbed sage
1/2 teaspoon pepper

In a large skillet, cook the sausage, onion and celery over medium heat until meat is no longer pink; drain. Transfer to a greased 5-qt. slow cooker. Stir in the remaining ingredients. Cover and cook on low for 4-5 hours or until heated through. **Yield:** 12 servings.

Beef 'n' Bean Torta

(Pictured below)

This zesty dish is a favorite of mine because it has a wonderful Southwestern taste and is easy to prepare. I serve it on nights when we have only a few minutes to eat before running off to meetings or sports events. —Joan Hallford
North Richland Hills, Texas

1 pound ground beef
1 small onion, chopped
1 can (15 ounces) pinto *or* black beans, rinsed and drained
1 can (10 ounces) diced tomatoes and green chilies, undrained
1 can (2-1/4 ounces) sliced ripe olives, drained
1-1/2 teaspoons chili powder
1/2 teaspoon salt
1/8 teaspoon pepper
3 drops hot pepper sauce
4 flour tortillas (8 inches)
1 cup (4 ounces) shredded cheddar cheese
Minced fresh cilantro, optional
Salsa, sour cream, shredded lettuce and chopped tomatoes, optional

Cut four 20-in. x 3-in. strips of heavy-duty foil; crisscross so they resemble spokes of a wheel. Place strips on the bottom and up the sides of a 5-qt. slow cooker. Coat strips with nonstick cooking spray.

In a large skillet, cook beef and onion over medium heat until meat is no longer pink; drain. Stir in the beans, tomatoes, olives, chili powder, salt, pepper and hot pepper sauce. Spoon about 1-2/3 cups into prepared slow cooker; top with one tortilla and 1/4 cup cheese. Repeat layers three times.

Cover and cook on low for 4-5 hours or until heated through. Using foil strips as handles, remove the tortilla stack to a platter. Sprinkle with cilantro. Serve with salsa, sour cream, lettuce and tomatoes if desired. **Yield:** 4 servings.

Warm Fruit Compote

I rely on the convenience of canned goods and my slow cooker to make this old-fashioned side dish. Full of peaches, pears, pineapple and apricots, it makes a heartwarming accompaniment to holiday menus.
—Mary Ann Jonns, Midlothian, Illinois

2 cans (29 ounces *each*) sliced peaches, drained
2 cans (29 ounces *each*) pear halves, drained and sliced
1 can (20 ounces) pineapple chunks, drained
1 can (15-1/4 ounces) apricot halves, drained and sliced
1 can (21 ounces) cherry pie filling

In a 5-qt. slow cooker, combine the peaches, pears, pineapple and apricots. Top with pie filling. Cover and cook on high for 2 hours or until heated through. Serve with a slotted spoon. **Yield:** 14-18 servings.

Beef 'n' Bean Torta

Spaghetti Pork Chops

(Pictured at right)

The moist chops simmer to perfection in a tangy sauce, then are served over pasta. This was one of my mother's most-loved recipes. —Ellen Gallavan, Midland, Michigan

- 3 cans (8 ounces *each*) tomato sauce
- 1 can (10-3/4 ounces) condensed tomato soup, undiluted
- 1 small onion, finely chopped
- 1 bay leaf
- 1 teaspoon celery seed
- 1/2 teaspoon Italian seasoning
- 6 bone-in pork chops (1 inch thick)
- 2 tablespoons olive *or* vegetable oil

Hot cooked spaghetti

In a 5-qt. slow cooker, combine the tomato sauce, soup, onion, bay leaf, celery seed and Italian seasoning. In a large skillet, brown pork chops in oil. Add to the slow cooker. Cover and cook on low for 6-8 hours or until meat is tender. Discard bay leaf. Serve chops and sauce over spaghetti. **Yield:** 6 servings.

Navy Bean Vegetable Soup

*My family likes bean soup, so I came up with this hearty version. Leftovers freeze well for first-rate future meals.
—Eleanor Mielke, Mitchell, South Dakota*

- 4 medium carrots, thinly sliced
- 2 celery ribs, chopped
- 1 medium onion, chopped
- 2 cups cubed fully cooked ham
- 1-1/2 cups dried navy beans
- 1 package (1.68 ounces) vegetable soup mix
- 1 envelope onion soup mix
- 1 bay leaf
- 1/2 teaspoon pepper
- 8 cups water

In a 5-qt. slow cooker, combine the first nine ingredients. Stir in water. Cover and cook on low for 9-10 hours or until beans are tender. Discard bay leaf. **Yield:** 12 servings.

Beef Burgundy

*Tender cubes of beef are treated to a burgundy wine sauce and savory vegetables in this robust entree. I made this often when I worked full-time. It's good over noodles or mashed potatoes.
—Sherri Mott
New Carlisle, Indiana*

- 6 bacon strips, diced
- 1 boneless beef chuck roast (3 pounds), cut into 1-1/2-inch cubes
- 1 can (10-1/2 ounces) condensed beef broth, undiluted
- 1 small onion, halved and sliced
- 1 medium carrot, sliced
- 2 tablespoons butter *or* margarine
- 1 tablespoon tomato paste
- 2 garlic cloves, minced

Spaghetti Pork Chops

- 3/4 teaspoon dried thyme
- 1/2 teaspoon salt
- 1/2 teaspoon pepper
- 1 bay leaf
- 1/2 pound fresh mushrooms, sliced
- 1/2 cup burgundy wine *or* beef broth
- 5 tablespoons all-purpose flour
- 2/3 cup cold water

Hot cooked noodles, optional

In a skillet, cook bacon over medium heat until crisp. Use a slotted spoon to remove to paper towels. In the drippings, brown the beef; drain. Place beef and bacon in a 5-qt. slow cooker. Add the broth, onion, carrot, butter, tomato paste, garlic, thyme, salt, pepper and bay leaf. Cover and cook on low for 7-8 hours or until meat is tender.

Add mushrooms and wine or broth. Combine flour and water until smooth; stir into slow cooker. Cover and cook on high for 30-45 minutes or until thickened. Discard bay leaf. Serve over noodles if desired. **Yield:** 8 servings.

Hot Chili Cheese Dip

I simplify party preparation by using my slow cooker to create this thick cheesy dip. Your guests won't believe how good it is. —Jeanie Carrigan, Madera, California

- 1 medium onion, finely chopped
- 2 garlic cloves, minced
- 2 teaspoons vegetable oil
- 2 cans (15 ounces *each*) chili without beans
- 2 cups salsa
- 2 packages (3 ounces *each*) cream cheese, cubed
- 2 cans (2-1/4 ounces *each*) sliced ripe olives, drained

Tortilla chips

In a skillet, saute onion and garlic in oil until tender. Transfer to a slow cooker. Stir in the chili, salsa, cream cheese and olives. Cover and cook on low for 4 hours or until heated through, stirring occasionally. Stir before serving with tortilla chips. **Yield:** 6 cups.

Great Grilling Recipes

AN OUTDOOR GRILL—whether gas or charcoal—can be a boon to busy cooks. It makes it quick and easy to cook an entire meal without heating up the kitchen, plus it leaves fewer pots and pans to wash.

So when time's tight, head to your backyard barbecue. Not only will you beat the heat, but you'll beat the clock and have the dinner bell ringing in a matter of minutes.

Grilled Hash Browns

(Pictured below)

Ready in 30 minutes or less

Since my husband and I love to grill meats, we're always looking for easy side dishes that cook on the grill, too. So I came up with this simple recipe for hash browns. There are never any leftovers. —Kelly Chastain
Bedford, Indiana

3-1/2 cups frozen cubed hash brown potatoes, thawed
   1 small onion, chopped
   1 tablespoon beef bouillon granules
Dash seasoned salt
Dash pepper
   1 tablespoon butter *or* margarine, melted

Grilled Hash Browns
Teriyaki Burgers

Place potatoes on a piece of heavy-duty foil (about 20 in. x 18 in.) coated with nonstick cooking spray. Sprinkle with onion, bouillon, seasoned salt and pepper; drizzle with butter.

Fold foil around potatoes and seal tightly. Grill, covered, over indirect medium heat for 10-15 minutes or until potatoes are tender, turning once. **Yield:** 4 servings.

Teriyaki Burgers

(Pictured below left)

Ready in 30 minutes or less

Water chestnuts add crunch to these moist patties. Top the burgers with additional teriyaki sauce for a flavorful alternative to ketchup. —Barb Schutz, Pandora, Ohio

✓ Uses less fat, sugar or salt. Includes Nutritional Analysis and Diabetic Exchanges.

   1 can (8 ounces) water chestnuts, drained and chopped
1/3 cup teriyaki sauce
   2 tablespoons chopped green onions
Salt and pepper to taste
1-1/2 pounds ground beef
   7 hamburger buns, split
  14 tomato slices
   7 lettuce leaves

In a large bowl, combine the water chestnuts, teriyaki sauce, onions, salt and pepper. Crumble beef over mixture and mix just until combined. Shape into seven 1/2-in.-thick patties. Grill, covered, over indirect medium heat for 6-8 minutes on each side or until meat is no longer pink. Serve on buns with tomato and lettuce. **Yield:** 7 burgers.

Nutritional Analysis: One burger with bun (prepared without salt) equals 321 calories, 11 g fat (4 g saturated fat), 35 mg cholesterol, 778 mg sodium, 28 g carbohydrate, 3 g fiber, 25 g protein. **Diabetic Exchanges:** 3 lean meat, 2 starch.

Lemon-Pepper Catfish

Plan ahead...needs to marinate

Nothing beats a late supper of tender and flavorful grilled catfish fillets after a hard day's work. It's easy to prepare and a favorite of our family during the summertime. —Regina Rosenberry, Greencastle, Pennsylvania

   6 tablespoons lemon juice
1/4 cup butter *or* margarine, melted
   2 teaspoons Worcestershire sauce
   4 catfish fillets (about 5 ounces *each*)
1/2 teaspoon salt
1/2 teaspoon lemon-pepper seasoning

In a shallow glass container, combine the lemon juice, butter and Worcestershire sauce; mix well. Add catfish and turn to coat. Cover and refrigerate for 1 hour, turning occasionally.

Coat grill rack with nonstick cooking spray before starting the grill. Drain and discard marinade. Sprinkle catfish with salt and lemon-pepper. Grill, covered, over

Herb Fryer Chicken

medium heat for 12-14 minutes or until fish flakes easily with a fork, turning once. **Yield:** 4 servings.

Herb Fryer Chicken

(Pictured above)

Plan ahead...needs to marinate

We use our grill all year long. Our boys love this chicken, and it's a hit with company, too. To really bring out the lemon flavor, I suggest piercing the chicken skin before marinating. —Charlene Sylvia, Sandy, Utah

1/3 cup lemon juice
1/4 cup olive *or* vegetable oil
1/4 cup minced fresh parsley
  2 tablespoons finely chopped onion
  3 garlic cloves, minced
  1 tablespoon grated lemon peel
  1 teaspoon minced fresh thyme
1/2 teaspoon salt
1/4 teaspoon pepper
  1 broiler/fryer chicken (3 pounds), cut up

In a large resealable plastic bag, combine the lemon juice, oil, parsley, onion, garlic, lemon peel, thyme, salt and pepper; add chicken. Seal bag and turn to coat; refrigerate overnight, turning occasionally. Drain and discard marinade. Grill chicken, covered, over medium heat for 35-40 minutes or until juices run clear, turning every 15 minutes. **Yield:** 6 servings.

Bacon Potato Bundles

Ready in 1 hour or less

I cut cleanup by grilling this versatile side dish in foil packets. Wrap the bacon around the veggies and secure it with a toothpick for a fun presentation. Add carrots,

squash or whatever vegetables you have on hand or are in season.   —Dorothy Sutherland, Seven Points, Texas

  4 large baking potatoes, peeled and
    quartered
  8 onion slices
  8 green pepper slices
  4 bacon strips
Salt and pepper to taste

Place the potatoes on four pieces of greased heavy-duty aluminum foil. Place onion and green pepper between potato quarters; top with bacon. Sprinkle with salt and pepper. Wrap in foil. Grill, covered, over medium-high heat for 40-50 minutes or until the potatoes are tender, turning once. **Yield:** 4 servings.

Hot Dogs with the Works

Ready in 30 minutes or less

What screams summer more than grilled hot dogs? I place hot dogs in buns before topping them with a zesty cheese sauce and grilling them in a double layer of foil.
    —Maria Regakis, Somerville, Massachusetts

1-1/2 cups (6 ounces) shredded pepper Jack *or*
    Monterey Jack cheese
  3/4 cup chopped seeded tomato
    3 tablespoons chopped onion
    2 tablespoons sweet pickle relish
    8 hot dogs
    8 hot dog buns

In a bowl, combine the cheese, tomato, onion and relish. Place hot dogs in buns; top with cheese mixture. Wrap hot dogs in a double layer of heavy-duty foil (about 12 in. x 10 in.). Grill, uncovered, over medium-hot heat for 8-10 minutes or until heated through and cheese is melted. **Yield:** 8 servings.

Chicken Pizza Packets

Carefully open each packet. Sprinkle with tomatoes and cheeses. Seal loosely; grill 2 minutes longer or until cheese is melted. **Yield:** 4 servings.

Bratwurst Supper

This meal-in-one grills to perfection in a heavy-duty foil bag and is ideal for camping. Loaded with chunks of bratwurst, red potatoes, mushrooms and carrots, it's easy to season with onion soup mix and a little soy sauce.
—Janice Meyer, Medford, Wisconsin

>   3 pounds uncooked bratwurst links
>   3 pounds small red potatoes, cut into wedges
>   1 pound baby carrots
>   1 large red onion, sliced and separated into rings
>   2 jars (4-1/2 ounces *each*) whole mushrooms, drained
>   1/4 cup butter *or* margarine, cubed
>   1 envelope onion soup mix
>   2 tablespoons soy sauce
>   1/2 teaspoon pepper

Cut bratwurst links into thirds. Place the bratwurst, potatoes, carrots, onion and mushrooms in a heavy-duty foil bag (17 in. x 15 in.). Dot with butter. Sprinkle with soup mix, soy sauce and pepper. Seal tightly; turn to coat.

Grill, covered, over medium heat for 45-55 minutes or until vegetables are tender and sausage is no longer pink, turning once. **Yield:** 12 servings.

Chicken Pizza Packets

(Pictured above)

Ready in 45 minutes or less

Basil, garlic, pepperoni and mozzarella give plenty of pizza flavor to chicken, green pepper, zucchini and cherry tomatoes in these individual foil dinners. This speedy grilled supper is a tasty way to get little ones to eat their veggies.
—Amber Zurbrugg, Alliance, Ohio

>   1 pound boneless skinless chicken breasts, cut into 1-inch pieces
>   2 tablespoons olive *or* vegetable oil
>   1 small zucchini, thinly sliced
>   16 pepperoni slices
>   1 small green pepper, julienned
>   1 small onion, sliced
>   1/2 teaspoon dried oregano
>   1/2 teaspoon dried basil
>   1/4 teaspoon salt
>   1/4 teaspoon garlic powder
>   1/4 teaspoon pepper
>   1 cup halved cherry tomatoes
>   1/2 cup shredded mozzarella cheese
>   1/2 cup shredded Parmesan cheese

In a large bowl, combine the first 11 ingredients. Coat four pieces of heavy-duty foil (about 12 in. square) with nonstick cooking spray. Place a quarter of the chicken mixture in the center of each piece. Fold foil around mixture and seal tightly. Grill, covered, over medium-hot heat for 15-18 minutes or until chicken juices run clear.

Jalapeno Chicken Wraps

Ready in 1 hour or less

These easy appetizers are always a hit at parties! Zesty strips of chicken and bits of onion sit in jalapeno halves that are wrapped in bacon and grilled. Serve them with blue cheese or ranch salad dressing for dipping.
—Leslie Buenz, Tinley Park, Illinois

>   1 pound boneless skinless chicken breasts
>   1 tablespoon garlic powder
>   1 tablespoon onion powder
>   1 tablespoon pepper
>   2 teaspoons seasoned salt
>   1 teaspoon paprika
>   1 small onion, cut into strips
>   15 jalapeno peppers, halved and seeded*
>   1 pound sliced bacon, halved widthwise
> Blue cheese salad dressing

Cut chicken into 2-in. x 1-1/2-in. strips. In a large resealable plastic bag, combine the garlic powder, onion powder, pepper, seasoned salt and paprika; add chicken and shake to coat. Place a chicken and onion strip in each jalapeno half. Wrap each with a piece of bacon and secure with toothpicks.

Grill, uncovered, over indirect medium heat for 18-20 minutes or until chicken juices run clear and bacon is crisp, turning once. Serve with blue cheese dressing. **Yield:** 2-1/2 dozen.

*Editor's Note: When cutting or seeding hot peppers, use rubber or plastic gloves to protect your hands. Avoid touching your face.

Southwestern Catfish

Ready in 45 minutes or less

Catfish fillets are rubbed with a blend that includes chili powder, cumin, coriander, cayenne and paprika, then topped with homemade salsa. A green salad, garlic bread and baked sweet potatoes round out the meal nicely.
—*Bruce Crittenden, Clinton, Mississippi*

   3 medium tomatoes, chopped
1/4 cup chopped onion
   2 jalapeno peppers, seeded and finely chopped*
   2 tablespoons white wine vinegar *or* cider vinegar
   3 teaspoons salt, *divided*
   3 teaspoons paprika
   3 teaspoons chili powder
   1 to 1-1/2 teaspoons ground cumin
   1 to 1-1/2 teaspoons ground coriander
3/4 to 1 teaspoon cayenne pepper
1/2 teaspoon garlic powder
   4 catfish fillets (6 ounces *each*)

For salsa, in a bowl, combine the tomatoes, onion, jalapenos, vinegar and 1 teaspoon salt. Cover and refrigerate for at least 30 minutes.

Combine the paprika, chili powder, cumin, coriander, cayenne, garlic powder and remaining salt; rub over catfish. Coat grill rack with nonstick cooking spray before starting the grill. Grill fillets, uncovered, over medium heat for 5 minutes on each side or until fish flakes easily with a fork. Serve with salsa. **Yield:** 4 servings.

*Editor's Note: When cutting or seeding hot peppers, use rubber or plastic gloves to protect your hands. Avoid touching your face.

Curried Peanut Chicken

Plan ahead...needs to marinate

This is a nice change from traditional grilled items. I sprinkle coconut and currants over a tasty combination of chicken and peppers.
—*Jennifer Myers Havertown, Pennsylvania*

1-1/2 cups orange juice
  3/4 cup peanut butter
    2 tablespoons curry powder
    4 boneless skinless chicken breast halves
    2 medium sweet red peppers, cut in half
  1/4 cup flaked coconut, toasted
  1/4 cup dried currants
Hot cooked rice

In a bowl, combine the orange juice, peanut butter and curry powder. Pour a third of the marinade into a large resealable plastic bag; add chicken. Seal bag and turn to coat; refrigerate for 8 hours or overnight. Cover and refrigerate remaining marinade.

Drain and discard marinade from chicken. Grill chicken and peppers over medium heat for 8-10 minutes on each side or until chicken juices run clear and peppers are tender. Warm the reserved marinade. Cut chicken and peppers into 1/2-in. strips; sprinkle with coconut and currants. Serve with rice and reserved marinade. **Yield:** 4 servings.

Chili Flank Steak

(Pictured below)

Plan ahead...needs to marinate

I started making this recipe when we moved from Idaho to Kentucky. It gets so hot here that we use our outdoor grill as often as possible to keep the kitchen cool. My husband loves this juicy steak and its tasty sauce. I like that I can have it ready to marinate in no time.
—*Karma Henry Glasgow, Kentucky*

2/3 cup packed brown sugar
2/3 cup V8 juice
2/3 cup soy sauce
1/2 cup olive *or* vegetable oil
  4 garlic cloves, chopped
  2 tablespoons chili powder
1/4 teaspoon ground cumin
  1 beef flank steak (about 1-1/2 pounds)

In a large bowl, combine the first seven ingredients; mix well. Pour half of the marinade into a large resealable bag; add the steak. Seal bag and turn to coat; refrigerate for 8 hours or overnight, turning occasionally. Cover and refrigerate remaining marinade.

Drain and discard marinade from steak. Grill steak, covered, over medium-hot heat for 6-10 minutes on each side or until meat reaches desired doneness (for rare, a meat thermometer should read 140°; medium, 160°; well-done, 170°). Serve with reserved marinade. **Yield:** 4-6 servings.

Chili Flank Steak

Cranberry Turkey Cutlets

saturated fat), 70 mg cholesterol, 252 mg sodium, 40 g carbohydrate, 4 g fiber, 29 g protein. **Diabetic Exchanges:** 3 very lean meat, 1-1/2 starch, 1 fruit.

Grilled Cheeseburger Pizza
(Pictured below)
Ready in 1 hour or less

I combined our daughter's two favorite foods—pizza and grilled cheeseburgers—to create this main dish. It's very simple to make, and she and her friends love it. If you don't like the toppings, replace them with whatever you prefer. —Tanya Gutierro, Beacon Falls, Connecticut

```
3/4 pound ground beef
  1 cup ketchup
  2 tablespoons prepared mustard
  1 prebaked Italian bread shell crust (14 ounces)
  1 cup shredded lettuce
  1 medium tomato, thinly sliced
1/8 teaspoon salt
1/8 teaspoon pepper
  1 small sweet onion, thinly sliced
1/2 cup dill pickle slices
  1 cup (4 ounces) shredded cheddar cheese
  1 cup (4 ounces) shredded mozzarella cheese
```

Shape beef into three 1/2-in.-thick patties. Grill, covered, over medium-hot heat for 5 minutes on each side or until meat is no longer pink. Meanwhile, combine ketchup and mustard; spread over the crust to within 1 in. of edge. Sprinkle with lettuce; top with tomato. Sprinkle with salt and pepper. When beef patties are cooked, cut into 1/2-in. pieces; arrange over tomato slices. Top with onion, pickles and cheeses.

Place pizza on a 16-in. square piece of heavy-duty foil; transfer to grill. Grill, covered, over indirect medium heat for 12-15 minutes or until cheese is melted and crust is lightly browned. Remove from the grill. Let stand for 5-10 minutes before slicing. **Yield:** 4-6 servings.

Cranberry Turkey Cutlets
(Pictured above)
Ready in 30 minutes or less

When our son-in-law brought home some wild turkey, we turned to this recipe. He took care of the grilling while I made the sauce, and we all enjoyed this healthy entree. —Marguerite Shaeffer, Sewell, New Jersey

✓ Uses less fat, sugar or salt. Includes Nutritional Analysis and Diabetic Exchanges.

```
  1 cup thinly sliced onion
  2 teaspoons vegetable or canola oil
  2 cups dried cranberries
  2 cups orange juice
1-1/2 teaspoons balsamic vinegar or cider vinegar
  6 turkey cutlets (4 ounces each and 1/2 inch
    thick)
1/2 teaspoon salt
1/2 teaspoon pepper
```

In a large skillet, saute onion in oil until lightly browned, about 6 minutes. Stir in the cranberries, orange juice and vinegar. Bring to a boil over medium heat; cook and stir until sauce begins to thicken. Set aside.

Coat grill rack with nonstick cooking spray before starting the grill. Sprinkle turkey cutlets with salt and pepper. Grill, covered, over indirect medium heat for 5-6 minutes on each side or until juices run clear. Top each cutlet with some of the cranberry sauce; grill 1-2 minutes longer. Serve with remaining cranberry sauce. **Yield:** 6 servings.

Nutritional Analysis: One serving (1 cutlet with 1/3 cup cranberry sauce) equals 309 calories, 2 g fat (trace

Grilled Cheeseburger Pizza

Warm Apple Topping

(Pictured at right)

Ready in 45 minutes or less

My husband and I love preparing entire meals on the grill, to the surprise and delight of company. We created this unique dessert for my mother, who can't eat most grain products. She was thrilled with the sweet fruit topping spooned over vanilla ice cream. —Sharon Manton
Harrisburg, Pennsylvania

Warm Apple Topping

      3 medium tart apples, peeled
  1/3 cup raisins
      1 tablespoon lemon juice
  1/3 cup packed brown sugar
  1/4 teaspoon ground cinnamon
  1/4 teaspoon ground cloves
  1/8 teaspoon salt
  1/8 teaspoon ground nutmeg
      2 tablespoons cold butter *or* margarine
  1/3 cup finely chopped walnuts
Vanilla ice cream

Cut each apple into 16 wedges; place all on an 18-in. square piece of heavy-duty foil. Sprinkle with raisins; drizzle with lemon juice. In a bowl, combine the brown sugar, cinnamon, cloves, salt and nutmeg; cut in the butter. Stir in the walnuts. Sprinkle over apples and raisins.

Fold foil around apple mixture and seal tightly. Grill over indirect medium heat for 18-22 minutes or until apples are tender. Serve over ice cream. **Yield:** 3 cups.

South Pacific Pork Kabobs

Plan ahead...needs to marinate

Try this tropical treat of pork marinated in a spicy soy mixture and topped with a peanut butter sauce. You can drizzle the sauce over the kabobs or put it in bowls for dipping. —Susan Putkonen, Gilbert, Minnesota

 Uses less fat, sugar or salt. Includes Nutritional Analysis and Diabetic Exchanges.

  1/4 cup sliced green onions
  1/4 cup water
  1/4 cup soy sauce
      3 tablespoons sugar
      1 tablespoon lemon juice
      1 garlic clove, minced
  1/2 teaspoon pepper
  1/4 teaspoon ground ginger *or* 1 teaspoon
         grated fresh gingerroot
      1 pound pork chop suey meat
PEANUT BUTTER SAUCE:
      1 teaspoon cornstarch
  1/4 teaspoon garlic salt
Dash pepper
  1/3 cup chicken broth
  1/3 cup milk
      3 tablespoons peanut butter
      2 tablespoons sliced green onion

In a large resealable bag, combine the first eight ingredients; add pork. Seal bag and turn to coat; refrigerate overnight.

Drain and discard marinade. Thread pork onto metal or soaked wooden skewers. Grill, covered, over indirect medium heat for 5-6 minutes on each side or until meat is no longer pink. In a saucepan, combine the cornstarch, garlic salt and pepper. Stir in broth until smooth. Add milk, peanut butter and onion; stir until blended. Bring to a boil; cook and stir for 2 minutes or until thickened. Serve with kabobs. **Yield:** 4 servings.

Nutritional Analysis: One kabob with 2 tablespoons sauce (prepared with lean pork loin, reduced-sodium soy sauce, fat-free milk and reduced-fat peanut butter) equals 286 calories, 10 g fat (3 g saturated fat), 63 mg cholesterol, 900 mg sodium, 18 g carbohydrate, 1 g fiber, 30 g protein. **Diabetic Exchanges:** 3 lean meat, 1 starch, 1 fat.

Coring Lettuce

IF LETTUCE is a popular part of your menus, try this tip. It makes it easy to remove the core from a head of iceberg lettuce.

Hold the head with both hands and firmly hit the head, core side down, against your kitchen countertop. Twist the core and it should come right out.

To clean the lettuce, run water into the area where the core was removed. Invert the lettuce and allow the water to drain out before using.

Summer Vegetable Medley

(Pictured below)

Ready in 30 minutes or less

This swift side dish is as beautiful as it is delicious. Red and yellow peppers, zucchini, corn and mushrooms are seasoned with garden-fresh herbs. Grilled in a foil pan, it's no-fuss cooking.
—Maria Regakis
Somerville, Massachusetts

1/2 cup butter *or* margarine, melted
1-1/4 teaspoons *each* minced fresh parsley, basil and chives
3/4 teaspoon salt
1/4 teaspoon pepper
3 medium ears sweet corn, husks removed, cut into 2-inch pieces
1 medium sweet red pepper, cut into 1-inch pieces
1 medium sweet yellow pepper, cut into 1-inch pieces
1 medium zucchini, cut into 1/4-inch slices
10 large fresh mushrooms

In a large bowl, combine the butter, parsley, basil, chives, salt and pepper. Add the vegetables; toss to coat. Place vegetables in a disposable foil pan. Grill, covered, over medium-high heat for 5 minutes; stir. Grill 5 minutes longer or until the vegetables are tender. **Yield:** 6-8 servings.

Summer Vegetable Medley

Onion-Smothered Sirloins

Friends and family love these savory steaks and sweet onions. The dinner is simple to prepare and the flavor is fantastic. I usually serve it with corn and baked potatoes cooked on the grill as well. For spicier steaks, increase the pepper flakes and cumin.
—Tina Michalicka
Hudson, Florida

1 teaspoon garlic powder
3/4 teaspoon salt, *divided*
1/2 teaspoon ground cumin
1/2 teaspoon dried oregano
1/4 teaspoon crushed red pepper flakes
4 boneless beef sirloin steaks (about 8 ounces *each* and 1 inch thick)
2 large sweet onions, cut into 1/2-inch slices and separated into rings
1/4 cup olive *or* vegetable oil
1/4 teaspoon pepper
1 medium lime, cut into quarters

In a bowl, combine the garlic powder, 1/2 teaspoon salt, cumin, oregano and pepper flakes. Rub over the steaks; set aside. Place onions in a disposable foil pan; add oil and toss to coat. Grill, covered, over medium heat for 30-40 minutes or until golden brown, stirring occasionally. Season onions with pepper, remaining salt and a squeeze of lime.

Grill steaks, uncovered, over medium heat for 7-10 minutes on each side or until meat reaches desired doneness (for rare, a meat thermometer should read 140°; medium, 160°; well-done, 170°). Squeeze remaining lime over the steaks; top with onions. **Yield:** 4 servings.

Deluxe Cheeseburgers

Ready in 30 minutes or less

I perk up ground beef with tomato paste, Worcestershire sauce, chopped onion, and Parmesan and cheddar cheeses. We love to grill these flavorful burgers in the summer and broil them in the winter.
—Kathleen Vashro
Corcoran, Minnesota

1 egg
1 can (6 ounces) tomato paste
1 tablespoon Worcestershire sauce
1 medium onion, chopped
1/2 cup grated Parmesan cheese
1/2 teaspoon seasoned salt
1/2 teaspoon salt
1/8 teaspoon pepper
2 pounds ground beef
8 slices cheddar cheese
8 hamburger buns, split

In a bowl, combine the first eight ingredients. Crumble beef over mixture and mix well. Shape into eight 3/4-in.-thick patties. Grill, covered, over medium heat for 5 minutes on each side. Top each burger with a cheese slice. Grill 1-2 minutes longer or until the cheese begins to melt. Serve on buns. **Yield:** 8 servings.

Italian Grilled Cheese

Italian Grilled Cheese

(Pictured above)

Ready in 15 minutes or less

Provolone cheese, tomato slices and basil leaves make up the satisfying filling for these flame-broiled sandwiches. Lightly brushed with Italian salad dressing, they're sure to become family favorites. —Melody Biddinger
Costa Mesa, California

  8 fresh basil leaves
  8 thin tomato slices
  4 slices provolone cheese
  4 slices Italian bread (1/4 inch thick)
  2 tablespoons prepared Italian salad dressing

Layer the basil, tomato and cheese on two slices of bread. Top with remaining bread. Brush outsides of sandwiches with salad dressing. Grill, uncovered, over medium heat for 3-4 minutes on each side. **Yield:** 2 servings.

Cheese-Topped Tomatoes

Ready in 30 minutes or less

Looking for a side dish to accompany grilled meat or chicken? I sprinkle blue cheese, bread crumbs and a few other ingredients over tomato halves, then grill them for delicious results. —Arlene Risius
Buffalo Center, Iowa

  8 plum tomatoes, halved lengthwise
3/4 teaspoon salt
1/4 cup dry bread crumbs

1/2 cup crumbled blue cheese *or* shredded
      cheddar cheese
1/4 cup grated onion
  2 tablespoons butter *or* margarine, melted

Sprinkle cut side of tomatoes with salt, bread crumbs, cheese and onion. Drizzle with butter. Grill, covered, over indirect medium heat for 6-8 minutes or until cheese is melted. **Yield:** 8 servings.

Artichoke Mushroom Caps

(Pictured below)

Ready in 45 minutes or less

These crumb-topped appetizers never last long at our get-togethers. The rich filling of cream cheese, artichoke hearts, Parmesan cheese and green onion is terrific. You can broil them in your oven to enjoy any time of year.
      —Ruth Lewis, West Newton, Pennsylvania

  1 package (3 ounces) cream cheese, softened
1/4 cup mayonnaise
  1 jar (6-1/2 ounces) marinated artichoke
      hearts, drained and finely chopped
1/4 cup grated Parmesan cheese
  2 tablespoons finely chopped green onion
 20 to 25 large fresh mushrooms, stems
      removed
1/4 cup seasoned bread crumbs
  2 teaspoons olive *or* vegetable oil

In a mixing bowl, beat cream cheese and mayonnaise until smooth. Beat in the artichokes, Parmesan cheese and onion. Lightly spray tops of mushrooms with non-stick cooking spray. Spoon cheese mixture into mushroom caps. Combine bread crumbs and oil; sprinkle over mushrooms. Grill, covered, over indirect medium heat for 8-10 minutes or until mushrooms are tender. **Yield:** about 2 dozen.

Artichoke Mushroom Caps

Bacon-Corn Stuffed Peppers

Sausage Vegetable Packets

Ready in 1 hour or less

We have so much squash in the summer, but we never tire of this recipe. We often leave the sausage out of the foil packets and just serve the veggies as a side dish. Even people who don't usually like zucchini enjoy it. —Kay Bish
Thompsonville, Illinois

  1/2 **pound fully cooked smoked sausage, cut into**
     1/2-inch pieces
    3 **medium zucchini, sliced**
    3 **medium tomatoes, sliced**
    1 **medium green pepper, sliced**
  1/4 **cup butter *or* margarine, melted**
    1 **envelope onion soup mix**
    1 **tablespoon brown sugar**
  1/4 **teaspoon salt**
  1/4 **teaspoon pepper**

In a large bowl, combine all of the ingredients. Divide between two pieces of double-layered heavy-duty foil (about 12 in. square). Fold foil around sausage mixture and seal tightly. Grill, covered, over medium heat for 25-30 minutes or until the vegetables are tender. **Yield:** 4 servings.

Bacon-Corn Stuffed Peppers

(Pictured above)

Ready in 45 minutes or less

Filled with corn, salsa, green onions, mozzarella cheese and bacon, these grilled pepper halves are sure to liven up your next cookout. They have a wonderful taste and are a fun alternative to the usual corn on the cob.
—Mitzi Sentiff, Alexandria, Virginia

✓ Uses less fat, sugar or salt. Includes Nutritional Analysis and Diabetic Exchanges.

    2 **cups frozen corn, thawed**
  1/3 **cup salsa**
    6 **green onions, chopped**
    1 **medium green pepper, halved and seeded**
    1 **medium sweet red pepper, halved and seeded**
  1/4 **cup shredded mozzarella cheese**
    2 **bacon strips, cooked and crumbled**
Additional salsa, optional

In a large bowl, combine the corn, salsa and onions. Spoon into pepper halves. Place each stuffed pepper half on a piece of heavy-duty foil (about 18 in. x 12 in.). Fold foil around peppers and seal tightly.

Grill, covered, over medium heat for 25-30 minutes or until peppers are crisp-tender. Carefully open packets. Sprinkle with cheese and bacon. Return to the grill for 3-5 minutes or until cheese is melted. Serve with additional salsa if desired. **Yield:** 4 servings.

Nutritional Analysis: One serving (prepared with part-skim mozzarella cheese and without additional salsa) equals 183 calories, 8 g fat (3 g saturated fat), 12 mg cholesterol, 270 mg sodium, 25 g carbohydrate, 4 g fiber, 6 g protein. **Diabetic Exchanges:** 2 vegetable, 1 starch, 1 fat.

Halibut with Cream Sauce

Ready in 45 minutes or less

This is definitely a family favorite. I serve the flaky fish and rich white sauce alongside rice pilaf.
—Ginny Eiseman, Ketchikan, Alaska

    5 **tablespoons butter *or* margarine, cubed**
    1 **medium onion, sliced and separated into**
     rings
1-1/2 **pounds halibut *or* salmon steaks**
  3/4 **cup mayonnaise**
  3/4 **cup sour cream**
  3/4 **teaspoon garlic powder**
  3/4 **teaspoon seasoned salt**
  3/4 **teaspoon dried basil**
  3/4 **teaspoon dried thyme**
  1/8 **teaspoon pepper**
  1/2 **cup dry bread crumbs**
    1 **cup shredded Parmesan cheese**

Place butter and onion on a double thickness of heavy-duty foil (about 24 in. x 18 in.). Cut fish into serving-size pieces, removing and discarding the bones. Place over the onion.

In a bowl, combine the mayonnaise, sour cream and seasonings. Set aside 1/2 cup for serving. Spoon the remaining sauce over fish. Sprinkle with bread crumbs and Parmesan cheese. Fold foil around fish and seal tightly. Grill, covered, over indirect medium heat for 15-20 minutes or until fish flakes easily with a fork. **Yield:** 6 servings.

Dressed-Up Bacon Burgers

(Pictured at right)

Ready in 45 minutes or less

The tangy homemade sauce that tops these mouth-watering burgers helps them stand out from the rest. This

recipe is a cinch to throw together. Because the bacon cooks on the grill alongside the burgers, cleanup is a breeze, too.
—Carol Mizell, Ruston, Louisiana

    3/4 cup mayonnaise
    3 tablespoons sweet pickle relish
    3 tablespoons ketchup
    1 tablespoon sugar
    1 tablespoon dried minced onion
    1 tablespoon Worcestershire sauce
    1/2 teaspoon salt
    1/4 teaspoon garlic powder
    1/4 teaspoon pepper
    2 pounds ground beef
    8 bacon strips
    8 slices cheddar cheese
    8 hamburger buns, split and toasted
Lettuce leaves

In a small bowl, whisk the mayonnaise, pickle relish, ketchup, sugar and onion until well blended. Cover and refrigerate. In a large bowl, combine the Worcestershire sauce, salt, garlic powder and pepper. Crumble beef over mixture; mix well. Shape into eight patties.

Place bacon on a piece of heavy-duty foil on one side of the grill. Place the patties on the other side of the grill. Grill, covered, over medium-hot heat for 20 minutes or until bacon is crisp and meat patties are no longer pink, turning once.

Drain bacon on paper towels. Place a cheese slice on each patty; cover and grill until cheese is melted. Layer bottom half of each bun with lettuce, patty, bacon and mayonnaise mixture. Add bun tops. **Yield:** 8 servings.

Honey Lemon Chicken

Honey Lemon Chicken

(Pictured above)

Plan ahead...needs to marinate

When I told our daughter, Amanda, that we were grilling chicken, she asked to make a marinade. Now we use her combination of honey, lemon, garlic and seasonings every time we grill chicken.
—*Tamara McFarlin*
Mondovi, Wisconsin

 Uses less fat, sugar or salt. Includes Nutritional Analysis and Diabetic Exchanges.

    1/2 cup lemon juice
    1/3 cup honey
    1/4 cup soy sauce
    2 tablespoons finely chopped onion
    4 garlic cloves, minced
    2 teaspoons dried parsley flakes
    2 teaspoons dried basil
    1 teaspoon salt-free seasoning blend
    1 teaspoon white pepper
    1 teaspoon lime juice
    6 boneless skinless chicken breast halves (5 ounces *each*)

In a bowl, combine the first 10 ingredients; mix well. Pour 2/3 cup marinade into a large resealable plastic bag; add the chicken. Seal bag and turn to coat; refrigerate for at least 4 hours or overnight. Cover and refrigerate remaining marinade.

Drain and discard marinade from chicken. Coat grill rack with nonstick cooking spray before starting the grill. Grill chicken, uncovered, over medium heat 12-15 minutes or until juices run clear, turning once and basting occasionally with reserved marinade. **Yield:** 6 servings.

Nutritional Analysis: One chicken breast (prepared with reduced-sodium soy sauce) equals 197 calories, 2 g fat (trace saturated fat), 82 mg cholesterol, 345 mg sodium, 10 g carbohydrate, trace fiber, 33 g protein.
Diabetic Exchanges: 4 very lean meat, 1/2 fruit.

Dressed-Up Bacon Burgers

Microwave Magic

LOOKING for fast-to-fix fare you can put on the table in a hurry? Take advantage of the ultimate time-easing tool—your microwave—and surprise your family with one of the following speedy specialties.

Chicken Divine

(Pictured below)

Ready in 30 minutes or less

I dress up a jar of creamy white pasta sauce, then cook it with chicken and vegetables. It's a swift and satisfying supper. —Shirley Miller, San Diego, California

        6 boneless skinless chicken breast halves
Dash pepper
        1 package (10 ounces) frozen chopped
             broccoli, thawed
        2 medium carrots, julienned
        2 tablespoons water
        1 jar (16 ounces) Parmesan and mozzarella
             pasta sauce*
        2 tablespoons sherry *or* chicken broth
    1/8 teaspoon ground nutmeg
Hot cooked noodles

Place chicken in a greased 11-in. x 7-in. x 2-in. microwave-safe dish; sprinkle with pepper. Cover with waxed paper. Microwave on high for 6-7 minutes or until juices run clear, rotating dish every 2 minutes; drain.

In a microwave-safe bowl, combine the broccoli, carrots and water. Cover and microwave on high for 3-4 minutes or until crisp-tender; drain. Spoon over chick-en. In a small bowl, combine the pasta sauce, sherry or broth and nutmeg; pour over chicken and vegetables. Cover and cook on high for 3 minutes or until heated through. Serve over noodles. **Yield:** 6 servings.

*Editor's Note: This recipe was tested with Ragu creamy pasta sauce.

Microwave Fried Rice

Ready in 30 minutes or less

I use my microwave to fix this full-flavored side dish. Since most any leftover meat, poultry or seafood can be added to the rice, it's versatile as well. —Merrill Powers Spearville, Kansas

        1 tablespoon vegetable oil
    1/2 cup sliced green onions
        1 medium carrot, shredded
        1 garlic clove, minced
        2 cups water
        1 cup uncooked long grain rice
        1 tablespoon beef *or* chicken bouillon granules
    3/4 cup frozen peas, thawed
        2 tablespoons soy sauce
1-1/4 cups chopped cooked ham, pork *or* shrimp,
             optional
        2 eggs

In a 2-qt. microwave-safe dish, combine the oil, onions, carrot and garlic. Cover and microwave on high for 3-4 minutes or until vegetables are crisp-tender. Stir in water, rice and bouillon. Cover and cook on high for 15-18 minutes or until rice is tender and liquid is absorbed, stirring once. Stir in the peas, soy sauce and ham if desired. Cover and let stand for 5 minutes.

Meanwhile, in a small microwave-safe bowl, beat the eggs. Cover and heat on high for 1-1/2 to 1-3/4 minutes or until firm. Cut into small pieces; stir into rice mixture. Serve immediately. **Yield:** 4 servings.

Peanut Butter Squares

Plan ahead...needs to chill

This recipe is so quick to make and uses ingredients usually found in ample supply in my cupboard. The chocolate-topped bars are a great take-along for potlucks and showers. —Marsha Murray, Niverville, Manitoba

    3/4 cup peanut butter
    1/2 cup packed brown sugar
    1/2 cup corn syrup
        1 tablespoon butter *or* margarine
        1 teaspoon vanilla extract
        2 cups cornflakes
        1 cup crisp rice cereal
1-1/2 cups semisweet chocolate chips

In a microwave-safe bowl, combine the peanut butter, brown sugar, corn syrup and butter. Microwave, uncovered, on high for 1 minute or until butter is melted. Stir in vanilla until combined. Add cereal; mix well. Spread into a greased 8-in. square pan.

In a microwave-safe bowl, melt the chocolate chips;

Chicken Divine

stir until smooth. Spread over the cereal mixture. Refrigerate until the chocolate is set. Cut into squares. **Yield:** about 1-1/2 dozen.

Strawberry Rhubarb Sauce

Pecan Cinnamon Fudge

Plan ahead...needs to chill

A handful of baking staples are all you'll need for this rich treat. It's the most fabulous fudge you will ever taste.
—Autumn Bradley-O'Rell, Lodi, Wisconsin

   1 teaspoon plus 1/2 cup butter (no substitutes), *divided*
1/4 cup milk
1-1/2 teaspoons vanilla extract
   3 cups confectioners' sugar
1/2 cup baking cocoa
   1 teaspoon ground cinnamon
   1 cup chopped pecans

Butter an 8-in. square dish with 1 teaspoon butter; set aside. In a microwave-safe bowl, combine milk and remaining butter. Microwave, uncovered, on high for 1-1/4 to 1-1/2 minutes or until butter is melted. Stir in vanilla.

In a bowl, combine the confectioners' sugar, cocoa and cinnamon; stir in milk mixture until blended. Stir in pecans. Pour into prepared pan. Refrigerate for 8 hours or overnight. Cut into squares. **Yield:** about 1-1/4 pounds.

Souped-Up Pork Supper

Ready in 45 minutes or less

Tomato soup, onion soup mix and fresh vegetables lend flavor to these speedy pork chops. You don't really have to watch them while they cook, so you can sit and visit...or fix the rest of the meal. —Myra Innes, Auburn, Kansas

   6 bone-in pork loin chops (1/2 inch thick)
   1 can (10-3/4 ounces) condensed tomato soup, undiluted
   1 envelope dry onion soup mix
   1 cup sliced onion
   1 cup sliced green pepper
   1 cup sliced fresh mushrooms
Hot cooked rice *or* noodles

Place pork chops in a microwave-safe dish with bone side facing the center. In a bowl, combine the soup, soup mix, onion, green pepper and mushrooms; pour over chops. Cover and microwave at 50% power for 30-34 minutes, turning dish every 5 minutes and turning chops once. Serve over rice or noodles. **Yield:** 6 servings.

Mushroom Chicken Roll-Ups

Ready in 30 minutes or less

After working all day, I can throw together these creamy chicken pinwheels in minutes. —Sandie Marroso
Henderson, Nevada

   4 boneless skinless chicken breast halves (8 ounces *each*)
   4 slices fully cooked ham
   1 cup (4 ounces) shredded mozzarella cheese
1/2 teaspoon garlic powder
1/2 teaspoon pepper
   2 tablespoons butter *or* margarine, melted
   1 can (10-3/4 ounces) condensed golden mushroom soup, undiluted
   1 jar (4-1/2 ounces) sliced mushrooms, drained
   3 tablespoons white wine *or* chicken broth
Hot cooked rice *or* noodles

Flatten chicken to 1/4-in. thickness. Place a slice of ham and 1/4 cup cheese on each piece; sprinkle with garlic powder and pepper. Roll up and secure with toothpicks. Place in a greased 2-qt. microwave-safe dish. Drizzle with butter. Microwave, uncovered, on high for 7 minutes, rotating dish a half turn twice.

Combine the soup, mushrooms and wine or broth; pour over chicken. Cover with waxed paper; cook on high for 4-5 minutes or until juices run clear, rotating a half turn twice. Let stand for 5 minutes. Discard toothpicks. Serve roll-ups with rice or noodles. **Yield:** 4 servings.

Strawberry Rhubarb Sauce

(Pictured above)

Ready in 30 minutes or less

This tangy-sweet sauce is delicious over ice cream and so easy to make. —Lorraine Guzek
Thief River Falls, Minnesota

   4 cups sliced fresh *or* frozen rhubarb, thawed
   1 package (10 ounces) frozen sweetened sliced strawberries, thawed
1/2 cup water
1/4 cup quick-cooking tapioca
   1 cup sugar
   4 drops red food coloring, optional

In a 2-qt. microwave-safe dish, combine the fruit, water and tapioca. Let stand for 5 minutes. Cover and microwave on high for 6 minutes. Stir; cook 4 minutes longer or until the rhubarb is tender. Stir in the sugar. Cover and microwave for 2 minutes. Stir in food coloring if desired. Serve warm or chilled. **Yield:** 4-1/2 cups.

Basil Brussels Sprouts
Potato Chip Chicken

Sour Cream Beef 'n' Beans

Ready in 30 minutes or less

I adjusted this favorite casserole for microwave use in the interest of speed and to save heating up the oven.
—Joyce Marten, Cottonwood, Arizona

    1 pound ground beef
    1 can (15 ounces) pinto beans, rinsed and
        drained
    1 can (15 ounces) enchilada sauce
1-1/2 cups (6 ounces) shredded cheddar cheese,
        divided
    1 can (4 ounces) chopped green chilies,
        undrained
1-1/2 cups crushed corn chips
    1 tablespoon dried minced onion
    1 cup (8 ounces) sour cream
Additional corn chips

Crumble beef into an ungreased 2-qt. microwave-safe dish; cover with waxed paper. Cook on high for 5 minutes or until meat is no longer pink, stirring twice; drain. Stir in the beans, enchilada sauce, 1 cup of cheese, chilies, crushed corn chips and onion; mix well. Cover and microwave on high for 3 minutes or until heated through, stirring once.

Top with the sour cream and remaining cheese. Heat, uncovered, at 70% power for 2-3 minutes or until cheese is melted. Serve with corn chips. **Yield:** 4-6 servings.

Broccoli Chicken Roll-Ups

Ready in 30 minutes or less

I roll cheese and broccoli into chicken breasts, zap them in the microwave, then drape them with a smooth sauce. I often make this dish with low-fat cheese and skim milk.
—Joyce Hooker, Knightstown, Indiana

    4 boneless skinless chicken breast halves
    2 slices process American cheese
    1 cup chopped fresh *or* frozen broccoli, thawed
    1 tablespoon all-purpose flour
1/2 cup milk
    1 tablespoon white wine *or* chicken broth
    1 teaspoon minced fresh parsley
1/4 teaspoon salt
1/8 teaspoon pepper

Flatten chicken to 1/4-in. thickness. Cut one cheese slice into four strips; place one strip in the center of each piece of chicken. Top with broccoli. Fold chicken in half and secure with wooden toothpicks. Place seam side down around the outside of a greased 8-in. square microwave-safe dish. Cover and microwave on high for 5-7 minutes or until chicken juices run clear; keep warm.

In a microwave-safe bowl, combine the flour, milk, wine or broth, parsley, salt and pepper until blended. Microwave, uncovered, on high for 1-1/2 to 2 minutes or until thickened. Dice remaining cheese slice; add to the sauce and stir until melted. Pour over chicken. Cook, uncovered, on high for 30 seconds or until heated through. **Yield:** 4 servings.

Basil Brussels Sprouts

(Pictured above)

Ready in 15 minutes or less

Our Test Kitchen created this simple side dish that takes advantage of the microwave.

    2 pounds brussels sprouts, trimmed and halved
    3 tablespoons water
1/4 cup butter *or* margarine, melted
1/2 teaspoon salt
1/2 teaspoon dried basil
1/2 teaspoon pepper

Place brussels sprouts and water in a 2-qt. microwave-safe dish. Cover; microwave on high for 6-8 minutes or until crisp-tender; drain. Combine remaining ingredients; drizzle over sprouts. Toss to coat. **Yield:** 4-6 servings.

Potato Chip Chicken

(Pictured above)

Ready in 15 minutes or less

This is one of the best recipes I've ever used. Not only is it quick and easy, but I think it tastes better than fried chicken. *—Jody Roberts, Hollister, California*

    1 cup coarsely crushed potato chips
    1 tablespoon minced fresh parsley
1/2 teaspoon salt
1/2 teaspoon paprika
1/4 teaspoon onion powder
    4 boneless skinless chicken breast halves
    2 tablespoons mayonnaise

In a large resealable plastic bag, combine the potato chips, parsley, salt, paprika and onion powder. Brush chicken with mayonnaise; add chicken to the crumb mixture and shake to coat. Place in an ungreased microwave-safe 11-in. x 7-in. x 2-in. dish. Cover with microwave-safe paper towels; cook on high for 8-10 minutes or until chicken juices run clear. **Yield:** 4 servings.

Butterscotch Peanut Fudge

Plan ahead…needs to chill

I found this fudge recipe in a very old book. It was written before microwaves, so I modified it to make a quick treat. —*Peggy Key, Grant, Alabama*

    1 can (14 ounces) sweetened condensed milk
    1 package (12 ounces) butterscotch chips
1-1/2 cups miniature marshmallows
  2/3 cup peanut butter
    1 teaspoon vanilla extract
    1 cup chopped salted peanuts

In a microwave-safe bowl, combine the milk, butterscotch chips and marshmallows. Microwave, uncovered, at 80% power for 3 minutes or until chips and marshmallows are melted, stirring frequently. Stir in peanut butter and vanilla until combined. Fold in the peanuts.

Pour into an 11-in. x 7-in. x 2-in. pan coated with nonstick cooking spray. Cover and refrigerate for 2 hours or until firm. Cut into squares. Store in the refrigerator. **Yield:** about 6-1/2 dozen.

Microwave Bread Pudding

Ready in 30 minutes or less

I came up with this warm dessert when baby-sitting. The kids were asking for something sweet, and I was craving bread pudding. —*Victoria Kvassay, Covina, California*

  3/4 cup heavy whipping cream
  1/2 cup semisweet chocolate chips
  1/4 cup whipped cream cheese
  1/4 cup sugar
    1 tablespoon butter *or* margarine
   10 slices white bread, cut into 1-inch cubes
   15 miniature peanut butter cups, quartered

In a large microwave-safe bowl, combine the cream, chocolate chips, cream cheese, sugar and butter. Cover and microwave on high for 3-4 minutes or until chips are melted; stir until smooth. Add the bread cubes; toss to coat.

Place half of the bread mixture in a greased 8-in. square microwave-safe dish. Sprinkle with peanut butter cups; top with the remaining bread mixture. Microwave, uncovered, on high for 2 minutes or until peanut butter cups are melted. Serve warm. **Yield:** 6-8 servings.

Parmesan Potato Wedges

Ready in 15 minutes or less

I often cube the potatoes before coating them to make flavorful nuggets. I find that children and adults alike enjoy them. —*Lois Lucas, Mt. Pleasant, Pennsylvania*

  1/3 cup dry bread crumbs
  1/4 cup grated Parmesan cheese
1-1/2 teaspoons onion salt
    1 teaspoon paprika
    2 medium potatoes, peeled and cut into wedges
    3 tablespoons all-purpose flour
  1/4 cup butter *or* margarine, melted

In a resealable plastic bag, combine the bread crumbs, Parmesan cheese, onion salt and paprika. Coat potatoes with flour; dip in butter. Add to bread crumb mixture; shake to coat evenly. Arrange on a microwave-safe plate.

Cover with waxed paper. Microwave on high for 4-6 minutes or until tender, rotating every 2 minutes. Let stand for 2 minutes. **Yield:** 3-4 servings.

Colorful Zucchini Boats

(Pictured below right)

Ready in 30 minutes or less

I hollow out zucchini, then fill the shells with an herb-seasoned stuffing for a colorful side dish. —*Shirley Glaab Hattiesburg, Mississippi*

    4 medium zucchini (about 7 inches *each*)
  1/4 pound fresh mushrooms, sliced
    1 small onion, chopped
  1/2 cup frozen corn, thawed
    1 tablespoon butter *or* margarine
  1/2 teaspoon dried thyme
  1/4 to 1/2 teaspoon dried basil
  1/4 teaspoon salt
  1/4 teaspoon pepper
    2 tablespoons prepared ranch salad dressing
  1/2 cup shredded cheddar cheese, *divided*
    4 cherry tomatoes, quartered

Cut a thin slice off bottom of zucchini so it sits flat. Cut a thin lengthwise slice from top of zucchini and discard. Scoop out pulp, leaving a 1/4-in. shell. Chop 1 cup pulp; set aside. Place zucchini shells in an ungreased 8-in. square microwave-safe dish. Cover and microwave on high for 3 minutes or until crisp-tender; drain and set aside.

In a microwave-safe bowl, combine mushrooms, onion and reserved zucchini pulp. Cover and microwave on high for 4 minutes; drain. Heat 1-2 minutes longer; drain thoroughly. Stir in the corn, butter, thyme, basil, salt and pepper. Cover and microwave on high for 1 minute. Stir in salad dressing and 1/4 cup cheese. Stuff into zucchini boats.

Microwave, uncovered, on high for 2-3 minutes. Sprinkle with the remaining cheese; top with tomatoes. Heat 1-2 minutes longer or until the vegetables are tender and the cheese is melted. Let stand for 3-5 minutes before serving. **Yield:** 4 servings.

Colorful Zucchini Boats

HERE'S a collection of theme-related recipes that taste terrific and are time-savers, too.

It's easy to dip into delicious dishes, like the sweet fondue treats at left, for your next gathering.

Lemons, blueberries, marshmallows and caramel are versatile ingredients that enhance meals and snacktimes throughout the day.

There's no pressure on you to get dinner done when a pressure cooker prepares a tempting recipe in mere minutes.

Savor the flavor of perfectly prepared pork and potatoes, creamy bagel spreads and appealing appetizers.

And if recipes that feed a crowd don't suit your smaller household, check out the rapid recipes here that are perfectly portioned to serve one or two.

FUN FONDUE. Warm Strawberry Fondue and Butterscotch Fondue (both recipes on p. 294).

Lemon Grilled Chicken
Lemon Cheesecake Dessert

Tangy Lemons

LOVELY LEMONS add an irresistible zest to effortless entrees, simple side dishes and desserts like these.

Lemon Grilled Chicken

(Pictured above)

Plan ahead...needs to marinate

My mother relied on this recipe. Its mild lemon taste reminds me of summertime. —*Ellen Seidl, Norfolk, Nebraska*

- 1/2 cup lemon juice
- 1/4 cup vegetable oil
- 3 tablespoons chopped onion
- 1/2 teaspoon salt
- 1/2 teaspoon pepper
- 1/2 teaspoon dried thyme
- 1 garlic clove, minced
- 1 broiler/fryer chicken (3 to 4 pounds), cut up

In a large resealable plastic bag, combine the first seven ingredients; mix well. Remove 1/4 cup for basting and refrigerate. Add chicken to the bag; seal and turn to coat. Refrigerate for 8 hours or overnight. Drain and discard marinade from chicken. Grill, covered, over medium heat for 20 minutes. Baste with reserved marinade. Grill 20-30 minutes longer or until juices run clear, basting and turning several times. **Yield:** 4 servings.

Editor's Note: This can also be made in the oven in a greased 13-in. x 9-in. x 2-in. baking dish. Bake, uncovered, at 350° for 50-60 minutes or until juices run clear.

Lemon Cheesecake Dessert

(Pictured above)

These light citrus squares are not too tart and not too sweet. —*Peggy Key, Grant, Alabama*

- 1-1/2 cups graham cracker crumbs (about 24 squares)
- 1/3 cup finely chopped pecans
- 1/3 cup sugar
- 1/3 cup butter *or* margarine, melted
- 2 packages (8 ounces *each*) cream cheese, softened
- 1 can (14 ounces) sweetened condensed milk
- 2 eggs
- 1/2 cup lemon juice

In a bowl, combine cracker crumbs, pecans and sugar. Add butter; mix well. Set aside 1/2 cup. Press the remaining crumb mixture into a greased 13-in. x 9-in. x 2-in. baking dish. Bake at 325° for 8 minutes. In a small mixing bowl, beat the cream cheese until smooth. Add the milk, eggs and lemon juice; beat until smooth. Spoon over crust. Sprinkle with the reserved crumb mixture. Bake for 30 minutes or until center is almost set. Cool on a wire rack. Store in the refrigerator. **Yield:** 16-20 servings.

Lemon Oregano Potatoes

These tender potatoes have been a family favorite for many years. —*Kate Hilts, Grand Rapids, Michigan*

- 3 large red potatoes, cut into 1/2-inch cubes
- 1/4 cup olive *or* vegetable oil
- 3 tablespoons lemon juice
- 1 teaspoon dried oregano
- 1/2 teaspoon salt

Place potatoes in a saucepan and cover with water. Bring to a boil over medium heat. Reduce heat. Simmer, uncovered, for 5-8 minutes or until potatoes are crisp-tender; drain. Add the oil, lemon juice, oregano and salt. Transfer to a greased 11-in. x 7-in. x 2-in. baking dish. Bake, uncovered, at 350° for 20-25 minutes or until potatoes are tender and lightly browned. **Yield:** 4 servings.

Lemon Bundt Cake

Convenient cake and pudding mixes hurry along this glazed cake. —*Ann Anderson, Andrews, North Carolina*

- 1 package (18-1/4 ounces) lemon cake mix
- 1 package (3.4 ounces) instant lemon pudding mix
- 4 eggs
- 1 cup water
- 1/3 cup vegetable oil
- 1 tablespoon butter *or* margarine, melted
- 1/4 cup orange juice
- 1 cup confectioners' sugar

In a mixing bowl, combine dry cake and pudding mixes, eggs, water and oil. Beat on medium speed 2 minutes. Pour into a greased and floured 10-in. fluted tube pan. Bake at 350° for 35-40 minutes or until a toothpick inserted near the center comes out clean. Cool on a wire rack 6-8 minutes.

Meanwhile, for glaze, combine butter and orange juice in a small bowl; stir in confectioners' sugar until smooth. Remove cake from pan to a serving platter; poke holes in cake with a meat fork. Slowly drizzle with glaze. Cool completely. **Yield:** 10-12 servings.

Pork and Potatoes

HERE, two culinary staples—pork and potatoes—are combined in three tasty time-saving ways.

Scalloped Pork Chop Combo

Ready in 1 hour or less

I create a meal-in-one by combining veggies, a box of scalloped potatoes and moist chops. —Sherry Schoneman Cedar Falls, Iowa

    6 bone-in pork loin chops (1/2 inch thick)
    2 tablespoons vegetable oil
    1 teaspoon salt
    2 cups water
    1 package (10 ounces) frozen French-style
      green beans
    1 cup thinly sliced carrots
    1 package (5 ounces) scalloped potatoes
    1 can (10-3/4 ounces) condensed cream of
      celery soup, undiluted
  2/3 cup milk
    2 tablespoons butter *or* margarine
  1/2 teaspoon Worcestershire sauce

In a skillet, brown pork chops in oil; sprinkle with salt. In a saucepan, bring the water to a boil; add beans, carrots, potatoes with contents of sauce packet, soup, milk, butter and Worcestershire sauce. Bring to a boil. Transfer to a greased 13-in. x 9-in. x 2-in. baking dish; top with pork chops. Cover; bake at 350° for 25 minutes. Uncover; bake 5 minutes longer or until pork and vegetables are tender. Let stand 10 minutes before serving. **Yield:** 6 servings.

Pork Hash Brown Bake

Ready in 1 hour or less

Chock-full of colorful vegetables and tender pork, this creamy casserole comes from our Test Kitchen staff.

  1/4 cup all-purpose flour
    2 teaspoons chicken bouillon granules
  1/2 teaspoon salt
    1 cup water
  1/2 cup milk
  1/4 cup sour cream
    3 cups frozen O'Brien hash brown potatoes,
      thawed
    2 cups cubed cooked pork
    1 package (10 ounces) frozen mixed
      vegetables, thawed
    1 can (4 ounces) mushroom stems and pieces,
      drained
  1/2 cup crushed cornflakes
    2 tablespoons butter *or* margarine, melted

In a saucepan, combine flour, bouillon, salt, water and milk until smooth. Bring to a boil; cook and stir for 2 minutes or until thickened. Remove from the heat; stir in sour cream.

In a large bowl, combine the potatoes, pork, vegetables and mushrooms. Add the sour cream mixture; stir to coat well. Transfer to a greased shallow 2-qt. baking dish. Toss cornflakes and butter; sprinkle over the top. Bake, uncovered, at 375° for 30-35 minutes or until heated through. **Yield:** 6 servings.

Potato Pork Skillet

(Pictured below)

Ready in 45 minutes or less

I always receive wonderful comments from everyone who tries this easy recipe. —Barbara Carlson
Brooklyn Park, Minnesota

✓ Uses less fat, sugar or salt. Includes Nutritional Analysis and Diabetic Exchanges.

    1 pound pork tenderloin, cut into 1/4-inch slices
    2 tablespoons butter *or* stick margarine
    1 can (14-1/2 ounces) chicken broth, *divided*
    8 small red potatoes, quartered
    1 tablespoon Dijon mustard
    2 teaspoons Worcestershire sauce
  1/4 teaspoon salt
  1/8 teaspoon pepper
    1 cup sliced fresh mushrooms
  1/2 cup sliced green onions
    2 tablespoons all-purpose flour

In a large skillet over medium-high heat, brown pork in butter on both sides. Remove and keep warm. Set aside 1/4 cup of broth. Add the potatoes, mustard, Worcestershire sauce, salt, pepper and remaining broth to the skillet. Bring to a boil. Reduce heat; cover and simmer for 15-17 minutes or until the potatoes are tender.

Stir in mushrooms, onions and pork. Cover and simmer 5 minutes longer or until meat is no longer pink. In a small bowl, combine the flour and reserved broth until smooth. Stir into pork mixture. Bring to a boil; cook and stir for 2 minutes or until thickened. **Yield:** 4 servings.

Nutritional Analysis: One serving (1-1/4 cups) equals 266 calories, 12 g fat (5 g saturated fat), 91 mg cholesterol, 828 mg sodium, 12 g carbohydrate, 4 g fiber, 28 g protein. **Diabetic Exchanges:** 3 lean meat, 1 starch, 1/2 fat.

Potato Pork Skillet

Marvelous Marshmallows

IT'S EASY to stir a little whimsy into snacks, salads and sweet sensations when you keep a bag of marshmallows on hand. These soft bites can swiftly sweeten up all sorts of dishes. Try one of the nifty no-bake recipes here.

Cathedral Window Cookies

(Pictured below)

Plan ahead...needs to chill

This treat is bound to become a family favorite. These cookies are great for bake sales and holidays. Kids of all ages love the colorful mini marshmallows, chocolate and chopped nuts.   —Diane Sequist Meriden, Connecticut

1 package (10-1/2 ounces) pastel miniature marshmallows
1 cup chopped walnuts, optional

Cathedral Window Cookies

2 cups (12 ounces) semisweet chocolate chips
1/2 cup butter *or* margarine, cubed

Place marshmallows and nuts if desired in a large bowl; set aside. In a heavy saucepan, melt chocolate chips and butter over medium-low heat. Pour over marshmallow mixture and mix well. Cover and refrigerate for 1 hour, stirring occasionally.

Shape marshmallow mixture into a 12-in. roll; wrap in waxed paper. Refrigerate for 4 hours or until firm. Unwrap and cut into 3/8-in. slices; cut slices in half. **Yield:** about 4-1/2 dozen.

Mallow Mint Dessert

Plan ahead...needs to chill

This minty marshmallow whip served on a cookie crumb crust will have folks asking for seconds. It's very light and refreshing. I like to top each serving with a dab of whipped cream and a maraschino cherry.
—Eleanor Mielke, Mitchell, South Dakota

32 large marshmallows
 1 cup evaporated milk
3/4 teaspoon mint extract
 3 drops green food coloring
 2 cups heavy whipping cream, whipped
1-3/4 cups crushed cream-filled chocolate
   sandwich cookies, *divided*
 2 tablespoons butter *or* margarine, melted

In a microwave-safe bowl, combine the marshmallows and milk. Microwave, uncovered, on high for 3 minutes or until marshmallows are melted. Stir until smooth. Cool to room temperature. Stir in the mint extract and food coloring. Fold in the whipped cream.

In a small bowl, combine 1-1/2 cups cookie crumbs and butter. Press into a greased 11-in. x 7-in. x 2-in. dish. Top with marshmallow mixture. Sprinkle with the remaining cookie crumbs. Cover and refrigerate for 4 hours before serving. **Yield:** 10 servings.

Marshmallow Fruit Salad

Ready in 15 minutes or less

I rely on convenient cans of pineapple chunks, fruit cocktail and mandarin oranges to speed up this marshmallow fluff. Dress up the salad a bit by stirring in rich sour cream and chopped pecans for a pleasant crunch.
—Christine Mills, Buffalo, New York

1 can (20 ounces) pineapple chunks, drained
1 can (15 ounces) fruit cocktail, drained
1 can (15 ounces) mandarin oranges, drained
1 cup chopped pecans
1 cup (8 ounces) sour cream
2-1/2 cups whipped topping
3 cups miniature marshmallows

In a large serving bowl, combine the fruit, pecans and sour cream. Fold in whipped topping and marshmallows. Cover and refrigerate until serving. **Yield:** 10-12 servings.

Spicy Steak Stew

Pressure Cooking

UNDER PRESSURE to get dinner on the table in a hurry? Try the speedy solution that's been a favorite of busy cooks for years—the pressure cooker.

Spicy Steak Stew

(Pictured above)

Ready in 45 minutes or less

This is a great last-minute meal that tastes very good.
—Wendy Hughes, Easton, Pennsylvania

    2 cups cubed beef flank steak (1/2-inch cubes)
    1 medium onion, sliced
    1 garlic clove, minced
    1 tablespoon vegetable oil
    1 can (14 ounces) onion-seasoned *or* regular
      beef broth
    1 can (14-1/2 ounces) Italian stewed tomatoes
    2 cups diced peeled potato
    1 cup coarsely chopped fresh broccoli
    1 celery rib, thinly sliced
  1/2 cup minced fresh parsley
    2 teaspoons Worcestershire sauce
  1/4 teaspoon *each* salt, pepper and crushed red
      pepper flakes
    1 tablespoon cornstarch
    1 tablespoon cold water

In a pressure cooker, cook steak, onion and garlic in oil until meat is no longer pink; drain. Add broth; simmer for 10 minutes. Add the vegetables, parsley, Worcestershire sauce and seasonings. Close cover securely; place pressure regulator on vent pipe. Bring cooker to full pressure over high heat. Reduce heat to medium; cook for 3 minutes. (Pressure regulator should maintain a slow steady rocking motion or release of steam; adjust heat if needed.)

Remove from the heat. Immediately cool according to manufacturer's directions until pressure is completely reduced. In a small bowl, combine cornstarch and water until smooth; stir into stew. Bring to a boil over medium heat; cook for 2 minutes or until thickened. **Yield:** 6 servings.

Editor's Note: This recipe was tested at 15 pounds pressure (psi).

Chicken Paprika

Ready in 30 minutes or less

I serve these tender chicken breasts with a rich paprika-seasoned sauce.   —Holly Ottum, Racine, Wisconsin

    4 bone-in chicken breast halves (3 pounds)
    1 medium onion, chopped
    2 tablespoons all-purpose flour
    1 cup chicken broth
    1 tablespoon tomato paste
    1 to 2 garlic cloves, minced
    1 tablespoon paprika
  1/2 teaspoon *each* salt and dried thyme
Dash hot pepper sauce
    1 cup (8 ounces) sour cream

Place chicken in a pressure cooker; top with onion. In a small bowl, whisk the flour, broth, tomato paste, garlic, and seasonings until smooth. Pour over chicken.

Close cover securely; place pressure regulator on vent pipe. Bring cooker to low pressure over high heat. Reduce heat to medium-high; cook for 12 minutes. (Pressure regulator should maintain a slow steady rocking motion or release of steam; adjust heat if needed.)

Remove from the heat. Immediately cool according to manufacturer's directions until pressure is completely reduced. Remove chicken and keep warm. Stir sour cream into cooking juices; serve over chicken. **Yield:** 4 servings.

Editor's Note: This recipe was tested at 10 pounds pressure (psi).

Porcupine Meatballs

Ready in 45 minutes or less

I occasionally use cream of mushroom soup instead of tomato soup.   —Mary Kelso, Hannibal, Missouri

    1 egg, lightly beaten
  1/2 cup uncooked instant rice
    2 tablespoons finely chopped onion
    1 tablespoon minced fresh parsley
  1/2 teaspoon salt
  1/4 teaspoon pepper
    1 pound lean ground beef
    1 can (10-3/4 ounces) condensed tomato
      soup, undiluted
    1 cup water
    1 teaspoon Worcestershire sauce

In a bowl, combine the first six ingredients. Crumble beef over mixture; mix well. Shape into 1-1/2-in. balls. Place on the rack in a pressure cooker. Combine soup, water and Worcestershire sauce; pour over meatballs.

Close cover securely; place pressure regulator on vent pipe. Bring cooker to full pressure over high heat. Reduce heat to medium; cook for 10 minutes. (Pressure regulator should maintain a slow steady rocking motion or release of steam; adjust heat if needed.) Remove from the heat. Immediately cool according to manufacturer's directions until pressure is completely reduced. **Yield:** 4 servings.

Editor's Note: This recipe was tested at 13 pounds pressure (psi).

Sour Cream Blueberry Muffins
Blueberry Cream Dessert

A Bounty of Blueberries

IT'S A BREEZE to brighten family meals when you turn to blueberries. These dishes are so good, you'll make them more than once in a blue moon!

Sour Cream Blueberry Muffins

(Pictured above)

Ready in 45 minutes or less

When we were growing up, my mom made these warm, delicious muffins on chilly mornings. —Tory Ross
Cincinnati, Ohio

    2 cups biscuit/baking mix
3/4 cup plus 2 tablespoons sugar, *divided*
    2 eggs
    1 cup (8 ounces) sour cream
    1 cup fresh *or* frozen blueberries*

In a bowl, combine the biscuit mix and 3/4 cup sugar. In another bowl, combine the eggs and sour cream; stir into the dry ingredients just until combined. Fold in the blueberries. Fill greased muffin cups three-fourths full. Sprinkle with the remaining sugar.
  Bake at 375° for 20-25 minutes or until a toothpick comes out clean. Cool for 5 minutes before removing from pan to a wire rack. **Yield:** 1 dozen.
  *Editor's Note: If using frozen blueberries, do not thaw before adding to the batter.

Blueberry Cream Dessert

(Pictured above)

A no-fuss crust spread with sweetened cream cheese is baked, then topped with convenient pie filling and whipped topping. —Mildred Sherrer, Bay City, Texas

1-1/2 cups graham cracker crumbs (about 24 squares)

    3/4 cup sugar, *divided*
    1/2 cup butter *or* margarine, melted
      1 package (8 ounces) cream cheese, softened
      2 eggs
      1 teaspoon vanilla extract
    1/2 teaspoon ground cinnamon
      1 can (21 ounces) blueberry pie filling
      1 carton (8 ounces) frozen whipped topping, thawed

In a bowl, combine the cracker crumbs, 1/4 cup sugar and butter. Press into a greased 13-in. x 9-in. x 2-in. baking dish. In a mixing bowl, beat the cream cheese and remaining sugar until smooth; add the eggs and vanilla. Pour over crust.
  Bake at 350° for 15-20 minutes or until set. Sprinkle with cinnamon. Cool on a wire rack. Spread with pie filling and whipped topping. Refrigerate until serving. **Yield:** 12-16 servings.

Blueberry Banana Salad

Ready in 15 minutes or less

We have several blueberry bushes in our yard, so using the bounty in this easy salad is a nice change from pies and muffins. —Yvonne Bellomo, Ebensburg, Pennsylvania

✓ Uses less fat, sugar or salt. Includes Nutritional Analysis and Diabetic Exchanges.

      2 cups sliced firm bananas
1-1/2 cups fresh blueberries
      1 can (11 ounces) mandarin oranges, drained
    1/2 cup miniature marshmallows
      2 tablespoons flaked coconut
    1/2 cup sour cream

In a bowl, combine the bananas, blueberries, oranges, marshmallows and coconut. Gently fold in the sour cream. Refrigerate leftovers. **Yield:** 6 servings.
  Nutritional Analysis: One 3/4-cup serving (prepared with reduced-fat sour cream) equals 125 calories, 2 g fat (1 g saturated fat), 7 mg cholesterol, 28 mg sodium, 27 g carbohydrate, 2 g fiber, 2 g protein. **Diabetic Exchange:** 1-1/2 starch.

Blueberry Sherbet

Plan ahead...needs to freeze

I like to garnish this refreshing dessert with whipped cream. It can also be made with raspberries or strawberries.
—Judith Rush, Newport, Rhode Island

      1 cup (8 ounces) sour cream
    3/4 cup sugar
      1 tablespoon lemon juice
    1/2 teaspoon vanilla extract
      3 cups fresh *or* frozen blueberries, thawed

In a blender or food processor, combine all ingredients; cover and process until smooth. Press through a sieve; discard the blueberry seeds and skin. Freeze for 8 hours or overnight. Remove from the freezer 30 minutes before serving. **Yield:** 2 cups.

Bagel Spreads

FIFTEEN minutes and a few ingredients are all you need to turn basic bagels into enticing edibles that satisfy the pickiest palates. Forget those costly supermarket spreads and whip up one of these quick creamy toppings today.

Seafood Avocado Spread

Ready in 15 minutes or less

Convenient canned shrimp, crabmeat and avocado chunks dress up salmon-flavored cream cheese in this spread. It's great on bagels, sandwich bread or crackers.
—Jeannie Phillips, Montesano, Washington

- 1 carton (8 ounces) spreadable salmon cream cheese
- 1 can (6 ounces) crabmeat, drained, flaked and cartilage removed
- 1 can (6 ounces) tiny shrimp, rinsed and drained
- 1 small ripe avocado, peeled and diced
- 1/2 cup mayonnaise *or* salad dressing
- 1/3 cup chopped celery
- 1/4 teaspoon salt
- 1/8 teaspoon pepper
- Bagels, split

In a bowl, combine the first eight ingredients; mix well. Toast bagels if desired; top with spread. **Yield:** 3 cups.

Cinnamon Spread

Ready in 15 minutes or less

Looking to make mornings a little sweeter? Try this streamlined version of cinnamon toast. —Kat Thompson Thermopolis, Wyoming

- 1/4 cup butter *or* margarine, softened
- 1/4 cup packed brown sugar
- 1 teaspoon ground cinnamon
- 1/4 teaspoon ground nutmeg
- Bagels, split

In a small bowl, combine the butter, brown sugar, cinnamon and nutmeg. Toast bagels if desired; top with spread. **Yield:** about 1/3 cup.

Garlic-Herb Bagel Spread

(Pictured at right)

Ready in 15 minutes or less

Our Test Kitchen staff mixed up this mouth-watering must-have, which is loaded with herbs and feta. The flavorful combo is perfect with toasted bagels or breadsticks.

 Uses less fat, sugar or salt. Includes Nutritional Analysis and Diabetic Exchanges.

- 1 package (3 ounces) cream cheese, softened
- 1/3 cup sour cream
- 1/4 cup crumbled feta cheese
- 2 garlic cloves, minced
- 1/2 teaspoon *each* garlic powder, dried oregano and basil
- Bagels, split

In a small mixing bowl, beat the cream cheese until smooth. Add the sour cream, feta cheese, garlic and seasonings; mix well. Toast bagels if desired; top with spread. **Yield:** 1 cup.

Nutritional Analysis: 2 tablespoons of spread (prepared with fat-free cream cheese and reduced-fat sour cream) equals 38 calories, 2 g fat (1 g saturated fat), 8 mg cholesterol, 117 mg sodium, 2 g carbohydrate, trace fiber, 3 g protein. **Diabetic Exchange:** 1 fat.

Ham Cream Cheese Spread

(Pictured below)

Ready in 15 minutes or less

I serve this fast fix on miniature bagels as a special-occasion appetizer. Full of ham and green onions, the hearty mixture comes together in no time and tastes terrific. —Donna Letts, Flint, Michigan

- 1 package (8 ounces) cream cheese, softened
- 1 cup (8 ounces) sour cream
- 1/4 teaspoon garlic powder
- 2 packages (2-1/2 ounces *each*) deli ham, chopped
- 2 to 3 green onions, thinly sliced
- Miniature bagels, split

In a small mixing bowl, combine the cream cheese, sour cream and garlic powder until smooth. Stir in ham and onions. Serve with bagels. **Yield:** about 2-1/2 cups.

Ham Cream Cheese Spread
Garlic-Herb Bagel Spread

Appealing Appetizers

NEED elegant hors d'oeuvres for a special event? Appealing appetizers for a casual get-together? Here you'll find streamlined snacks that taste terrific but won't fritter away your free time.

Mushroom Broccoli Cups

(Pictured below)

Ready in 1 hour or less

This is my very favorite appetizer and the one all my friends and family ask me to make. —Linda Senuta
Gettysburg, Pennsylvania

 24 slices bread
  1 egg
  1 egg white
 1/3 cup milk
  1 teaspoon dried parsley flakes
 1/2 teaspoon salt
 1/4 teaspoon baking powder
 1/8 teaspoon dried thyme
Dash pepper
 1/3 cup finely chopped fresh broccoli
 1/3 cup shredded cheddar cheese
 1/4 cup finely chopped fresh mushrooms
  1 tablespoon finely chopped onion

With a rolling pin, roll bread flat; cut with a 2-1/2-in. biscuit cutter. (Discard bread scraps or save for another use.) Press bread rounds into miniature muffin cups coated with nonstick cooking spray. Broil 6 in. from the heat until golden brown, about 2-3 minutes. Cool in pans on a wire rack.

In a bowl, beat egg, egg white, milk, parsley, salt, baking powder, thyme and pepper. Stir in broccoli, cheese, mushrooms and onion. Spoon about 1 teaspoonful in-to each toast cup. Bake at 350° for 15-20 minutes or until set. Serve immediately. **Yield:** 2 dozen.

Zippy Shrimp Spread

(Pictured below left)

Plan ahead...needs to chill

Horseradish adds kick to the seafood sauce in this shrimp spread. It's a must at Christmas and other special occasions. —Leigh Hein, Vernon, Connecticut

  2 packages (8 ounces *each*) cream cheese, softened
  1 teaspoon seasoned salt
  1 teaspoon Worcestershire sauce
 1/2 teaspoon onion powder
  1 bottle (12 ounces) seafood sauce
  1 tablespoon prepared horseradish
  2 cans (6 ounces *each*) tiny shrimp, rinsed and drained
Minced fresh parsley
Assorted crackers

In a mixing bowl, beat cream cheese until smooth. Beat in seasoned salt, Worcestershire sauce and onion powder. Spread onto a 13-in. platter. Combine seafood sauce and horseradish; spread over cream cheese layer. Sprinkle with shrimp and parsley. Cover; chill for at least 1 hour. Serve with crackers. **Yield:** 3-1/2 cups.

Ginger Meatballs

Ready in 1 hour or less

These sweet and tangy meatballs have caused many guests to ask, "What is that delicious flavor?"
—Sybil Leson, Houston, Texas

✓ Uses less fat, sugar or salt. Includes Nutritional Analysis and Diabetic Exchanges.

  1 egg
 1/2 cup finely crushed gingersnaps (about 11 cookies)
  1 teaspoon salt
1-1/2 pounds ground beef
  1 cup ketchup
 1/4 cup packed brown sugar
  2 tablespoons Dijon mustard
 1/2 teaspoon ground ginger

In a large bowl, combine egg, cookie crumbs and salt. Crumble beef over mixture and mix well. Shape into 1-in. balls. Place 1 in. apart in ungreased 15-in. x 10-in. x 1-in. baking pans. Bake, uncovered, at 350° for 15-20 minutes or until no longer pink; drain.

In a large skillet, combine ketchup, brown sugar, mustard and ginger. Add meatballs. Simmer, uncovered, for 15-20 minutes or until heated through, gently stirring several times. **Yield:** about 3-1/2 dozen.

Nutritional Analysis: One serving (2 meatballs, prepared with lean ground beef) equals 97 calories, 4 g fat (1 g saturated fat), 22 mg cholesterol, 322 mg sodium, 8 g carbohydrate, trace fiber, 7 g protein. **Diabetic Exchanges:** 1 lean meat, 1/2 starch.

Zippy Shrimp Spread
Mushroom Broccoli Cups

Cinnamon Caramel Apples
Caramel Pecan Delight

Gooey Good Caramel

WITH a convenient package of chewy caramels or a jar of luscious caramel ice cream topping, you're well on your way to whipping up a tempting treat.

Cinnamon Caramel Apples

(Pictured above)

Our Test Kitchen staff used cinnamon and chocolate to give a fun and tasty twist to traditional caramel apples. Rolled in nuts, coconut or colorful candies, they'll delight kids of all ages.

  2 packages (14 ounces *each*) caramels
  3 tablespoons milk chocolate chips
  3 tablespoons water
  1 teaspoon ground cinnamon
3/4 teaspoon vanilla extract
  8 Popsicle sticks
  8 large tart apples
Chocolate-covered toffee bits, finely chopped salted peanuts and cashews, flaked coconut, M&M miniature baking bits *and/or* chocolate sprinkles

In a microwave-safe bowl, combine the caramels, chocolate chips, water, cinnamon and vanilla. Microwave, uncovered, on high for 2 minutes; stir. Microwave 1 minute longer or until caramels are melted.

Insert Popsicle sticks into the apples; dip into caramel mixture, turning to coat. Roll in or press on desired toppings. Place on waxed paper; let stand until set. **Yield:** 8 servings.

Editor's Note: This recipe was tested with Hershey caramels in an 850-watt microwave.

Caramel Pecan Delight

(Pictured at left)

Plan ahead…needs to chill

After one bite of this rich caramel-drizzled dessert, you'll move it to the top of your recipe file. A buttery crust of crushed pecan cookies complements the cheesecake-like filling. It's a glorious treat.
—Judy Atwell
Aptos, California

  1 package (16 ounces) pecan cookies, crushed
1/2 cup butter *or* margarine, melted
  2 packages (8 ounces *each*) cream cheese, softened
  1 jar (12 ounces) caramel ice cream topping, *divided*
1-1/2 cups cold milk
  1 package (5.1 ounces) instant vanilla pudding mix
3/4 cup chopped pecans

In a bowl, combine cookie crumbs and butter. Press into a greased 13-in. x 9-in. x 2-in. baking dish. Bake at 375° for 10 minutes. Cool on a wire rack.

In a large mixing bowl, beat cream cheese and 1/2 cup caramel topping until smooth. In a bowl, whisk milk and pudding mix for 2 minutes; fold into cream cheese mixture. Spread over the cooled crust. Sprinkle with pecans. Cover and refrigerate for at least 6 hours. Cut into squares; drizzle with remaining caramel topping. **Yield:** 12-15 servings.

Walnut Caramel Cake

I once enjoyed a nutty chocolate-caramel cake at a teahouse. I eventually happened upon a similar recipe that dresses up a boxed cake mix. The moist cake is a hit, especially with chocolate lovers, whenever I serve it.
—Deanna Richter, Elmore, Minnesota

  1 package (18-1/4 ounces) German chocolate cake mix
  1 package (14 ounces) caramels*
3/4 cup butter *or* margarine, cubed
  3 tablespoons milk
  1 cup chopped walnuts
  1 cup (6 ounces) semisweet chocolate chips

Prepare cake mix according to package directions. Pour half of the batter into a greased 13-in. x 9-in. x 2-in. baking pan. Bake at 350° for 18 minutes. Meanwhile, in a large saucepan, combine the caramels, butter and milk. Cook and stir over medium-low heat until melted. Pour over warm cake.

Sprinkle with the walnuts and chocolate chips. Pour the remaining batter over chips. Bake 35-40 minutes longer or until cake is set and pulls away from sides of pan. Cool on a wire rack. **Yield:** 12-15 servings.

*Editor's Note: This recipe was tested with Hershey caramels.

Warm Strawberry Fondue
Butterscotch Fondue

Festive Fondue

THROWING A PARTY is a cinch with recipes that are quick, creative and crowd-pleasing. Fondue is a perfect example. It's a snap to stir up, fun to eat and easy to serve because guests do the dipping.

Fondue easily fits into most menus, whether served as a rich cheesy appetizer, savory main dish or delicious dessert. Consider one or more of the following fondues for your next get-together.

Warm Strawberry Fondue

(Pictured above and on page 285)

Ready in 15 minutes or less

For a delightful dessert, I need only a handful of ingredients to fix this unusual fruit fondue. Use grapes, bananas, strawberries and angel food cake cubes as dippers.
—Sharon Mensing
Greenfield, Iowa

✓ Uses less fat, sugar or salt. Includes Nutritional Analysis and Diabetic Exchanges.

 1 package (10 ounces) frozen sweetened
 sliced strawberries, thawed
 1/4 cup half-and-half cream
 1 teaspoon cornstarch
 1/2 teaspoon lemon juice
Angel food cake cubes and fresh fruit

In a food processor or blender, combine the strawberries, cream, cornstarch and lemon juice; cover and process until smooth. Pour into a saucepan. Bring to a boil; cook and stir for 2 minutes or until slightly thickened. Transfer to a fondue pot or mini slow cooker; keep warm. Serve with cake and fruit. **Yield:** 1-1/2 cups.

Nutritional Analysis: One serving (2 tablespoons, prepared with fat-free half-and-half; calculated without cake and fruit) equals 27 calories, trace fat (0 saturated fat), 0 cholesterol, 6 mg sodium, 7 g carbohydrate, trace fiber, trace protein. **Diabetic Exchange:** 1/2 fruit.

Butterscotch Fondue

(Pictured at left and on page 284)

Ready in 30 minutes or less

Folks of all ages will enjoy dipping into a pot filled with this yummy concoction from our Test Kitchen. The combination of brown sugar, sweetened condensed milk and toffee bits has lovely flavor. Use it to cap off a meal...or serve it as a sweet snack. Paired with cubes of angel food cake or fruit, it's a deliciously different treat.

 1/2 cup butter *or* margarine, cubed
 2 cups packed brown sugar
 1 can (14 ounces) sweetened condensed milk
 1 cup light corn syrup
 2 tablespoons water
 1/4 cup English toffee bits *or* almond brickle
 chips
 1 teaspoon vanilla extract
Angel food cake cubes and fresh fruit

In a large saucepan, combine the butter, brown sugar, milk, corn syrup and water. Cook and stir over medium heat until smooth. Remove from the heat. Stir in toffee bits and vanilla. Transfer to a fondue pot or mini slow cooker; keep warm. Serve with cake and fruit. **Yield:** 4 cups.

Parmesan Fondue

Ready in 15 minutes or less

This wonderful recipe was given to me many years ago at a New Year's Eve potluck. Since then, it has been a tradition to serve it at our holiday open house. The creamy mixture is always a hit.
—Gwynne Fleener
Coeur d'Alene, Idaho

1-1/2 to 2 cups milk
 2 packages (8 ounces *each*) cream cheese,
 cubed
1-1/2 cups grated Parmesan cheese
 1/2 teaspoon garlic salt
 1 loaf (1 pound) French bread, cubed

In a large saucepan, cook and stir the milk and cream cheese over low heat until cheese is melted. Stir in Parmesan cheese and garlic salt; cook and stir until heated through. Transfer to a fondue pot or mini slow cooker; keep warm. Serve with bread cubes. **Yield:** about 3-1/2 cups.

Dinner Duets

SPEEDY SUPPERS that feed a crowd can hit the right note for large households, family gatherings and church potlucks. But for some folks with just one or two in their home, large-quantity recipes don't fit their needs.

So our Test Kitchen came up with recipes for main dishes that serve just two people. (These recipes are also great for singles...just refrigerate the extras to enjoy the next day.)

Greek Pita Pizzas

Pineapple Pork Kabobs

(Pictured below)

Plan ahead...needs to marinate

Pork tenderloin is marinated and grilled to tender perfection in these eye-catching kabobs. Enjoy the skewers with strawberry gelatin and chocolate cupcakes for dessert.

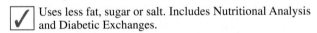 Uses less fat, sugar or salt. Includes Nutritional Analysis and Diabetic Exchanges.

- **1 can (8 ounces) unsweetened pineapple chunks**
- **2 tablespoons plus 1-1/2 teaspoons cider vinegar**
- **2 tablespoons brown sugar**
- **Dash pepper**
- **1/2 pound pork tenderloin, cut into 1-inch pieces**
- **1/2 small sweet red pepper, cut into 1-inch chunks**
- **1/2 small green pepper, cut into 1-inch chunks**
- **Hot cooked rice, optional**

Drain pineapple, reserving juice; set pineapple aside. In a bowl, combine the pineapple juice, vinegar, brown sugar and pepper. Pour half of the marinade into a large resealable plastic bag; add the pork. Seal and turn to coat; refrigerate for 4 hours. Cover and refrigerate remaining marinade for basting.

Drain and discard marinade from pork. On metal or soaked wooden skewers, alternately thread the pork, pineapple and peppers. Grill kabobs, covered, over medium heat for 10-15 minutes or until vegetables are tender and pork is no longer pink, turning and basting occasionally with reserved marinade. Serve with rice if desired. **Yield:** 2 servings.

Nutritional Analysis: One serving (calculated without rice) equals 266 calories, 4 g fat (1 g saturated fat), 74 mg cholesterol, 72 mg sodium, 33 g carbohydrate, 2 g fiber, 24 g protein. **Diabetic Exchanges:** 3 lean meat, 2 fruit.

Greek Pita Pizzas

(Pictured above)

Ready in 15 minutes or less

Pita bread is the crust for these single-serving pizzas that get Mediterranean flair from olives, spinach and feta cheese. Breadsticks and a wedge of iceberg lettuce drizzled with salad dressing make fine pizza partners.

- **2 whole pita breads**
- **2 tablespoons olive *or* vegetable oil, *divided***
- **1/4 cup sliced stuffed olives**
- **2 teaspoons red wine vinegar *or* cider vinegar**
- **1 garlic clove, minced**
- **1/2 teaspoon dried oregano**
- **1/4 teaspoon dried basil**
- **Dash pepper**
- **1/2 cup torn fresh spinach**
- **1/3 cup crumbled feta cheese**
- **1 small tomato, seeded and chopped**
- **1/4 cup shredded Parmesan cheese**

Brush pitas with 1 tablespoon oil. Place on a baking sheet. Broil 4 in. from the heat for 2 minutes. Meanwhile, in a bowl, combine the olives, vinegar, garlic, oregano, basil, pepper and remaining oil. Spread over pitas; top with spinach, feta cheese, tomato and Parmesan cheese. Broil 3 minutes longer or until cheese is melted. **Yield:** 2 servings.

Pineapple Pork Kabobs

Manicotti for Two

(Pictured below)

Ready in 1 hour or less

Manicotti shells are filled with a three-cheese mixture, then topped with store-bought spaghetti sauce beefed up with flavorful sausage. Enjoy them with sliced canned pears and frozen garlic bread...or accompany the entree with steamed fresh green beans and warm Italian bread.

4 uncooked manicotti shells
1/2 pound bulk Italian sausage
1-1/2 cups meatless spaghetti sauce
1 cup ricotta cheese
1/2 cup shredded mozzarella cheese, *divided*
1/4 cup grated Parmesan cheese
1/2 teaspoon Italian seasoning
1/4 teaspoon garlic powder
1/4 teaspoon pepper

Cook manicotti according to package directions. Meanwhile, in a skillet, cook the sausage over medium heat until no longer pink; drain. Stir in spaghetti sauce.

Drain manicotti and rinse with cold water. In a bowl, combine the ricotta cheese, 1/4 cup of mozzarella cheese, Parmesan cheese, Italian seasoning, garlic powder and pepper. Carefully stuff manicotti. Place in a greased 11-in. x 7-in. x 2-in. baking dish. Top with sausage mixture.

Bake, uncovered, at 350° for 30-35 minutes or until heated through. Sprinkle with remaining mozzarella. Bake 3-5 minutes longer or until cheese is melted. **Yield:** 2 servings.

Pilaf-Stuffed Pork Chops

Pilaf-Stuffed Pork Chops

(Pictured above)

Ready in 1 hour or less

A quick homemade gravy adds the finishing touch to these tender pork chops stuffed with rice and colorful vegetables. Serve them with corn on the cob and Key lime pie or complete the meal with applesauce and bakery cookies.

1/2 cup water
1/2 cup uncooked instant rice
1/4 cup shredded carrot
1/4 cup shredded zucchini
1/4 teaspoon onion salt
1/4 teaspoon pepper, *divided*
2 bone-in pork loin chops (1-1/2 inches thick)
1/8 teaspoon salt
1 tablespoon butter *or* margarine
3/4 cup beef broth
1 tablespoon cornstarch
3 tablespoons cold water
1/4 teaspoon browning sauce, optional

In a saucepan, bring water to a boil. Add rice. Remove from the heat; cover and let stand for 5 minutes. Fluff with a fork. Stir in the carrot, zucchini, onion salt and 1/8 teaspoon pepper; set aside.

Cut a pocket in each pork chop; sprinkle with salt and remaining pepper. In a skillet, brown chops in butter. Cool for 5 minutes. Stuff with pilaf. Place in an ungreased 11-in. x 7-in. x 2-in. baking dish. Pour broth into dish. Cover and bake at 350° for 25-30 minutes or until a meat thermometer inserted into the meat reads 160°.

Remove chops and keep warm. Pour cooking juices into a saucepan. Combine cornstarch and cold water until smooth; stir into juices. Bring to a boil; cook and stir for 1 minute or until thickened. Stir in browning sauce if desired. Serve over pork chops. **Yield:** 2 servings.

Manicotti for Two

Steak and Onions

Ready in 45 minutes or less

Sweet caramelized onions add great flavor to these rose-mary-rubbed steaks. Serve them with baked potatoes and a Caesar salad. Or complement the entree with cooked carrot sticks and apple pie a la mode.

    1 **large onion, halved and sliced**
    2 **tablespoons butter *or* margarine**
 1/3 **cup white wine *or* chicken broth**
    1 **garlic clove, minced**
 1/2 **teaspoon dried rosemary, crushed**
 1/4 **teaspoon salt**
 1/4 **teaspoon pepper**
    2 **beef tenderloin steaks (1-1/2 to 2 inches thick)**

In a large skillet, cook onion in butter over medium heat for 15-20 minutes or until onion is golden brown, stirring frequently. Stir in wine or broth and garlic. Bring to boil. Reduce heat; simmer, uncovered, for 3-4 minutes or until liquid has evaporated.

Meanwhile, combine the rosemary, salt and pepper; rub over steaks. Broil 4 in. from the heat for 7-9 minutes on each side or until meat reaches desired doneness (for rare, a meat thermometer should read 140°; medium, 160°; well-done, 170°). Serve with caramelized onions. **Yield:** 2 servings.

Pepper Jack Stuffed Chicken

(Pictured below)

Ready in 45 minutes or less

The spicy cheese and Mexican seasoning give plenty of zip to these tender chicken rolls. Round out the meal with rice pilaf and pineapple tidbits. Or microwave frozen broccoli and serve peppermint stick ice cream for dessert.

    2 **ounces pepper Jack cheese**
    2 **boneless skinless chicken breast halves**
    1 **teaspoon Mexican *or* taco seasoning**
    1 **tablespoon vegetable oil**

Cut cheese into two 2-1/4-in. x 1-in. x 3/4-in. strips. Flatten chicken to 1/4-in. thickness. Place a strip of cheese down the center of each chicken breast half; fold chicken over cheese and secure with toothpicks. Rub Mexican seasoning over chicken.

In a large skillet, brown chicken in oil on all sides. Transfer to a greased 8-in. square baking dish. Bake, uncovered, at 350° for 25-30 minutes or until chicken juices run clear. Discard toothpicks. **Yield:** 2 servings.

Flattening Chicken

FLATTENING or pounding meat can serve several purposes. It is typically done for quicker, more even cooking and to produce an attractive appearance.

When tender cuts of meat or poultry are flattened, it's best to put them inside a heavy-duty resealable plastic bag or between two sheets of heavy plastic wrap to prevent messy splatters. Use only the smooth side of a meat mallet to gently pound them to the desired thickness. This will prevent the meat from shredding.

When tougher cuts of meat need tenderizing, they are pounded with the ridged side of a meat mallet to break up the connective tissue.

Pepper Jack-Stuffed Chicken

Chapter 20

298

NO TIME to entertain? Think again! An elaborate meal can have time-saving elements that make hosting a gathering a snap—and a lot of fun—for the hostess.

Here, fellow busy cooks share an assortment of favorite, fast-to-fix recipes they like to prepare for guests.

Our Test Kitchen staff combined some of these timely dishes to create six complete menus that will keep your kitchen time to a minimum and impress family and friends.

Plus, you'll see how to add special touches to your table with easy and inexpensive garnishes and table decorations.

GREAT FOR GUESTS. Clockwise from upper right: Roasted Veggie Platter, Green Peas Supreme, Crab Mornay and Peanut Butter Cup Pie (all recipes on p. 309).

Show Your Love with Valentine's Day Dinner

HERE, our home economists compiled a heartwarming meal that streamlines entertaining for the host while making the guests feel special. (Turn to page 312 for sweet garnishes that dress up individual dessert plates...and other ways to add inviting touches to your table.)

Crab Au Gratin Spread

Ready in 45 minutes or less

For a warm and winning appetizer, I serve this special cracker spread. It's rich tasting and easy to whip up.
            —Suzanne Zick, Lincolnton, North Carolina

    2 tablespoons plus 1 teaspoon butter *or* margarine, *divided*
    3 tablespoons all-purpose flour
  1/2 teaspoon salt
  1/8 teaspoon paprika
  1/2 cup half-and-half cream
  1/2 cup milk
  1/4 cup white wine *or* chicken broth
    1 can (6 ounces) crabmeat, drained, flaked and cartilage removed *or* 2/3 cup chopped imitation crabmeat
    1 can (4 ounces) mushroom stems and pieces, drained and chopped
1-1/2 teaspoons snipped chives
  1/2 cup shredded cheddar cheese
    1 tablespoon dry bread crumbs
Assorted crackers

In a saucepan, melt 2 tablespoons butter. Stir in the flour, salt and paprika until smooth. Gradually add cream, milk and wine or broth. Bring to a boil; cook and stir for 1-2 minutes or until thickened. Stir in the crab, mushrooms and chives; heat through. Stir in cheese just until melted.

Transfer to a greased shallow 1-qt. baking dish. Melt remaining butter; toss with bread crumbs. Sprinkle over crab mixture. Bake, uncovered, at 400° for 10-15 minutes or until bubbly. Let stand for 5 minutes. Serve with crackers. **Yield:** about 2 cups.

Poppy Seed Salad Dressing

Ready in 15 minutes or less

This sweet simple dressing is especially good on a spinach or lettuce salad topped with fresh orange sections and sliced strawberries. We also like it on a tossed vegetable salad.   —Debbie Snyder, Kalispell, Montana

    1 cup vegetable oil
  1/3 cup cider vinegar
  1/2 cup sugar
    1 tablespoon poppy seeds
    1 teaspoon salt
    1 teaspoon ground mustard
Salad greens and vegetables of your choice

In a jar with a tight-fitting lid, combine first six ingredients; shake until sugar is dissolved. Shake again before serving. Drizzle over tossed salad. **Yield:** 1-1/3 cups.

Chicken with Oriental Stuffing

Ready in 1 hour or less

With unusual ingredients like bean sprouts and water chestnuts, this dressing is my favorite, baked along with moist leg quarters.   —Pam Szmon, Dauphin, Manitoba

  3/4 cup finely chopped onion
1-1/4 cups butter *or* margarine, *divided*
    3 bacon strips, cooked and crumbled
    1 can (14 ounces) bean sprouts, drained
    1 can (8 ounces) sliced water chestnuts, drained
    1 can (4 ounces) mushroom stems and pieces, drained and chopped
    1 tablespoon Worcestershire sauce
  1/8 teaspoon ground ginger
   10 cups cubed day-old bread
  1/2 to 3/4 teaspoon salt
Pepper to taste
    8 chicken leg quarters

In a large saucepan, saute onion in 1 cup butter until tender. Add bacon, bean sprouts, water chestnuts, mushrooms, Worcestershire sauce and ginger. Cook and stir over medium heat for 1 minute. Remove from the heat; stir in the bread cubes, salt and pepper. Transfer to a greased 3-qt. baking dish.

Place the chicken in a greased 15-in. x 10-in. x 1-in. baking pan. Melt the remaining butter; brush over chicken. Bake at 350° for 40-45 minutes or until a meat thermometer reads 180°. Bake the stuffing alongside for 30-35 minutes or until heated through. **Yield:** 8 servings.

Raspberry Mousse Pie

Plan ahead...needs to chill

For a fast finishing touch, place luscious slices of this pie on dessert plates decorated with melted chocolate (see how-to photos on page 312). —Mary Fuller, Le Mars, Iowa

1-1/2 cups cold milk
    1 package (3.4 ounces) instant cheesecake *or* vanilla pudding mix
    1 chocolate crumb crust (9 inches)
1-1/2 teaspoons unflavored gelatin
    2 tablespoons cold water
  1/2 cup seedless raspberry jam
    1 teaspoon lemon juice
    1 carton (8 ounces) frozen whipped topping, thawed
Fresh raspberries and mint, optional

In a mixing bowl, beat milk and pudding mix on low speed for 2 minutes. Pour into crust. Cover; refrigerate.

In a microwave-safe bowl, sprinkle gelatin over cold water; let stand for 1 minute. Microwave on high for 20-30 seconds; stir until dissolved. Gradually whisk in jam and lemon juice. Chill for 10 minutes. Fold in the whipped topping. Spread over pudding.

Refrigerate for 2 hours or until set. Garnish with raspberries and mint if desired. **Yield:** 6-8 servings.

Editor's Note: This recipe was tested in an 850-watt microwave.

Celebrate Spring with Streamlined Supper

ENTERTAINING is a breeze when your menu features delightful dishes that look impressive yet are easy to prepare. Turn to page 313 for tips on slicing the cake and sea-inspired table decor.

Creamy Dill Salmon Steaks

Ready in 30 minutes or less

These moist salmon steaks and simple sauce are cooked in the same skillet for easy prep and cleanup. Friends have found this dinner to be elegant and delicious.
—Valerie Hutson, Byron, Minnesota

1/2 cup chopped green onions
1 tablespoon butter *or* margarine
1 can (10-3/4 ounces) condensed cream of chicken soup, undiluted
1/2 cup half-and-half cream
2 tablespoons white wine *or* chicken broth
2 tablespoons chopped fresh dill *or* 2 teaspoons dill weed
4 salmon steaks (1 inch thick)

In a large skillet, saute the onions in butter. Add the soup, cream, wine or broth and dill. Place salmon steaks on top. Cover and simmer for 15 minutes or until fish flakes easily with a fork. **Yield:** 4 servings.

Spring Vegetable Medley

Ready in 45 minutes or less

Seasoned with Dijon mustard and thyme, these savory buttered vegetables are perfect when served with seafood, poultry or beef. They're a colorful and tasty combination.
—Edna Hoffman, Hebron, Indiana

✓ Uses less fat, sugar or salt. Includes Nutritional Analysis and Diabetic Exchanges.

2 cups quartered small red potatoes
1 cup fresh baby carrots
1/2 cup water
1/2 teaspoon chicken bouillon granules
2 cups cut fresh asparagus (2-inch pieces)
1 medium zucchini, cut into 1/4-inch pieces
1 tablespoon butter *or* stick margarine, melted
1-1/2 teaspoons Dijon mustard
1/2 teaspoon dried thyme
1/4 teaspoon salt, optional

In a large saucepan, bring the potatoes, carrots, water and bouillon to a boil. Reduce heat; cover and simmer for 10 minutes. Add the asparagus and zucchini; cover and simmer for 10 minutes or until crisp-tender. Combine the butter, mustard, thyme and salt if desired; pour over vegetables and toss to coat. **Yield:** 4 servings.

Nutritional Analysis: One 1-cup serving (prepared without salt) equals 95 calories, 3 g fat (2 g saturated fat), 8 mg cholesterol, 244 mg sodium, 14 g carbohydrate, 6 g fiber, 5 g protein. **Diabetic Exchange:** 1 starch.

Italian Mini Loaves

Guests will reach for seconds once they sample a slice from one of these fragrant little loaves. You can also make breadsticks with this dough.
—Debra Hartze
Zeeland, North Dakota

2 to 2-1/4 cups bread flour
4-1/2 teaspoons sugar
1 package (1/4 ounce) quick-rise yeast
1 teaspoon garlic salt
1/2 teaspoon Italian seasoning
1/2 teaspoon dried parsley flakes
1/2 cup milk
1/4 cup water
2 tablespoons butter *or* margarine, *divided*
1 egg
6 tablespoons grated Parmesan cheese, *divided*

In a mixing bowl, combine 3/4 cup flour, sugar, yeast, garlic salt, Italian seasoning and parsley. In a saucepan, heat milk, water and 1 tablespoon butter to 120°-130°. Add to dry ingredients; beat just until moistened. Add egg, 4 tablespoons Parmesan cheese and enough remaining flour to form a soft dough; beat until smooth. Turn onto a floured surface; knead until smooth and elastic, about 5 minutes. Place in a greased bowl, turning once to grease top. Cover and let rise in a warm place for 15 minutes.

Punch dough down. Turn onto a lightly floured surface. Divide into thirds; shape into loaves. Place in three greased 5-3/4-in. x 3-in. x 2-in. loaf pans. Cover and let rise until doubled, about 25 minutes. Melt remaining butter; brush over dough. Sprinkle with remaining Parmesan cheese. Bake at 350° for 20-25 minutes or until golden brown. Remove from pans to wire racks. **Yield:** 3 loaves.

Chocolate Cream Torte

This cake is so good, I can serve it as an everyday dessert or for special occasions.
—Dorothy Monroe
Pocatello, Idaho

1 package (18-1/4 ounces) chocolate cake mix
1-1/2 cups heavy whipping cream
1/3 cup confectioners' sugar
FROSTING:
1 package (8 ounces) cream cheese, softened
1/4 cup butter *or* margarine, softened
2 teaspoons vanilla extract
2 cups confectioners' sugar
3 tablespoons baking cocoa

Prepare and bake cake according to package directions, using two greased and floured 9-in. round baking pans. Cool 10 minutes before remove from pans to wire racks. When cool, split each cake in half horizontally.

In a small mixing bowl, beat cream until soft peaks form; fold in confectioners' sugar; spread between layers. In another mixing bowl, beat cream cheese, butter and vanilla. Gradually beat in confectioners' sugar and cocoa. Frost the top of the torte. Store in the refrigerator. **Yield:** 12-16 servings.

Fast-to-Fix Fare Is Pleasing Patio Meal

HERE'S a memorable menu that that makes entertaining outdoors easy. Dining on the patio is a breeze with fast-to-fix fare like a creamy make-ahead appetizer, a savory salad, pleasing grilled beef pinwheels and a no-fuss rich chocolate mousse.

Turn to page 314 for an easy way to hollow out a round bread loaf and other tips that will perk up your table.

Bread Bowl Appetizer

Plan ahead...needs to chill

This dip is a favorite at potlucks and picnics. Although it's terrific as an appetizer, we often turn the creamy mixture into a sandwich by spreading it on slices of crusty baguettes. —Melissa Cook, Chico, California

1-3/4 cups sour cream
1-3/4 cups mayonnaise
   3/4 cup shredded cheddar cheese
   1/4 pound deli pastrami, finely chopped
   1/4 pound deli ham, finely chopped
   1/4 pound deli corned beef, finely chopped
     3 tablespoons finely chopped green onions
     2 teaspoons onion powder
     2 teaspoons celery seed
     1 unsliced round bread (1 pound)
Crackers *and/or* raw vegetables

In a bowl, combine the first nine ingredients; cover and chill for 8 hours or overnight. To serve dip, cut the top fourth off the loaf of bread. Carefully hollow out bottom of loaf, leaving a 1/2-in. shell (see page 314). (Save top and removed bread for another use.) Fill shell with dip. Serve with crackers and/or vegetables. **Yield:** 6 cups dip.

Something Special Salad

Ready in 30 minutes or less

This is a good choice when a run-of-the-mill salad isn't special enough. I cook a pound of bacon at a time and keep it in the freezer. With the added convenience of shredded cheese and packaged salad greens, there isn't much preparation time required. —Linda Wright, Okemos, Michigan

   3/4 cup vegetable oil
     2 tablespoons lemon juice
     3 garlic cloves, minced
   1/4 teaspoon salt
Dash pepper
     5 cups torn romaine
     2 medium tomatoes, cut into wedges
   3/4 cup shredded Swiss cheese
   1/3 cup shredded Parmesan cheese
     1 cup seasoned salad croutons
   2/3 cup slivered almonds, toasted
     4 bacon strips, cooked and crumbled

In a jar with a tight-fitting lid, combine the oil, lemon juice, garlic, salt and pepper; shake well. In a large bowl, combine the romaine, tomatoes and cheeses. Drizzle with dressing and toss to coat. Sprinkle with the croutons, almonds and bacon. **Yield:** 6 servings.

Spinach Steak Pinwheels

Ready in 30 minutes or less

Bacon and spinach bring plenty of flavor to these sirloin spirals. It's an easy dish to make and great to grill at a backyard cookout. I get lots of compliments on it. —Helen Vail, Glenside, Pennsylvania

1-1/2 pounds boneless beef sirloin steak
     8 bacon strips, cooked and drained
     1 package (10 ounces) frozen chopped spinach, thawed and squeezed dry
   1/4 cup grated Parmesan cheese
   1/2 teaspoon salt
   1/8 teaspoon cayenne pepper

Make diagonal cuts in steak at 1-in. intervals to within 1/2 in. of bottom of meat. Repeat cuts in opposite direction. Pound to 1/2-in. thickness. Place bacon down the center of the meat. In a bowl, combine the spinach, Parmesan cheese, salt and cayenne; spoon over bacon. Roll up and secure with toothpicks. Cut into six slices.

Grill, uncovered, over medium heat for 6 minutes on each side or until meat reaches desired doneness (for rare, a meat thermometer should read 140°; medium, 160°; well-done, 170°). Discard toothpicks. **Yield:** 6 servings.

Creamy Chocolate Mousse

Ready in 1 hour or less

This fluffy dessert is sure to satisfy chocolate cravings. I like to garnish servings of the mousse with strawberries. —Joan Schroeder, Pinedale, Wyoming

1-1/2 cups heavy whipping cream
     3 tablespoons sugar
1-1/2 teaspoons vanilla extract
   1/3 cup chocolate syrup
     3 tablespoons baking cocoa
Maraschino cherries and fresh mint, optional

In a chilled mixing bowl, beat cream until soft peaks form. Gradually add sugar and vanilla, beating until stiff peaks form. Fold in chocolate syrup and cocoa. Spoon into dessert dishes. Refrigerate until serving. Garnish with cherries and mint if desired. **Yield:** 6 servings.

Timely Tips

● I write the date on all of my dry goods, including cake mixes, spices and baking powder, before adding them to the pantry. It helps remind me how long I've had ingredients on hand. I always date my packages of meat before I put them in the freezer, too, so that I can use the oldest items first. —*Betty Stephens Sedan, Kansas*

● To save time and to keep your sink sparkling clean, put the stoppers from your sink in the dishwasher each time you run it. It's easy and you'll love the results. —*Jean Keiser West Chester, Pennsylvania*

Simple Summer Supper Tempts Taste Buds

MENUS that prompt praise from guests shouldn't require hours in a hot kitchen. Preparing backyard fare that's full-flavored, festive *and* fuss-free is easy with this selection of recipes.

Marinated grilled ribs, two stovetop side dishes and a fruit-topped cake that starts with a box mix make a meal you'll be pleased to prepare and serve.

Country Pork Ribs

Plan ahead...needs to marinate

These hearty ribs feature a lip-smacking sauce that's deliciously tangy with just the right hint of sweetness. The marinade is absolutely terrific for country-style ribs, but I've found it's great with other meats, too. —*Brian Johnson LaGrange, Georgia*

  1 cup grapefruit *or* orange juice
  1 cup ketchup
  1/2 cup cider vinegar
  1/4 cup soy sauce
  1/4 cup Worcestershire sauce
  2 tablespoons prepared horseradish
  2 tablespoons prepared mustard
  2 teaspoons ground ginger
  1 to 2 teaspoons hot pepper sauce
  1/2 teaspoon garlic powder
  4 to 5 pounds country-style pork ribs
  1/4 cup honey
  2 tablespoons brown sugar

In a bowl, combine the first 10 ingredients; mix well. Pour 1-1/2 cups marinade into a large resealable plastic bag; add the ribs. Seal and turn to coat; refrigerate for at least 4 hours. Cover and refrigerate remaining marinade.

Drain and discard marinade from the ribs. Grill, covered, over indirect medium heat for 20 minutes on each side. Meanwhile, in a saucepan, combine the honey, brown sugar and reserved marinade. Bring to a boil; cook and stir for 2 minutes or until slightly thickened.

Baste ribs with some of the sauce. Grill 15-20 minutes longer or until a meat thermometer reads 160°, turning and basting occasionally. Serve with the remaining sauce. **Yield:** 8 servings.

Garlic Parsley Spaghetti

Ready in 30 minutes or less

This recipe calls for only a few ingredients. I combine pasta, garlic and parsley to create the savory dish. —*Evelyn Sparish Cumberland, Wisconsin*

  1 package (16 ounces) thin spaghetti
  4 garlic cloves, minced
  1/2 cup olive *or* vegetable oil
  1/2 cup minced fresh parsley
Salt and pepper to taste

Cook spaghetti according to package directions. Meanwhile, in a large skillet, lightly brown garlic in oil over medium heat. Drain spaghetti and add to the skillet. Sprinkle with parsley, salt and pepper; toss to coat. **Yield:** 8-10 servings.

Sesame Broccoli

Ready in 15 minutes or less

For a time-saving addition to supper, I season broccoli spears with lemon, soy sauce and sesame seeds. It's a nice change from plain broccoli. —*Myra Innes, Auburn, Kansas*

✓ Uses less fat, sugar or salt. Includes Nutritional Analysis and Diabetic Exchanges.

  1 cup water
  1 pound fresh broccoli, cut into spears
  1 tablespoon sesame seeds
  4 teaspoons olive *or* canola oil, *divided*
  1 tablespoon sugar
  1 tablespoon lemon juice
  1 tablespoon soy sauce

In a large saucepan, bring water to a boil. Add broccoli. Reduce heat; cover and simmer for 5-7 minutes or until crisp-tender. Meanwhile, in a small skillet, saute sesame seeds in 1 teaspoon oil until lightly browned. Remove from the heat. Stir in the sugar, lemon juice, soy sauce and remaining oil. Drain broccoli; toss with sesame seed mixture. **Yield:** 8 servings.

Nutritional Analysis: One 1/2-cup serving (prepared with reduced-sodium soy sauce) equals 49 calories, 3 g fat (trace saturated fat), 0 cholesterol, 97 mg sodium, 5 g carbohydrate, 2 g fiber, 2 g protein. **Diabetic Exchanges:** 1 vegetable, 1/2 fat.

Orange Angel Food Cake

Our Test Kitchen staff concludes this fast-to-fix feast with slices of delicate orange cake topped with a dreamy citrus sauce and colorful fruit.

  1 can (15 ounces) mandarin oranges
3/4 to 1 cup orange juice
  1 package (16 ounces) angel food cake mix
3/4 teaspoon orange extract
  3 drops yellow food coloring, optional
  3 drops red food coloring, optional
  5 teaspoons cornstarch
1/4 cup cold water
Blueberries and sliced peaches, strawberries and kiwifruit

Drain oranges, reserving juice in a 2-cup measuring cup; add enough orange juice to measure 1-3/4 cups. Set aside. Finely chop oranges; drain well and set aside. Prepare cake batter according to package directions, adding the orange extract and food coloring if desired with the water. Fold in the chopped oranges. Pour into an ungreased 10-in. tube pan. Bake according to package directions.

In a saucepan, combine the cornstarch and cold water until smooth. Gradually add the reserved orange juice mixture. Bring to a boil; cook and stir for 2 minutes or until slightly thickened. Cool to room temperature. Slice cake; serve with fruit and orange sauce. **Yield:** 12-16 servings.

Freezer Is Key to Fast, Flavorful Feast

YOUR FREEZER will hurry along three of the four recipes that make up this impressive meal, which is sure to be a delight. It's so easy, you'll feel like a guest at your own party.

Crab Mornay

Ready in 30 minutes or less

I sometimes have unexpected dinner guests, so I keep the ingredients for this easy microwave entree on hand. Prepared pastry shells overflow with a creamy combination of canned crab and mushrooms. I serve this with a packaged salad and receive lots of compliments on the meal.
—Beverly Callison, Memphis, Tennessee

   1 package (10 ounces) frozen pastry shells
1/2 cup butter *or* margarine, cubed
   1 jar (6 ounces) sliced mushrooms, drained
   6 green onions, sliced
   1 jar (4 ounces) diced pimientos, drained
   2 tablespoons all-purpose flour
   1 can (12 ounces) evaporated milk
   2 cups (8 ounces) shredded Swiss cheese
   3 cans (6 ounces *each*) crabmeat, drained, flaked and cartilage removed
   1 teaspoon salt
1/8 teaspoon cayenne pepper
1/3 cup minced fresh parsley

Bake pastry shells according to package directions. Meanwhile, place butter in a 2-qt. microwave-safe dish. Cover and microwave on high for 1 minute or until melted. Add the mushrooms, onions and pimientos. Cook on high for 4 minutes or until vegetables are crisp-tender.

   Combine the flour and milk until smooth; stir into the vegetable mixture. Microwave, uncovered, on high for 4 minutes or until thickened, stirring every minute. Add the cheese, crab, salt and cayenne. Cook on high for 2 minutes or until the cheese is melted. Spoon into the pastry shells; sprinkle with parsley. **Yield:** 6 servings.

Roasted Veggie Platter

Ready in 30 minutes or less

This combination of colorful vegetables is so good when baked in the oven. They make a lovely presentation when threaded on skewers before roasting, too.
—Margaret Allen, Abingdon, Virginia

✓ Uses less fat, sugar or salt. Includes Nutritional Analysis and Diabetic Exchanges.

   1 medium sweet red pepper, cut into 1-1/2-inch pieces
   1 medium red onion, cut into wedges
   1 medium yellow summer squash, cut into 1/2-inch slices
1/2 pound whole fresh mushrooms
1/4 pound fresh green beans, trimmed
1/4 cup Italian salad dressing
1/4 teaspoon dried basil
1/4 teaspoon dried thyme
1/4 teaspoon dried rosemary, crushed

Place the vegetables in a greased 15-in. x 10-in. x 1-in. baking pan. Drizzle with salad dressing and sprinkle with herbs. Bake, uncovered, at 425° for 15-20 minutes or until vegetables are crisp-tender. **Yield:** 6 servings.

   Nutritional Analysis: One 1/2-cup serving (prepared with fat-free salad dressing) equals 41 calories, trace fat (trace saturated fat), trace cholesterol, 146 mg sodium, 8 g carbohydrate, 3 g fiber, 2 g protein. **Diabetic Exchange:** 1 vegetable.

Green Peas Supreme

Ready in 30 minutes or less

Canadian bacon and pearl onions are tasty additions to this simple stovetop side dish made with convenient frozen peas. I always get requests for second helpings.
—Marlene Muckenhirn, Delano, Minnesota

   4 ounces Canadian bacon, diced
   1 tablespoon butter *or* margarine
   3 cups frozen peas
  12 pearl onions, peeled
1/2 cup water
1/2 teaspoon sugar
1/2 teaspoon salt
1/4 teaspoon pepper

In a large skillet, cook bacon in butter until lightly browned. Add the peas, onions, water, sugar, salt and pepper. Cover and cook over medium heat until vegetables are tender, about 10-15 minutes; drain. **Yield:** 6 servings.

Peanut Butter Cup Pie

Plan ahead...needs to freeze

I can put this pie together in 10 minutes and just pull it out of the freezer when we're ready for a scrumptious dessert. Feel free to substitute different flavors of pudding mix and candy bars, such as butterscotch pudding and Butterfinger candy bars.
—Tammy Casaletto, Goshen, Indiana

1-1/2 cups cold milk
   1 package (3.9 ounces) instant chocolate pudding mix
   1 cup plus 2 tablespoons chopped peanut butter cups, *divided*
   1 carton (8 ounces) frozen whipped topping, thawed
   1 chocolate crumb crust (8 *or* 9 inches)

In a bowl, whisk the milk and pudding mix for 2 minutes. Let stand for 2 minutes or until soft-set. Fold in 1 cup of chopped peanut butter cups. Fold in whipped topping. Spoon into crust. Cover and freeze for 6 hours or overnight.

   Remove from the freezer 15-20 minutes before serving. Garnish with the remaining peanut butter cups. **Yield:** 6-8 servings.

Seasonal Supper
Welcomes Guests

STREAMLINED SELECTIONS like these are sure to please a crowd. Give yourself a head start by cooking the tortellini for the salad a day early. Store it in the refrigerator until you're ready to combine it with the other salad ingredients.

Five items are all you need for the glazed ham. While it's baking, assemble the sweet potato side dish. Since the sweet potatoes call for the same oven temperature as the entree, you can pop them in the oven alongside the ham during the last half hour or so of baking.

For an easy but impressive dessert, set out luscious napoleons that are a snap to assemble when it's time to serve. Baking the pastry and preparing the rich chocolate filling earlier in the day leaves time to visit with guests.

Tortellini Spinach Salad

Ready in 15 minutes or less

I create a unique salad by tossing bright green spinach leaves with delicious cheese tortellini and Parmesan cheese. Bottled poppy seed salad dressing makes it a snap to put together. —Janet DuBau, Naperville, Illinois

✓ Uses less fat, sugar or salt. Includes Nutritional Analysis and Diabetic Exchanges.

- 12 cups fresh baby spinach
- 1-1/2 cups cooked cheese tortellini
- 3/4 cup shredded Parmesan cheese
- 3/4 cup poppy seed salad dressing

In a salad bowl, combine the spinach, tortellini and Parmesan cheese. Drizzle with dressing; toss to coat. **Yield:** 12 servings.

Nutritional Analysis: One 3/4-cup serving (prepared with fat-free salad dressing) equals 71 calories, 2 g fat (1 g saturated fat), 6 mg cholesterol, 419 mg sodium, 8 g carbohydrate, 1 g fiber, 5 g protein. **Diabetic Exchanges:** 1 lean meat, 1 vegetable.

Citrus Sweet Potatoes

A mild orange glaze lets the taste of sweet potatoes shine through in this nut-topped side dish. When I was dating my husband, my mother would make this whenever he'd come for Sunday dinner. We've been married more than 40 years and he thinks I can make it almost as good as Mom did. —Pauline Kelley
St. Peters, Missouri

- 6 medium sweet potatoes, peeled
- 1/3 cup packed brown sugar
- 1 tablespoon cornstarch
- 1 cup orange juice concentrate
- 2 teaspoons grated lemon peel
- 1/2 cup chopped pecans, optional

Place sweet potatoes in a large saucepan and cover with water. Bring to a boil. Reduce heat; cover and simmer for 40-45 minutes or until tender. Drain and cool. Cut into 1/2-in. slices. Place in a greased 13-in. x 9-in. x 2-in. baking dish.

In a small saucepan, combine brown sugar and cornstarch. Whisk in orange juice concentrate and lemon peel. Bring to a boil; cook and stir for 1-2 minutes or until thickened. Pour over sweet potatoes. Sprinkle with pecans if desired. Bake, uncovered, at 325° for 30-35 minutes or until sweet potatoes are heated through and sauce is bubbly. **Yield:** 12 servings.

Marmalade Baked Ham

My family loves the flavor that orange marmalade, beer and brown sugar give this ham. I score the ham and inserts whole cloves for an appealing look with little effort.
—Clo Runco, Punxsutawney, Pennsylvania

- 1 boneless fully cooked ham (3 to 4 pounds)
- 12 to 15 whole cloves
- 1 can (12 ounces) beer *or* beef broth
- 1/4 cup packed brown sugar
- 1/2 cup orange marmalade

Place ham on a rack in a shallow roasting pan. Score the surface of the ham, making diamond shapes 1/2 in. deep; insert a clove in each diamond. Pour beer or broth over ham. Rub brown sugar over surface of ham. Cover and bake at 325° for 1-1/4 hours. Spread with marmalade. Bake, uncovered, for 15-25 minutes or until a meat thermometer reads 140° and ham is heated through. **Yield:** 12-14 servings.

Chocolate Napoleons

Ready in 45 minutes or less

People will think you fussed over these impressive desserts. I use frozen puff pastry for the flaky shells and dress up pudding mix for the yummy chocolate filling.
—Roberta Strohmaier
Lebanon, New Jersey

- 1 sheet frozen puff pastry, thawed
- 2 cups cold milk
- 2 cups (16 ounces) sour cream
- 2 packages (3.9 ounces *each*) instant chocolate pudding mix

TOPPING:
- 1 cup confectioners' sugar
- 2 tablespoons milk
- 2 squares (1 ounce *each*) semisweet chocolate, melted and cooled

On a lightly floured surface, roll pastry into a 12-in. square. With a sharp knife, cut into twelve 4-in. x 3-in. rectangles. Place on ungreased baking sheets. Bake at 400° for 9-12 minutes or until puffed and golden brown. Remove to wire racks to cool.

In a small bowl, whisk milk and sour cream until smooth. Add pudding mix; whisk for 2 minutes or until blended. Refrigerate for 5 minutes. To assemble, split each pastry in half. Spoon pudding mixture over bottom halves and replace tops. Combine confectioners' sugar and milk until smooth; drizzle over top. Drizzle with melted chocolate. Serve immediately. **Yield:** 12 servings.

Table Toppers

WHEN company's coming, take a little extra time to dress up your table. Our kitchen staff came up with these inexpensive ideas for attractive table toppers, neat napkin folds and fancy food presentation.

Create Party Favor with Paper Napkin

SERVING sweets to guests at your table? Present them in a heart-shaped holder that's a snap to create with a paper napkin.

To begin, place a square paper beverage napkin diagonally on a flat surface. Bring the two outside corners to meet in the center. Lightly press the folds.

1. Use a glue stick to run a line of glue along the center on one side of napkin.

2. Fold the napkin in half at the center, so the glue is pressed to the napkin on the other side of the center line. Press firmly along the glue line.

3. Use your fingers to open and shape the curves on both sides of the heart.

Place candy holder on each guest's plate and fill with after-dinner mints, valentine conversation hearts or candies of your choice (see photo above right).

Turn CDs into Cute Beverage Coasters

KEEP your dining table free from stains and water damage with these easy-to-make beverage coasters that you can create with compact discs, colorful craft foam and just a few other items.

We took advantage of promotional CDs received in the mail for Internet service providers. But you can use old CDs or buy inexpensive recordable CDs from a discount or office supply store.

Find craft foam at fabric and craft stores. It's sold as 8-1/2-inch by 11-inch sheets with or without an adhesive backing. It also comes in precut shapes.

To make the bottom of the coaster, place a CD on a sheet of adhesive craft foam and trace around it. Then use a scissors or X-acto knife to cut out the circle and attach it to one side of the CD. (If you can't find adhesive craft foam, simply use a glue stick.)

After lining the bottom of the CD, use a glue stick to attach precut foam hearts to the top in a pleasing pattern. (Watch how you place the shapes, so the base of a drinking glass will rest evenly on the foam.)

Melted Chocolate Is a Sweet Garnish

DRESS UP dessert plates in a dash with simple chocolate garnishes that are sure to melt hearts. The two-tone designs are the perfect plate decoration for individual slices of Raspberry Mousse Pie (page 301).

In a microwave-safe bowl, heat 1/2 cup vanilla chips and 1/2 teaspoon shortening at 70% power for 45 seconds; stir. Microwave 10-20 seconds longer or until chips are melted. Transfer to a resealable plastic bag.

In another microwave-safe bowl, heat 3 tablespoons semisweet chocolate chips and 1/4 teaspoon shortening until melted. Transfer to a resealable plastic bag.

Snip a corner from the bag holding white chocolate; pipe circles about 1 inch wide along the edge of each dessert plate.

1. Snip a corner from bag of semisweet chocolate; pipe smaller circles on top of white chocolate but a little off-center.

2. Carefully place the tip of a wooden skewer or toothpick in semisweet chocolate closest to outer edge of white chocolate. To create the "top" of the heart, pull the skewer through the semisweet chocolate. Continue dragging it to the opposite side of the white chocolate to create the heart's "tail".

Repeat with remaining circles of chocolate.

Bring the Beach Back to Your Table

FEW THINGS are more relaxing than strolling along a sandy beach at sunset. You can capture that magic with a homemade centerpiece (see photo below right).

Simply fill a clear glass vase with white scenic sand available at craft stores. Use the sand to support a votive or small pillar candle, and surround the candle with decorative sea glass and small seashells—also found at craft stores.

We chose two small rectangular vases for our luminaries. You can use whatever glass vases or containers you'd like, as long as they can safely hold lit candles.

We found that 2-3/4 pounds of scenic sand was enough for our display, but the amount may vary depending on your containers.

Candles and sea glass come in many colors and styles. Choose those that match your dinnerware, and your centerpiece will go over "swimmingly" with friends and family.

Napkin Rings Tie to Seaside Supper

WHY "knot" tie a little fun into your maritime meal? It's a cinch with speedy square knot napkin rings.

To resemble yacht rope, we used white upholstery cable cord. Feel free to use whatever clean cord or narrow rope you have on hand.

For each napkin ring, cut 20 inches of cord and place it horizontally on a surface. Then fold a square cloth napkin in half and roll it. Place the rolled napkin in the center of the rope.

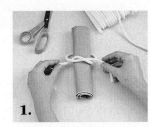

1. Grab an end of the rope in each hand. Place the left end of the rope over the right. Tuck it under and then pull through, making a loose knot that rests on top of the napkin.

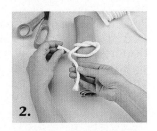

2. You now have two ends of rope on either side of the napkin. Place the

rope on the right side of the napkin beneath the rope on the left side. Next, take the rope that is now beneath the left rope, and bring it up and over the left rope and pull it through the loop.

3. Gently pull both ends of the rope to create the square knot. Do not tie the knot too tight. It should be easy for guests to remove the napkin from the napkin ring. Adjust the knot and napkin as necessary and place on a dinner plate (as shown at right).

Shake Things Up with Shell Servers

HERE'S an idea that's sure to have guests buzzing about your creativity. Make your own salt and pepper servers with seashells purchased from a craft store.

Begin by washing the shells with warm soapy water. Scrub shells thoroughly with a kitchen brush before setting them in a deep pan. Cover the shells with boiling water and allow them to soak for at least 10 minutes.

Dry the shells thoroughly. Fill one with table salt and one with pepper. Add small salt spoons to each and set them on the table for an easy elegant alternative to traditional salt and pepper shakers (see photo below).

Layered Cake Is Doubly Delightful

TURNING a boxed mix into a sweet treat that's eye-appealing, too, is easy when you make Chocolate Cream Torte (photo and recipe on pages 302-303).

The torte looks luscious when two cake layers are sliced into four layers and spread with sweetened whipped cream. But you don't have to split hairs to split the cakes into layers. Just follow these steps:

After the cake layers have cooled, insert toothpicks around the outside of each layer halfway up the side. Make sure the toothpicks are at the same level and lined up evenly around the cake.

Place a long serrated knife at the edge of one cake layer, gently resting the blade flat on the toothpicks. Carefully slice the cake horizontally, keeping the cake in place with your other hand. Use the toothpicks as guides to keep the layers even while cutting.

Repeat with second cake layer. Discard toothpicks and finish as recipe directs.

Bread Loaf Makes Cute Dip Container

HOLLOWING OUT a round loaf of bread to create the bowl is easy to do. First, cut off the top fourth of the loaf. Use a knife to cut around the perimeter of the bread, about 1/2 inch from the crust.

Insert your fingers along the cut and loosen the bread from the bottom of loaf. Remove the bread. (Cut it into cubes to serve with the dip or save for another use, such as making croutons.)

Then fill the hollow loaf with a savory dip (see the recipe on page 305) or most any spread for vegetables or crackers.

Silverware Bouquet Is Pretty, Practical

YOU won't need a whole garden of fresh flowers—just a few blooms—to create this simple centerpiece that's perfect for an outdoor dinner.

To assemble it, gather a cloth napkin, a place setting of silverware and a flower for each diner.

We picked bright green napkins to complement the table setting and help create the look of leaves and stems for our bouquet.

When choosing flowers, you'll find tall single-stem flowers work best. We used tulips, but gerbera daisies or roses would look lovely as well.

1. To begin, arrange a napkin on a diagonal, then place a fork, knife and spoon in the middle. Fold the bottom tip of the napkin over the silverware handles. Starting at one side, begin folding or rolling the edge of the napkin toward the center.

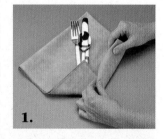

2. Once the silverware is rolled into the napkin, place a flower on top and continue rolling. (Be sure to pat dry the flower stem with a paper towel, so it doesn't dampen the napkin.)

Repeat with remaining napkins, silverware and flowers. Arrange napkin bundles in a flowerpot or vase to create a centerpiece...or place one on each diner's plate (see photo top right).

You'll want to create this bouquet right before dinner so the flowers don't wilt. Or buy water tubes from a florist. The plastic vials have a hole in the top, so you can fill them with water, insert a flower stem and keep your blooms fresh longer.

Spruce Up Platter with Pen and Paint

DON'T have a serving platter that matches your favorite set of dishware? You can create one in a jiffy when you start with a clear glass serving platter, a paint pen and some spray paint.

Cover your work area with newspaper or a large piece of cardboard to protect the surface. Place plate upside down.

1. Use an opaque paint pen from a craft or stationery store to draw a design on the rim of the underside of the platter. We used a fine-line navy blue paint pen to mimic the subtle swirls on some of the napkins in our centerpiece.

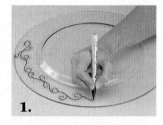

2. Once the design on the underside of the rim is dry, spray the entire underside of the plate with several light coats of spray paint. We used a can of latex spray paint in pale green to contrast with our blue design.

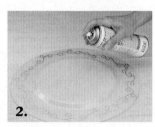

Allow the paint to dry completely between coats.

Once it's dry, turn the plate over to display the two-tone design. (You can see just the edge of our platter peeking out from under the vegetables in the photo above.)

You may want to seal the back of the plate with a clear acrylic. Whether you seal it or not, be sure to wash your platter by hand.

Simple Centerpiece Is Country-Inspired

FLOWERS brighten up any dining experience, particularly when they're held in a vase that matches the table setting. Creating such a vase is a cinch when you use a cloth napkin to disguise a plain jar or container.

We chose a blue napkin with a simple design that complements our dishes. If your napkin has a design, be sure that it's printed on both sides of the cloth.

We used a 20-inch square napkin, but any size will work as long as it's large enough to cover your jar.

Our vase was made from a 1-quart mason jar. An empty peanut butter container, instant coffee canister or mayonnaise jar would also work.

1. Start by unfolding a cloth napkin and setting it on your surface. Place your empty jar in the middle of the napkin and lift up the edges of the napkin, gathering them around the top.

2. Slip a rubber band around the napkin-wrapped jar, adjusting it so it holds the gathered napkin securely near the mouth of the jar.

Fold down the edges of the napkin and arrange them so the rubber band can't be seen. (If your napkin is not large enough to hide the rubber band, tie strands of raffia, ribbon or yarn over the rubber band.)

3. Fill the jar with water, then arrange fresh flowers in your new vase. The flowers you choose should reflect the season and the atmosphere of your gathering. The daisies we selected are a cheerful option for a casual cookout on a warm summer evening.

Place Markers Are Stone's Throw Away

SINCE summer is the time for outdoor dining, why not create place markers with items from your own backyard? Smooth pretty stones not only designate where guests sit, they're a great way to hold down paper napkins if breezes blow.

Using an opaque paint pen from a craft or stationery store, write the name of each dinner guest on a clean dry stone. Feel free to include a design or small drawing, too. Once the paint dries, the stones are ready to be set on your table.

We wanted our place markers to coordinate with our table (see photo at far right), so we wrote guests' names

with a blue paint pen and used a white pen to draw a tiny flower on each stone.

If you're unable to find enough smooth stones, you can buy small bags of them from the floral departments of craft stores and many department and discount retailers.

Heavenly Servings Slice Up Easily

DUE to its light-as-air texture, angel food cake can be a challenge to slice. All too often, cutting the classic cake results in squashed slices that look less than appetizing. Using the right knife, however, can make a world of difference.

The next time you serve a delicate dessert such as Orange Angel Food Cake (recipe on page 307), reach for a serrated knife. A knife with a blade at least 10 inches long will cut through angel food and other foam cakes easily.

Simply set the cake on a cutting board and gently hold the dessert in place with one hand. Using a sawing motion, slice the cake with the serrated knife, keeping the cut pieces in place until you're done.

If you have an electric knife, you can give that a try instead. You will find that it also cuts through angel food cake without "squeezing" the air out of the cake, giving you tall clean slices.

Summer Squash Gets a Groovy Treatment

FRESH vegetables can add brilliant color to most any menu. But they can lend a decorative look, too, when "grooved" with a handy kitchen tool.

A citrus stripper or lemon zester (or even a sharp paring knife) is key to this time-saving trick for squash.

Use the tool to remove strips of peel down the length of the squash, making evenly spaced vertical notches. Discard the strips, then slice the squash widthwise to showcase the effect.

It works nicely with zucchini and the yellow summer squash used in the Roasted Veggie Platter (see photo and recipe on pages 308 and 309).

Or try this technique on other produce, such as fresh cucumbers for vegetable trays or citrus fruits like oranges, lemons and limes for garnishes.

Houseplants Enhance Pretty Place Mats

YOU don't need to head to the garden or flower shop to add bright touches of greenery to your table. By trimming a few trailing vines from an everyday houseplant, you can dress up plain place mats with ease. Plus, the treatment will protect your place mats from spills.

To start, you will need some solid-colored cloth place mats, clear self-adhesive shelf paper and a lush houseplant—like the ivy we use here—that has pretty shaped leaves that aren't too thick. (If you don't have an ivy, try silk ivy leaves or other silk foliage instead.)

1. To begin, unroll the shelf paper, placing it with the paper backing facing up. Put a place mat on top, aligning it on two sides. Use a pencil to mark the cutting lines for the remaining two sides. Set the place mat aside and cut along the lines with scissors.

2. With the shelf paper cut to the size of the place mat, peel off the paper backing and discard it. Place the shelf paper on your work surface with the adhesive facing up.

Remove leaves of different sizes from your plant, then place them in a pleasing pattern along each end of the shelf paper. Be sure to press down the leaves firmly so they stick.

3. Starting at one end of the place mat, press the shelf paper on top of the place mat with the adhesive side down. Don't worry if you see some wrinkles or bubbles. They're easy to remove; simply lift the paper up again, then smooth it down with your hand as you go.

Place your completed place mat on your dining table as shown in the photo above. You can easily wipe off any spills after each use and continue to use the place mats until the ivy turns brown. Just peel off the shelf paper and leaves, and your place mats are as good as new!

Ivy Napkin Rings Tie the Look Together

ADD fresh flair to your table with time to spare when you create quick napkin rings using trailing strands of vine from a houseplant. The rich green foliage circling each napkin ties in nicely with the ivy-covered place mats also featured here.

The napkin rings are a snap to make. Simply cut a short length of ivy from your plant and wrap it around a cloth napkin that's been gathered into a loose casual bundle. Or, fold the napkin into quarters and roll it for a more formal look.

Then place the napkin on a plate, tucking the loose ends of the vine underneath the napkin to keep them in place (see photo above).

Dazzle Diners with Simple Centerpiece

MAKE the most of this year's holiday greeting cards by displaying favorites on your dinner table. To create the appealing centerpiece shown in the photo below right, you'll need a bowl, a wire photograph holder, Christmas cards, ornaments and a garland.

We selected items to match the colors of our place setting. We picked a silver bowl, a silver wire photo holder, metallic glass ornaments and matching bead garland.

When choosing cards for your arrangement, consider ones that work with your color scheme and have appealing designs or sentiments. To keep your centerpiece from looking too "busy", select cards that focus on simple artwork.

1. First, place the photo holder in the center of the bowl. To keep it from tipping, use reusable adhesive (like Fun-Tak) to secure the base of the photo holder to the bottom of the bowl. (If you don't have any reusable adhesive, use florist's clay or do without, taking extra care when moving your centerpiece.)

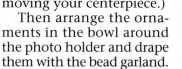

Then arrange the ornaments in the bowl around the photo holder and drape them with the bead garland.

2. Next, arrange your cards in the arms of the photo holder, placing the smaller cards in front. To avoid a crowded look, don't place a card in every arm. Our photo holder had 10 arms, but we displayed only five cards.

Because this arrangement is one-sided, you may want to place similar-sized Christmas cards back-to-back, so the arrangement is pleasing from both sides.

Feel free to adapt this idea to birthdays, graduations and other special events throughout the year.

Set the Scene with Easy Place Markers

RECYCLE old Christmas cards by turning them into personal place markers. Careful cutting showcases the card's design by making it "pop up" above the place marker.

For best results, select cards that have space at the bottom to write a guest's name. To make the cutting easier, choose those with designs that are evenly framed by a plain area.

1. Remove the back of the card and discard it. Measure the height of the card and mark the midpoint on both sides of the design. These marks, placed where the border and design meet, designate the

starting points of the "pop-up" cut.

2. Set the card on a cutting board or work surface. Starting at one of the pencil marks, use a craft knife to cut up and around the top half of the design. (Do not cut on the fold line or around the bottom half of the design.) Use a ruler to ensure straight edges as you continue to cut around the design to the other marked midpoint.

3. Write the name of a guest on the bottom of the card. Then carefully fold the card in half at the midpoint, except for the design, which should pop up.

Repeat these steps for each place card. Then arrange one at each place setting for a holiday table your guests will not soon forget.

Wrap Napkins with Festive Garland

DECK your table with nifty napkin rings that take seconds to assemble using a tree-trimming garland.

For each napkin ring, simply snip off a 10-inch piece of bead garland and wrap it around a folded napkin a few times. Tuck the garland's ends underneath the napkin before setting it on the plate.

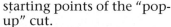

Chapter 21

Back to the Basics

DURING THE WEEK, many people barely have a spare moment to sit and relax, much less spend time cooking.

But on those slower-paced weekends, when you do have a few minutes to spare, why not head to the kitchen for a refresher on common cooking techniques or for a chance to tackle recipes that are a little more challenging?

Whether you want to review the basics for making satisfying stir-fries, creating old-fashioned cream puffs and preparing various types of marinades, or you'd like to learn how to stock your pantry, prepare delicious deep-fried foods and make terrific Christmas candies, the easy-to-follow recipes and helpful hints here will sharpen your culinary skills.

SWEETEN THE SEASON. Peppery Peanut Brittle and Crunchy Peanut Butter Balls (recipes on pp. 330 & 331).

Satisfying Stir-Fry Suppers

LIVELY LIFESTYLES call for dishes that cook in no time but don't skimp on taste. And when agendas get active, nothing beats a streamlined stir-fry.

Stir-frying cooks bite-size pieces of meat and vegetables over medium-high heat in a small amount of oil. It's a boon to busy folks because it's fast, preserves flavors and nutrients and can easily be customized to suit family tastes. Since it usually requires just one pan, cleanup's a snap, too.

When it comes to stir-fries, the possible meat-and-vegetable combinations are endless. Sirloin, chicken breast and shrimp are all great options, but you can get creative with turkey sausage, cubed pork, imitation crab or last night's leftovers. Plus, there's a multitude of fresh or frozen veggies to chose from.

Because stir-fried foods cook extremely fast, they need to be stirred almost constantly. That's why it's best to have all of your ingredients cut and measured before you begin.

Stir-fries were originally eaten with chopsticks, so items are typically cut into bite-size pieces. Slicing meat into small pieces ensures thorough cooking in a short period of time.

Similarly, vegetables should be cut into small pieces that are equal in size to ensure even cooking.

Stir-Frying Made Simple

1. Chop and measure all of the ingredients, keeping them close at hand. Begin by heating a small amount of oil over medium-high heat. Add the meat, poultry or seafood to the hot oil and stir.

2. When it's cooked through, remove the meat from the skillet. Cover and keep warm. Stir-fry the vegetables, adding more oil if necessary.

3. Return the meat to the skillet. Stir the sauce mixture, then add to skillet. Complete the stir-fry by adding the softer fast-cooking vegetables like tomatoes.

If you're racing against the clock, consider using frozen veggies. Many varieties are already cut into perfect portions, with some blends specifically prepared for stir-fries.

One item common to most every stir-fry is oil. That oil, however, can vary according to taste. Vegetable, olive and canola oils are the most popular, but sesame and peanut oils add flavors that many stir-fry specialists enjoy.

Regardless of the oil used, it's important to warm it in the pan over medium-high heat before you begin. A wok—a deep, bowl-shaped pan—is commonly used for stir-frying. If you don't own one, a large skillet or saute pan works just as well.

Once the oil is heated, add the meat, poultry or seafood and start stirring. Remove pieces from the pan as soon as they're cooked through, and then give vegetables their turn.

Adding different vegetables to the pan at different times prevents some veggies from overcooking. Start with denser produce, such as broccoli, carrots and cauliflower, because it takes longer for them to become crisp-tender.

Items that cook more quickly—mushrooms and peppers, for example—can be added to the skillet shortly after. Green onions, peas and other rapid-cooking veggies should be tossed in near the end of the process.

Personalize your dish with a favorite herb or spice. Garlic and ginger are standard seasonings in a stir-fry, but cayenne pepper, curry and red pepper flakes are wonderful ways to give the final feast a little kick.

Seasonings and herbs are usually added to the meat or vegetables while stir-frying, but they can also be combined with a sauce.

Whip up your own sauce with broth, seasonings, teriyaki or soy sauce and cornstarch for thickening. Shortly before the vegetables are done, return the meat to the pan and stir in the sauce mixture.

After the sauce has thickened, add any vegetables that simply need to be warmed, such as tomatoes. Then you're ready to put dinner on the table.

Some stir-fries stand on their own, but most are served over rice, pasta or chow mein noodles.

See what you have on hand to stir-fry tonight. Or, consider the following reader recipes. They're sure to lead to stir-fry success.

Chicken Noodle Stir-Fry

Ready in 30 minutes or less

A frozen pasta-vegetable blend and ramen noodles make this specialty a cinch to toss together. This filling meal is so easy to fix that teenagers can make it themselves.
—Lois McAtee, Oceanside, California

    1 **pound boneless skinless chicken breasts, cut into strips**
    2 **tablespoons vegetable oil**
1-1/2 **cups water**
    2 **garlic cloves, minced**
    2 **packages (3 ounces *each*) chicken ramen noodles**

1 package (16 ounces) frozen Oriental *or*
   garlic pasta-vegetable blend
1 sweet red pepper, julienned
2 tablespoons soy sauce

In a large skillet or wok, stir-fry the chicken in oil. Add water and garlic; bring to a boil. Add the noodles and contents of seasoning packets, vegetables, red pepper and soy sauce. Cover and simmer for 7-9 minutes or until noodles and vegetables are tender. **Yield:** 4 servings.

Scallops with Spaghetti

(Pictured at right)

Ready in 30 minutes or less

My mom used to serve this speedy stir-fry when I was young. Now it's one of my family's most-requested dinners. It tastes great with shrimp, too. —Susan D'Amore
West Chester, Pennsylvania

1 package (7 ounces) spaghetti
1 pound sea scallops
4 garlic cloves, minced
2 tablespoons olive *or* vegetable oil
1 tablespoon butter *or* margarine
1-1/2 cups julienned carrots
1-1/2 cups frozen French-style green beans,
   thawed
1 sweet red pepper, julienned
2 tablespoons lemon juice
1 tablespoon minced fresh parsley
1 tablespoon minced fresh basil *or* 1 teaspoon
   dried basil
1/4 teaspoon salt
1/8 teaspoon pepper

Cook spaghetti according to package directions. Meanwhile, in a large skillet or wok, stir-fry scallops and garlic in oil and butter for 5 minutes or until scallops are opaque; remove and keep warm.

In the same skillet, stir-fry the carrots, beans and red pepper until crisp-tender. Stir in the lemon juice, parsley, basil, salt and pepper. Drain spaghetti. Add scallops and spaghetti to the vegetable mixture; toss to coat. **Yield:** 4 servings.

Vegetable Steak Stir-Fry

(Pictured above right)

Ready in 30 minutes or less

Sirloin steak and fresh vegetables take center stage in this showstopper. While I don't have much time to cook, I like to experiment with food. This quick dish is a favorite.
—Pamela Brandal, Park City, Illinois

✓ Uses less fat, sugar or salt. Includes Nutritional Analysis and Diabetic Exchanges.

3/4 pound boneless beef sirloin steak, cubed
3 teaspoons canola *or* vegetable oil, *divided*
2 cups broccoli florets
2 cups cauliflowerets
2 cups julienned carrots

Scallops with Spaghetti
Vegetable Steak Stir-Fry

6 garlic cloves, minced
1 tablespoon cornstarch
3/4 cup beef broth
1/3 cup sherry *or* additional broth
1 tablespoon water
1-1/2 teaspoons soy sauce
1/4 teaspoon ground ginger
2 medium tomatoes, cut into wedges
Hot cooked rice, optional

In a large skillet or wok, stir-fry steak in 2 teaspoons oil until no longer pink. Remove and keep warm. In the same pan, heat the remaining oil. Add broccoli, cauliflower, carrots and garlic; stir-fry until vegetables are crisp-tender.

In a bowl, combine cornstarch, broth, sherry or additional broth, water, soy sauce and ginger until smooth. Return beef to the pan. Stir cornstarch mixture and add to pan. Bring to a boil; cook and stir for 2 minutes or until thickened. Add tomatoes; heat through. Serve over rice if desired. **Yield:** 4 servings.

Nutritional Analysis: One 1-cup serving (prepared with reduced-sodium soy sauce; calculated without rice) equals 251 calories, 9 g fat (2 g saturated fat), 50 mg cholesterol, 364 mg sodium, 18 g carbohydrate, 5 g fiber, 23 g protein. **Diabetic Exchanges:** 3 lean meat, 3 vegetable, 1/2 fat.

Cream Puffs Filled with Fun

IF YOU'VE avoided baking cream puffs because you thought they were too time-consuming, read on! You'll see that the pretty puffs are easy, impressive and anything but intimidating.

Cream puffs are golden pastries made from a speedy stovetop dough. When baked, the dough forms a crisp exterior and a nearly hollow interior that is ideal for holding various fillings, both sweet and savory.

Preparing the crowd-pleasing treats involves three simple steps: forming the dough, baking the puffs and adding fillings and toppings.

Cream puffs are made from a French pastry dough sometimes referred to as "choux" (pronounced "shoo"). The thick sticky dough is also used for making eclairs and similar sweets.

This kind of dough does not call for leavening (like baking powder) to make it rise. The steam that builds up inside of the pastry shells during the baking process gives them their deliciously light and airy texture.

Prepared on the stovetop over medium heat, the basic dough comes together easily with flour, eggs and butter.

When making the dough, be sure to add all of the flour at once, stirring until it forms a ball. Remove the saucepan from the heat and let the dough cool slightly before adding the eggs.

Eggs should be added one at a time, beating well after each addition. This will produce a smooth shiny ball of dough that's ready to turn into palate-pleasing puffs.

Once the dough is formed, you're ready to begin baking.

For regular size puffs, drop heaping tablespoons of dough onto greased baking sheets. The dough will expand as it bakes, so leave 3 inches of space between each portion of dough.

For a fancier look, pipe the dough onto baking sheets using a pastry bag and 1/2-inch star tip. Or, place tablespoons of dough side by side on a baking sheet to form a pretty pastry ring for a unique after-dinner delight.

It's easy to make miniature cream puffs by using smaller amounts of dough and decreasing the baking time. If you aren't following a recipe specifically for mini puffs, be sure to watch them so they don't burn or dry out.

Regardless of the size and shape of the cream puffs, bake them until they are golden on all sides. Under-baking can cause the puffs to collapse.

After removing the pastries from the oven, prick them with a sharp knife or slice them in half. This allows the steam to escape so the puffs won't become soggy. Remove the soft dough from inside the halves with a fork and discard it.

Don't have time to fill the puffs right away? Cooled puffs can be frozen in freezer bags or freezer containers up to 6 months. Thaw in the refrigerator a day early, then simply fill before serving.

Since cream puff pastry is not sweetened, it's versatile and can hold a variety of fillings. Savory mixtures—like chicken, tuna or seafood salad—are perfect fillings for elegant luncheons or special-occasion appetizers.

Sweet centers—such as custard, whipped cream, mousse or instant pudding—are popular for dessert puffs.

For fast final touches, busy bakers no longer rely solely on confectioners' sugar to jazz up cream puffs. Whipped cream and sliced berries are a few of the items used to garnish puffs with effortless yet unforgettable flair.

In addition, toppings like fudge sauce bring homemade pizzazz to cream puffs purchased from a bakery or a grocer's frozen food aisle.

Serve the cream puffs immediately after filling or topping them so they don't become spongy.

Ready to get started? Try a few of the following cream puff recipes...the spectacular results are sure to impress!

Cream Puff Pointers

THINKING of trying your hand at baking a tempting batch of cream puffs? Keep the following steps in mind and you'll be enjoying them in no time.

1. In a saucepan, bring the water, butter and salt to a boil. Add the flour all at once, stirring quickly until the mixture forms a smooth ball.

2. Remove the saucepan from the heat for 5 minutes. Add the eggs one at a time, beating well after each addition. Beat the dough until it is smooth and shiny.

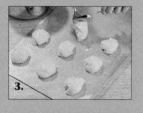

3. Drop portions of the dough onto a greased baking sheet, leaving 3 inches of space between each. Bake as directed.

4. Remove baked puffs to a wire rack and immediately split each puff so the steam escapes. Remove the soft dough from inside the halves with a fork. Cool puffs before adding filling.

Crab-Stuffed Mini Puffs

Ready in 1 hour or less

These tender puffs from our home economists feature a fast mouth-watering seafood filling.

    1 cup water
1/2 cup butter (no substitutes)
1/4 teaspoon salt
    1 cup all-purpose flour
    4 eggs
CRAB FILLING:
    1 cup mayonnaise
1/2 cup sour cream
    2 tablespoons finely chopped onion
    1 teaspoon salt
    1 teaspoon dill weed
    1 teaspoon lemon juice
1/4 teaspoon pepper
    2 packages (8 ounces *each*) flaked imitation
      crabmeat, shredded

In a heavy saucepan over medium heat, bring water, butter and salt to a boil. Add flour all at once; stir until a smooth ball forms. Remove from the heat; let stand for 5 minutes. Add eggs, one at a time, beating well after each addition. Beat until smooth and shiny.

Drop by tablespoonfuls 3 in. apart onto greased baking sheets. Bake at 400° for 25-30 minutes or until golden brown. Remove to wire racks. Immediately split puffs open; remove and discard soft dough from inside. Cool puffs completely.

For filling, combine the mayonnaise, sour cream, onion, salt, dill, lemon juice and pepper in a bowl. Fold in the crab. Fill bottom halves of puffs; replace tops. Serve immediately. **Yield:** 2 dozen.

Chocolate Cream Puffs

(Pictured above right)

Ready in 1 hour or less

A bit of cocoa turns traditional cream puffs into these extraordinary desserts. Guests will think you spent hours fussing over the tender chocolate pastries, which are filled with a rich creamy mixture and fresh strawberries.

    1 cup water
1/2 cup butter (no substitutes)
1/4 teaspoon salt
    1 cup all-purpose flour
    3 tablespoons baking cocoa
    4 eggs
    2 packages (8 ounces *each*) cream cheese,
      softened
    1 cup sugar
    2 cups heavy whipping cream, whipped
    3 cups coarsely chopped fresh strawberries

In a heavy saucepan over medium heat, bring water, butter and salt to a boil. Add the flour and cocoa all at once; stir until a smooth ball forms. Remove from the heat; let stand for 5 minutes. Add eggs, one at a time, beating well after each. Beat until smooth and shiny.

Cream Puff Pyramids
Chocolate Cream Puffs

Drop by heaping tablespoonfuls 3 in. apart onto greased baking sheets. Bake at 400° for 30-35 minutes or until set and browned. Remove to wire racks. Immediately split puffs open; remove and discard soft dough from inside. Cool puffs completely.

In a small mixing bowl, beat the cream cheese and sugar until fluffy. Fold in whipped cream and strawberries. Fill bottom halves of puffs; replace tops. Serve immediately. **Yield:** 15 servings.

Cream Puff Pyramids

(Pictured above)

Ready in 15 minutes or less

I celebrate holidays by topping store-bought miniature cream puffs with canned pie filling and melted chocolate. These quick-to-assemble desserts call for only five ingredients. Nothing could be simpler or more elegant.
—Saundra Busby, West Columbia, South Carolina

    2 cans (21 ounces *each*) cherry pie filling
24 to 32 frozen cream-filled miniature cream
      puffs,* thawed
    1 cup (6 ounces) semisweet chocolate chips,
      melted
    3 tablespoons confectioners' sugar
Whipped cream in a can

In a saucepan, warm cherry pie filling over medium-low heat just until heated through. Place three or four cream puffs on each dessert plate.

Place melted chocolate in a small resealable plastic bag; cut a small hole in a corner of the bag. Spoon about 1/4 cup of warm pie filling over cream puffs; drizzle with chocolate. Dust with confectioners' sugar; garnish with whipped cream. **Yield:** 8 servings.

*Editor's Note: This recipe was tested with Delizza frozen cream-filled miniature cream puffs.

Stocked Pantry Simplifies Mealtime

Italian Noodle Casserole

DO YOU MARVEL at cooks who can throw together a complete meal at the drop of a hat? Do you wonder what their secret is? Chances are, it's a well-stocked pantry. Menu planning and meal preparation are easier when you have all the ingredients you need at your fingertips. For a handy pantry list, see the box at far right.

Having these items on hand makes it simpler to put together quick meals because you can choose recipes that suit your timetable and your tastes.

Besides simplifying menu planning, there are several other reasons to keep your pantry stocked:

• It saves time because you can avoid last-minute trips to the store, which is especially helpful if the closest store is several miles away or the weather conditions are poor.

• It makes it easier to entertain drop-in guests, because you can put together an easy appetizer or even an entire meal with ingredients you have on hand.

• It eliminates the frustration you feel when you really want to try a new recipe but can't because you're missing an ingredient or two.

• It saves money, because you can take advantage of sales to stock up on ingredients you'll need to buy sooner or later.

To avoid one huge grocery bill, consider adding to your shortcut pantry gradually. Buy items when you have a coupon or when they're on special.

And be sure to buy only what you'll use in a timely manner. You won't save time or money if the food spoils before you can use it.

Salad dressing, peanut butter and whole wheat flour can be stored for up to 6 months while canned goods, dry pasta, convenience mixes and many baking supplies can be kept for up to 1 year. When in doubt, check the expiration date on the item.

Also, don't forget to rotate the canned goods in your pantry, bringing the older cans forward and putting the new cans in back to ensure foods are used by their expiration date.

Peanut Butter Fudge Bars

(Pictured at left)

I rely on a cake mix and other pantry staples to make these rich crumb-topped treats. —Peggy Murray, Enfield, Maine

        1 package (18-1/4 ounces) yellow cake mix
        1 cup creamy peanut butter
        1 egg
    1/2 cup vegetable oil
        1 can (14 ounces) sweetened condensed milk
        1 cup (6 ounces) semisweet chocolate chips
        2 tablespoons butter *or* margarine

In a bowl, combine cake mix, peanut butter, egg and oil. Press two-thirds of the mixture into a greased 13-in. x 9-in. x 2-in. baking pan. Bake at 350° for 10 minutes. Cool on a wire rack for 5 minutes.

In a heavy saucepan, heat the milk, chocolate chips and butter over low heat; stir until blended. Pour over crust. Sprinkle with remaining crumb mixture. Bake for 20-25 minutes or until golden brown. Cool on a wire rack. Cut into bars. **Yield:** 2-1/2 dozen.

Peanut Butter Fudge Bars

Italian Noodle Casserole

(Pictured at left)

Ready in 1 hour or less

Canned goods make it a snap to assemble this hearty Italian dish. —Joann Hosbach, Las Cruces, New Mexico

- 1 pound ground beef
- 1 package (8 ounces) wide egg noodles
- 1 tablespoon olive *or* vegetable oil
- 2 cups (8 ounces) shredded Colby cheese, *divided*
- 2 cans (15 ounces *each*) tomato sauce
- 1 can (15 ounces) great northern beans, rinsed and drained
- 1 can (14-1/2 ounces) Italian stewed tomatoes
- 1 can (10-3/4 ounces) condensed tomato soup, undiluted
- 2 teaspoons Italian seasoning
- 2 teaspoons dried parsley flakes
- 1/8 teaspoon *each* onion salt, garlic salt and pepper
- 2 tablespoons grated Parmesan cheese

In a large skillet, cook beef over medium heat until no longer pink; drain. Meanwhile, cook the noodles according to package directions; drain. In a large bowl, combine the beef, noodles, oil, 1-1/2 cups Colby cheese, tomato sauce, beans, tomatoes, soup and seasonings.

Transfer to a greased 13-in. x 9-in. x 2-in. baking dish. Cover and bake at 350° for 30 minutes. Uncover; sprinkle with Parmesan cheese and remaining Colby cheese. Bake 5-10 minutes longer or until the cheese is melted. **Yield:** 6-8 servings.

Soothing Chicken Soup

Ready in 30 minutes or less

I made a few improvements to a fast-to-fix recipe to create this comforting soup. It's easy to stir up with broth, soup mix and instant rice. —Kris Countryman
Joliet, Illinois

 Uses less fat, sugar or salt. Includes Nutritional Analysis and Diabetic Exchanges.

- 2 cups sliced celery
- 3 quarts chicken broth
- 4 cups cubed cooked chicken
- 1 can (10-3/4 ounces) condensed cream of mushroom soup, undiluted
- 1 cup uncooked instant rice
- 1 envelope onion soup mix
- 1 teaspoon poultry seasoning
- 1/2 teaspoon seasoned salt, optional
- 1/2 teaspoon dried thyme
- 1/2 teaspoon pepper

In a Dutch oven or soup kettle, simmer celery in broth until tender. Stir in the remaining ingredients. Bring to a boil. Reduce heat; cover and simmer for 6-8 minutes or until the rice is tender. **Yield:** 16 servings (4 quarts).

Nutritional Analysis: One 1-cup serving (prepared with reduced-sodium broth, reduced-sodium reduced-fat cream of mushroom soup and reduced-sodium onion soup mix and without seasoned salt) equals 98 calories, 3 g fat (1 g saturated fat), 26 mg cholesterol, 295 mg sodium, 10 g carbohydrate, trace fiber, 9 g protein. **Diabetic Exchanges:** 1 lean meat, 1/2 starch.

Handy Pantry List

LIKE to make meals in a hurry? Then you may want to stock your "shortcut pantry" with some of the following items.

Baking

Baking chips (butterscotch, milk chocolate, semisweet, white, etc.)
Baking chocolate squares (semisweet, unsweetened, white)
Baking cocoa
Baking powder
Baking soda
Biscuit/baking mix
Canned frosting
Coconut
Corn syrup
Cornstarch
Cream of tartar
Dried fruit (apricots, cranberries, raisins)
Extracts (almond, mint, vanilla)
Flour (all-purpose, bread, whole wheat)
Food coloring
Gelatin
Honey
Instant pudding
Marshmallows
Milk (evaporated, sweetened condensed)
Mixes (brownie, cake, corn bread, muffin, quick bread, etc.)
Nonfat dry milk powder
Nonstick cooking spray
Nuts (almonds, pecans, walnuts)
Oil (olive, vegetable)
Pie filling
Quick-cooking oats
Quick-cooking tapioca
Salt
Shortening
Sugar (brown, confectioners, granulated)

Canned/jarred goods

Applesauce
Beans (black, great northern, kidney, etc.)
Broth (beef, chicken)
Cream soups (chicken, mushroom, etc.)
Fruits (fruit cocktail, pineapple, etc.)
Green chilies
Ketchup
Mushrooms
Olives
Peanut butter
Salsa
Sauces (Alfredo, picante, process cheese, spaghetti, taco, etc.)
Tomatoes (diced, paste, sauce, stewed)
Tuna

Seasonings

Bouillon granules (beef, chicken)
Hot pepper sauce
Onion soup mix
Taco seasoning
Vinegar (cider, red wine, white, etc.)
Worcestershire sauce

Starches

Bread (pita, sandwich)
Crackers
Croutons
Dried beans (kidney, navy, pinto)
Dry bread crumbs
Noodle mixes
Pasta (egg noodles, macaroni, penne, small shells, spaghetti, etc.)
Rice (instant, long grain)
Rice mixes
Stuffing mix

Marinades Give Fast Fare Flair

LOOKING to punch up the flavor of steaks, chops or chicken before quickly cooking them on the grill? Then stir up a marinade! Although marinades sometimes require advance planning, they're easy to throw together with on-hand ingredients, they increase the flavor of food and they can tenderize it, too.

Many folks depend on these simple blends to boost the taste of meats and poultry before grilling. But marinades are so versatile, you can use them on fish, seafood and vegetables as well as foods that are broiled in the oven or cooked on the stovetop.

Marinades usually consist of oil, an acidic ingredient and various herbs, spices and seasonings. (See box at far right for seasoning suggestions.)

Oil adds moisture and helps distribute flavors while the acid acts as a tenderizing agent on meats by breaking down the fibers. Common acidic ingredients are vinegar, wine, yogurt, and pineapple, lime, orange and lemon juices.

It's best to marinate foods in heavy-duty plastic bags or glass dishes. The acid in the marinade can react with aluminum pans, altering the flavor of the food and discoloring the pan.

A general guide is 1 cup of marinade per pound of meat when marinated in a heavy-duty plastic bag and 2 cups per pound of meat marinated in a flat dish.

The marinade should completely cover the food. If there isn't enough marinade to cover it, turn the food occasionally to ensure even distribution of flavors.

The advantages of marinating in a plastic bag are that less marinade is needed, the bag can be turned over easily to distribute the marinade, and when you're done, the bag can simply be thrown away.

Marinating times depend on the type of food and the amount of flavor you want. Delicate seafood and tender cuts of meat pick up great flavor when marinated from 15 minutes to 2 hours.

Less tender cuts can be marinated from 6 hours to overnight. (Marinating longer than 24 hours is not recommended because it can cause the surface of the meat to become mushy.)

To help tenderize meat and to increase flavor, cut meat into serving-size pieces before marinating so it will absorb more of the marinade.

Although a marinade can help tenderize meat, it will not turn a tough cut of meat into a tender one. (A better way to tenderize a tough cut of meat is by cooking it with moist heat, such as braising or slow cooking, then slicing it across the grain.)

And don't forget—foods should be covered and refrigerated while they're marinating.

To get the most flavor out of your marinade, consider reserving a portion of it before adding it to the meat to serve as a sauce with the food. Or double the marinade recipe and reserve half of it for basting, then discard the amount used to marinate the food.

If you'd rather not discard the marinade after draining it from the uncooked meat, put it in a saucepan and bring it to a full rolling boil for 1 minute before using it to baste the food. This will ensure that it's food-safe.

Before basting meats, first cook the food on one side for 5 minutes. Then turn and baste on the cooked side of the meat to prevent cross-contamination from raw meat to the marinade.

If the food can't be turned on the grill (because it's too delicate or too large, for example), simply spoon the marinade or basting sauce over it.

Once you're done basting, discard any remaining marinade.

When cooking foods that have been marinated in a sugary mixture, keep a close eye on them. The high sugar content will cause them to brown (and burn) more quickly, especially when grilling.

Sirloin Squash Shish Kabobs

(Pictured at left)

Plan ahead…needs to marinate

When our grill comes out in the spring, this is the first recipe my family asks me to make. You can also use this marinade on six pork chops or a large piece of round steak cut into serving-size pieces.
— *Ronda Karbo, Russell, Minnesota*

  1 cup packed brown sugar
  1 cup soy sauce
  1 teaspoon *each* garlic powder, ground
      mustard and ground ginger
  1 pound boneless beef sirloin steak, cut
      into 1-inch pieces
  1 medium zucchini, cut into 1/4-inch slices

Sirloin Squash Shish Kabobs

1 medium yellow summer squash, cut into
   1/4-inch slices
1 medium sweet red pepper, cut into 1-inch
   pieces
1 medium red onion, cut into eight wedges,
   optional

In a bowl, combine the brown sugar, soy sauce, garlic powder, mustard and ginger. Place beef in a large resealable plastic bag; add 1 cup marinade. Seal bag and toss to coat. Place zucchini, yellow squash, red pepper and onion if desired in another resealable bag; add remaining marinade and toss to coat. Refrigerate beef and vegetables for at least 4 hours, turning occasionally.

Drain and discard marinade. On eight metal or soaked wooden skewers, alternately thread beef and vegetables. Grill, covered, over medium-hot heat or broil 4-6 in. from the heat for 10 minutes or until meat reaches desired doneness, turning occasionally. **Yield:** 4 servings.

Chili Barbecue Chops

Chili Barbecue Chops

(Pictured above right)

Plan ahead...needs to marinate

I jazz up store-bought Italian salad dressing with barbecue sauce and chili powder to make the easy marinade for these pork chops. They're simmered on the stovetop for just a few minutes, so they're on the table in no time.
—Tonya Fitzgerald, West Monroe, Louisiana

1/2 cup Italian salad dressing
1/2 cup barbecue sauce
  2 teaspoons chili powder
  4 bone-in pork chops (3/4 inch thick)

In a bowl, combine the salad dressing, barbecue sauce and chili powder; mix well. Pour 1/2 cup marinade into a large resealable plastic bag; add the pork chops. Seal bag and turn to coat; refrigerate for at least 1 hour. Cover and refrigerate remaining marinade.

Drain and discard marinade from pork. In a large skillet coated with nonstick cooking spray, brown chops on both sides over medium heat; drain. Add reserved marinade. Bring to a boil. Reduce heat; cover and simmer for 5-7 minutes or until a meat thermometer reads 160°. **Yield:** 4 servings.

Spicy Bacon-Wrapped Shrimp

Plan ahead...needs to marinate

This grilling recipe has been in our family for many years and always gets rave reviews. I combine tender marinated shrimp with bacon strips to produce these delightful appetizers that will surely disappear in a hurry.
—Jane Bone, Cape Coral, Florida

1/4 cup sugar
1/4 cup lemon juice
  2 tablespoons olive *or* vegetable oil
  4 teaspoons paprika
  1 teaspoon *each* salt, pepper, curry powder,
     ground cumin and ground coriander
1/2 to 1 teaspoon cayenne pepper

18 uncooked jumbo shrimp, peeled and
   deveined
 9 bacon strips, halved lengthwise

In a bowl, combine the sugar, lemon juice, oil and seasonings; mix well. Pour 1/4 cup marinade into a large resealable plastic bag; add the shrimp. Seal bag and turn to coat; refrigerate for 30-60 minutes. Cover and refrigerate remaining marinade for basting.

In a skillet, cook bacon over medium heat until cooked but not crisp. Drain on paper towels. Remove shrimp from marinade; discard the marinade. Wrap each shrimp with a piece of bacon and secure with a toothpick.

Grill bacon-wrapped shrimp, uncovered, over medium heat for 7-10 minutes or until shrimp turn pink, turning and basting with reserved marinade. **Yield:** 1-1/2 dozen.

Have Your Say in the Seasonings!

FEEL FREE to experiment when preparing marinades. If you're in a hurry, a prepared salad dressing like zesty Italian makes a great marinade for a variety of meats, poultry and vegetables.

If you have a few minutes, create your own marinade with your favorite seasonings. Different herbs and spices round out the flavor of some foods better than others. Here are some suggestions to try in your marinades:

Beef and pork—basil, crushed red pepper flakes, cumin, garlic, ginger, ground mustard, oregano, pepper, sage, tarragon, thyme.

Chicken—basil, cumin, oregano, rosemary, sage, tarragon, thyme.

Fish—curry powder, dill weed, garlic, ginger, oregano, pepper, rosemary, thyme.

Vegetables—chili powder, cloves, curry powder, dill weed, ginger, ground mustard, nutmeg, oregano, pepper, rosemary.

While these are general guidelines, remember that marinades are very versatile; your favorite beef marinade will likely taste just as good on chicken, pork or even vegetables. So give one a try.

Deep-Fry a Bite When Time's Tight

NO LONGER reserved for French fries and onion rings, deep-fat frying can help busy cooks prepare golden family favorites in a snap. Whether you use a countertop deep fryer, electric skillet or large pot, deep-frying is easy to do.

By completely submerging food in hot oil for mere minutes, this cooking method seals in flavors and juices. And since the items to be fried are often coated in breading or batter first, they stay moist inside but have a wonderful crunchy exterior after deep-frying.

If you deep-fry foods often, you may want to consider one of the many countertop deep-fat fryers available today. These handy appliances usually include adjustable temperature gauges and baskets to safely retrieve fried items.

While they can make it easier, they aren't a necessity for cooking great-tasting fried foods. An electric skillet or deep pot or saucepan used on the stovetop works just as well.

Electric skillets can be set to a specific temperature. But if you're using a pot or skillet, you'll need a deep-fat thermometer. (For more on deep-fat thermometers, see the box below left.)

Pots and saucepans must be deep enough to contain the splatters and bubbling of the oil when heated. In addition, pots should be slightly wider than the stovetop's burner or electric coil, so spilled fat is less likely to come in contact with the heat source.

Once you have the equipment to deep-fry, it's time to select the type of oil you'd like to use.

Oils have different smoke points—the temperature at which it begins to smoke and give foods an unpleasant flavor. The higher the smoke point, the better suited an oil is for deep-fat frying.

Vegetable oils such as corn, peanut and canola have high smoke points, making them ideal for deep-frying. Butter and margarine, on the other hand, have low smoke points and are not recommended for this cooking method.

If you're frying with an electric skillet, pot or saucepan, don't use too much oil or it may boil over or spill when the food is added. A good guideline is to fill the pot no more than halfway with oil. For a countertop fryer, follow the manufacturer's directions.

The temperature of the oil is extremely important when deep-frying. If the temperature is too low, the food absorbs too much oil and becomes greasy. If the temperature is too high, the outside of the food may burn before the inside is completely cooked.

Most deep-frying recipes call for the oil to be heated between 365° and 375°. Carefully add your food only when the desired temperature is reached.

When items are added to the oil, the temperature of the oil decreases. By frying foods in smaller batches, however, the oil should return quickly to the proper temperature.

Continue to regulate the temperature while frying, and turn the food frequently with long-handled metal tongs so it cooks evenly. Once the items are cooked through, remove them in the order that they were added to the oil.

Tongs are handy for retrieving large items while mesh skimmers or heat-resistant slotted spoons are great for removing smaller foods. Place the fried items on paper plates lined with paper towels to soak up excess fat.

After each batch of food is removed from the fryer, wait until the oil returns to the proper cooking temperature before adding the next batch.

When you're done frying, the oil can be saved to reuse at a later time. Simply allow it to cool to room temperature and strain it through cheesecloth into an airtight container.

It can be kept in the refrigerator for up to 6 months but should be discarded after it's used three times.

Deep-Frying Facts

KEEPING the oil at the proper temperature and checking for doneness are vital points for delicious deep-fried fare. Follow these tips and you're sure to succeed.

- Deep-fat thermometers are often used interchangeably with candy thermometers because both read high temperatures. Many styles clip onto the pan so the temperature of the oil can continually be monitored. For accurate readings, be sure the tip of the thermometer doesn't touch the sides or bottom of the pot.
- If the item you're frying includes uncooked ingredients such as eggs or meat, be sure its center is cooked. Fry a few pieces and remove from the fryer to check for doneness. When they're done, note the time and temperature to use when you fry the rest of the batch.
- Foods that are wet or moist will tend to make the oil splatter. When appropriate, pat foods dry with a paper towel before frying.
- Don't season foods while they're frying. If an item is breaded, try mixing herbs into the breading, or season items immediately after they have been removed from the fryer.

Fried Mushrooms Marinara

(Pictured above right)

Ready in 45 minutes or less

Offer this eye-appealing appetizer at your next party and get ready to hand out the recipe. I deep-fry breaded mushrooms before adding them to a bed of spaghetti sauce. —Barbara McCalley, Allison Park, Pennsylvania

    1 cup all-purpose flour
    1/2 teaspoon salt
    1/4 teaspoon pepper
    3 eggs
    1 tablespoon water
    1 cup seasoned bread crumbs
    1 pound medium fresh mushrooms, stems removed
Oil for deep-fat frying
    1 jar (26 ounces) marinara sauce *or* meatless spaghetti sauce
    1 cup (4 ounces) shredded mozzarella cheese
    1/4 cup grated Parmesan cheese

In a large resealable plastic bag, combine the flour, salt and pepper. In a shallow dish, beat the eggs and water. Place the bread crumbs in another shallow dish. Add mushrooms to the flour mixture; seal and shake to coat. Dip in egg mixture, then coat with bread crumbs. Let stand for 15 minutes.

In a deep saucepan, electric skillet or deep-fat fryer, heat oil to 375°. Fry mushrooms, six to eight at a time, for 1-2 minutes or until golden brown, turning occasionally. Drain on paper towels.

Pour spaghetti sauce into an ungreased 13-in. x 9-in. x 2-in. baking dish. Top with the mushrooms. Sprinkle with cheeses. Bake, uncovered, at 350° for 4-6 minutes or until cheese is melted. **Yield:** about 2 dozen.

Shrimp Egg Rolls

(Pictured above right)

Ready in 1 hour or less

My friend Yi owns a Chinese restaurant and taught me that Chinese cooking is simple if you have great recipes. She uses shrimp, bean sprouts, cabbage and carrot for these crispy egg rolls served with a homemade sweet-and-sour sauce. —Rose Bialowas, New Port Richey, Florida

4-1/2 teaspoons cornstarch
    1/2 cup sugar
    1 cup pineapple juice
    1/2 cup white vinegar
    2 tablespoons ketchup
    1 teaspoon soy sauce
    1 can (6 ounces) small shrimp, rinsed and drained *or* 1 cup frozen small cooked shrimp, chopped
    1 cup canned bean sprouts, chopped
    1 cup shredded cabbage
    1 cup chopped onion
    1/2 cup grated carrot
    1 tablespoon vegetable oil
    1/2 teaspoon pepper
    1/4 teaspoon salt
    12 egg roll wrappers
Additional oil for deep-fat frying

For sweet-sour sauce, combine the cornstarch, sugar, pineapple juice, vinegar, ketchup and soy sauce in a

Fried Mushrooms Marinara
Shrimp Egg Rolls

saucepan until smooth. Bring to a boil; cook and stir for 1-2 minutes or until thickened. Remove from the heat; set aside.

In a large skillet, stir-fry the shrimp, bean sprouts, cabbage, onion and carrot in oil until crisp-tender; cool slightly. Stir in pepper and salt. Position egg roll wrappers with a long edge facing you. Spoon 1/4 cup of shrimp mixture on the bottom third of each wrapper. Fold bottom over filling; fold sides over filling toward center. Moisten top edge with water; roll up tightly to seal.

In a deep saucepan, electric skillet or deep-fat fryer, heat oil to 375°. Fry egg rolls, a few at a time, for 4-5 minutes or until golden brown, turning often. Drain on paper towels. Serve with sweet-sour sauce. **Yield:** 1 dozen.

Apple Puffs

Ready in 45 minutes or less

The recipe for these golden sugar-topped puffs comes from my mother. They are a great way to warm up a cool day. I like to fry them up when friends come for coffee. —Pat Klingler, Ashtabula, Ohio

    3 cups all-purpose flour
    1/2 cup sugar
1-1/2 teaspoons baking powder
    2 teaspoons ground cinnamon
    1 egg
1-1/2 cups milk
    4 medium tart apples, peeled and chopped
Confectioners' sugar
Oil for deep-fat frying

In a large bowl, combine the flour, sugar, baking powder and cinnamon. In another bowl, beat the egg and milk; stir into dry ingredients just until moistened. Fold in apples. In a deep saucepan, electric skillet or deep-fat fryer, heat oil to 375°. Drop batter by rounded tablespoonfuls into oil. Fry until golden brown on both sides. Drain on paper towels. Dust with confectioners' sugar. Serve warm. **Yield:** about 4 dozen.

Fix Crowd-Pleasing Christmas Candies

WHAT'S Christmas without candy? This taste-tempting treat is even better when it's homemade. If you're thinking about stirring up some gifts from your kitchen for loved ones this holiday season, review these techniques for creating sensational sweets.

With a little planning, even busy cooks can find time to make a batch or two of candy. First, choose a day when the humidity is less than 60%, because high humidity can affect the texture of sugar syrup candies like soft caramels, peanut brittle and hard candy.

When cooking candy on the stovetop, use a heavy saucepan that's deep enough for the sugar mixture to bubble without nearing the top of the pan. If you're making candy in the microwave, use a microwave-safe glass bowl.

Many cooked candies require using a thermometer designed for candy making. To test its accuracy before each use, place it in a saucepan of boiling water; the thermometer should read 212°. If it doesn't, adjust your recipe temperature based on the results of the test.

When using it, attach the candy thermometer to the side of the saucepan if possible, but don't let the bulb touch the bottom of the pan. Read the thermometer at eye level. To avoid breaking it, let it cool before washing it.

The candy thermometer helps gauge the consistency of the sugar syrup. At higher temperatures, the syrup is more concentrated and the final candy will be harder. However, if you don't have a candy thermometer, you can use a cold-water test (see box below right) to determine the syrup concentration.

Chocolate is popular in candy making, whether used as an ingredient in fudges and truffles or used to coat other candies. There are several types of chocolate, including baking chocolate, candy coating and chocolate chips.

Baking chocolate is typically found in 8-ounce packages that are divided into 1- or 2-ounce squares. Candy coating—also known as almond bark or confectionery coating—usually comes in 1-1/2- to 2-pound blocks or in bags of small flat disks. Chocolate chips usually come in 6-, 12- or 24-ounce bags.

Melting chocolate can be challenging because it scorches easily. On the stovetop, melt chocolate over low heat in a heavy saucepan, or melt it in the top of a double boiler over hot (not boiling) water. In the microwave, heat 6 ounces of chopped semisweet chocolate or chips on high (100% power) for 1 minute, then stir. Continue to heat and stir at 10- to 15-second intervals until melted and smooth.

When melting white or milk chocolate, white candy coating, or vanilla, butterscotch or milk chocolate chips in the microwave, follow the same method but heat on medium-high (70% power).

It is important to keep moisture away from melted chocolate. Even a small drop of water can make the chocolate seize (clump and harden). If this happens, stir in 1 tablespoon of vegetable oil for each 6 ounces of chocolate. However, if chocolate seizes due to excessive heat, it can't be saved.

When dipping candies in chocolate, it's best to use candy coating because it becomes firm at room temperature. But you can use chocolate chips instead. Simply stir in 1 tablespoon of shortening to every 6 ounces of chips when melting.

Peppery Peanut Brittle
Crunchy Peanut Butter Balls

Peppery Peanut Brittle

(Pictured at left and on page 318)

Ready in 1 hour or less

A touch of hot pepper sauce gives a unique zip to this crunchy confection. We call it blistering brittle. The mixture reaches hard-crack stage in the microwave, so you don't even need a candy thermometer.
—Janie Sanders, Vicksburg, Mississippi

1-1/4 cups salted dry roasted peanuts
1-1/2 teaspoons hot pepper sauce
1/4 teaspoon ground allspice
1 cup sugar
1/2 cup light corn syrup
1 teaspoon butter (no substitutes)
1-1/2 teaspoons baking soda
1 teaspoon vanilla extract

Coat a 15-in. x 10-in. x 1-in. pan and metal spatula with nonstick cooking spray; set aside. In a bowl, toss the peanuts, hot pepper sauce and allspice until evenly coated; set aside.

In a 2-qt. microwave-safe glass bowl, combine sugar and corn syrup. Microwave, uncovered, on high for 4 minutes; stir. Add peanut mixture; stir until blended.

Heat on high 4-5 minutes longer or until mixture turns a light amber color (mixture will be very hot). Stir in butter. Microwave 45 seconds longer. Quickly stir in baking soda and vanilla until mixture foams and becomes light-colored.

Immediately pour mixture onto prepared pan and spread as thin as possible with prepared spatula. Cool. Break into pieces. **Yield:** about 1 pound.

Editor's Note: This recipe was tested in an 850-watt microwave.

Crunchy Peanut Butter Balls

(Pictured below left and on page 319)

Ready in 1 hour or less

The first time I made this candy, I knew it was going to be a big hit. My husband and friends agree it's the best they've ever tasted. It's so quick and simple to prepare. I've been asked for the recipe countless times.
—Janice Brightwell, Jeffersonville, Indiana

```
1 cup peanut butter*
1 jar (7 ounces) marshmallow creme
1-1/2 cups crisp rice cereal
1-1/2 cups semisweet chocolate chips
4 teaspoons shortening
```

In a large bowl, combine the peanut butter and marshmallow creme; add cereal and stir until well coated. In a small microwave-safe bowl, combine chocolate chips and shortening. Microwave, uncovered, for 1-2 minutes or until chips are melted; stir until smooth.

Roll cereal mixture into 1-in. balls; dip in chocolate. Place on a waxed paper-lined pan. Refrigerate until set. **Yield:** 2-1/2 dozen.

*Editor's Note: Reduced-fat or generic brands of peanut butter are not recommended for this recipe.

Apricot White Fudge

Plan ahead...needs to chill

This fudge has become a family favorite because of the luscious blending of flavors. I try to make it for gifts at Christmastime. Use a candy thermometer or the cold-water test to make sure the mixture reaches soft-ball stage, then chill until set.
—Debbie Purdue
Freeland, Michigan

```
1-1/2 teaspoons plus 1/2 cup butter (no
       substitutes), divided
   2 cups sugar
 3/4 cup sour cream
  12 squares (1 ounce each) white baking
       chocolate, chopped
   1 jar (7 ounces) marshmallow creme
 3/4 cup chopped dried apricots
 3/4 cup chopped walnuts
```

Line a 9-in. square pan with foil and grease with 1-1/2 teaspoons butter; set aside. In a heavy saucepan, combine sugar, sour cream and remaining butter. Bring to a boil over medium heat, stirring constantly. Cook and stir until a candy thermometer reads 234° (soft-ball stage), about 5-1/2 minutes.

Remove from heat. Stir in chocolate until melted. Stir in marshmallow creme until blended. Fold in apricots and walnuts. Pour into prepared pan. Cover and refrigerate overnight. Using foil, lift fudge out of pan. Discard foil; cut fudge into 1-in. squares. **Yield:** about 2 pounds.

Cold-Water Test for Candy

IF YOU do not have a candy thermometer, you can determine the temperature range or stage of your candy mixture by testing it in a small glass bowl filled with cold water. Dip a metal spoon into the hot candy mixture and drop it into the cold water.

Thread stage (230°-233°): The mixture should fall off the spoon and into the water in a fine thread.

Soft-ball stage (234°-240°): When cooled and removed from the water, the ball will run over your finger.

Firm-ball stage (244°-248°): When cooled and removed from the water, the ball will hold its shape.

Hard-ball stage (250°-266°): When cooled and removed from the water, the candy will form a hard yet pliable ball.

Soft-crack stage (270°-290°): When cooled and removed from the water, the candy will separate into hard pliable threads.

Hard-crack stage (300°-310°): When cooled and removed from the water, the candy will separate into hard brittle threads.

General Recipe Index

This handy index lists every recipe by food category, major ingredient and/or cooking method, so you can easily locate recipes to suit your needs.

✓ *Recipe includes Nutritional Analysis and Diabetic Exchanges*

✓ Recipe includes Nutritional Analysis and Diabetic Exchanges

✓ Recipe includes Nutritional Analysis and Diabetic Exchanges

✓ Recipe includes Nutritional Analysis and Diabetic Exchanges

✓ Recipe includes Nutritional Analysis and Diabetic Exchanges

✓ Recipe includes Nutritional Analysis and Diabetic Exchanges

✓ Recipe includes Nutritional Analysis and Diabetic Exchanges

✓ Recipe includes Nutritional Analysis and Diabetic Exchanges

✓ *Recipe includes Nutritional Analysis and Diabetic Exchanges*

Italian Meatball Seasoning, 86
✓Life Preserver Meat Loaves, 43
✓Little Meat Loaves, 230
Meatball Sandwich Slices, 189
Meatball Stroganoff, 148
Meatballs Monte Carlo, 153
Meatballs with Gravy, 107
Melt-in-Your-Mouth Meat
   Loaf, 266
Onion Turkey Meatballs, 151
Pasta Meatball Soup, 25
Porcupine Meatballs, 289
✓Tender Turkey Meatballs, 224
Turkey Ham Loaf, 111
✓Turkey Meatball Soup, 192

MEAT PIES
Bean 'n' Beef Crescent Pie, 92
Chicken Potpie, 114
Hot Dog Pie, 255
✓Taco Pie, 72
Two-Tater Shepherd's Pie, 251

MICROWAVE RECIPES
Desserts
   Butterscotch Peanut
      Fudge, 283
   Microwave Bread
      Pudding, 283
   Microwave Cake Mix, 86
   Peanut Butter Squares, 280
   Pecan Cinnamon Fudge, 281
   Strawberry Rhubarb
      Sauce, 281
Main Dishes
   Broccoli Chicken Roll-Ups, 282
   Chicken Divine, 280
   Crab Mornay, 309
   Microwave Fried Rice, 280
   Microwave Red Snapper, 65
   Mushroom Chicken
      Roll-Ups, 281
   Potato Chip Chicken, 282
   Snow Pea Pork Medley, 97
   Souped-Up Pork Supper, 281
   Sour Cream Beef 'n' Beans, 282
   Tomato Macaroni
      Casserole, 50
Side Dishes
   Basil Brussels Sprouts, 282
   Colorful Zucchini Boats, 283
   ✓Glazed Spiced Apples, 231
   Maple Baked Beans, 57
   Parmesan Potato Wedges, 283

MINT
Chocolate Chip Mint
   Cookies, 212
Chocolate Mint Torte, 119
Grasshopper Pie, 201
Mallow Mint Dessert, 288
Mint Cake, 202
Mint Candy Cookies, 198

MUFFINS
✓Almond Bran Muffins, 233
✓Applesauce Oat Muffins, 228
✓Apricot Oat Muffins, 221
Banana Meringue Muffins, 157
Butter Muffin Mix, 88
✓ Chip Muffins, 159
✓Confetti Corn Muffins, 162
Frosted Pumpkin Muffins, 166
Ham Muffinwiches, 78
Honey Chip Muffins, 164
Kiwifruit Muffins, 163
Maple Bacon Muffins, 129
✓Mexicorn Muffins, 160
Orange Mini Muffins, 156
Pepperoni Pizza Muffins, 164
Raisin Bran Muffin Mix, 84
Sour Cream Blueberry
   Muffins, 290

MUSHROOMS
Artichoke Mushroom Caps, 277
Fried Mushrooms Marinara, 328
Mushroom Broccoli Cups, 292
Mushroom Chicken
   Cacciatore, 258
Mushroom Chicken Roll-Ups, 281
Mushroom Crab Melts, 185
Mushroom Ham Fettuccine, 240
Mushroom Pasta Sauce, 112
Mushroom Potatoes, 266
Mushroom Sausage Omelets, 30
Swiss Mushroom Pie, 54

MUSTARD
Honey Mustard Chicken, 52
Honey-Mustard Potatoes, 56

NUTS (also see Peanut Butter)
Breads
   ✓Almond Bran Muffins, 233
   Almond-Honey Wheat
      Bread, 172
   Cherry Pistachio Bread, 164
   Nutty Peach Quick Bread, 163

Pecan Apricot Bread, 156
Pecan Sweet Roll Rings, 126
Pecan Zucchini Bread, 160
Tropical Sweet Bread, 169
Walnut Date Loaf, 159
Desserts
   Banana Nut Cupcakes, 213
   Butterscotch Peanut Treats, 58
   Caramel Pecan Delight, 293
   Chewy Walnut Bars, 215
   Cocoa Cola Cake, 74
   Coconut Macadamia Bars, 22
   Heavenly Hash Bars, 61
   Macadamia Berry Dessert, 118
   Macadamia Cocoa
      Cookies, 202
   Peanutty Chocolate
      Cookies, 214
   Pecan Cereal Clusters, 252
   Pecan Pie Bars, 217
   Walnut Caramel Cake, 293
   Walnut Carrot Cake, 76
   Warm Apple Topping, 275
Main Dishes
   Cashew Chicken, 138
   Curried Peanut Chicken, 273
Salads
   Apple Peanut Salad, 255
   Banana Nut Salad, 251
Sandwich
   Chicken Pecan Wraps, 69
Snacks
   Butterscotch Peanut
      Fudge, 283
   Honey Peanut Apple Dip, 68
   Kiddie Crunch Mix, 215
   Pecan Cinnamon Fudge, 281
   Peppery Peanut Brittle, 330
   Reindeer Snack Mix, 47
   Sweet Snack Mix, 212

OATS
✓Applesauce Oat Muffins, 228
✓Apricot Oat Muffins, 221
Cereal Cookie Bars, 217
Oatmeal Spice Mix, 84
Orange Cranberry Oatmeal, 133
Peanut Butter Oat Bread, 167
Scotch Teas, 53

ONIONS & LEEKS
✓Apple-Onion Pork Chops, 233
Barbecued Onion Meat
   Loaves, 22

✓ Recipe includes Nutritional Analysis and Diabetic Exchanges

✓ Recipe includes Nutritional Analysis and Diabetic Exchanges

✓ *Recipe includes Nutritional Analysis and Diabetic Exchanges*

✓ Recipe includes Nutritional Analysis and Diabetic Exchanges

✓ Recipe includes Nutritional Analysis and Diabetic Exchanges

✓ Recipe includes Nutritional Analysis and Diabetic Exchanges

✓ Recipe includes Nutritional Analysis and Diabetic Exchanges

Alphabetical Index

This handy index lists every recipe in alphabetical order so you can easily find your favorite recipes.

✓ Recipe includes Nutritional Analysis and Diabetic Exchanges

✓ *Recipe includes Nutritional Analysis and Diabetic Exchanges*

Frosted Cake Brownies, 214
Frosted Pumpkin Muffins, 166
Frosty Peanut Butter Pie, 11
Frozen Fudge Pops, 87
Fruit Medley, 26
✓Fruit Slush Cups, 126
Fruited Cranberry Gelatin, 51
Fruited Sausage, 133
Fudgy Brownies, 94
Fudgy Peanut Butter Cake, 265

G

✓Garden Frittata, 229
Garlic Butter Shrimp, 59
Garlic Chicken 'n' Pasta, 54
✓Garlic Green Beans, 233
✓Garlic-Herb Bagel Spread, 291
Garlic Parsley Spaghetti, 307
German Chocolate Bars, 59
Ginger Fruit Sundaes, 68
✓Ginger Meatballs, 292
✓Glazed Spiced Apples, 231
Golden Pan Rolls, 173
Grandma's Spoiler Sandwich, 246
✓Gran's Apple Cake, 232
Grape Ice, 121
Grapefruit Orange Medley, 134
Grasshopper Pie, 201
Greek Ham Wraps, 93
Greek Pasta Salad, 182
Greek Pita Pizzas, 295
Green 'n' Gold Veggies, 28
Green Chili Rice Casserole, 57
Green Peas Supreme, 309
Grilled Cheese with Tomato, 65
Grilled Cheeseburger Pizza, 274
Grilled Chicken Salad, 98
✓Grilled Fish Sandwiches, 190
Grilled Hash Browns, 270
Grilled Roast Beef Sandwiches, 180
✓Grilled Salmon Steaks, 232
Grilled Sesame Chicken, 98
Ground Beef Mix, 106
Gumdrop Cereal Bars, 213

H

Halibut with Cream Sauce, 278
Halloween Cake Cookies, 253
Ham and Bean Bake, 138
Ham and Bean Stew, 262
Ham 'n' Broccoli Hash, 50
Ham 'n' Cheese Quiche, 108
Ham 'n' Cheese Stromboli, 176
✓Ham and Corn Chowder, 180

Ham 'n' Corn Scrambled Eggs, 67
Ham and Pea Salad, 179
Ham Coleslaw, 66
Ham Cream Cheese Spread, 291
Ham Griddle Cakes, 129
Ham Muffinwiches, 78
✓Ham Noodle Casserole, 223
Ham Spaghetti Skillet, 153
Hamburger Goulash, 111
Hamburger Rice Skillet, 150
Hamburger Stew, 116
✓Harvest Soup, 229
Hash Brown Pizza, 75
Hawaiian Ham Steaks, 31
Hearty Beans with Beef, 261
Hearty German Potato Salad, 96
Hearty Grilled Cheese, 176
Hearty Pancake Mix, 86
Heavenly Hash Bars, 61
Herb Fryer Chicken, 271
Herb Sausage Biscuits, 167
Herbed French Bread, 25
✓Herbed Orange Roughy, 28
Herbed Pork and Potatoes, 96
Herbed Sandwich Buns, 170
Ho-Ho-Ho Sandwiches, 47
Holiday Sugar Cookies, 209
Homemade Hash Browns, 99
Homemade Pizza Sauce, 100
Homemade Refried Beans, 92
Hominy Beef Bake, 139
✓Honey Chicken Stir-Fry, 231
Honey Chip Muffins, 164
Honey Corn Bread, 156
✓Honey Lemon Chicken, 279
Honey Mustard Chicken, 52
Honey-Mustard Potatoes, 56
Honey Peanut Apple Dip, 68
Hot Chili Cheese Dip, 269
Hot Cranberry Drink, 241
Hot Dog Pie, 255
Hot Dogs with the Works, 271
Hot Pizza Sub, 187
Hot Roll Mix, 88
Hurry-Up Tuna Supper, 151

I

Ice Cream Party Roll, 120
Ice Cream Sandwiches, 29
Italian Beef Sandwiches, 27
Italian Bow Tie Bake, 143
Italian Bread Salad, 68
Italian Chicken Rice Soup, 190
✓Italian Chicken Stew, 148

Italian Chicken Strips, 108
Italian Grilled Cheese, 277
Italian Meatball Seasoning, 86
Italian Mini Loaves, 303
Italian Noodle Casserole, 325
✓Italian Peasant Soup, 181
Italian Salad Croutons, 58

J

Jack-o'-Lantern Brownies, 206
Jalapeno Chicken Wraps, 272

K

Kiddie Crunch Mix, 215
Kiwifruit Muffins, 163

L

Lamb with Sauteed Veggies, 24
✓Late-Night Breadsticks, 37
Lemon Blueberry Coffee Cake, 158
Lemon Bundt Cake, 286
Lemon Cheese Bars, 240
Lemon Cheesecake Dessert, 286
Lemon Grilled Chicken, 286
Lemon Lime Dessert, 116
Lemon Oregano Potatoes, 286
Lemon-Pepper Catfish, 270
Lemon-Pepper Veggies, 32
Lemon Pineapple Fizz, 251
✓Life Preserver Meat Loaves, 43
✓Light Chicken Cordon Bleu, 226
Lime Sherbet, 238
Lime Sherbet Molded Salad, 80
✓Little Meat Loaves, 230
✓Lo-Cal Cheese Dip, 222
Lobster Newburg, 147

M

Macadamia Berry Dessert, 118
Macadamia Cocoa Cookies, 202
Mallow Mint Dessert, 288
Mandarin Cookie Salad, 54
Manicotti for Two, 296
Maple Bacon Muffins, 129
Maple Baked Beans, 57
Maple Breakfast Rolls, 125
Marmalade Baked Ham, 311
Marshmallow Fruit Salad, 288
Marshmallow Treat Pops, 245
Meatball Sandwich Slices, 189
Meatball Stroganoff, 148
Meatballs Monte Carlo, 153
Meatballs with Gravy, 107
✓Melon with Ice Cream, 224
Melt-in-Your-Mouth Meat Loaf, 266

✓ Recipe includes Nutritional Analysis and Diabetic Exchanges

✓ Recipe includes Nutritional Analysis and Diabetic Exchanges

✓ Recipe includes Nutritional Analysis and Diabetic Exchanges